Dutch-English Dictionary

Engels-Nederlands Woordenboek

Berlitz Dictionaries

Dansk	Engelsk, Fransk, Italiensk, Spansk, Tysk
Deutsch	Dänisch, Englisch, Finnisch, Französisch, Italienisch Niederländisch, Norwegisch, Portugiesisch, Schwedisch, Spanisch
English	Danish, Dutch, Finnish, French, German, Italian, Norwegian, Portuguese, Spanish, Swedish
Español	Alemán, Danés, Finlandés, Francés, Holandés, Inglés, Noruego, Sueco
Français	Allemand, Anglais, Danois, Espagnol, Finnois, Italien, Néerlandais, Norvégien, Portugais, Suédois
Italiano	Danese, Finlandese, Francese, Inglese, Norvegese Olandese, Svedese, Tedesco
Nederlands	Duits, Engels, Frans, Italiaans, Portugees, Spaans
Norsk	Engelsk, Fransk, Italiensk, Spansk, Tysk
Português	Alemão, Francês, Holandês, Inglês, Sueco
Suomi	Englanti, Espanja, Italia, Ranska, Ruotsi, Saksa
Svenska	Engelska, Finska, Franska, Italienska, Portugisiska Spanska, Tyska

Dutch-English
Dictionary

Engels-Nederlands
Woordenboek

Berlitz Publishing Company, Inc.

Princeton   Mexico City   Dublin   Eschborn   Singapore

Library of Congress Catalog Card Number: 78-78084
2nd revised edition 1994–3rd printing December 1999

ISBN 2-8315-6306-2

Printed in the Netherlands

Inhoud

Contents

Voorwoord

Bij het selecteren van de 12 500 woordbegrippen in beide talen voor dit woordenboek stond de redactie in de allereerste plaats de behoeften van de reiziger voor ogen. Dit boekje zal van grote waarde blijken te zijn voor de vele reizigers, toeristen en zakenmensen die het waarderen zich verzekerd te weten van een klein en praktisch woordenboek. Het biedt hen – evenals aan beginners en gevorderden – de benodigde woordenschat, alsook sleutelwoorden en uitdrukkingen voor dagelijks gebruik.

Zoals onze succesvolle taal- en reisgidsen, zijn deze woordenboekjes – tot stand gekomen met behulp van een computer data bank – speciaal ontworpen om in jaszak of handtas gestoken te worden.

Behalve wat u normaliter in woordenboeken vindt, biedt Berlitz nog de volgende extra's:

- een transcriptie van elk grondwoord in het internationale fonetische alfabet (IPA), hetgeen het uitspreken van woorden waarvan de spelling moeilijk lijkt vergemakkelijkt

- een unieke, praktische woordenlijst van culinaire begrippen om het lezen van een menu in een buitenlands restaurant te vereenvoudigen en de mysteries te ontrafelen van bijzondere gerechten

- nuttige informatie over tijdsaanduiding, getallen, de vervoeging van onregelmatige werkwoorden, veel gebruikte afkortingen en een lijst van veel voorkomende uitdrukkingen.

Hoewel geen enkel woordenboek van dit formaat kan pretenderen volledig te zijn, verwachten wij toch dat de gebruiker van dit boek zich goed uitgerust zal voelen om buitenlandse reizen met vertrouwen te ondernemen. Wij zouden het evenwel op prijs stellen opmerkingen, kritiek of suggesties te ontvangen, die mogelijkerwijs kunnen helpen bij het voorbereiden van toekomstige uitgaven.

Preface

In selecting the 12.500 word-concepts in each language for this dictionary, the editors have had the traveller's needs foremost in mind. This book will prove invaluable to all the millions of travellers, tourists and business people who appreciate the reassurance a small and practical dictionary can provide. It offers them—as it does beginners and students—all the basic vocabulary they are going to encounter and to have to use, giving the key words and expressions to allow them to cope in everyday situations.

Like our successful phrase books and travel guides, these dictionaries—created with the help of a computer data bank—are designed to slip into pocket or purse, and thus have a role as handy companions at all times.

Besides just about everything you normally find in dictionaries, there are these Berlitz bonuses:

- imitated pronunciation next to each foreign-word entry, making it easy to read and enunciate words whose spelling may look forbidding

- a unique, practical glossary to simplify reading a foreign restaurant menu and to take the mystery out of complicated dishes and indecipherable names on bills of fare

- useful information on how to tell the time and how to count, on conjugating irregular verbs, commonly seen abbreviations and converting to the metric system, in addition to basic phrases.

While no dictionary of this size can pretend to completeness, we expect the user of this book will feel well armed to affront foreign travel with confidence. We should, however, be very pleased to receive comments, criticism and suggestions that you think may be of help in preparing future editions.

dutch-english

---

nederlands-engels

Afkortingen

adj	bijvoeglijk naamwoord	*p*	verleden tijd
adv	bijwoord	*pl*	meervoud
Am	Amerikaans	*plAm*	meervoud (Amerikaans)
art	lidwoord	*pp*	voltooid deelwoord
c	gemeenslachtig	*pr*	tegenwoordige tijd
conj	voegwoord	*pref*	voorvoegsel
n	zelfstandig naamwoord	*prep*	voorzetsel
nAm	zelfstandig naamwoord	*pron*	voornaamwoord
	(Amerikaans)	*v*	werkwoord
nt	onzijdig	*vAm*	werkwoord
num	telwoord		(Amerikaans)

Inleiding

Het woordenboek is zodanig opgezet, dat het zoveel mogelijk beantwoordt aan de eisen van de praktijk. Onnodige taalkundige aanduidingen zijn achterwege gelaten. De volgorde van de woorden is strikt alfabetisch, ook als het samengestelde woorden of woorden met een koppelteken betreft. Als enige uitzondering op deze regel zijn enkele idiomatische uitdrukkingen opgenomen als een afzonderlijk artikel, waarbij het meest toonaangevende woord van de uitdrukking bepalend is voor de alfabetische rangschikking. Wanneer bij een grondwoord nog daarvan afgeleide samenstellingen of uitdrukkingen zijn gegeven, staan ook deze weer in alfabetische volgorde.

Achter elk grondwoord vindt u een fonetische transcriptie (zie de Gids voor de uitspraak) en vervolgens, wanneer van toepassing, de woordsoort. Wanneer bij hetzelfde grondwoord meerdere woordsoorten behoren, zijn de vertalingen telkens naar de woordsoort gegroepeerd.

Het meervoud van zelfstandige naamwoorden is altijd opgenomen, wanneer dat onregelmatig is; tevens is het meervoud gegeven van bepaalde woorden waarover de gebruiker in twijfel zou kunnen verkeren.

Wanneer in onregelmatige meervoudsvormen of in afgeleide samenstellingen en uitdrukkingen het teken ∼ wordt gebruikt, duidt dit een herhaling aan van het grondwoord als geheel.

In onregelmatige meervoudsvormen van samengestelde woorden wordt alleen het gedeelte, dat verandert, voluit geschreven en het onveranderde deel aangegeven door een liggend streepje (-).

Een sterretje (*) voor een werkwoord geeft aan, dat dit werkwoord onregelmatig is. Voor nadere bijzonderheden kunt u de lijst van onregelmatige werkwoorden raadplegen.

Dit woordenboek is gebaseerd op de Britse spelling. Alle woorden en woordbetekenissen die overwegend Amerikaans zijn, zijn als zodanig aangegeven (zie lijst van gebezigde afkortingen).

Uitspraak

Elk trefwoord in dit deel van het woordenboek wordt gevolgd door een transcriptie in het internationale fonetische alfabet (IPA). In dit alfabet vertegenwoordigt elk teken altijd dezelfde klank. Letters die hieronder niet beschreven zijn worden min of meer op dezelfde wijze uitgesproken als in het Nederlands.

Medeklinkers

b	nooit scherp zoals in heb
d	nooit scherp zoals in raad
ð	als de z in zee, maar lispend uitgesproken
g	als een zachte k, zoals in het Franse garçon
ŋ	als de ng in bang
r	plaats de tong eerst als voor de ʒ (zie beneden), open dan de mond enigszins en beweeg de tong daarbij naar beneden
ʃ	als de sj in sjofel
θ	als de s in samen, maar lispend uitgesproken
v	als de w in waar
w	een korte, zwakke oe-klank
ʒ	als de g in etage

N.B. De lettergroep **sj** moet worden uitgesproken als een **s** gevolgd door een **j**-klank, maar *niet* als in **sj**ofel.

Klinkers

ɑ:	als de aa in maat
æ	een klank tussen de a in als en de e in best
ʌ	min of meer als de a in als
e	als in best
ɛ	als de e in best, maar met de tong wat lager
ə	als de e in achter
ɔ	min of meer als de o in pot
u	als de oe in goed, maar korter

1) Een dubbele punt (:) geeft aan dat de voorafgaande klinker lang is.

2) Enkele aan het Frans ontleende Engelse woorden bevatten neusklanken, die aangegeven worden d.m.v. een tilde boven de klinker (b.v. ã). Deze worden door de neus en de mond tegelijkertijd uitgesproken.

Tweeklanken

Een tweeklank bestaat uit twee klinkers, waarvan er één sterk is (beklemtoond) en de andere zwak (niet beklemtoond) en die samen als één klinker worden uitgesproken, zoals **ei** in het Nederlands. In het Engels is de tweede klinker altijd zwak. Een tweeklank kan soms gevolgd worden door een [ə]. In dergelijke gevallen heeft de tweede klinker van de tweeklank de neiging zeer zwak te worden.

Klemtoon

Het teken (') geeft aan dat de klemtoon op de volgende lettergreep valt. Als in een woord meer dan één lettergreep wordt beklemtoond, wordt het teken (ˌ) geplaatst vóór de lettergreep, waarop de bijklemtoon valt.

Amerikaanse uitspraak

Onze transcriptie geeft de gebruikelijke Engelse uitspraak aan. De Amerikaanse uitspraak verschilt in enkele opzichten van het Britse Engels en kent daarbij nog belangrijke regionale verschillen. Hier volgen enkele van de meest opvallende afwijkingen:

1) In tegenstelling tot in het Britse Engels wordt de **r** ook uitgesproken voor een medeklinker en aan het einde van een woord.

2) In vele woorden (b.v. *ask*, *castle*, *laugh* enz.) wordt [ɑː] uitgesproken als [æː].

3) De [ɔ]-klank wordt in het Amerikaans uitgesproken als [ɑ], vaak ook als [ɔː].

4) In woorden als *duty*, *tune*, *new* enz. valt in het Amerikaans de [j]-klank voor de [uː] vaak weg.

5) Bovendien wordt bij een aantal woorden in het Amerikaans de klemtoon anders gelegd.

A

a [ei,ə] *art* (an) een *art*

abbey ['æbi] *n* abdij *c*

abbreviation [ə,bri:vi'eiʃən] *n* afkorting *c*

aberration [,æbə'reiʃən] *n* afwijking *c*

ability [ə'biləti] *n* bekwaamheid *c*; vermogen *nt*

able ['eibəl] *adj* in staat; capabel, bekwaam; *be ~ to* in staat *zijn om; *kunnen

abnormal [æb'nɔ:məl] *adj* abnormaal

aboard [ə'bɔ:d] *adv* aan boord

abolish [ə'bɔliʃ] *v* afschaffen

abortion [ə'bɔ:ʃən] *n* abortus *c*

about [ə'baut] *prep* over; betreffende, omtrent; om; *adv* omstreeks, ongeveer; omheen

above [ə'bʌv] *prep* boven; *adv* boven

abroad [ə'brɔ:d] *adv* naar het buitenland, in het buitenland

abscess ['æbses] *n* abces *nt*

absence ['æbsəns] *n* afwezigheid *c*

absent ['æbsənt] *adj* afwezig

absolutely ['æbsəlu:tli] *adv* absoluut

abstain from [əb'stein] zich *onthouden van

abstract ['æbstrækt] *adj* abstract

absurd [əb'sə:d] *adj* absurd, ongerijmd

abundance [ə'bʌndəns] *n* overvloed *c*

abundant [ə'bʌndənt] *adj* overvloedig

abuse [ə'bju:s] *n* misbruik *nt*

abyss [ə'bis] *n* afgrond *c*

academy [ə'kædəmi] *n* academie *c*

accelerate [ək'seləreit] *v* versnellen

accelerator [ək'seləreitə] *n* gaspedaal *nt*

accent ['æksənt] *n* accent *nt*; nadruk *c*

accept [ək'sept] *v* aanvaarden, *aannemen; accepteren

access ['ækses] *n* toegang *c*

accessary [ək'sesəri] *n* medeplichtige *c*

accessible [ək'sesəbəl] *adj* toegankelijk

accessories [ək'sesəriz] *pl* toebehoren *pl*, accessoires *pl*

accident ['æksidənt] *n* ongeluk *nt*, ongeval *nt*

accidental [,æksi'dentəl] *adj* toevallig

accommodate [ə'kɔmədeit] *v* *onderbrengen

accommodation [ə,kɔmə'deiʃən] *n* accommodatie *c*, logies *nt*, onderdak *nt*

accompany [ə'kʌmpəni] *v* vergezellen; begeleiden

accomplish [ə'kʌmpliʃ] *v* *volbrengen; bereiken

in accordance with [in ə'kɔ:dəns wið] ingevolge

according to [ə'kɔ:diŋ tu:] volgens; overeenkomstig

account [ə'kaunt] *n* rekening *c*; verslag *nt*; ~ **for** verantwoorden; **on** ~ **of** vanwege

accountable [ə'kauntəbəl] *adj* verklaarbaar

accurate ['ækjurət] *adj* nauwkeurig

accuse [ə'kju:z] *v* beschuldigen; aanklagen

accused [ə'kju:zd] *n* verdachte *c*

accustom [ə'kʌstəm] *v* wennen; **accustomed** gewoon, gewend

ache [eik] *v* pijn *doen; *n* pijn *c*

achieve [ə'tʃi:v] *v* bereiken; presteren

achievement [ə'tʃi:vmənt] *n* prestatie *c*

acid ['æsid] *n* zuur *nt*

acknowledge [ək'nɔlidʒ] *v* erkennen; *toegeven; bevestigen

acne ['ækni] *n* acne *c*

acorn ['eikɔ:n] *n* eikel *c*

acquaintance [ə'kweintəns] *n* bekende *c*, kennis *c*

acquire [ə'kwaiə] *v* *verwerven

acquisition [,ækwi'ziʃən] *n* acquisitie *c*

acquittal [ə'kwitəl] *n* vrijspraak *c*

across [ə'krɔs] *prep* over; aan de andere kant van; *adv* aan de overkant

act [ækt] *n* daad *c*; bedrijf *nt*, akte *c*; nummer *nt*; *v* *optreden, handelen; zich *gedragen; toneelspelen

action ['ækʃən] *n* actie *c*, handeling *c*

active ['æktiv] *adj* actief; bedrijvig

activity [æk'tivəti] *n* activiteit *c*

actor ['æktə] *n* acteur *c*, toneelspeler *c*

actress ['æktris] *n* actrice *c*, toneelspeelster *c*

actual ['æktʃuəl] *adj* eigenlijk, werkelijk

actually ['æktʃuəli] *adv* feitelijk

acute [ə'kju:t] *adj* acuut

adapt [ə'dæpt] *v* aanpassen

adaptor [ə'dæptə] *n* verbindingsstuk *nt*

add [æd] *v* optellen; toevoegen

addition [ə'diʃən] *n* optelling *c*; toevoeging *c*

additional [ə'diʃənəl] *adj* extra; bijkomend; bijkomstig

address [ə'dres] *n* adres *nt*; *v* adresseren; *aanspreken

addressee [,ædre'si:] *n* geadresseerde *c*

adequate ['ædikwət] *adj* toereikend; adequaat, passend

adjective ['ædʒiktiv] *n* bijvoeglijk naamwoord

adjourn [ə'dʒə:n] *v* uitstellen

adjust [ə'dʒʌst] *v* afstellen; aanpassen

administer [əd'ministə] *v* toedienen

administration [əd,mini'streiʃən] *n* administratie *c*; beheer *nt*

administrative [əd'ministrətiv] *adj* administratief; bestuurlijk; ~ **law** bestuursrecht *nt*

admiral ['ædmərəl] *n* admiraal *c*

admiration [,ædmə'reiʃən] *n* bewondering *c*

admire [əd'maiə] *v* bewonderen

admission [əd'miʃən] *n* toegang *c*; toelating *c*

admit [əd'mit] *v* *toelaten; *toegeven, bekennen

admittance [əd'mitəns] *n* toegang *c*; **no** ~ verboden toegang

adopt [ə'dɔpt] *v* adopteren; *aannemen

adult ['ædʌlt] *n* volwassene *c*; *adj* volwassen

advance [əd'vɑ:ns] *n* vooruitgang *c*; voorschot *nt*; *v* *vooruitgaan; *voorschieten; **in** ~ vooruit, van tevoren

advanced [əd'vɑ:nst] *adj* gevorderd

advantage [əd'vɑ:ntidʒ] *n* voordeel *nt*

advantageous [,ædvən'teidʒəs] *adj* voordelig

adventure [əd'ventʃə] *n* avontuur *nt*

adverb ['ædvə:b] *n* bijwoord *nt*

advertisement [əd'və:tismənt] *n* advertentie *c*; annonce *c*

advertising ['ædvətaizɪŋ] *n* reclame *c*

advice [əd'vais] *n* advies *nt*, raad *c*

advise [əd'vaiz] *v* adviseren, *aanraden

advocate ['ædvəkət] *n* voorstander *c*

aerial ['ɛəriəl] *n* antenne *c*

aeroplane ['ɛərəplein] *n* vliegtuig *nt*

affair [ə'fɛə] *n* aangelegenheid *c*; verhouding *c*, affaire *c*

affect [ə'fekt] *v* beïnvloeden; *betreffen

affected [ə'fektid] *adj* geaffecteerd

affection [ə'fekʃən] *n* aandoening *c*; genegenheid *c*

affectionate [ə'fekʃənit] *adj* lief, aanhankelijk

affiliated [ə'filieitid] *adj* aangesloten

affirmative [ə'fə:mətiv] *adj* bevestigend

affliction [ə'flikʃən] *n* leed *nt*

afford [ə'fɔ:d] *v* zich veroorloven

afraid [ə'freid] *adj* angstig, bang; *be ~ bang *zijn

Africa ['æfrikə] Afrika

African ['æfrikən] *adj* Afrikaans; *n* Afrikaan *c*

after ['ɑ:ftə] *prep* na; achter; *conj* nadat

afternoon [,ɑ:ftə'nu:n] *n* middag *c*, namiddag *c*; **this** ~ vanmiddag

afterwards ['ɑ:ftəwədz] *adv* later; nadien, naderhand

again [ə'gen] *adv* weer; opnieuw; ~ **and again** telkens

against [ə'genst] *prep* tegen

age [eidʒ] *n* leeftijd *c*; ouderdom *c*; **of** ~ meerderjarig; **under** ~ minderjarig

aged ['eidʒid] *adj* bejaard; oud

agency ['eidʒənsi] *n* agentschap *nt*; bureau *nt*; vertegenwoordiging *c*

agenda [ə'dʒendə] *n* agenda *c*

agent ['eidʒənt] *n* vertegenwoordiger

c, agent *c*

aggressive [ə'gresiv] *adj* agressief

ago [ə'gou] *adv* geleden

agrarian [ə'grɛəriən] *adj* agrarisch, landbouw-

agree [ə'gri:] *v* het eens *zijn; toestemmen; *overeenkomen

agreeable [ə'gri:əbəl] *adj* aangenaam

agreement [ə'gri:mənt] *n* contract *nt*; akkoord *nt*, overeenkomst *c*

agriculture ['ægrikʌltʃə] *n* landbouw *c*

ahead [ə'hed] *adv* vooruit; ~ **of** voor; ***go** ~ *doorgaan; **straight** ~ rechtuit

aid [eid] *n* hulp *c*; *v* *bijstaan, *helpen

AIDS [eidz] *n* AIDS

ailment ['eilmənt] *n* kwaal *c*; ziekte *c*

aim [eim] *n* doel *nt*; ~ **at** richten op, mikken op; beogen, nastreven

air [ɛə] *n* lucht *c*; *v* luchten

air-conditioning ['ɛəkən,diʃəniŋ] *n* luchtverversing *c*; **air-conditioned** *adj* air conditioned

aircraft ['ɛəkrɑ:ft] *n* (pl ~) vliegtuig *nt*; toestel *nt*

airfield ['ɛəfi:ld] *n* vliegveld *nt*

air-filter ['ɛə,filtə] *n* luchtfilter *nt*

airline ['ɛəlain] *n* luchtvaartmaatschappij *c*

airmail ['ɛəmeil] *n* luchtpost *c*

airplane ['ɛəplein] *nAm* vliegtuig *nt*

airport ['ɛəpɔ:t] *n* luchthaven *c*

air-sickness ['ɛə,siknəs] *n* luchtziekte *c*

airtight ['ɛətait] *adj* luchtdicht

airy ['ɛəri] *adj* luchtig

aisle [ail] *n* zijbeuk *c*; gangpad *nt*

alarm [ə'lɑ:m] *n* alarm *nt*; *v* alarmeren

alarm-clock [ə'lɑ:mklɔk] *n* wekker *c*

album ['ælbəm] *n* album *nt*

alcohol ['ælkəhɔl] *n* alcohol *c*

alcoholic [,ælkə'hɔlik] *adj* alcoholisch

ale [eil] *n* bier *nt*

algebra ['ældʒibrə] *n* algebra *c*

Algeria [æl'dʒiəriə] Algerije

Algerian [æl'dʒiəriən] *adj* Algerijns; *n* Algerijn *c*

alien ['eiliən] *n* buitenlander *c*; vreemdeling *c*; *adj* buitenlands

alike [ə'laik] *adj* eender, gelijk

alimony ['æliməni] *n* alimentatie *c*

alive [ə'laiv] *adj* in leven, levend

all [ɔ:l] *adj* al; ~ **in** alles inbegrepen; ~ **right!** goed!; **at** ~ helemaal

allergic [ə'lədʒik] *adj* allergisch

allergy ['ælədʒi] *n* allergie *c*

alley ['æli] *n* steeg *c*

alliance [ə'laiəns] *n* bondgenootschap *nt*

allot [ə'lɔt] *v* *toewijzen

allow [ə'lau] *v* veroorloven, *toestaan; ~ **to** *laten; *be allowed *mogen; *be allowed to *mogen

allowance [ə'lauəns] *n* toelage *c*

all-round [ˌɔ:l'raund] *adj* veelzijdig

almanac ['ɔ:lmənæk] *n* almanak *c*

almond ['ɑ:mənd] *n* amandel *c*

almost ['ɔ:lmoust] *adv* bijna; haast

alone [ə'loun] *adv* alleen

along [ə'lɔŋ] *prep* langs

aloud [ə'laud] *adv* hardop

alphabet ['ælfəbet] *n* alfabet *nt*

already [ɔ:l'redi] *adv* reeds, al

also ['ɔ:lsou] *adv* ook; tevens, eveneens

altar ['ɔ:ltə] *n* altaar *nt*

alter ['ɔ:ltə] *v* wijzigen, veranderen

alteration [ˌɔ:ltə'reiʃən] *n* wijziging *c*, verandering *c*

alternate [ɔ:l'tə:nət] *adj* afwisselend

alternative [ɔ:l'tə:nətiv] *n* alternatief *nt*

although [ɔ:l'ðou] *conj* ofschoon, hoewel

altitude ['æltitju:d] *n* hoogte *c*

alto ['æltou] *n* (pl ~s) alt *c*

altogether [ˌɔ:ltə'geðə] *adv* helemaal;

in totaal

always ['ɔ:lweiz] *adv* altijd

am [æm] *v* (pr be)

amaze [ə'meiz] *v* verwonderen, verbazen

amazement [ə'meizmənt] *n* verbazing *c*

ambassador [æm'bæsədə] *n* ambassadeur *c*

amber ['æmbə] *n* barnsteen *nt*

ambiguous [æm'bigjuəs] *adj* dubbelzinnig; onduidelijk

ambitious [æm'biʃəs] *adj* ambitieus; eerzuchtig

ambulance ['æmbjuləns] *n* ziekenauto *c*, ambulance *c*

ambush ['æmbuʃ] *n* hinderlaag *c*

America [ə'merikə] Amerika

American [ə'merikən] *adj* Amerikaans; *n* Amerikaan *c*

amethyst ['æmiθist] *n* amethist *c*

amid [ə'mid] *prep* onder; tussen, midden in, te midden van

ammonia [ə'mouniə] *n* ammonia *c*

amnesty ['æmnisti] *n* amnestie *c*

among [ə'mʌŋ] *prep* te midden van; tussen, onder; ~ **other things** onder andere

amount [ə'maunt] *n* hoeveelheid *c*; som *c*, bedrag *nt*; ~ **to** *bedragen

amuse [ə'mju:z] *v* amuseren, vermaken

amusement [ə'mju:zmənt] *n* amusement *nt*, vermaak *nt*

amusing [ə'mju:ziŋ] *adj* amusant

anaemia [ə'ni:miə] *n* bloedarmoede *c*

anaesthesia [ˌænis'θi:ziə] *n* verdoving *c*

anaesthetic [ˌænis'θetik] *n* pijnstillend middel

analyse ['ænəlaiz] *v* ontleden, analyseren

analysis [ə'næləsis] *n* (pl -ses) analyse *c*

analyst ['ænəlist] *n* analist *c*; analyticus *c*

anarchy ['ænəki] *n* anarchie *c*

anatomy [ə'nætəmi] *n* anatomie *c*

ancestor ['ænsestə] *n* voorvader *c*

anchor ['æŋkə] *n* anker *nt*

anchovy ['æntʃəvi] *n* ansjovis *c*

ancient ['einʃənt] *adj* oud; ouderwets, verouderd; oeroud

and [ænd, ənd] *conj* en

angel ['eindʒəl] *n* engel *c*

anger ['æŋgə] *n* toorn *c*, boosheid *c*; woede *c*

angle ['æŋgəl] *v* hengelen; *n* hoek *c*

angry ['æŋgri] *adj* kwaad

animal ['æniməl] *n* dier *nt*

ankle ['æŋkəl] *n* enkel *c*

annex[1] ['æneks] *n* bijgebouw *nt*; bijlage *c*

annex[2] [ə'neks] *v* annexeren

anniversary [,æni'və:səri] *n* verjaardag *c*

announce [ə'nauns] *v* bekendmaken, aankondigen

announcement [ə'naunsmənt] *n* aankondiging *c*, bekendmaking *c*

annoy [ə'nɔi] *v* irriteren, ergeren

annoyance [ə'nɔiəns] *n* ergernis *c*

annoying [ə'nɔiiŋ] *adj* vervelend, hinderlijk

annual ['ænjuəl] *adj* jaarlijks; *n* jaarboek *nt*

per annum [pər 'ænəm] jaarlijks

anonymous [ə'nɔniməs] *adj* anoniem

another [ə'nʌðə] *adj* nog een; een ander

answer ['ɑ:nsə] *v* antwoorden; beantwoorden; *n* antwoord *nt*

ant [ænt] *n* mier *c*

anthology [æn'θɔlədʒi] *n* bloemlezing *c*

antibiotic [,æntibai'ɔtik] *n* antibioticum *nt*

anticipate [æn'tisipeit] *v* verwachten,
*voorzien; *voorkomen

antifreeze ['æntifri:z] *n* antivries *c*

antipathy [æn'tipəθi] *n* afkeer *c*

antique [æn'ti:k] *adj* antiek; *n* antiquiteit *c*; ~ **dealer** antiquair *c*

antiquity [æn'tikwəti] *n* Oudheid *c*; **antiquities** *pl* oudheden *pl*

antiseptic [,ænti'septik] *n* antiseptisch middel

antlers ['æntləz] *pl* gewei *nt*

anxiety [æŋ'zaiəti] *n* bezorgdheid *c*

anxious ['æŋkʃəs] *adj* verlangend; bezorgd

any ['eni] *adj* enig

anybody ['enibɔdi] *pron* wie dan ook

anyhow ['enihau] *adv* hoe dan ook

anyone ['eniwʌn] *pron* iedereen

anything ['eniθiŋ] *pron* wat dan ook

anyway ['eniwei] *adv* in elk geval

anywhere ['eniwɛə] *adv* waar dan ook; overal

apart [ə'pɑ:t] *adv* apart, afzonderlijk; ~ **from** afgezien van

apartment [ə'pɑ:tmənt] *nAm* appartement *nt*, flat *c*; etage *c*; ~ **house** *Am* flatgebouw *nt*

aperitif [ə'perətiv] *n* aperitief *nt/c*

apologize [ə'pɔlədʒaiz] *v* zich verontschuldigen

apology [ə'pɔlədʒi] *n* excuus *nt*, verontschuldiging *c*

apparatus [,æpə'reitəs] *n* apparaat *nt*, toestel *nt*

apparent [ə'pærənt] *adj* schijnbaar; duidelijk

apparently [ə'pærəntli] *adv* blijkbaar; klaarblijkelijk

apparition [,æpə'riʃən] *n* verschijning *c*

appeal [ə'pi:l] *n* beroep *nt*

appear [ə'piə] *v* *lijken, *schijnen; *blijken; *verschijnen; *optreden

appearance [ə'piərəns] *n* voorkomen *nt*; aanblik *c*; optreden *nt*

appendicitis [ə‚pendi'saitis] *n* blinde-darmontsteking *c*

appendix [ə'pendiks] *n* (pl -dices, -dixes) blindedarm *c*

appetite ['æpətait] *n* trek *c*, eetlust *c*

appetizer ['æpətaizə] *n* borrelhapje *nt*

appetizing ['æpətaizin] *adj* smakelijk

applause [ə'plɔ:z] *n* applaus *nt*

apple ['æpəl] *n* appel *c*

appliance [ə'plaiəns] *n* toestel *nt*, apparaat *nt*

application [‚æpli'keiʃən] *n* toepassing *c*; aanvraag *c*; sollicitatie *c*

apply [ə'plai] *v* toepassen; gebruiken; solliciteren; *gelden

appoint [ə'pɔint] *v* aanstellen, benoemen

appointment [ə'pɔintmənt] *n* afspraak *c*; benoeming *c*

appreciate [ə'pri:ʃieit] *v* schatten; waarderen, op prijs stellen

appreciation [ə‚pri:ʃi'eiʃən] *n* schatting *c*; waardering *c*

approach [ə'proutʃ] *v* naderen; *n* aanpak *c*; toegang *c*

appropriate [ə'proupriət] *adj* juist, geschikt, passend

approval [ə'pru:vəl] *n* goedkeuring *c*; instemming *c*; **on** ~ op zicht

approve [ə'pru:v] *v* goedkeuren; ~ **of** instemmen met

approximate [ə'prɔksimət] *adj* bij benadering

approximately [ə'prɔksimətli] *adv* circa, ongeveer

apricot ['eiprikɔt] *n* abrikoos *c*

April ['eiprəl] april

apron ['eiprən] *n* schort *c*

Arab ['ærəb] *adj* Arabisch; *n* Arabier *c*

arbitrary ['ɑ:bitrəri] *adj* willekeurig

arcade [ɑ:'keid] *n* zuilengang *c*, galerij *c*

arch [ɑ:tʃ] *n* boog *c*; gewelf *nt*

archaeologist [‚ɑ:ki'ɔlədʒist] *n* archeoloog *c*

archaeology [‚ɑ:ki'ɔlədʒi] *n* oudheidkunde *c*, archeologie *c*

archbishop [‚ɑ:tʃ'biʃəp] *n* aartsbisschop *c*

arched [ɑ:tʃt] *adj* boogvormig

architect ['ɑ:kitekt] *n* architect *c*

architecture ['ɑ:kitektʃə] *n* bouwkunde *c*, architectuur *c*

archives ['ɑ:kaivz] *pl* archief *nt*

are [ɑ:] *v* (pr be)

area ['ɛəriə] *n* streek *c*; gebied *nt*; oppervlakte *c*; ~ **code** netnummer *nt*

Argentina [‚ɑ:dʒən'ti:nə] Argentinië

Argentinian [‚ɑ:dʒən'tiniən] *adj* Argentijns; *n* Argentijn *c*

argue ['ɑ:gju:] *v* argumenteren, debatteren, discussiëren; redetwisten

argument ['ɑ:gjumənt] *n* argument *nt*; discussie *c*; woordenwisseling *c*

arid ['ærid] *adj* dor

***arise** [ə'raiz] *v* *oprijzen, *ontstaan

arithmetic [ə'riθmətik] *n* rekenkunde *c*

arm [ɑ:m] *n* arm *c*; wapen *nt*; leuning *c*; *v* bewapenen

armchair ['ɑ:mtʃɛə] *n* fauteuil *c*, leunstoel *c*

armed [ɑ:md] *adj* gewapend; ~ **forces** strijdkrachten *pl*

armour ['ɑ:mə] *n* harnas *nt*

army ['ɑ:mi] *n* leger *nt*

aroma [ə'roumə] *n* aroma *nt*

around [ə'raund] *prep* om, rond; *adv* rondom

arrange [ə'reindʒ] *v* rangschikken, ordenen; regelen

arrangement [ə'reindʒmənt] *n* regeling *c*

arrest [ə'rest] *v* arresteren; *n* aanhouding *c*, arrestatie *c*

arrival [ə'raivəl] *n* aankomst *c*; komst *c*

arrive [ə'raiv] *v* *aankomen

arrow ['ærou] *n* pijl *c*

art [ɑ:t] *n* kunst *c*; vaardigheid *c*; ~
collection kunstverzameling *c*; ~
exhibition kunsttentoonstelling *c*;
~ **gallery** kunstgalerij *c*; ~ **history**
kunstgeschiedenis *c*; **arts and
crafts** kunstnijverheid *c*; ~ **school**
kunstacademie *c*

artery ['ɑ:təri] *n* slagader *c*

artichoke ['ɑ:titʃouk] *n* artisjok *c*

article ['ɑ:tikəl] *n* artikel *nt*; lidwoord
nt

artifice ['ɑ:tifis] *n* list *c*

artificial [,ɑ:ti'fiʃəl] *adj* kunstmatig

artist ['ɑ:tist] *n* kunstenaar *c*; kunstenares *c*

artistic [ɑ:'tistik] *adj* artistiek, kunstzinnig

as [æz] *conj* als, zoals; even; aangeze-
zien, omdat; ~ **from** vanaf; met ingang van; ~ **if** alsof

asbestos [æz'bestɔs] *n* asbest *nt*

ascend [ə'send] *v* omhoog *gaan; *opstijgen; *beklimmen

ascent [ə'sent] *n* stijging *c*; beklimming *c*

ascertain [,æsə'tein] *v* constateren;
zich vergewissen van, zich vergewissen van

ash [æʃ] *n* as *c*

ashamed [ə'ʃeimd] *adj* beschaamd;
*be ~ zich schamen

ashore [ə'ʃɔ:] *adv* aan land

ashtray ['æʃtrei] *n* asbak *c*

Asia ['eiʃə] Azië

Asian ['eiʃən] *adj* Aziatisch; *n* Aziaat
c

aside [ə'said] *adv* opzij, terzijde

ask [ɑ:sk] *v* *vragen; *verzoeken; uitnodigen

asleep [ə'sli:p] *adj* in slaap

asparagus [ə'spærəgəs] *n* asperge *c*

aspect ['æspekt] *n* aspect *nt*

asphalt ['æsfælt] *n* asfalt *nt*

aspire [ə'spaiə] *v* streven

aspirin ['æspərin] *n* aspirine *c*

ass [æs] *n* ezel *c*

assassination [ə,sæsi'neiʃən] *n* moord
c

assault [ə'sɔ:lt] *v* *aanvallen; aanranden

assemble [ə'sembəl] *v* *bijeenbrengen;
in elkaar zetten, monteren

assembly [ə'sembli] *n* vergadering *c*,
bijeenkomst *c*

assignment [ə'sainmənt] *n* opdracht *c*

assign to [ə'sain] *opdragen aan;
*toeschrijven aan

assist [ə'sist] *v* *bijstaan, *helpen; ~
at bijwonen

assistance [ə'sistəns] *n* hulp *c*; steun
c, bijstand *c*

assistant [ə'sistənt] *n* assistent *c*

associate [ə'souʃiət] *n* partner *c*, vennoot *c*; bondgenoot *c*; lid *nt*; *v* associëren; ~ **with** *omgaan met

association [ə,sousi'eiʃən] *n* genootschap *nt*, vereniging *c*

assort [ə'sɔ:t] *v* sorteren

assortment [ə'sɔ:tmənt] *n* assortiment
nt, sortering *c*

assume [ə'sju:m] *v* *aannemen, veronderstellen

assure [ə'ʃuə] *v* verzekeren

asthma ['æsmə] *n* astma *nt*

astonish [ə'stɔniʃ] *v* verbazen

astonishing [ə'stɔniʃin] *adj* verbazend

astonishment [ə'stɔniʃmənt] *n* verbazing *c*

astronomy [ə'strɔnəmi] *n* sterrenkunde
c

asylum [ə'sailəm] *n* asiel *nt*; gesticht
nt, tehuis *nt*

at [æt] *prep* in, bij, op; naar

ate [et] *v* (p eat)

atheist ['eiθiist] *n* atheïst *c*

athlete ['æθli:t] *n* atleet *c*

athletics [æθ'letiks] *pl* atletiek *c*

Atlantic [ət'læntik] Atlantische Oceaan

atmosphere ['ætməsfiə] *n* atmosfeer *c*; sfeer *c*, stemming *c*

atom ['ætəm] *n* atoom *nt*

atomic [ə'tɔmik] *adj* atomisch; atoom-

atomizer ['ætəmaizə] *n* sproeier *c*; spuitbus *c*, verstuiver *c*

attach [ə'tætʃ] *v* hechten, vastmaken; aanhechten; bijvoegen; **attached to** gehecht aan

attack [ə'tæk] *v* *aanvallen; *n* aanval *c*

attain [ə'tein] *v* bereiken

attainable [ə'teinəbəl] *adj* haalbaar; bereikbaar

attempt [ə'tempt] *v* proberen, trachten; beproeven; *n* poging *c*

attend [ə'tend] *v* bijwonen; ~ **on** bedienen; ~ **to** passen op, zich *bezighouden met; letten op, aandacht besteden aan

attendance [ə'tendəns] *n* opkomst *c*

attendant [ə'tendənt] *n* oppasser *c*

attention [ə'tenʃən] *n* aandacht *c*; *pay ~ opletten

attentive [ə'tentiv] *adj* oplettend

attic ['ætik] *n* zolder *c*

attitude ['ætitjuːd] *n* houding *c*

attorney [ə'təːni] *n* advocaat *c*

attract [ə'trækt] *v* *aantrekken

attraction [ə'trækʃən] *n* attractie *c*; aantrekking *c*, bekoring *c*

attractive [ə'træktiv] *adj* aantrekkelijk

auburn ['ɔːbən] *adj* kastanjebruin

auction ['ɔːkʃən] *n* veiling *c*

audible ['ɔːdibəl] *adj* hoorbaar

audience ['ɔːdiəns] *n* publiek *nt*

auditor ['ɔːditə] *n* toehoorder *c*

auditorium [ˌɔːdi'tɔːriəm] *n* aula *c*

August ['ɔːgəst] augustus

aunt [ɑːnt] *n* tante *c*

Australia [ɔ'streiliə] Australië

Australian [ɔ'streiliən] *adj* Australisch; *n* Australiër *c*

Austria ['ɔstriə] Oostenrijk

Austrian ['ɔstriən] *adj* Oostenrijks; *n* Oostenrijker *c*

authentic [ɔː'θentik] *adj* authentiek; echt

author ['ɔːθə] *n* auteur *c*, schrijver *c*

authoritarian [ɔːˌθɔri'teəriən] *adj* autoritair

authority [ɔː'θɔrəti] *n* gezag *nt*; macht *c*; **authorities** *pl* autoriteiten *pl*, overheid *c*

authorization [ˌɔːθərai'zeiʃən] *n* machtiging *c*; toestemming *c*

automatic [ˌɔːtə'mætik] *adj* automatisch; ~ **teller** geldautomaat

automation [ˌɔːtə'meiʃən] *n* automatisering *c*

automobile ['ɔːtəməbiːl] *n* auto *c*; ~ **club** automobielclub *c*

autonomous [ɔː'tɔnəməs] *adj* autonoom

autopsy ['ɔːtɔpsi] *n* autopsie *c*

autumn ['ɔːtəm] *n* najaar *nt*, herfst *c*

available [ə'veiləbəl] *adj* verkrijgbaar, voorhanden, beschikbaar

avalanche ['ævəlɑːnʃ] *n* lawine *c*

avaricious [ˌævə'riʃəs] *adj* gierig

avenue ['ævənjuː] *n* laan *c*

average ['ævəridʒ] *adj* gemiddeld; *n* gemiddelde *nt*; **on the ~** gemiddeld

averse [ə'vəːs] *adj* afkerig

aversion [ə'vəːʃən] *n* tegenzin *c*

avert [ə'vəːt] *v* afwenden

avoid [ə'vɔid] *v* *vermijden; *ontwijken

await [ə'weit] *v* wachten op, afwachten

awake [ə'weik] *adj* wakker

awake [ə'weik] *v* wekken

award [ə'wɔːd] *n* prijs *c*; *v* toekennen

aware [ə'weə] *adj* bewust

away [ə'wei] *adv* weg; *go ~ *weggaan

awful ['ɔːfəl] *adj* afschuwelijk, ver-

schrikkelijk
awkward ['ɔ:kwəd] *adj* pijnlijk; onhandig
awning ['ɔ:niŋ] *n* zonnescherm *nt*
axe [æks] *n* bijl *c*
axle ['æksəl] *n* as *c*

B

baby ['beibi] *n* baby *c*; ~ **carriage** *Am* kinderwagen *c*
babysitter ['beibi,sitə] *n* babysitter *c*
bachelor ['bætʃələ] *n* vrijgezel *c*
back [bæk] *n* rug *c*; *adv* terug; *go* ~ *teruggaan
backache ['bækeik] *n* rugpijn *c*
backbone ['bækboun] *n* ruggegraat *c*
background ['bækgraund] *n* achtergrond *c*; vorming *c*
backwards ['bækwədz] *adv* achteruit
bacon ['beikən] *n* spek *nt*
bacterium [bæk'ti:riəm] *n* (pl -ria) bacterie *c*
bad [bæd] *adj* slecht; ernstig, erg; stout
bag [bæg] *n* zak *c*; tas *c*, handtas *c*; koffer *c*
baggage ['bægidʒ] *n* bagage *c*; ~ **deposit office** *Am* bagagedepot *nt*; **hand** ~ *Am* handbagage *c*
bail [beil] *n* borgsom *c*
bailiff ['beilif] *n* deurwaarder *c*
bait [beit] *n* aas *nt*
bake [beik] *v* *bakken
baker ['beikə] *n* bakker *c*
bakery ['beikəri] *n* bakkerij *c*
balance ['bæləns] *n* evenwicht *nt*; balans *c*; saldo *nt*
balcony ['bælkəni] *n* balkon *nt*
bald [bɔ:ld] *adj* kaal
ball [bɔ:l] *n* bal *c*; bal *nt*
ballet ['bælei] *n* ballet *nt*

balloon [bə'lu:n] *n* ballon *c*
ballpoint-pen ['bɔ:lpointpen] *n* ballpoint *c*
ballroom ['bɔ:lru:m] *n* danszaal *c*
bamboo [bæm'bu:] *n* (pl ~s) bamboe *nt*
banana [bə'nɑ:nə] *n* banaan *c*
band [bænd] *n* orkest *nt*; band *c*
bandage ['bændidʒ] *n* verband *nt*
bandit ['bændit] *n* bandiet *c*
bangle ['bæŋgəl] *n* armband *c*
banisters ['bænistəz] *pl* trapleuning *c*
bank [bæŋk] *n* oever *c*; bank *c*; *v* deponeren; ~ **account** bankrekening *c*
banknote ['bæŋknout] *n* bankbiljet *nt*
bank-rate ['bæŋkreit] *n* disconto *nt*
bankrupt ['bæŋkrʌpt] *adj* failliet, bankroet
banner ['bænə] *n* vaandel *nt*
banquet ['bæŋkwit] *n* banket *nt*
banqueting-hall ['bæŋkwitiŋhɔ:l] *n* banketzaal *c*
baptism ['bæptizəm] *n* doopsel *nt*, doop *c*
baptize [bæp'taiz] *v* dopen
bar [bɑ:] *n* bar *c*; stang *c*; tralie *c*
barber ['bɑ:bə] *n* kapper *c*
bare [bɛə] *adj* naakt, bloot; kaal
barely ['bɛəli] *adv* nauwelijks
bargain ['bɑ:gin] *n* koopje *nt*; *v* *afdingen
baritone ['bæritoun] *n* bariton *c*
bark [bɑ:k] *n* bast *c*; *v* blaffen
barley ['bɑ:li] *n* gerst *c*
barmaid ['bɑ:meid] *n* barjuffrouw *c*
barman ['bɑ:mən] *n* (pl -men) barman *c*
barn [bɑ:n] *n* schuur *c*
barometer [bə'rɔmitə] *n* barometer *c*
baroque [bə'rɔk] *adj* barok
barracks ['bærəks] *pl* kazerne *c*
barrel ['bærəl] *n* ton *c*, vat *nt*
barrier ['bæriə] *n* barrière *c*; slagboom

c

barrister ['bæristə] n advocaat c

bartender ['ba:,tendə] n barman c

base [beis] n basis c; grondslag c; v baseren

baseball ['beisbɔ:l] n honkbal nt

basement ['beismənt] n souterrain c

basic ['beisik] adj fundamenteel

basilica [bə'zilikə] n basiliek c

basin ['beisən] n kom c, bekken nt

basis ['beisis] n (pl bases) grondslag c, basis c

basket ['ba:skit] n mand c

bass[1] [beis] n bas c

bass[2] [bæs] n (pl ~) baars c

bastard ['ba:stəd] n bastaard c; schoft c

batch [bætʃ] n partij c

bath [ba:θ] n bad nt; ~ **salts** badzout nt; ~ **towel** badhanddoek c

bathe [beið] v baden, een bad *nemen

bathing-cap ['beiðiŋkæp] n badmuts c

bathing-suit ['beiðiŋsu:t] n badpak nt; zwembroek c

bathing-trunks ['beiðiŋtrʌŋks] n zwembroek c

bathrobe ['ba:θroub] n badjas c

bathroom ['ba:θru:m] n badkamer c; toilet nt

batter ['bætə] n beslag nt

battery ['bætəri] n batterij c; accu c

battle ['bætəl] n slag c; strijd c, gevecht nt; v *vechten

bay [bei] n baai c; v blaffen

***be** [bi:] v *zijn

beach [bi:tʃ] n strand nt; **nudist** ~ naaktstrand nt

bead [bi:d] n kraal c; **beads** pl kralensnoer nt; rozenkrans c

beak [bi:k] n snavel c; bek c

beam [bi:m] n straal c; balk c

bean [bi:n] n boon c

bear [beə] n beer c

***bear** [beə] v *dragen; dulden; *ver-

dragen

beard [biəd] n baard c

bearer ['beərə] n drager c

beast [bi:st] n beest nt; ~ **of prey** roofdier nt

***beat** [bi:t] v *slaan; *verslaan

beautiful ['bju:tifəl] adj mooi

beauty ['bju:ti] n schoonheid c; ~ **parlour** schoonheidssalon c; ~ **salon** schoonheidssalon c; ~ **treatment** schoonheidsbehandeling c

beaver ['bi:və] n bever c

because [bi'kɔz] conj omdat; aangezien; ~ **of** vanwege, wegens

***become** [bi'kʌm] v *worden; goed *staan

bed [bed] n bed nt; ~ **and board** vol pension, kost en inwoning; ~ **and breakfast** logies en ontbijt

bedding ['bediŋ] n beddegoed nt

bedroom ['bedru:m] n slaapkamer c

bee [bi:] n bij c

beech [bi:tʃ] n beuk c

beef [bi:f] n rundvlees nt

beehive ['bi:haiv] n bijenkorf c

been [bi:n] v (pp be)

beer [biə] n bier nt; pils nt

beet [bi:t] n biet c

beetle ['bi:təl] n kever c

beetroot ['bi:tru:t] n beetwortel c

before [bi'fɔ:] prep voor; conj voordat; adv van tevoren; eerder, tevoren

beg [beg] v bedelen; smeken; *vragen

beggar ['begə] n bedelaar c

***begin** [bi'gin] v *beginnen; *aanvangen

beginner [bi'ginə] n beginneling c

beginning [bi'giniŋ] n begin nt; aanvang c

on behalf of [ɔn bi'ha:f ɔv] namens, in naam van; ten behoeve van

behave [bi'heiv] v zich *gedragen

behaviour [bi'heivjə] n gedrag nt

behind [bi'haind] *prep* achter; *adv* achteraan

beige [beiʒ] *adj* beige

being ['bi:iŋ] *n* wezen *nt*

Belgian ['beldʒən] *adj* Belgisch; *n* Belg *c*

Belgium ['beldʒəm] België

belief [bi'li:f] *n* geloof *nt*

believe [bi'li:v] *v* geloven

bell [bel] *n* klok *c*; bel *c*

bellboy ['belbɔi] *n* piccolo *c*

belly ['beli] *n* buik *c*

belong [bi'lɔŋ] *v* toebehoren

belongings [bi'lɔŋiŋz] *pl* bezittingen *pl*

beloved [bi'lʌvd] *adj* bemind

below [bi'lou] *prep* onder; beneden; *adv* onderaan, beneden

belt [belt] *n* riem *c*; **garter ~** *Am* jarretelgordel *c*

bench [bentʃ] *n* bank *c*

bend [bend] *n* bocht *c*; kromming *c*

*bend [bend] *v* *buigen; **~ down** zich bukken

beneath [bi'ni:θ] *prep* onder; *adv* beneden

benefit ['benifit] *n* winst *c*, baat *c*; voordeel *nt*; *v* profiteren

bent [bent] *adj* (pp bend) krom

beret ['berei] *n* baret *c*

berry ['beri] *n* bes *c*

berth [bə:θ] *n* couchette *c*; kooi *c*

beside [bi'said] *prep* naast

besides [bi'saidz] *adv* bovendien; trouwens; *prep* behalve

best [best] *adj* best

bet [bet] *n* weddenschap *c*; inzet *c*

*bet [bet] *v* wedden

betray [bi'trei] *v* *verraden

better ['betə] *adj* beter

between [bi'twi:n] *prep* tussen

beverage ['bevəridʒ] *n* drank *c*

beware [bi'weə] *v* zich hoeden, oppassen

bewitch [bi'witʃ] *v* beheksen, betoveren

beyond [bi'jɔnd] *prep* verder dan; voorbij; behalve; *adv* verder

bible ['baibəl] *n* bijbel *c*

bicycle ['baisikəl] *n* fiets *c*; rijwiel *nt*

big [big] *adj* groot; omvangrijk; dik; gewichtig

bile [bail] *n* gal *c*

bilingual [bai'liŋgwəl] *adj* tweetalig

bill [bil] *n* rekening *c*; nota *c*; *v* factureren

billiards ['biljədz] *pl* biljart *nt*

*bind [baind] *v* *binden

binoculars [bi'nɔkjələz] *pl* verrekijker *c*; toneelkijker *c*

biology [bai'ɔlədʒi] *n* biologie *c*

birch [bə:tʃ] *n* berk *c*

bird [bə:d] *n* vogel *c*

Biro ['bairou] *n* ballpoint *c*

birth [bə:θ] *n* geboorte *c*

birthday ['bə:θdei] *n* verjaardag *c*

biscuit ['biskit] *n* koekje *nt*

bishop ['biʃəp] *n* bisschop *c*

bit [bit] *n* stukje *nt*; beetje *nt*

bitch [bitʃ] *n* teef *c*

bite [bait] *n* hap *c*; beet *c*; steek *c*

*bite [bait] *v* *bijten

bitter ['bitə] *adj* bitter

black [blæk] *adj* zwart; **~ market** zwarte markt

blackberry ['blækbəri] *n* braam *c*

blackbird ['blækbə:d] *n* merel *c*

blackboard ['blækbɔ:d] *n* schoolbord *nt*

black-currant [,blæk'kʌrənt] *n* zwarte bes

blackmail ['blækmeil] *n* chantage *c*; *v* chanteren

blacksmith ['blæksmiθ] *n* smid *c*

bladder ['blædə] *n* blaas *c*

blade [bleid] *n* lemmet *nt*; **~ of grass** grasspriet *c*

blame [bleim] *n* schuld *c*; verwijt *nt*; *v* de schuld *geven aan, beschuldigen

blank [blæŋk] *adj* blanco

blanket ['blæŋkit] *n* deken *c*

blast [blɑːst] *n* explosie *c*

blazer ['bleizə] *n* sportjasje *nt*, blazer *c*

bleach [bliːtʃ] *v* bleken

bleak [bliːk] *adj* guur

*bleed [bliːd] *v* bloeden; **uitzuigen

bless [bles] *v* zegenen

blessing ['blesiŋ] *n* zegen *c*

blind [blaind] *n* rolgordijn *nt*, jaloezie *c*; *adj* blind; *v* verblinden

blister ['blistə] *n* blaar *c*, blaas *c*

blizzard ['blizəd] *n* sneeuwstorm *c*

block [blɔk] *v* versperren, blokkeren; *n* blok *nt*; ~ **of flats** flatgebouw *nt*

blonde [blɔnd] *n* blondine *c*

blood [blʌd] *n* bloed *nt*; ~ **pressure** bloeddruk *c*

blood-poisoning ['blʌd,pɔizəniŋ] *n* bloedvergiftiging *c*

blood-vessel ['blʌd,vesəl] *n* bloedvat *nt*

blot [blɔt] *n* vlek *c*; smet *c*; **blotting paper** vloeipapier *nt*

blouse [blauz] *n* blouse *c*

blow [blou] *n* klap *c*, slag *c*; windvlaag *c*

*blow [blou] *v* *blazen; **waaien

blow-out ['blouaut] *n* bandepech *c*

blue [bluː] *adj* blauw; neerslachtig

blunt [blʌnt] *adj* bot; stomp

blush [blʌʃ] *v* blozen

board [bɔːd] *n* plank *c*; bord *nt*; pension *nt*; bestuur *nt*; ~ **and lodging** vol pension, kost en inwoning

boarder ['bɔːdə] *n* kostganger *c*

boarding-house ['bɔːdiŋhaus] *n* pension *nt*

boarding-school ['bɔːdiŋskuːl] *n* internaat *nt*

boast [boust] *v* opscheppen

boat [bout] *n* schip *nt*, boot *c*

body ['bɔdi] *n* lichaam *nt*; lijf *nt*

bodyguard ['bɔdigɑːd] *n* lijfwacht *c*

bog [bɔg] *n* moeras *nt*

boil [bɔil] *v* koken; *n* steenpuist *c*

bold [bould] *adj* stoutmoedig; vrijpostig, brutaal

Bolivia [bə'liviə] Bolivië

Bolivian [bə'liviən] *adj* Boliviaans; *n* Boliviaan *c*

bolt [boult] *n* grendel *c*; bout *c*

bomb [bɔm] *n* bom *c*; *v* bombarderen

bond [bɔnd] *n* obligatie *c*

bone [boun] *n* been *nt*, bot *nt*; graat *c*; *v* uitbenen

bonnet ['bɔnit] *n* motorkap *c*

book [buk] *n* boek *nt*; *v* reserveren, boeken; **inschrijven

booking ['bukiŋ] *n* reservering *c*, bespreking *c*

bookseller ['buk,selə] *n* boekhandelaar *c*

bookstand ['bukstænd] *n* boekenstalletje *nt*

bookstore ['bukstɔː] *n* boekwinkel *c*, boekhandel *c*

boot [buːt] *n* laars *c*; bagageruimte *c*

booth [buːð] *n* kraam *c*; hokje *nt*

border ['bɔːdə] *n* grens *c*; rand *c*

bore[1] [bɔː] *v* vervelen; boren; *n* zeurpiet *c*

bore[2] [bɔː] *v* (p bear)

boring ['bɔːriŋ] *adj* vervelend, saai

born [bɔːn] *adj* geboren

borrow ['bɔrou] *v* lenen; ontlenen

bosom ['buzəm] *n* borst *c*

boss [bɔs] *n* chef *c*, baas *c*

botany ['bɔtəni] *n* plantkunde *c*

both [bouθ] *adj* beide; **both ... and** zowel ... als

bother ['bɔðə] *v* vervelen, hinderen; moeite *doen; *n* last *c*

bottle ['bɔtəl] *n* fles *c*; ~ **opener** flesopener *c*; **hot-water** ~ warmwaterkruik *c*

bottleneck ['bɔtəlnek] *n* flessehals *c*

bottom ['bɔtəm] n bodem c; achterwerk nt, zitvlak nt; adj onderst

bough [bau] n tak c

bought [bɔ:t] v (p, pp buy)

boulder ['bouldə] n rotsblok nt

bound [baund] n grens c; *be ~ to *moeten; ~ for op weg naar

boundary ['baundəri] n grens c; landsgrens c

bouquet [bu'kei] n boeket nt

bourgeois ['buəʒwa:] adj burgerlijk

boutique [bu'ti:k] n boutique c

bow¹ [bau] v *buigen

bow² [bou] n boog c; ~ tie vlinderdasje nt, strikje nt

bowels [bauəlz] pl darmen, ingewanden pl

bowl [boul] n schaal c

bowling ['boulin] n bowling c, kegelspel nt; ~ alley kegelbaan c

box¹ [bɔks] v boksen; **boxing match** bokswedstrijd c

box² [bɔks] n doos c

box-office ['bɔks,ɔfis] n plaatskaartenbureau nt, kassa c

boy [bɔi] n jongen c; joch nt, knaap c; bediende c; ~ scout padvinder c

bra [bra:] n beha c, bustehouder c

bracelet ['breislit] n armband c

braces ['breisiz] pl bretels pl

brain [brein] n hersenen pl; verstand nt

brain-wave ['breinweiv] n inval c

brake [breik] n rem c; ~ drum remtrommel c; ~ lights remlichten pl

branch [bra:ntʃ] n tak c; filiaal nt

brand [brænd] n merk nt; brandmerk nt

brand-new [,brænd'nju:] adj splinternieuw

brass [bra:s] n messing nt; koper nt, geelkoper nt; ~ band n fanfarekorps nt

brassiere ['bræziə] n bustehouder c, beha c

brassware ['bra:swɛə] n koperwerk nt

brave [breiv] adj moedig, dapper; flink

Brazil [brə'zil] Brazilië

Brazilian [brə'ziljən] adj Braziliaans; n Braziliaan c

breach [bri:tʃ] n bres c

bread [bred] n brood nt; **wholemeal ~** volkorenbrood nt

breadth [bredθ] n breedte c

break [breik] n breuk c; pauze c

***break** [breik] v *breken; ~ down stuk *gaan; ontleden

breakdown ['breikdaun] n panne c, motorpech c

breakfast ['brekfəst] n ontbijt nt

bream [bri:m] n (pl ~) brasem c

breast [brest] n borst c

breaststroke ['breststrouk] n schoolslag c

breath [breθ] n adem c; lucht c

breathe [bri:ð] v ademen

breathing ['bri:ðin] n ademhaling c

breed [bri:d] n ras nt; soort c/nt

***breed** [bri:d] v fokken

breeze [bri:z] n bries c

brew [bru:] v brouwen

brewery ['bru:əri] n brouwerij c

bribe [braib] v *omkopen

bribery ['braibəri] n omkoping c

brick [brik] n steen c, baksteen c

bricklayer ['brik,leiə] n metselaar c

bride [braid] n bruid c

bridegroom ['braidgru:m] n bruidegom c

bridge [bridʒ] n brug c; bridge nt

brief [bri:f] adj kort; beknopt

briefcase ['bri:fkeis] n aktentas c

briefs [bri:fs] pl slip c, onderbroek c

bright [brait] adj helder; blinkend; snugger, pienter

brill [bril] n griet c

brilliant ['briljənt] *adj* schitterend; briljant

brim [brim] *n* rand *c*

*****bring** [briŋ] *v* *brengen; *meebrengen; ~ **back** *terugbrengen; ~ **up** opvoeden, *grootbrengen; ter sprake *brengen

brisk [brisk] *adj* levendig

Britain ['britən] Engeland

British ['britiʃ] *adj* Brits; Engels

Briton ['britən] *n* Brit *c*; Engelsman *c*

broad [brɔːd] *adj* breed; ruim, wijd; globaal

broadcast ['brɔːdkɑːst] *n* uitzending *c*

*****broadcast** ['brɔːdkɑːst] *v* *uitzenden

brochure ['brouʃuə] *n* brochure *c*

broke[1] [brouk] *v* (p break)

broke[2] [brouk] *adj* platzak

broken ['broukən] *adj* (pp break) stuk, kapot

broker ['broukə] *n* makelaar *c*

bronchitis [brɔŋ'kaitis] *n* bronchitis *c*

bronze [brɔnz] *n* brons *nt*; *adj* bronzen

brooch [broutʃ] *n* broche *c*

brook [bruk] *n* beek *c*

broom [bruːm] *n* bezem *c*

brothel ['brɔθəl] *n* bordeel *nt*

brother ['brʌðə] *n* broer *c*; broeder *c*

brother-in-law ['brʌðərinlɔː] *n* (pl brothers-) zwager *c*

brought [brɔːt] *v* (p, pp bring)

brown [braun] *adj* bruin

bruise [bruːz] *n* blauwe plek, kneuzing *c*; *v* kneuzen

brunette [bruː'net] *n* brunette *c*

brush [brʌʃ] *n* borstel *c*; kwast *c*; *v* poetsen, borstelen

brutal ['bruːtəl] *adj* beestachtig

bubble ['bʌbəl] *n* bel *c*

bucket ['bʌkit] *n* emmer *c*

buckle ['bʌkəl] *n* gesp *c*

bud [bʌd] *n* knop *c*

budget ['bʌdʒit] *n* begroting *c*, budget *nt*

buffet ['bufei] *n* buffet *nt*

bug [bʌg] *n* wandluis *c*; kever *c*; *nAm* insekt *nt*

*****build** [bild] *v* bouwen

building ['bildiŋ] *n* gebouw *nt*

bulb [bʌlb] *n* bol *c*; bloembol *c*; **light** ~ gloeilamp *c*

Bulgaria [bʌl'geəriə] Bulgarije

Bulgarian [bʌl'geəriən] *adj* Bulgaars; *n* Bulgaar *c*

bulk [bʌlk] *n* omvang *c*; massa *c*; meerderheid *c*

bulky ['bʌlki] *adj* lijvig, omvangrijk

bull [bul] *n* stier *c*

bullet ['bulit] *n* kogel *c*

bullfight ['bulfait] *n* stierengevecht *nt*

bullring ['bulriŋ] *n* arena *c*

bump [bʌmp] *v* *stoten; botsen; bonzen; *n* stoot *c*, bons *c*

bumper ['bʌmpə] *n* bumper *c*

bumpy ['bʌmpi] *adj* hobbelig

bun [bʌn] *n* broodje *nt*

bunch [bʌntʃ] *n* bos *c*; groep *c*

bundle ['bʌndəl] *n* bundel *c*; *v* *samenbinden, bundelen

bunk [bʌŋk] *n* kooi *c*

buoy [bɔi] *n* boei *c*

burden ['bəːdən] *n* last *c*

bureau ['bjuərou] *n* (pl ~x, ~s) bureau *nt*, schrijftafel *c*; *nAm* commode *c*

bureaucracy [bjuə'rɔkrəsi] *n* bureaucratie *c*

burglar ['bəːglə] *n* inbreker *c*

burgle ['bəːgəl] *v* *inbreken

burial ['beriəl] *n* teraardebestelling *c*, begrafenis *c*

burn [bəːn] *n* brandwond *c*

*****burn** [bəːn] *v* branden; verbranden; aanbranden

*****burst** [bəːst] *v* *barsten; *breken

bury ['beri] *v* *begraven; *bedelven

bus [bʌs] *n* bus *c*

bush [buʃ] *n* struik *c*

business ['biznəs] *n* zaken *pl*, handel *c*; bedrijf *nt*, zaak *c*; werk *nt*; aangelegenheid *c*; ~ **hours** openingstijden *pl*, kantooruren *pl*; ~ **trip** zakenreis *c*; **on** ~ voor zaken

business-like ['biznislaik] *adj* zakelijk

businessman ['biznəsmən] *n* (pl -men) zakenman *c*

bust [bʌst] *n* buste *c*

bustle ['bʌsəl] *n* drukte *c*

busy ['bizi] *adj* bezig; druk

but [bʌt] *conj* maar; doch; *prep* behalve

butcher ['butʃə] *n* slager *c*

butter ['bʌtə] *n* boter *c*

butterfly ['bʌtəflai] *n* vlinder *c*; ~ **stroke** vlinderslag *c*

buttock ['bʌtək] *n* bil *c*

button ['bʌtən] *n* knoop *c*; *v* knopen

buttonhole ['bʌtənhoul] *n* knoopsgat *nt*

*buy [bai] *v* *kopen; aanschaffen

buyer ['baiə] *n* koper *c*

by [bai] *prep* door; met, per; bij

by-pass ['baipɑːs] *n* ringweg *c*; *v* passeren

C

cab [kæb] *n* taxi *c*

cabaret ['kæbərei] *n* cabaret *nt*; nachtclub *c*

cabbage ['kæbidʒ] *n* kool *c*

cab-driver ['kæb,draivə] *n* taxichauffeur *c*

cabin ['kæbin] *n* cabine *c*; hut *c*; kleedhokje *nt*; kajuit *c*

cabinet ['kæbinət] *n* kabinet *nt*

cable ['keibəl] *n* kabel *c*; telegram *nt*; *v* telegraferen

cadre ['kɑːdə] *n* kader *nt*

café ['kæfei] *n* café *nt*

cafeteria [,kæfə'tiəriə] *n* cafetaria *c*

caffeine ['kæfiːn] *n* coffeïne *c*

cage [keidʒ] *n* kooi *c*

cake [keik] *n* cake *c*; gebak *nt*, taart *c*, koek *c*

calamity [kə'læməti] *n* onheil *nt*, ramp *c*

calcium ['kælsiəm] *n* calcium *nt*

calculate ['kælkjuleit] *v* uitrekenen, berekenen

calculation [,kælkju'leiʃən] *n* berekening *c*

calculator ['kælkju'leitə] *n* rekenmachine *c*

calendar ['kæləndə] *n* kalender *c*

calf [kɑːf] *n* (pl calves) kalf *nt*; kuit *c*; ~ **skin** kalfsleer *nt*

call [kɔːl] *v* *roepen; noemen; opbellen; *n* roep *c*; visite *c*, bezoek *nt*; telefoontje *nt*; ***be called** *heten; ~ **names** *uitschelden; ~ **on** *bezoeken; ~ **up** *Am* opbellen

callus ['kæləs] *n* eelt *nt*

calm [kɑːm] *adj* rustig, kalm; ~ **down** kalmeren; bedaren

calorie ['kæləri] *n* calorie *c*

came [keim] *v* (p come)

camel ['kæməl] *n* kameel *c*

cameo ['kæmiou] *n* (pl ~s) camee *c*

camera ['kæmərə] *n* fototoestel *nt*; filmcamera *c*; ~ **shop** fotowinkel *c*

camp [kæmp] *n* kamp *nt*; *v* kamperen

campaign [kæm'pein] *n* campagne *c*

camp-bed [,kæmp'bed] *n* veldbed *nt*, stretcher *c*

camper ['kæmpə] *n* kampeerder *c*

camping ['kæmpiŋ] *n* camping *c*; ~ **site** camping *c*, kampeerterrein *nt*

camshaft ['kæmʃɑːft] *n* nokkenas *c*

can [kæn] *n* blik *nt*; ~ **opener** blikopener *c*

*can [kæn] *v* *kunnen

Canada ['kænədə] Canada

Canadian [kə'neidiən] *adj* Canadees;

n Canadees *c*

canal [kə'næl] *n* kanaal *nt*; gracht *c*, singel *c*

canary [kə'neəri] *n* kanarie *c*

cancel ['kænsəl] *v* annuleren; *afzeggen

cancellation [ˌkænsə'leiʃən] *n* annulering *c*

cancer ['kænsə] *n* kanker *c*

candelabrum [ˌkændə'lɑ:brəm] *n* (pl -bra) kandelaber *c*

candidate ['kændidət] *n* kandidaat *c*, gegadigde *c*

candle ['kændəl] *n* kaars *c*

candy ['kændi] *nAm* snoepje *nt*; snoep *nt*, snoepgoed *nt*; ~ **store** *Am* snoepwinkel *c*

cane [kein] *n* riet *nt*; stok *c*

canister ['kænistə] *n* trommel *c*, bus *c*

canoe [kə'nu:] *n* kano *c*

canteen [kæn'ti:n] *n* kantine *c*

canvas ['kænvəs] *n* tentdoek *nt*

cap [kæp] *n* pet *c*, muts *c*

capable ['keipəbəl] *adj* kundig, bekwaam

capacity [kə'pæsəti] *n* capaciteit *c*; vermogen *nt*; bekwaamheid *c*

cape [keip] *n* cape *c*; kaap *c*

capital ['kæpitəl] *n* hoofdstad *c*; kapitaal *nt*; *adj* belangrijk, hoofd-; ~ **letter** hoofdletter *c*

capitalism ['kæpitəlizəm] *n* kapitalisme *nt*

capitulation [kəˌpitju'leiʃən] *n* capitulatie *c*

capsule ['kæpsju:l] *n* capsule *c*

captain ['kæptin] *n* kapitein *c*; gezagvoerder *c*

capture ['kæptʃə] *v* gevangen *nemen, *vangen; *innemen; *n* vangst *c*; inneming *c*

car [kɑ:] *n* auto *c*; ~ **hire** autoverhuur *c*; ~ **park** parkeerplaats *c*; ~ **rental** *Am* autoverhuur *c*

carafe [kə'ræf] *n* karaf *c*

caramel ['kærəməl] *n* karamel *c*

carat ['kærət] *n* karaat *nt*

caravan ['kærəvæn] *n* caravan *c*; woonwagen *c*

carburettor [ˌkɑ:bju'retə] *n* carburateur *c*

card [kɑ:d] *n* kaart *c*; briefkaart *c*

cardboard ['kɑ:dbɔ:d] *n* karton *nt*; *adj* kartonnen

cardigan ['kɑ:digən] *n* vest *nt*

cardinal ['kɑ:dinəl] *n* kardinaal *c*; *adj* kardinaal, hoofd-

care [keə] *n* verzorging *c*; zorg *c*; ~ **about** zich bekommeren om; ~ **for** *houden van; *take ~ **of** zorgen voor, verzorgen

career [kə'riə] *n* loopbaan *c*, carrière *c*

carefree ['keəfri:] *adj* onbezorgd

careful ['keəfəl] *adj* voorzichtig; zorgvuldig, nauwkeurig

careless ['keələs] *adj* achteloos, slordig

caretaker ['keəˌteikə] *n* concierge *c*

cargo ['kɑ:gou] *n* (pl ~es) lading *c*, vracht *c*

carnival ['kɑ:nivəl] *n* carnaval *nt*

carp [kɑ:p] *n* (pl ~) karper *c*

carpenter ['kɑ:pintə] *n* timmerman *c*

carpet ['kɑ:pit] *n* vloerkleed *nt*, tapijt *nt*

carriage ['kæridʒ] *n* wagon *c*; koets *c*, rijtuig *nt*

carriageway ['kæridʒwei] *n* rijbaan *c*

carrot ['kærət] *n* peen *c*, wortel *c*

carry ['kæri] *v* *dragen; voeren; ~ **on** voortzetten; *doorgaan; ~ **out** uitvoeren

carry-cot ['kærikɔt] *n* reiswieg *c*

cart [kɑ:t] *n* kar *c*, wagen *c*

cartilage ['kɑ:tilidʒ] *n* kraakbeen *nt*

carton ['kɑ:tən] *n* kartonnen doos; slof *c*

cartoon [kɑ:'tu:n] *n* tekenfilm *c*

cartridge ['kɑ:tridʒ] *n* patroon *c*

carve [kɑːv] v *snijden; kerven, *houtsnijden

carving ['kɑːviŋ] n houtsnijwerk nt

case [keis] n geval nt; zaak c; koffer c; etui nt; **attaché ~** aktentas c; **in ~** indien; **in ~ of** in geval van

cash [kæʃ] n contanten pl, contant geld; v verzilveren, incasseren, innen; **~ dispenser** geldautomaat

cashier [kæ'ʃiə] n kassier c; caissière c

cashmere ['kæʃmiə] n kasjmier nt

casino [kə'siːnou] n (pl ~s) casino nt

cask [kɑːsk] n ton c, vat nt

cast [kɑːst] n worp c

***cast** [kɑːst] v gooien, *werpen; **cast iron** gietijzer nt

castle ['kɑːsəl] n slot nt, kasteel nt

casual ['kæʒuəl] adj ongedwongen; terloops, toevallig

casualty ['kæʒuəlti] n slachtoffer nt

cat [kæt] n kat c

catacomb ['kætəkoum] n catacombe c

catalogue ['kætələɡ] n catalogus c

catarrh [kə'tɑː] n catarre c

catastrophe [kə'tæstrəfi] n catastrofe c

***catch** [kætʃ] v *vangen; *grijpen; betrappen; *nemen, halen

category ['kætigəri] n categorie c

cathedral [kə'θiːdrəl] n dom c, kathedraal c

catholic ['kæθəlik] adj katholiek

cattle ['kætəl] pl vee nt

caught [kɔːt] v (p, pp catch)

cauliflower ['kɔliflauə] n bloemkool c

cause [kɔːz] v veroorzaken; aanrichten; n oorzaak c; beweegreden c, aanleiding c; zaak c; **~ to** *doen

causeway ['kɔːzwei] n straatweg c

caution ['kɔːʃən] n voorzichtigheid c; v waarschuwen

cautious ['kɔːʃəs] adj bedachtzaam

cave [keiv] n grot c; spelonk c

cavern ['kævən] n hol nt

caviar ['kæviɑː] n kaviaar c

cavity ['kævəti] n holte c

cease [siːs] v *ophouden

ceiling ['siːliŋ] n plafond nt

celebrate ['selibreit] v vieren

celebration [,seli'breiʃən] n viering c

celebrity [si'lebrəti] n roem c

celery ['seləri] n selderij c

celibacy ['selibəsi] n celibaat nt

cell [sel] n cel c

cellar ['selə] n kelder c

cellophane ['seləfein] n cellofaan nt

cement [si'ment] n cement nt

cemetery ['semitri] n begraafplaats c, kerkhof nt

censorship ['sensəʃip] n censuur c

centigrade ['sentigreid] adj celsius

centimetre ['sentimiːtə] n centimeter c

central ['sentrəl] adj centraal; **~ heating** centrale verwarming; **~ station** centraal station

centralize ['sentrəlaiz] v centraliseren

centre ['sentə] n centrum nt; middelpunt nt

century ['sentʃəri] n eeuw c

ceramics [si'ræmiks] pl aardewerk nt, ceramiek c

ceremony ['serəməni] n ceremonie c

certain ['səːtən] adj zeker; bepaald

certificate [sə'tifikət] n certificaat nt; attest nt, akte c, diploma nt, getuigschrift nt

chain [tʃein] n keten c, ketting c

chair [tʃeə] n stoel c; zetel c

chairman ['tʃeəmən] n (pl -men) voorzitter c

chalet ['ʃælei] n chalet nt

chalk [tʃɔːk] n krijt nt

challenge ['tʃæləndʒ] v uitdagen; n uitdaging c

chamber ['tʃeimbə] n kamer c

chambermaid ['tʃeimbəmeid] n kamermeisje nt

champagne [ʃæm'pein] n champagne

c

champion ['tʃæmpjən] n kampioen c; voorvechter c

chance [tʃɑːns] n toeval nt; kans c, gelegenheid c; risico nt; gok c; **by ~** toevallig

change [tʃeindʒ] v wijzigen, veranderen; wisselen; zich verkleden; overstappen; n wijziging c, verandering c; wisselgeld nt, kleingeld nt

channel ['tʃænəl] n kanaal nt; **English Channel** het Kanaal

chaos ['keiɔs] n chaos c

chaotic [kei'ɔtik] adj chaotisch

chap [tʃæp] n vent c

chapel ['tʃæpəl] n kerk c, kapel c

chaplain ['tʃæplin] n kapelaan c

character ['kærəktə] n karakter nt

characteristic [,kærəktə'ristik] adj kenmerkend, karakteristiek; n kenmerk nt; karaktertrek c

characterize ['kærəktəraiz] v kenmerken

charcoal ['tʃɑːkoul] n houtskool c

charge [tʃɑːdʒ] v berekenen; belasten; aanklagen; *laden; n prijs c; belasting c, lading c, last c; aanklacht c; **~ plate** Am credit card; **free of ~** kosteloos; **in ~ of** belast met; ***take ~ of** op zich *nemen

charity ['tʃærəti] n liefdadigheid c

charm [tʃɑːm] n bekoring c, charme c; amulet c

charming ['tʃɑːmiŋ] adj charmant

chart [tʃɑːt] n tabel c; grafiek c; zeekaart c; **conversion ~** omrekentabel c

chase [tʃeis] v *najagen; *verdrijven, *verjagen; n jacht c

chasm ['kæzəm] n kloof c

chassis ['ʃæsi] n (pl ~) chassis c

chaste [tʃeist] adj kuis

chat [tʃæt] v kletsen, babbelen; n babbeltje nt, praatje nt, geklets nt

chatterbox ['tʃætəbɔks] n babbelkous c

chauffeur ['ʃoufə] n chauffeur c

cheap [tʃiːp] adj goedkoop; voordelig

cheat [tʃiːt] v *bedriegen; oplichten

check [tʃek] v controleren, *nakijken; n ruit c; nAm rekening c; cheque c; **check!** schaak!; **~ in** zich *inschrijven

check-book ['tʃekbuk] nAm chequeboekje nt

checkerboard ['tʃekəbɔːd] nAm schaakbord nt

checkers ['tʃekəz] plAm damspel nt

checkroom ['tʃekruːm] nAm garderobe c

check-up ['tʃekʌp] n onderzoek nt

cheek [tʃiːk] n wang c

cheek-bone ['tʃiːkboun] n jukbeen c

cheer [tʃiə] v juichen; **~ up** opvrolijken

cheerful ['tʃiəfəl] adj opgewekt, vrolijk

cheese [tʃiːz] n kaas c

chef [ʃef] n chef-kok c

chemical ['kemikəl] adj scheikundig, chemisch

chemist ['kemist] n apotheker c; **chemist's** apotheek c; drogisterij c

chemistry ['kemistri] n scheikunde c, chemie c

cheque [tʃek] n cheque c

cheque-book ['tʃekbuk] n chequeboekje nt

chequered ['tʃekəd] adj geruit, geblokt

cherry ['tʃeri] n kers c

chess [tʃes] n schaakspel nt

chest [tʃest] n borst c; borstkas c; kist c; **~ of drawers** ladenkast c

chestnut ['tʃesnʌt] n kastanje c

chew [tʃuː] v kauwen

chewing-gum ['tʃuːiŋɡʌm] n kauwgom c/nt

chicken ['tʃikin] n kip c; kuiken nt

chickenpox ['tʃikinpɔks] n waterpokken *pl*

chief [tʃi:f] *n* chef *c*; *adj* hoofd-, voornaamst

chieftain ['tʃi:ftən] *n* opperhoofd *nt*

child [tʃaild] *n* (pl children) kind *nt*

childbirth ['tʃaildbə:θ] *n* bevalling *c*

childhood ['tʃaildhud] *n* jeugd *c*

Chile ['tʃili] Chili

Chilean ['tʃiliən] *adj* Chileens; *n* Chileen *c*

chill [tʃil] *n* rilling *c*

chilly ['tʃili] *adj* kil

chimes [tʃaimz] *pl* carillon *nt*

chimney ['tʃimni] *n* schoorsteen *c*

chin [tʃin] *n* kin *c*

China ['tʃainə] China

china ['tʃainə] *n* porselein *nt*

Chinese [tʃai'ni:z] *adj* Chinees; *n* Chinees *c*

chink [tʃiŋk] *n* kier *c*

chip [tʃip] *n* schilfer *c*; fiche *c*; *v* *afsnijden, *afbreken; **chips** frites *pl*

chiropodist [ki'rɔpədist] *n* pedicure *c*

chisel ['tʃizəl] *n* beitel *c*

chives [tʃaivz] *pl* bieslook *nt*

chlorine ['klɔ:ri:n] *n* chloor *nt*

chock-full [tʃɔk'ful] *adj* afgeladen, stampvol

chocolate ['tʃɔklət] *n* chocola *c*; bonbon *c*; chocolademelk *c*

choice [tʃɔis] *n* keuze *c*; keus *c*

choir [kwaiə] *n* koor *nt*

choke [tʃouk] *v* stikken; wurgen; *n* choke *c*

***choose** [tʃu:z] *v* *kiezen

chop [tʃɔp] *n* kotelet *c*, karbonade *c*; *v* hakken

Christ [kraist] Christus

christen ['krisən] *v* dopen

christening ['krisəniŋ] *n* doop *c*

Christian ['kristʃən] *adj* christelijk; *n* christen *c*; ~ **name** voornaam *c*

Christmas ['krisməs] Kerstmis

chromium ['kroumiəm] *n* chroom *nt*

chronic ['krɔnik] *adj* chronisch

chronological [,krɔnə'lɔdʒikəl] *adj* chronologisch

chuckle ['tʃʌkəl] *v* grinniken

chunk [tʃʌŋk] *n* stuk *nt*

church [tʃə:tʃ] *n* kerk *c*

churchyard ['tʃə:tʃɑ:d] *n* kerkhof *nt*

cigar [si'gɑ:] *n* sigaar *c*; ~ **shop** sigarenwinkel *c*

cigarette [,sigə'ret] *n* sigaret *c*; ~ **tobacco** shag *c*

cigarette-case [,sigə'retkeis] *n* sigarettenkoker *c*

cigarette-holder [,sigə'ret,houldə] *n* sigarettepijpje *nt*

cigarette-lighter [,sigə'ret,laitə] *n* aansteker *c*

cinema ['sinəmə] *n* bioscoop *c*

cinnamon ['sinəmən] *n* kaneel *c*

circle ['sə:kəl] *n* cirkel *c*; kring *c*; balkon *nt*; *v* omringen, *omgeven

circulation [,sə:kju'leiʃən] *n* circulatie *c*; bloedsomloop *c*; omloop *c*

circumstance ['sə:kəmstæns] *n* omstandigheid *c*

circus ['sə:kəs] *n* circus *nt*

citizen ['sitizən] *n* burger *c*

citizenship ['sitizənʃip] *n* staatsburgerschap *nt*

city ['siti] *n* stad *c*

civic ['sivik] *adj* burger-

civil ['sivəl] *adj* civiel; beleefd; ~ **law** burgerlijk recht; ~ **servant** ambtenaar *c*

civilian [si'viljən] *adj* burger-; *n* burger *c*

civilization [,sivəlai'zeiʃən] *n* beschaving *c*

civilized ['sivəlaizd] *adj* beschaafd

claim [kleim] *v* vorderen, opeisen; beweren; *n* eis *c*, aanspraak *c*

clamp [klæmp] *n* klem *c*; klemschroef *c*

clap [klæp] *v* applaudisseren, klappen

clarify ['klærifai] v ophelderen, verduidelijken

class [klɑ:s] n rang c, klasse c; klas c

classical ['klæsikəl] adj klassiek

classify ['klæsifai] v indelen

class-mate ['klɑ:smeit] n klasgenoot c

classroom ['klɑ:sru:m] n leslokaal nt

clause [klɔ:z] n clausule c

claw [klɔ:] n klauw c

clay [klei] n klei c

clean [kli:n] adj zuiver, schoon; v schoonmaken, reinigen

cleaning ['kli:niŋ] n schoonmaak c, reiniging c; ~ **fluid** reinigingsmiddel nt

clear [kliə] adj helder; duidelijk; v opruimen

clearing ['kliəriŋ] n open plaats

cleft [kleft] n kloof c

clergyman ['klə:dʒimən] n (pl -men) dominee c, predikant c; geestelijke c

clerk [klɑ:k] n kantoorbediende c, beambte c; klerk c; secretaris c

clever ['klevə] adj intelligent; slim, pienter, knap

client ['klaiənt] n klant c; cliënt c

cliff [klif] n rots c, klip c

climate ['klaimit] n klimaat nt

climb [klaim] v *klimmen; *stijgen; n stijging c

clinic ['klinik] n kliniek c

cloak [klouk] n mantel c

cloakroom ['kloukru:m] n garderobe c

clock [klɔk] n klok c; **at ... o'clock** om ... uur

cloister ['klɔistə] n klooster nt

close¹ [klouz] v *sluiten; **closed** adj toe, dicht, gesloten

close² [klous] adj nabij

closet ['klɔzit] n kast c; nAm kleerkast c

cloth [klɔθ] n stof c; doek c

clothes [klouðz] pl kleding c, kleren pl

clothes-brush ['klouðzbrʌʃ] n kleerborstel c

clothing ['klouðiŋ] n kleding c

cloud [klaud] n wolk c; **clouds** bewolking c

cloud-burst ['klaudbə:st] n wolkbreuk c

cloudy ['klaudi] adj betrokken, bewolkt

clover ['klouvə] n klaver c

clown [klaun] n clown c

club [klʌb] n club c; sociëteit c, vereniging c; knots c, knuppel c

clumsy ['klʌmzi] adj onhandig

clutch [klʌtʃ] n koppeling c; greep c

coach [koutʃ] n bus c; rijtuig nt; koets c; trainer c

coachwork ['koutʃwə:k] n carrosserie c

coagulate [kou'ægjuleit] v stollen

coal [koul] n kolen pl

coarse [kɔ:s] adj grof

coast [koust] n kust c

coat [kout] n mantel c, jas c

coat-hanger ['kout,hæŋə] n kleerhanger c

cobweb ['kɔbweb] n spinneweb nt

cocaine [kou'kein] n cocaïne c

cock [kɔk] n haan c

cocktail ['kɔkteil] n cocktail c

coconut ['koukənʌt] n kokosnoot c

cod [kɔd] n (pl ~) kabeljauw c

code [koud] n code c

coffee ['kɔfi] n koffie c

cognac ['kɔnjæk] n cognac c

coherence [kou'hiərəns] n samenhang c

coin [kɔin] n munt c; geldstuk nt, muntstuk nt

coincide [,kouin'said] v *samenvallen

cold [kould] adj koud; n kou c; verkoudheid c; **catch a** ~ kou vatten

collapse [kə'læps] v *bezwijken, instorten

collar ['kɔlə] n halsband c; boord nt/c, kraag c; ~ **stud** boordeknoopje nt

collarbone ['kɔləboun] n sleutelbeen nt

colleague ['kɔli:g] n collega c

collect [kə'lekt] v verzamelen; ophalen, afhalen; collecteren

collection [kə'lekʃən] n collectie c, verzameling c; lichting c

collective [kə'lektiv] adj collectief

collector [kə'lektə] n verzamelaar c; collectant c

college ['kɔlidʒ] n instelling voor hoger onderwijs; school c

collide [kə'laid] v botsen

collision [kə'liʒən] n aanrijding c, botsing c; aanvaring c

Colombia [kə'lɔmbiə] Colombia

Colombian [kə'lɔmbiən] adj Colombiaans; n Colombiaan c

colonel ['kə:nəl] n kolonel c

colony ['kɔləni] n kolonie c

colour ['kʌlə] n kleur c; v kleuren; ~ **film** kleurenfilm c

colourant ['kʌlərənt] n kleurstof c

colour-blind ['kʌləblaind] adj kleurenblind

coloured ['kʌləd] adj gekleurd

colourful ['kʌləfəl] adj bont, kleurrijk

column ['kɔləm] n pilaar c, zuil c; kolom c; rubriek c; kolonne c

coma ['koumə] n coma nt

comb [koum] v kammen; n kam c

combat ['kɔmbæt] n strijd c, gevecht nt; v *bestrijden, *vechten

combination [,kɔmbi'neiʃən] n combinatie c

combine [kəm'bain] v combineren; *samenbrengen

*come [kʌm] v *komen; ~ across *tegenkomen; *vinden

comedian [kə'mi:diən] n toneelspeler c; komiek c

comedy ['kɔmədi] n blijspel nt, komedie c; **musical** ~ musical c

comfort ['kʌmfət] n gemak nt, komfort nt, gerief nt; troost c; v troosten

comfortable ['kʌmfətəbəl] adj geriefelijk, comfortabel

comic ['kɔmik] adj komisch

comics ['kɔmiks] pl stripverhaal nt

coming ['kʌmiŋ] n komst c

comma ['kɔmə] n komma c

command [kə'mɑ:nd] v *bevelen; n bevel nt

commander [kə'mɑ:ndə] n bevelhebber c

commemoration [kə,memə'reiʃən] n herdenking c

commence [kə'mens] v *beginnen

comment ['kɔment] n commentaar nt; v aanmerken

commerce ['kɔmə:s] n handel c

commercial [kə'mə:ʃəl] adj handels-, commercieel; n reclamespot c; ~ **law** handelsrecht nt

commission [kə'miʃən] n commissie c

commit [kə'mit] v toevertrouwen; plegen, *begaan

committee [kə'miti] n commissie c, comité nt

common ['kɔmən] adj gemeenschappelijk; gebruikelijk, gewoon; ordinair

commune ['kɔmju:n] n commune c

communicate [kə'mju:nikeit] v meedelen, mededelen

communication [kə,mju:ni'keiʃən] n communicatie c; mededeling c

communiqué [kə'mju:nikei] n communiqué c

communism ['kɔmjunizəm] n communisme nt

communist ['kɔmjunist] n communist c

community [kə'mju:nəti] n samenleving c, gemeenschap c

commuter [kə'mju:tə] n forens c

compact ['kɔmpækt] adj compact

compact disc ['kɔmpækt disk] n compact disk c; ~ player compact disk speler

companion [kəm'pænjən] n metgezel c

company ['kʌmpəni] n gezelschap nt; maatschappij c; firma c

comparative [kəm'pærətiv] adj relatief

compare [kəm'pɛə] v *vergelijken

comparison [kəm'pærisən] n vergelijking c

compartment [kəm'pɑ:tmənt] n coupé c

compass ['kʌmpəs] n kompas nt

compel [kəm'pel] v *dwingen

compensate ['kɔmpənseit] v compenseren

compensation [,kɔmpən'seiʃən] n compensatie c; schadevergoeding c

compete [kəm'pli:t] v wedijveren

competition [,kɔmpə'tiʃən] n wedstrijd c; concurrentie c

competitor [kəm'petitər] n concurrent c

compile [kəm'pail] v samenstellen

complain [kəm'plein] v klagen

complaint [kəm'pleint] n klacht c

complete [kəm'pli:t] adj compleet, volledig; v voltooien

completely [kəm'pli:tli] adv helemaal, volkomen, geheel

complex ['kɔmpleks] adj ingewikkeld

complexion [kəm'plekʃən] n teint c

complicated ['kɔmplikeitid] adj gecompliceerd, ingewikkeld

compliment ['kɔmplimənt] n compliment nt; v gelukwensen, feliciteren

compose [kəm'pouz] v samenstellen

composer [kəm'pouzə] n componist c

composition [,kɔmpə'ziʃən] n compositie c; samenstelling c

comprehensive [,kɔmpri'hensiv] adj uitgebreid

comprise [kəm'praiz] v omvatten

compromise ['kɔmprəmaiz] n compromis nt

compulsory [kəm'pʌlsəri] adj verplicht

computer [kəm'pjutə] n computer

comrade ['kɔmreid] n kameraad c

conceal [kən'si:l] v *verbergen

conceited [kən'si:tid] adj verwaand

conceive [kən'si:v] v opvatten

concentrate ['kɔnsəntreit] v concentreren

concentration [,kɔnsən'treiʃən] n concentratie c

conception [kən'sepʃən] n begrip nt; conceptie c

concern [kən'sə:n] v *aangaan, *betreffen; n zorg c; aangelegenheid c; bedrijf nt, onderneming c

concerned [kən'sə:nd] adj bezorgd; betrokken

concerning [kən'sə:niŋ] prep omtrent, betreffende

concert ['kɔnsət] n concert nt; ~ hall concertzaal c

concession [kən'seʃən] n concessie c

concise [kən'sais] adj beknopt, summier

conclusion [kəŋ'klu:ʒən] n gevolgtrekking c, conclusie c

concrete ['kɔŋkri:t] adj concreet; n beton nt

concurrence [kəŋ'kʌrəns] n samenloop c

concussion [kəŋ'kʌʃən] n hersenschudding c

condition [kən'diʃən] n voorwaarde c; toestand c; omstandigheid c

conditional [kən'diʃənəl] adj voorwaardelijk

conditioner [kən'diʃənə] n conditioner

condom ['kɔndəm] n condoom nt

conduct¹ ['kɔndʌkt] n gedrag nt

conduct² [kən'dʌkt] v leiden; begeleiden; dirigeren

conductor [kən'dʌktə] *n* conducteur *c*; dirigent *c*

confectioner [kən'fekʃənə] *n* banketbakker *c*

conference ['kɔnfərəns] *n* conferentie *c*

confess [kən'fes] *v* bekennen; biechten; *belijden

confession [kən'feʃən] *n* bekentenis *c*; biecht *c*

confidence ['kɔnfidəns] *n* vertrouwen *nt*

confident ['kɔnfidənt] *adj* gerust

confidential [,kɔnfi'denʃəl] *adj* vertrouwelijk

confirm [kən'fə:m] *v* bevestigen

confirmation [,kɔnfə'meiʃən] *n* bevestiging *c*

confiscate ['kɔnfiskeit] *v* vorderen, beslag leggen op

conflict ['kɔnflikt] *n* conflict *nt*

confuse [kən'fju:z] *v* verwarren

confusion [kən'fju:ʒən] *n* verwarring *c*

congratulate [kən'grætʃuleit] *v* feliciteren, gelukwensen

congratulation [kən,grætʃu'leiʃən] *n* felicitatie *c*, gelukwens *c*

congregation [,kɔŋgri'geiʃən] *n* gemeente *c*; orde *c*, congregatie *c*

congress ['kɔŋgres] *n* congres *nt*; bijeenkomst *c*

connect [kə'nekt] *v* *verbinden; *aansluiten

connection [kə'nekʃən] *n* relatie *c*; verband *nt*; aansluiting *c*, verbinding *c*

connoisseur [,kɔnə'sə:] *n* kenner *c*

connotation [,kɔnə'teiʃən] *n* bijbetekenis *c*

conquer ['kɔŋkə] *v* veroveren; *overwinnen

conqueror ['kɔŋkərə] *n* veroveraar *c*

conquest ['kɔŋkwest] *n* verovering *c*

conscience ['kɔnʃəns] *n* geweten *nt*

conscious ['kɔnʃəs] *adj* bewust

consciousness ['kɔnʃəsnəs] *n* bewustzijn *nt*

conscript ['kɔnskript] *n* dienstplichtige *c*

consent [kən'sent] *v* toestemmen; instemmen; *n* instemming *c*, toestemming *c*

consequence ['kɔnsikwəns] *n* consequentie *c*, gevolg *nt*

consequently ['kɔnsikwəntli] *adv* bijgevolg

conservative [kən'sə:vətiv] *adj* behoudend, conservatief

consider [kən'sidə] *v* beschouwen; *overwegen; menen, *vinden

considerable [kən'sidərəbəl] *adj* aanzienlijk; flink, aanmerkelijk

considerate [kən'sidərət] *adj* attent

consideration [kən,sidə'reiʃən] *n* overweging *c*; consideratie *c*, aandacht *c*

considering [kən'sidəriŋ] *prep* gezien

consignment [kən'sainmənt] *n* zending *c*

consist of [kən'sist] *bestaan uit

conspire [kən'spaiə] *v* *samenzweren

constant ['kɔnstənt] *adj* aanhoudend

constipation [,kɔnsti'peiʃən] *n* obstipatie *c*, constipatie *c*

constituency [kən'stitʃuənsi] *n* kiesdistrict *nt*

constitution [,kɔnsti'tju:ʃən] *n* grondwet *c*

construct [kən'strʌkt] *v* bouwen; opbouwen, construeren

construction [kən'strʌkʃən] *n* constructie *c*; opbouw *c*; gebouw *nt*, bouw *c*

consul ['kɔnsəl] *n* consul *c*

consulate ['kɔnsjulət] *n* consulaat *nt*

consult [kən'sʌlt] *v* raadplegen

consultation [,kɔnsəl'teiʃən] *n* raadple-

ging *c*; consult *nt*; ~ **hours** *n*
spreekuur *nt*

consumer [kən'sju:mə] *n* verbruiker *c*,
consument *c*

contact ['kɔntækt] *n* contact *nt*; aanraking *c*; *v* zich in verbinding stellen met; ~ **lenses** contactlenzen *pl*

contagious [kən'teidʒəs] *adj* aanstekelijk, besmettelijk

contain [kən'tein] *v* bevatten; *inhouden

container [kən'teinə] *n* reservoir *nt*;
container *c*

contemporary [kən'tempərəri] *adj*
eigentijds; toenmalig; hedendaags;
n tijdgenoot *c*

contempt [kən'tempt] *n* verachting *c*,
minachting *c*

content [kən'tent] *adj* tevreden

contents ['kɔntents] *pl* inhoud *c*

contest ['kɔntest] *n* strijd *c*; wedstrijd
c

continent ['kɔntinənt] *n* continent *nt*,
werelddeel *nt*; vasteland *nt*

continental [,kɔnti'nentəl] *adj* continentaal

continual [kən'tinjuəl] *adj* voortdurend; **continually** *adv* steeds

continue [kən'tinju:] *v* voortzetten,
vervolgen; *voortgaan, *doorgaan

continuous [kən'tinjuəs] *adj* voortdurend, doorlopend, onafgebroken

contour ['kɔntuə] *n* omtrek *c*

contraceptive [,kɔntrə'septiv] *n* voorbehoedmiddel *nt*

contract[1] ['kɔntrækt] *n* contract *nt*

contract[2] [kən'trækt] *v* *oplopen

contractor [kən'træktə] *n* aannemer *c*

contradict [,kɔntrə'dikt] *v* *tegenspre-
ken

contradictory [,kɔntrə'diktəri] *adj* tegenstrijdig

contrary ['kɔntrəri] *n* tegendeel *nt*;
adj tegengesteld; **on the** ~ integendeel

contrast ['kɔntrɑ:st] *n* contrast *nt*;
verschil *nt*, tegenstelling *c*

contribution [,kɔntri'bju:ʃən] *n* bijdrage *c*

control [kən'troul] *n* controle *c*; *v*
controleren

controversial [,kɔntrə'və:ʃəl] *adj* controversieel, omstreden

convenience [kən'vi:njəns] *n* gemak *nt*

convenient [kən'vi:njənt] *adj* geriefelijk; geschikt, passend, gemakkelijk

convent ['kɔnvənt] *n* klooster *nt*

conversation [,kɔnvə'seiʃən] *n* conversatie *c*, gesprek *nt*

convert [kən'və:t] *v* bekeren; omrekenen

convict[1] [kən'vikt] *v* schuldig *bevinden

convict[2] ['kɔnvikt] *n* veroordeelde *c*

conviction [kən'vikʃən] *n* overtuiging
c; veroordeling *c*

convince [kən'vins] *v* overtuigen

convulsion [kən'vʌlʃən] *n* kramp *c*

cook [kuk] *n* kok *c*; *v* koken; bereiden, klaarmaken

cookbook ['kukbuk] *nAm* kookboek
nt

cooker ['kukə] *n* fornuis *nt*; **gas** ~
gasfornuis *nt*

cookery-book ['kukəribuk] *n* kookboek *nt*

cookie ['kuki] *nAm* biscuit *nt*

cool [ku:l] *adj* koel; **cooling system**
koelsysteem *nt*

co-operation [kou,ɔpə'reiʃən] *n* samenwerking *c*; medewerking *c*

co-operative [kou'ɔpərətiv] *adj* coöperatief; gewillig, bereidwillig; *n* coöperatie *c*

co-ordinate [kou'ɔ:dineit] *v* coördineren

co-ordination [kou,ɔ:di'neiʃən] *n* coördinatie *c*

copper ['kɔpə] n roodkoper nt, koper nt

copy ['kɔpi] n kopie c; afschrift nt; exemplaar nt; v kopiëren; namaken; carbon ~ doorslag c

coral ['kɔrəl] n koraal c

cord [kɔ:d] n koord nt; snoer nt

cordial ['kɔ:diəl] adj hartelijk

corduroy ['kɔ:dərɔi] n ribfluweel nt

core [kɔ:] n kern c; klokhuis nt

cork [kɔ:k] n kurk c; stop c

corkscrew ['kɔ:kskru:] n kurketrekker c

corn [kɔ:n] n korrel c; graan nt, koren nt; eksteroog nt, likdoorn c; ~ on the cob maïskolf c

corner ['kɔ:nə] n hoek c

cornfield ['kɔ:nfi:ld] n korenveld nt

corpse [kɔ:ps] n lijk nt

corpulent ['kɔ:pjulənt] adj corpulent; gezet, dik

correct [kə'rekt] adj goed, correct, juist; v corrigeren, verbeteren

correction [kə'rekʃən] n correctie c; verbetering c

correctness [kə'rektnəs] n juistheid c

correspond [,kɔri'spɔnd] v corresponderen; *overeenkomen

correspondence [,kɔri'spɔndəns] n briefwisseling c, correspondentie c

correspondent [,kɔri'spɔndənt] n correspondent c

corridor ['kɔridɔ:] n gang c

corrupt [kə'rʌpt] adj corrupt; v *omkopen

corruption [kə'rʌpʃən] n omkoping c

corset ['kɔ:sit] n korset nt

cosmetics [kɔz'metiks] pl kosmetica pl, schoonheidsmiddelen pl

cost [kɔst] n kosten pl; prijs c

*cost [kɔst] v kosten

cosy ['kouzi] adj knus, gezellig

cot [kɔt] nAm stretcher c

cottage ['kɔtidʒ] n buitenhuis nt

cotton ['kɔtən] n katoen nt/c; katoenen

cotton-wool ['kɔtənwul] n watten pl

couch [kautʃ] n divan c

cough [kɔf] n hoest c; v hoesten

could [kud] v (p can)

council ['kaunsəl] n raad c

councillor ['kaunsələ] n raadslid nt

counsel ['kaunsəl] n raad c

counsellor ['kaunsələ] n raadsman c

count [kaunt] v tellen; optellen; meetellen; achten; n graaf c

counter ['kauntə] n toonbank c; balie c

counterfeit ['kauntəfi:t] v vervalsen

counterfoil ['kauntəfɔil] n controlestrook c

counterpane ['kauntəpein] n sprei c

countess ['kauntis] n gravin c

country ['kʌntri] n land nt; platteland nt; streek c; ~ house landhuis nt

countryman ['kʌntrimən] n (pl -men) landgenoot c

countryside ['kʌntrisaid] n platteland nt

county ['kaunti] n graafschap nt

couple ['kʌpəl] n paar nt

coupon ['ku:pɔn] n coupon c, bon c

courage ['kʌridʒ] n dapperheid c, moed c

courageous [kə'reidʒəs] adj dapper, moedig

course [kɔ:s] n koers c; gang c; loop c; cursus c; intensive ~ spoedcursus c; of ~ uiteraard, natuurlijk

court [kɔ:t] n rechtbank c; hof nt

courteous ['kə:tiəs] adj hoffelijk

cousin ['kʌzən] n nicht c, neef c

cover ['kʌvə] v bedekken; n schuilplaats c, beschutting c; deksel nt; omslag c/nt

cow [kau] n koe c

coward ['kauəd] n lafaard c

cowardly ['kauədli] adj laf

cow-hide ['kauhaid] *n* koeiehuid *c*

crab [kræb] *n* krab *c*

crack [kræk] *n* gekraak *nt*; barst *c*; *v* kraken; *breken, barsten

cracker ['krækə] *nAm* koekje *nt*

cradle ['kreidəl] *n* wieg *c*; bakermat *c*

cramp [kræmp] *n* kramp *c*

crane [krein] *n* hijskraan *c*

crankcase ['kræŋkkeis] *n* carter *nt*

crankshaft ['kræŋkʃɑ:ft] *n* krukas *c*

crash [kræʃ] *n* botsing *c*; *v* botsen; neerstorten; ~ **barrier** vangrail *c*

crate [kreit] *n* krat *nt*

crater ['kreitə] *n* krater *c*

crawl [krɔ:l] *v* *kruipen; *n* crawl *c*

craze [kreiz] *n* rage *c*

crazy ['kreizi] *adj* gek; dwaas, krankzinnig

creak [kri:k] *v* kraken

cream [kri:m] *n* crème *c*; room *c*; *adj* roomkleurig

creamy ['kri:mi] *adj* romig

crease [kri:s] *v* kreuken; *n* vouw *c*; plooi *c*

create [kri'eit] *v* *scheppen; creëren

creature ['kri:tʃə] *n* schepsel *nt*; wezen *nt*

credible ['kredibəl] *adj* geloofwaardig

credit ['kredit] *n* krediet *nt*; *v* crediteren; ~ **card** credit card

creditor ['kreditə] *n* schuldeiser *c*

credulous ['kredjuləs] *adj* goedgelovig

creek [kri:k] *n* inham *c*, kreek *c*

*creep** [kri:p] *v* *kruipen

creepy ['kri:pi] *adj* eng, griezelig

cremate [kri'meit] *v* cremeren

cremation [kri'meiʃən] *n* crematie *c*

crew [kru:] *n* bemanning *c*

cricket ['krikit] *n* cricket *nt*; krekel *c*

crime [kraim] *n* misdaad *c*

criminal ['kriminəl] *n* delinquent *c*, misdadiger *c*; *adj* crimineel, misdadig; ~ **law** strafrecht *nt*

criminality [ˌkrimi'næləti] *n* criminali-teit *c*

crimson ['krimzən] *adj* vuurrood

crippled ['kripəld] *adj* kreupel

crisis ['kraisis] *n* (pl crises) crisis *c*

crisp [krisp] *adj* croquant, knappend

critic ['kritik] *n* criticus *c*

critical ['kritikəl] *adj* kritisch; kritiek, hachelijk, zorgwekkend

criticism ['kritisizəm] *n* kritiek *c*

criticize ['kritisaiz] *v* bekritiseren

crochet ['krouʃei] *v* haken

crockery ['krɔkəri] *n* aardewerk *nt*, vaatwerk *nt*

crocodile ['krɔkədail] *n* krokodil *c*

crooked ['krukid] *adj* verdraaid, krom; oneerlijk

crop [krɔp] *n* oogst *c*

cross [krɔs] *v* *oversteken; *adj* kwaad, boos; *n* kruis *nt*

cross-eyed ['krɔsaid] *adj* scheel

crossing ['krɔsiŋ] *n* overtocht *c*; kruising *c*; oversteekplaats *c*; overweg *c*

crossroads ['krɔsroudz] *n* kruispunt *nt*

crosswalk ['krɔswɔ:k] *nAm* zebrapad *nt*

crow [krou] *n* kraai *c*

crowbar ['kroubɑ:] *n* breekijzer *nt*

crowd [kraud] *n* massa *c*, menigte *c*

crowded ['kraudid] *adj* druk; overvol

crown [kraun] *n* kroon *c*; *v* kronen; bekronen

crucifix ['kru:sifiks] *n* kruisbeeld *nt*

crucifixion [ˌkru:si'fikʃən] *n* kruisiging *c*

crucify ['kru:sifai] *v* kruisigen

cruel [kruəl] *adj* wreed

cruise [kru:z] *n* boottocht *c*, cruise *c*

crumb [krʌm] *n* kruimel *c*

crusade [kru:'seid] *n* kruistocht *c*

crust [krʌst] *n* korst *c*

crutch [krʌtʃ] *n* kruk *c*

cry [krai] *v* huilen; schreeuwen; *roepen; *n* kreet *c*, schreeuw *c*; roep *c*

crystal ['kristəl] n kristal nt; adj kristallen

Cuba ['kju:bə] Cuba

Cuban ['kju:bən] adj Cubaans; n Cubaan c

cube [kju:b] n kubus c; blokje nt

cuckoo ['kuku:] n koekoek c

cucumber ['kju:kəmbə] n komkommer c

cuddle ['kʌdəl] v knuffelen

cudgel ['kʌdʒəl] n knuppel c

cuff [kʌf] n manchet c

cuff-links ['kʌfliŋks] pl manchetknopen pl

cul-de-sac ['kʌldəsæk] n doodlopende weg

cultivate ['kʌltiveit] v bebouwen; verbouwen, kweken

culture ['kʌltʃə] n cultuur c; beschaving c

cultured ['kʌltʃəd] adj beschaafd

cunning ['kʌniŋ] adj sluw

cup [kʌp] n kopje nt; beker c

cupboard ['kʌbəd] n kast c

curb [kə:b] n trottoirband c; v beteugelen

cure [kjuə] v *genezen; n kuur c; genezing c

curio ['kjuəriou] n (pl ~s) rariteit c

curiosity [,kjuəri'ɔsəti] n nieuwsgierigheid c

curious ['kjuəriəs] adj benieuwd, nieuwsgierig; raar

curl [kə:l] v krullen; n krul c

curler ['kə:lə] n krulspeld c

curling-tongs ['kə:liŋtɔnz] pl krultang c

curly ['kə:li] adj krullend

currant ['kʌrənt] n krent c; bes c

currency ['kʌrənsi] n valuta c; **foreign** ~ buitenlands geld

current ['kʌrənt] n stroming c; stroom c; adj gangbaar, huidig; **alternating** ~ wisselstroom c; **direct** ~ gelijkstroom c

curry ['kʌri] n kerrie c

curse [kə:s] v vloeken; vervloeken; n vloek c

curtain ['kə:tən] n gordijn nt; doek nt

curve [kə:v] n kromming c; bocht c

curved [kə:vd] adj krom, gebogen

cushion ['kuʃən] n kussen nt

custodian [kʌ'stoudiən] n suppoost c

custody ['kʌstədi] n hechtenis c; hoede c; voogdij c

custom ['kʌstəm] n gewoonte c; gebruik nt

customary ['kʌstəməri] adj gebruikelijk, gewoon, gewoonlijk

customer ['kʌstəmə] n klant c; cliënt c

Customs ['kʌstəmz] pl douane c; ~ **duty** accijns c; ~ **officer** douanebeambte c

cut [kʌt] n snee c; snijwond c

cut [kʌt] v *snijden; knippen; verlagen; ~ **off** *afsnijden; afknippen; *afsluiten; ~ **class** mengen

cutlery ['kʌtləri] n bestek nt

cutlet ['kʌtlət] n karbonade c

cycle ['saikəl] n fiets c; rijwiel nt; kringloop c, cyclus c

cyclist ['saiklist] n fietser c; wielrijder c

cylinder ['silində] n cilinder c; ~ **head** cilinderkop c

cynical ['sinikəl] adj cynisch

cystitis [si'staitis] n blaasontsteking c

Czech [tʃek] adj Tsjechisch; n Tsjech c

D

dad [dæd] n vader c

daddy ['dædi] n papa c

daffodil ['dæfədil] *n* narcis *c*
daily ['deili] *adj* dagelijks; *n* dagblad *nt*
dairy ['dɛəri] *n* zuivelwinkel *c*
dam [dæm] *n* dam *c*; dijk *c*
damage ['dæmidʒ] *n* schade *c*; *v* beschadigen
damp [dæmp] *adj* vochtig; nat; *n* vocht *nt*; *v* bevochtigen
dance [dɑ:ns] *v* dansen; *n* dans *c*
dandelion ['dændilaiən] *n* paardebloem *c*
dandruff ['dændrəf] *n* roos *c*
Dane [dein] *n* Deen *c*
danger ['deindʒə] *n* gevaar *nt*
dangerous ['deindʒərəs] *adj* gevaarlijk
Danish ['deiniʃ] *adj* Deens
dare [dɛə] *v* wagen, durven; uitdagen
daring ['dɛəriŋ] *adj* gedurfd
dark [dɑ:k] *adj* duister, donker; *n* duisternis *c*
darling ['dɑ:liŋ] *n* schat *c*, lieveling *c*
darn [dɑ:n] *v* stoppen
dash [dæʃ] *v* snellen; *n* gedachtenstreepje *nt*
dashboard ['dæʃbɔ:d] *n* dashboard *nt*
data ['deitə] *pl* gegeven *nt*
date[1] [deit] *n* datum *c*; afspraak *c*; *v* dateren; **out of ~** ouderwets
date[2] [deit] *n* dadel *c*
daughter ['dɔ:tə] *n* dochter *c*
dawn [dɔ:n] *n* ochtendschemering *c*; dageraad *c*
day [dei] *n* dag *c*; **by ~** overdag; **~ trip** excursie *c*; **per ~** per dag; **the ~ before yesterday** eergisteren
daybreak ['deibreik] *n* dageraad *c*
daylight ['deilait] *n* daglicht *nt*
dead [ded] *adj* dood; gestorven
deaf [def] *adj* doof
deal [di:l] *n* transactie *c*, affaire *c*
*deal [di:l] *v* uitdelen; **~ with** *v* te maken *hebben met; zaken *doen met

dealer ['di:lə] *n* koopman *c*, handelaar *c*
dear [diə] *adj* lief; duur; dierbaar
death [deθ] *n* dood *c*; **~ penalty** doodstraf *c*
debate [di'beit] *n* debat *nt*
debit ['debit] *n* debet *nt*
debt [det] *n* schuld *c*
decaffeinated [di:'kæfineitid] *adj* coffeïnevrij
deceit [di'si:t] *n* bedrog *nt*
deceive [di'si:v] *v* *bedriegen
December [di'sembə] december
decency ['di:sənsi] *n* fatsoen *nt*
decent ['di:sənt] *adj* fatsoenlijk
decide [di'said] *v* beslissen, *besluiten
decision [di'siʒən] *n* beslissing *c*, besluit *nt*
deck [dek] *n* dek *nt*; **~ cabin** dekhut *c*; **~ chair** ligstoel *c*
declaration [,deklə'reiʃən] *n* verklaring *c*; aangifte *c*
declare [di'klɛə] *v* verklaren; *opgeven; *aangeven
decoration [,dekə'reiʃən] *n* versiering *c*
decrease [di:'kri:s] *v* verminderen; *afnemen; *n* vermindering *c*
dedicate ['dedikeit] *v* toewijden
deduce [di'dju:s] *v* afleiden
deduct [di'dʌkt] *v* *aftrekken
deed [di:d] *n* handeling *c*, daad *c*
deep [di:p] *adj* diep
deep-freeze [,di:p'fri:z] *n* diepvrieskast *c*
deer [diə] *n* (pl ~) hert *nt*
defeat [di'fi:t] *v* *verslaan; *n* nederlaag *c*
defective [di'fektiv] *adj* gebrekkig, defect
defence [di'fens] *n* verdediging *c*; defensie *c*
defend [di'fend] *v* verdedigen
deficiency [di'fiʃənsi] *n* gebrek *nt*
deficit ['defisit] *n* tekort *nt*

define [di'fain] v *omschrijven, bepalen, definiëren

definite ['definit] adj bepaald; vastomlijnd

definition [,defi'niʃən] n bepaling c, definitie c

deformed [di'fɔ:md] adj misvormd, mismaakt

degree [di'gri:] n graad c; titel c

delay [di'lei] v vertragen; uitstellen; n oponthoud nt, vertraging c; uitstel nt

delegate ['deligət] n gedelegeerde c

delegation [,deli'geiʃən] n delegatie c, afvaardiging c

deliberate¹ [di'libəreit] v beraadslagen, overleggen

deliberate² [di'libərət] adj opzettelijk

deliberation [di,libə'reiʃən] n beraad nt, overleg nt

delicacy ['delikəsi] n lekkernij c

delicate ['delikət] adj fijn; teder; delikaat

delicatessen [,delikə'tesən] n delicatessen pl; delicatessenwinkel c

delicious [di'liʃəs] adj lekker, heerlijk

delight [di'lait] n genot nt, verrukking c; v in verrukking *brengen; **delighted** opgetogen

delightful [di'laitfəl] adj heerlijk, verrukkelijk

deliver [di'livə] v afleveren, bezorgen; verlossen

delivery [di'livəri] n levering c, bezorging c; bevalling c; verlossing c; ~ **van** bestelauto c

demand [di'ma:nd] v vereisen, eisen; n eis c; navraag c

democracy [di'mɔkrəsi] n democratie c

democratic [,demə'krætik] adj democratisch

demolish [di'mɔliʃ] v slopen

demolition [,demə'liʃən] n afbraak c

demonstrate ['demənstreit] v aantonen; demonstreren, betogen

demonstration [,demən'streiʃən] n demonstratie c; betoging c

den [den] n hol nt

Denmark ['denma:k] Denemarken

denomination [di,nɔmi'neiʃən] n benaming c

dense [dens] adj dicht

dent [dent] n deuk c

dentist ['dentist] n tandarts c

denture ['dentʃə] n kunstgebit nt

deny [di'nai] v ontkennen; *onthouden, weigeren, *ontzeggen

deodorant [di:'oudərənt] n deodorant c

depart [di'pa:t] v *heengaan, *vertrekken; *overlijden

department [di'pa:tmənt] n departement nt, afdeling c; ~ **store** warenhuis nt

departure [di'pa:tʃə] n vertrek nt

dependant [di'pendənt] adj afhankelijk

depend on [di'pend] *afhangen van

deposit [di'pɔzit] n storting c; statiegeld nt; bezinksel nt, afzetting c; v storten

depository [di'pɔzitəri] n bergplaats c

depot ['depou] n opslagplaats c; nAm station nt

depress [di'pres] v deprimeren

depressed [di'prest] adj neerslachtig

depressing [di'presiŋ] adj triest

depression [di'preʃən] n neerslachtigheid c; depressie c; teruggang c

deprive of [di'praiv] *ontnemen

depth [depθ] n diepte c

deputy ['depjuti] n afgevaardigde c; plaatsvervanger c

descend [di'send] v dalen

descendant [di'sendənt] n afstammeling c

descent [di'sent] n afdaling c

describe [di'skraib] v *beschrijven

description [di'skripʃən] n beschrijving

c; signalement *nt*

desert[1] ['dezət] *n* woestijn *c*; *adj* woest, verlaten

desert[2] [di'zə:t] *v* deserteren; *verlaten

deserve [di'zə:v] *v* verdienen

design [di'zain] *v* *ontwerpen; *n* ontwerp *nt*; doel *nt*

designate ['dezigneit] *v* *aanwijzen

desirable [di'zaiərəbəl] *adj* begeerlijk, wenselijk

desire [di'zaiə] *n* wens *c*; zin *c*, begeerte *c*; *v* begeren, verlangen, wensen

desk [desk] *n* bureau *nt*; lessenaar *c*; schoolbank *c*

despair [di'spɛə] *n* wanhoop *c*; *v* wanhopen

despatch [di'spætʃ] *v* *verzenden

desperate ['despərət] *adj* wanhopig

despise [di'spaiz] *v* verachten

despite [di'spait] *prep* ondanks

dessert [di'zə:t] *n* dessert *nt*

destination [,desti'neiʃən] *n* bestemming *c*

destine ['destin] *v* bestemmen

destiny ['destini] *n* noodlot *nt*, lot *nt*

destroy [di'strɔi] *v* vernielen, vernietigen

destruction [di'strʌkʃən] *n* vernietiging *c*; ondergang *c*

detach [di'tætʃ] *v* losmaken

detail ['di:teil] *n* bijzonderheid *c*, detail *nt*

detailed ['di:teild] *adj* uitvoerig, gedetailleerd

detect [di'tekt] *v* ontdekken

detective [di'tektiv] *n* detective *c*; ~ story detectiveroman *c*

detergent [di'tə:dʒənt] *n* wasmiddel *nt*

determine [di'tə:min] *v* vaststellen, bepalen

determined [di'tə:mind] *adj* vastbesloten

detour ['di:tuə] *n* omweg *c*; omleiding *c*

devaluation [,di:vælju'eiʃən] *n* devaluatie *c*

devalue [,di:'vælju:] *v* devalueren

develop [di'veləp] *v* ontwikkelen

development [di'veləpmənt] *n* ontwikkeling *c*

deviate [di'vieit] *v* *afwijken

devil ['devəl] *n* duivel *c*

devise [di'vaiz] *v* beramen

devote [di'vout] *v* wijden

dew [dju:] *n* dauw *c*

diabetes [,daiə'bi:ti:z] *n* diabetes *c*, suikerziekte *c*

diabetic [,daiə'betik] *n* suikerzieke *c*, diabeticus *c*

diagnose [,daiəg'nouz] *v* een diagnose stellen; constateren

diagnosis [,daiəg'nousis] *n* (pl -ses) diagnose *c*

diagonal [dai'ægənəl] *n* diagonaal *c*; *adj* diagonaal

diagram ['daiəgræm] *n* schema *nt*; figuur *c*, grafiek *c*

dialect ['daiəlekt] *n* dialect *c*

diamond ['daiəmənd] *n* diamant *c*

diaper ['daiəpə] *nAm* luier *c*

diaphragm ['daiəfræm] *n* tussenschot *nt*

diarrhoea [,daiə'riə] *n* diarree *c*

diary ['daiəri] *n* agenda *c*; dagboek *nt*

dictaphone ['diktəfoun] *n* dictafoon *c*

dictate [dik'teit] *v* dicteren

dictation [dik'teiʃən] *n* dictaat *nt*; dictee *nt*

dictator [dik'teitə] *n* dictator *c*

dictionary ['dikʃənəri] *n* woordenboek *nt*

did [did] *v* (p do)

die [dai] *v* *sterven; *overlijden

diesel ['di:zəl] *n* diesel *c*

diet ['daiət] *n* dieet *nt*

differ ['difə] *v* verschillen

difference ['difərəns] n verschil nt; onderscheid nt

different ['difərənt] adj verschillend; ander

difficult ['difikəlt] adj moeilijk; lastig

difficulty ['difikəlti] n moeilijkheid c; moeite c

*dig [dig] v *graven; *delven

digest [di'dʒest] v verteren

digestible [di'dʒestəbəl] adj verteerbaar

digestion [di'dʒestʃən] n spijsvertering c

digit ['didʒit] n cijfer nt

digital [didʒitəl] adj digitaal

dignified ['dignifaid] adj waardig

dike [daik] n dijk c; dam c

dilapidated [di'læpideitid] adj bouwvallig

diligence ['dilidʒəns] n vlijt c, ijver c

diligent ['dilidʒənt] adj vlijtig, ijverig

dilute [dai'lju:t] v aanlengen, verdunnen

dim [dim] adj dof, mat; donker, zwak

dine [dain] v warm *eten

dinghy ['diŋgi] n bootje nt

dining-car ['dainiŋka:] n restauratiewagen c

dining-room ['dainiŋru:m] n eetkamer c; eetzaal c

dinner ['dinə] n warme maaltijd; avondeten nt, middageten nt

dinner-jacket ['dinə,dʒækit] n smoking c

dinner-service ['dinə,sə:vis] n eetservies nt

diphtheria [dif'θiəriə] n difterie c

diploma [di'ploumə] n diploma nt

diplomat ['dipləmæt] n diplomaat c

direct [di'rekt] adj rechtstreeks, direct; v richten; *wijzen; leiden; regisseren

direction [di'rekʃən] n richting c; instructie c; regie c; bestuur nt; di-

rectional signal Am richtingaanwijzer c; **directions for use** gebruiksaanwijzing c

directive [di'rektiv] n richtlijn c

director [di'rektə] n directeur c; regisseur c

dirt [də:t] n vuil nt

dirty ['də:ti] adj smerig, vies, vuil

disabled [di'seibəld] adj gehandicapt, invalide

disadvantage [,disəd'va:ntidʒ] n nadeel nt

disagree [,disə'gri:] v het oneens *zijn, van mening verschillen

disagreeable [,disə'gri:əbəl] adj onaangenaam

disappear [,disə'piə] v *verdwijnen

disappoint [,disə'pɔint] v teleurstellen; ***be disappointing** *tegenvallen

disappointment [,disə'pɔintmənt] n teleurstelling c

disapprove [,disə'pru:v] v afkeuren

disaster [di'za:stə] n ramp c; catastrofe c, onheil nt

disastrous [di'za:strəs] adj rampzalig

disc [disk] n schijf c; grammofoonplaat c; **slipped ~** hernia c

discard [di'ska:d] v afdanken

discharge [dis'tʃa:dʒ] v lossen, *uitladen; **~ of** *ontheffen van

discipline ['disiplin] n discipline c

discolour [di'skʌlə] v verkleuren

disconnect [,diskə'nekt] v ontkoppelen; uitschakelen

discontented [,diskən'tentid] adj ontevreden

discontinue [,diskən'tinju:] v *opheffen, staken

discount ['diskaunt] n korting c, reductie c

discover [di'skʌvə] v ontdekken

discovery [di'skʌvəri] n ontdekking c

discuss [di'skʌs] v *bespreken; discussiëren

discussion [di'skʌʃən] n discussie c; gesprek nt, bespreking c, debat nt

disease [di'zi:z] n ziekte c

disembark [ˌdisim'bɑ:k] v van boord *gaan, ontschepen

disgrace [dis'greis] n schande c

disguise [dis'gaiz] v zich vermommen; n vermomming c

disgusting [dis'gʌstiŋ] adj misselijk, walgelijk

dish [diʃ] n bord nt; schotel c, schaal c; gerecht nt

dishonest [di'sɔnist] adj oneerlijk

disinfect [ˌdisin'fekt] v ontsmetten

disinfectant [ˌdisin'fektənt] n ontsmettingsmiddel nt

dislike [di'slaik] v een hekel *hebben aan, niet *houden van; n afkeer c, hekel c, antipathie c

dislocated [dislokeitid] adj ontwricht

dismiss [dis'mis] v *wegzenden; *ontslaan

disorder [di'sɔ:də] n wanorde c

dispatch [di'spætʃ] v versturen, *verzenden

display [di'splei] v vertonen; tonen; n tentoonstelling c, expositie c

displease [di'spli:z] v ontstemmen, mishagen

disposable [di'spouzəbəl] adj wegwerp-

disposal [di'spouzəl] n beschikking c

dispose of [di'spouz] beschikken over

dispute [di'spju:t] n onenigheid c; ruzie c, geschil nt; v twisten, betwisten

dissatisfied [di'sætisfaid] adj ontevreden

dissolve [di'zɔlv] v oplossen; *ontbinden

dissuade from [di'sweid] *afraden

distance ['distəns] n afstand c; ~ in kilometres kilometertal nt

distant ['distənt] adj ver

distinct [di'stiŋkt] adj duidelijk; verschillend

distinction [di'stiŋkʃən] n onderscheid nt, verschil nt

distinguish [di'stiŋgwiʃ] v onderscheid maken, *onderscheiden

distinguished [di'stiŋgwiʃt] adj voornaam

distress [di'stres] n nood c; ~ signal noodsein nt

distribute [di'stribju:t] v uitdelen

distributor [di'stribjutə] n agent c; stroomverdeler c

district ['distrikt] n district nt; streek c; wijk c

disturb [di'stə:b] v storen, verstoren

disturbance [di'stə:bəns] n storing c; verwarring c

ditch [ditʃ] n greppel c, sloot c

dive [daiv] v *duiken

diversion [dai'və:ʃən] n wegomlegging c; afleiding c

divide [di'vaid] v delen; verdelen; *scheiden

divine [di'vain] adj goddelijk

division [di'viʒən] n deling c; scheiding c; afdeling c

divorce [di'vɔ:s] n echtscheiding c; v *scheiden

dizziness ['dizinəs] n duizeligheid c

dizzy ['dizi] adj duizelig

*** do** [du:] v *doen; voldoende *zijn

dock [dɔk] n dok nt; kade c; v aanleggen

docker ['dɔkə] n havenarbeider c

doctor ['dɔktə] n arts c, dokter c; doctor c

document ['dɔkjumənt] n document nt

dog [dɔg] n hond c

dogged ['dɔgid] adj hardnekkig

doll [dɔl] n pop c

dome [doum] n koepel c

domestic [də'mestik] adj huiselijk; binnenlands; n bediende c

domicile ['dɔmisail] n woonplaats c

domination [ˌdɔmi'neiʃən] *n* overheersing *c*

dominion [də'minjən] *n* heerschappij *c*

donate [dou'neit] *v* *schenken

donation [dou'neiʃən] *n* schenking *c*, gift *c*

done [dʌn] *v* (pp do)

donkey ['dɔŋki] *n* ezel *c*

donor ['dounə] *n* donateur *c*

door [dɔː] *n* deur *c*; **revolving ~** draaideur *c*; **sliding ~** schuifdeur *c*

doorbell ['dɔːbel] *n* deurbel *c*

door-keeper ['dɔːˌkiːpə] *n* portier *c*

doorman ['dɔːmən] *n* (pl -men) portier *c*

dormitory ['dɔːmitri] *n* slaapzaal *c*

dose [dous] *n* dosis *c*

dot [dɔt] *n* punt *c*

double ['dʌbəl] *adj* dubbel

doubt [daut] *v* betwijfelen, twijfelen; *n* twijfel *c*; **without ~** zonder twijfel

doubtful ['dautfəl] *adj* twijfelachtig; onzeker

dough [dou] *n* deeg *nt*

down[1] [daun] *adv* neer; omlaag, naar beneden, omver; *adj* neerslachtig; *prep* langs, van … af; **~ payment** aanbetaling *c*

down[2] [daun] *n* dons *nt*

downpour ['daunpɔː] *n* stortbui *c*

downstairs [ˌdaun'steəz] *adv* naar beneden, beneden

downstream [ˌdaun'striːm] *adv* stroomafwaarts

down-to-earth [ˌdauntu'ə:θ] *adj* nuchter

downwards ['daunwədz] *adv* neer, naar beneden

dozen ['dʌzən] *n* (pl ~, ~s) dozijn *nt*

draft [drɑːft] *n* wissel *c*

drag [dræg] *v* slepen

dragon ['drægən] *n* draak *c*

drain [drein] *v* droogleggen; afwate-

ren; *n* afvoer *c*

drama ['drɑːmə] *n* drama *nt*; treurspel *nt*; toneel *nt*

dramatic [drə'mætik] *adj* dramatisch

dramatist ['dræmətist] *n* toneelschrijver *c*

drank [dræŋk] *v* (p drink)

draper ['dreipə] *n* manufacturier *c*

drapery ['dreipəri] *n* stoffen

draught [drɑːft] *n* tocht *c*; **draughts** damspel *nt*

draught-board ['drɑːftbɔːd] *n* dambord *nt*

draw [drɔː] *n* trekking *c*

*draw [drɔː] *v* tekenen; *trekken; *opnemen; **~ up** opstellen

drawbridge ['drɔːbridʒ] *n* ophaalbrug *c*

drawer ['drɔːə] *n* la *c*, lade *c*; **drawers** onderbroek *c*

drawing ['drɔːiŋ] *n* tekening *c*

drawing-pin ['drɔːiŋpin] *n* punaise *c*

drawing-room ['drɔːiŋruːm] *n* salon *c*

dread [dred] *v* vrezen; *n* vrees *c*

dreadful ['dredfəl] *adj* vreselijk, ontzettend

dream [driːm] *n* droom *c*

*dream [driːm] *v* dromen

dress [dres] *v* aankleden; zich kleden, zich aankleden; *verbinden; *n* japon *c*, jurk *c*

dressing-gown ['dresiŋgaun] *n* kamerjas *c*

dressing-room ['dresiŋruːm] *n* kleedkamer *c*

dressing-table ['dresiŋteibəl] *n* toilettafel *c*

dressmaker ['dresˌmeikə] *n* naaister *c*

drill [dril] *v* boren; trainen; *n* boor *c*

drink [driŋk] *n* borrel *c*, drank *c*

*drink [driŋk] *v* *drinken

drinking-water ['driŋkiŋˌwɔːtə] *n* drinkwater *nt*

drip-dry [ˌdrip'drai] *adj* zelfstrijkend,

no-iron

drive [draiv] *n* rijweg *c*; autorit *c*

*drive [draiv] *v* *rijden; besturen

driver ['draivə] *n* chauffeur *c*

drizzle ['drizəl] *n* motregen *c*

drop [drɔp] *v* *laten vallen; *n* druppel *c*

drought [draut] *n* droogte *c*

drown [draun] *v* *verdrinken; ***be drowned** *verdrinken

drug [drʌg] *n* verdovend middel; geneesmiddel *nt*

drugstore ['drʌgstɔ:] *nAm* drogisterij *c*, apotheek *c*; warenhuis *nt*

drum [drʌm] *n* trommel *c*

drunk [drʌŋk] *adj* (pp drink) dronken

dry [drai] *adj* droog; *v* drogen; afdrogen

dry-clean [,drai'kli:n] *v* chemisch reinigen

dry-cleaner's [,drai'kli:nəz] *n* stomerij *c*

dryer ['draiə] *n* centrifuge *c*

duchess [dʌtʃis] *n* hertogin *c*

duck [dʌk] *n* eend *c*

due [dju:] *adj* verwacht; verschuldigd; vervallen

dues [dju:z] *pl* schulden *pl*

dug [dʌg] *v* (p, pp dig)

duke [dju:k] *n* hertog *c*

dull [dʌl] *adj* vervelend, saai; flets, mat; bot

dumb [dʌm] *adj* stom; suf, dom

dune [dju:n] *n* duin *nt*

dung [dʌŋ] *n* mest *c*

dunghill ['dʌŋhil] *n* mesthoop *c*

duration [dju'reiʃən] *n* duur *c*

during ['djuərin] *prep* gedurende, tijdens

dusk [dʌsk] *n* avondschemering *c*

dust [dʌst] *n* stof *nt*

dustbin ['dʌstbin] *n* vuilnisbak *c*

dusty ['dʌsti] *adj* stoffig

Dutch [dʌtʃ] *adj* Nederlands, Hollands

Dutchman ['dʌtʃmən] *n* (pl -men) Nederlander *c*, Hollander *c*

dutiable ['dju:tiəbəl] *adj* belastbaar

duty ['dju:ti] *n* plicht *c*; taak *c*; invoerrecht *nt*; **Customs ~** accijns *c*

duty-free [,dju:ti'fri:] *adj* belastingvrij

dwarf [dwɔ:f] *n* dwerg *c*

dye [dai] *v* verven; *n* verf *c*

dynamo ['dainəmou] *n* (pl ~s) dynamo *c*

dysentery ['disəntri] *n* dysenterie *c*

E

each [i:tʃ] *adj* elk, ieder; **~ other** elkaar

eager ['i:gə] *adj* verlangend, ongeduldig

eagle ['i:gəl] *n* arend *c*

ear [iə] *n* oor *nt*

earache ['iəreik] *n* oorpijn *c*

ear-drum ['iədrʌm] *n* trommelvlies *nt*

earl [ə:l] *n* graaf *c*

early ['ə:li] *adj* vroeg

earn [ə:n] *v* verdienen

earnest ['ə:nist] *n* ernst *c*

earnings ['ə:niŋz] *pl* inkomsten *pl*, verdiensten *pl*

earring ['iəriŋ] *n* oorbel *c*

earth [ə:θ] *n* aarde *c*; grond *c*

earthenware ['ə:θənwɛə] *n* aardewerk *nt*

earthquake ['ə:θkweik] *n* aardbeving *c*

ease [i:z] *n* ongedwongenheid *c*, gemak *nt*

east [i:st] *n* oost *c*, oosten *nt*

Easter ['i:stə] Pasen

easterly ['i:stəli] *adj* oostelijk

eastern ['i:stən] *adj* oost-, oostelijk

easy ['i:zi] *adj* gemakkelijk; geriefelijk; **~ chair** leunstoel *c*

easy-going ['i:zi,gouiŋ] *adj* ontspannen

* **eat** [i:t] *v* *eten

eavesdrop ['i:vzdrɔp] *v* afluisteren

ebony ['ebəni] *n* ebbehout *nt*

eccentric [ik'sentrik] *adj* excentriek

echo ['ekou] *n* (pl ~es) weerklank *c*, echo *c*

eclipse [i'klips] *n* verduistering *c*

economic [,i:kə'nɔmik] *adj* economisch

economical [,i:kə'nɔmikəl] *adj* spaarzaam, zuinig

economist [i'kɔnəmist] *n* econoom *c*

economize [i'kɔnəmaiz] *v* sparen

economy [i'kɔnəmi] *n* economie *c*

ecstasy ['ekstəzi] *n* extase *c*

Ecuador ['ekwədɔ:] Ecuador

Ecuadorian [,ekwə'dɔ:riən] *n* Ecuadoriaan *c*

eczema ['eksimə] *n* eczeem *nt*

edge [edʒ] *n* kant *c*, rand *c*

edible ['edibəl] *adj* eetbaar

edition [i'diʃən] *n* editie *c*, uitgave *c*; **morning** ~ ochtendeditie *c*

editor ['editə] *n* redakteur *c*

educate ['edʒukeit] *v* opleiden, opvoeden

education [,edʒu'keiʃən] *n* onderwijs *nt*; opvoeding *c*

eel [i:l] *n* aal *c*, paling *c*

effect [i'fekt] *n* gevolg *nt*, effect *nt*; *v* *teweegbrengen; **in** ~ feitelijk

effective [i'fektiv] *adj* doeltreffend, effectief

efficient [i'fiʃənt] *adj* efficiënt, doelmatig

effort ['efət] *n* inspanning *c*; poging *c*

egg [eg] *n* ei *nt*

egg-cup ['egkʌp] *n* eierdopje *nt*

eggplant ['egpla:nt] *n* aubergine *c*

egg-yolk ['egjouk] *n* eierdooier *c*

egoistic [,egou'istik] *adj* zelfzuchtig

Egypt ['i:dʒipt] Egypte

Egyptian [i'dʒipʃən] *adj* Egyptisch; *n* Egyptenaar *c*

eiderdown ['aidədaun] *n* donzen dekbed

eight [eit] *num* acht

eighteen [,ei'ti:n] *num* achttien

eighteenth [,ei'ti:nθ] *num* achttiende

eighth [eitθ] *num* achtste

eighty ['eiti] *num* tachtig

either ['aiðə] *pron* een van beide; **either ... or** hetzij ... hetzij, of ... of

elaborate [i'læbəreit] *v* uitwerken

elastic [i'læstik] *adj* elastisch; rekbaar; elastiek *nt*

elasticity [,elæ'stisəti] *n* rek *c*

elbow ['elbou] *n* elleboog *c*

elder ['eldə] *adj* ouder

elderly ['eldəli] *adj* bejaard

eldest ['eldist] *adj* oudst

elect [i'lekt] *v* *kiezen, *verkiezen

election [i'lekʃən] *n* verkiezing *c*

electric [i'lektrik] *adj* elektrisch; ~ **razor** scheerapparaat *nt*; ~ **cord** snoer *nt*

electrician [,ilek'triʃən] *n* elektricien *c*

electricity [,ilek'trisəti] *n* elektriciteit *c*

electronic [ilek'trɔnik] *adj* elektronisch; ~ **game** elektronisch spel

elegance ['eligəns] *n* elegantie *c*

elegant ['eligənt] *adj* elegant

element ['elimənt] *n* bestanddeel *nt*, element *c*

elephant ['elifənt] *n* olifant *c*

elevator ['eliveitə] *nAm* lift *c*

eleven [i'levən] *num* elf

eleventh [i'levənθ] *num* elfde

elf [elf] *n* (pl elves) elf *c*

eliminate [i'limineit] *v* elimineren

elm [elm] *n* iep *c*

else [els] *adv* anders

elsewhere [,el'sweə] *adv* elders

emancipation [i,mænsi'peiʃən] *n* emancipatie *c*

embankment [im'bæŋkmənt] *n* kade *c*

embargo [em'ba:gou] *n* (pl ~es) embargo *nt*

embark [im'ba:k] v inschepen; instappen

embarkation [,emba:'keiʃən] n inscheping c

embarrass [im'bærəs] v in verwarring brengen; in verlegenheid *brengen; hinderen; **embarrassed** verlegen, gegeneerd; **embarrassing** pijnlijk

embassy ['embəsi] n ambassade c

emblem ['embləm] n embleem nt

embrace [im'breis] v omhelzen; n omhelzing c

embroider [im'brɔidə] v borduren

embroidery [im'brɔidəri] n borduurwerk nt

emerald ['emərəld] n smaragd nt

emergency [i'mə:dʒənsi] n spoedgeval nt, noodgeval nt; noodtoestand c; ~ **exit** nooduitgang c

emigrant ['emigrənt] n emigrant c

emigrate ['emigreit] v emigreren

emigration [,emi'greiʃən] n emigratie c

emotion [i'mouʃən] n ontroering c, emotie c

emperor ['empərə] n keizer c

emphasize ['emfəsaiz] v benadrukken

empire ['empaiə] n keizerrijk nt, rijk nt

employ [im'plɔi] v tewerkstellen; gebruiken

employee [,emplɔi'i:] n werknemer c, employé c

employer [im'plɔiə] n werkgever c

employment [im'plɔimənt] n tewerkstelling c, werk nt; ~ **exchange** arbeidsbureau nt

empress ['empris] n keizerin c

empty ['empti] adj leeg; v ledigen

enable [i'neibəl] v in staat stellen

enamel [i'næməl] n email nt

enamelled [i'næməld] adj geëmailleerd

enchanting [in'tʃa:ntiŋ] adj prachtig, betoverend

encircle [in'sə:kəl] v omcirkelen, omringen; *insluiten

enclose [iŋ'klouz] v *bijsluiten, *insluiten

enclosure [iŋ'klouʒə] n bijlage c

encounter [iŋ'kauntə] v ontmoeten; n ontmoeting c

encourage [iŋ'kʌridʒ] v aanmoedigen

encyclopaedia [en,saiklə'pi:diə] n encyclopedie c

end [end] n einde nt; slot nt; v beëindigen; *aflopen

ending ['endiŋ] n einde nt

endless ['endləs] adj oneindig

endorse [in'dɔ:s] v aftekenen, endosseren

endure [in'djuə] v *verdragen

enemy ['enəmi] n vijand c

energetic [,enə'dʒetik] adj energiek

energy ['enədʒi] n energie c; kracht c

engage [in'geidʒ] v in dienst *nemen; *bespreken; zich *verbinden; **engaged** verloofd; bezig, bezet

engagement [in'geidʒmənt] n verloving c; verplichting c; afspraak c; ~ **ring** verlovingsring c

engine ['endʒin] n machine c, motor c; locomotief c

engineer [,endʒi'niə] n ingenieur c

England ['iŋglənd] Engeland

English ['iŋgliʃ] adj Engels

Englishman ['iŋgliʃmən] n (pl -men) Engelsman c

engrave [iŋ'greiv] v graveren

engraver [iŋ'greivə] n graveur c

engraving [iŋ'greiviŋ] n prent c; gravure c

enigma [i'nigmə] n raadsel nt

enjoy [in'dʒɔi] v *genieten van

enjoyable [in'dʒɔiəbəl] adj fijn, prettig, leuk; lekker

enjoyment [in'dʒɔimənt] n genot nt

enlarge [in'la:dʒ] v vergroten; uitbreiden

enlargement [in'la:dʒmənt] n vergroting *c*

enormous [i'nɔ:məs] *adj* reusachtig, enorm

enough [i'nʌf] *adv* genoeg; *adj* voldoende

enquire [iŋ'kwaiə] *v* informeren; *onderzoeken

enquiry [iŋ'kwaiəri] *n* informatie *c*; onderzoek *nt*; enquête *c*

enter ['entə] *v* *betreden, *binnengaan; *inschrijven

enterprise ['entəpraiz] *n* onderneming *c*

entertain [,entə'tein] *v* vermaken, *onderhouden; *ontvangen

entertainer [,entə'teinə] *n* conferencier *c*

entertaining [,entə'teiniŋ] *adj* vermakelijk, amusant

entertainment [,entə'teinmənt] *n* vermaak *nt*, amusement *nt*

enthusiasm [in'θju:ziæzəm] *n* enthousiasme *nt*

enthusiastic [in,θju:zi'æstik] *adj* enthousiast

entire [in'taiə] *adj* heel, geheel

entirely [in'taiəli] *adv* helemaal

entrance ['entrəns] *n* ingang *c*; toegang *c*; binnenkomst *c*

entrance-fee ['entrənsfi:] *n* entree *c*

entry ['entri] *n* ingang *c*, entree *c*; toegang *c*; post *c*; **no ~** verboden toegang

envelope ['envəloup] *n* envelop *c*

envious ['enviəs] *adj* afgunstig, jaloers

environment [in'vaiərənmənt] *n* milieu *nt*; omgeving *c*

envoy ['envɔi] *n* gezant *c*

envy ['envi] *n* afgunst *c*; *v* benijden

epic ['epik] *n* epos *nt*; *adj* episch

epidemic [,epi'demik] *n* epidemie *c*

epilepsy ['epilepsi] *n* epilepsie *c*

epilogue ['epilɔg] *n* epiloog *c*

episode ['episoud] *n* episode *c*

equal ['i:kwəl] *adj* gelijk; *v* evenaren

equality [i'kwɔləti] *n* gelijkheid *c*

equalize ['i:kwəlaiz] *v* gelijk maken

equally ['i:kwəli] *adv* even

equator [i'kweitə] *n* evenaar *c*

equip [i'kwip] *v* uitrusten

equipment [i'kwipmənt] *n* uitrusting *c*

equivalent [i'kwivələnt] *adj* equivalent, gelijkwaardig

eraser [i'reizə] *n* gom *c/nt*

erect [i'rekt] *v* opbouwen, oprichten; *adj* overeind, rechtopstaand

err [ə:] *v* zich vergissen; dwalen

errand ['erənd] *n* boodschap *c*

error ['erə] *n* fout *c*, vergissing *c*

escalator ['eskəleitə] *n* roltrap *c*

escape [i'skeip] *v* ontsnappen; vluchten, ontvluchten, *ontgaan; *n* ontsnapping *c*

escort¹ ['eskɔ:t] *n* escorte *nt*

escort² [i'skɔ:t] *v* escorteren

especially [i'speʃəli] *adv* voornamelijk, vooral

esplanade [,esplə'neid] *n* promenade *c*

essay ['esei] *n* essay *nt*; verhandeling *c*, opstel *nt*

essence ['esəns] *n* essentie *c*; kern *c*, wezen *nt*

essential [i'senʃəl] *adj* onontbeerlijk; wezenlijk, essentieel

essentially [i'senʃəli] *adv* vooral

establish [i'stæbliʃ] *v* vestigen; vaststellen

estate [i'steit] *n* landgoed *nt*

esteem [i'sti:m] *n* respect *nt*, achting *c*; *v* achten

estimate¹ ['estimeit] *v* taxeren, schatten

estimate² ['estimət] *n* schatting *c*

estuary ['estʃuəri] *n* riviermonding *c*

etcetera [et'setərə] enzovoort

etching ['etʃiŋ] *n* ets *c*

eternal [i'tə:nəl] *adj* eeuwig

eternity [i'tə:nəti] *n* eeuwigheid *c*

ether ['i:θə] *n* ether *c*
Ethiopia [iθi'oupiə] Ethiopië
Ethiopian [iθi'oupiən] *adj* Ethiopisch;
n Ethiopiër *c*
Europe ['juərəp] Europa
European [juərə'pi:ən] *adj* Europees;
n Europeaan *c*
European Union [juərə'pi:ən 'ju:njən]
Europese Unie
evacuate [i'vækjueit] *v* evacueren
evaluate [i'væljueit] *v* schatten
evaporate [i'væpəreit] *v* verdampen
even ['i:vən] *adj* effen, plat, gelijk;
constant; even; *adv* zelfs
evening ['i:vniŋ] *n* avond *c*; ~ **dress**
avondkleding *c*
event [i'vent] *n* gebeurtenis *c*; geval
nt
eventual [i'ventʃuəl] *adj* eventueel;
uiteindelijk
ever ['evə] *adv* ooit; altijd
every ['evri] *adj* ieder, elk
everybody ['evri,bɔdi] *pron* iedereen
everyday ['evridei] *adj* alledaags
everyone ['evriwʌn] *pron* ieder, iedereen
everything ['evriθiŋ] *pron* alles
everywhere ['evriwɛə] *adv* overal
evidence ['evidəns] *n* bewijs *nt*
evident ['evidənt] *adj* duidelijk
evil ['i:vəl] *n* kwaad *nt*; *adj* slecht
evolution [,i:və'lu:ʃən] *n* evolutie *c*
exact [ig'zækt] *adj* nauwkeurig, precies
exactly [ig'zæktli] *adv* precies
exaggerate [ig'zædʒəreit] *v* *overdrijven
examination [ig,zæmi'neiʃən] *n* examen
nt; onderzoek *nt*; verhoor *nt*
examine [ig'zæmin] *v* *onderzoeken
example [ig'za:mpəl] *n* voorbeeld *nt*;
for ~ bijvoorbeeld
exceed [ik'si:d] *v* *overschrijden;
*overtreffen
excel [ik'sel] *v* *uitblinken

excellent ['eksələnt] *adj* voortreffelijk,
uitstekend
except [ik'sept] *prep* uitgezonderd, behalve
exception [ik'sepʃən] *n* uitzondering *c*
exceptional [ik'sepʃənəl] *adj* buitengewoon, uitzonderlijk
excerpt ['eksə:pt] *n* passage *c*
excess [ik'ses] *n* exces *nt*
excessive [ik'sesiv] *adj* buitensporig
exchange [iks'tʃeindʒ] *v* uitwisselen,
wisselen, ruilen; *n* ruil *c*; beurs *c*;
~ **office** wisselkantoor *nt*; ~ **rate**
koers *c*
excite [ik'sait] *v* *opwinden
excitement [ik'saitmənt] *n* drukte *c*,
opwinding *c*
exciting [ik'saitiŋ] *adj* spannend
exclaim [ik'skleim] *v* *uitroepen
exclamation [,eksklə'meiʃən] *n* uitroep
c
exclude [ik'sklu:d] *v* *uitsluiten
exclusive [ik'sklu:siv] *adj* exclusief
exclusively [ik'sklu:sivli] *adv* uitsluitend
excursion [ik'skə:ʃən] *n* uitstapje *nt*,
excursie *c*
excuse[1] [ik'skju:s] *n* excuus *nt*
excuse[2] [ik'skju:z] *v* verontschuldigen,
excuseren
execute ['eksikju:t] *v* uitvoeren
execution [,eksi'kju:ʃən] *n* terechtstelling *c*
executioner [,eksi'kju:ʃənə] *n* beul *c*
executive [ig'zekjutiv] *adj* uitvoerend;
n uitvoerende macht; directeur *c*
exempt [ig'zempt] *v* *ontheffen, vrijstellen; *adj* vrijgesteld
exemption [ig'zempʃən] *n* vrijstelling *c*
exercise ['eksəsaiz] *n* oefening *c*; thema *nt*; *v* oefenen; uitoefenen
exhale [eks'heil] *v* uitademen
exhaust [ig'zɔ:st] *n* uitlaatpijp *c*, uitlaat *c*; *v* uitputten; ~ **gases** uit-

exhibit 53 extraordinary

laatgassen *pl*

exhibit [ig'zibit] *v* tentoonstellen; vertonen

exhibition [,eksi'biʃən] *n* expositie *c*, tentoonstelling *c*

exile ['eksail] *n* ballingschap *c*; balling *c*

exist [ig'zist] *v* *bestaan

existence [ig'zistəns] *n* bestaan *nt*

exit ['eksit] *n* uitgang *c*; uitrit *c*

exotic [ig'zɔtik] *adj* exotisch

expand [ik'spænd] *v* uitbreiden; uitspreiden; ontplooien

expect [ik'spekt] *v* verwachten

expectation [,ekspek'teiʃən] *n* verwachting *c*

expedition [,ekspə'diʃən] *n* verzending *c*; expeditie *c*

expel [ik'spel] *v* *uitwijzen

expenditure [ik'spenditʃə] *n* kosten *pl*, uitgave *c*

expense [ik'spens] *n* uitgave *c*; **expenses** *pl* onkosten *pl*

expensive [ik'spensiv] *adj* prijzig, duur; kostbaar

experience [ik'spiəriəns] *n* ervaring *c*; *v* *ervaren, *ondervinden, beleven; **experienced** ervaren

experiment [ik'sperimənt] *n* proef *c*, experiment *nt*; *v* experimenteren

expert ['ekspɔ:t] *n* deskundige *c*, vakman *c*, expert *c*; *adj* deskundig

expire [ik'spaiə] *v* *vervallen, *aflopen, *verstrijken; uitademen; **expired** vervallen

expiry [ik'spaiəri] *n* vervaldag *c*, afloop *c*

explain [ik'splein] *v* verklaren, uitleggen

explanation [,eksplə'neiʃən] *n* toelichting *c*, uitleg *c*, verklaring *c*

explicit [ik'splisit] *adj* uitdrukkelijk, expliciet

explode [ik'sploud] *v* ontploffen

exploit [ik'splɔit] *v* uitbuiten, exploiteren

explore [ik'splɔ:] *v* verkennen, *onderzoeken

explosion [ik'splouʒən] *n* explosie *c*

explosive [ik'splousiv] *adj* explosief; *n* springstof *c*

export[1] [ik'spɔ:t] *v* uitvoeren, exporteren

export[2] ['ekspɔ:t] *n* export *c*

exportation [,ekspɔ:'teiʃən] *n* uitvoer *c*

exports ['ekspɔ:ts] *pl* export *c*

exposition [,ekspə'ziʃən] *n* tentoonstelling *c*

exposure [ik'spouʒə] *n* blootstelling *c*; belichting *c*; ~ **meter** belichtingsmeter *c*

express [ik'spres] *v* uitdrukken; betuigen, uiten; *adj* expresse-; uitdrukkelijk; ~ **train** sneltrein *c*

expression [ik'spreʃən] *n* uitdrukking *c*; uiting *c*

exquisite [ik'skwizit] *adj* voortreffelijk

extend [ik'stend] *v* verlengen; uitbreiden; verlenen

extension [ik'stenʃən] *n* verlenging *c*; uitbreiding *c*; toestel *nt*; ~ **cord** verlengsnoer *nt*

extensive [ik'stensiv] *adj* omvangrijk; veelomvattend, uitgebreid

extent [ik'stent] *n* omvang *c*

exterior [ek'stiəriə] *adj* uiterlijk; *n* buitenkant *c*

external [ek'stə:nəl] *adj* uiterlijk

extinguish [ik'stingwiʃ] *v* blussen, doven

extort [ik'stɔ:t] *v* *afdwingen

extortion [ik'stɔ:ʃən] *n* afpersing *c*

extra ['ekstrə] *adj* extra

extract[1] [ik'strækt] *v* *uittrekken, *trekken

extract[2] ['ekstrækt] *n* fragment *nt*

extradite ['ekstrədait] *v* uitleveren

extraordinary [ik'strɔ:dənri] *adj* bui-

tengewoon
extravagant [ik'strævəgənt] *adj* overdreven, extravagant
extreme [ik'stri:m] *adj* extreem;
hoogst, uiterst; *n* uiterste *nt*
exuberant [ig'zju:bərənt] *adj* uitbundig
eye [ai] *n* oog *nt*
eyebrow ['aibrau] *n* wenkbrauw *c*
eyelash ['ailæʃ] *n* wimper *c*
eyelid ['ailid] *n* ooglid *nt*
eye-pencil ['ai,pensəl] *n* wenkbrauwstift *c*
eye-shadow ['ai,ʃædou] *n* ogenschaduw *c*
eye-witness ['ai,witnəs] *n* ooggetuige *c*

F

fable ['feibəl] *n* fabel *c*
fabric ['fæbrik] *n* stof *c*; structuur *c*
façade [fə'sɑ:d] *n* gevel *c*
face [feis] *n* gezicht *nt*; *v* het hoofd
*bieden aan; ~ **massage** gezichtsmassage *c*; **facing** tegenover
face-cream ['feiskri:m] *n* gezichtscrème *c*
face-pack ['feispæk] *n* schoonheidsmasker *nt*
face-powder ['feis,paudə] *n* gezichtspoeder *nt/c*
facility [fə'siləti] *n* faciliteit *c*
fact [fækt] *n* feit *nt*; **in ~** in feite
factor ['fæktə] *n* factor *c*
factory ['fæktəri] *n* fabriek *c*
factual ['fæktʃuəl] *adj* feitelijk
faculty ['fækəlti] *n* vermogen *nt*; gave
c, talent *nt*, bekwaamheid *c*; faculteit *c*
fad [fæd] *n* gril *c*
fade [feid] *v* verkleuren, *verschieten
faience [fai'ɑ:s] *n* aardewerk *nt*, faience *c*

fail [feil] *v* falen; tekort *schieten;
*ontbreken; *nalaten; zakken;
without ~ beslist
failure ['feiljə] *n* mislukking *c*; fiasco
c
faint [feint] *v* *flauwvallen; *adj* zwak,
vaag, flauw
fair [feə] *n* kermis *c*; beurs *c*; *adj* billijk, eerlijk; blond; mooi
fairly ['feəli] *adv* vrij, nogal, tamelijk
fairy ['feəri] *n* fee *c*
fairytale ['feəriteil] *n* sprookje *nt*
faith [feiθ] *n* geloof *nt*; vertrouwen *nt*
faithful ['feiθful] *adj* trouw
fake [feik] *n* vervalsing *c*
fall [fɔ:l] *n* val *c*; *nAm* herfst *c*
***fall** [fɔ:l] *v* *vallen
false [fɔ:ls] *adj* vals; verkeerd, onwaar, onecht; ~ **teeth** kunstgebit
nt
falter ['fɔ:ltə] *v* wankelen; stamelen
fame [feim] *n* faam *c*, roem *c*; reputatie *c*
familiar [fə'miljə] *adj* vertrouwd; familiaar
family ['fæməli] *n* gezin *nt*; familie *c*;
~ **name** achternaam *c*
famous ['feiməs] *adj* beroemd
fan [fæn] *n* ventilator *c*; waaier *c*; fan
c; ~ **belt** ventilatorriem *c*
fanatical [fə'nætikəl] *adj* fanatiek
fancy ['fænsi] *v* lusten, zin *hebben
in; zich verbeelden, zich voorstellen; *n* gril *c*; fantasie *c*
fantastic [fæn'tæstik] *adj* fantastisch
fantasy ['fæntəzi] *n* fantasie *c*
far [fɑ:] *adj* ver; *adv* veel; **by ~** verreweg; **so ~** tot nu toe
far-away ['fɑ:rəwei] *adj* ver
farce [fɑ:s] *n* klucht *c*, farce *c*
fare [feə] *n* reiskosten *pl*, tarief *nt*;
kost *c*, voedsel *nt*
farm [fɑ:m] *n* boerderij *c*
farmer ['fɑ:mə] *n* boer *c*; **farmer's**

wife boerin *c*
farmhouse ['fɑːmhaus] *n* boerderij *c*
far-off ['fɑːrɔf] *adj* afgelegen
fascinate ['fæsineit] *v* boeien
fascism ['fæʃizəm] *n* fascisme *nt*
fascist ['fæʃist] *adj* fascistisch; *n* fascist *c*
fashion ['fæʃən] *n* mode *c*; manier *c*
fashionable ['fæʃənəbəl] *adj* modieus
fast [fɑːst] *adj* vlug, snel; vast
fasten ['fɑːsən] *v* vastmaken, bevestigen; *sluiten
fastener ['fɑːsənə] *n* sluiting *c*
fat [fæt] *adj* vet, dik; *n* vet *nt*
fatal ['feitəl] *adj* fataal, dodelijk, noodlottig
fate [feit] *n* lot *nt*, noodlot *nt*
father ['fɑːðə] *n* vader *c*; pater *c*
father-in-law ['fɑːðərinlɔː] *n* (pl fathers-) schoonvader *c*
fatherland ['fɑːðələnd] *n* vaderland *nt*
fatness ['fætnəs] *n* dikte *c*
fatty ['fæti] *adj* vettig
faucet ['fɔːsit] *nAm* kraan *c*
fault [fɔːlt] *n* schuld *c*; fout *c*, defect *nt*, gebrek *nt*
faultless ['fɔːltləs] *adj* foutloos; feilloos
faulty ['fɔːlti] *adj* gebrekkig, defect
favour ['feivə] *n* gunst *c*; *v* begunstigen, bevoorrechten
favourable ['feivərəbəl] *adj* gunstig
favourite ['feivərit] *n* lieveling *c*, favoriet *c*; *adj* lievelings-
fawn [fɔːn] *adj* lichtbruin; *n* reekalf *nt*
fax [fæks] *n* fax *c*; send a ~ een fax versturen
fear [fiə] *n* vrees *c*, angst *c*; *v* vrezen
feasible ['fiːzəbəl] *adj* uitvoerbaar
feast [fiːst] *n* feest *nt*
feat [fiːt] *n* prestatie *c*
feather ['feðə] *n* veer *c*
feature ['fiːtʃə] *n* kenmerk *nt*; gelaats-

trek *c*
February ['februəri] februari
federal ['fedərəl] *adj* federaal
federation [ˌfedə'reiʃən] *n* federatie *c*; bond *c*
fee [fiː] *n* honorarium *nt*
feeble ['fiːbəl] *adj* zwak
*feed [fiːd] *v* voeden; fed up with beu
*feel [fiːl] *v* voelen; betasten; ~ like zin *hebben in
feeling ['fiːliŋ] *n* gevoel *nt*
fell [fel] *v* (p fall)
fellow ['felou] *n* kerel *c*
felt¹ [felt] *n* vilt *nt*
felt² [felt] *v* (p, pp feel)
female ['fiːmeil] *adj* vrouwelijk
feminine ['feminin] *adj* vrouwelijk
fence [fens] *n* omheining *c*; hek *nt*; *v* schermen
fender ['fendə] *n* bumper *c*
ferment [fə'ment] *v* gisten
ferry-boat ['feribout] *n* veerboot *c*
fertile ['fəːtail] *adj* vruchtbaar
festival ['festivəl] *n* festival *nt*
festive ['festiv] *adj* feestelijk
fetch [fetʃ] *v* halen; afhalen
feudal ['fjuːdəl] *adj* feodaal
fever ['fiːvə] *n* koorts *c*
feverish ['fiːvəriʃ] *adj* koortsig
few [fjuː] *adj* weinig
fiancé [fi'ɑ̃ːsei] *n* verloofde *c*
fiancée [fi'ɑ̃ːsei] *n* verloofde *c*
fibre ['faibə] *n* vezel *c*
fiction ['fikʃən] *n* fictie *c*, verzinsel *nt*
field [fiːld] *n* akker *c*, veld *nt*; gebied *nt*; ~ glasses veldkijker *c*
fierce [fiəs] *adj* wild; woest, fel
fifteen [ˌfif'tiːn] *num* vijftien
fifteenth [ˌfif'tiːnθ] *num* vijftiende
fifth [fifθ] *num* vijfde
fifty ['fifti] *num* vijftig
fig [fig] *n* vijg *c*
fight [fait] *n* strijd *c*, gevecht *nt*

*fight [fait] v *strijden, *vechten

figure ['figə] n gestalte c, figuur c; cijfer nt

file [fail] n vijl c; dossier nt; rij c

Filipino [,fili'pi:nou] n Filippijn c

fill [fil] v vullen; ~ **in** invullen; **filling station** benzinestation nt; ~ **out** Am invullen; ~ **up** opvullen

filling ['filiŋ] n vulling c

film [film] n film c; v filmen

filter ['filtə] n filter nt

filthy ['filθi] adj smerig, vuil

final ['fainəl] adj laatst

finance [fai'næns] v financieren

finances [fai'nænsiz] pl financiën pl

financial [fai'nænʃəl] adj financieel

finch [fintʃ] n vink c

*find [faind] v *vinden

fine [fain] n boete c; adj fijn; mooi; uitstekend, prachtig; ~ **arts** schone kunsten

finger ['fiŋgə] n vinger c; **little** ~ pink c

fingerprint ['fiŋgəprint] n vingerafdruk c

finish ['finiʃ] v afmaken, beëindigen; eindigen; n einde nt; eindstreep c; **finished** af; op

Finland ['finlənd] Finland

Finn [fin] n Fin c

Finnish ['finiʃ] adj Fins

fire [faiə] n vuur nt; brand c; v *schieten; *ontslaan

fire-alarm ['faiərə,lɑ:m] n brandalarm nt

fire-brigade ['faiəbri,geid] n brandweer c

fire-escape ['faiəri,skeip] n brandtrap c

fire-extinguisher ['faiərik,stiŋgwiʃə] n brandblusapparaat nt

fireplace ['faiəpleis] n haard c

fireproof ['faiəpru:f] adj brandvrij; vuurvast

firm [fə:m] adj vast; stevig; n firma c

first [fə:st] num eerst; **at** ~ eerst; aanvankelijk; ~ **name** voornaam c

first-aid [,fə:st'eid] n eerste hulp; ~ **kit** verbandkist c; ~ **post** eerste hulppost

first-class [,fə:st'klɑ:s] adj eersteklas

first-rate [,fə:st'reit] adj eersterangs, prima

fir-tree ['fə:tri:] n denneboom c, den c

fish¹ [fiʃ] n (pl ~, ~es) vis c; ~ **shop** viswinkel c

fish² [fiʃ] v vissen; hengelen; **fishing gear** vistuig nt; **fishing hook** vishaak c; **fishing industry** visserij c; **fishing licence** visakte c; **fishing line** vislijn c; **fishing net** visnet nt; **fishing rod** hengel c; **fishing tackle** vistuig nt

fishbone ['fiʃboun] n graat c, visgraat c

fisherman ['fiʃəmən] n (pl -men) visser c

fist [fist] n vuist c

fit [fit] adj geschikt; n aanval c; v passen; **fitting room** paskamer c

five [faiv] num vijf

fix [fiks] v repareren

fixed [fikst] adj vast

fizz [fiz] n prik c

fjord [fjɔ:d] n fjord c

flag [flæg] n vlag c

flame [fleim] n vlam c

flamingo [flə'miŋgou] n (pl ~s, ~es) flamingo c

flannel ['flænəl] n flanel nt

flash [flæʃ] n flits c

flash-bulb ['flæʃbʌlb] n flitslampje nt

flash-light ['flæʃlait] n zaklantaarn c

flask [flɑ:sk] n flacon c; **thermos** ~ thermosfles c

flat [flæt] adj vlak, plat; n flat c; ~ **tyre** lekke band

flavour ['fleivə] n smaak c; v kruiden

fleet [fli:t] n vloot c

flesh [fleʃ] n vlees nt

flew [flu:] v (p fly)

flex [fleks] n snoer nt

flexible ['fleksibəl] adj buigbaar; soepel

flight [flait] n vlucht c; **charter ~** chartervlucht c

flint [flint] n vuursteen c

float [flout] v *drijven; n vlotter c

flock [flɔk] n kudde c

flood [flʌd] n overstroming c; vloed c

floor [flɔ:] n vloer c; etage c, verdieping c; **~ show** floor-show c

florist ['flɔrist] n bloemist c

flour [flauə] n bloem c, meel nt

flow [flou] v vloeien, stromen

flower [flauə] n bloem c

flowerbed ['flauəbed] n bloemperk nt

flower-shop ['flauəʃɔp] n bloemenwinkel c

flown [floun] v (pp fly)

flu [flu:] n griep c

fluent ['flu:ənt] adj vloeiend

fluid ['flu:id] adj vloeibaar; n vloeistof c

flute [flu:t] n fluit c

fly [flai] n vlieg c; gulp c

***fly** [flai] v *vliegen

foam [foum] n schuim nt; v schuimen

foam-rubber ['foum,rʌbə] n schuimrubber nt

focus ['foukəs] n brandpunt nt

fog [fɔg] n mist c

foggy ['fɔgi] adj mistig

foglamp ['fɔglæmp] n mistlamp c

fold [fould] v *vouwen; *opvouwen; n vouw c

folk [fouk] n volk nt; **~ song** volkslied nt

folk-dance ['foukdɑ:ns] n volksdans c

folklore ['fouklɔ:] n folklore c

follow ['fɔlou] v volgen; **following** adj eerstvolgend, volgend

***be fond of** [bi: fɔnd ɔv] *houden van

food [fu:d] n voedsel nt; eten nt, kost c; **~ poisoning** voedselvergiftiging c

foodstuffs ['fu:dstʌfs] pl levensmiddelen pl

fool [fu:l] n gek c, dwaas c; v foppen

foolish ['fu:liʃ] adj mal, dwaas

foot [fut] n (pl feet) voet c; **~ powder** voetpoeder nt/c; **on ~** te voet

football ['futbɔ:l] n voetbal c; **~ match** voetbalwedstrijd c

foot-brake ['futbreik] n voetrem c

footpath ['futpɑ:θ] n voetpad nt

footwear ['futweə] n schoeisel nt

for [fɔ:, fə] prep voor; gedurende; naar; vanwege, wegens, uit; conj want

***forbid** [fə'bid] v *verbieden

force [fɔ:s] v noodzaken, *dwingen; forceren; n macht c, kracht c; geweld nt; **by ~** noodgedwongen; **driving ~** drijfkracht c

ford [fɔ:d] n doorwaadbare plaats

forecast ['fɔ:kɑ:st] n voorspelling c; v voorspellen

foreground ['fɔ:graund] n voorgrond c

forehead ['fɔred] n voorhoofd nt

foreign ['fɔrin] adj buitenlands; vreemd

foreigner ['fɔrinə] n buitenlander c; vreemdeling c

foreman ['fɔ:mən] n (pl -men) voorman c

foremost ['fɔ:moust] adj hoogst

foresail ['fɔ:seil] n fok c

forest ['fɔrist] n woud nt, bos nt

forester ['fɔristə] n boswachter c

forge [fɔ:dʒ] v vervalsen

***forget** [fə'get] v *vergeten

forgetful [fə'getfəl] adj vergeetachtig

***forgive** [fə'giv] v *vergeven

fork [fɔ:k] n vork c; tweesprong c; v zich splitsen

form [fɔ:m] n vorm c; formulier nt;

klas *c*; *v* vormen

formal ['fɔ:məl] *adj* formeel

formality [fɔ:'mæləti] *n* formaliteit *c*

former ['fɔ:mə] *adj* voormalig; vroeger; **formerly** voorheen, vroeger

formula ['fɔ:mjulə] *n* (pl ~e, ~s) formule *c*

fort [fɔ:t] *n* fort *nt*

fortnight ['fɔ:tnait] *n* veertien dagen

fortress ['fɔ:tris] *n* vesting *c*

fortunate ['fɔ:tʃənət] *adj* gelukkig

fortune ['fɔ:tʃu:n] *n* fortuin *nt*; lot *nt*, geluk *nt*

forty ['fɔ:ti] *num* veertig

forward ['fɔ:wəd] *adv* vooruit, voorwaarts; *v* *nazenden

foster-parents ['fɔstə,pɛərənts] *pl* pleegouders *pl*

fought [fɔ:t] *v* (p, pp fight)

foul [faul] *adj* smerig; gemeen

found[1] [faund] *v* (p, pp find)

found[2] [faund] *v* oprichten, stichten

foundation [faun'deiʃən] *n* stichting *c*; ~ **cream** basiscrème *c*

fountain ['fauntin] *n* fontein *c*; bron *c*

fountain-pen ['fauntinpen] *n* vulpen *c*

four [fɔ:] *num* vier

fourteen [,fɔ:'ti:n] *num* veertien

fourteenth [,fɔ:'ti:nθ] *num* veertiende

fourth [fɔ:θ] *num* vierde

fowl [faul] *n* (pl ~s, ~) gevogelte *nt*

fox [fɔks] *n* vos *c*

foyer ['fɔiei] *n* foyer *c*

fraction ['frækʃən] *n* fractie *c*

fracture ['fræktʃə] *v* *breken; *n* breuk *c*

fragile ['frædʒail] *adj* breekbaar; broos

fragment ['frægmənt] *n* fragment *nt*; stuk *nt*

frame [freim] *n* lijst *c*; montuur *nt*

France [fra:ns] Frankrijk

franchise ['fræntʃaiz] *n* kiesrecht *nt*

fraternity [frə'tə:nəti] *n* broederschap *c*

fraud [frɔ:d] *n* fraude *c*, bedrog *nt*

fray [frei] *v* rafelen

free [fri:] *adj* vrij; gratis; ~ **of charge** gratis; ~ **ticket** vrijkaart *c*

freedom ['fri:dəm] *n* vrijheid *c*

*****freeze** [fri:z] *v* *vriezen; *bevriezen

freezing ['fri:ziŋ] *adj* ijskoud

freezing-point ['fri:ziŋpoint] *n* vriespunt *nt*

freight [freit] *n* lading *c*, vracht *c*

freight-train ['freittrein] *nAm* goederentrein *c*

French [frentʃ] *adj* Frans

Frenchman ['frentʃmən] *n* (pl -men) Fransman *c*

frequency ['fri:kwənsi] *n* frequentie *c*

frequent ['fri:kwənt] *adj* veelvuldig, frequent; **frequently** dikwijls

fresh [freʃ] *adj* vers; fris; ~ **water** zoet water

friction ['frikʃən] *n* wrijving *c*

Friday ['fraidi] vrijdag *c*

fridge [fridʒ] *n* koelkast *c*, ijskast *c*

friend [frend] *n* vriend *c*; vriendin *c*

friendly ['frendli] *adj* vriendelijk; amicaal, vriendschappelijk

friendship ['frendʃip] *n* vriendschap *c*

fright [frait] *n* angst *c*, schrik *c*

frighten ['fraitən] *v* *doen schrikken

frightened ['fraitənd] *adj* bang; *be ~ *schrikken

frightful ['fraitfəl] *adj* verschrikkelijk, vreselijk

fringe [frindʒ] *n* franje *c*

frock [frɔk] *n* jurk *c*

frog [frɔg] *n* kikker *c*

from [frɔm] *prep* van; uit; vanaf

front [frʌnt] *n* voorkant *c*; **in ~ of** voor

frontier ['frʌntiə] *n* grens *c*

frost [frɔst] *n* vorst *c*

froth [frɔθ] *n* schuim *nt*

frozen ['frouzən] *adj* bevroren; ~ **food** diepvries produkten

fruit [fru:t] n fruit nt; vrucht c

fry [frai] v *bakken; *braden

frying-pan ['fraiiŋpæn] n koekepan c

fuel ['fju:əl] n brandstof c; benzine c; ~ **pump** Am benzinepomp c

full [ful] adj vol; ~ **board** vol pension; ~ **stop** punt c; ~ **up** vol

fun [fʌn] n plezier nt, pret c; lol c

function ['fʌŋkʃən] n functie c

fund [fʌnd] n fonds nt

fundamental [,fʌndə'mentəl] adj fundamenteel

funeral ['fju:nərəl] n begrafenis c

funnel ['fʌnəl] n trechter c

funny ['fʌni] adj leuk, grappig; zonderling

fur [fə:] n pels c; ~ **coat** bontjas c; **furs** bont nt

furious ['fjuəriəs] adj razend, woedend

furnace ['fə:nis] n oven c

furnish ['fə:niʃ] v leveren, verschaffen; inrichten, meubileren; ~ **with** *voorzien van

furniture ['fə:nitʃə] n meubilair nt

furrier ['fʌriə] n bontwerker c

further ['fə:ðə] adj verder; nader

furthermore ['fə:ðəmɔ:] adv bovendien

furthest ['fə:ðist] adj verst

fuse [fju:z] n zekering c; lont c

fuss [fʌs] n drukte c; ophef c, herrie c

future ['fju:tʃə] n toekomst c; adj toekomstig

G

gable ['geibəl] n geveltop c

gadget ['gædʒit] n technisch snufje nt

gaiety ['geiəti] n vrolijkheid c, pret c

gain [gein] v *winnen; n winst c

gait [geit] n gang c, loop c

gale [geil] n storm c

gall [gɔ:l] n gal c; ~ **bladder** galblaas c

gallery ['gæləri] n galerij c

gallop ['gæləp] n galop c

gallows ['gælouz] pl galg c

gallstone ['gɔ:lstoun] n galsteen c

game [geim] n spel nt; wild nt; ~ **reserve** wildpark nt

gang [gæŋ] n bende c; ploeg c

gangway ['gæŋwei] n loopplank c

gaol [dʒeil] n gevangenis c

gap [gæp] n bres c

garage ['gæra:ʒ] n garage c; v stallen

garbage ['ga:bidʒ] n vuilnis nt, afval nt

garden ['ga:dən] n tuin c; **public** ~ plantsoen nt; **zoological gardens** dierentuin c

gardener ['ga:dənə] n tuinman c

gargle ['ga:gəl] v gorgelen

garlic ['ga:lik] n knoflook nt/c

gas [gæs] n gas nt; nAm benzine c; ~ **cooker** gasstel nt; ~ **pump** Am benzinepomp c; ~ **station** Am benzinestation nt; ~ **stove** gaskachel c

gasoline ['gæsəli:n] nAm benzine c

gastric ['gæstrik] adj maag-; ~ **ulcer** maagzweer c

gasworks ['gæswə:ks] n gasfabriek c

gate [geit] n poort c; hek nt

gather ['gæðə] v verzamelen; *bijeenkomen; oogsten

gauge [geidʒ] n meter c

gauze [gɔ:z] n gaas nt

gave [geiv] v (p give)

gay [gei] adj vrolijk; bont

gaze [geiz] v staren

gear [giə] n versnelling c; uitrusting c; **change** ~ schakelen; ~ **lever** versnellingspook c

gear-box ['giəbɔks] n versnellingsbak c

gem [dʒem] n juweel nt, edelsteen c; kleinood nt

gender ['dʒendə] n geslacht nt

general ['dʒenərəl] adj algemeen; n
generaal c; ~ practitioner huisarts
c; in ~ in het algemeen

generate ['dʒenəreit] v verwekken

generation [,dʒenə'reiʃən] n generatie
c

generator ['dʒenəreitər] n generator c

generosity [,dʒenə'rɔsəti] n edelmoedigheid c

generous ['dʒenərəs] adj gul, royaal

genital ['dʒenitəl] adj geslachtelijk

genius ['dʒi:niəs] n genie nt

gentle ['dʒentəl] adj zacht; teer, licht;
voorzichtig

gentleman ['dʒentəlmən] n (pl -men)
heer c

genuine ['dʒenjuin] adj echt

geography [dʒi'ɔgrəfi] n aardrijkskunde c

geology [dʒi'ɔlədʒi] n geologie c

geometry [dʒi'ɔmətri] n meetkunde c

germ [dʒə:m] n bacil c; kiem c

German ['dʒə:mən] adj Duits; n Duitser c

Germany ['dʒə:məni] Duitsland

gesticulate [dʒi'stikjuleit] v gebaren

*get [get] v *krijgen; halen; *wor-
den; ~ back *teruggaan; ~ off uitstappen; ~ on instappen; vorderen; ~ up *opstaan

ghost [goust] n spook nt; geest c

giant ['dʒaiənt] n reus c

giddiness ['gidinəs] n duizeligheid c

giddy ['gidi] adj duizelig

gift [gift] n geschenk nt, cadeau nt;
gave c

gifted ['giftid] adj begaafd

gigantic [dʒai'gæntik] adj reusachtig

giggle ['gigəl] v giechelen

gill [gil] n kieuw c

gilt [gilt] adj verguld

ginger ['dʒindʒə] n gember c

gipsy ['dʒipsi] n zigeuner c

girdle ['gə:dəl] n step-in c

girl [gə:l] n meisje nt; ~ guide padvindster c

*give [giv] v *geven; *aangeven; ~
away verklappen; ~ in *toegeven;
~ up *opgeven

glacier ['glæsiə] n gletsjer c

glad [glæd] adj verheugd, blij; gladly
graag, gaarne

gladness ['glædnəs] n vreugde c

glamorous ['glæmərəs] adj betoverend,
fascinerend

glamour ['glæmə] n charme c

glance [glɑ:ns] n blik c; v een blik
*werpen

gland [glænd] n klier c

glare [gleə] n scherp licht; schittering
c

glaring ['gleəriŋ] adj verblindend

glass [glɑ:s] n glas nt; glazen; glasses bril c; magnifying ~ vergrootglas nt

glaze [gleiz] v emailleren

glen [glen] n bergkloof c

glide [glaid] v *glijden

glider ['glaidə] n zweefvliegtuig nt

glimpse [glimps] n blik c; glimp c; v
even *zien

global ['gloubəl] adj wereldomvattend

globe [gloub] n wereldbol c, aardbol c

gloom [glu:m] n duister c

gloomy ['glu:mi] adj somber

glorious ['glɔ:riəs] adj prachtig

glory ['glɔ:ri] n glorie c, roem c; eer c,
lof c

gloss [glɔs] n glans c

glossy ['glɔsi] adj glanzend

glove [glʌv] n handschoen c

glow [glou] v gloeien; n gloed c

glue [glu:] n lijm c

*go [gou] v *gaan; *lopen; *worden;
~ ahead *doorgaan; ~ away *weggaan; ~ back *teruggaan; ~ home
naar huis *gaan; ~ in *binnengaan;

~ **on** *doorgaan; ~ **out** *uitgaan;
~ **through** meemaken, doormaken

goal [goul] n doel nt; doelpunt nt

goalkeeper ['goul,ki:pə] n doelman c

goat [gout] n bok c, geit c

god [gɔd] n god c

goddess ['gɔdis] n godin c

godfather ['gɔd,fa:ðə] n peetvader c

goggles ['gɔgəlz] pl duikbril c

gold [gould] n goud nt; ~ **leaf** blad-goud nt

golden ['gouldən] adj gouden

goldmine ['gouldmain] n goudmijn c

goldsmith ['gouldsmiθ] n goudsmid c

golf [gɔlf] n golf nt

golf-club ['gɔlfklʌb] n golfclub c

golf-course ['gɔlfkɔ:s] n golfbaan c

golf-links ['gɔlflinks] n golfbaan c

gondola ['gɔndələ] n gondel c

gone [gɔn] adv (pp go) weg

good [gud] adj goed; lekker; zoet, braaf

good-bye! [,gud'bai] dag!

good-humoured [,gud'hju:məd] adj op-geruimd

good-looking [,gud'lukin] adj knap

good-natured [,gud'neitʃəd] adj goed-hartig

goods [gudz] pl waren pl, goederen pl; ~ **train** goederentrein c

good-tempered [,gud'tempəd] adj goedgestemd

goodwill [,gud'wil] n welwillendheid c

goose [gu:s] n (pl geese) gans c

gooseberry ['guzbəri] n kruisbes c

goose-flesh ['gu:sfleʃ] n kippevel nt

gorge [gɔ:dʒ] n ravijn c

gorgeous ['gɔ:dʒəs] adj prachtig

gospel ['gɔspəl] n evangelie nt

gossip ['gɔsip] n geroddel nt; v rodde-len

got [gɔt] v (p, pp get)

gourmet ['guəmei] n fijnproever c

gout [gaut] n jicht c

govern ['gʌvən] v regeren

governess ['gʌvənis] n gouvernante c

government ['gʌvənmənt] n bewind nt, regering c

governor ['gʌvənə] n gouverneur c

gown [gaun] n japon c

grab [græb] n greep c; roof c

grace [greis] n gratie c; genade c

graceful ['greisfəl] adj bevallig

grade [greid] n graad c; v rangschik-ken

gradient ['greidiənt] n helling c

gradual ['grædʒuəl] adj geleidelijk; **gradually** adv langzamerhand

graduate ['grædʒueit] v een diploma behalen

grain [grein] n korrel c, graan nt, ko-ren nt

gram [græm] n gram c

grammar ['græmə] n grammatica c

grammatical [grə'mætikəl] adj gram-maticaal

grand [grænd] adj groots

granddad ['grændæd] n opa c

granddaughter ['græn,dɔ:tə] n klein-dochter c

grandfather ['græn,fa:ðə] n grootvader c; opa c

grandmother ['græn,mʌðə] n groot-moeder c; oma c

grandparents ['græn,pɛərənts] pl groot-ouders pl

grandson ['grænsʌn] n kleinzoon c

granite ['grænit] n graniet nt

grant [gra:nt] v gunnen, verlenen; in-willigen; n toelage c, beurs c

grapefruit ['greipfru:t] n pompelmoes c

grapes [greips] pl druiven pl

graph [græf] n grafiek c

graphic ['græfik] adj grafisch

grasp [gra:sp] v *grijpen; n greep c

grass [gra:s] n gras nt

grasshopper ['grɑːsˌhɔpə] n sprink-haan c

grate [greit] n rooster nt; v raspen

grateful ['greitfəl] adj erkentelijk, dankbaar

grater ['greitə] n rasp c

gratis ['grætis] adj gratis

gratitude ['grætitjuːd] n dankbaarheid c

gratuity [grə'tjuːəti] n fooi c

grave [greiv] n graf nt; adj ernstig

gravel ['grævəl] n kiezel c, grind nt

gravestone ['greivstoun] n grafsteen c

graveyard ['greivjɑːd] n kerkhof nt

gravity ['grævəti] n zwaartekracht c; ernst c

gravy ['greivi] n jus c

graze [greiz] v grazen; n schaafwond c

grease [griːs] n vet nt; v smeren

greasy ['griːsi] adj vet, vettig

great [greit] adj groot; **Great Britain** Groot-Brittannië

Greece [griːs] Griekenland

greed [griːd] n hebzucht c

greedy ['griːdi] adj hebzuchtig; gulzig

Greek [griːk] adj Grieks; n Griek c

green [griːn] adj groen; ~ **card** groene kaart

greengrocer ['griːnˌgrousə] n groente-boer c

greenhouse ['griːnhaus] n broeikas c, kas c

greens [griːnz] pl groente c

greet [griːt] v groeten

greeting ['griːtiŋ] n groet c

grey [grei] adj grijs; grauw

greyhound ['greihaund] n hazewind c

grief [griːf] n verdriet nt; bedroefd-heid c, smart c

grieve [griːv] v treuren

grill [gril] n grill c; v roosteren

grill-room ['grilruːm] n grillroom c

grin [grin] v grijnzen; n grijns c

*grind [graind] v *malen; fijnmalen

grip [grip] v *grijpen; n houvast nt, greep c; nAm handkoffertje nt

grit [grit] n gruis nt

groan [groun] v kreunen

grocer ['grousə] n kruidenier c; **gro-cer's** kruidenierswinkel c

groceries ['grousəriz] pl kruideniers-waren pl

groin [grɔin] n lies c

groove [gruːv] n groef c

gross[1] [grous] n (pl ~) gros nt

gross[2] [grous] adj grof; bruto

grotto ['grɔtou] n (pl ~es, ~s) grot c

ground[1] [graund] n bodem c, grond c; ~ **floor** begane grond; **grounds** ter-rein nt

ground[2] [graund] v (p, pp grind)

group [gruːp] n groep c

grouse [graus] n (pl ~) korhoen nt

grove [grouv] n bosje nt

*grow [grou] v groeien; kweken; *worden

growl [graul] v grommen

grown-up ['grounʌp] adj volwassen; n volwassene c

growth [grouθ] n groei c; gezwel nt

grudge [grʌdʒ] v misgunnen

grumble ['grʌmbəl] v mopperen

guarantee [ˌgærən'tiː] n garantie c; waarborg c; v garanderen

guarantor [ˌgærən'tɔː] n borg c

guard [gɑːd] n bewaker c; v bewaken

guardian ['gɑːdiən] n voogd c

guess [ges] v *raden; *denken, gis-sen; n gissing c

guest [gest] n logé c, gast c

guest-house ['gesthaus] n pension nt

guest-room ['gestruːm] n logeerkamer c

guide [gaid] n gids c; v leiden

guidebook ['gaidbuk] n gids c

guide-dog ['gaiddɔg] n geleidehond c

guilt [gilt] n schuld c

guilty ['gilti] *adj* schuldig
guinea-pig ['ginipig] *n* cavia *c*
guitar [gi'tɑ:] *n* gitaar *c*
gulf [gʌlf] *n* golf *c*
gull [gʌl] *n* meeuw *c*
gum [gʌm] *n* tandvlees *nt*; gom *c*; lijm *c*
gun [gʌn] *n* geweer *nt*, revolver *c*; kanon *nt*
gunpowder ['gʌn,paudə] *n* kruit *nt*
gust [gʌst] *n* windstoot *c*
gusty ['gʌsti] *adj* winderig
gut [gʌt] *n* darm *c*; **guts** lef *c*
gutter ['gʌtə] *n* goot *c*
guy [gai] *n* vent *c*
gymnasium [dʒim'neiziəm] *n* (pl ~s, -sia) gymnastiekzaal *c*
gymnast ['dʒimnæst] *n* gymnast *c*
gymnastics [dʒim'næstiks] *pl* gymnastiek *c*
gynaecologist [,gainə'kɔlədʒist] *n* gynaecoloog *c*, vrouwenarts *c*

H

haberdashery ['hæbədæʃəri] *n* garenen bandwinkel
habit ['hæbit] *n* gewoonte *c*
habitable ['hæbitəbəl] *adj* bewoonbaar
habitual [hə'bitʃuəl] *adj* gewoon
had [hæd] *v* (p, pp have)
haddock ['hædək] *n* (pl ~) schelvis *c*
haemorrhage ['heməridʒ] *n* bloeding *c*
haemorrhoids ['hemərɔidz] *pl* aambeien *pl*
hail [heil] *n* hagel *c*
hair [heə] *n* haar *nt*; ~ **cream** haarcrème *c*; ~ **gel** haargel; ~ **piece** haarstukje *nt*; ~ **tonic** haartonic *c*
hairbrush ['heəbrʌʃ] *n* haarborstel *c*
hair-do ['heədu:] *n* kapsel *nt*, coiffure *c*

hairdresser ['heə,dresə] *n* kapper *c*
hair-dryer ['heədraiə] *n* haardroger *c*
hair-grip ['heəgrip] *n* haarspeld *c*
hair-net ['heənet] *n* haarnetje *nt*
hair-oil ['heərɔil] *n* haarolie *c*
hairpin ['heəpin] *n* haarspeld *c*
hair-spray ['heəsprei] *n* haarlak *c*
hairy ['heəri] *adj* harig
half¹ [hɑ:f] *adj* half
half² [hɑ:f] *n* (pl halves) helft *c*
half-time [,hɑ:f'taim] *n* rust *c*
halfway [,hɑ:f'wei] *adv* halverwege
halibut ['hælibət] *n* (pl ~) heilbot *c*
hall [hɔ:l] *n* hal *c*; zaal *c*
halt [hɔ:lt] *v* stoppen
halve [hɑ:v] *v* halveren
ham [hæm] *n* ham *c*
hamlet ['hæmlət] *n* gehucht *nt*
hammer ['hæmə] *n* hamer *c*
hammock ['hæmɔk] *n* hangmat *c*
hamper ['hæmpə] *n* mand *c*
hand [hænd] *n* hand *c*; *v* *aangeven; ~ **cream** handcrème *c*
handbag ['hændbæg] *n* handtas *c*
handbook ['hændbuk] *n* handboek *nt*
hand-brake ['hændbreik] *n* handrem *c*
handcuffs ['hændkʌfs] *pl* handboeien *pl*
handful ['hændful] *n* handvol *c*
handicraft ['hændikrɑ:ft] *n* handenarbeid *c*; handwerk *nt*
handkerchief ['hæŋkətʃif] *n* zakdoek *c*
handle ['hændəl] *n* steel *c*, handvat *nt*; *v* hanteren; behandelen
hand-made [,hænd'meid] *adj* met de hand gemaakt
handshake ['hændʃeik] *n* handdruk *c*
handsome ['hænsəm] *adj* knap
handwork ['hændwə:k] *n* handwerk *nt*
handwriting ['hænd,raitiŋ] *n* handschrift *nt*
handy ['hændi] *adj* handig
*****hang** [hæŋ] *v* *ophangen; *hangen
hanger ['hæŋə] *n* kleerhanger *c*

hangover ['hæŋ,ouvə] *n* kater *c*

happen ['hæpən] *v* *voorkomen, gebeuren

happening ['hæpəniŋ] *n* gebeurtenis *c*

happiness ['hæpinəs] *n* geluk *nt*

happy ['hæpi] *adj* blij, gelukkig

harbour ['ha:bə] *n* haven *c*

hard [ha:d] *adj* hard; moeilijk; **hardly** nauwelijks

hardware ['ha:dwɛə] *n* ijzerwaren *pl*; ~ **store** handel in ijzerwaren

hare [hɛə] *n* haas *c*

harm [ha:m] *n* schade *c*; kwaad *nt*; *v* schaden

harmful ['ha:mfəl] *adj* nadelig, schadelijk

harmless ['ha:mləs] *adj* onschadelijk

harmony ['ha:məni] *n* harmonie *c*

harp [ha:p] *n* harp *c*

harpsichord ['ha:psiko:d] *n* clavecimbel *c*

harsh [ha:ʃ] *adj* ruw; streng; wreed

harvest ['ha:vist] *n* oogst *c*

has [hæz] *v* (pr have)

haste [heist] *n* spoed *c*, haast *c*

hasten ['heisən] *v* zich haasten

hasty ['heisti] *adj* haastig

hat [hæt] *n* hoed *c*; ~ **rack** kapstok *c*

hatch [hætʃ] *n* luik *nt*

hate [heit] *v* een hekel *hebben aan; haten; *n* haat *c*

hatred ['heitrid] *n* haat *c*

haughty ['hɔ:ti] *adj* hooghartig

haul [hɔ:l] *v* slepen

have [hæv] *v* *hebben; *laten; ~ **to** *moeten

haversack ['hævəsæk] *n* broodzak *c*

hawk [hɔ:k] *n* havik *c*; valk *c*

hay [hei] *n* hooi *nt*; ~ **fever** hooikoorts *c*

hazard ['hæzəd] *n* risico *nt*

haze [heiz] *n* nevel *c*; waas *nt*

hazelnut ['heizəlnʌt] *n* hazelnoot *c*

hazy ['heizi] *adj* heiig; wazig

he [hi:] *pron* hij

head [hed] *n* hoofd *nt*; kop *c*; *v* leiden; ~ **of state** staatshoofd *nt*; ~ **teacher** schoolhoofd *nt*, hoofdonderwijzer *c*

headache ['hedeik] *n* hoofdpijn *c*

heading ['hediŋ] *n* titel *c*

headlamp ['hedlæmp] *n* koplamp *c*

headland ['hedlənd] *n* landtong *c*

headlight ['hedlait] *n* koplamp *c*

headline ['hedlain] *n* kop *c*

headmaster [,hed'ma:stə] *n* schoolhoofd *nt*; rector *c*, directeur *c*

headquarters [,hed'kwɔ:təz] *pl* hoofdkwartier *nt*

head-strong ['hedstrɔŋ] *adj* koppig

head-waiter [,hed'weitə] *n* maître d'hôtel

heal [hi:l] *v* *genezen

health [helθ] *n* gezondheid *c*; ~ **centre** consultatiebureau *nt*; ~ **certificate** gezondheidsattest *nt*

healthy ['helθi] *adj* gezond

heap [hi:p] *n* stapel *c*, hoop *c*

hear [hiə] *v* horen

hearing ['hiəriŋ] *n* gehoor *c*

heart [ha:t] *n* hart *nt*; kern *c*; **by** ~ uit het hoofd; ~ **attack** hartaanval *c*

heartburn ['ha:tbə:n] *n* maagzuur *nt*

hearth [ha:θ] *n* haard *c*

heartless ['ha:tləs] *adj* harteloos

hearty ['ha:ti] *adj* hartelijk

heat [hi:t] *n* warmte *c*, hitte *c*; *v* verwarmen; **heating pad** elektrisch kussen

heater ['hi:tə] *n* kachel *c*; **immersion** ~ dompelaar *c*

heath [hi:θ] *n* heide *c*

heathen ['hi:ðən] *n* heiden *c*; heidens

heather ['heðə] *n* heide *c*

heating ['hi:tiŋ] *n* verwarming *c*

heaven ['hevən] *n* hemel *c*

heavy ['hevi] *adj* zwaar

Hebrew ['hiːbruː] n Hebreeuws nt	**hill** [hil] n heuvel c
hedge [hedʒ] n heg c	**hillock** ['hilək] n lage heuvel nt
hedgehog ['hedʒhɔg] n egel c	**hillside** ['hilsaid] n helling c
heel [hiːl] n hiel c; hak c	**hilltop** ['hiltɔp] n heuveltop c
height [hait] n hoogte c; toppunt nt, hoogtepunt nt	**hilly** ['hili] adj heuvelachtig
hell [hel] n hel c	**him** [him] pron hem
hello! [heˈlou] hallo! ; dag!	**himself** [himˈself] pron zich; zelf
helm [helm] n roer nt	**hinder** ['hində] v hinderen
helmet ['helmit] n helm c	**hinge** [hindʒ] n scharnier nt
helmsman ['helmzmən] n stuurman c	**hip** [hip] n heup c
help [help] v *helpen; n hulp c	**hire** [haiə] v huren; **for** ~ te huur
helper ['helpə] n helper c	**hire-purchase** [ˌhaiəˈpəːtʃəs] n huurkoop c
helpful ['helpfəl] adj hulpvaardig	**his** [hiz] adj zijn
helping ['helpiŋ] n portie c	**historian** [hiˈstɔːriən] n geschiedkundige c
hem [hem] n zoom c	**historic** [hiˈstɔrik] adj historisch
hemp [hemp] n hennep c	**historical** [hiˈstɔrikəl] adj geschiedkundig
hen [hen] n hen c; kip c	**history** ['histəri] n geschiedenis c
henceforth [ˌhensˈfɔːθ] adv voortaan	**hit** [hit] n hit c
her [həː] pron haar	***hit** [hit] v *slaan; raken, *treffen
herb [həːb] n kruid nt	**hitchhike** ['hitʃhaik] v liften
herd [həːd] n kudde c	**hitchhiker** ['hitʃˌhaikə] n lifter c
here [hiə] adv hier; ~ **you are** alstublieft	**hoarse** [hɔːs] adj schor, hees
hereditary [hiˈreditəri] adj erfelijk	**hobby** ['hɔbi] n liefhebberij c, hobby c
hernia ['həːniə] n breuk c	**hobby-horse** ['hɔbihɔːs] n stokpaardje nt
hero ['hiərou] n (pl ~es) held c	**hockey** ['hɔki] n hockey nt
heron ['herən] n reiger c	**hoist** [hɔist] v *hijsen
herring ['heriŋ] n (pl ~, ~s) haring c	**hold** [hould] n ruim nt
herself [həːˈself] pron zich; zelf	***hold** [hould] v *vasthouden, *houden; bewaren; ~ **on** zich *vasthouden; ~ **up** ondersteunen
hesitate ['heziteit] v aarzelen	**hold-up** ['houldʌp] n overval c
heterosexual [ˌhetərəˈsekʃuəl] adj heteroseksueel	**hole** [houl] n kuil c, gat nt
hiccup ['hikʌp] n hik c	**holiday** ['hɔlədi] n vakantie c; feestdag c; ~ **camp** vakantiekamp nt; ~ **resort** vakantieoord nt; **on** ~ met vakantie
hide [haid] n huid c	**Holland** ['hɔlənd] Holland
***hide** [haid] v *verbergen; verstoppen	**hollow** ['hɔlou] adj hol
hideous ['hidiəs] adj afschuwelijk	**holy** ['houli] adj heilig
hierarchy ['haiərɑːki] n hiërarchie c	**homage** ['hɔmidʒ] n hulde c
high [hai] adj hoog	
highway ['haiwei] n hoofdweg c; nAm autoweg c	
hijack ['haidʒæk] v kapen	
hijacker ['haidʒækə] n kaper c	
hike [haik] v *trekken	

home [houm] *n* thuis *nt*; tehuis *nt*, huis *nt*; *adv* thuis, naar huis; **at ~** thuis

home-made [‚houm'meid] *adj* eigengemaakt

homesickness ['houm‚siknəs] *n* heimwee *nt*

homosexual [‚houmə'sekʃuəl] *adj* homoseksueel

honest ['ɔnist] *adj* eerlijk; oprecht

honesty ['ɔnisti] *n* eerlijkheid *c*

honey ['hʌni] *n* honing *c*

honeymoon ['hʌnimu:n] *n* huwelijksreis *c*, wittebroodsweken *pl*

honk [hʌŋk] *vAm* claxonneren

honour ['ɔnə] *n* eer *c*; *v* eren, huldigen

honourable ['ɔnərəbəl] *adj* eervol, eerzaam; rechtschapen

hood [hud] *n* kap *c*; *nAm* motorkap *c*

hoof [hu:f] *n* hoef *c*

hook [huk] *n* haak *c*

hoot [hu:t] *v* claxonneren

hooter ['hu:tə] *n* claxon *c*

hoover ['hu:və] *v* stofzuigen

hop[1] [hɔp] *v* huppelen; *n* sprong *c*

hop[2] [hɔp] *n* hop *c*

hope [houp] *n* hoop *c*; *v* hopen

hopeful ['houpfəl] *adj* hoopvol

hopeless ['houpləs] *adj* hopeloos

horizon [hə'raizən] *n* kim *c*, horizon *c*

horizontal [‚hɔri'zɔntəl] *adj* horizontaal

horn [hɔ:n] *n* hoorn *c*; claxon *c*

horrible ['hɔribəl] *adj* vreselijk; verschrikkelijk, gruwelijk, afschuwelijk

horror ['hɔrə] *n* afgrijzen *nt*, afschuw *c*

hors-d'œuvre [ɔ:'də:vr] *n* hors d'œuvre *c*, voorgerecht *nt*

horse [hɔ:s] *n* paard *nt*

horseman ['hɔ:smən] *n* (pl -men) ruiter *c*

horsepower ['hɔ:s‚pauə] *n* paardekracht *c*

horserace ['hɔ:sreis] *n* harddraverij *c*

horseradish ['hɔ:s‚rædiʃ] *n* mierikswortel *c*

horseshoe ['hɔ:sʃu:] *n* hoefijzer *nt*

horticulture ['hɔ:tikʌltʃə] *n* tuinbouw *c*

hosiery ['houʒəri] *n* tricotgoederen *pl*

hospitable ['hɔspitəbəl] *adj* gastvrij

hospital ['hɔspitəl] *n* hospitaal *nt*, ziekenhuis *nt*

hospitality [‚hɔspi'tæləti] *n* gastvrijheid *c*

host [houst] *n* gastheer *c*

hostage ['hɔstidʒ] *n* gijzelaar *c*

hostel ['hɔstəl] *n* herberg *c*

hostess ['houstis] *n* gastvrouw *c*

hostile ['hɔstail] *adj* vijandig

hot [hɔt] *adj* warm, heet

hotel [hou'tel] *n* hotel *nt*

hot-tempered [‚hɔt'tempəd] *adj* driftig

hour [auə] *n* uur *nt*

hourly ['auəli] *adj* uur-

house [haus] *n* huis *nt*; woning; pand *nt*; **~ agent** makelaar *c*; **~ block** *Am* huizenblok *nt*; **public ~** kroeg *c*

houseboat ['hausbout] *n* woonboot *c*

household ['haushould] *n* huishouden *nt*

housekeeper ['haus‚ki:pə] *n* huishoudster *c*

housekeeping ['haus‚ki:piŋ] *n* huishouden *nt*

housemaid ['hausmeid] *n* meid *c*

housewife ['hauswaif] *n* huisvrouw *c*

housework ['hauswə:k] *n* huishouden *nt*

how [hau] *adv* hoe; wat; **~ many** hoeveel; **~ much** hoeveel

however [hau'evə] *conj* evenwel, echter

hug [hʌg] *v* omhelzen; *n* omhelzing *c*

huge [hju:dʒ] *adj* geweldig, enorm, reusachtig

hum [hʌm] v neuriën
human ['hju:mən] adj menselijk; ~ **being** menselijk wezen
humanity [hju'mænəti] n mensheid c
humble ['hʌmbəl] adj nederig
humid ['hju:mid] adj vochtig
humidity [hju'midəti] n vochtigheid c
humorous ['hju:mərəs] adj grappig, geestig, humoristisch
humour ['hju:mə] n humor c
hundred ['hʌndrəd] n honderd
Hungarian [hʌŋ'gɛəriən] adj Hongaars; n Hongaar c
Hungary ['hʌŋgəri] Hongarije
hunger ['hʌŋgə] n honger c
hungry ['hʌŋgri] adj hongerig
hunt [hʌnt] v jagen; n jacht c; ~ **for** *zoeken
hunter ['hʌntə] n jager c
hurricane ['hʌrikən] n orkaan c; ~ **lamp** stormlamp c
hurry ['hʌri] v *opschieten, zich haasten; n haast c; **in a** ~ haastig
***hurt** [hə:t] v pijn *doen, bezeren; kwetsen
hurtful ['hə:tfəl] adj schadelijk
husband ['hʌzbənd] n echtgenoot c, man c
hut [hʌt] n hut c
hydrogen ['haidrədʒən] n waterstof c
hygiene ['haidʒi:n] n hygiëne c
hygienic [hai'dʒi:nik] adj hygiënisch
hymn [him] n gezang nt
hyphen ['haifən] n koppelteken nt
hypocrisy [hi'pɔkrəsi] n huichelarij c
hypocrite ['hipəkrit] n huichelaar c
hypocritical [,hipə'kritikəl] adj huichelachtig, hypocriet, schijnheilig
hysterical [hi'sterikəl] adj hysterisch

I

I [ai] pron ik
ice [ais] n ijs nt
ice-bag ['aisbæg] n koeltas c
ice-cream ['aiskri:m] n ijs nt, ijsje nt
Iceland ['aisland] IJsland
Icelander ['aisləndə] n IJslander c
Icelandic [ais'lændik] adj IJslands
icon ['aikɔn] n ikoon c
idea [ai'diə] n idee nt/c; inval c, gedachte c; denkbeeld nt, begrip nt
ideal [ai'diəl] adj ideaal; n ideaal nt
identical [ai'dentikəl] adj identiek
identification [ai,dentifi'keifən] n identificatie c
identify [ai'dentifai] v identificeren
identity [ai'dentəti] n identiteit c; ~ **card** identiteitskaart c
idiom ['idiəm] n idioom nt
idiomatic [,idiə'mætik] adj idiomatisch
idiot ['idiət] n idioot c
idiotic [,idi'ɔtik] adj idioot
idle ['aidəl] adj werkeloos; lui; ijdel
idol ['aidəl] n afgod c; idool nt
if [if] conj als; indien
ignition [ig'nifən] n ontsteking c; ~ **coil** ontsteking c
ignorant ['ignərənt] adj onwetend
ignore [ig'nɔ:] v negeren
ill [il] adj ziek; slecht; kwaad
illegal [i'li:gəl] adj illegaal, onwettig
illegible [i'ledʒəbəl] adj onleesbaar
illiterate [i'litərət] n analfabeet c
illness ['ilnəs] n ziekte c
illuminate [i'lu:mineit] v verlichten
illumination [i,lu:mi'neifən] n verlichting c
illusion [i'lu:ʒən] n illusie c; droombeeld nt
illustrate ['iləstreit] v illustreren
illustration [,ilə'streifən] n illustratie c
image ['imidʒ] n beeld nt

imaginary [i'mædʒinəri] *adj* denkbeeldig

imagination [i,mædʒi'neiʃən] *n* verbeelding *c*

imagine [i'mædʒin] *v* zich voorstellen; zich verbeelden; zich *indenken

imitate ['imiteit] *v* nabootsen, imiteren

imitation [,imi'teiʃən] *n* namaak *c*, imitatie *c*

immediate [i'mi:djət] *adj* onmiddellijk

immediately [i'mi:djətli] *adv* meteen, dadelijk, onmiddellijk

immense [i'mens] *adj* oneindig, reusachtig, onmetelijk

immigrant ['imigrənt] *n* immigrant *c*

immigrate ['imigreit] *v* immigreren

immigration [,imi'greiʃən] *n* immigratie *c*

immodest [i'mɔdist] *adj* onbescheiden

immunity [i'mju:nəti] *n* immuniteit *c*

immunize ['imjunaiz] *v* immuun maken

impartial [im'pɑ:ʃəl] *adj* onpartijdig

impassable [im'pɑ:səbəl] *adj* onbegaanbaar

impatient [im'peiʃənt] *adj* ongeduldig

impede [im'pi:d] *v* belemmeren

impediment [im'pedimənt] *n* beletsel *nt*

imperfect [im'pə:fikt] *adj* onvolmaakt

imperial [im'piəriəl] *adj* keizerlijk; rijks-

impersonal [im'pə:sənəl] *adj* onpersoonlijk

impertinence [im'pə:tinəns] *n* onbeschaamdheid *c*

impertinent [im'pə:tinənt] *adj* brutaal, onbeschoft, onbeschaamd

implement[1] ['implimənt] *n* werktuig *nt*, gereedschap *nt*

implement[2] ['impliment] *v* uitvoeren

imply [im'plai] *v* impliceren; *inhouden

impolite [,impə'lait] *adj* onbeleefd

import[1] [im'pɔ:t] *v* invoeren, importeren

import[2] ['impɔ:t] *n* import *c*, invoer *c*; ~ **duty** invoerrecht *nt*

importance [im'pɔ:təns] *n* belang *nt*

important [im'pɔ:tənt] *adj* gewichtig, belangrijk

importer [im'pɔ:tə] *n* importeur *c*

imposing [im'pouziŋ] *adj* indrukwekkend

impossible [im'pɔsəbəl] *adj* onmogelijk

impotence ['impətəns] *n* impotentie *c*

impotent ['impətənt] *adj* impotent

impound [im'paund] *v* beslag leggen op

impress [im'pres] *v* imponeren, indruk maken op

impression [im'preʃən] *n* indruk *c*

impressive [im'presiv] *adj* indrukwekkend

imprison [im'prizən] *v* gevangen zetten

imprisonment [im'prizənmənt] *n* gevangenschap *c*

improbable [im'prɔbəbəl] *adj* onwaarschijnlijk

improper [im'prɔpə] *adj* ongepast

improve [im'pru:v] *v* verbeteren

improvement [im'pru:vmənt] *n* verbetering *c*

improvise ['imprəvaiz] *v* improviseren

impudent ['impjudənt] *adj* onbeschaamd

impulse ['impʌls] *n* impuls *c*; prikkel *c*

impulsive [im'pʌlsiv] *adj* impulsief

in [in] *prep* in; over, op; *adv* binnen

inaccessible [i,næk'sesəbəl] *adj* ontoegankelijk

inaccurate [i'nækjurət] *adj* onnauwkeurig

inadequate [i'nædikwət] *adj* onvoldoende

incapable [iŋ'keipəbəl] *adj* onbekwaam

incense ['insens] *n* wierook *c*

incident ['insidənt] n incident nt

incidental [,insi'dentəl] adj toevallig

incite [in'sait] v aansporen

inclination [,iŋkli'neiʃən] n neiging c

incline [iŋ'klain] n helling c

inclined [iŋ'klaind] adj genegen, geneigd; *be ~ to v neigen

include [iŋ'klu:d] v bevatten, *insluiten; included inbegrepen

inclusive [iŋ'klu:siv] adj inclusief

income ['iŋkəm] n inkomen nt

income-tax ['iŋkəmtæks] n inkomstenbelasting c

incompetent [iŋ'kɔmpətənt] adj onbekwaam

incomplete [,iŋkəm'pli:t] adj onvolledig, incompleet

inconceivable [,iŋkən'si:vəbəl] adj ondenkbaar

inconspicuous [,iŋkən'spikjuəs] adj onopvallend

inconvenience [,iŋkən'vi:njəns] n ongemak nt, ongerief nt

inconvenient [,iŋkən'vi:njənt] adj ongelegen; lastig

incorrect [,iŋkə'rekt] adj onnauwkeurig, onjuist

increase¹ [iŋ'kri:s] v vermeerderen; *oplopen, *toenemen

increase² ['iŋkri:s] n toename c; verhoging c

incredible [iŋ'kredəbəl] adj ongelofelijk

incurable [iŋ'kjuərəbəl] adj ongeneeslijk

indecent [in'di:sənt] adj onfatsoenlijk

indeed [in'di:d] adv inderdaad

indefinite [in'definit] adj onbepaald

indemnity [in'demnəti] n schadeloosstelling c, schadevergoeding c

independence [,indi'pendəns] n onafhankelijkheid c

independent [,indi'pendənt] adj onafhankelijk; zelfstandig

index ['indeks] n register nt, index c; ~ finger wijsvinger c

India ['indiə] India

Indian ['indiən] adj Indisch; Indiaans; n Indiër c; Indiaan c

indicate ['indikeit] v *aangeven, aanduiden

indication [,indi'keiʃən] n teken nt, aanwijzing c

indicator ['indikeitə] n richtingaanwijzer c

indifferent [in'difərənt] adj onverschillig

indigestion [,indi'dʒestʃən] n indigestie c

indignation [,indig'neiʃən] n verontwaardiging c

indirect [,indi'rekt] adj indirect

individual [,indi'vidʒuəl] adj afzonderlijk, individueel; n enkeling c, individu nt

Indonesia [,ində'ni:ziə] Indonesië

Indonesian [,ində'ni:ziən] adj Indonesisch; n Indonesiër c

indoor ['indɔ:] adj binnen

indoors [,in'dɔ:z] adv binnen

indulge [in'dʌldʒ] v *toegeven

industrial [in'dʌstriəl] adj industrieel; ~ area industriegebied nt

industrious [in'dʌstriəs] adj vlijtig

industry ['indəstri] n industrie c

inedible [i'nedibəl] adj oneetbaar

inefficient [,ini'fiʃənt] adj ondoeltreffend

inevitable [i'nevitəbəl] adj onvermijdelijk

inexpensive [,inik'spensiv] adj goedkoop

inexperienced [,inik'spiəriənst] adj onervaren

infant ['infənt] n zuigeling c

infantry ['infəntri] n infanterie c

infect [in'fekt] v besmetten, *aansteken

infection [in'fekʃən] *n* infectie *c*

infectious [in'fekʃəs] *adj* besmettelijk

infer [in'fə:] *v* afleiden

inferior [in'fiəriə] *adj* inferieur, minderwaardig; lager

infinite ['infinət] *adj* oneindig

infinitive [in'finitiv] *n* onbepaalde wijs

infirmary [in'fə:məri] *n* ziekenzaal *c*

inflammable [in'flæməbəl] *adj* ontvlambaar

inflammation [,inflə'meiʃən] *n* ontsteking *c*

inflatable [in'fleitəbəl] *adj* opblaasbaar

inflate [in'fleit] *v* *opblazen

inflation [in'fleiʃən] *n* inflatie *c*

influence ['influəns] *n* invloed *c*; *v* beïnvloeden

influential [,influ'enʃəl] *adj* invloedrijk

influenza [,influ'enzə] *n* griep *c*

inform [in'fɔ:m] *v* informeren; inlichten, mededelen

informal [in'fɔ:məl] *adj* informeel

information [,infə'meiʃən] *n* informatie *c*; inlichting *c*, mededeling *c*; ~ **bureau** inlichtingenkantoor *nt*

infra-red [,infrə'red] *adj* infrarood

infrequent [in'fri:kwənt] *adj* zeldzaam

ingredient [iŋ'gri:diənt] *n* ingrediënt *nt*, bestanddeel *nt*

inhabit [in'hæbit] *v* bewonen

inhabitable [in'hæbitəbəl] *adj* bewoonbaar

inhabitant [in'hæbitənt] *n* inwoner *c*; bewoner *c*

inhale [in'heil] *v* inademen

inherit [in'herit] *v* erven

inheritance [in'heritəns] *n* erfenis *c*

initial [i'niʃəl] *adj* begin-, eerst; *n* voorletter *c*; *v* paraferen

initiative [i'niʃətiv] *n* initiatief *nt*

inject [in'dʒekt] *v* *inspuiten

injection [in'dʒekʃən] *n* injectie *c*

injure ['indʒə] *v* verwonden, kwetsen; krenken

injured ['indʒəd] *adj* gewond

injury ['indʒəri] *n* verwonding *c*; letsel *nt*, blessure *c*

injustice [in'dʒʌstis] *n* onrecht *nt*

ink [iŋk] *n* inkt *c*

inlet ['inlet] *n* inham *c*

inn [in] *n* herberg *c*

inner ['inə] *adj* inwendig; ~ **tube** binnenband *c*

inn-keeper ['in,ki:pə] *n* herbergier *c*

innocence ['inəsəns] *n* onschuld *c*

innocent ['inəsənt] *adj* onschuldig

inoculate [i'nɔkjuleit] *v* inenten

inoculation [i,nɔkju'leiʃən] *n* inenting *c*

inquire [iŋ'kwaiə] *v* *navragen, informatie *inwinnen

inquiry [iŋ'kwaiəri] *n* vraag *c*, navraag *c*; onderzoek *nt*; ~ **office** informatiebureau *nt*

inquisitive [iŋ'kwizətiv] *adj* nieuwsgierig

insane [in'sein] *adj* krankzinnig

inscription [in'skripʃən] *n* inscriptie *c*

insect ['insekt] *n* insekt *nt*; ~ **repellent** insektenwerend middel

insecticide [in'sektisaid] *n* insekticide *c*

insensitive [in'sensətiv] *adj* ongevoelig

insert [in'sə:t] *v* invoegen

inside [,in'said] *n* binnenkant *c*; *adj* binnenst; *adv* binnen; van binnen; *prep* in, binnen; ~ **out** binnenste buiten; **insides** ingewanden *pl*

insight ['insait] *n* inzicht *nt*

insignificant [,insig'nifikənt] *adj* onbelangrijk; onbeduidend, nietsbetekenend; nietig

insist [in'sist] *v* *aandringen; *aanhouden, *volhouden

insolence ['insələns] *n* onbeschaamdheid *c*

insolent ['insələnt] *adj* brutaal, onbeschaamd

insomnia [in'sɔmniə] *n* slapeloosheid *c*

inspect [in'spekt] v inspecteren

inspection [in'spekʃən] n inspectie c; controle c

inspector [in'spektə] n inspecteur c

inspire [in'spaiə] v bezielen

install [in'stɔ:l] v installeren

installation [,instə'leiʃən] n installatie c

instalment [in'stɔ:lmənt] n afbetaling c

instance ['instəns] n voorbeeld nt; geval nt; **for ~** bijvoorbeeld

instant ['instənt] n ogenblik nt

instantly ['instəntli] adv ogenblikkelijk, onmiddellijk, meteen

instead of [in'sted ɔv] in plaats van

instinct ['instiŋkt] n instinct nt

institute ['instiʈju:t] n instituut nt; instelling c; v instellen

institution [,insti'ʈju:ʃən] n inrichting c, instelling c

instruct [in'strʌkt] v onderrichten

instruction [in'strʌkʃən] n onderwijs nt

instructive [in'strʌktiv] adj leerzaam

instructor [in'strʌktə] n leraar c

instrument ['instrumənt] n instrument nt; **musical ~** muziekinstrument nt

insufficient ['insə'fiʃənt] adj onvoldoende

insulate ['insjuleit] v isoleren

insulation [,insju'leiʃən] n isolatie c

insulator ['insjuleitə] n isolator c

insult¹ [in'sʌlt] v beledigen

insult² ['insʌlt] n belediging c

insurance [in'ʃuərəns] n assurantie c, verzekering c; **~ policy** verzekeringspolis c

insure [in'ʃuə] v verzekeren

intact [in'tækt] adj intact

intellect ['intəlekt] n intellect nt

intellectual [,intə'lektʃuəl] adj intellectueel

intelligence [in'telidʒəns] n intelligen-

tie c

intelligent [in'telidʒənt] adj intelligent

intend [in'tend] v van plan *zijn, bedoelen

intense [in'tens] adj intens; hevig

intention [in'tenʃən] n bedoeling c

intentional [in'tenʃənəl] adj opzettelijk

intercourse ['intəkɔ:s] n omgang c

interest ['intrəst] n interesse c, belangstelling c; belang nt; rente c; v interesseren; **interested** geïnteresseerd, belangstellend

interesting ['intrəstiŋ] adj interessant

interfere [,intə'fiə] v tussenbeide *komen; **~ with** zich bemoeien met

interference [,intə'fiərəns] n inmenging c

interim ['intərim] n tussentijd c

interior [in'tiəriə] n binnenkant c

interlude ['intəlu:d] n intermezzo nt

intermediary [,intə'mi:djəri] n tussenpersoon c

intermission [,intə'miʃən] n pauze c

internal [in'tə:nəl] adj intern, inwendig

international [,intə'næʃənəl] adj internationaal

interpret [in'tə:prit] v tolken; vertolken

interpreter [in'tə:pritə] n tolk c

interrogate [in'terəgeit] v *ondervragen

interrogation [in,terə'geiʃən] n verhoor nt

interrogative [,intə'rɔgətiv] adj vragend

interrupt [,intə'rʌpt] v *onderbreken

interruption [,intə'rʌpʃən] n onderbreking c

intersection [,intə'sekʃən] n kruispunt nt

interval ['intəvəl] n pauze c; tussenpoos c

intervene [,intə'vi:n] v *ingrijpen

interview ['intəvju:] n interview nt, vraaggesprek nt

intestine [in'testin] n darm c; **intestines** ingewanden pl

intimate ['intimət] adj intiem

into ['intu] prep in

intolerable [in'tɔlərəbəl] adj onuitstaanbaar

intoxicated [in'tɔksikeitid] adj dronken

intrigue [in'tri:g] n komplot nt

introduce [,intrə'dju:s] v introduceren, voorstellen; inleiden; invoeren

introduction [,intrə'dʌkʃən] n inleiding c

invade [in'veid] v *binnenvallen

invalid¹ [in'vəli:d] n invalide c; adj invalide

invalid² [in'vælid] adj ongeldig

invasion [in'veiʒən] n inval c, invasie c

invent [in'vent] v *uitvinden; *verzinnen

invention [in'venʃən] n uitvinding c

inventive [in'ventiv] adj vindingrijk

inventor [in'ventə] n uitvinder c

inventory ['invəntri] n inventaris c

invert [in'və:t] v omdraaien

invest [in'vest] v investeren; beleggen

investigate [in'vestigeit] v *onderzoeken

investigation [in,vesti'geiʃən] n onderzoek nt

investment [in'vestmənt] n investering c; belegging c, geldbelegging c

investor [in'vestə] n investeerder c

invisible [in'vizəbəl] adj onzichtbaar

invitation [,invi'teiʃən] n uitnodiging c

invite [in'vait] v inviteren, uitnodigen

invoice ['invɔis] n factuur c

involve [in'vɔlv] v impliceren; **involved** betrokken

inwards ['inwədz] adv naar binnen

iodine ['aiədi:n] n jodium nt

Iran [i'rɑ:n] Iran

Iranian [i'reiniən] adj Iraans; n Iraniër c

Iraq [i'rɑ:k] Irak

Iraqi [i'rɑ:ki] adj Iraaks; n Irakees c

irascible [i'ræsibəl] adj driftig

Ireland ['aiələnd] Ierland

Irish ['aiəriʃ] adj Iers

Irishman ['aiəriʃmən] n (pl -men) Ier c

iron ['aiən] n ijzer nt; strijkijzer nt; ijzeren; v *strijken

ironical [ai'rɔnikəl] adj ironisch

ironworks ['aiənwə:ks] n hoogovens pl

irony ['aiərəni] n ironie c

irregular [i'regjulə] adj onregelmatig

irreparable [i'repərəbəl] adj onherstelbaar

irrevocable [i'revəkəbəl] adj onherroepelijk

irritable ['iritəbəl] adj prikkelbaar

irritate ['iriteit] v prikkelen, irriteren

is [iz] v (pr be)

island ['ailənd] n eiland nt

isolate ['aisəleit] v isoleren

isolation [,aisə'leiʃən] n isolement nt; isolatie c

Israel ['izreil] Israël

Israeli [iz'reili] adj Israëlisch; n Israëliër c

issue ['iʃu:] v *uitgeven; n uitgifte c, oplage c, uitgave c; kwestie c, punt nt; uitkomst c, resultaat nt, gevolg nt, slot nt, einde nt; uitgang c

isthmus ['isməs] n landengte c

it [it] pron het

Italian [i'tæljən] adj Italiaans; n Italiaan c

italics [i'tæliks] pl cursiefschrift nt

Italy ['itəli] Italië

itch [itʃ] n jeuk c; kriebel c; v jeuken

item ['aitəm] n artikel nt; punt nt

itinerant [ai'tinərənt] adj rondreizend

itinerary [ai'tinərəri] n reisplan nt, reisroute c

ivory ['aivəri] n ivoor nt

ivy ['aivi] n klimop c

J

jack [dʒæk] n krik c

jacket ['dʒækit] n jasje nt, colbert c, vest nt; omslag c/nt

jade [dʒeid] n jade nt/c

jail [dʒeil] n gevangenis c

jailer ['dʒeilə] n cipier c

jam [dʒæm] n jam c; verkeersopstopping c

janitor ['dʒænitə] n concierge c

January ['dʒænjuəri] januari

Japan [dʒə'pæn] Japan

Japanese [,dʒæpə'ni:z] adj Japans; n Japanner c

jar [dʒɑ:] n pot c

jaundice ['dʒɔ:ndis] n geelzucht c

jaw [dʒɔ:] n kaak c

jealous ['dʒeləs] adj jaloers

jealousy ['dʒeləsi] n jaloezie c

jeans [dʒi:nz] pl spijkerbroek c

jelly ['dʒeli] n gelei c

jelly-fish ['dʒelifiʃ] n kwal c

jersey ['dʒə:zi] n jersey c; trui c

jet [dʒet] n straal c; straalvliegtuig nt

jetty ['dʒeti] n pier c

Jew [dʒu:] n jood c

jewel ['dʒu:əl] n juweel nt

jeweller ['dʒu:ələ] n juwelier c

jewellery ['dʒu:əlri] n juwelen; bijouterie c

Jewish ['dʒu:iʃ] adj joods

job [dʒɔb] n karwei nt; betrekking c, baan c

jockey ['dʒɔki] n jockey c

join [dʒɔin] v *verbinden; zich voegen bij, zich *aansluiten bij; samenvoegen, verenigen

joint [dʒɔint] n gewricht nt; las c; adj verenigd, gezamenlijk

jointly ['dʒɔintli] adv gezamenlijk

joke [dʒouk] n mop c, grap c

jolly ['dʒɔli] adj leuk

Jordan ['dʒɔ:dən] Jordanië

Jordanian [dʒɔ:'deiniən] adj Jordaans; n Jordaniër c

journal ['dʒə:nəl] n tijdschrift nt

journalism ['dʒə:nəlizəm] n journalistiek c

journalist ['dʒə:nəlist] n journalist c

journey ['dʒə:ni] n reis c

joy [dʒɔi] n genot nt, vreugde c

joyful ['dʒɔifəl] adj blij, vrolijk

jubilee ['dʒu:bili:] n jubileum nt

judge [dʒʌdʒ] n rechter c; v oordelen; beoordelen

judgment ['dʒʌdʒmənt] n oordeel nt; beoordeling c

jug [dʒʌg] n kan c

juggle ['dʒʌgəl] v jongleren, goochelen

juice [dʒu:s] n sap nt

juicy ['dʒu:si] adj sappig

July [dʒu'lai] juli

jump [dʒʌmp] v *springen; n sprong c

jumper ['dʒʌmpə] n jumper c

junction ['dʒʌŋkʃən] n kruising c; knooppunt nt

June [dʒu:n] juni

jungle ['dʒʌŋgəl] n oerwoud nt, jungle c

junior ['dʒu:njə] adj jonger

junk [dʒʌŋk] n rommel c

jury ['dʒuəri] n jury c

just [dʒʌst] adj terecht, rechtvaardig; juist; adv pas; precies; alleen, slechts

justice ['dʒʌstis] n recht nt; gerechtigheid c, rechtvaardigheid c

juvenile ['dʒu:vənail] adj jeugdig

K

kangaroo [,kæŋgə'ru:] *n* kangoeroe *c*

keel [ki:l] *n* kiel *c*

keen [ki:n] *adj* enthousiast; scherp

* **keep** [ki:p] *v* *houden; bewaren; *blijven; ~ **away from** niet *betreden; ~ **off** *afblijven; ~ **on** *doorgaan met; ~ **quiet** *zwijgen; ~ **up** *volhouden; ~ **up with** *bijhouden

keg [keg] *n* vaatje *nt*

kennel ['kenəl] *n* hondehok *nt*; kennel *c*

Kenya ['kenjə] Kenya

kerosene ['kerəsi:n] *n* petroleum *c*

kettle ['ketəl] *n* ketel *c*

key [ki:] *n* sleutel *c*

keyhole ['ki:houl] *n* sleutelgat *nt*

khaki ['ka:ki] *n* kaki *nt*

kick [kik] *v* trappen, schoppen; *n* trap *c*, schop *c*

kick-off [,ki'kɔf] *n* aftrap *c*

kid [kid] *n* kind *nt*; geiteleer *nt*; *v* *beetnemen

kidney ['kidni] *n* nier *c*

kill [kil] *v* *ombrengen, doden

kilogram ['kiləgræm] *n* kilo *c*

kilometre ['kilə,mi:tə] *n* kilometer *c*

kind [kaind] *adj* aardig, vriendelijk; goed; *n* soort *c/nt*

kindergarten ['kində,ga:tən] *n* kleuterschool *c*

king [kiŋ] *n* koning *c*

kingdom ['kiŋdəm] *n* koninkrijk *nt*; rijk *nt*

kiosk ['ki:ɔsk] *n* kiosk *c*

kiss [kis] *n* zoen *c*, kus *c*; *v* kussen

kit [kit] *n* uitrusting *c*

kitchen ['kitʃin] *n* keuken *c*; ~ **garden** moestuin *c*

knapsack ['næpsæk] *n* knapzak *c*

knave [neiv] *n* boer *c*

knee [ni:] *n* knie *c*

kneecap ['ni:kæp] *n* knieschijf *c*

* **kneel** [ni:l] *v* knielen

knew [nju:] *v* (p know)

knickers ['nikəz] *pl* onderbroek *c*

knife [naif] *n* (pl knives) mes *nt*

knight [nait] *n* ridder *c*

* **knit** [nit] *v* breien

knob [nɔb] *n* knop *c*

knock [nɔk] *v* kloppen; *n* klop *c*; ~ **against** *stoten tegen; ~ **down** *neerslaan

knot [nɔt] *n* knoop *c*; *v* knopen

* **know** [nou] *v* *weten, kennen

knowledge ['nɔlidʒ] *n* kennis *c*

knuckle ['nʌkəl] *n* knokkel *c*

L

label ['leibəl] *n* etiket *nt*; *v* etiketteren

laboratory [lə'bɔrətəri] *n* laboratorium *nt*

labour ['leibə] *n* werk *nt*, arbeid *c*; weeën *pl*; *v* zwoegen; **labor permit** *Am* werkvergunning *c*

labourer ['leibərə] *n* arbeider *c*

labour-saving ['leibə,seiviŋ] *adj* arbeidbesparend

labyrinth ['læbərinθ] *n* doolhof *c*

lace [leis] *n* kant *nt*; veter *c*

lack [læk] *n* gemis *nt*, gebrek *nt*; *v* missen

lacquer ['lækə] *n* lak *c*

lad [læd] *n* jongen *c*, joch *nt*

ladder ['lædə] *n* ladder *c*

lady ['leidi] *n* dame *c*; **ladies' room** damestoilet *c*

lagoon [lə'gu:n] *n* lagune *c*

lake [leik] *n* meer *nt*

lamb [læm] *n* lam *nt*; lamsvlees *nt*

lame [leim] *adj* lam, mank, kreupel

lamentable ['læməntəbəl] *adj* erbarmelijk

lamp [læmp] *n* lamp *c*

lamp-post ['læmppoust] *n* lantaarnpaal *c*

lampshade ['læmpʃeid] *n* lampekap *c*

land [lænd] *n* land *nt*; *v* landen; aan land *gaan

landlady ['lænd,leidi] *n* hospita *c*

landlord ['lændlɔ:d] *n* huisbaas *c*; hospes *c*

landmark ['lændmɑ:k] *n* baken *nt*; mijlpaal *c*

landscape ['lændskeip] *n* landschap *nt*

lane [lein] *n* steeg *c*, pad *nt*; rijstrook *c*

language ['læŋgwidʒ] *n* taal *c*; ~ **laboratory** talenpracticum *nt*

lantern ['læntən] *n* lantaarn *c*

lapel [lə'pel] *n* revers *c*

larder ['lɑ:də] *n* provisiekast *c*

large [lɑ:dʒ] *adj* groot; ruim

lark [lɑ:k] *n* leeuwerik *c*

laryngitis [,lærin'dʒaitis] *n* keelontsteking *c*

last [lɑ:st] *adj* laatst; vorig; *v* duren; **at** ~ eindelijk; tenslotte, uiteindelijk

lasting ['lɑ:stiŋ] *adj* blijvend, duurzaam

latchkey ['lætʃki:] *n* huissleutel *c*

late [leit] *adj* laat; te laat

lately ['leitli] *adv* de laatste tijd, onlangs, laatst

lather ['lɑ:ðə] *n* schuim *nt*

Latin America ['lætin ə'merikə] Latijns-Amerika

Latin-American [,lætinə'merikən] *adj* Latijns-Amerikaans

latitude ['lætitju:d] *n* breedtegraad *c*

laugh [lɑ:f] *v* *lachen; *n* lach *c*

laughter ['lɑ:ftə] *n* gelach *nt*

launch [lɔ:ntʃ] *v* inzetten; lanceren; *n* motorschip *nt*

launching ['lɔ:ntʃiŋ] *n* tewaterlating *c*

launderette [,lɔ:ndə'ret] *n* wasserette *c*

laundry ['lɔ:ndri] *n* wasserij *c*; was *c*

lavatory ['lævətəri] *n* toilet *nt*

lavish ['læviʃ] *adj* kwistig

law [lɔ:] *n* wet *c*; recht *nt*; ~ **court** gerecht *nt*

lawful ['lɔ:fəl] *adj* wettig

lawn [lɔ:n] *n* grasveld *nt*, gazon *nt*

lawsuit ['lɔ:su:t] *n* proces *nt*, geding *nt*

lawyer ['lɔ:jə] *n* advocaat *c*; jurist *c*

laxative ['læksətiv] *n* laxeermiddel *nt*

*lay [lei] *v* plaatsen, zetten, leggen; ~ **bricks** metselen

layer [leiə] *n* laag *c*

layman ['leimən] *n* leek *c*

lazy ['leizi] *adj* lui

lead¹ [li:d] *n* voorsprong *c*; leiding *c*; riem *c*

lead² [led] *n* lood *nt*

*lead [li:d] *v* leiden

leader ['li:də] *n* aanvoerder *c*, leider *c*

leadership ['li:dəʃip] *n* leiderschap *nt*

leading ['li:diŋ] *adj* vooraanstaand, voornaamst

leaf [li:f] *n* (pl leaves) blad *nt*

league [li:g] *n* bond *c*

leak [li:k] *v* lekken; *n* lek *nt*

leaky ['li:ki] *adj* lek

lean [li:n] *adj* mager

*lean [li:n] *v* leunen

leap [li:p] *n* sprong *c*

*leap [li:p] *v* *springen

leap-year ['li:pjiə] *n* schrikkeljaar *nt*

*learn [lə:n] *v* leren

learner ['lə:nə] *n* beginneling *c*, beginner *c*

lease [li:s] *n* huurcontract *nt*; pacht *c*; *v* verpachten, verhuren; huren

leash [li:ʃ] *n* lijn *c*

least [li:st] *adj* geringst, minst; kleinst; **at** ~ minstens; tenminste

leather ['leðə] *n* leer *nt*; lederen, leren

leave [li:v] *n* verlof *nt*

*leave [li:v] v *vertrekken, *verlaten; *laten; ~ behind *achterlaten; ~ out *weglaten

Lebanese [,lebə'ni:z] adj Libanees; n Libanees c

Lebanon ['lebənən] Libanon

lecture ['lektʃə] n college nt, lezing c

left[1] [left] adj links

left[2] [left] v (p, pp leave)

left-hand ['lefthænd] adj links

left-handed [,left'hændid] adj linkshandig

leg [leg] n poot c, been nt

legacy ['legəsi] n erfenis c

legal ['li:gəl] adj wettig, wettelijk; juridisch

legalization [,li:gəlai'zeifən] n legalisatie c

legation [li'geifən] n legatie c

legible ['ledʒibəl] adj leesbaar

legitimate [li'dʒitimət] adj wettig

leisure ['leʒə] n vrije tijd; gemak nt

lemon ['lemən] n citroen c

lemonade [,lemə'neid] n limonade c

*lend [lend] v lenen, uitlenen

length [leŋθ] n lengte c

lengthen ['leŋθən] v verlengen

lengthways ['leŋθweiz] adv in de lengte

lens [lenz] n lens c; telephoto ~ telelens c; zoom ~ zoomlens c

leprosy ['leprəsi] n lepra c

less [les] adv minder

lessen ['lesən] v verminderen

lesson ['lesən] n les c

*let [let] v *laten; verhuren; ~ down teleurstellen

letter ['letə] n brief c; letter c; ~ of credit kredietbrief c; ~ of recommendation aanbevelingsbrief c

letter-box ['letəbɔks] n brievenbus c

lettuce ['letis] n sla c

level ['levəl] adj egaal; plat, vlak, effen, gelijk; n peil nt, niveau nt; waterpas c; v egaliseren, nivelleren; ~ crossing overweg c

lever ['li:və] n hefboom c, hendel c

Levis ['li:vaiz] pl jeans pl

liability [,laiə'biləti] n aansprakelijkheid c

liable ['laiəbəl] adj aansprakelijk; ~ to onderhevig aan

liberal ['libərəl] adj liberaal; mild, royaal, vrijgevig

liberation [,libə'reifən] n bevrijding c

Liberia [lai'biəriə] Liberia

Liberian [lai'biəriən] adj Liberiaans; n Liberiaan c

liberty ['libəti] n vrijheid c

library ['laibrəri] n bibliotheek c

licence ['laisəns] n licentie c; vergunning c; driving ~ rijbewijs nt; ~ number Am kenteken nt; ~ plate Am nummerbord nt

license ['laisəns] v een vergunning verlenen

lick [lik] v likken

lid [lid] n deksel nt

lie [lai] v *liegen; n leugen c

*lie [lai] v *liggen; ~ down *gaan liggen

life [laif] n (pl lives) leven nt; ~ insurance levensverzekering c

lifebelt ['laifbelt] n reddingsgordel c

lifetime ['laiftaim] n leven nt

lift [lift] v optillen; n lift c

light [lait] n licht nt; adj licht; ~ bulb peer c

*light [lait] v *aansteken

lighter ['laitə] n aansteker c

lighthouse ['laithaus] n vuurtoren c

lighting ['laitiŋ] n verlichting c

lightning ['laitniŋ] n bliksem c

like [laik] v *houden van; *mogen, lusten; adj gelijk; conj zoals; prep als

likely ['laikli] adj waarschijnlijk

like-minded [,laik'maindid] adj gelijkgezind

likewise ['laikwaiz] *adv* evenzo, eveneens

lily ['lili] *n* lelie *c*

limb [lim] *n* ledemaat *c*

lime [laim] *n* kalk *c*; linde *c*; limoen *c*

limetree ['laimtri:] *n* linde *c*

limit ['limit] *n* limiet *c*; *v* beperken

limp [limp] *v* hinken; *adj* slap

line [lain] *n* regel *c*; streep *c*; snoer *nt*; lijn *c*; rij *c*; **stand in ~** *Am* in de rij *staan

linen ['linin] *n* linnen *nt*; linnengoed *nt*

liner ['lainə] *n* lijnboot *c*

lingerie ['lɔ̃ʒəri:] *n* lingerie *c*

lining ['lainiŋ] *n* voering *c*

link [liŋk] *v* *verbinden; *n* verbinding *c*; schakel *c*

lion ['laiən] *n* leeuw *c*

lip [lip] *n* lip *c*

lipsalve ['lipsa:v] *n* lippenboter *c*

lipstick ['lipstik] *n* lippenstift *c*

liqueur [li'kjuə] *n* likeur *c*

liquid ['likwid] *adj* vloeibaar; *n* vloeistof *c*

liquor ['likə] *n* sterke drank

liquorice ['likəris] *n* drop *c*

list [list] *n* lijst *c*; *v* noteren

listen ['lisən] *v* aanhoren, luisteren

listener ['lisnə] *n* luisteraar *c*

literary ['litrəri] *adj* letterkundig, literair

literature ['litrətʃə] *n* literatuur *c*

litre ['li:tə] *n* liter *c*

litter ['litə] *n* afval *nt*; rommel *c*; nest *nt*

little ['litəl] *adj* klein; weinig

live[1] [liv] *v* leven; wonen

live[2] [laiv] *adj* levend

livelihood ['laivlihud] *n* kost *c*

lively ['laivli] *adj* levendig

liver ['livə] *n* lever *c*

living-room ['liviŋru:m] *n* huiskamer *c*,

woonkamer *c*

load [loud] *n* lading *c*; last *c*; *v* *laden

loaf [louf] *n* (pl loaves) brood *nt*

loan [loun] *n* lening *c*

lobby ['lɔbi] *n* hal *c*; foyer *c*

lobster ['lɔbstə] *n* kreeft *c*

local ['loukəl] *adj* lokaal, plaatselijk; **~ call** lokaal gesprek; **~ train** stoptrein *c*

locality [lou'kæləti] *n* plaats *c*

locate [lou'keit] *v* plaatsen

location [lou'keiʃən] *n* ligging *c*

lock [lɔk] *v* op slot *doen; *n* slot *nt*; sluis *c*; **~ up** *opsluiten

locomotive [,loukə'moutiv] *n* locomotief *c*

lodge [lɔdʒ] *v* herbergen; *n* jachthuis *nt*

lodger ['lɔdʒə] *n* kamerbewoner *c*

lodgings ['lɔdʒiŋz] *pl* logies *nt*

log [lɔg] *n* houtblok *c*

logic ['lɔdʒik] *n* logica *c*

logical ['lɔdʒikəl] *adj* logisch

lonely ['lounli] *adj* eenzaam

long [lɔŋ] *adj* lang; langdurig; **~ for** verlangen naar; **no longer** niet meer

longing ['lɔŋiŋ] *n* verlangen *nt*

longitude ['lɔndʒitju:d] *n* lengtegraad *c*

look [luk] *v* *kijken; *lijken, er uit *zien; *n* kijkje *nt*, blik *c*; uiterlijk *nt*, voorkomen *nt*; **~ after** verzorgen, zorgen voor, passen op; **~ at** *aankijken, *kijken naar; **~ for** *zoeken; **~ out** *uitkijken, oppassen; **~ up** *opzoeken

looking-glass ['lukiŋglɑ:s] *n* spiegel *c*

loop [lu:p] *n* lus *c*

loose [lu:s] *adj* los

loosen ['lu:sən] *v* losmaken

lord [lɔ:d] *n* lord *c*

lorry ['lɔri] *n* vrachtwagen *c*

***lose** [lu:z] *v* kwijtraken, *verliezen

loss [lɔs] *n* verlies *nt*

lost [lɔst] *adj* verdwaald; weg; ~ **and found** gevonden voorwerpen; ~ **property office** bureau voor gevonden voorwerpen

lot [lɔt] *n* lot *nt*; hoop *c*, boel *c*

lotion ['louʃən] *n* lotion *c*; **aftershave** ~ after shave

lottery ['lɔtəri] *n* loterij *c*

loud [laud] *adj* hard, luid

loud-speaker [,laud'spi:kə] *n* luidspreker *c*

lounge [laundʒ] *n* salon *c*

louse [laus] *n* (pl lice) luis *c*

love [lʌv] *v* *houden van, *liefhebben; *n* liefde *c*; **in** ~ verliefd

lovely ['lʌvli] *adj* heerlijk, prachtig, mooi

lover ['lʌvə] *n* minnaar *c*

love-story ['lʌv,stɔ:ri] *n* liefdesgeschiedenis *c*

low [lou] *adj* laag; diep; neerslachtig; ~ **tide** eb *c*

lower ['louə] *v* *neerlaten; verlagen; *strijken; *adj* onderst, lager

lowlands ['loulandz] *pl* laagland *nt*

loyal ['lɔiəl] *adj* loyaal

lubricate ['lu:brikeit] *v* oliën, smeren

lubrication [,lu:bri'keiʃən] *n* smering *c*; ~ **oil** smeerolie *c*; ~ **system** smeersysteem *nt*

luck [lʌk] *n* geluk *nt*; toeval *nt*; **bad** ~ pech *c*

lucky charm amulet *c*

ludicrous ['lu:dikrəs] *adj* belachelijk, bespottelijk

luggage ['lʌgidʒ] *n* bagage *c*; **hand** ~ handbagage *c*; **left** ~ **office** bagagedepot *nt*; ~ **rack** bagagerek *nt*, bagagenet *nt*; ~ **van** bagagewagen *c*

lukewarm ['lu:kwɔ:m] *adj* lauw

lumbago [lʌm'beigou] *n* spit *nt*

luminous ['lu:minəs] *adj* lichtgevend

lump [lʌmp] *n* brok *nt*, klont *c*, stuk

nt; bult *c*; ~ **of sugar** suikerklontje *nt*; ~ **sum** ronde som

lumpy ['lʌmpi] *adj* klonterig

lunacy ['lu:nəsi] *n* krankzinnigheid *c*

lunatic ['lu:nətik] *adj* krankzinnig; *n* krankzinnige *c*

lunch [lʌntʃ] *n* lunch *c*, middageten *nt*

luncheon ['lʌntʃən] *n* middageten *nt*

lung [lʌŋ] *n* long *c*

lust [lʌst] *n* wellust *c*

luxurious [lʌg'ʒuəriəs] *adj* luxueus

luxury ['lʌkʃəri] *n* luxe *c*

M

machine [mə'ʃi:n] *n* apparaat *nt*, machine *c*

machinery [mə'ʃi:nəri] *n* machinerie *c*; mechanisme *nt*

mackerel ['mækrəl] *n* (pl ~) makreel *c*

mackintosh ['mækintɔʃ] *n* regenjas *c*

mad [mæd] *adj* krankzinnig, waanzinnig, gek; kwaad

madam ['mædəm] *n* mevrouw

madness ['mædnəs] *n* waanzin *c*

magazine [,mægə'zi:n] *n* blad *nt*

magic ['mædʒik] *n* toverkunst *c*, magie *c*; *adj* tover-

magician [mə'dʒiʃən] *n* goochelaar *c*

magistrate ['mædʒistreit] *n* magistraat *c*

magnetic [mæg'netik] *adj* magnetisch

magneto [mæg'ni:tou] *n* (pl ~s) magneet *c*

magnificent [mæg'nifisənt] *adj* prachtig; groots, luisterrijk

magpie ['mægpai] *n* ekster *c*

maid [meid] *n* meid *c*

maiden name ['meidən neim] meisjesnaam *c*

mail [meil] *n* post *c*; *v* posten; ~ **order** *Am* postwissel *c*

mailbox ['meilbɔks] *nAm* brievenbus *c*
main [mein] *adj* hoofd-, voornaamst; grootst; ~ **deck** bovendek *nt*; ~ **line** hoofdlijn *c*; ~ **road** hoofdweg *c*; ~ **street** hoofdstraat *c*
mainland ['meinlənd] *n* vasteland *nt*
mainly ['meinli] *adv* hoofdzakelijk
mains [meinz] *pl* hoofdleiding *c*
maintain [mein'tein] *v* handhaven
maintenance ['meintənəns] *n* onderhoud *nt*
maize [meiz] *n* maïs *c*
major ['meidʒə] *adj* groter; grootst; *n* majoor *c*
majority [mə'dʒɔrəti] *n* meerderheid *c*
*make [meik] *v* maken; verdienen; halen; ~ **do with** zich **behelpen met; ~ **good** vergoeden; ~ **up** opstellen
make-up ['meikʌp] *n* make-up *c*
malaria [mə'leəriə] *n* malaria *c*
Malay [mə'lei] *n* Maleis *nt*
Malaysia [mə'leiziə] Maleisië
Malaysian [mə'leiziən] *adj* Maleisisch
male [meil] *adj* mannelijk
malicious [mə'liʃəs] *adj* boosaardig
malignant [mə'lignənt] *adj* kwaadaardig
mallet ['mælit] *n* houten hamer
malnutrition [,mælnju'triʃən] *n* ondervoeding *c*
mammal ['mæməl] *n* zoogdier *nt*
mammoth ['mæməθ] *n* mammoet *c*
man [mæn] *n* (pl men) man *c*; mens *c*; **men's room** herentoilet *nt*
manage ['mænidʒ] *v* beheren; slagen
manageable ['mænidʒəbəl] *adj* hanteerbaar
management ['mænidʒmənt] *n* directie *c*; beheer *nt*
manager ['mænidʒə] *n* chef *c*, directeur *c*
mandarin ['mændərin] *n* mandarijn *c*
mandate ['mændeit] *n* mandaat *nt*

manger ['meindʒə] *n* kribbe *c*
manicure ['mænikjuə] *n* manicure *c*; *v* manicuren
mankind [mæn'kaind] *n* mensheid *c*
mannequin ['mænəkin] *n* mannequin *c*
manner ['mænə] *n* wijze *c*, manier *c*; **manners** *pl* manieren
man-of-war [,mænəv'wɔ:] *n* oorlogsschip *nt*
manor-house ['mænəhaus] *n* herenhuis *nt*
mansion ['mænʃən] *n* herenhuis *nt*
manual ['mænjuəl] *adj* hand-
manufacture [,mænju'fæktʃə] *v* vervaardigen, fabriceren
manufacturer [,mænju'fæktʃərə] *n* fabrikant *c*
manure [mə'njuə] *n* mest *c*
manuscript ['mænjuskript] *n* manuscript *nt*
many ['meni] *adj* veel
map [mæp] *n* kaart *c*; landkaart *c*; plattegrond *c*
maple ['meipəl] *n* esdoorn *c*
marble ['ma:bəl] *n* marmer *nt*; knikker *c*
March [ma:tʃ] maart
march [ma:tʃ] *v* marcheren; *n* mars *c*
mare [meə] *n* merrie *c*
margarine [,ma:dʒə'ri:n] *n* margarine *c*
margin ['ma:dʒin] *n* kantlijn *c*, marge *c*
maritime ['mæritaim] *adj* maritiem
mark [ma:k] *v* aankruisen; merken; kenmerken; *n* merkteken *nt*; cijfer *nt*; schietschijf *c*
market ['ma:kit] *n* markt *c*
market-place ['ma:kitpleis] *n* marktplein *nt*
marmalade ['ma:məleid] *n* marmelade *c*
marriage ['mæridʒ] *n* huwelijk *nt*

marrow ['mærou] *n* merg *nt*

marry ['mæri] *v* huwen, trouwen;
married couple echtpaar *nt*

marsh [mɑːʃ] *n* moeras *nt*

marshy ['mɑːʃi] *adj* moerassig

martyr ['mɑːtə] *n* martelaar *c*

marvel ['mɑːvəl] *n* wonder *nt*; *v* zich
verbazen

marvellous ['mɑːvələs] *adj* prachtig

mascara [mæ'skɑːrə] *n* mascara *c*

masculine ['mæskjulin] *adj* mannelijk

mash [mæʃ] *v* fijnstampen

mask [mɑːsk] *n* masker *nt*

Mass [mæs] *n* mis *c*

mass [mæs] *n* massa *c*; ~ production
massaproduktie *c*

massage ['mæsɑːʒ] *n* massage *c*; *v*
masseren

masseur [mæ'səː] *n* masseur *c*

massive ['mæsiv] *adj* massief

mast [mɑːst] *n* mast *c*

master ['mɑːstə] *n* meester *c*; baas *c*;
leraar *c*, onderwijzer *c*; *v* beheersen

masterpiece ['mɑːstəpiːs] *n* meesterwerk *nt*

mat [mæt] *n* mat *c*; *adj* mat, dof

match [mætʃ] *n* lucifer *c*; wedstrijd *c*;
v passen bij

match-box ['mætʃbɔks] *n* lucifersdoosje *nt*

material [mə'tiəriəl] *n* materiaal *nt*;
stof *c*; *adj* stoffelijk, materieel

mathematical [,mæθə'mætikəl] *adj*
wiskundig

mathematics [,mæθə'mætiks] *n* wiskunde *c*

matrimonial [,mætri'mouniəl] *adj* echtelijk

matrimony ['mætriməni] *n* echt *c*

matter ['mætə] *n* stof *c*, materie *c*;
aangelegenheid *c*, kwestie *c*, zaak *c*;
v van belang *zijn; as a ~ of fact
feitelijk, eigenlijk

matter-of-fact [,mætərəv'fækt] *adj*

nuchter

mattress ['mætrəs] *n* matras *c*

mature [mə'tjuə] *adj* rijp

maturity [mə'tjuərəti] *n* rijpheid *c*

mausoleum [,mɔːsə'liːəm] *n* mausoleum *nt*

mauve [mouv] *adj* lichtpaars

May [mei] mei

*may [mei] *v* *kunnen; *mogen

maybe ['meibiː] *adv* misschien

mayor [mɛə] *n* burgemeester *c*

maze [meiz] *n* doolhof *nt*

me [miː] *pron* me

meadow ['medou] *n* wei *c*

meal [miːl] *n* maaltijd *c*, maal *nt*

mean [miːn] *adj* gemeen; *n* gemiddelde *nt*

*mean [miːn] *v* betekenen; bedoelen;
menen

meaning ['miːniŋ] *n* betekenis *c*

meaningless ['miːniŋləs] *adj* nietszeggend

means [miːnz] *n* middel *nt*; by no ~
zeker niet, geenszins

in the meantime [in ðə 'miːntaim] inmiddels, ondertussen

meanwhile ['miːnwail] *adv* intussen,
ondertussen

measles ['miːzəlz] *n* mazelen *pl*

measure ['meʒə] *v* *meten; *n* maat *c*;
maatregel *c*

meat [miːt] *n* vlees *nt*

mechanic [mi'kænik] *n* monteur *c*

mechanical [mi'kænikəl] *adj* mechanisch

mechanism ['mekənizəm] *n* mechanisme *nt*

medal ['medəl] *n* medaille *c*

mediaeval [,medi'iːvəl] *adj* middeleeuws

mediate ['miːdieit] *v* bemiddelen

mediator ['miːdieitə] *n* bemiddelaar *c*

medical ['medikəl] *adj* geneeskundig,
medisch

medicine ['medsin] n geneesmiddel nt; geneeskunde c

meditate ['mediteit] v mediteren

Mediterranean [,meditə'reiniən] Middellandse Zee

medium ['mi:diəm] adj middelmatig, gemiddeld, midden-

*meet [mi:t] v ontmoeten; *tegenkomen

meeting ['mi:tiŋ] n vergadering c, bijeenkomst c: ontmoeting c

meeting-place ['mi:tiŋpleis] n trefpunt nt

melancholy ['melənkəli] n weemoed c

mellow ['melou] adj zacht

melodrama ['melə,drɑ:mə] n melodrama nt

melody ['melədi] n melodie c

melon ['melən] n meloen c

melt [melt] v *smelten

member ['membə] n lid nt; **Member of Parliament** kamerlid nt

membership ['membəʃip] n lidmaatschap nt

memo ['memou] n (pl ~s) memorandum nt

memorable ['memərəbəl] adj gedenkwaardig

memorial [mə'mɔ:riəl] n gedenkteken nt

memorize ['meməraiz] v uit het hoofd leren

memory ['meməri] n geheugen nt; herinnering c; nagedachtenis c

mend [mend] v herstellen, repareren

menstruation [,menstru'eiʃən] n menstruatie c

mental ['mentəl] adj geestelijk

mention ['menʃən] v noemen, vermelden; n melding c, vermelding c

menu ['menju:] n spijskaart c, menukaart c

merchandise ['mə:tʃəndaiz] n handelswaar c, koopwaar c

merchant ['mə:tʃənt] n handelaar c, koopman c

merciful ['mə:sifəl] adj barmhartig

mercury ['mə:kjuri] n kwik nt

mercy ['mə:si] n genade c, clementie c

mere [miə] adj louter

merely ['miəli] adv slechts

merger ['mə:dʒə] n fusie c

merit ['merit] v verdienen; n verdienste c

mermaid ['mə:meid] n zeemeermin c

merry ['meri] adj vrolijk

merry-go-round ['merigou,raund] n draaimolen c

mesh [meʃ] n maas c

mess [mes] n rommel c, warboel c; ~ up *bederven

message ['mesidʒ] n boodschap c, bericht nt

messenger ['mesindʒə] n bode c

metal ['metəl] n metaal nt; metalen

meter ['mi:tə] n meter c

method ['meθəd] n aanpak c, methode c; orde c

methodical [mə'θɔdikəl] adj methodisch

methylated spirits ['meθəleitid 'spirits] brandspiritus c

metre ['mi:tə] n meter c

metric ['metrik] adj metrisch

Mexican ['meksikən] adj Mexicaans; n Mexicaan c

Mexico ['meksikou] Mexico

mezzanine ['mezəni:n] n entresol c

microphone ['maikrəfoun] n microfoon c

midday ['middei] n middag c

middle ['midəl] n midden nt; adj middelst; **Middle Ages** middeleeuwen pl; **middle-class** adj burgerlijk

midnight ['midnait] n middernacht c

midst [midst] n midden nt

midsummer ['mid,sʌmə] n midzomer c

midwife ['midwaif] n (pl -wives) vroedvrouw *c*

might [mait] *n* macht *c*

*might [mait] *v* *kunnen

mighty ['maiti] *adj* machtig

migraine ['migrein] *n* migraine *c*

mild [maild] *adj* zacht

mildew ['mildju] *n* schimmel *c*

mile [mail] *n* mijl *c*

mileage ['mailidʒ] *n* afstand in mijlen

milepost ['mailpoust] *n* wegwijzer *c*

milestone ['mailstoun] *n* mijlpaal *c*

milieu ['mi:ljə] *n* milieu *nt*

military ['militəri] *adj* militair; ~ **force** krijgsmacht *c*

milk [milk] *n* melk *c*

milkman ['milkmən] *n* (pl -men) melkboer *c*

milk-shake ['milkʃeik] *n* milk shake *c*

mill [mil] *n* molen *c*; fabriek *c*

miller ['milə] *n* molenaar *c*

milliner ['milinə] *n* modiste *c*

million ['miljən] *n* miljoen *nt*

millionaire [,miljə'neə] *n* miljonair *c*

mince [mins] *v* fijnhakken

mind [maind] *n* geest *c*; *v* bezwaar *hebben tegen; letten op, *geven om

mine [main] *n* mijn *c*

miner ['mainə] *n* mijnwerker *c*

mineral ['minərəl] *n* delfstof *c*, mineraal *nt*; ~ **water** mineraalwater *nt*

miniature ['minjətʃə] *n* miniatuur *c*

minimum ['miniməm] *n* minimum *nt*

mining ['mainiŋ] *n* mijnbouw *c*

minister ['ministə] *n* minister *c*; predikant *c*; **Prime Minister** premier *c*

ministry ['ministri] *n* ministerie *nt*

mink [miŋk] *n* nerts *nt*

minor ['mainə] *adj* klein, gering, kleiner; ondergeschikt; *n* minderjarige *c*

minority [mai'nɔrəti] *n* minderheid *c*

mint [mint] *n* munt *c*

minus ['mainəs] *prep* min

minute¹ ['minit] *n* minuut *c*; **minutes** notulen *pl*

minute² [mai'nju:t] *adj* minuscuul

miracle ['mirəkəl] *n* wonder *nt*

miraculous [mi'rækjuləs] *adj* wonderbaarlijk

mirror ['mirə] *n* spiegel *c*

misbehave [,misbi'heiv] *v* zich *misdragen

miscarriage [mis'kæridʒ] *n* miskraam *c*

miscellaneous [,misə'leiniəs] *adj* gemengd

mischief ['mistʃif] *n* kattekwaad *nt*; onheil *nt*, schade *c*, kwaad *nt*

mischievous ['mistʃivəs] *adj* ondeugend

miserable ['mizərəbəl] *adj* beroerd, ellendig

misery ['mizəri] *n* narigheid *c*, ellende *c*; nood *c*

misfortune [mis'fɔ:tʃen] *n* tegenslag *c*, ongeluk *nt*

*mislay [mis'lei] *v* kwijtraken

misplaced [mis'pleist] *adj* misplaatst

mispronounce [,misprə'nauns] *v* verkeerd *uitspreken

miss¹ [mis] mejuffrouw, juffrouw *c*

miss² [mis] *v* missen

missing ['misiŋ] *adj* ontbrekend; ~ **person** vermiste *c*

mist [mist] *n* nevel *c*, mist *c*

mistake [mi'steik] *n* abuis *nt*, vergissing *c*, fout *c*

*mistake [mi'steik] *v* verwarren

mistaken [mi'steikən] *adj* fout; *be ~ zich vergissen

mister ['mistə] meneer, mijnheer

mistress ['mistrəs] *n* vrouw des huizes; meesteres *c*; maîtresse *c*

mistrust [mis'trʌst] *v* wantrouwen

misty ['misti] *adj* mistig

*misunderstand [,misʌndə'stænd] *v* *misverstaan

misunderstanding [‚misʌndə'stændiŋ] *n* misverstand *nt*

misuse [mis'ju:s] *n* misbruik *nt*

mittens ['mitənz] *pl* wanten *pl*

mix [miks] *v* mengen; ~ **with** *omgaan met

mixed [mikst] *adj* gemêleerd, gemengd

mixer ['miksə] *n* mixer *c*

mixture ['mikstʃə] *n* mengsel *nt*

moan [moun] *v* kreunen

moat [mout] *n* gracht *c*

mobile ['moubail] *adj* beweeglijk, mobiel

mock [mɔk] *v* bespotten

mockery ['mɔkəri] *n* spot *c*

model ['mɔdəl] *n* model *nt*; mannequin *c*; *v* modelleren, boetseren

moderate ['mɔdərət] *adj* gematigd, matig; middelmatig

modern ['mɔdən] *adj* modern

modest ['mɔdist] *adj* discreet, bescheiden

modesty ['mɔdisti] *n* bescheidenheid *c*

modify ['mɔdifai] *v* wijzigen

mohair ['mouheə] *n* mohair *nt*

moist [mɔist] *adj* nat, vochtig

moisten ['mɔisən] *v* bevochtigen

moisture ['mɔistʃə] *n* vochtigheid *c*; **moisturizing cream** vochtinbrengende crème

molar ['moulə] *n* kies *c*

moment ['moumənt] *n* moment *nt*, ogenblik *nt*

momentary ['moumentəri] *adj* kortstondig

monarch ['mɔnək] *n* vorst *c*

monarchy ['mɔnəki] *n* monarchie *c*

monastery ['mɔnəstri] *n* klooster *nt*

Monday ['mʌndi] maandag *c*

monetary ['mʌnitəri] *adj* monetair; ~ **unit** munteenheid *c*

money ['mʌni] *n* geld *nt*; ~ **exchange** wisselkantoor *nt*; ~ **order** overschrijving *c*

monk [mʌŋk] *n* monnik *c*

monkey ['mʌŋki] *n* aap *c*

monologue ['mɔnolɔg] *n* monoloog *c*

monopoly [mə'nɔpəli] *n* monopolie *nt*

monotonous [mə'nɔtənəs] *adj* eentonig

month [mʌnθ] *n* maand *c*

monthly ['mʌnθli] *adj* maandelijks; ~ **magazine** maandblad *c*

monument ['mɔnjumənt] *n* gedenkteken *nt*, monument *nt*

mood [mu:d] *n* humeur *nt*, stemming *c*

moon [mu:n] *n* maan *c*

moonlight ['mu:nlait] *n* maanlicht *nt*

moor [muə] *n* heide *c*, veen *nt*

moose [mu:s] *n* (pl ~, ~s) eland *c*

moped ['mouped] *n* bromfiets *c*

moral ['mɔrəl] *n* moraal *c*; *adj* zedelijk, moreel; **morals** zeden *pl*

morality [mə'ræləti] *n* moraliteit *c*

more [mɔ:] *adj* meer; **once** ~ nogmaals

moreover [mɔ:'rouvə] *adv* voorts, bovendien

morning ['mɔ:niŋ] *n* ochtend *c*, morgen *c*; ~ **paper** ochtendblad *nt*; **this** ~ vanmorgen

Moroccan [mə'rɔkən] *adj* Marokkaans; *n* Marokkaan *c*

Morocco [mə'rɔkou] Marokko

morphia ['mɔ:fiə] *n* morfine *c*

morphine ['mɔ:fi:n] *n* morfine *c*

morsel ['mɔ:səl] *n* brok *c*

mortal ['mɔ:təl] *adj* dodelijk, sterfelijk

mortgage ['mɔ:gidʒ] *n* hypotheek *c*

mosaic [mə'zeiik] *n* mozaïek *nt*

mosque [mɔsk] *n* moskee *c*

mosquito [mə'ski:tou] *n* (pl ~es) mug *c*; muskiet *c*

mosquito-net [mə'ski:tounet] *n* muskietennet *nt*

moss [mɔs] *n* mos *nt*

most [moust] *adj* meest; **at** ~ hoogstens, hooguit; ~ **of all** vooral

mostly ['moustli] adv meestal

motel [mou'tel] n motel nt

moth [moθ] n mot c

mother ['mʌðə] n moeder c; ~ tongue moedertaal c

mother-in-law ['mʌðərinlɔ:] n (pl mothers-) schoonmoeder c

mother-of-pearl [,mʌðərəv'pə:l] n paarlemoer nt

motion ['mouʃən] n beweging c; motie c

motive ['moutiv] n motief nt

motor ['moutə] n motor c; v *autorij-den; ~ body Am carrosserie c; starter ~ startmotor c

motorbike ['moutəbaik] nAm brom-mer c

motor-boat ['moutəbout] n motorboot c

motor-car ['moutəka:] n auto c

motor-cycle ['moutə,saikəl] n motor-fiets c

motoring ['moutəriŋ] n automobilisme nt

motorist ['moutərist] n automobilist c

motorway ['moutəwei] n snelweg c

motto ['motou] n (pl ~es, ~s) devies nt

mouldy ['mouldi] adj beschimmeld

mound [maund] n heuvel c

mount [maunt] v *bestijgen; n berg c

mountain ['mauntin] n berg c; ~ pass bergpas c; ~ range bergketen c

mountaineering [,maunti'niəriŋ] n bergsport c

mountainous ['mauntinəs] adj berg-achtig

mourning ['mɔ:niŋ] n rouw c

mouse [maus] n (pl mice) muis c

moustache [mə'sta:ʃ] n snor c

mouth [mauθ] n mond c; muil c, bek c; monding c

mouthwash ['mauθwɔʃ] n mondspoe-ling c

movable ['mu:vəbəl] adj roerend

move [mu:v] v *bewegen; verplaat-sen; verhuizen; ontroeren; n zet c, stap c; verhuizing c

movement ['mu:vmənt] n beweging c

movie ['mu:vi] n film c; movies Am bioscoop c; ~ theater Am bios-coop c

much [mʌtʃ] adj veel; as ~ evenveel; evenzeer

muck [mʌk] n drek c

mud [mʌd] n modder c

muddle ['mʌdəl] n wirwar c, warboel c; v verknoeien

muddy ['mʌdi] adj modderig

mud-guard ['mʌdga:d] n spatbord nt

muffler ['mʌflə] nAm knalpot c

mug [mʌg] n beker c, kroes c

mulberry ['mʌlbəri] n moerbei c

mule [mju:l] n muildier nt, muilezel c

mullet ['mʌlit] n mul c

multiplication [,mʌltipli'keiʃən] n ver-menigvuldiging c

multiply ['mʌltiplai] v vermenigvuldi-gen

mumps [mʌmps] n bof c

municipal [mju:'nisipəl] adj gemeente-lijk

municipality [mju:,nisi'pæləti] n ge-meentebestuur nt

murder ['mə:də] n moord c; v ver-moorden

murderer ['mə:dərə] n moordenaar c

muscle ['mʌsəl] n spier c

muscular ['mʌskjulə] adj gespierd

museum [mju:'zi:əm] n museum nt

mushroom ['mʌʃru:m] n champignon c; paddestoel c

music ['mju:zik] n muziek c; ~ acad-emy conservatorium nt

musical ['mju:zikəl] adj muzikaal; n musical c

music-hall ['mju:zikhɔ:l] n variététhea-ter nt

musician [mju:'ziʃən] *n* musicus *c*
muslin ['mʌzlin] *n* mousseline *c*
mussel ['mʌsəl] *n* mossel *c*
* **must** [mʌst] *v* *moeten
mustard ['mʌstəd] *n* mosterd *c*
mute [mju:t] *adj* stom
mutiny ['mju:tini] *n* muiterij *c*
mutton ['mʌtən] *n* schapevlees *nt*
mutual ['mju:tʃuəl] *adj* onderling, wederzijds
my [mai] *adj* mijn
myself [mai'self] *pron* me; zelf
mysterious [mi'stiəriəs] *adj* mysterieus, geheimzinnig
mystery ['mistəri] *n* raadsel *nt*, mysterie *nt*
myth [miθ] *n* mythe *c*

N

nail [neil] *n* nagel *c*; spijker *c*
nailbrush ['neilbrʌʃ] *n* nagelborstel *c*
nail-file ['neilfail] *n* nagelvijl *c*
nail-polish ['neil,poliʃ] *n* nagellak *c*
nail-scissors ['neil,sizəz] *pl* nagelschaar *c*
naïve [nɑ:'i:v] *adj* naïef
naked ['neikid] *adj* bloot, naakt; kaal
name [neim] *n* naam *c*; *v* noemen; **in the ~ of** namens
namely ['neimli] *adv* namelijk
nap [næp] *n* dutje *nt*
napkin ['næpkin] *n* servet *nt*
nappy ['næpi] *n* luier *c*
narcosis [nɑ:'kousis] *n* (pl -ses) narcose *c*
narcotic [nɑ:'kɔtik] *n* narcoticum *nt*
narrow ['nærou] *adj* eng, smal, nauw
narrow-minded [,nærou'maindid] *adj* bekrompen
nasty ['nɑ:sti] *adj* naar, akelig
nation ['neiʃən] *n* natie *c*; volk *nt*

national ['næʃənəl] *adj* nationaal; volks-; staats-; ~ **anthem** volkslied *nt*; ~ **dress** nationale klederdracht; ~ **park** natuurreservaat *nt*
nationality [,næʃə'næləti] *n* nationaliteit *c*
nationalize ['næʃənəlaiz] *v* nationaliseren
native ['neitiv] *n* inboorling *c*; *adj* inheems; ~ **country** vaderland *nt*, geboorteland *nt*; ~ **language** moedertaal *c*
natural ['nætʃərəl] *adj* natuurlijk; aangeboren
naturally ['nætʃərəli] *adv* natuurlijk, uiteraard
nature ['neitʃə] *n* natuur *c*; aard *c*
naughty ['nɔ:ti] *adj* ondeugend, stout
nausea ['nɔ:siə] *n* misselijkheid *c*
naval ['neivəl] *adj* marine-
navel ['neivəl] *n* navel *c*
navigable ['nævigəbəl] *adj* bevaarbaar
navigate ['nævigeit] *v* *varen; sturen
navigation [,nævi'geiʃən] *n* navigatie *c*; scheepvaart *c*
navy ['neivi] *n* marine *c*
near [niə] *prep* bij; *adj* nabij, dichtbij
nearby ['niəbai] *adj* nabijzijnd
nearly ['niəli] *adv* haast, bijna
neat [ni:t] *adj* keurig, net; puur
necessary ['nesəsəri] *adj* nodig, noodzakelijk
necessity [nə'sesəti] *n* noodzaak *c*
neck [nek] *n* hals *c*; **nape of the ~** nek *c*
necklace ['nekləs] *n* halsketting *c*
necktie ['nektai] *n* das *c*
need [ni:d] *v* hoeven, behoeven, nodig *hebben; *n* nood *c*, behoefte *c*; noodzaak *c*; ~ **to** *moeten
needle ['ni:dəl] *n* naald *c*
needlework ['ni:dəlwə:k] *n* handwerk *nt*
negative ['negətiv] *adj* ontkennend,

negatief; *n* negatief *nt*
neglect [ni'glekt] *v* verwaarlozen; *n* verwaarlozing *c*
neglectful [ni'glektfəl] *adj* nalatig
negligee ['negliʒei] *n* negligé *nt*
negotiate [ni'gouʃieit] *v* onderhandelen
negotiation [ni,gouʃi'eiʃən] *n* onderhandeling *c*
Negro ['ni:grou] *n* (pl ~es) neger *c*
neighbour ['neibə] *n* buur *c*, buurman *c*
neighbourhood ['neibəhud] *n* buurt *c*
neighbouring ['neibəriŋ] *adj* aangrenzend, naburig
neither ['naiðə] *pron* geen van beide; **neither ... nor** noch ... noch
neon ['ni:ɔn] *n* neon *nt*
nephew ['nefju:] *n* neef *c*
nerve [nə:v] *n* zenuw *c*; durf *c*
nervous ['nə:vəs] *adj* nerveus, zenuwachtig
nest [nest] *n* nest *nt*
net [net] *n* net *nt*; *adj* netto
the Netherlands ['neðələndz] Nederland
network ['netwə:k] *n* netwerk *nt*
neuralgia [njuə'rældʒə] *n* zenuwpijn *c*
neurosis [njuə'rousis] *n* neurose *c*
neuter ['nju:tə] *adj* onzijdig
neutral ['nju:trəl] *adj* neutraal
never ['nevə] *adv* nimmer, nooit
nevertheless [,nevəðə'les] *adv* niettemin
new [nju:] *adj* nieuw; **New Year** nieuwjaar
news [nju:z] *n* nieuwsberichten *pl*, nieuws *nt*; journaal *nt*
newsagent ['nju:,zeidʒənt] *n* krantenverkoper *c*
newspaper ['nju:z,peipə] *n* krant *c*
newsreel ['nju:zri:l] *n* filmjournaal *nt*
newsstand ['nju:zstænd] *n* krantenkiosk *c*

New Zealand [nju: 'zi:lənd] Nieuw-Zeeland
next [nekst] *adj* volgend; ~ **to** naast
nice [nais] *adj* aardig, mooi, prettig; lekker; sympathiek
nickel ['nikəl] *n* nikkel *nt*
nickname ['nikneim] *n* bijnaam *c*
nicotine ['nikəti:n] *n* nicotine *c*
niece [ni:s] *n* nicht *c*
Nigeria [nai'dʒiəriə] Nigeria
Nigerian [nai'dʒiəriən] *adj* Nigeriaans; *n* Nigeriaan *c*
night [nait] *n* nacht *c*; avond *c*; **by** ~ 's nachts; ~ **flight** nachtvlucht *c*; ~ **rate** nachttarief *nt*; ~ **train** nachttrein *c*
nightclub ['naitklʌb] *n* nachtclub *c*
night-cream ['naitkri:m] *n* nachtcrème *c*
nightdress ['naitdres] *n* nachtjapon *c*
nightingale ['naitiŋgeil] *n* nachtegaal *c*
nightly ['naitli] *adj* nachtelijk
nil [nil] niets
nine [nain] *num* negen
nineteen [,nain'ti:n] *num* negentien
nineteenth [,nain'ti:nθ] *num* negentiende
ninety ['nainti] *num* negentig
ninth [nainθ] *num* negende
nitrogen ['naitrədʒən] *n* stikstof *c*
no [nou] neen, nee; *adj* geen; ~ **one** niemand
nobility [nou'biləti] *n* adel *c*
noble ['noubəl] *adj* adellijk; edel
nobody ['noubɔdi] *pron* niemand
nod [nɔd] *n* knik *c*; *v* knikken
noise [nɔiz] *n* geluid *nt*; herrie *c*, rumoer *nt*, lawaai *nt*
noisy ['nɔizi] *adj* lawaaierig; gehorig
nominal ['nɔminəl] *adj* nominaal
nominate ['nɔmineit] *v* benoemen
nomination [,nɔmi'neiʃən] *n* nominatie *c*; benoeming *c*
none [nʌn] *pron* geen

nonsense ['nɔnsəns] *n* onzin *c*

noon [nu:n] *n* middag *c*

normal ['nɔ:məl] *adj* gewoon, normaal

north [nɔ:θ] *n* noorden *nt*; noord *c*; *adj* noordelijk; **North Pole** noordpool *c*

north-east [,nɔ:θ'i:st] *n* noordoosten *nt*

northerly ['nɔ:ðəli] *adj* noordelijk

northern ['nɔ:ðən] *adj* noordelijk

north-west [,nɔ:θ'west] *n* noordwesten *nt*

Norway ['nɔ:wei] Noorwegen

Norwegian [nɔ:'wi:dʒən] *adj* Noors; *n* Noor *c*

nose [nouz] *n* neus *c*

nosebleed ['nouzbli:d] *n* neusbloeding *c*

nostril ['nɔstril] *n* neusgat *nt*

not [nɔt] *adv* niet

notary ['noutəri] *n* notaris *c*

note [nout] *n* aantekening *c*, notitie *c*; noot *c*; toon *c*; *v* noteren; opmerken, constateren

notebook ['noutbuk] *n* notitieboek *nt*

noted ['noutid] *adj* befaamd

notepaper ['nout,peipə] *n* schrijfpapier *nt*, briefpapier *nt*

nothing ['nʌθiŋ] *n* niks, niets

notice ['noutis] *v* bemerken, merken, opmerken; *zien; *n* aankondiging *c*, bericht *nt*; notitie *c*, aandacht *c*

noticeable ['noutisəbəl] *adj* merkbaar; opmerkelijk

notify ['noutifai] *v* mededelen; waarschuwen

notion ['nouʃən] *n* begrip *nt*, notie *c*

notorious [nou'tɔ:riəs] *adj* berucht

nougat ['nu:ga:] *n* noga *c*

nought [nɔ:t] *n* nul *c*

noun [naun] *n* zelfstandig naamwoord *c*

nourishing ['nʌriʃiŋ] *adj* voedzaam

novel ['nɔvəl] *n* roman *c*

novelist ['nɔvəlist] *n* romanschrijver *c*

November [nou'vembə] november

now [nau] *adv* nu; thans; ~ **and then** nu en dan

nowadays ['nauədeiz] *adv* tegenwoordig

nowhere ['nouwɛə] *adv* nergens

nozzle ['nɔzəl] *n* tuit *c*

nuance [nju:'ã:s] *n* nuance *c*

nuclear ['nju:kliə] *adj* kern-, nucleair; ~ **energy** kernenergie *c*

nucleus ['nju:kliəs] *n* kern *c*

nude [nju:d] *adj* naakt; *n* naakt *nt*

nuisance ['nju:səns] *n* last *c*

numb [nʌm] *adj* gevoelloos; verstijfd

number ['nʌmbə] *n* nummer *nt*; cijfer *nt*, getal *nt*; aantal *nt*

numeral ['nju:mərəl] *n* telwoord *nt*

numerous ['nju:mərəs] *adj* talrijk

nun [nʌn] *n* non *c*

nunnery ['nʌnəri] *n* nonnenklooster *nt*

nurse [nə:s] *n* zuster *c*, verpleegster *c*; kinderjuffrouw *c*; *v* verplegen; zogen

nursery ['nə:səri] *n* kinderkamer *c*; crèche *c*; boomkwekerij *c*

nut [nʌt] *n* noot *c*; moer *c*

nutcrackers ['nʌt,krækəz] *pl* notekraker *c*

nutmeg ['nʌtmeg] *n* nootmuskaat *c*

nutritious [nju:'triʃəs] *adj* voedzaam

nutshell ['nʌtʃel] *n* notedop *c*

nylon ['nailən] *n* nylon *c*

O

oak [ouk] *n* eik *c*

oar [ɔ:] *n* roeiriem *c*

oasis [ou'eisis] *n* (pl oases) oase *c*

oath [ouθ] *n* eed *c*

oats [outs] *pl* haver *c*

obedience [ə'bi:diəns] *n* gehoorzaamheid *c*

obedient [ə'bi:diənt] *adj* gehoorzaam

obey [ə'bei] *v* gehoorzamen

object[1] ['ɔbdʒikt] *n* object *nt*; voorwerp *nt*; doel *nt*

object[2] [əb'dʒekt] *v* *tegenwerpen; ~ **to** bezwaar *hebben tegen

objection [əb'dʒekʃən] *n* bezwaar *nt*, tegenwerping *c*

objective [əb'dʒektiv] *adj* objectief; *n* doel *nt*

obligatory [ə'bligətəri] *adj* verplicht

oblige [ə'blaidʒ] *v* verplichten; ***be obliged to** verplicht *zijn om; *moeten

obliging [ə'blaidʒiŋ] *adj* voorkomend

oblong ['ɔblɔŋ] *adj* langwerpig; *n* rechthoek *c*

obscene [əb'si:n] *adj* obsceen

obscure [əb'skjuə] *adj* obscuur, duister

observation [ˌɔbzə'veiʃən] *n* observatie *c*, waarneming *c*

observatory [əb'zə:vətri] *n* observatorium *nt*

observe [əb'zə:v] *v* observeren, *waarnemen

obsession [əb'seʃən] *n* obsessie *c*

obstacle ['ɔbstəkəl] *n* hindernis *c*

obstinate ['ɔbstinət] *adj* koppig; hardnekkig

obtain [əb'tein] *v* behalen, *verkrijgen

obtainable [əb'teinəbəl] *adj* verkrijgbaar

obvious ['ɔbviəs] *adj* duidelijk

occasion [ə'keiʒən] *n* gelegenheid *c*; aanleiding *c*

occasionally [ə'keiʒənəli] *adv* af en toe, nu en dan

occupant ['ɔkjupənt] *n* bewoner *c*

occupation [ˌɔkju'peiʃən] *n* werk *nt*; bezetting *c*

occupy ['ɔkjupai] *v* *innemen, bezetten; **occupied** *adj* bezet

occur [ə'kə:] *v* gebeuren, *voorkomen, zich *voordoen

occurrence [ə'kʌrəns] *n* gebeurtenis *c*

ocean ['ouʃən] *n* oceaan *c*

October [ɔk'toubə] oktober

octopus ['ɔktəpəs] *n* octopus *c*

oculist ['ɔkjulist] *n* oogarts *c*

odd [ɔd] *adj* raar, vreemd; oneven

odour ['oudə] *n* geur *c*

of [ɔv, əv] *prep* van

off [ɔf] *adv* af; weg; *prep* van

offence [ə'fens] *n* overtreding *c*; belediging *c*, aanstoot *c*

offend [ə'fend] *v* krenken, beledigen; *overtreden

offensive [ə'fensiv] *adj* offensief; beledigend, aanstootgevend; *n* offensief *nt*

offer ['ɔfə] *v* *aanbieden; *bieden; *n* aanbieding *c*, aanbod *nt*

office ['ɔfis] *n* bureau *nt*, kantoor *nt*; ambt *nt*; ~ **hours** kantooruren *pl*

officer ['ɔfisə] *n* officier *c*

official [ə'fiʃəl] *adj* officieel

off-licence ['ɔf,laisəns] *n* slijterij *c*

often ['ɔfən] *adv* vaak, dikwijls

oil [ɔil] *n* olie *c*; **fuel** ~ stookolie *c*; ~ **filter** oliefilter *nt*; ~ **pressure** oliedruk *c*

oil-painting [ˌɔil'peintiŋ] *n* olieverfschilderij *nt*

oil-refinery ['ɔilri,fainəri] *n* olieraffinaderij *c*

oil-well ['ɔilwel] *n* oliebron *c*

oily ['ɔili] *adj* olieachtig

ointment ['ɔintmənt] *n* zalf *c*

okay! [ˌou'kei] in orde!

old [ould] *adj* oud; ~ **age** ouderdom *c*

old-fashioned [ˌould'fæʃənd] *adj* ouderwets

olive ['ɔliv] *n* olijf *c*; ~ **oil** olijfolie *c*

omelette ['ɔmlət] *n* omelet *nt*

ominous ['ɔminəs] *adj* onheilspellend

omit [ə'mit] *v* *weglaten

omnipotent [ɔm'nipətənt] *adj* almachtig

on [ɔn] *prep* op; aan
once [wʌns] *adv* eenmaal, eens; **at ~** meteen, dadelijk; **~ more** nog eens
oncoming [ˈɔnˌkʌmiŋ] *adj* tegemoetkomend, naderend
one [wʌn] *num* een; *pron* men
oneself [wʌnˈself] *pron* zelf
onion [ˈʌnjən] *n* ui *c*
only [ˈounli] *adj* enig; *adv* slechts, alleen, maar; *conj* maar
onwards [ˈɔnwədz] *adv* voorwaarts
onyx [ˈɔniks] *n* onyx *nt*
opal [ˈoupəl] *n* opaal *c*
open [ˈoupən] *v* openen; *adj* open; openhartig
opening [ˈoupəniŋ] *n* opening *c*
opera [ˈɔpərə] *n* opera *c*; **~ house** opera *c*
operate [ˈɔpəreit] *v* opereren, werken
operation [ˌɔpəˈreiʃən] *n* werking *c*; operatie *c*
operator [ˈɔpəreitə] *n* telefoniste *c*
operetta [ˌɔpəˈretə] *n* operette *c*
opinion [əˈpinjən] *n* opinie *c*, mening *c*
opponent [əˈpounənt] *n* tegenstander *c*
opportunity [ˌɔpəˈtjuːnəti] *n* gelegenheid *c*, kans *c*
oppose [əˈpouz] *v* zich verzetten
opposite [ˈɔpəzit] *prep* tegenover; *adj* tegengesteld
opposition [ˌɔpəˈziʃən] *n* oppositie *c*
oppress [əˈpres] *v* beklemmen, verdrukken
optician [ɔpˈtiʃən] *n* opticien *c*
optimism [ˈɔptimizəm] *n* optimisme *nt*
optimist [ˈɔptimist] *n* optimist *c*
optimistic [ˌɔptiˈmistik] *adj* optimistisch
optional [ˈɔpʃənəl] *adj* facultatief
or [ɔː] *conj* of
oral [ˈɔːrəl] *adj* mondeling
orange [ˈɔrindʒ] *n* sinaasappel *c*; *adj* oranje
orchard [ˈɔːtʃəd] *n* boomgaard *c*

orchestra [ˈɔːkistrə] *n* orkest *nt*; **~ seat** *Am* stalles *pl*
order [ˈɔːdə] *v* *bevelen; bestellen; *n* volgorde *c*, orde *c*; opdracht *c*, bevel *nt*; bestelling *c*; **in ~** in orde; **in ~ to** om te; **made to ~** op maat gemaakt; **out of ~** buiten werking; **postal ~** postwissel *c*
order-form [ˈɔːdəfɔːm] *n* bestelformulier *nt*
ordinary [ˈɔːdənri] *adj* alledaags, gewoon
ore [ɔː] *n* erts *nt*
organ [ˈɔːgən] *n* orgaan *nt*; orgel *nt*
organic [ɔːˈgænik] *adj* organisch
organization [ˌɔːgənaiˈzeiʃən] *n* organisatie *c*
organize [ˈɔːgənaiz] *v* organiseren
Orient [ˈɔːriənt] *n* Oosten *nt*
oriental [ˌɔːriˈentəl] *adj* oosters
orientate [ˈɔːriənteit] *v* zich oriënteren
origin [ˈɔridʒin] *n* origine *c*, oorsprong *c*; afstamming *c*, herkomst *c*
original [əˈridʒinəl] *adj* oorspronkelijk, origineel
originally [əˈridʒinəli] *adv* aanvankelijk
orlon [ˈɔːlɔn] *n* orlon *nt*
ornament [ˈɔːnəmənt] *n* versiersel *nt*
ornamental [ˌɔːnəˈmentəl] *adj* ornamenteel
orphan [ˈɔːfən] *n* wees *c*
orthodox [ˈɔːθədɔks] *adj* orthodox
ostrich [ˈɔstritʃ] *n* struisvogel *c*
other [ˈʌðə] *adj* ander
otherwise [ˈʌðəwaiz] *conj* anders
*ought to [ɔːt] *moeten
our [auə] *adj* ons
ourselves [auəˈselvz] *pron* ons; zelf
out [aut] *adv* buiten, uit; **~ of** buiten, uit
outbreak [ˈautbreik] *n* uitbarsting *c*
outcome [ˈautkʌm] *n* resultaat *nt*
*outdo [ˌautˈduː] *v* *overtreffen

outdoors [,aut'dɔ:z] *adv* buiten

outfit ['autfit] *n* uitrusting *c*

outline ['autlain] *n* omtrek *c*; *v* schetsen

outlook ['autluk] *n* verwachting *c*; zienswijze *c*

output ['autput] *n* produktie *c*

outrage ['autreidʒ] *n* gewelddaad *c*

outside [,aut'said] *adv* buiten; *prep* buiten; *n* uiterlijk *nt*, buitenkant *c*

outsize ['autsaiz] *n* extra grote maat

outskirts ['autskə:ts] *pl* buitenwijk *c*

outstanding [,aut'stændiŋ] *adj* eminent, vooraanstaand

outward ['autwəd] *adj* uiterlijk

outwards ['autwədz] *adv* naar buiten

oval ['ouvəl] *adj* ovaal

oven ['ʌvən] *n* oven *c*; **microwave ~** mikrogolf oven

over ['ouvə] *prep* boven, over; meer dan; *adv* over; omver; *adj* voorbij; **~ there** ginds

overall ['ouvərɔ:l] *adj* totaal

overalls ['ouvərɔ:lz] *pl* overall *c*

overcast ['ouvəka:st] *adj* betrokken

overcoat ['ouvəkout] *n* overjas *c*

* **overcome** [,ouvə'kʌm] *v* *overwinnen

overdue [,ouvə'dju:] *adj* te laat; achterstallig

overgrown [,ouvə'groun] *adj* begroeid

overhaul [,ouvə'hɔ:l] *v* reviseren

overlook [,ouvə'luk] *v* over het hoofd *zien

overnight [,ouvə'nait] *adv* 's nachts

overseas [,ouvə'si:z] *adj* overzees

oversight ['ouvəsait] *n* vergissing *c*

* **oversleep** [,ouvə'sli:p] *v* zich *verslapen

overstrung [,ouvə'strʌŋ] *adj* overspannen

* **overtake** [,ouvə'teik] *v* inhalen; **no overtaking** inhalen verboden

over-tired [,ouvə'taiəd] *adj* oververmoeid

overture ['ouvətʃə] *n* ouverture *c*

overweight ['ouvəweit] *n* bagageoverschot *nt*

overwhelm [,ouvə'welm] *v* onthutsen, overweldigen

overwork [,ouvə'wə:k] *v* zich overwerken

owe [ou] *v* verschuldigd *zijn, schuldig *zijn; te danken *hebben aan; **owing to** vanwege, ten gevolge van

owl [aul] *n* uil *c*

own [oun] *v* *bezitten; *adj* eigen

owner ['ounə] *n* bezitter *c*, eigenaar *c*

ox [ɔks] *n* (pl oxen) os *c*

oxygen ['ɔksidʒən] *n* zuurstof *c*

oyster ['ɔistə] *n* oester *c*

P

pace [peis] *n* gang *c*; schrede *c*, stap *c*; tempo *nt*

Pacific Ocean [pə'sifik 'ouʃən] Stille Oceaan

pacifism ['pæsifizəm] *n* pacifisme *nt*

pacifist ['pæsifist] *n* pacifist *c*; pacifistisch

pack [pæk] *v* inpakken; **~ up** inpakken

package ['pækidʒ] *n* pak *nt*

packet ['pækit] *n* pakje *nt*

packing ['pækiŋ] *n* verpakking *c*

pad [pæd] *n* kussentje *nt*; blocnote *c*

paddle ['pædəl] *n* peddel *c*

padlock ['pædlɔk] *n* hangslot *nt*

pagan ['peigən] *adj* heidens; *n* heiden *c*

page [peidʒ] *n* pagina *c*, bladzijde *c*

page-boy ['peidʒbɔi] *n* piccolo *c*

pail [peil] *n* emmer *c*

pain [pein] *n* pijn *c*; **pains** moeite *c*

painful ['peinfəl] *adj* pijnlijk

painless ['peinləs] *adj* pijnloos

paint [peint] n verf c; v schilderen; verven

paint-box ['peintbɔks] n verfdoos c

paint-brush ['peintbrʌʃ] n penseel nt

painter ['peintə] n schilder c

painting ['peintiŋ] n schilderij nt

pair [peə] n paar nt

Pakistan [‚pɑːki'stɑːn] Pakistan

Pakistani [‚pɑːki'stɑːni] adj Pakistaans; n Pakistaan c

palace ['pæləs] n paleis nt

pale [peil] adj bleek; licht

palm [pɑːm] n palm c; handpalm c

palpable ['pælpəbəl] adj tastbaar

palpitation [‚pælpi'teiʃən] n hartklopping c

pan [pæn] n pan c

pane [pein] n ruit c

panel ['pænəl] n paneel nt

panelling ['pænəliŋ] n lambrizering c

panic ['pænik] n paniek c

pant [pænt] v hijgen

panties ['pæntiz] pl onderbroek c, slip c

pants [pænts] pl onderbroek c; plAm broek c

pant-suit ['pæntsuːt] n broekpak nt

panty-hose ['pæntihouz] n panty c

paper ['peipə] n papier nt; krant c; papieren; **carbon** ~ carbonpapier nt; ~ **bag** papieren zak; ~ **napkin** papieren servet; **typing** ~ schrijfmachinepapier nt; **wrapping** ~ pakpapier nt

paperback ['peipəbæk] n pocketboek nt

paper-knife ['peipənaif] n briefopener c

parade [pə'reid] n parade c, optocht c

paraffin ['pærəfin] n petroleum c

paragraph ['pærəgrɑːf] n alinea c, paragraaf c

parakeet ['pærəkiːt] n parkiet c

paralise ['pærəlaiz] v verlammen

parallel ['pærəlel] adj evenwijdig, parallel; n parallel c

parcel ['pɑːsəl] n pakket nt, pakje nt

pardon ['pɑːdən] n vergiffenis c; gratie c

parents ['peərənts] pl ouders pl

parents-in-law ['peərəntsinlɔː] pl schoonouders pl

parish ['pæriʃ] n parochie c

park [pɑːk] n park nt; v parkeren; **no parking** verboden te parkeren; **parking fee** parkeertarief nt; **parking light** stadslicht nt; **parking lot** Am parkeerplaats c; **parking meter** parkeermeter c; **parking zone** parkeerzone c

parliament ['pɑːləmənt] n parlement nt

parliamentary [‚pɑːlə'mentəri] adj parlementair

parrot ['pærət] n papegaai c

parsley ['pɑːsli] n peterselie c

parson ['pɑːsən] n dominee c

parsonage ['pɑːsənidʒ] n pastorie c

part [pɑːt] n gedeelte nt, deel nt; stuk nt; v *scheiden; **spare** ~ onderdeel nt

partial ['pɑːʃəl] adj gedeeltelijk; partijdig

participant [pɑː'tisipənt] n deelnemer c

participate [pɑː'tisipeit] v *deelnemen

particular [pə'tikjulə] adj bijzonder, speciaal; kieskeurig; **in** ~ in het bijzonder

parting ['pɑːtiŋ] n afscheid nt; scheiding c

partition [pɑː'tiʃən] n tussenschot nt

partly ['pɑːtli] adv deels, gedeeltelijk

partner ['pɑːtnə] n partner c; compagnon c

partridge ['pɑːtridʒ] n patrijs c

party ['pɑːti] n partij c; fuif c, feestje nt; groep c

pass [pɑ:s] v *voorbijgaan, passeren; *aangeven; slagen; vAm inhalen; **no passing** Am inhalen verboden; ~ **by** passeren; ~ **through** *gaan door

passage ['pæsidʒ] n doorgang c; overtocht c; passage c; doorreis c

passenger ['pæsəndʒə] n passagier c; ~ **car** Am wagon c; ~ **train** personentrein c

passer-by [,pɑ:sə'bai] n voorbijganger c

passion ['pæʃən] n hartstocht c, passie c; drift c

passionate ['pæʃənət] adj hartstochtelijk

passive ['pæsiv] adj passief

passport ['pɑ:spɔ:t] n paspoort nt; ~ **control** paspoortcontrole c; ~ **photograph** pasfoto c

password ['pɑ:swə:d] n wachtwoord nt

past [pɑ:st] n verleden nt; adj vorig, afgelopen, voorbij; prep langs, voorbij

paste [peist] n pasta c; v plakken

pastry ['peistri] n gebak nt; ~ **shop** banketbakkerij c

pasture ['pɑ:stʃə] n weiland nt

patch [pætʃ] v verstellen

patent ['peitənt] n patent nt, octrooi nt

path [pɑ:θ] n pad nt

patience ['peiʃəns] n geduld nt

patient ['peiʃənt] adj geduldig; n patiënt c

patriot ['peitriət] n patriot c

patrol [pə'troul] n patrouille c; v patrouilleren; surveilleren

pattern ['pætən] n motief nt, patroon nt

pause [pɔ:z] n pauze c; v pauzeren

pave [peiv] v plaveien, bestraten

pavement ['peivmənt] n trottoir nt;

plaveisel nt

pavilion [pə'viljən] n paviljoen nt

paw [pɔ:] n poot c

pawn [pɔ:n] v verpanden; n pion c

pawnbroker ['pɔ:n,broukə] n pandjesbaas c

pay [pei] n salaris nt, loon nt

*pay [pei] v betalen; lonen; ~ **attention to** letten op; **paying** rendabel; ~ **off** aflossen; ~ **on account** afbetalen

pay-desk ['peidesk] n kassa c

payee [pei'i:] n begunstigde c

payment ['peimənt] n betaling c

pea [pi:] n erwt c

peace [pi:s] n vrede c

peaceful ['pi:sfəl] adj vreedzaam

peach [pi:tʃ] n perzik c

peacock ['pi:kɔk] n pauw c

peak [pi:k] n top c; spits c; ~ **hour** spitsuur nt; ~ **season** hoogseizoen nt

peanut ['pi:nʌt] n pinda c

pear [pɛə] n peer c

pearl [pə:l] n parel c

peasant ['pezənt] n boer c

pebble ['pebəl] n kiezel c

peculiar [pi'kju:ljə] adj eigenaardig; speciaal, bijzonder

peculiarity [pi,kju:li'ærəti] n eigenaardigheid c

pedal ['pedəl] n pedaal nt/c

pedestrian [pi'destriən] n voetganger c; **no pedestrians** verboden voor voetgangers; ~ **crossing** zebrapad nt

pedicure ['pedikjuə] n pedicure c

peel [pi:l] v schillen c; n schil c

peep [pi:p] v gluren

peg [peg] n klerenhaak c

pelican ['pelikən] n pelikaan c

pelvis ['pelvis] n bekken nt

pen [pen] n pen c

penalty ['penəlti] n boete c; straf c; ~

kick strafschop c

pencil ['pensəl] n potlood nt

pencil-sharpener ['pensəl‚ʃɑ:pnə] n puntenslijper c

penetrate ['penitreit] v *doordringen

penguin ['peŋgwin] n pinguin c

penicillin [‚peni'silin] n penicilline c

peninsula [pə'ninsjulə] n schiereiland nt

penknife ['pennaif] n (pl -knives) zakmes nt

pension¹ ['pɑ̃:siɔ̃:] n pension nt

pension² ['penʃən] n pensioen nt

people ['pi:pəl] pl mensen; n volk nt

pepper ['pepə] n peper c

peppermint ['pepəmint] n pepermunt c

perceive [pə'si:v] v bemerken

percent [pə'sent] n procent nt

percentage [pə'sentidʒ] n percentage nt

perceptible [pə'septibəl] adj merkbaar

perception [pə'sepʃən] n gewaarwording c

perch [pə:tʃ] (pl ~) baars c

percolator ['pə:kəleitə] n percolator c

perfect ['pə:fikt] adj volkomen, volmaakt

perfection [pə'fekʃən] n perfectie c, volmaaktheid c

perform [pə'fɔ:m] v uitvoeren, verrichten

performance [pə'fɔ:məns] n voorstelling c

perfume ['pə:fju:m] n parfum nt

perhaps [pə'hæps] adv misschien; wellicht

peril ['peril] n gevaar nt

perilous ['periləs] adj gevaarlijk

period ['piəriəd] n tijdperk nt, periode c; punt c

periodical [‚piəri'ɔdikəl] n tijdschrift nt; adj periodiek

perish ['periʃ] v *omkomen

perishable ['periʃəbəl] adj aan bederf onderhevig

perjury ['pə:dʒəri] n meineed c

permanent ['pə:mənənt] adj blijvend, permanent, duurzaam; bestendig, vast; ~ **press** plooihoudend; ~ **wave** permanent c

permission [pə'miʃən] n toestemming c, permissie c; verlof nt, vergunning c

permit¹ [pə'mit] v *toestaan, veroorloven

permit² ['pə:mit] n vergunning c

peroxide [pə'rɔksaid] n waterstofperoxyde nt

perpendicular [‚pə:pən'dikjulə] adj loodrecht

Persia ['pə:ʃə] Perzië

Persian ['pə:ʃən] adj Perzisch; n Pers c

person ['pə:sən] n persoon c; **per ~** per persoon

personal ['pə:sənəl] adj persoonlijk

personality [‚pə:sə'næləti] n persoonlijkheid c

personnel [‚pə:sə'nel] n personeel nt

perspective [pə'spektiv] n perspectief nt

perspiration [‚pə:spə'reiʃən] n transpiratie c, zweet nt

perspire [pə'spaiə] v transpireren, zweten

persuade [pə'sweid] v overreden, overhalen; overtuigen

persuasion [pə'sweiʒən] n overtuiging c

pessimism ['pesimizəm] n pessimisme nt

pessimist ['pesimist] n pessimist c

pessimistic [‚pesi'mistik] adj pessimistisch

pet [pet] n huisdier nt; lieveling c

petal ['petəl] n bloemblad nt

petition [pi'tiʃən] n petitie c

petrol ['petrəl] n benzine c; **unleaded ~** loodvrije benzine c; **~ pump** benzinepomp c; **~ station** benzine-station nt; **~ tank** benzinetank c

petroleum [pi'trouliəm] n petroleum c

petty ['peti] adj klein, nietig, onbeduidend; **~ cash** kleingeld nt

pewter ['pju:tə] n tin nt

phantom ['fæntəm] n spook nt

pharmacology [,fɑ:mə'kɔlədʒi] n farmacologie c

pharmacy ['fɑ:məsi] n apotheek c; drogisterij c

phase [feiz] n fase c

pheasant ['fezənt] n fazant c

Philippine ['filipain] adj Filippijns

Philippines ['filipi:nz] pl Filippijnen pl

philosopher [fi'lɔsəfə] n wijsgeer c, filosoof c

philosophy [fi'lɔsəfi] n wijsbegeerte c, filosofie c

phone [foun] n telefoon c; v opbellen, telefoneren

phonetic [fə'netik] adj fonetisch

photo ['foutou] n (pl ~s) foto c

photocopy ['foutəkɔpi] n fotocopie c

photograph ['foutəgrɑ:f] n foto c; v fotograferen

photographer [fə'tɔgrəfə] n fotograaf c

photography [fə'tɔgrəfi] n fotografie c

phrase [freiz] n uitdrukking c

phrase-book ['freizbuk] n taalgids c

physical ['fizikəl] adj fysiek

physician [fi'ziʃən] n dokter c

physicist ['fizisist] n natuurkundige c

physics ['fiziks] n fysica c, natuurkunde c

physiology [,fizi'ɔlədʒi] n fysiologie c

pianist ['pi:ənist] n pianist c

piano [pi'ænou] n piano c; **grand ~** vleugel c

pick [pik] v plukken; *kiezen; n keus c; **~ up** oprapen; ophalen; **pick-up**

van bestelauto c

pick-axe ['pikæks] n houweel nt

pickles ['pikəlz] pl zoetzuur nt, pickles pl

picnic ['piknik] n picknick c; v picknicken

picture ['piktʃə] n schilderij nt; plaat c, prent c; beeld nt, afbeelding c; **~ postcard** ansichtkaart c, prent-briefkaart c; **pictures** bioscoop c

picturesque [,piktʃə'resk] adj pittoresk, schilderachtig

piece [pi:s] n stuk nt

pier [piə] n pier c

pierce [piəs] v doorboren

pig [pig] n varken nt; zwijn nt

pigeon ['pidʒən] n duif c

pig-headed [,pig'hedid] adj eigenwijs

piglet ['piglət] n big c

pigskin ['pigskin] n varkensleer nt

pike [paik] n (pl ~) snoek c

pile [pail] n stapel c; v opstapelen; **piles** pl aambeien pl

pilgrim ['pilgrim] n pelgrim c

pilgrimage ['pilgrimidʒ] n bedevaart c

pill [pil] n pil c

pillar ['pilə] n zuil c, pilaar c

pillar-box ['piləbɔks] n brievenbus c

pillow ['pilou] n kussen nt, hoofdkussen nt

pillow-case ['piloukeis] n kussensloop c/nt

pilot ['pailət] n piloot c; loods c

pimple ['pimpəl] n puistje c

pin [pin] n speld c; v vastspelden; **bobby ~** Am haarspeld c

pincers ['pinsəz] pl nijptang c

pinch [pintʃ] v *knijpen

pineapple ['pai,næpəl] n ananas c

ping-pong ['piŋpɔŋ] n tafeltennis nt

pink [piŋk] adj roze

pioneer [,paiə'niə] n pionier c

pious ['paiəs] adj vroom

pip [pip] n pit c

pipe [paip] *n* pijp *c*; leiding *c*; ~ **cleaner** pijpestoker *c*; ~ **tobacco** pijptabak *c*

pirate ['paiərət] *n* piraat *c*

pistol ['pistəl] *n* pistool *nt*

piston ['pistən] *n* zuiger *c*; ~ **ring** zuigerring *c*

piston-rod ['pistənrɔd] *n* zuigerstang *c*

pit [pit] *n* kuil *c*; groeve *c*

pitcher ['pitʃə] *n* kruik *c*

pity ['piti] *n* medelijden *nt*; *v* medelijden *hebben met, beklagen; **what a pity!** jammer!

placard ['plækɑ:d] *n* aanplakbiljet *nt*

place [pleis] *n* plaats *c*; *v* zetten, plaatsen; ~ **of birth** geboorteplaats *c*; *take* ~ *plaatshebben

plague [pleig] *n* plaag *c*

plaice [pleis] (pl ~) schol *c*

plain [plein] *adj* duidelijk; gewoon, eenvoudig; *n* vlakte *c*

plan [plæn] *n* plan *nt*; plattegrond *c*; *v* plannen

plane [plein] *adj* vlak; *n* vliegtuig *nt*; ~ **crash** vliegramp *c*

planet ['plænit] *n* planeet *c*

planetarium [,plæni'teəriəm] *n* planetarium *nt*

plank [plæŋk] *n* plank *c*

plant [plɑ:nt] *n* plant *c*; bedrijf *nt*; *v* planten

plantation [plæn'teiʃən] *n* plantage *c*

plaster ['plɑ:stə] *n* pleister *nt*, gips *nt*; pleister *c*

plastic ['plæstik] *adj* plastic; *n* plastic *nt*

plate [pleit] *n* bord *nt*; plaat *c*

plateau ['plætou] *n* (pl ~x, ~s) hoogvlakte *c*

platform ['plætfɔ:m] *n* perron *nt*; ~ **ticket** perronkaartje *nt*

platinum ['plætinəm] *n* platina *nt*

play [plei] *v* spelen; bespelen; *n* spel *nt*; toneelstuk *nt*; **one-act** ~ eenakter *c*; ~ **truant** spijbelen

player [pleiə] *n* speler *c*

playground ['pleigraund] *n* speelplaats *c*

playing-card ['pleiiŋkɑ:d] *n* speelkaart *c*

playwright ['pleirait] *n* toneelschrijver *c*

plea [pli:] *n* pleidooi *nt*

plead [pli:d] *v* pleiten

pleasant ['plezənt] *adj* prettig, aardig, aangenaam

please [pli:z] alstublieft; *v* *bevallen; **pleased** ingenomen; **pleasing** aangenaam

pleasure ['pleʒə] *n* genoegen *nt*, pret *c*, plezier *nt*

plentiful ['plentifəl] *adj* overvloedig

plenty ['plenti] *n* overvloed *c*; heleboel *c*

pliers [plaiəz] *pl* tang *c*

plimsolls ['plimsəlz] *pl* gymschoenen *pl*

plot [plɔt] *n* samenzwering *c*, komplot *nt*; handeling *c*; perceel *nt*

plough [plau] *n* ploeg *c*; *v* ploegen

plucky ['plʌki] *adj* flink

plug [plʌg] *n* stekker *c*; ~ **in** inschakelen

plum [plʌm] *n* pruim *c*

plumber ['plʌmə] *n* loodgieter *c*

plump [plʌmp] *adj* mollig

plural ['pluərəl] *n* meervoud *nt*

plus [plʌs] *prep* plus

pneumatic [nju:'mætik] *adj* pneumatisch

pneumonia [nju:'mouniə] *n* longontsteking *c*

poach [poutʃ] *v* stropen

pocket ['pɔkit] *n* zak *c*

pocket-book ['pɔkitbuk] *n* portefeuille *c*

pocket-comb ['pɔkitkoum] *n* zakkam *c*

pocket-knife ['pɔkitnaif] *n* (pl -knives)

zakmes *nt*

pocket-watch ['pɔkitwɔtʃ] *n* zakhorloge *nt*

poem ['pouim] *n* gedicht *nt*

poet ['pouit] *n* dichter *c*

poetry ['pouitri] *n* dichtkunst *c*

point [pɔint] *n* punt *nt*; punt *c*; *v* *wijzen; ~ of view standpunt *nt*; ~ out *aanwijzen

pointed ['pɔintid] *adj* spits

poison ['pɔizən] *n* vergif *nt*; *v* vergiftigen

poisonous ['pɔizənəs] *adj* giftig

Poland ['poulənd] Polen

Pole [poul] *n* Pool *c*

pole [poul] *n* paal *c*

police [pə'li:s] *pl* politie *c*

policeman [pə'li:smən] *n* (pl -men) agent *c*, politieagent *c*

police-station [pə'li:s,steiʃən] *n* politiebureau *nt*

policy ['pɔlisi] *n* beleid *nt*, politiek *c*; polis *c*

polio ['pouliou] *n* polio *c*, kinderverlamming *c*

Polish ['pouliʃ] *adj* Pools

polish ['pɔliʃ] *v* poetsen

polite [pə'lait] *adj* beleefd

political [pə'litikəl] *adj* politiek

politician [,pɔli'tiʃən] *n* politicus *c*

politics ['pɔlitiks] *n* politiek *c*

pollution [pə'lu:ʃən] *n* vervuiling *c*, verontreiniging *c*

pond [pɔnd] *n* vijver *c*

pony ['pouni] *n* pony *c*

poor [puə] *adj* arm; armoedig; slecht

pope [poup] *n* paus *c*

poplin ['pɔplin] *n* popeline *nt/c*

pop music [pop 'mju:zik] popmuziek *c*

poppy ['pɔpi] *n* klaproos *c*; papaver *c*

popular ['pɔpjulə] *adj* populair; volks-

population [,pɔpju'leiʃən] *n* bevolking *c*

populous ['pɔpjuləs] *adj* dichtbevolkt

porcelain ['pɔ:səlin] *n* porselein *nt*

porcupine ['pɔ:kjupain] *n* stekelvarken *nt*

pork [pɔ:k] *n* varkensvlees *nt*

port [pɔ:t] *n* haven *c*; bakboord *nt*

portable ['pɔ:təbəl] *adj* draagbaar

porter ['pɔ:tə] *n* kruier *c*; portier *c*

porthole ['pɔ:thoul] *n* patrijspoort *c*

portion ['pɔ:ʃən] *n* portie *c*

portrait ['pɔ:trit] *n* portret *nt*

Portugal ['pɔ:tjugəl] Portugal

Portuguese [,pɔ:tju'gi:z] *adj* Portugees; *n* Portugees *c*

position [pə'ziʃən] *n* positie *c*; houding *c*; betrekking *c*

positive ['pɔzətiv] *adj* positief; *n* positief *nt*

possess [pə'zes] *v* *bezitten; possessed *adj* bezeten

possession [pə'zeʃən] *n* bezit *nt*; possessions eigendom *nt*

possibility [,pɔsə'biləti] *n* mogelijkheid *c*

possible ['pɔsəbəl] *adj* mogelijk; eventueel

post [poust] *n* paal *c*; betrekking *c*; post *c*; *v* posten; post-office postkantoor *nt*

postage ['poustidʒ] *n* frankering *c*; ~ paid franko; ~ stamp postzegel *c*

postcard ['poustka:d] *n* briefkaart *c*; ansichtkaart *c*

poster ['poustə] *n* affiche *nt*, poster *c*

poste restante [poust re'stã:t] poste restante

postman ['poustmən] *n* (pl -men) postbode *c*

post-paid [,poust'peid] *adj* franko

postpone [pə'spoun] *v* uitstellen

pot [pot] *n* pot *c*

potato [pə'teitou] *n* (pl ~es) aardappel *c*

pottery ['pɔtəri] *n* aardewerk *nt*

pouch [pautʃ] *n* buidel *c*

poulterer ['poultərə] n poelier c
poultry ['poultri] n gevogelte nt
pound [paund] n pond nt
pour [pɔ:] v *inschenken, *schenken, *gieten
poverty ['pɒvəti] n armoede c
powder ['paudə] n poeder nt/c; ~ compact poederdoos c; talc ~ talkpoeder nt/c
powder-puff ['paudəpʌf] n poederdons c
powder-room ['paudəru:m] n damestoilet nt
power [pauə] n kracht c; energie c; macht c; mogendheid c
powerful ['pauəfəl] adj machtig; sterk
powerless ['pauələs] adj machteloos
power-station ['pauə,steiʃən] n elektriciteitscentrale c
practical ['præktikəl] adj praktisch
practically ['præktikli] adv vrijwel
practice ['præktis] n praktijk c
practise ['præktis] v beoefenen; oefenen
praise [preiz] v *prijzen; n lof c
pram [præm] n kinderwagen c
prawn [prɔ:n] n garnaal c, steurgarnaal c
pray [prei] v *bidden
prayer [prɛə] n gebed nt
preach [pri:tʃ] v preken
precarious [pri'kɛəriəs] adj hachelijk
precaution [pri'kɔ:ʃən] n voorzorg c; voorzorgsmaatregel c
precede [pri'si:d] v *voorafgaan
preceding [pri'si:diŋ] adj voorgaand
precious ['preʃəs] adj kostbaar; dierbaar
precipice ['presipis] n afgrond c
precipitation [pri,sipi'teiʃən] n neerslag c
precise [pri'sais] adj precies, exact, nauwkeurig; secuur
predecessor ['pri:disesə] n voorganger

c
predict [pri'dikt] v voorspellen
prefer [pri'fə:] v de voorkeur *geven aan, liever *hebben
preferable ['prefərəbəl] adj te verkiezen, verkieslijker, de voorkeur verdienend
preference ['prefərəns] n voorkeur c
prefix ['pri:fiks] n voorvoegsel nt
pregnant ['pregnənt] adj in verwachting, zwanger
prejudice ['predʒədis] n vooroordeel nt
preliminary [pri'liminəri] adj inleidend; voorlopig
premature ['premətʃuə] adj voorbarig
premier ['premiə] n premier c
premises ['premisiz] pl pand nt
premium ['pri:miəm] n premie c
prepaid [,pri:'peid] adj vooruitbetaald
preparation [,prepə'reiʃən] n voorbereiding c
prepare [pri'pɛə] v voorbereiden; klaarmaken
prepared [pri'pɛəd] adj bereid
preposition [,prepə'ziʃən] n voorzetsel nt
prescribe [pri'skraib] v *voorschrijven
prescription [pri'skripʃən] n recept nt
presence ['prezəns] n aanwezigheid c; tegenwoordigheid c
present¹ ['prezənt] n geschenk nt, cadeau nt; heden nt; adj tegenwoordig; aanwezig
present² [pri'zent] v voorstellen; *aanbieden
presently ['prezəntli] adv meteen, dadelijk
preservation [,prezə'veiʃən] n bewaring c
preserve [pri'zə:v] v bewaren; inmaken
president ['prezidənt] n president c; voorzitter c
press [pres] n pers c; v indrukken,

drukken; persen; ~ **conference**
persconferentie *c*

pressing ['presiŋ] *adj* urgent, dringend

pressure ['preʃə] *n* druk *c*; spanning
c; **atmospheric** ~ luchtdruk *c*

pressure-cooker ['preʃə,kukə] *n* snelkookpan *c*

prestige [pre'sti:ʒ] *n* prestige *nt*

presumable [pri'zju:məbəl] *adj* vermoedelijk

presumptuous [pri'zʌmpʃəs] *adj* overmoedig; arrogant

pretence [pri'tens] *n* voorwendsel *nt*

pretend [pri'tend] *v* *doen alsof, voorwenden

pretext ['pri:tekst] *n* voorwendsel *nt*

pretty ['priti] *adj* mooi, knap; *adv*
vrij, tamelijk, nogal

prevent [pri'vent] *v* beletten, verhinderen; *voorkomen

preventive [pri'ventiv] *adj* preventief

previous ['pri:viəs] *adj* verleden, vroeger, voorgaand

pre-war [,pri:'wɔ:] *adj* vooroorlogs

price [prais] *v* prijzen; ~ **list** prijslijst
c

priceless ['praisləs] *adj* onschatbaar

price-list ['prais,list] *n* prijs *c*

prick [prik] *v* prikken

pride [praid] *n* trots *c*

priest [pri:st] *n* priester *c*

primary ['praiməri] *adj* primair; eerst,
hoofd-; elementair

prince [prins] *n* prins *c*

princess [prin'ses] *n* prinses *c*

principal ['prinsəpəl] *adj* voornaamst;
n rector *c*, directeur *c*

principle ['prinsəpəl] *n* beginsel *nt*,
principe *nt*

print [print] *v* drukken; *n* afdruk *c*;
prent *c*; **printed matter** drukwerk
nt

prior [praiə] *adj* vroeger

priority [prai'ɔrəti] *n* prioriteit *c*, voor-

rang *c*

prison ['prizən] *n* gevangenis *c*

prisoner ['prizənə] *n* gedetineerde *c*,
gevangene *c*; ~ **of war** krijgsgevangene *c*

privacy ['praivəsi] *n* privacy *c*, privéleven *nt*

private ['praivit] *adj* particulier, privé;
persoonlijk

privilege ['privilidʒ] *n* voorrecht *nt*

prize [praiz] *n* prijs *c*; beloning *c*

probable ['prɔbəbəl] *adj* vermoedelijk,
waarschijnlijk

probably ['prɔbəbli] *adv* waarschijnlijk

problem ['prɔbləm] *n* probleem *nt*;
vraagstuk *nt*

procedure [prə'si:dʒə] *n* procedure *c*

proceed [prə'si:d] *v* *voortgaan; te
werk *gaan

process ['prouses] *n* proces *nt*, procédé *nt*

procession [prə'seʃən] *n* processie *c*,
stoet *c*

proclaim [prə'kleim] *v* afkondigen

produce[1] [prə'dju:s] *v* produceren

produce[2] ['prɔdju:s] *n* opbrengst *c*,
produkt *c*

producer [prə'dju:sə] *n* producent *c*

product ['prɔdʌkt] *n* produkt *nt*

production [prə'dʌkʃən] *n* produktie *c*

profession [prə'feʃən] *n* vak *nt*, beroep
nt

professional [prə'feʃənəl] *adj* beroeps-

professor [prə'fesə] *n* hoogleraar *c*,
professor *c*

profit ['prɔfit] *n* voordeel *nt*, winst *c*;
baat *c*; *v* profiteren

profitable ['prɔfitəbəl] *adj* winstgevend

profound [prə'faund] *adj* diepzinnig

programme ['prougræm] *n* programma
nt

progress[1] ['prougres] *n* vooruitgang *c*

progress[2] [prə'gres] *v* vorderen

progressive [prə'gresiv] *adj* vooruitstrevend, progressief; toenemend

prohibit [prə'hibit] v *verbieden

prohibition [,proui'biʃən] n verbod nt

prohibitive [prə'hibitiv] adj onoverkomelijk

project ['prɔdʒekt] n plan nt, project nt

promenade [,prɔmə'na:d] n promenade c

promise ['prɔmis] n belofte c; v beloven

promote [prə'mout] v bevorderen

promotion [prə'mouʃən] n promotie c

prompt [prɔmpt] adj onmiddellijk, prompt

pronoun ['prounaun] n voornaamwoord nt

pronounce [prə'nauns] v *uitspreken

pronunciation [,prənʌnsi'eiʃən] n uitspraak c

proof [pru:f] n bewijs nt

propaganda [,prɔpə'gændə] n propaganda c

propel [prə'pel] v *aandrijven

propeller [prə'pelə] n schroef c, propeller c

proper ['prɔpə] adj juist; behoorlijk, passend, geschikt, gepast

property ['prɔpəti] n bezit nt, eigendom nt; eigenschap c

prophet ['prɔfit] n profeet c

proportion [prə'pɔ:ʃən] n proportie c

proportional [prə'pɔ:ʃənəl] adj evenredig

proposal [prə'pouzəl] n voorstel nt

propose [prə'pouz] v voorstellen

proposition [,prɔpə'ziʃən] n voorstel nt

proprietor [prə'praiətə] n eigenaar c

prospect ['prɔspekt] n vooruitzicht nt

prospectus [prə'spektəs] n prospectus c

prosperity [prɔ'sperəti] n voorspoed c, welvaart c

prosperous ['prɔspərəs] adj welvarend

prostitute ['prɔstitju:t] n prostituée c

protect [prə'tekt] v beschermen

protection [prə'tekʃən] n bescherming c

protein ['prouti:n] n eiwit nt

protest[1] ['proutest] n protest nt

protest[2] [prə'test] v protesteren

Protestant ['prɔtistənt] adj protestants

proud [praud] adj trots; hoogmoedig

prove [pru:v] v aantonen, *bewijzen; *blijken

proverb ['prɔvə:b] n spreekwoord nt

provide [prə'vaid] v leveren, verschaffen; **provided that** mits

province ['prɔvins] n provincie c; gewest nt

provincial [prə'vinʃəl] adj provinciaal

provisional [prə'viʒənəl] adj voorlopig

provisions [prə'viʒənz] pl voorraad c

prune [pru:n] n pruim c

psychiatrist [sai'kaiətrist] n psychiater c

psychic ['saikik] adj psychisch

psychoanalyst [,saikou'ænəlist] n analyticus c

psychological [,saikə'lɔdʒikəl] adj psychologisch

psychologist [sai'kɔlədʒist] n psycholoog c

psychology [sai'kɔlədʒi] n psychologie c

pub [pʌb] n café nt; kroeg c

public ['pʌblik] adj publiek, openbaar; algemeen; n publiek nt; ~ **garden** plantsoen nt; ~ **house** café nt

publication [,pʌbli'keiʃən] n publikatie c

publicity [pʌ'blisəti] n reclame c

publish ['pʌbliʃ] v publiceren, *uitgeven

publisher ['pʌbliʃə] n uitgever c

puddle ['pʌdəl] n plas c

pull [pul] v *trekken; ~ **out** *vertrekken; ~ **up** stoppen

pulley ['puli] *n* (pl ~s) katrol *c*

Pullman ['pulmən] *n* slaaprijtuig *nt*

pullover ['pu,louvə] *n* pullover *c*

pulpit ['pulpit] *n* kansel *c*, preekstoel *c*

pulse [pʌls] *n* polsslag *c*, pols *c*

pump [pʌmp] *n* pomp *c*; *v* pompen

punch [pʌntʃ] *v* stompen; *n* vuistslag *c*

punctual ['pʌŋktʃuəl] *adj* stipt, punctueel

puncture ['pʌŋktʃə] *n* lekke band, bandepech *c*

punctured ['pʌŋktʃəd] *adj* lek

punish ['pʌniʃ] *v* straffen

punishment ['pʌniʃmənt] *n* straf *c*

pupil ['pju:pəl] *n* leerling *c*

puppet-show ['pʌpitʃou] *n* poppenkast *c*

purchase ['pə:tʃəs] *v* *kopen; *n* aankoop *c*, koop *c*; ~ **price** koopprijs *c*; ~ **tax** ómzetbelasting *c*

purchaser ['pə:tʃəsə] *n* koper *c*

pure [pjuə] *adj* rein, zuiver

purple ['pə:pəl] *adj* paars

purpose ['pə:pəs] *n* bedoeling *c*, doel *nt*; **on** ~ opzettelijk

purse [pə:s] *n* beurs *c*, portemonnee *c*

pursue [pə'sju:] *v* vervolgen; nastreven

pus [pʌs] *n* etter *c*

push [puʃ] *n* zet *c*, duw *c*; *v* duwen; *schuiven; *dringen

push-button ['puʃ,bʌtən] *n* drukknop *c*

*** put** [put] *v* plaatsen, leggen, zetten; stoppen; stellen; ~ **away** *opbergen; ~ **off** opschorten; ~ **on** *aantrekken; ~ **out** *uitdoen

puzzle ['pʌzəl] *n* puzzel *c*; raadsel *nt*; *v* in verwarring *brengen; **jigsaw** ~ legpuzzel *c*

puzzling ['pʌzliŋ] *adj* onbegrijpelijk

pyjamas [pə'dʒɑ:məz] *pl* pyjama *c*

Q

quack [kwæk] *n* kwakzalver *c*, charlatan *c*

quail [kweil] *n* (pl ~, ~s) kwartel *c*

quaint [kweint] *adj* raar; ouderwets

qualification [,kwɔlifi'keiʃən] *n* bevoegdheid *c*; voorbehoud *nt*, restriktie *c*

qualified ['kwɔlifaid] *adj* gediplomeerd; bevoegd

qualify ['kwɔlifai] *v* geschikt *zijn

quality ['kwɔləti] *n* kwaliteit *c*; eigenschap *c*

quantity ['kwɔntəti] *n* hoeveelheid *c*; aantal *nt*

quarantine ['kwɔrənti:n] *n* quarantaine *c*

quarrel ['kwɔrəl] *v* twisten, ruzie maken; *n* twist *c*, ruzie *c*

quarry ['kwɔri] *n* steengroeve *c*

quarter ['kwɔ:tə] *n* kwart *nt*; kwartaal *nt*; wijk *c*; ~ **of an hour** kwartier *nt*

quarterly ['kwɔ:təli] *adj* driemaandelijks

quay [ki:] *n* kade *c*

queen [kwi:n] *n* koningin *c*

queer [kwiə] *adj* zonderling, raar; vreemd

query ['kwiəri] *n* vraag *c*; *v* *navragen; betwijfelen

question ['kwestʃən] *n* vraag *c*; kwestie *c*, vraagstuk *nt*; *v* *ondervragen; in twijfel *trekken; ~ **mark** vraagteken *nt*

queue [kju:] *n* rij *c*; *v* in de rij *staan

quick [kwik] *adj* vlug

quick-tempered [,kwik'tempəd] *adj* driftig

quiet ['kwaiət] *adj* stil, kalm, bedaard, rustig; *n* stilte *c*, rust *c*

quilt [kwilt] *n* sprei *c*

quinine [kwi'ni:n] *n* kinine *c*

quit [kwit] *v* *ophouden met, *uitscheiden

quite [kwait] *adv* helemaal; tamelijk, vrij, nogal; zeer, heel

quiz [kwiz] *n* (pl ~zes) quiz *c*

quota ['kwoutə] *n* quota *c*

quotation [kwou'teiʃən] *n* citaat *nt*; ~ **marks** aanhalingstekens *pl*

quote [kwout] *v* citeren, aanhalen

R

rabbit ['ræbit] *n* konijn *nt*

rabies ['reibiz] *n* hondsdolheid *c*

race [reis] *n* wedloop *c*, race *c*; ras *nt*

race-course ['reiskɔ:s] *n* renbaan *c*

race-horse ['reishɔ:s] *n* renpaard *nt*

race-track ['reistræk] *n* renbaan *c*

racial ['reiʃəl] *adj* rassen-

racket ['rækit] *n* kabaal *nt*

racquet ['rækit] *n* racket *c*

radiator ['reidieitə] *n* radiator *c*

radical ['rædikəl] *adj* radicaal

radio ['reidiou] *n* radio *c*

radish ['rædiʃ] *n* radijs *c*

radius ['reidiəs] *n* (pl radii) straal *c*

raft [rɑ:ft] *n* vlot *nt*

rag [ræg] *n* vod *nt*

rage [reidʒ] *n* razernij *c*, woede *c*; *v* razen, woeden

raid [reid] *n* inval *c*

rail [reil] *n* leuning *c*, reling *c*

railing ['reiliŋ] *n* hek *nt*

railroad ['reilroud] *nAm* spoorbaan *c*, spoorweg *c*

railway ['reilwei] *n* spoorweg *c*, spoorbaan *c*

rain [rein] *n* regen *c*; *v* regenen

rainbow ['reinbou] *n* regenboog *c*

raincoat ['reinkout] *n* regenjas *c*

rainproof ['reinpru:f] *adj* waterdicht

rainy ['reini] *adj* regenachtig

raise [reiz] *v* optillen; verhogen; *grootbrengen, verbouwen, fokken; *heffen; *nAm* loonsverhoging *c*, opslag *c*

raisin ['reizən] *n* rozijn *c*

rake [reik] *n* hark *c*

rally ['ræli] *n* bijeenkomst *c*

ramp [ræmp] *n* glooiing *c*

ramshackle ['ræm,ʃækəl] *adj* gammel

rancid ['rænsid] *adj* ranzig

rang [ræŋ] *v* (p ring)

range [reindʒ] *n* bereik *nt*

range-finder ['reindʒ,faində] *n* afstandsmeter *c*

rank [ræŋk] *n* rang *c*; rij *c*

ransom ['rænsəm] *n* losgeld *nt*

rape [reip] *v* verkrachten

rapid ['ræpid] *adj* vlug, snel

rapids ['ræpidz] *pl* stroomversnelling *c*

rare [rɛə] *adj* zeldzaam

rarely ['rɛəli] *adv* zelden

rascal ['rɑ:skəl] *n* schelm *c*, deugniet *c*

rash [ræʃ] *n* uitslag *c*, huiduitslag *c*; *adj* overhaast, onbezonnen

raspberry ['rɑ:zbəri] *n* framboos *c*

rat [ræt] *n* rat *c*

rate [reit] *n* prijs *c*, tarief *nt*; snelheid *c*; **at any ~** hoe dan ook, in elk geval; ~ **of exchange** wisselkoers *c*

rather ['rɑ:ðə] *adv* vrij, tamelijk, nogal; liever, eerder

ration ['ræʃən] *n* rantsoen *nt*

rattan [ræ'tæn] *n* rotan *c*

raven ['reivən] *n* raaf *c*

raw [rɔ:] *adj* rauw; ~ **material** grondstof *c*

ray [rei] *n* straal *c*

rayon ['reiɔn] *n* kunstzijde *c*

razor ['reizə] *n* scheerapparaat *nt*

razor-blade ['reizəbleid] *n* scheermesje *nt*

reach [ri:tʃ] *v* bereiken; *n* bereik *nt*

reaction [ri'ækʃən] n reactie c

* **read** [ri:d] v *lezen

reading-lamp ['ri:diŋlæmp] n leeslamp c

reading-room ['ri:diŋru:m] n leeszaal c

ready ['redi] adj gereed, klaar

ready-made [,redi'meid] adj confectie-

real [riəl] adj echt

reality [ri'æləti] n werkelijkheid c

realizable ['riəlaizəbəl] adj haalbaar

realize ['riəlaiz] v beseffen; tot stand *brengen, verwezenlijken

really ['riəli] adv echt, werkelijk; eigenlijk

rear [riə] n achterkant c; v *groot-brengen

rear-light [riə'lait] n achterlicht nt

reason ['ri:zən] n oorzaak c, reden c; verstand nt, rede c; v redeneren

reasonable ['ri:zənəbəl] adj redelijk; billijk

reassure [,ri:ə'ʃuə] v geruststellen

rebate ['ri:beit] n korting c, reductie c

rebellion [ri'beljən] n opstand c, op-roer nt

recall [ri'kɔ:l] v zich herinneren; *te-rugroepen; *herroepen

receipt [ri'si:t] n kwitantie c, reçu nt; ontvangst c

receive [ri'si:v] v *krijgen, *ontvangen

receiver [ri'si:və] n telefoonhoorn c

recent ['ri:sənt] adj recent

recently ['ri:səntli] adv kort geleden, onlangs

reception [ri'sepʃən] n ontvangst c; onthaal nt; ~ **office** receptie c

receptionist [ri'sepʃənist] n receptioni-ste c

recession [ri'seʃən] n teruggang c

recipe ['resipi] n recept nt

recital [ri'saitəl] n recital nt

reckon ['rekən] v rekenen; beschou-wen; *denken

recognition [,rekəg'niʃən] n erkenning c

recognize ['rekəgnaiz] v herkennen; erkennen

recollect [,rekə'lekt] v zich herinneren

recommence [,ri:kə'mens] v hervatten

recommend [,rekə'mend] v *aanprij-zen, *aanbevelen; *aanraden

recommendation [,rekəmen'deiʃən] n aanbeveling c

reconciliation [,rekənsili'eiʃən] n ver-zoening c

record¹ ['rekɔ:d] n grammofoonplaat c; record nt; register nt

record² [ri'kɔ:d] v aantekenen

recorder [ri'kɔ:də] n bandrecorder c

recording [ri'kɔ:diŋ] n opname c

record-player ['rekɔ:d,pleiə] n platen-speler c, pick-up c

recover [ri'kʌvə] v *terugvinden; zich herstellen, *genezen

recovery [ri'kʌvəri] n genezing c, her-stel nt

recreation [,rekri'eiʃən] n recreatie c, ontspanning c; ~ **centre** recreatie-centrum nt; ~ **ground** speelterrein nt

recruit [ri'kru:t] n rekruut c

rectangle ['rektæŋgəl] n rechthoek c

rectangular [rek'tæŋgjulə] adj recht-hoekig

rectory ['rektəri] n pastorie c

rectum ['rektəm] n endeldarm c

recyclable [,ri:'saikləbəl] adj recycleer-baar

recycle [,ri:'saikəl] v recycleren

red [red] adj rood

redeem [ri'di:m] v verlossen

reduce [ri'dju:s] v reduceren, vermin-deren, verlagen

reduction [ri'dʌkʃən] n korting c, re-ductie c

redundant [ri'dʌndənt] adj overbodig

reed [ri:d] n riet nt

reef [ri:f] n rif nt

reference ['refrəns] n referentie c, verwijzing c; betrekking c; **with ~ to** met betrekking tot

refer to [ri'fə:] *verwijzen naar

refill ['ri:fil] n vulling c

refinery [ri'fainəri] n raffinaderij c

reflect [ri'flekt] v weerkaatsen

reflection [ri'flekʃən] n weerkaatsing c; spiegelbeeld nt

reflector [ri'flektə] n reflector c

reformation [,refə'meiʃən] n reformatie c

refresh [ri'freʃ] v verfrissen

refreshment [ri'freʃmənt] n verfrissing c

refrigerator [ri'fridʒəreitə] n koelkast c, ijskast c

refund¹ [ri'fʌnd] v terugbetalen

refund² ['ri:fʌnd] n terugbetaling c

refusal [ri'fju:zəl] n weigering c

refuse¹ [ri'fju:z] v weigeren

refuse² ['refju:s] n afval nt

regard [ri'ga:d] v beschouwen; *bekijken; n respect nt; **as regards** betreffende, aangaande, wat betreft

regarding [ri'ga:din] prep met betrekking tot, betreffende; ten aanzien van

regatta [ri'gætə] n regatta c

régime [rei'ʒi:m] n regime nt

region ['ri:dʒən] n streek c; gebied nt

regional ['ri:dʒənəl] adj plaatselijk

register ['redʒistə] v zich *inschrijven; aantekenen; **registered letter** aangetekende brief

registration [,redʒi'streiʃən] n registratie c; ~ **form** inschrijvingsformulier nt; ~ **number** kenteken nt; ~ **plate** nummerbord nt

regret [ri'gret] v betreuren; n spijt c

regular ['regjulə] adj geregeld, regelmatig; gewoon, normaal

regulate ['regjuleit] v regelen

regulation [,regju'leiʃən] n reglement

nt, voorschrift nt; regeling c

rehabilitation [,ri:hə,bili'teiʃən] n revalidatie c

rehearsal [ri'hə:səl] n repetitie c

rehearse [ri'hə:s] v repeteren

reign [rein] n regering c; v regeren

reimburse [,ri:im'bə:s] v terugbetalen, vergoeden

reindeer ['reindiə] n (pl ~) rendier nt

reject [ri'dʒekt] v *afwijzen, *verwerpen; afkeuren

relate [ri'leit] v vertellen

related [ri'leitid] adj verwant

relation [ri'leiʃən] n relatie c, verband nt; verwante c

relative ['relətiv] n familielid nt; adj betrekkelijk, relatief

relax [ri'læks] v zich ontspannen

relaxation [,rilæk'seiʃən] n ontspanning c

reliable [ri'laiəbəl] adj betrouwbaar

relic ['relik] n relikwie c

relief [ri'li:f] n verademing c, verlichting c; steun c; reliëf nt

relieve [ri'li:v] v verlichten; aflossen

religion [ri'lidʒən] n godsdienst c

religious [ri'lidʒəs] adj godsdienstig

rely on [ri'lai] vertrouwen op

remain [ri'mein] v *blijven; *overblijven

remainder [ri'meində] n restant nt, rest c

remaining [ri'meinin] adj overig, overblijvend

remark [ri'ma:k] n opmerking c; v opmerken

remarkable [ri'ma:kəbəl] adj opmerkelijk

remedy ['remədi] n geneesmiddel nt; middel nt

remember [ri'membə] v zich herinneren; *onthouden

remembrance [ri'membrəns] n aandenken nt, herinnering c

remind [ri'maind] v herinneren

remit [ri'mit] v overmaken

remittance [ri'mitəns] n storting c

remnant ['remnənt] n overblijfsel nt, restant nt, rest c

remote [ri'mout] adj afgelegen, ver

removal [ri'mu:vəl] n verwijdering c

remove [ri'mu:v] v verwijderen

remunerate [ri'mju:nəreit] v vergoeden

remuneration [ri,mju:nə'reiʃən] n vergoeding c

renew [ri'nju:] v vernieuwen; verlengen

rent [rent] v huren; n huur c

repair [ri'pɛə] v herstellen, repareren; n herstel c

reparation [,repə'reiʃən] n reparatie c

*repay [ri'pei] v terugbetalen

repayment [ri'peimənt] n terugbetaling c

repeat [ri'pi:t] v herhalen

repellent [ri'pelənt] adj weerzinwekkend, afstotelijk

repentance [ri'pentəns] n berouw nt

repertory ['repətəri] n repertoire nt

repetition [,repə'tiʃən] n herhaling c

replace [ri'pleis] v *vervangen

reply [ri'plai] v antwoorden; n antwoord nt; **in ~** als antwoord

report [ri'pɔ:t] v rapporteren; melden; zich aanmelden; n verslag nt, rapport nt

reporter [ri'pɔ:tə] n verslaggever c

represent [,repri'zent] v vertegenwoordigen; voorstellen

representation [,reprizen'teiʃən] n vertegenwoordiging c

representative [,repri'zentətiv] adj representatief

reprimand ['reprima:nd] v berispen

reproach [ri'proutʃ] n verwijt nt; v *verwijten

reproduce [,ri:prə'dju:s] v reproduceren

reproduction [,ri:prə'dʌkʃən] n reproductie c

reptile ['reptail] n reptiel nt

republic [ri'pʌblik] n republiek c

republican [ri'pʌblikən] adj republikeins

repulsive [ri'pʌlsiv] adj weerzinwekkend

reputation [,repju'teiʃən] n reputatie c; naam c

request [ri'kwest] n verzoek nt; v *verzoeken

require [ri'kwaiə] v vereisen

requirement [ri'kwaiəmənt] n vereiste c

requisite ['rekwizit] adj vereist

rescue ['reskju:] v redden; n redding c

research [ri'sə:tʃ] n onderzoek nt

resemblance [ri'zembləns] n gelijkenis c

resemble [ri'zembəl] v *lijken op

resent [ri'zent] v kwalijk *nemen

reservation [,rezə'veiʃən] n reservering c

reserve [ri'zə:v] v reserveren; *bespreken; n reserve c

reserved [ri'zə:vd] adj gereserveerd

reservoir ['rezəvwa:] n reservoir nt

reside [ri'zaid] v wonen

residence ['rezidəns] n woonplaats c; **~ permit** verblijfsvergunning c

resident ['rezidənt] n inwoner c; adj woonachtig; intern

resign [ri'zain] v ontslag *nemen

resignation [,rezig'neiʃən] n ontslagneming c

resin ['rezin] n hars nt/c

resist [ri'zist] v zich verzetten

resistance [ri'zistəns] n verzet nt

resolute ['rezəlu:t] adj resoluut, vastberaden

respect [ri'spekt] n respect nt; ontzag nt, achting c, eerbied c; v respecteren

respectable [ri'spektəbəl] *adj* eerzaam, respectabel

respectful [ri'spektfəl] *adj* eerbiedig

respective [ri'spektiv] *adj* respectievelijk

respiration [,respə'reiʃən] *n* ademhaling *c*

respite ['respait] *n* uitstel *nt*

responsibility [ri,sponsə'biləti] *n* verantwoordelijkheid *c*; aansprakelijkheid *c*

responsible [ri'sponsəbəl] *adj* verantwoordelijk; aansprakelijk

rest [rest] *n* rust *c*; rest *c*; *v* uitrusten, rusten

restaurant ['restərɔ̃:] *n* restaurant *nt*

restful ['restfəl] *adj* rustig

rest-home ['resthoum] *n* rusthuis *nt*

restless ['restləs] *adj* onrustig; ongedurig

restrain [ri'strein] *v* *inhouden, *weerhouden

restriction [ri'strikʃən] *n* beperking *c*

result [ri'zʌlt] *n* resultaat *nt*; gevolg *nt*; uitslag *c*; *v* resulteren

resume [ri'zju:m] *v* hervatten

résumé ['rezjumei] *n* samenvatting *c*

retail ['ri:teil] *v* in het klein *verkopen; ~ **trade** kleinhandel *c*, detailhandel *c*

retailer ['ri:teilə] *n* detaillist *c*, kleinhandelaar *c*; wederverkoper *c*

retina ['retinə] *n* netvlies *nt*

retired [ri'taiəd] *adj* gepensioneerd

return [ri'tə:n] *v* *terugkomen, terugkeren; *n* terugkeer *c*; ~ **flight** retourvlucht *c*; ~ **journey** terugreis *c*

reunite [,ri:ju:'nait] *v* herenigen

reveal [ri'vi:l] *v* openbaren, onthullen

revelation [,revə'leiʃən] *n* onthulling *c*

revenge [ri'vendʒ] *n* wraak *c*

revenue ['revənju:] *n* inkomen *nt*

reverse [ri'və:s] *n* tegendeel *nt*; keerzijde *c*; omkeer *c*, tegenslag *c*; *adj* omgekeerd; *v* *achteruitrijden

review [ri'vju:] *n* bespreking *c*; tijdschrift *nt*

revise [ri'vaiz] *v* *herzien

revision [ri'viʒən] *n* herziening *c*

revival [ri'vaivəl] *n* herstel *nt*

revolt [ri'voult] *v* in opstand *komen; *n* opstand *c*, oproer *nt*

revolting [ri'voultiŋ] *adj* walgelijk, stuitend, weerzinwekkend

revolution [,revə'lu:ʃən] *n* revolutie *c*; omwenteling *c*

revolutionary [,revə'lu:ʃənəri] *adj* revolutionair

revolver [ri'volvə] *n* revolver *c*

revue [ri'vju:] *n* revue *c*

reward [ri'wɔ:d] *n* beloning *c*; *v* belonen

rheumatism ['ru:mətizəm] *n* reumatiek *c*

rhinoceros [rai'nosərəs] *n* (pl ~, ~es) neushoorn *c*

rhubarb ['ru:bɑ:b] *n* rabarber *c*

rhyme [raim] *n* rijm *nt*

rhythm ['riðəm] *n* ritme *nt*

rib [rib] *n* rib *c*

ribbon ['ribən] *n* lint *c*

rice [rais] *n* rijst *c*

rich [ritʃ] *adj* rijk

riches ['ritʃiz] *pl* rijkdom *c*

riddle ['ridəl] *n* raadsel *nt*

ride [raid] *n* rit *c*

*****ride** [raid] *v* *rijden; *paardrijden

rider ['raidə] *n* ruiter *c*

ridge [ridʒ] *n* bergrug *c*

ridicule ['ridikju:l] *v* bespotten

ridiculous [ri'dikjuləs] *adj* bespottelijk, belachelijk

riding ['raidiŋ] *n* paardesport *c*

riding-school ['raidiŋsku:l] *n* manege *c*

rifle ['raifəl] *v* geweer *nt*

right [rait] *n* recht *nt*; *adj* goed, juist; recht; rechts; billijk, rechtvaardig; **all right!** in orde!; * **be** ~ gelijk *hebben; ~ **of way** voorrang c

righteous ['raitʃəs] adj rechtvaardig

right-hand ['raithænd] adj rechter, rechts

rightly ['raitli] adv terecht

rim [rim] n velg c; rand c

ring [riŋ] n ring c; kring c; piste c

*ring [riŋ] v bellen; ~ **up** opbellen

rinse [rins] v spoelen; n spoeling c

riot ['raiət] n rel c

rip [rip] v scheuren

ripe [raip] adj rijp

rise [raiz] n opslag c, verhoging c; stijging c; opkomst c

*rise [raiz] v *opstaan; *opgaan; *stijgen

rising ['raiziŋ] n opstand c

risk [risk] n risico nt; gevaar nt; v wagen

risky ['riski] adj gewaagd, riskant

rival ['raivəl] n rivaal c; concurrent c; v rivaliseren

rivalry ['raivəlri] n rivaliteit c; concurrentie c

river ['rivə] n rivier c; ~ **bank** oever c

riverside ['rivəsaid] n rivieroever c

roach [routʃ] n (pl ~) blankvoren c

road [roud] n straat c, weg c; ~ **fork** n tweesprong c; ~ **map** wegenkaart c; ~ **system** wegennet nt; ~ **up** werk in uitvoering

roadhouse ['roudhaus] n wegrestaurant nt

roadside ['roudsaid] n wegkant c; ~ **restaurant** wegrestaurant nt

roadway ['roudwei] nAm rijbaan c

roam [roum] v *zwerven

roar [rɔː] v loeien, brullen; n gebrul nt, geraas nt

roast [roust] v *braden, roosteren

rob [rɔb] v beroven

robber ['rɔbə] n dief c

robbery ['rɔbəri] n roof c, diefstal c, beroving c

robe [roub] n jurk c; gewaad nt

robin ['rɔbin] n roodborstje nt

robust [rou'bʌst] adj fors

rock [rɔk] n rots c; v schommelen

rocket ['rɔkit] n raket c

rock-'n-roll [,rɔkən'roul] n rock en roll c

rocky ['rɔki] adj rotsachtig

rod [rɔd] n stang c, roede c

roe [rou] n kuit c, viskuit c

roll [roul] v rollen; n rol c; broodje nt

Roman Catholic ['roumən 'kæθəlik] rooms-katholiek

romance [rə'mæns] n romance c

romantic [rə'mæntik] adj romantisch

roof [ruːf] n dak nt; **thatched** ~ strodak nt

room [ruːm] n vertrek nt, kamer c; ruimte c, plaats c; ~ **and board** kost en inwoning; ~ **service** bediening op de kamer; ~ **temperature** kamertemperatuur c

roomy ['ruːmi] adj ruim

root [ruːt] n wortel c

rope [roup] n touw c

rosary ['rouzəri] n rozenkrans c

rose [rouz] n roos c; adj roze

rotten ['rɔtən] adj rot

rouge [ruːʒ] n rouge c/nt

rough [rʌf] adj ruw

roulette [ruː'let] n roulette c

round [raund] adj rond; prep rondom, om; n ronde c; ~ **trip** Am retour

roundabout ['raundəbaut] n rotonde c

rounded ['raundid] adj afgerond

route [ruːt] n route c

routine [ruː'tiːn] n routine c

row¹ [rou] n rij c; v roeien

row² [rau] n ruzie c

rowdy ['raudi] adj baldadig

rowing-boat ['rouiŋbout] n roeiboot c

royal ['rɔiəl] adj koninklijk

rub [rʌb] v *wrijven

rubber ['rʌbə] n rubber nt; vlakgom

c/nt ; ~ **band** elastiek *nt*
rubbish ['rʌbiʃ] *n* afval *nt* ; geklets *nt*, onzin *c* ; **talk** ~ kletsen
rubbish-bin ['rʌbiʃbin] *n* vuilnisbak *c*
ruby ['ru:bi] *n* robijn *c*
rucksack ['rʌksæk] *n* rugzak *c*
rudder ['rʌdə] *n* roer *nt*
rude [ru:d] *adj* grof
rug [rʌg] *n* kleedje *nt*
ruin ['ru:in] *v* ruïneren ; *n* ondergang *c* ; **ruins** ruïne *c*
ruination [,ru:i'neiʃən] *n* ondergang *c*
rule [ru:l] *n* regel *c* ; bewind *nt*, bestuur *nt*, heerschappij *c* ; *v* heersen, regeren ; **as a** ~ gewoonlijk, in de regel
ruler ['ru:lə] *n* vorst *c*, heerser *c* ; liniaal *c*
Rumania [ru:'meiniə] Roemenië
Rumanian [ru:'meiniən] *adj* Roemeens ; *n* Roemeen *c*
rumour ['ru:mə] *n* gerucht *nt*
*run** [rʌn] *v* rennen ; ~ **into** *tegenkomen
runaway ['rʌnəwei] *n* ontsnapte gevangene
rung [rʌn] *v* (pp ring)
runway ['rʌnwei] *n* startbaan *c*
rural ['ruərəl] *adj* plattelands-
ruse [ru:z] *n* list *c*
rush [rʌʃ] *v* zich haasten ; *n* bies *c*
rush-hour ['rʌʃauə] *n* spitsuur *nt*
Russia ['rʌʃə] Rusland
Russian ['rʌʃən] *adj* Russisch ; *n* Rus *c*
rust [rʌst] *n* roest *nt*
rustic ['rʌstik] *adj* rustiek
rusty ['rʌsti] *adj* roestig

S

saccharin ['sækərin] *n* sacharine *c*
sack [sæk] *n* zak *c*
sacred ['seikrid] *adj* heilig
sacrifice ['sækrifais] *n* offer *nt* ; *v* opofferen
sacrilege ['sækrilidʒ] *n* heiligschennis *c*
sad [sæd] *adj* bedroefd ; verdrietig, droevig, treurig
saddle ['sædəl] *n* zadel *nt*
sadness ['sædnəs] *n* bedroefdheid *c*
safe [seif] *adj* veilig ; *n* brandkast *c*, kluis *c*
safety ['seifti] *n* veiligheid *c*
safety-belt ['seiftibelt] *n* veiligheidsgordel *c*
safety-pin ['seiftipin] *n* veiligheidsspeld *c*
safety-razor ['seifti,reizə] *n* scheerapparaat *nt*
sail [seil] *v* *bevaren, *varen ; *n* zeil *nt*
sailing-boat ['seilinbout] *n* zeilboot *c*
sailor ['seilə] *n* matroos *c*
saint [seint] *n* heilige *c*
salad ['sæləd] *n* sla *c*
salad-oil ['sælədoil] *n* slaolie *c*
salary ['sæləri] *n* loon *nt*, salaris *nt*
sale [seil] *n* verkoop *c* ; **clearance** ~ opruiming *c* ; **for** ~ te koop ; **sales** uitverkoop *c* ; **sales tax** omzetbelasting *c*
saleable ['seiləbəl] *adj* verkoopbaar
salesgirl ['seilzgə:l] *n* verkoopster *c*
salesman ['seilzmən] *n* (pl -men) verkoper *c*
salmon ['sæmən] *n* (pl ~) zalm *c*
salon ['sælɔ̃:] *n* salon *c*
saloon [sə'lu:n] *n* bar *c*
salt [sɔ:lt] *n* zout *nt*
salt-cellar ['sɔ:lt,selə] *n* zoutvaatje *nt*
salty ['sɔ:lti] *adj* zout

salute [sə'lu:t] v groeten

salve [sɑ:v] n zalf c

same [seim] adj zelfde

sample ['sɑ:mpəl] n monster nt

sanatorium [,sænə'tɔ:riəm] n (pl ~s, -ria) sanatorium nt

sand [sænd] n zand nt

sandal ['sændəl] n sandaal c

sandpaper ['sænd,peipə] n schuurpapier nt

sandwich ['sænwidʒ] n boterham c

sandy ['sændi] adj zanderig

sanitary ['sænitəri] adj sanitair; ~ towel maandverband nt

sapphire ['sæfaiə] n saffier nt

sardine [sɑ:'di:n] n sardine c

satchel ['sætʃəl] n schooltas c

satellite ['sætəlait] n satelliet c

satin ['sætin] n satijn nt

satisfaction [,sætis'fækʃən] n bevrediging c, voldoening c

satisfy ['sætisfai] v bevredigen; satisfied voldaan, tevreden

Saturday ['sætədi] zaterdag c

sauce [sɔ:s] n saus c

saucepan ['sɔ:spən] n steelpan c

saucer ['sɔ:sə] n schoteltje nt

Saudi Arabia [,saudiə'reibiə] Saoedi-Arabië

Saudi Arabian [,saudiə'reibiən] adj Saoedi-Arabisch

sauna ['sɔ:nə] n sauna c

sausage ['sɔsidʒ] n worst c

savage ['sævidʒ] adj wild

save [seiv] v redden; sparen

savings ['seivinz] pl spaargeld nt; ~ bank spaarbank c

saviour ['seivjə] n redder c

savoury ['seivəri] adj smakelijk; pikant

saw[1] [sɔ:] v (p see)

saw[2] [sɔ:] n zaag c

sawdust ['sɔ:dʌst] n zaagsel nt

saw-mill ['sɔ:mil] n houtzagerij c

* say [sei] v *zeggen

scaffolding ['skæfəldiŋ] n steigers pl

scale [skeil] n schaal c; toonladder c; schub c; scales pl weegschaal c

scandal ['skændəl] n schandaal c

Scandinavia [,skændi'neiviə] Scandinavië

Scandinavian [,skændi'neiviən] adj Scandinavisch; n Scandinaviër c

scapegoat ['skeipgout] n zondebok c

scar [skɑ:] n litteken nt

scarce [skɛəs] adj schaars

scarcely ['skɛəsli] adv nauwelijks

scarcity ['skɛəsəti] n schaarste c

scare [skɛə] v *doen schrikken; n schrik c

scarf [skɑ:f] n (pl ~s, scarves) das c, sjaal c

scarlet ['skɑ:lət] adj vuurrood

scary ['skɛəri] adj griezelig

scatter ['skætə] v verspreiden

scene [si:n] n scène c

scenery ['si:nəri] n landschap nt

scenic ['si:nik] adj schilderachtig

scent [sent] n geur c

schedule ['ʃedju:l] n dienstregeling c, rooster nt

scheme [ski:m] n schema nt; plan nt

scholar ['skɔlə] n geleerde c; leerling c

scholarship ['skɔləʃip] n studiebeurs c

school [sku:l] n school c

schoolboy ['sku:lbɔi] n schooljongen c

schoolgirl ['sku:lgə:l] n schoolmeisje nt

schoolmaster ['sku:l,mɑ:stə] n onderwijzer c, meester c

schoolteacher ['sku:l,ti:tʃə] n onderwijzer c

science ['saiəns] n wetenschap c

scientific [,saiən'tifik] adj wetenschappelijk

scientist ['saiəntist] n geleerde c

scissors ['sizəz] pl schaar c

scold [skould] v berispen; *schelden

scooter ['sku:tə] n scooter c; autoped c

score [skɔ:] n stand c; v scoren

scorn [skɔ:n] n hoon c, verachting c; v verachten

Scot [skɔt] n Schot c

Scotch [skɔtʃ] adj Schots; **scotch tape** plakband nt

Scotland ['skɔtlənd] Schotland

Scottish ['skɔtiʃ] adj Schots

scout [skaut] n padvinder c

scrap [skræp] n snipper c

scrap-book ['skræpbuk] n plakboek nt

scrape [skreip] v schrappen

scrap-iron ['skræpaiən] n schroot nt

scratch [skrætʃ] v krassen, krabben; n kras c, schram c

scream [skri:m] v gillen, schreeuwen; n gil c, schreeuw c

screen [skri:n] n scherm nt; beeldscherm nt

screw [skru:] n schroef c; v schroeven

screw-driver ['skru:,draivə] n schroevedraaier c

scrub [skrʌb] v schrobben; n struik c

sculptor ['skʌlptə] n beeldhouwer c

sculpture ['skʌlptʃə] n beeldhouwwerk nt

sea [si:] n zee c

sea-bird ['si:bə:d] n zeevogel c

sea-coast ['si:koust] n zeekust c

seagull ['si:gʌl] n meeuw c, zeemeeuw c

seal [si:l] n zegel nt; rob c, zeehond c

seam [si:m] n naad c

seaman ['si:mən] n (pl -men) zeeman c

seamless ['si:mləs] adj naadloos

seaport ['si:pɔ:t] n zeehaven c

search [sə:tʃ] v *zoeken; fouilleren, *doorzoeken

searchlight ['sə:tʃlait] n schijnwerper c

seascape ['si:skeip] n zeegezicht nt

sea-shell ['si:ʃel] n zeeschelp c

seashore ['si:ʃɔ:] n kust c

seasick ['si:sik] adj zeeziek

seasickness ['si:,siknəs] n zeeziekte c

seaside ['si:said] n kust c; ~ **resort** badplaats c

season ['si:zən] n jaargetijde nt, seizoen nt; **high** ~ hoogseizoen nt; **low** ~ naseizoen nt; **off** ~ buiten het seizoen

season-ticket ['si:zən,tikit] n abonnementskaart c

seat [si:t] n stoel c; plaats c, zitplaats c; zetel c

seat-belt ['si:tbelt] n veiligheidsgordel c

sea-urchin ['si:,ə:tʃin] n zeeëgel c

sea-water ['si:,wɔ:tə] n zeewater nt

second ['sekənd] num tweede; n seconde c; tel c

secondary ['sekəndəri] adj secundair, ondergeschikt; ~ **school** middelbare school

second-hand [,sekənd'hænd] adj tweedehands

secret ['si:krət] n geheim nt; adj geheim

secretary ['sekrətri] n secretaresse c; secretaris c

section ['sekʃən] n sectie c; afdeling c, vak nt

secure [si'kjuə] adj veilig; v bemachtigen

security [si'kjuərəti] n veiligheid c; pand nt

sedate [si'deit] adj kalm

sedative ['sedətiv] n kalmerend middel c

seduce [si'dju:s] v verleiden

* **see** [si:] v *zien; *begrijpen, *inzien; ~ **to** zorgen voor

seed [si:d] n zaad nt

* **seek** [si:k] v *zoeken

seem [si:m] v *lijken, *schijnen

seen [si:n] v (pp see)

seesaw ['si:sɔ:] *n* wip *c*

seize [si:z] *v* *grijpen

seldom ['seldəm] *adv* zelden

select [si'lekt] *v* selecteren, *uitkiezen ; adj* select, uitgelezen

selection [si'lekʃən] *n* keuze *c*, selectie *c*

self-centred [,self'sentəd] *adj* egocentrisch

self-employed [,selfim'plɔid] *adj* zelfstandig

self-evident [,sel'fevidənt] *adj* vanzelfsprekend

self-government [,self'gʌvəmənt] *n* zelfbestuur *nt*

selfish ['selfiʃ] *adj* egoïstisch

selfishness ['selfiʃnəs] *n* egoïsme *nt*

self-service [,self'sə:vis] *n* zelfbediening *c* ; ~ **restaurant** zelfbedieningsrestaurant *nt*

***sell** [sel] *v* *verkopen

semblance ['sembləns] *n* schijn *c*

semi- ['semi] half

semicircle ['semi,sə:kəl] *n* halve cirkel

semi-colon [,semi'koulən] *n* puntkomma *c*

senate ['senət] *n* senaat *c*

senator ['senətə] *n* senator *c*

***send** [send] *v* sturen, *zenden ; ~ **back** terugsturen, *terugzenden ; ~ **for** *laten halen ; ~ **off** versturen

senile ['si:nail] *adj* seniel

sensation [sen'seiʃən] *n* sensatie *c* ; gewaarwording *c*, gevoel *nt*

sensational [sen'seiʃənəl] *adj* sensationeel, opzienbarend

sense [sens] *n* zintuig *nt* ; gezond verstand, rede *c* ; zin *c*, betekenis *c* ; *v* voelen ; ~ **of honour** eergevoel *nt*

senseless ['sensləs] *adj* zinloos

sensible ['sensəbəl] *adj* verstandig

sensitive ['sensitiv] *adj* gevoelig

sentence ['sentəns] *n* zin *c* ; vonnis *nt* ; *v* veroordelen

sentimental [,senti'mentəl] *adj* sentimenteel

separate[1] ['sepəreit] *v* *scheiden

separate[2] ['sepərət] *adj* afzonderlijk, gescheiden

separately ['sepərətli] *adv* apart

September [sep'tembə] september

septic ['septik] *adj* septisch ; *become ~ *ontsteken

sequel ['si:kwəl] *n* vervolg *nt*

sequence ['si:kwəns] *n* volgorde *c* ; reeks *c*

serene [sə'ri:n] *adj* kalm ; helder

serial ['siəriəl] *n* feuilleton *nt*

series ['siəri:z] *n* (pl ~) reeks *c*, serie *c*

serious ['siəriəs] *adj* serieus, ernstig

seriousness ['siəriəsnəs] *n* ernst *c*

sermon ['sə:mən] *n* preek *c*

serum ['siərəm] *n* serum *nt*

servant ['sə:vənt] *n* bediende *c*

serve [sə:v] *v* bedienen

service ['sə:vis] *n* dienst *c* ; bediening *c* ; ~ **charge** bedieningsgeld *nt* ; ~ **station** benzinestation *nt*

serviette [,sə:vi'et] *n* servet *nt*

session ['seʃən] *n* zitting *c*

set [set] *n* stel *nt*, groep *c*

***set** [set] *v* zetten ; ~ **menu** vast menu ; ~ **out** *vertrekken

setting ['setiŋ] *n* omgeving *c* ; ~ **lotion** haarversteviger *c*

settle ['setəl] *v* afhandelen, regelen ; ~ **down** zich vestigen

settlement ['setəlmənt] *n* regeling *c*, schikking *c*, overeenkomst *c*

seven ['sevən] *num* zeven

seventeen [,sevən'ti:n] *num* zeventien

seventeenth [,sevən'ti:nθ] *num* zeventiende

seventh ['sevənθ] *num* zevende

seventy ['sevənti] *num* zeventig

several ['sevərəl] *adj* ettelijk, verscheidene

severe [si'viə] *adj* hevig, streng, ernstig

sew [sou] v naaien; ~ **up** hechten

sewer ['su:ə] n riool nt

sewing-machine ['souiŋmə,ʃi:n] n naaimachine c

sex [seks] n geslacht nt; sex c

sexton ['sekstən] n koster c

sexual ['sekʃuəl] adj seksueel

sexuality [,sekʃu'æləti] n seksualiteit c

shade [ʃeid] n schaduw c; tint c

shadow ['ʃædou] n schaduw c

shady ['ʃeidi] adj schaduwrijk

*****shake** [ʃeik] v schudden

shaky ['ʃeiki] adj gammel

*****shall** [ʃæl] v *zullen; *moeten

shallow ['ʃælou] adj ondiep

shame [ʃeim] n schaamte c; schande c; shame! foei!

shampoo [ʃæm'pu:] n shampoo c

shamrock ['ʃæmrɔk] n klaver c

shape [ʃeip] n vorm c; v vormen

share [ʃeə] v delen; n deel nt; aandeel nt

shark [ʃɑ:k] n haai c

sharp [ʃɑ:p] adj scherp

sharpen ['ʃɑ:pən] v *slijpen

shave [ʃeiv] v zich *scheren

shaver ['ʃeivə] n scheerapparaat nt

shaving-brush ['ʃeiviŋbrʌʃ] n scheerkwast c

shaving-cream ['ʃeiviŋkri:m] n scheercrème c

shaving-soap ['ʃeiviŋsoup] n scheerzeep c

shawl [ʃɔ:l] n omslagdoek c, sjaal c

she [ʃi:] pron ze

shed [ʃed] n schuur c

*****shed** [ʃed] v storten; verspreiden

sheep [ʃi:p] n (pl ~) schaap nt

sheer [ʃiə] adj absoluut, puur; dun, doorzichtig

sheet [ʃi:t] n laken nt; blad nt; plaat c

shelf [ʃelf] n (pl shelves) plank c

shell [ʃel] n schelp c; dop c

shellfish ['ʃelfiʃ] n schaaldier nt

shelter ['ʃeltə] n beschutting c, schuilplaats c; v beschutten

shepherd ['ʃepəd] n herder c

shift [ʃift] n ploeg c

*****shine** [ʃain] v *schijnen; glanzen, *blinken

ship [ʃip] n schip nt; v verschepen; **shipping line** scheepvaartlijn c

shipowner ['ʃi,pounə] n reder c

shipyard ['ʃipjɑ:d] n scheepswerf c

shirt [ʃə:t] n hemd nt, overhemd nt

shiver ['ʃivə] v bibberen, rillen; n rilling c

shivery ['ʃivəri] adj rillerig

shock [ʃɔk] n schok c; v schokken; ~ **absorber** schokbreker c

shocking ['ʃɔkiŋ] adj schokkend

shoe [ʃu:] n schoen c; **gym shoes** gymschoenen pl; ~ **polish** schoensmeer c

shoe-lace ['ʃu:leis] n schoenveter c

shoemaker ['ʃu:,meikə] n schoenmaker c

shoe-shop ['ʃu:ʃɔp] n schoenwinkel c

shook [ʃuk] v (p shake)

*****shoot** [ʃu:t] v *schieten

shop [ʃɔp] n winkel c; v winkelen; ~ **assistant** verkoper c; **shopping bag** boodschappentas c; **shopping centre** winkelcentrum nt

shopkeeper ['ʃɔp,ki:pə] n winkelier c

shop-window [,ʃɔp'windou] n etalage c

shore [ʃɔ:] n oever c, kust c

short [ʃɔ:t] adj kort; klein; ~ **circuit** kortsluiting c

shortage ['ʃɔ:tidʒ] n tekort nt, gebrek nt

shortcoming ['ʃɔ:t,kʌmiŋ] n tekortkoming c

shorten ['ʃɔ:tən] v verkorten

shorthand ['ʃɔ:thænd] n stenografie c

shortly ['ʃɔ:tli] adv weldra, binnenkort, spoedig

shorts [ʃɔːts] *pl* korte broek; *plAm* onderbroek *c*

short-sighted [ˌʃɔːtˈsaitid] *adj* bijziend

shot [ʃɔt] *n* schot *nt*; injectie *c*; opname *c*

***should** [ʃud] *v* *moeten

shoulder [ˈʃouldə] *n* schouder *c*

shout [ʃaut] *v* schreeuwen, *roepen; *n* schreeuw *c*

shovel [ˈʃʌvəl] *n* schop *c*

show [ʃou] *n* voorstelling *c*; tentoonstelling *c*

***show** [ʃou] *v* tonen; *laten zien, tentoonstellen; aantonen

show-case [ˈʃoukeis] *n* vitrine *c*

shower [ʃauə] *n* douche *c*; bui *c*, regenbui *c*

showroom [ˈʃouruːm] *n* toonzaal *c*

shriek [ʃriːk] *v* gillen; *n* gil *c*

shrimp [ʃrimp] *n* garnaal *c*

shrine [ʃrain] *n* heiligdom *nt*, schrijn *c*

***shrink** [ʃriŋk] *v* *krimpen

shrinkproof [ˈʃriŋkpruːf] *adj* krimpvrij

shrub [ʃrʌb] *n* struik *c*

shudder [ˈʃʌdə] *n* rilling *c*

shuffle [ˈʃʌfəl] *v* schudden

***shut** [ʃʌt] *v* *sluiten; **shut** dicht, gesloten; ~ **in** *insluiten

shutter [ˈʃʌtə] *n* luik *nt*, blind *nt*

shy [ʃai] *adj* schuw, verlegen

shyness [ˈʃainəs] *n* verlegenheid *c*

Siam [saiˈæm] Siam

Siamese [ˌsaiəˈmiːz] *adj* Siamees; *n* Siamees *c*

sick [sik] *adj* ziek; misselijk

sickness [ˈsiknəs] *n* ziekte *c*; misselijkheid *c*

side [said] *n* kant *c*, zijde *c*; partij *c*; **one-sided** *adj* eenzijdig

sideburns [ˈsaidbəːnz] *pl* bakkebaarden *pl*

sidelight [ˈsaidlait] *n* zijlicht *nt*

side-street [ˈsaidstriːt] *n* zijstraat *c*

sidewalk [ˈsaidwɔːk] *nAm* stoep *c*, trottoir *nt*

sideways [ˈsaidweiz] *adv* opzij

siege [siːdʒ] *n* belegering *c*

sieve [siv] *n* zeef *c*; *v* zeven

sift [sift] *v* zeven

sight [sait] *n* zicht *nt*; gezicht *nt*, aanblik *c*; bezienswaardigheid *c*

sign [sain] *n* teken *nt*; gebaar *nt*, wenk *c*; *v* ondertekenen, tekenen

signal [ˈsignəl] *n* signaal *nt*; sein *nt*, teken *nt*; *v* seinen

signature [ˈsignətʃə] *n* handtekening

significant [sigˈnifikənt] *adj* veelbetekenend

signpost [ˈsainpoust] *n* wegwijzer *c*

silence [ˈsailəns] *n* stilte *c*; *v* tot zwijgen *brengen

silencer [ˈsailənsə] *n* knalpot *c*

silent [ˈsailənt] *adj* zwijgend, stil; *be ~ *zwijgen

silk [silk] *n* zijde *c*

silken [ˈsilkən] *adj* zijden

silly [ˈsili] *adj* mal, dwaas

silver [ˈsilvə] *n* zilver *nt*; zilveren

silversmith [ˈsilvəsmiθ] *n* zilversmid *c*

silverware [ˈsilvəwɛə] *n* zilverwerk *nt*

similar [ˈsimilə] *adj* dergelijk, overeenkomstig

similarity [ˌsimiˈlærəti] *n* gelijkenis *c*

simple [ˈsimpəl] *adj* simpel, eenvoudig; gewoon

simply [ˈsimpli] *adv* eenvoudig, gewoonweg

simulate [ˈsimjuleit] *v* huichelen

simultaneous [ˌsiməlˈteiniəs] *adj* gelijktijdig; **simultaneously** *adv* tegelijkertijd

sin [sin] *n* zonde *c*

since [sins] *prep* sedert; *adv* sindsdien; *conj* sinds; aangezien

sincere [sinˈsiə] *adj* oprecht

sinew [ˈsinjuː] *n* pees *c*

***sing** [siŋ] *v* *zingen

singer [ˈsiŋə] *n* zanger *c*; zangeres *c*

single ['singəl] *adj* enkel; ongetrouwd
singular ['singjulə] *n* enkelvoud *nt*;
  adj eigenaardig
sinister ['sinistə] *adj* onheilspellend
sink [siŋk] *n* gootsteen *c*
* **sink** [siŋk] *v* *zinken
sip [sip] *n* slokje *nt*
siphon ['saifən] *n* sifon *c*
sir [sə:] meneer
siren ['saiərən] *n* sirene *c*
sister ['sistə] *n* zuster *c*, zus *c*
sister-in-law ['sistərinlɔ:] *n* (pl sisters-)
  schoonzuster *c*
* **sit** [sit] *v* *zitten; ~ **down** *gaan zitten
site [sait] *n* plaats *c*; ligging *c*
sitting-room ['sitiŋru:m] *n* zitkamer *c*
situated ['sitʃueitid] *adj* gelegen
situation [,sitʃu'eiʃən] *n* situatie *c*; ligging *c*
six [siks] *num* zes
sixteen [,siks'ti:n] *num* zestien
sixteenth [,siks'ti:nθ] *num* zestiende
sixth [siksθ] *num* zesde
sixty ['siksti] *num* zestig
size [saiz] *n* grootte *c*, maat *c*; afmeting *c*, omvang *c*; formaat *nt*
skate [skeit] *v* schaatsen; *n* schaats *c*
skating-rink ['skeitiŋriŋk] *n* kunstijsbaan *c*, ijsbaan *c*
skeleton ['skelitən] *n* skelet *nt*, geraamte *nt*
sketch [sketʃ] *n* tekening *c*, schets *c*;
  v tekenen, schetsen
sketch-book ['sketʃbuk] *n* schetsboek
  nt
ski[1] [ski:] *v* skiën
ski[2] [ski:] *n* (pl ~, ~s) ski *c*; ~ **boots**
  skischoenen *pl*; ~ **pants** skibroek
  c; ~ **poles** *Am* skistokken *pl*; ~
  sticks skistokken *pl*
skid [skid] *v* slippen
skier ['ski:ə] *n* skiër *c*
skilful ['skilfəl] *adj* bekwaam, behen-

dig, vaardig
ski-lift ['ski:lift] *n* skilift *c*
skill [skil] *n* vaardigheid *c*
skilled [skild] *adj* vaardig, vakkundig
skin [skin] *n* vel *nt*, huid *c*; schil *c*; ~
  cream huidcrème *c*
skip [skip] *v* huppelen; *overslaan
skirt [skə:t] *n* rok *c*
skull [skʌl] *n* schedel *c*
sky [skai] *n* hemel *c*; lucht *c*
skyscraper ['skai,skreipə] *n* wolkenkrabber *c*
slack [slæk] *adj* traag
slacks [slæks] *pl* broek *c*
slam [slæm] *v* *dichtslaan
slander ['slɑ:ndə] *n* laster *c*
slant [slɑ:nt] *v* hellen
slanting ['slɑ:ntiŋ] *adj* schuin, hellend,
  scheef
slap [slæp] *v* *slaan; *n* klap *c*
slate [sleit] *n* lei *nt*
slave [sleiv] *n* slaaf *c*
sledge [sledʒ] *n* slee *c*, slede *c*
sleep [sli:p] *n* slaap *c*
* **sleep** [sli:p] *v* *slapen
sleeping-bag ['sli:piŋbæg] *n* slaapzak *c*
sleeping-car ['sli:piŋkɑ:] *n* slaapwagen
  c
sleeping-pill ['sli:piŋpil] *n* slaappil *c*
sleepless ['sli:pləs] *adj* slapeloos
sleepy ['sli:pi] *adj* slaperig
sleeve [sli:v] *n* mouw *c*; hoes *c*
sleigh [slei] *n* slee *c*, ar *c*
slender ['slendə] *adj* slank
slice [slais] *n* snee *c*
slide [slaid] *n* glijbaan *c*; dia *c*
* **slide** [slaid] *v* *glijden
slight [slait] *adj* licht; gering
slim [slim] *adj* slank; *v* vermageren
slip [slip] *v* slippen, *uitglijden; ontglippen; *n* misstap *c*; onderrok *c*
slipper ['slipə] *n* slof *c*, pantoffel *c*
slippery ['slipəri] *adj* glibberig, glad
slogan ['slougən] *n* leus *c*, slagzin *c*

slope [sloup] *n* helling *c*; *v* glooien

sloping ['sloupiŋ] *adj* afhellend

sloppy ['slɔpi] *adj* slordig

slot [slɔt] *n* gleuf *c*

slot-machine ['slɔt,məʃi:n] *n* automaat *c*

slovenly ['slʌvənli] *adj* slordig

slow [slou] *adj* traag, langzaam; ~ **down** vertragen; afremmen

sluice [slu:s] *n* sluis *c*

slum [slʌm] *n* achterbuurt *c*

slump [slʌmp] *n* prijsdaling *c*

slush [slʌʃ] *n* sneeuwslik *nt*

sly [slai] *adj* listig

smack [smæk] *v* *slaan; *n* klap *c*

small [smɔ:l] *adj* klein; gering

smallpox ['smɔ:lpɔks] *n* pokken *pl*

smart [smɑ:t] *adj* chic; knap, pienter

smell [smel] *n* geur *c*

***smell** [smel] *v* *ruiken; *stinken

smelly ['smeli] *adj* stinkend

smile [smail] *v* glimlachen; *n* glimlach *c*

smith [smiθ] *n* smid *c*

smoke [smouk] *v* roken; *n* rook *c*; **no smoking** verboden te roken

smoker ['smoukə] *n* roker *c*; rookcoupé *c*

smoking-compartment ['smoukiŋkəm,pɑ:tmənt] *n* coupé voor rokers

smoking-room ['smoukiŋru:m] *n* rookkamer *c*

smooth [smu:ð] *adj* effen, vlak, glad; zacht

smuggle ['smʌgəl] *v* smokkelen

snack [snæk] *n* snack *c*

snack-bar ['snækbɑ:] *n* snackbar *c*

snail [sneil] *n* slak *c*

snake [sneik] *n* slang *c*

snapshot ['snæpʃɔt] *n* kiekje *nt*, momentopname *c*

sneakers ['sni:kəz] *plAm* gymschoenen *pl*

sneeze [sni:z] *v* niezen

sniper ['snaipə] *n* sluipschutter *c*

snooty ['snu:ti] *adj* verwaand

snore [snɔ:] *v* snurken

snorkel ['snɔ:kəl] *n* snorkel *c*

snout [snaut] *n* snuit *c*

snow [snou] *n* sneeuw *c*; *v* sneeuwen

snowstorm ['snoustɔ:m] *n* sneeuwstorm *c*

snowy ['snoui] *adj* besneeuwd

so [sou] *conj* dus; *adv* zo; dermate; **and** ~ **on** enzovoort; ~ **far** tot zover; ~ **that** zodat, opdat

soak [souk] *v* weken, doorweken

soap [soup] *n* zeep *c*; ~ **powder** zeeppoeder *nt*

sober ['soubə] *adj* nuchter; bezonnen

so-called [,sou'kɔ:ld] *adj* zogenaamd

soccer ['sɔkə] *n* voetbal *nt*; ~ **team** elftal *nt*

social ['souʃəl] *adj* maatschappelijk, sociaal

socialism ['souʃəlizəm] *n* socialisme *nt*

socialist ['souʃəlist] *adj* socialistisch; *n* socialist *c*

society [sə'saiəti] *n* maatschappij *c*; genootschap *nt*, vereniging *c*; gezelschap *nt*

sock [sɔk] *n* sok *c*

socket ['sɔkit] *n* fitting *c*

soda-water ['soudə,wɔ:tə] *n* spuitwater *nt*, sodawater *nt*

sofa ['soufə] *n* sofa *c*

soft [sɔft] *adj* zacht; ~ **drink** frisdrank *c*

soften ['sɔfən] *v* verzachten

soil [sɔil] *n* grond *c*; bodem *c*, aarde *c*

soiled [sɔild] *adj* bevuild

sold [sould] *v* (p, pp sell); ~ **out** uitverkocht

solder ['sɔldə] *v* solderen

soldering-iron ['sɔldəriŋaiən] *n* soldeerbout *c*

soldier ['souldʒə] *n* militair *c*, soldaat *c*

sole¹ [soul] *adj* enig

sole² [soul] *n* zool *c*; tong *c*

solely ['soulli] *adv* uitsluitend

solemn ['soləm] *adj* plechtig

solicitor [sə'lisitə] *n* raadsman *c*, advocaat *c*

solid ['sɔlid] *adj* stevig, solide; massief; *n* vaste stof

soluble ['sɔljubəl] *adj* oplosbaar

solution [sə'lu:ʃən] *n* oplossing *c*

solve [sɔlv] *v* oplossen

sombre ['sɔmbə] *adj* somber

some [sʌm] *adj* enige, enkele; *pron* sommige; iets; ~ **day** eens; ~ **more** nog wat; ~ **time** eens

somebody ['sʌmbədi] *pron* iemand

somehow ['sʌmhau] *adv* op de een of andere manier

someone ['sʌmwʌn] *pron* iemand

something ['sʌmθiŋ] *pron* iets

sometimes ['sʌmtaimz] *adv* soms

somewhat ['sʌmwɔt] *adv* enigszins

somewhere ['sʌmwɛə] *adv* ergens

son [sʌn] *n* zoon *c*

song [sɔŋ] *n* lied *nt*

son-in-law ['sʌninlɔ:] *n* (pl sons-) schoonzoon *c*

soon [su:n] *adv* vlug, gauw, weldra, spoedig; **as ~ as** zodra

sooner ['su:nə] *adv* liever

sore [sɔ:] *adj* pijnlijk, zeer; *n* zere plek; zweer *c*; ~ **throat** keelpijn *c*

sorrow ['sɔrou] *n* droefheid *c*, leed *nt*, verdriet *nt*

sorry ['sɔri] *adj* bedroefd; **sorry!** neem me niet kwalijk!, sorry!, pardon!

sort [sɔ:t] *v* sorteren, rangschikken; *n* slag *nt*, soort *c/nt*; **all sorts of** allerlei

soul [soul] *n* ziel *c*; geest *c*

sound [saund] *n* klank *c*, geluid *nt*; *v* *klinken; *adj* degelijk

soundproof ['saundpru:f] *adj* geluiddicht

soup [su:p] *n* soep *c*

soup-plate ['su:ppleit] *n* soepbord *nt*

soup-spoon ['su:pspu:n] *n* soeplepel *c*

sour [sauə] *adj* zuur

source [sɔ:s] *n* bron *c*

south [sauθ] *n* zuid *c*, zuiden *nt*; **South Pole** zuidpool *c*

South Africa [sauθ 'æfrikə] Zuid-Afrika

south-east [,sauθ'i:st] *n* zuidoosten *nt*

southerly ['sʌðəli] *adj* zuidelijk

southern ['sʌðən] *adj* zuidelijk

south-west [,sauθ'west] *n* zuidwesten *nt*

souvenir ['su:vəniə] *n* souvenir *nt*; ~ **shop** souvenirwinkel *c*

sovereign ['sɔvrin] *n* vorst *c*

Soviet ['souviət] *adj* Sovjet-

***sow** [sou] *v* zaaien

spa [spa:] *n* geneeskrachtige bron

space [speis] *n* ruimte *c*; afstand *c*, tussenruimte *c*; *v* spatiëren

spacious ['speiʃəs] *adj* ruim

spade [speid] *n* schop *c*, spade *c*

Spain [spein] Spanje

Spaniard ['spænjəd] *n* Spanjaard *c*

Spanish ['spæniʃ] *adj* Spaans

spanking ['spæŋkiŋ] *n* pak slaag

spanner ['spænə] *n* schroefsleutel *c*; moersleutel *c*

spare [spɛə] *adj* reserve-, extra; *v* missen; ~ **part** onderdeel *nt*; ~ **room** logeerkamer *c*; ~ **time** vrije tijd; ~ **tyre** reserveband *c*; ~ **wheel** reservewiel *nt*

spark [spa:k] *n* vonk *c*

sparking-plug ['spa:kiŋplʌg] *n* bougie *c*

sparkling ['spa:kliŋ] *adj* fonkelend; mousserend

sparrow ['spærou] *n* mus *c*

***speak** [spi:k] *v* *spreken

spear [spiə] *n* speer *c*

special ['speʃəl] *adj* bijzonder, spe-

ciaal; ~ **delivery** expresse-
specialist ['speʃəlist] n specialist c
speciality [,speʃi'æləti] n specialiteit c
specialize ['speʃəlaiz] v zich specialiseren
specially ['speʃəli] adv in het bijzonder
species ['spi:ʃi:z] n (pl ~) soort c/nt
specific [spə'sifik] adj specifiek
specimen ['spesimən] n exemplaar nt, specimen nt
speck [spek] n spat c
spectacle ['spektəkəl] n schouwspel nt; **spectacles** bril c
spectator [spek'teitə] n kijker c, toeschouwer c
speculate ['spekjuleit] v speculeren
speech [spi:tʃ] n spraak c; rede c, toespraak c; taal c
speechless ['spi:tʃləs] adj sprakeloos
speed [spi:d] n snelheid c; vaart c, spoed c; **cruising** ~ kruissnelheid c; ~ **limit** maximum snelheid, snelheidsbeperking c
* **speed** [spi:d] v hard *rijden; te hard *rijden
speeding ['spi:diŋ] n snelheidsovertreding c
speedometer [spi:'dɔmitə] n snelheidsmeter c
spell [spel] n betovering c
* **spell** [spel] v spellen
spelling ['speliŋ] n spelling c
* **spend** [spend] v *uitgeven, besteden; *doorbrengen
sphere [sfiə] n bol c; sfeer c
spice [spais] n specerij c; **spices** kruiden
spiced [spaist] adj gekruid
spicy ['spaisi] adj pikant
spider ['spaidə] n spin c; **spider's web** spinneweb nt
* **spill** [spil] v morsen
* **spin** [spin] v *spinnen; draaien
spinach ['spinidʒ] n spinazie c

spine [spain] n ruggegraat c
spinster ['spinstə] n oude vrijster
spire [spaiə] n spits c
spirit ['spirit] n geest c; bui c; **spirits** sterke drank; stemming c; ~ **stove** spiritusbrander c
spiritual ['spiritʃuəl] adj geestelijk
spit [spit] n spuug nt, speeksel nt; spit nt
* **spit** [spit] v spuwen
in spite of [in spait ɔv] ongeacht, ondanks
spiteful ['spaitfəl] adj hatelijk
splash [splæʃ] v spatten
splendid ['splendid] adj schitterend, prachtig
splendour ['splendə] n pracht c
splint [splint] n spalk c
splinter ['splintə] n splinter c
* **split** [split] v *splijten
* **spoil** [spɔil] v *bederven; verwennen
spoke[1] [spouk] v (p speak)
spoke[2] [spouk] n spaak c
sponge [spʌndʒ] n spons c
spook [spu:k] n spook nt
spool [spu:l] n spoel c
spoon [spu:n] n lepel c
sport [spɔ:t] n sport c
sports-car ['spɔ:tska:] n sportwagen c
sports-jacket ['spɔ:ts,dʒækit] n sportjasje nt
sportsman ['spɔ:tsmən] n (pl -men) sportman c
sportswear ['spɔ:tswɛə] n sportkleding c
spot [spɔt] n spat c, vlek c; plek c, plaats c
spotless ['spɔtləs] adj vlekkeloos
spotlight ['spɔtlait] n schijnwerper c
spotted ['spɔtid] adj gespikkeld
spout [spaut] n straal c
sprain [sprein] v verstuiken, verzwikken; n verstuiking c
* **spread** [spred] v spreiden

spring [sprɪŋ] n voorjaar nt, lente c; veer c; bron c

springtime ['sprɪŋtaim] n voorjaar nt

sprouts [sprauts] pl spruitjes pl

spy [spai] n spion c

squadron ['skwɔdrən] n eskader nt

square [skweə] adj vierkant; n kwadraat nt, vierkant nt; plein c

squash [skwɔʃ] n vruchtensap nt

squirrel ['skwirəl] n eekhoorn c

squirt [skwə:t] n straal c

stable ['steibəl] adj stabiel; n stal c

stack [stæk] n stapel c

stadium ['steidiəm] n stadion nt

staff [stɑ:f] n staf c

stage [steidʒ] n toneel nt; fase c, stadium nt; etappe c

stain [stein] v vlekken; n spat c, vlek c; **stained glass** gebrandschilderd glas; ~ **remover** vlekkenwater nt

stainless ['steinləs] adj vlekkeloos; ~ **steel** roestvrij staal

staircase ['steəkeis] n trap c

stairs [steəz] pl trap c

stale [steil] adj oudbakken

stall [stɔ:l] n kraam c; stalles pl

stamina ['stæminə] n uithoudingsvermogen nt

stamp [stæmp] n postzegel c; stempel c; v frankeren; stampen; ~ **machine** postzegelautomaat c

stand [stænd] n kraam c; tribune c

*stand [stænd] v *staan

standard ['stændəd] n norm c, maatstaf c; standaard-; ~ **of living** levensstandaard c

stanza ['stænzə] n couplet nt

staple ['steipəl] n nietje nt

star [stɑ:] n ster c

starboard ['stɑ:bəd] n stuurboord nt

starch [stɑ:tʃ] n stijfsel nt; v *stijven

stare [steə] v staren

starling ['stɑ:liŋ] n spreeuw c

start [stɑ:t] v *beginnen; n begin nt;

starter motor startmotor c

starting-point ['stɑ:tiŋpɔint] n uitgangspunt nt

state [steit] n staat c; toestand c; v verklaren

the States Verenigde Staten

statement ['steitmənt] n verklaring c

statesman ['steitsmən] n (pl -men) staatsman c

station ['steiʃən] n station nt; plaats c

stationary ['steiʃənəri] adj stilstaand

stationer's ['steiʃənəz] n kantoorboekhandel c

stationery ['steiʃənəri] n schrijfbehoeften pl

station-master ['steiʃən,mɑ:stə] n stationschef c

statistics [stə'tistiks] pl statistiek c

statue ['stætʃu:] n standbeeld nt

stay [stei] v *blijven; logeren, *verblijven; n verblijf nt

steadfast ['stedfɑ:st] adj standvastig

steady ['stedi] adj vast

steak [steik] n biefstuk c

*steal [sti:l] v *stelen

steam [sti:m] n stoom c

steamer ['sti:mə] n stoomboot c

steel [sti:l] n staal nt

steep [sti:p] adj steil

steeple ['sti:pəl] n kerktoren c

steering-column ['stiəriŋ,kɔləm] n stuurkolom c

steering-wheel ['stiəriŋwi:l] n stuurwiel nt

steersman ['stiəzmən] n (pl -men) stuurman c

stem [stem] n steel c

stenographer [ste'nɔgrəfə] n stenograaf c

step [step] n pas c, stap c, trede c; v stappen

stepchild ['steptʃaild] n (pl -children) stiefkind nt

stepfather ['step,fɑ:ðə] n stiefvader c

stepmother ['step,mʌðə] *n* stiefmoeder *c*

sterile ['sterail] *adj* steriel

sterilize ['sterilaiz] *v* steriliseren

steward ['stju:əd] *n* steward *c*

stewardess ['stju:ədes] *n* stewardess *c*

stick [stik] *n* stok *c*

***stick** [stik] *v* kleven, plakken

sticky ['stiki] *adj* kleverig

stiff [stif] *adj* stijf

still [stil] *adv* nog; toch; *adj* stil

stillness ['stilnəs] *n* stilte *c*

stimulant ['stimjulənt] *n* stimulerend middel

stimulate ['stimjuleit] *v* stimuleren

sting [stiŋ] *n* prik *c*, steek *c*

***sting** [stiŋ] *v* *steken

stingy ['stindʒi] *adj* gierig

***stink** [stiŋk] *v* *stinken

stipulate ['stipjuleit] *v* bepalen

stipulation [,stipju'leiʃən] *n* bepaling *c*

stir [stə:] *v* *bewegen; roeren

stirrup ['stirəp] *n* stijgbeugel *c*

stitch [stitʃ] *n* steek *c*; hechting *c*

stock [stɔk] *n* voorraad *c*; *v* in voorraad *hebben; ~ **exchange** effectenbeurs *c*, beurs *c*; ~ **market** effectenbeurs *c*; **stocks and shares** effecten

stocking ['stɔkiŋ] *n* kous *c*

stole[1] [stoul] *v* (p steal)

stole[2] [stoul] *n* stola *c*

stomach ['stʌmək] *n* maag *c*

stomach-ache ['stʌməkeik] *n* buikpijn *c*, maagpijn *c*

stone [stoun] *n* steen *c*; edelsteen *c*; pit *c*; stenen; **pumice ~** puimsteen *nt*

stood [stud] *v* (p, pp stand)

stop [stɔp] *v* stoppen; *ophouden met, staken; *n* halte *c*; **stop!** halt!

stopper ['stɔpə] *n* stop *c*

storage ['stɔ:ridʒ] *n* opslag *c*

store [stɔ:] *n* voorraad *c*; winkel *c*; *v* *opslaan

store-house ['stɔ:haus] *n* magazijn *nt*

storey ['stɔ:ri] *n* etage *c*, verdieping *c*

stork [stɔ:k] *n* ooievaar *c*

storm [stɔ:m] *n* storm *c*

stormy ['stɔ:mi] *adj* stormachtig

story ['stɔ:ri] *n* verhaal *nt*

stout [staut] *adj* dik, gezet, corpulent

stove [stouv] *n* kachel *c*; fornuis *nt*

straight [streit] *adj* recht; eerlijk; *adv* recht; ~ **ahead** rechtdoor; ~ **away** direct, meteen; ~ **on** rechtdoor

strain [strein] *n* inspanning *c*; spanning *c*; *v* forceren; zeven

strainer ['streinə] *n* vergiet *nt*

strange [streindʒ] *adj* vreemd; raar

stranger ['streindʒə] *n* vreemdeling *c*; vreemde *c*

strangle ['stræŋgəl] *v* wurgen

strap [stræp] *n* riem *c*

straw [strɔ:] *n* stro *nt*

strawberry ['strɔ:bəri] *n* aardbei *c*

stream [stri:m] *n* beek *c*; stroom *c*; *v* stromen

street [stri:t] *n* straat *c*

streetcar ['stri:tka:] *nAm* tram *c*

street-organ ['stri:,tɔ:gən] *n* draaiorgel *nt*

strength [streŋθ] *n* sterkte *c*, kracht *c*

stress [stres] *n* spanning *c*; nadruk *c*; *v* benadrukken

stretch [stretʃ] *v* rekken; *n* stuk *nt*

strict [strikt] *adj* strikt; streng

strife [straif] *n* strijd *c*

strike [straik] *n* staking *c*

***strike** [straik] *v* *slaan; *toeslaan; *treffen; staken; *strijken

striking ['straikiŋ] *adj* frappant, opmerkelijk, opvallend

string [striŋ] *n* touw *nt*; snaar *c*

strip [strip] *n* strook *c*

stripe [straip] *n* streep *c*

striped [straipt] *adj* gestreept

stroke [strouk] *n* beroerte *c*

stroll [stroul] *v* wandelen; *n* wandeling *c*

strong [strɔŋ] *adj* sterk; krachtig

stronghold ['strɔŋhould] *n* burcht *c*

structure ['strʌktʃə] *n* structuur *c*

struggle ['strʌgəl] *n* strijd *c*, worsteling *c*; *v* worstelen, *strijden

stub [stʌb] *n* controlestrook *c*

stubborn ['stʌbən] *adj* hardnekkig

student ['stju:dənt] *n* student *c*; studente *c*

study ['stʌdi] *v* studeren; *n* studie *c*; studeerkamer *c*

stuff [stʌf] *n* stof *c*; spul *nt*

stuffed [stʌft] *adj* gevuld

stuffing ['stʌfiŋ] *n* vulling *c*

stuffy ['stʌfi] *adj* benauwd

stumble ['stʌmbəl] *v* struikelen

stung [stʌŋ] *v* (p, pp sting)

stupid ['stju:pid] *adj* dom

style [stail] *n* stijl *c*

subject[1] ['sʌbdʒikt] *n* onderwerp *nt*; onderdaan *c*; ~ **to** onderhevig aan

subject[2] [səb'dʒekt] *v* *onderwerpen

submit [səb'mit] *v* zich *onderwerpen

subordinate [sə'bɔ:dinət] *adj* ondergeschikt; bijkomstig

subscriber [səb'skraibə] *n* abonnee *c*

subscription [səb'skripʃən] *n* abonnement *nt*

subsequent ['sʌbsikwənt] *adj* volgend

subsidy ['sʌbsidi] *n* subsidie *c*

substance ['sʌbstəns] *n* substantie *c*

substantial [səb'stænʃəl] *adj* stoffelijk; werkelijk; aanzienlijk

substitute ['sʌbstitju:t] *v* *vervangen; *n* vervanging *c*; plaatsvervanger *c*

subtitle ['sʌb,taitəl] *n* ondertitel *c*

subtle ['sʌtəl] *adj* subtiel

subtract [səb'trækt] *v* *aftrekken

suburb ['sʌbə:b] *n* buitenwijk *c*, voorstad *c*

suburban [sə'bə:bən] *adj* van de voorstad

subway ['sʌbwei] *nAm* ondergrondse *c*

succeed [sək'si:d] *v* slagen; opvolgen

success [sək'ses] *n* succes *nt*

successful [sək'sesfəl] *adj* succesvol

succumb [sə'kʌm] *v* *bezwijken

such [sʌtʃ] *adj* dergelijk, zulk; *adv* zo; ~ **as** zoals

suck [sʌk] *v* *zuigen

sudden ['sʌdən] *adj* plotseling

suddenly ['sʌdənli] *adv* opeens

suede [sweid] *n* suède *nt/c*

suffer ['sʌfə] *v* *lijden; *ondergaan

suffering ['sʌfəriŋ] *n* lijden *nt*

suffice [sə'fais] *v* voldoende *zijn

sufficient [sə'fiʃənt] *adj* voldoende, genoeg

suffrage ['sʌfridʒ] *n* stemrecht *nt*, kiesrecht *nt*

sugar ['ʃugə] *n* suiker *c*

suggest [sə'dʒest] *v* voorstellen

suggestion [sə'dʒestʃən] *n* voorstel *nt*

suicide ['su:isaid] *n* zelfmoord *c*

suit [su:t] *v* schikken; aanpassen; goed *staan; *n* kostuum *nt*

suitable ['su:təbəl] *adj* gepast, geschikt

suitcase ['su:tkeis] *n* koffer *c*

suite [swi:t] *n* suite *c*

sum [sʌm] *n* som *c*

summary ['sʌməri] *n* resumé *nt*, samenvatting *c*

summer ['sʌmə] *n* zomer *c*; ~ **time** zomertijd *c*

summit ['sʌmit] *n* top *c*

summons ['sʌmənz] *n* (pl ~es) dagvaarding *c*

sun [sʌn] *n* zon *c*

sunbathe ['sʌnbeið] *v* zonnebaden

sunburn ['sʌnbə:n] *n* zonnebrand *c*

Sunday ['sʌndi] *n* zondag *c*

sun-glasses ['sʌn,glɑ:siz] *pl* zonnebril *c*

sunlight ['sʌnlait] *n* zonlicht *nt*

sunny ['sʌni] *adj* zonnig

sunrise ['sʌnraiz] n zonsopgang c
sunset ['sʌnset] n zonsondergang c
sunshade ['sʌnʃeid] n parasol c
sunshine ['sʌnʃain] n zonneschijn c
sunstroke ['sʌnstrouk] n zonnesteek c
suntan oil ['sʌntænɔil] zonnebrandolie c
superb [su'pə:b] adj groots, prachtig
superficial [,su:pə'fiʃəl] adj oppervlakkig
superfluous [su'pə:fluəs] adj overbodig
superior [su'piəriə] adj beter, groter, hoger, superieur
superlative [su'pə:lətiv] adj overtreffend; n superlatief c
supermarket ['su:pə,ma:kit] n supermarkt c
superstition [,su:pə'stiʃən] n bijgeloof nt
supervise ['su:pəvaiz] v toezicht *houden op
supervision [,su:pə'viʒən] n controle c, toezicht nt
supervisor ['su:pəvaizə] n opzichter c
supper ['sʌpə] n avondeten nt
supple ['sʌpəl] adj soepel, lenig, buigzaam
supplement ['sʌplimənt] n supplement nt
supply [sə'plai] n aanvoer c, levering c; voorraad c; aanbod nt; v leveren, bezorgen
support [sə'pɔ:t] v ondersteunen, steunen; n steun c; ~ hose steunkousen pl
supporter [sə'pɔ:tə] n supporter c
suppose [sə'pouz] v *aannemen, veronderstellen; supposing that aangenomen dat
suppository [sə'pɔzitəri] n zetpil c
suppress [sə'pres] v onderdrukken
surcharge ['sə:tʃa:dʒ] n toeslag c
sure [ʃuə] adj zeker
surely ['ʃuəli] adv zeker

surface ['sə:fis] n oppervlakte c
surf-board ['sə:fbɔ:d] n surfplank c
surgeon ['sə:dʒən] n chirurg c; veterinary ~ veearts c
surgery ['sə:dʒəri] n operatie c; spreekkamer c
surname ['sə:neim] n achternaam c
surplus ['sə:pləs] n overschot nt
surprise [sə'praiz] n verrassing c; verbazing c; v verrassen; verbazen
surrender [sə'rendə] v zich *overgeven; n overgave c
surround [sə'raund] v omringen, *omgeven
surrounding [sə'raundiŋ] adj omliggend
surroundings [sə'raundiŋz] pl omgeving c
survey ['sə:vei] n overzicht nt
survival [sə'vaivəl] n overleving c
survive [sə'vaiv] v overleven
suspect[1] [sə'spekt] v *verdenken; vermoeden
suspect[2] ['sʌspekt] n verdachte c
suspend [sə'spend] v schorsen
suspenders [sə'spendəz] plAm bretels pl; suspender belt jarretelgordel c
suspension [sə'spenʃən] n vering c, ophanging c; ~ bridge hangbrug c
suspicion [sə'spiʃən] n verdenking c; wantrouwen nt, argwaan c
suspicious [sə'spiʃəs] adj verdacht; argwanend, achterdochtig
sustain [sə'stein] v *verdragen
Swahili [swɑ'hi:li] n Swahili nt
swallow ['swɔlou] v inslikken, slikken; n zwaluw c
swam [swæm] v (p swim)
swamp [swɔmp] n moeras nt
swan [swɔn] n zwaan c
swap [swɔp] v ruilen
*swear [swɛə] v *zweren; vloeken
sweat [swet] n zweet nt; v zweten
sweater ['swetə] n sweater c

Swede [swi:d] n Zweed c
Sweden ['swi:dən] Zweden
Swedish ['swi:diʃ] adj Zweeds
*** sweep** [swi:p] v vegen
sweet [swi:t] adj zoet; lief; n snoepje nt; toetje nt; **sweets** snoep nt, snoepgoed c
sweeten ['swi:tən] v zoet maken
sweetheart ['swi:thɑ:t] n liefje nt, lieveling c
sweetshop ['swi:tʃɔp] n snoepwinkel c
swell [swel] adj prachtig
*** swell** [swel] v *zwellen
swelling ['swelin] n zwelling c
swift [swift] adj snel
*** swim** [swim] v *zwemmen
swimmer ['swimə] n zwemmer c
swimming ['swimin] n zwemsport c; ~ **pool** zwembad nt
swimming-trunks ['swimintrʌŋks] n zwembroek c
swim-suit ['swimsu:t] n zwempak nt
swindle ['swindəl] v oplichten; n zwendelarij c
swindler ['swindlə] n oplichter c
swing [swin] n schommel c
*** swing** [swin] v zwaaien; schommelen
Swiss [swis] adj Zwitsers; n Zwitser c
switch [switʃ] n schakelaar c; v omwisselen; ~ **off** uitschakelen; ~ **on** inschakelen
switchboard ['switʃbɔ:d] n schakelbord nt
Switzerland ['switsələnd] Zwitserland
sword [sɔ:d] n zwaard nt
swum [swʌm] v (pp swim)
syllable ['siləbəl] n lettergreep c
symbol ['simbəl] n symbool nt
sympathetic [,simpə'θetik] adj hartelijk, begrijpend
sympathy ['simpəθi] n sympathie c; medegevoel nt
symphony ['simfəni] n symfonie c
symptom ['simtəm] n symptoom nt

synagogue ['sinəgɔg] n synagoge c
synonym ['sinənim] n synoniem nt
synthetic [sin'θetik] adj synthetisch
syphon ['saifən] n sifon c
Syria ['siriə] Syrië
Syrian ['siriən] adj Syrisch; n Syriër c
syringe [si'rindʒ] n spuit c
syrup ['sirəp] n stroop c, siroop c
system ['sistəm] n systeem nt; stelsel nt; **decimal** ~ tientallig stelsel
systematic [,sistə'mætik] adj systematisch

T

table ['teibəl] n tafel c; tabel c; ~ **of contents** inhoudsopgave c; ~ **tennis** tafeltennis nt
table-cloth ['teibəlklɔθ] n tafellaken nt
tablespoon ['teibəlspu:n] n eetlepel c
tablet ['tæblit] n tablet nt
taboo [tə'bu:] n taboe nt
tactics ['tæktiks] pl tactiek c
tag [tæg] n etiket nt
tail [teil] n staart c
tail-light ['teillait] n achterlicht nt
tailor ['teilə] n kleermaker c
tailor-made ['teiləmeid] adj op maat gemaakt
*** take** [teik] v *nemen; pakken; *brengen; *begrijpen, snappen; ~ **away** *meenemen; *afnemen, *wegnemen; ~ **off** starten; ~ **out** *wegnemen; ~ **over** *overnemen; ~ **place** *plaatshebben; ~ **up** *innemen
take-off ['teikɔf] n start c
tale [teil] n verhaal nt, vertelling c
talent ['tælənt] n aanleg c, talent nt
talented ['tæləntid] adj begaafd
talk [tɔ:k] v *spreken, praten; n gesprek nt

talkative ['tɔ:kətiv] *adj* spraakzaam
tall [tɔ:l] *adj* hoog; lang, groot
tame [teim] *adj* mak, tam; *v* temmen
tampon ['tæmpən] *n* tampon *c*
tangerine [,tændʒə'ri:n] *n* mandarijn *c*
tangible ['tændʒibəl] *adj* tastbaar
tank [tæŋk] *n* tank *c*
tanker ['tæŋkə] *n* tankschip *nt*
tanned [tænd] *adj* gebruind
tap [tæp] *n* kraan *c*; klop *c*; *v* kloppen
tape [teip] *n* band *c*; lint *nt*; **adhesive** ~ plakband *nt*; hechtpleister *c*
tape-measure ['teip,meʒə] *n* centimeter *c*
tape-recorder ['teipri,kɔ:də] *n* bandrecorder *c*
tapestry ['tæpistri] *n* wandkleed *nt*, gobelin *c*
tar [ta:] *n* teer *c/nt*
target ['ta:git] *n* doel *nt*, mikpunt *nt*
tariff ['tærif] *n* tarief *nt*
tarpaulin [ta:'pɔ:lin] *n* dekzeil *nt*
task [ta:sk] *n* taak *c*
taste [teist] *n* smaak *c*; *v* smaken; proeven
tasteless ['teistləs] *adj* smakeloos
tasty ['teisti] *adj* lekker, smakelijk
taught [tɔ:t] *v* (p, pp teach)
tavern ['tævən] *n* herberg *c*
tax [tæks] *n* belasting *c*; *v* belasten
taxation [tæk'seiʃən] *n* belasting *c*
tax-free ['tæksfri:] *adj* belastingvrij
taxi ['tæksi] *n* taxi *c*; ~ **rank** taxistandplaats *c*; ~ **stand** *Am* taxistandplaats *c*
taxi-driver ['tæksi,draivə] *n* taxichauffeur *c*
taxi-meter ['tæksi,mi:tə] *n* taximeter *c*
tea [ti:] *n* thee *c*
*teach [ti:tʃ] *v* leren, *onderwijzen
teacher ['ti:tʃə] *n* docent *c*, leraar *c*; lerares *c*; onderwijzer *c*, meester *c*, schoolmeester *c*

teachings ['ti:tʃiŋz] *pl* leer *c*
tea-cloth ['ti:klɔθ] *n* theedoek *c*
teacup ['ti:kʌp] *n* theekopje *nt*
team [ti:m] *n* equipe *c*, ploeg *c*
teapot ['ti:pɔt] *n* theepot *c*
tear¹ [tiə] *n* traan *c*
tear² [teə] *n* scheur *c*; ***tear** *v* scheuren
tear-jerker ['tiə,dʒə:kə] *n* smartlap *c*
tease [ti:z] *v* plagen
tea-set ['ti:set] *n* theeservies *nt*
tea-shop ['ti:ʃɔp] *n* tearoom *c*
teaspoon ['ti:spu:n] *n* theelepel *c*
teaspoonful ['ti:spu:n,ful] *n* theelepel *c*
technical ['teknikəl] *adj* technisch
technician [tek'niʃən] *n* technicus *c*
technique [tek'ni:k] *n* techniek *c*
technology [tek'nɔlədʒi] *n* technologie *c*
teenager ['ti:,neidʒə] *n* tiener *c*
teetotaller [ti:'toutələ] *n* geheelonthouder *c*
telegram ['teligræm] *n* telegram *nt*
telegraph ['teligra:f] *v* telegraferen
telepathy [ti'lepəθi] *n* telepathie *c*
telephone ['telifoun] *n* telefoon *c*; ~ **book** *Am* telefoongids *c*, telefoonboek *nt*; ~ **booth** telefooncel *c*; ~ **call** telefoongesprek *nt*; ~ **directory** telefoonboek *nt*, telefoongids *c*; ~ **operator** telefoniste *c*
television ['teliviʒən] *n* televisie *c*; ~ **set** televisietoestel *nt*; **cable** ~ kabel-tv; **satellite** ~ satelliet-tv
telex ['teleks] *n* telex *c*
*tell [tel] *v* *zeggen; vertellen
temper ['tempə] *n* boosheid *c*
temperature ['temprətʃə] *n* temperatuur *c*
tempest ['tempist] *n* storm *c*
temple ['tempəl] *n* tempel *c*; slaap *c*
temporary ['tempərəri] *adj* voorlopig, tijdelijk

tempt [tempt] v *aantrekken

temptation [temp'teiʃən] n verleiding c

ten [ten] num tien

tenant ['tenənt] n huurder c

tend [tend] v de neiging *hebben; verzorgen; ~ **to** neigen tot

tendency ['tendənsi] n neiging c, tendens c

tender ['tendə] adj teder, teer; mals

tendon ['tendən] n pees c

tennis ['tenis] n tennis nt; ~ **shoes** tennisschoenen

tennis-court ['teniskɔ:t] n tennisbaan c

tense [tens] adj gespannen

tension ['tenʃən] n spanning c

tent [tent] n tent c

tenth [tenθ] num tiende

tepid ['tepid] adj lauw

term [tə:m] n term c; periode c, termijn c; voorwaarde c

terminal ['tə:minəl] n eindpunt nt

terrace ['terəs] n terras nt

terrain [te'rein] n terrein nt

terrible ['teribəl] adj verschrikkelijk, ontzettend, vreselijk

terrific [tə'rifik] adj geweldig

terrify ['terifai] v schrik *aanjagen; **terrifying** angstwekkend

territory ['teritəri] n gebied nt

terror ['terə] n angst c

terrorism ['terərizəm] n terrorisme nt, terreur c

terrorist ['terərist] n terrorist c

terylene ['terəli:n] n terylene nt

test [test] n proef c, test c; v proberen, testen

testify ['testifai] v getuigen

text [tekst] n tekst c

textbook ['teksbuk] n leerboek nt

textile ['tekstail] n textiel c/nt

texture ['tekstʃə] n structuur c

Thai [tai] adj Thailands; n Thailander c

Thailand ['tailænd] Thailand

than [ðæn] conj dan

thank [θæŋk] v bedanken, danken; ~ **you** dank u

thankful ['θæŋkfəl] adj dankbaar

that [ðæt] adj die, dat; conj dat

thaw [θɔ:] v dooien, ontdooien; n dooi c

the [ðə,ði] art de art; **the ... the** hoe ... hoe

theatre ['θiətə] n schouwburg c, theater nt

theft [θeft] n diefstal c

their [ðeə] adj hun

them [ðem] pron hen

theme [θi:m] n thema nt, onderwerp nt

themselves [ðəm'selvz] pron zich; zelf nt

then [ðen] adv toen; vervolgens, dan

theology [θi'ɔlədʒi] n theologie c

theoretical [θiə'retikəl] adj theoretisch

theory ['θiəri] n theorie c

therapy ['θerəpi] n therapie c

there [ðeə] adv daar; daarheen

therefore ['ðeəfɔ:] conj daarom

thermometer [θə'mɔmitə] n thermometer c

thermostat ['θə:məstæt] n thermostaat c

these [ði:z] adj deze

thesis ['θi:sis] n (pl theses) stelling c

they [ðei] pron ze

thick [θik] adj dik; dicht

thicken ['θikən] v verdikken

thickness ['θiknəs] n dikte c

thief [θi:f] n (pl thieves) dief c

thigh [θai] n dij c

thimble ['θimbəl] n vingerhoed c

thin [θin] adj dun; mager

thing [θiŋ] n ding nt

*think [θiŋk] v *denken; *nadenken; ~ **of** *denken aan; *bedenken; ~ **over** *overdenken

thinker ['θiŋkə] n denker c

third [θə:d] *num* derde

thirst [θə:st] *n* dorst *c*

thirsty ['θə:sti] *adj* dorstig

thirteen [,θə:'ti:n] *num* dertien

thirteenth [,θə:'ti:nθ] *num* dertiende

thirtieth ['θə:tiəθ] *num* dertigste

thirty ['θə:ti] *num* dertig

this [ðis] *adj* dit, deze

thistle ['θisəl] *n* distel *c*

thorn [θɔ:n] *n* doorn *c*

thorough ['θʌrə] *adj* grondig, degelijk

thoroughbred ['θʌrəbred] *adj* volbloed

thoroughfare ['θʌrəfeə] *n* hoofdweg *c*, hoofdstraat *c*

those [ðouz] *adj* die

though [ðou] *conj* hoewel, ofschoon, alhoewel; *adv* overigens

thought¹ [θɔ:t] *v* (p, pp think)

thought² [θɔ:t] *n* gedachte *c*

thoughtful ['θɔ:tfəl] *adj* nadenkend; zorgzaam

thousand ['θauzənd] *num* duizend

thread [θred] *n* draad *c*; garen *nt*; *v* *rijgen

threadbare ['θredbeə] *adj* versleten

threat [θret] *n* dreigement *nt*, bedreiging *c*

threaten ['θretən] *v* dreigen, bedreigen; **threatening** dreigend

three [θri:] *num* drie

three-quarter [,θri:'kwɔ:tə] *adj* driekwart

threshold ['θreʃould] *n* drempel *c*

threw [θru:] *v* (p throw)

thrifty ['θrifti] *adj* zuinig

throat [θrout] *n* keel *c*; hals *c*

throne [θroun] *n* troon *c*

through [θru:] *prep* door

throughout [θru:'aut] *adv* overal

throw [θrou] *n* gooi *c*

*throw [θrou] *v* *werpen, gooien

thrush [θrʌʃ] *n* lijster *c*

thumb [θʌm] *n* duim *c*

thumbtack ['θʌmtæk] *nAm* punaise *c*

thump [θʌmp] *v* stampen

thunder ['θʌndə] *n* donder *c*; *v* donderen

thunderstorm ['θʌndəstɔ:m] *n* onweer *nt*

thundery ['θʌndəri] *adj* onweerachtig

Thursday ['θə:zdi] donderdag *c*

thus [ðʌs] *adv* zo

thyme [taim] *n* tijm *c*

tick [tik] *n* streepje *nt*; ~ **off** aanstrepen

ticket ['tikit] *n* kaartje *nt*; bon *c*; ~ **collector** conducteur *c*; ~ **machine** kaartenautomaat *c*

tickle ['tikəl] *v* kietelen

tide [taid] *n* getij *nt*; **high** ~ hoog water; **low** ~ laag water

tidings ['taidiŋz] *pl* nieuws *nt*

tidy ['taidi] *adj* net; ~ **up** opruimen

tie [tai] *v* knopen, *binden; *n* das *c*

tiger ['taigə] *n* tijger *c*

tight [tait] *adj* strak; nauw, krap; *adv* vast

tighten ['taitən] *v* aanhalen, *aantrekken; strakker maken; strakker *worden

tights [taits] *pl* maillot *c*

tile [tail] *n* tegel *c*; dakpan *c*

till [til] *prep* tot aan, tot; *conj* tot, totdat

timber ['timbə] *n* timmerhout *nt*

time [taim] *n* tijd *c*; maal *c*, keer *c*; **all the** ~ aldoor; **in** ~ op tijd; ~ **of arrival** aankomsttijd *c*; ~ **of departure** vertrektijd *c*

time-saving ['taim,seiviŋ] *adj* tijdbesparend

timetable ['taim,teibəl] *n* dienstregeling *c*

timid ['timid] *adj* bedeesd

timidity [ti'midəti] *n* verlegenheid *c*

tin [tin] *n* tin *nt*; bus *c*, blik *nt*; **tinned food** conserven *pl*

tinfoil ['tinfɔil] *n* zilverpapier *nt*

tin-opener ['ti,noupənə] *n* blikopener *c*
tiny ['taini] *adj* minuscuul
tip [tip] *n* punt *c*; fooi *c*
tire[1] [taiə] *n* band *c*
tire[2] [taiə] *v* vermoeien
tired [taiəd] *adj* vermoeid, moe; ~ **of** beu
tiring ['taiəriŋ] *adj* vermoeiend
tissue ['tiʃu:] *n* weefsel *nt*; papieren zakdoek
title ['taitəl] *n* titel *c*
to [tu:] *prep* tot; aan, voor, bij, naar; om te
toad [toud] *n* pad *c*
toadstool ['toudstu:l] *n* paddestoel *c*
toast [toust] *n* toast *c*
tobacco [tə'bækou] *n* (pl ~s) tabak *c*; ~ **pouch** tabakszak *c*
tobacconist [tə'bækənist] *n* sigarenwinkelier *c*; **tobacconist's** tabakswinkel *c*
today [tə'dei] *adv* vandaag
toddler ['tɔdlə] *n* peuter *c*
toe [tou] *n* teen *c*
toffee ['tɔfi] *n* toffee *c*
together [tə'geðə] *adv* bijeen, samen
toilet ['tɔilət] *n* toilet *nt*; ~ **case** toilettas *c*
toilet-paper ['tɔilət,peipə] *n* closetpapier *nt*, toiletpapier *nt*
toiletry ['tɔilətri] *n* toiletbenodigdheden *pl*
token ['toukən] *n* teken *nt*; bewijs *nt*; munt *c*
told [tould] *v* (p, pp tell)
tolerable ['tɔlərəbəl] *adj* draaglijk
toll [toul] *n* tol *c*
tomato [tə'mɑ:tou] *n* (pl ~es) tomaat *c*
tomb [tu:m] *n* graf *nt*
tombstone ['tu:mstoun] *n* grafsteen *c*
tomorrow [tə'mɔrou] *adv* morgen
ton [tʌn] *n* ton *c*
tone [toun] *n* toon *c*; klank *c*

tongs [tɔŋz] *pl* tang *c*
tongue [tʌŋ] *n* tong *c*
tonic ['tɔnik] *n* tonicum *nt*
tonight [tə'nait] *adv* vannacht, vanavond
tonsilitis [,tɔnsə'laitis] *n* amandelontsteking *c*
tonsils ['tɔnsəlz] *pl* amandelen
too [tu:] *adv* te; ook
took [tuk] *v* (p take)
tool [tu:l] *n* werktuig *nt*, gereedschap *nt*; ~ **kit** gereedschapskist *c*
toot [tu:t] *vAm* claxonneren
tooth [tu:θ] *n* (pl teeth) tand *c*
toothache ['tu:θeik] *n* tandpijn *c*
toothbrush ['tu:θbrʌʃ] *n* tandenborstel *c*
toothpaste ['tu:θpeist] *n* tandpasta *c*/*nt*
toothpick ['tu:θpik] *n* tandestoker *c*
toothpowder ['tu:θ,paudə] *n* tandpoeder *nt*/*c*
top [tɔp] *n* top *c*; bovenkant *c*; deksel *nt*; bovenst; **on** ~ **of** bovenop; ~ **side** bovenkant *c*
topcoat ['tɔpkout] *n* overjas *c*
topic ['tɔpik] *n* onderwerp *nt*
topical ['tɔpikəl] *adj* actueel
torch [tɔ:tʃ] *n* fakkel *c*; zaklantaarn *c*
torment[1] [tɔ:'ment] *v* kwellen
torment[2] ['tɔ:ment] *n* kwelling *c*
torture ['tɔ:tʃə] *n* marteling *c*; *v* martelen
toss [tɔs] *v* gooien
tot [tɔt] *n* kleuter *c*
total ['toutəl] *adj* totaal; geheel, volslagen; *n* totaal *nt*
totalitarian [,toutæli'teəriən] *adj* totalitair
totalizator ['toutəlaizeitə] *n* totalisator *c*
touch [tʌtʃ] *v* aanraken; *betreffen; *n* contact *nt*, aanraking *c*; tastzin *c*
touching ['tʌtʃiŋ] *adj* aandoenlijk

tough [tʌf] *adj* taai
tour [tuə] *n* rondreis *c*
tourism ['tuərizəm] *n* toerisme *nt*
tourist ['tuərist] *n* toerist *c*; ~ **class** toeristenklasse *c*; ~ **office** verkeersbureau *nt*
tournament ['tuənəmənt] *n* toernooi *nt*
tow [tou] *v* slepen
towards [tə'wɔ:dz] *prep* naar; jegens
towel [tauəl] *n* handdoek *c*
towelling ['tauəliŋ] *n* badstof *c*
tower [tauə] *n* toren *c*
town [taun] *n* stad *c*; ~ **centre** stadscentrum *nt*; ~ **hall** stadhuis *nt*
townspeople ['taunz,pi:pəl] *pl* stadsmensen *pl*
toxic ['tɔksik] *adj* vergiftig
toy [tɔi] *n* speelgoed *nt*
toyshop ['tɔiʃɔp] *n* speelgoedwinkel *c*
trace [treis] *n* spoor *nt*; *v* opsporen
track [træk] *n* spoor *nt*; renbaan *c*
tractor ['træktə] *n* tractor *c*
trade [treid] *n* koophandel *c*, handel *c*; ambacht *nt*, vak *nt*; *v* handel *drijven
trademark ['treidma:k] *n* handelsmerk *nt*
trader ['treidə] *n* handelaar *c*
tradesman ['treidzmən] *n* (pl -men) handelaar *c*
trade-union [,treid'ju:njən] *n* vakbond *c*
tradition [trə'diʃən] *n* traditie *c*
traditional [trə'diʃənəl] *adj* traditioneel
traffic ['træfik] *n* verkeer *nt*; ~ **jam** verkeersopstopping *c*; ~ **light** stoplicht *nt*
trafficator ['træfikeitə] *n* richtingaanwijzer *c*
tragedy ['trædʒədi] *n* tragedie *c*
tragic ['trædʒik] *adj* tragisch
trail [treil] *n* spoor *nt*, pad *nt*
trailer ['treilə] *n* aanhangwagen *c*;

nAm kampeerwagen *c*
train [trein] *n* trein *c*; *v* dresseren, trainen; **stopping** ~ stoptrein *c*; **through** ~ doorgaande trein
training ['treiniŋ] *n* training *c*
trait [treit] *n* trek *c*
traitor ['treitə] *n* verrader *c*
tram [træm] *n* tram *c*
tramp [træmp] *n* landloper *c*, vagebond *c*; *v* *rondtrekken
tranquil ['træŋkwil] *adj* rustig
tranquillizer ['træŋkwilaizə] *n* kalmerend middel
transaction [træn'zækʃən] *n* transactie *c*
transatlantic [,trænzət'læntik] *adj* transatlantisch
transfer [træns'fə:] *v* *overbrengen
transform [træns'fɔ:m] *v* veranderen
transformer [træns'fɔ:mə] *n* transformator *c*
transition [træn'siʃən] *n* overgang *c*
translate [træns'leit] *v* vertalen
translation [træns'leiʃən] *n* vertaling *c*
translator [træns'leitə] *n* vertaler *c*
transmission [trænz'miʃən] *n* uitzending *c*
transmit [trænz'mit] *v* *uitzenden
transmitter [trænz'mitə] *n* zender *c*
transparent [træn'speərənt] *adj* doorzichtig
transport[1] ['trænspɔ:t] *n* vervoer *nt*
transport[2] [træn'spɔ:t] *v* transporteren
transportation [,trænspɔ:'teiʃən] *n* transport *nt*
trap [træp] *n* val *c*
trash [træʃ] *n* rommel *c*; ~ **can** *Am* vuilnisbak *c*
travel ['trævəl] *v* reizen; ~ **agency** reisbureau *nt*; ~ **agent** reisagent *c*; ~ **insurance** reisverzekering *c*; **travelling expenses** reiskosten *pl*
traveller ['trævələ] *n* reiziger *c*; **traveller's cheque** reischeque *c*

tray [trei] n dienblad nt

treason ['tri:zən] n verraad nt

treasure ['treʒə] n schat c

treasurer ['treʒərə] n penningmeester c

treasury ['treʒəri] n schatkist c

treat [tri:t] v behandelen

treatment ['tri:tmənt] n behandeling c

treaty ['tri:ti] n verdrag nt

tree [tri:] n boom c

tremble ['trembəl] v rillen, beven; trillen

tremendous [tri'mendəs] adj enorm

trespasser ['trespəsə] n indringer c

trial [traiəl] n rechtszaak c; proef c

triangle ['traiæŋgəl] n driehoek c

triangular [trai'æŋgjulə] adj driehoekig

tribe [traib] n stam c

tributary ['tribjutəri] n zijrivier c

tribute ['tribju:t] n hulde c

trick [trik] n streek c; foefje nt, kunstje nt

trigger ['trigə] n trekker c

trim [trim] v bijknippen

trip [trip] n uitstapje nt, reis c

triumph ['traiəmf] n triomf c; v zegevieren

triumphant [trai'ʌmfənt] adj triomfantelijk

trolley-bus ['trɔlibʌs] n trolleybus c

troops [tru:ps] pl troepen pl

tropical ['trɔpikəl] adj tropisch

tropics ['trɔpiks] pl tropen pl

trouble ['trʌbəl] n zorg c, moeite c, last c; v storen

troublesome ['trʌbəlsəm] adj lastig

trousers ['trauzəz] pl broek c

trout [traut] n (pl ~) forel c

truck [trʌk] nAm vrachtwagen c

true [tru:] adj waar; werkelijk, echt; getrouw, trouw

trumpet ['trʌmpit] n trompet c

trunk [trʌŋk] n koffer c; stam c; nAm kofferruimte c; **trunks** pl

gymnastiekbroek c

trunk-call ['trʌŋkkɔ:l] n interlokaal gesprek

trust [trʌst] v vertrouwen; n vertrouwen nt

trustworthy ['trʌst,wə:ði] adj betrouwbaar

truth [tru:θ] n waarheid c

truthful ['tru:θfəl] adj waarheidsgetrouw

try [trai] v proberen; trachten, pogen; n poging c; ~ **on** passen

tube [tju:b] n pijp c, buis c; tube c

tuberculosis [tju:,bə:kju'lousis] n tuberculose c

Tuesday ['tju:zdi] dinsdag c

tug [tʌg] v slepen; n sleepboot c; ruk c

tuition [tju:'iʃən] n onderwijs nt

tulip ['tju:lip] n tulp c

tumbler ['tʌmblə] n beker c

tumour ['tju:mə] n gezwel nt, tumor c

tuna ['tju:nə] n (pl ~, ~s) tonijn c

tune [tju:n] n wijs c, melodie c; ~ **in** afstemmen

tuneful ['tju:nfəl] adj melodieus

tunic ['tju:nik] n tuniek c

Tunisia [tju:'niziə] Tunesië

Tunisian [tju:'niziən] adj Tunesisch; n Tunesiër c

tunnel ['tʌnəl] n tunnel c

turbine ['tə:bain] n turbine c

turbojet [,tə:bou'dʒet] n straalvliegtuig nt

Turk [tə:k] n Turk c

Turkey ['tə:ki] Turkije

turkey ['tə:ki] n kalkoen c

Turkish ['tə:kiʃ] adj Turks; ~ **bath** Turks bad

turn [tə:n] v draaien, keren; omkeren, omdraaien; n wending c, draai c; bocht c; beurt c; ~ **back** terugkeren; ~ **down** *verwerpen; ~ **into** veranderen in; ~ **off** dichtdraaien;

~ **on** aanzetten; opendraaien; ~
over omkeren; ~ **round** omkeren;
zich omdraaien

turning ['tə:niŋ] *n* bocht *c*

turning-point ['tə:niŋpɔint] *n* keerpunt
nt

turnover ['tə:,nouvə] *n* omzet *c*; ~ **tax**
omzetbelasting *c*

turnpike ['tə:npaik] *nAm* tolweg *c*

turpentine ['tə:pəntain] *n* terpentijn *c*

turtle ['tə:təl] *n* schildpad *c*

tutor ['tju:tə] *n* huisonderwijzer *c*;
voogd *c*

tuxedo [tʌk'si:dou] *nAm* (pl ~s, ~es)
smoking *c*

tweed [twi:d] *n* tweed *nt*

tweezers ['twi:zəz] *pl* pincet *c*

twelfth [twelfθ] *num* twaalfde

twelve [twelv] *num* twaalf

twentieth ['twentiəθ] *num* twintigste

twenty ['twenti] *num* twintig

twice [twais] *adv* tweemaal

twig [twig] *n* twijg *c*

twilight ['twailait] *n* schemering *c*

twine [twain] *n* touw *nt*

twins [twinz] *pl* tweeling *c*; **twin beds**
lits-jumeaux *nt*

twist [twist] *v* *winden; draaien; *n*
draai *c*

two [tu:] *num* twee

two-piece [,tu:'pi:s] *adj* tweedelig

type [taip] *v* tikken, typen; *n* type *nt*

typewriter ['taipraitə] *n* schrijfmachine *c*

typewritten ['taipritən] getypt

typhoid ['taifɔid] *n* tyfus *c*

typical ['tipikəl] *adj* kenmerkend, typisch

typist ['taipist] *n* typiste *c*

tyrant ['taiərənt] *n* tiran *c*

tyre [taiə] *n* band *c*; ~ **pressure** bandenspanning *c*

U

ugly ['ʌgli] *adj* lelijk

ulcer ['ʌlsə] *n* zweer *c*

ultimate ['ʌltimət] *adj* laatst

ultraviolet [,ʌltrə'vaiələt] *adj* ultraviolet

umbrella [ʌm'brelə] *n* paraplu *c*

umpire ['ʌmpaiə] *n* scheidsrechter *c*

unable [ʌ'neibəl] *adj* onbekwaam

unacceptable [,ʌnək'septəbəl] *adj* onaanvaardbaar

unaccountable [,ʌnə'kauntəbəl] *adj* onverklaarbaar

unaccustomed [,ʌnə'kʌstəmd] *adj* niet
gewend

unanimous [ju:'næniməs] *adj* unaniem

unanswered [,ʌ'nɑ:nsəd] *adj* onbeantwoord

unauthorized [,ʌ'nɔ:θəraizd] *adj* onbevoegd

unavoidable [,ʌnə'vɔidəbəl] *adj* onvermijdelijk

unaware [,ʌnə'weə] *adj* onbewust

unbearable [ʌn'beərəbəl] *adj* ondraaglijk

unbreakable [,ʌn'breikəbəl] *adj* onbreekbaar

unbroken [,ʌn'broukən] *adj* heel

unbutton [,ʌn'bʌtən] *v* losknopen

uncertain [ʌn'sə:tən] *adj* onzeker

uncle ['ʌŋkəl] *n* oom *c*

unclean [,ʌn'kli:n] *adj* onrein

uncomfortable [ʌn'kʌmfətəbəl] *adj* ongemakkelijk

uncommon [ʌn'kɔmən] *adj* ongewoon,
zeldzaam

unconditional [,ʌnkən'diʃənəl] *adj* onvoorwaardelijk

unconscious [ʌn'kɔnʃəs] *adj* bewusteloos

uncork [,ʌn'kɔ:k] *v* ontkurken

uncover [ʌn'kʌvə] *v* blootleggen

uncultivated [ˌʌn'kʌltiveitid] *adj* onbebouwd

under ['ʌndə] *prep* beneden, onder

undercurrent ['ʌndə.kʌrənt] *n* onderstroom *c*

underestimate [ˌʌndə'restimeit] *v* onderschatten

underground ['ʌndəgraund] *adj* ondergronds; *n* metro *c*

underline [ˌʌndə'lain] *v* onderstrepen

underneath [ˌʌndə'ni:θ] *adv* beneden

underpants ['ʌndəpænts] *plAm* onderbroek *c*

undershirt ['ʌndəʃə:t] *n* hemd *nt*

undersigned ['ʌndəsaind] *n* ondergetekende *c*

*****understand** [ˌʌndə'stænd] *v* *begrijpen

understanding [ˌʌndə'stændiŋ] *n* begrip *nt*

*****undertake** [ˌʌndə'teik] *v* *ondernemen

undertaking [ˌʌndə'teikiŋ] *n* onderneming *c*

underwater ['ʌndə.wɔ:tə] *adj* onderwater-

underwear ['ʌndəweə] *n* ondergoed *nt*

undesirable [ˌʌndi'zaiərəbəl] *adj* ongewenst

*****undo** [ˌʌn'du:] *v* losmaken

undoubtedly [ʌn'dautidli] *adv* ongetwijfeld

undress [ˌʌn'dres] *v* zich uitkleden

undulating ['ʌndjuleitiŋ] *adj* golvend

unearned [ˌʌ'nə:nd] *adj* onverdiend

uneasy [ʌ'ni:zi] *adj* onbehaaglijk

uneducated [ˌʌ'nedjukeitid] *adj* ongeschoold

unemployed [ˌʌnim'plɔid] *adj* werkeloos

unemployment [ˌʌnim'plɔimənt] *n* werkeloosheid *c*

unequal [ˌʌ'ni:kwəl] *adj* ongelijk

uneven [ˌʌ'ni:vən] *adj* ongelijk, oneffen

unexpected [ˌʌnik'spektid] *adj* onvoorzien, onverwacht

unfair [ˌʌn'feə] *adj* oneerlijk, onbillijk

unfaithful [ˌʌn'feiθfəl] *adj* ontrouw

unfamiliar [ˌʌnfə'miljə] *adj* onbekend

unfasten [ˌʌn'fɑ:sən] *v* losmaken

unfavourable [ˌʌn'feivərəbəl] *adj* ongunstig

unfit [ˌʌn'fit] *adj* ongeschikt

unfold [ʌn'fould] *v* ontvouwen

unfortunate [ʌn'fɔ:tʃənət] *adj* ongelukkig

unfortunately [ʌn'fɔ:tʃənətli] *adv* helaas, ongelukkigerwijs

unfriendly [ˌʌn'frendli] *adj* onvriendelijk

unfurnished [ˌʌn'fə:niʃt] *adj* ongemeubileerd

ungrateful [ʌn'greitfəl] *adj* ondankbaar

unhappy [ʌn'hæpi] *adj* ongelukkig

unhealthy [ʌn'helθi] *adj* ongezond

unhurt [ˌʌn'hə:t] *adj* heelhuids

uniform ['ju:nifɔ:m] *n* uniform *nt/c*; *adj* uniform

unimportant [ˌʌnim'pɔ:tənt] *adj* onbelangrijk

uninhabitable [ˌʌnin'hæbitəbəl] *adj* onbewoonbaar

uninhabited [ˌʌnin'hæbitid] *adj* onbewoond

unintentional [ˌʌnin'tenʃənəl] *adj* onopzettelijk

union ['ju:njən] *n* vereniging *c*; verbond *nt*, unie *c*

unique [ju:'ni:k] *adj* uniek

unit ['ju:nit] *n* eenheid *c*

unite [ju:'nait] *v* verenigen

United States [ju:'naitid steits] Verenigde Staten

unity ['ju:nəti] *n* eenheid *c*

universal [ˌju:ni'və:səl] *adj* algemeen, universeel

universe ['ju:nivɔ:s] *n* heelal *nt*

university [ju:ni'vɔ:sɔti] *n* universiteit *c*

unjust [,ʌn'dʒʌst] *adj* onrechtvaardig

unkind [ʌn'kaind] *adj* onaardig, onvriendelijk

unknown [,ʌn'noun] *adj* onbekend

unlawful [,ʌn'lɔ:fəl] *adj* onwettig

unlearn [,ʌn'lɔ:n] *v* afleren

unless [ən'les] *conj* tenzij

unlike [,ʌn'laik] *adj* verschillend

unlikely [ʌn'laikli] *adj* onwaarschijnlijk

unlimited [ʌn'limitid] *adj* grenzeloos, onbeperkt

unload [,ʌn'loud] *v* lossen, *uitladen

unlock [,ʌn'lɔk] *v* openen

unlucky [ʌn'lʌki] *adj* ongelukkig

unnecessary [ʌn'nesəsəri] *adj* onnodig

unoccupied [,ʌ'nɔkjupaid] *adj* onbezet

unofficial [,ʌnə'fiʃəl] *adj* officieus

unpack [,ʌn'pæk] *v* uitpakken

unpleasant [ʌn'plezənt] *adj* onaangenaam, onplezierig; naar, vervelend

unpopular [,ʌn'pɔpjulə] *adj* impopulair, onbemind

unprotected [,ʌnprə'tektid] *adj* onbeschermd

unqualified [,ʌn'kwɔlifaid] *adj* onbevoegd

unreal [,ʌn'riəl] *adj* onwerkelijk

unreasonable [ʌn'ri:zənəbəl] *adj* onredelijk

unreliable [,ʌnri'laiəbəl] *adj* onbetrouwbaar

unrest [,ʌn'rest] *n* onrust *c*; rusteloosheid *c*

unsafe [,ʌn'seif] *adj* onveilig

unsatisfactory [,ʌnsætis'fæktəri] *adj* onbevredigend

unscrew [,ʌn'skru:] *v* losschroeven

unselfish [,ʌn'selfiʃ] *adj* onzelfzuchtig

unskilled [,ʌn'skild] *adj* ongeschoold

unsound [,ʌn'saund] *adj* ongezond

unstable [,ʌn'steibəl] *adj* labiel

unsteady [,ʌn'stedi] *adj* wankel, onvast; onevenwichtig

unsuccessful [,ʌnsək'sesfəl] *adj* mislukt

unsuitable [,ʌn'su:təbəl] *adj* ongepast

unsurpassed [,ʌnsə'pɑ:st] *adj* onovertroffen

untidy [ʌn'taidi] *adj* slordig

untie [,ʌn'tai] *v* losknopen

until [ən'til] *prep* tot

untrue [,ʌn'tru:] *adj* onwaar

untrustworthy [,ʌn'trʌst,wə:ði] *adj* onbetrouwbaar

unusual [ʌn'ju:ʒuəl] *adj* ongebruikelijk, ongewoon

unwell [,ʌn'wel] *adj* onwel

unwilling [,ʌn'wiliŋ] *adj* onwillig

unwise [,ʌn'waiz] *adj* onverstandig

unwrap [,ʌn'ræp] *v* uitpakken

up [ʌp] *adv* naar boven, omhoog, op

upholster [ʌp'houlstə] *v* bekleden

upkeep ['ʌpki:p] *n* onderhoud *nt*

uplands ['ʌpləndz] *pl* hoogvlakte *c*

upon [ə'pɔn] *prep* op

upper ['ʌpə] *adj* hoger, bovenst

upright ['ʌprait] *adj* rechtopstaand; *adv* overeind

upset [ʌp'set] *v* verstoren; *adj* overstuur

upside-down [,ʌpsaid'daun] *adv* ondersteboven

upstairs [,ʌp'steəz] *adv* boven; naar boven

upstream [,ʌp'stri:m] *adv* stroomopwaarts

upwards ['ʌpwədz] *adv* naar boven

urban ['ɔ:bən] *adj* stedelijk

urge [ɔ:dʒ] *v* aansporen; *n* drang *c*

urgency ['ɔ:dʒənsi] *n* urgentie *c*

urgent ['ɔ:dʒənt] *adj* dringend

urine ['juərin] *n* urine *c*

Uruguay ['juərəgwai] Uruguay

Uruguayan [juərə'gwaiən] *adj* Uru-

guayaans; *n* Uruguayaan *c*
us [ʌs] *pron* ons
usable ['ju:zəbəl] *adj* bruikbaar
usage ['ju:zidʒ] *n* gebruik *nt*
use[1] [ju:z] *v* gebruiken; *be used to
gewoon *zijn; ~ up verbruiken
use[2] [ju:s] *n* gebruik *nt*; nut *nt*; *be
of ~ baten
useful ['ju:sfəl] *adj* bruikbaar, nuttig
useless ['ju:sləs] *adj* nutteloos
user ['ju:zə] *n* gebruiker *c*
usher ['ʌʃə] *n* suppoost *c*
usherette [,ʌʃə'ret] *n* ouvreuse *c*
usual ['ju:ʒuəl] *adj* gebruikelijk
usually ['ju:ʒuəli] *adv* gewoonlijk
utensil [ju:'tensəl] *n* gereedschap *nt*,
werktuig *nt*; gebruiksvoorwerp *nt*
utility [ju:'tiləti] *n* nut *nt*
utilize ['ju:tilaiz] *v* benutten
utmost ['ʌtmoust] *adj* uiterst
utter ['ʌtə] *adj* volslagen, totaal; *v* uiten

V

vacancy ['veikənsi] *n* vacature *c*
vacant ['veikənt] *adj* vacant
vacate [və'keit] *v* ontruimen
vacation [və'keiʃən] *n* vakantie *c*
vaccinate ['væksineit] *v* inenten
vaccination [,væksi'neiʃən] *n* inenting
c
vacuum ['vækjuəm] *n* vacuüm *nt*;
vAm stofzuigen; ~ **cleaner** stofzuiger *c*; ~ **flask** thermosfles *c*
vagrancy ['veigrənsi] *n* landloperij *c*
vague [veig] *adj* vaag
vain [vein] *adj* ijdel; vergeefs; **in ~**
vergeefs, tevergeefs
valet ['vælit] *n* bediende *c*
valid ['vælid] *adj* geldig
valley ['væli] *n* dal *nt*, vallei *c*

valuable ['væljubəl] *adj* waardevol,
kostbaar; **valuables** *pl* kostbaarheden *pl*
value ['vælju:] *n* waarde *c*; *v* schatten
valve [vælv] *n* ventiel *nt*
van [væn] *n* bestelauto *c*
vanilla [və'nilə] *n* vanille *c*
vanish ['væniʃ] *v* *verdwijnen
vapour ['veipə] *n* damp *c*
variable ['veəriəbəl] *adj* veranderlijk
variation [,veəri'eiʃən] *n* afwisseling *c*;
verandering *c*
varied ['veərid] *adj* gevarieerd
variety [və'raiəti] *n* verscheidenheid *c*;
~ **show** variétévoorstelling *c*; ~
theatre variététheater *nt*
various ['veəriəs] *adj* allerlei, verscheidene
varnish ['va:niʃ] *n* lak *c*, vernis *nt/c*;
v lakken
vary ['veəri] *v* variëren, afwisselen;
veranderen; verschillen
vase [va:z] *n* vaas *c*
vaseline ['væsəli:n] *n* vaseline *c*
vast [va:st] *adj* onmetelijk, uitgestrekt
vault [vɔ:lt] *n* gewelf *nt*; kluis *c*
veal [vi:l] *n* kalfsvlees *nt*
vegetable ['vedʒətəbəl] *n* groente *c*; ~
merchant groenteboer *c*
vegetarian [,vedʒi'teəriən] *n* vegetariër
c
vegetation [,vedʒi'teiʃən] *n* plantengroei *c*
vehicle ['vi:əkəl] *n* voertuig *nt*
veil [veil] *n* sluier *c*
vein [vein] *n* ader *c*; **varicose ~** spatader *c*
velvet ['velvit] *n* fluweel *nt*
velveteen [,velvi'ti:n] *n* katoenfluweel
nt
venerable ['venərəbəl] *adj* eerbiedwaardig
venereal disease [vi'niəriəl di'zi:z] geslachtsziekte *c*

Venezuela [,veni'zweilə] Venezuela

Venezuelan [,veni'zweilən] *adj* Venezolaans; *n* Venezolaan *c*

ventilate ['ventileit] *v* ventileren; luchten

ventilation [,venti'leifən] *n* ventilatie *c*; luchtverversing *c*

ventilator ['ventileitə] *n* ventilator *c*

venture ['ventfə] *v* wagen

veranda [və'rændə] *n* veranda *c*

verb [və:b] *n* werkwoord *nt*

verbal ['və:bəl] *adj* mondeling

verdict ['və:dikt] *n* vonnis *nt*, uitspraak *c*

verge [və:dʒ] *n* rand *c*

verify ['verifai] *v* verifiëren

verse [və:s] *n* vers *nt*

version ['və:fən] *n* versie *c*; vertaling *c*

versus ['və:səs] *prep* contra

vertical ['və:tikəl] *adj* verticaal

vertigo ['və:tigou] *n* duizeling *c*

very ['veri] *adv* erg, zeer; *adj* precies, waar, werkelijk; uiterst

vessel ['vesəl] *n* vaartuig *nt*, schip *nt*; vat *nt*

vest [vest] *n* hemd *nt*; *nAm* vest *nt*

veterinary surgeon ['vetrinəri 'sə:dʒən] dierenarts *c*

via [vaiə] *prep* via

viaduct ['vaiədʌkt] *n* viaduct *c/nt*

vibrate [vai'breit] *v* trillen

vibration [vai'breifən] *n* vibratie *c*

vicinity [vi'sinəti] *n* nabijheid *c*, buurt *c*

vicious ['vifəs] *adj* boosaardig

victim ['viktim] *n* slachtoffer *nt*; dupe *c*

victory ['viktəri] *n* overwinning *c*

video ['vidiou] *n* video *c*; ~ **camera** video camera; ~ **cassette** video cassette; ~ **recorder** video recorder

view [vju:] *n* uitzicht *nt*; opvatting *c*, mening *c*; *v* *bekijken

view-finder ['vju:,faində] *n* zoeker *c*

vigilant ['vidʒilənt] *adj* waakzaam

villa ['vilə] *n* villa *c*

village ['vilidʒ] *n* dorp *nt*

villain ['vilən] *n* boef *c*

vine [vain] *n* wijnstok *c*

vinegar ['vinigə] *n* azijn *c*

vineyard ['vinjəd] *n* wijngaard *c*

vintage ['vintidʒ] *n* wijnoogst *c*

violation [vaiə'leifən] *n* schending *c*

violence ['vaiələns] *n* geweld *nt*

violent ['vaiələnt] *adj* gewelddadig; hevig, heftig

violet ['vaiələt] *n* viooltje *nt*; *adj* violet

violin [vaiə'lin] *n* viool *c*

virgin ['və:dʒin] *n* maagd *c*

virtue ['və:tfu:] *n* deugd *c*

visa ['vi:zə] *n* visum *nt*

visibility [,vizə'biləti] *n* zicht *nt*

visible ['vizəbəl] *adj* zichtbaar

vision ['viʒən] *n* visie *c*

visit ['vizit] *v* *bezoeken; *n* visite *c*, bezoek *nt*; **visiting hours** bezoekuren *pl*

visiting-card ['vizitiŋkɑ:d] *n* visitekaartje *nt*

visitor ['vizitə] *n* bezoeker *c*

vital ['vaitəl] *adj* essentieel

vitamin ['vitəmin] *n* vitamine *c*

vivid ['vivid] *adj* levendig

vocabulary [və'kæbjuləri] *n* vocabulaire *nt*, woordenschat *c*; woordenlijst *c*

vocal ['voukəl] *adj* vocaal

vocalist ['voukəlist] *n* zanger *c*

voice [vɔis] *n* stem *c*

void [vɔid] *adj* nietig

volcano [vɔl'keinou] *n* (pl ~es, ~s) vulkaan *c*

volt [voult] *n* volt *c*

voltage ['voultidʒ] *n* voltage *c/nt*

volume ['vɔljum] *n* volume *nt*; deel

voluntary ['vɔləntəri] *adj* vrijwillig

volunteer [,vɔlən'tiə] *n* vrijwilliger *c*

vomit ['vɔmit] *v* braken, *overgeven

vote [vout] *v* stemmen; *n* stem *c*; stemming *c*

voucher ['vautʃə] *n* bon *c*, bewijs *nt*

vow [vau] *n* gelofte *c*, eed *c*; *v* *zweren

vowel [vauəl] *n* klinker *c*

voyage ['vɔiidʒ] *n* reis *c*

vulgar ['vʌlgə] *adj* vulgair; volks-, ordinair

vulnerable ['vʌlnərəbəl] *adj* kwetsbaar

vulture ['vʌltʃə] *n* gier *c*

W

wade [weid] *v* waden

wafer ['weifə] *n* wafel *c*

waffle ['wɔfəl] *n* wafel *c*

wages ['weidʒiz] *pl* loon *nt*

waggon ['wægən] *n* wagon *c*

waist [weist] *n* taille *c*, middel *nt*

waistcoat ['weiskout] *n* vest *nt*

wait [weit] *v* wachten; ~ **on** bedienen

waiter ['weitə] *n* ober *c*, kelner *c*

waiting *n* het wachten

waiting-list ['weitiŋlist] *n* wachtlijst *c*

waiting-room ['weitiŋru:m] *n* wachtkamer *c*

waitress ['weitris] *n* serveerster *c*

***wake** [weik] *v* wekken; ~ **up** ontwaken, wakker *worden

walk [wɔ:k] *v* *lopen; wandelen; *n* wandeling *c*; loop *c*; **walking** te voet

walker ['wɔ:kə] *n* wandelaar *c*

walking-stick ['wɔ:kiŋstik] *n* wandelstok *c*

wall [wɔ:l] *n* muur *c*; wand *c*

wallet ['wɔlit] *n* portefeuille *c*

wallpaper ['wɔ:l,peipə] *n* behang *nt*

walnut ['wɔ:lnʌt] *n* walnoot *c*

waltz [wɔ:ls] *n* wals *c*

wander ['wɔndə] *v* *rondzwerven, *zwerven

want [wɔnt] *v* *willen; wensen; *n* behoefte *c*; gebrek *nt*, gemis *nt*

war [wɔ:] *n* oorlog *c*

warden ['wɔ:dən] *n* bewaker *c*, opzichter *c*

wardrobe ['wɔ:droub] *n* klerenkast *c*, garderobe *c*

warehouse ['wɛəhaus] *n* magazijn *nt*, pakhuis *nt*

wares [wɛəz] *pl* waren *pl*

warm [wɔ:m] *adj* heet, warm; *v* verwarmen

warmth [wɔ:mθ] *n* warmte *c*

warn [wɔ:n] *v* waarschuwen

warning ['wɔ:niŋ] *n* waarschuwing *c*

wary ['wɛəri] *adj* behoedzaam

was [wɔz] *v* (p be)

wash [wɔʃ] *v* *wassen; ~ **and wear** zelfstrijkend; ~ **up** afwassen

washable ['wɔʃəbəl] *adj* wasbaar

wash-basin ['wɔʃ,beisən] *n* wasbekken *nt*

washing ['wɔʃiŋ] *n* was *c*; wasgoed *nt*

washing-machine ['wɔʃiŋmə,ʃi:n] *n* wasmachine *c*

washing-powder ['wɔʃiŋ,paudə] *n* waspoeder *nt*

washroom ['wɔʃru:m] *nAm* toilet *nt*

wash-stand ['wɔʃstænd] *n* wastafel *c*

wasp [wɔsp] *n* wesp *c*

waste [weist] *v* verspillen; *n* verspilling *c*; *adj* braak

wasteful ['weistfəl] *adj* verkwistend

wastepaper-basket [weist'peipə,ba:-skit] *n* prullenmand *c*

watch [wɔtʃ] *v* *kijken naar, *gadeslaan; letten op; *n* horloge *nt*; ~ **for** *uitkijken naar; ~ **out** *uitkijken

watch-maker ['wɔtʃ,meikə] *n* horlogemaker c

watch-strap ['wɔtʃstræp] n horloge-bandje nt

water ['wɔːtə] n water nt; **iced ~** ijs-water nt; **running ~** stromend water; **~ pump** waterpomp c; **~ ski** waterski c

water-colour ['wɔːtə,kʌlə] n waterverf c; aquarel c

watercress ['wɔːtəkres] n waterkers c

waterfall ['wɔːtəfɔːl] n waterval c

watermelon ['wɔːtə,melən] n watermeloen c

waterproof ['wɔːtəpruːf] adj waterdicht

water-softener [,wɔːtə,sɔfnə] n wasverzachter c

waterway ['wɔːtəwei] n vaarwater nt

watt [wɔt] n watt c

wave [weiv] n golf c; v zwaaien

wave-length ['weivleŋθ] n golflengte c

wavy ['weivi] adj golvend

wax [wæks] n was c

waxworks ['wækswəːks] pl wassenbeeldenmuseum nt

way [wei] n manier c, wijze c; weg c; kant c, richting c; afstand c; **any ~** hoe dan ook; **by the ~** tussen twee haakjes; **one-way traffic** eenrichtingsverkeer nt; **out of the ~** afgelegen; **the other ~ round** andersom; **~ back** terugweg c; **~ in** ingang c; **~ out** uitgang c

wayside ['weisaid] n wegkant c

we [wiː] pron we

weak [wiːk] adj zwak; slap

weakness ['wiːknəs] n zwakheid c

wealth [welθ] n rijkdom c

wealthy ['welθi] adj rijk

weapon ['wepən] n wapen nt

***wear** [weə] v *aanhebben, *dragen; **~ out** *verslijten

weary ['wiəri] adj moe, vermoeid

weather ['weðə] n weer nt; **~ fore-**

cast weerbericht nt

***weave** [wiːv] v *weven

weaver ['wiːvə] n wever c

wedding ['wediŋ] n huwelijk nt, bruiloft c

wedding-ring ['wediŋriŋ] n trouwring c

wedge [wedʒ] n wig c

Wednesday ['wenzdi] woensdag c

weed [wiːd] n onkruid nt

week [wiːk] n week c

weekday ['wiːkdei] n weekdag c

weekly ['wiːkli] adj wekelijks

***weep** [wiːp] v huilen

weigh [wei] v *wegen

weighing-machine ['weiiŋmə,ʃiːn] n weegschaal c

weight [weit] n gewicht c

welcome ['welkəm] adj welkom; n welkom nt; v verwelkomen

weld [weld] v lassen

welfare ['welfeə] n welzijn nt

well[1] [wel] adv goed; adj gezond; **as ~** ook, eveneens; **as ~ as** evenals; **well!** welnu!

well[2] [wel] n bron c, put c

well-founded [,wel'faundid] adj gegrond

well-known ['welnoun] adj bekend

well-to-do [,weltə'duː] adj bemiddeld

went [went] v (p go)

were [wəː] v (p be)

west [west] n west c, westen nt

westerly ['westəli] adj westelijk

western ['westən] adj westers

wet [wet] adj nat; vochtig

whale [weil] n walvis c

wharf [wɔːf] n (pl ~s, wharves) kade c

what [wɔt] pron wat; **~ for** waarom

whatever [wɔ'tevə] pron wat dan ook

wheat [wiːt] n tarwe c

wheel [wiːl] n wiel nt

wheelbarrow ['wiːl,bærou] n kruiwagen c

wheelchair ['wi:ltʃeə] n rolstoel c

when [wen] adv wanneer; conj als, toen, wanneer

whenever [we'nevə] conj wanneer ook

where [weə] adv waar; conj waar

wherever [weə'revə] conj waar ook

whether ['weðə] conj of; **whether ... or** of ... of

which [witʃ] pron welk; dat

whichever [wi'tʃevə] adj welk ook

while [wail] conj terwijl; n poosje nt

whilst [wailst] conj terwijl

whim [wim] n gril c, bevlieging c

whip [wip] n zweep c; v kloppen

whiskers ['wiskəz] pl bakkebaarden pl

whisper ['wispə] v fluisteren; n gefluister nt

whistle ['wisəl] v *fluiten; n fluitje nt

white [wait] adj wit; blank

whitebait ['waitbeit] n witvis c

whiting ['waitiŋ] n (pl ~) wijting c

Whitsun ['witsən] Pinksteren

who [hu:] pron wie; die

whoever [hu:'evə] pron wie ook

whole [houl] adj geheel, heel; n geheel nt

wholesale ['houlseil] n groothandel c; ~ **dealer** grossier c

wholesome ['houlsəm] adj gezond

wholly ['houlli] adv helemaal

whom [hu:m] pron wie

whore [hɔ:] n hoer c

whose [hu:z] pron wiens; van wie

why [wai] adv waarom

wicked ['wikid] adj slecht

wide [waid] adj wijd, breed

widen ['waidən] v verwijden

widow ['widou] n weduwe c

widower ['widouə] n weduwnaar c

width [widθ] n breedte c

wife [waif] n (pl wives) echtgenote c, vrouw c

wig [wig] n pruik c

wild [waild] adj wild; woest

will [wil] n wil c; testament nt

***will** [wil] v *willen; *zullen

willing ['wiliŋ] adj bereid

willingly ['wiliŋli] adv graag

will-power ['wilpauə] n wilskracht c

***win** [win] v *winnen

wind [wind] n wind c

***wind** [waind] v kronkelen; *opwinden, *winden

winding ['waindiŋ] adj kronkelig

windmill ['windmil] n molen c, windmolen c

window ['windou] n raam nt

window-sill ['windousil] n vensterbank c

windscreen ['windskri:n] n voorruit c; ~ **wiper** ruitenwisser c

windshield ['windʃi:ld] nAm voorruit c; ~ **wiper** Am ruitenwisser c

windy ['windi] adj winderig

wine [wain] n wijn c

wine-cellar ['wain,selə] n wijnkelder c

wine-list ['wainlist] n wijnkaart c

wine-merchant ['wain,mə:tʃənt] n wijnkoper c

wine-waiter ['wain,weitə] n wijnkelner c

wing [wiŋ] n vleugel c

winkle ['wiŋkəl] n alikruik c

winner ['winə] n winnaar c

winning ['winiŋ] adj winnend; **winnings** pl winst c

winter ['wintə] n winter c; ~ **sports** wintersport c

wipe [waip] v vegen, afvegen

wire [waiə] n draad c; ijzerdraad nt

wireless ['waiələs] n radio c

wisdom ['wizdəm] n wijsheid c

wise [waiz] adj wijs

wish [wiʃ] v verlangen, wensen; n verlangen nt, wens c

witch [witʃ] n heks c

with [wið] prep met; bij; van

***withdraw** [wið'drɔ:] v *terugtrekken

within [wi'ðin] *prep* binnen; *adv* van binnen

without [wi'ðaut] *prep* zonder

witness ['witnəs] *n* getuige *c*

wits [wits] *pl* verstand *nt*

witty ['witi] *adj* geestig

wolf [wulf] *n* (pl wolves) wolf *c*

woman ['wumən] *n* (pl women) vrouw *c*

womb [wu:m] *n* baarmoeder *c*

won [wʌn] *v* (p, pp win)

wonder ['wʌndə] *n* wonder *nt*; verwondering *c*; *v* zich *afvragen

wonderful ['wʌndəfəl] *adj* prachtig, verrukkelijk; heerlijk

wood [wud] *n* hout *nt*; bos *nt*

wood-carving ['wud,ka:viŋ] *n* houtsnijwerk *nt*

wooded ['wudid] *adj* bebost

wooden ['wudən] *adj* houten; ~ **shoe** klomp *c*

woodland ['wudlənd] *n* bebost gebied

wool [wul] *n* wol *c*; **darning** ~ stopgaren *nt*

woollen ['wulən] *adj* wollen

word [wə:d] *n* woord *nt*

wore [wɔ:] *v* (p wear)

work [wə:k] *n* werk *nt*; arbeid *c*; *v* werken; functioneren; **working day** werkdag *c*; ~ **of art** kunstwerk *nt*; ~ **permit** werkvergunning *c*

worker ['wə:kə] *n* arbeider *c*

working ['wə:kiŋ] *n* werking *c*

workman ['wə:kmən] *n* (pl -men) arbeider *c*

works [wə:ks] *pl* fabriek *c*

workshop ['wə:kʃɔp] *n* werkplaats *c*

world [wə:ld] *n* wereld *c*; ~ **war** wereldoorlog *c*

world-famous [,wə:ld'feiməs] *adj* wereldberoemd

world-wide ['wə:ldwaid] *adj* wereldomvattend

worm [wə:m] *n* worm *c*

worn [wɔ:n] *adj* (pp wear) versleten

worn-out [,wɔ:n'aut] *adj* versleten

worried ['wʌrid] *adj* ongerust

worry ['wʌri] *v* zich ongerust maken; *n* zorg *c*, bezorgdheid *c*

worse [wə:s] *adj* slechter; *adv* erger

worship ['wə:ʃip] *v* *aanbidden; *n* eredienst *c*

worst [wə:st] *adj* slechtst; *adv* ergst

worsted ['wustid] *n* kamgaren *nt*

worth [wə:θ] *n* waarde *c*; *be ~ waard *zijn; *be worth-while de moeite waard *zijn

worthless ['wə:θləs] *adj* waardeloos

worthy of ['wə:ði əv] waard

would [wud] *v* (p will) gewoon *zijn

wound¹ [wu:nd] *n* wond *c*; *v* kwetsen, verwonden

wound² [waund] *v* (p, pp wind)

wrap [ræp] *v* inpakken

wreck [rek] *n* wrak *nt*; *v* vernielen

wrench [rentʃ] *n* sleutel *c*; ruk *c*; *v* verdraaien

wrinkle ['riŋkəl] *n* rimpel *c*

wrist [rist] *n* pols *c*

wrist-watch ['ristwɔtʃ] *n* polshorloge *nt*

***write** [rait] *v* *schrijven; **in writing** schriftelijk; ~ **down** *opschrijven

writer ['raitə] *n* schrijver *c*

writing-pad ['raitiŋpæd] *n* blocnote *c*, schrijfblok *nt*

writing-paper ['raitiŋ,peipə] *n* schrijfpapier *nt*

written ['ritən] *adj* (pp write) schriftelijk

wrong [rɔŋ] *adj* verkeerd, fout; *n* onrecht *nt*; *v* onrecht *aandoen; *be ~ ongelijk *hebben

wrote [rout] *v* (p write)

X

Xmas ['krisməs] Kerstmis
X-ray ['eksrei] *n* röntgenfoto *c*; *v* doorlichten

Y

yacht [jɔt] *n* jacht *nt*
yacht-club ['jɔtklʌb] *n* zeilclub *c*
yachting ['jɔtiŋ] *n* zeilsport *c*
yard [jɑːd] *n* erf *nt*
yarn [jɑːn] *n* garen *nt*
yawn [jɔːn] *v* gapen, geeuwen
year [jiə] *n* jaar *nt*
yearly ['jiəli] *adj* jaarlijks
yeast [jiːst] *n* gist *c*
yell [jel] *v* gillen; *n* gil *c*
yellow ['jelou] *adj* geel
yes [jes] ja
yesterday ['jestədi] *adv* gisteren
yet [jet] *adv* nog; *conj* toch, echter, maar
yield [jiːld] *v* *opbrengen; *toegeven
yoke [jouk] *n* juk *nt*

yolk [jouk] *n* dooier *c*
you [juː] *pron* je; jou; u; jullie
young [jʌŋ] *adj* jong
your [jɔː] *adj* uw; jouw; jullie
yourself [jɔː'self] *pron* je; zelf
yourselves [jɔː'selvz] *pron* je; zelf
youth [juːθ] *n* jeugd *c*; ~ **hostel** jeugdherberg *c*

Z

Zaire [zaː'iə] Zaïre
zeal [ziːl] *n* ijver *c*
zealous ['zeləs] *adj* ijverig
zebra ['ziːbrə] *n* zebra *c*
zenith ['zeniθ] *n* zenit *nt*; toppunt *nt*
zero ['ziərou] *n* (pl ~s) nul *c*
zest [zest] *n* animo *c*
zinc [ziŋk] *n* zink *nt*
zip [zip] *n* ritssluiting *c*; ~ **code** *Am* postcode *c*
zipper ['zipə] *n* ritssluiting *c*
zodiac ['zoudiæk] *n* dierenriem *c*
zombie ['zɔmbi] *n* levend lijk *nt*
zone [zoun] *n* zone *c*; gebied *nt*
zoo [zuː] *n* (pl ~s) dierentuin *c*
zoology [zou'ɔlədʒi] *n* zoölogie *c*

Culinaire woordenlijst

Spijzen

almond amandel
anchovy ansjovis
angel food cake witte, ronde cake, gemaakt van suiker, eiwit en bloem
angels on horseback geroosterde, met spek omwikkelde oesters
appetizer borrelhapje
apple appel
~ **charlotte** lagen van appels en sneetjes boord met vanille en slagroom
~ **dumpling** appelbol
~ **sauce** appelmoes
apricot abrikoos
Arbroath smoky gerookte schelvis
artichoke artisjok
asparagus asperge
~ **tip** aspergepunt
aspic koude schotel in gelei
assorted gevarieerd, gemengd
bacon spek
~ **and eggs** spiegeleieren met spek
bagel klein kransvormig broodje
baked in de oven gebakken, gebraden
~ **Alaska** omelette sibérienne
~ **beans** witte bonen in tomatensaus

~ **potato** hele, ongeschilde aardappel, in de oven gebakken
Bakewell tart amandeltaart met jam
baloney worstsoort
banana banaan
~ **split** in de lengte gehalveerde banaan met ijs, noten en overgoten met vruchtensiroop of vloeibare chocolade
barbecue 1) gehakt rundvlees in tomatensaus in een broodje geserveerd 2) maaltijd van geroosterd vlees in de open lucht
~ **sauce** zeer scherpe tomatensaus
barbecued geroosterd op houtskool
basil basilicum
bass baars
bean boon
beef rundvlees
~ **olive** blinde vink
beefburger gehakte, geroosterde biefstuk geserveerd in een broodje
beet, beetroot rode biet
bilberry blauwe bosbes
bill rekening
~ **of fare** menu

biscuit 1) koekje (GB) 2) broodje (US)

black pudding bloedworst

blackberry braam

blackcurrant zwarte bes

bloater verse bokking

blood sausage bloedworst

blueberry blauwe bosbes

boiled gekookt

Bologna (sausage) worstsoort

bone bot

boned ontbeend

Boston baked beans witte bonen met stukjes spek en stroop

Boston cream pie taart met vla-vulling en chocoladeglazuur

brains hersenen

braised gestoofd

bramble pudding bramenpudding, vaak met schijfjes appel erin

braunschweiger gerookte lever-worst

bread brood

breaded gepaneerd

breakfast ontbijt

bream brasem

breast borst (stuk)

brisket borststuk

broad bean tuinboon

broth bouillon

brown Betty afwisselende lagen appel, perzik of kers en paneer-meel, met suiker en kruiderijen, in de oven gebakken

brunch ontbijt en lunch gecombi-neerd

brussels sprout spruitje

bubble and squeak soort panne-koek van gebakken aardappe-len en kool, soms met vlees

bun 1) krentebroodje (GB) 2) klein, luchtig broodje (US)

butter boter

buttered beboterd

cabbage kool

Caesar salad sla met gerooster-de, naar knoflook smakende brooddobbelsteentjes, anjovis en geraspte kaas

cake gebak, koek, cake, taart

cakes koekjes, taartjes

calf kalfsvlees

Canadian bacon gerookt spek in dikke plakken gesneden

canapé belegd sneetje brood

cantaloupe wratmeloen, kante-loep

caper kappertje

capercaillie, capercailzie auer-hoen

carp karper

carrot wortel

cashew vrucht van de cajouboom

casserole gestoofd

catfish meerval (vis)

catsup ketchup

cauliflower bloemkool

celery selderie

cereal graansoorten voor bij het ontbijt, zoals maïsvlokken, ha-vermout, met melk en suiker
hot ~ havermoutpap

chateaubriand dubbele biefstuk van de haas

check rekening

Cheddar (cheese) stevige kaas met een milde, zurige smaak

cheese kaas
~ **board** kaasassortiment
~ **cake** kaaskoekje

cheeseburger gehakte, gerooster-de biefstuk met schijfje kaas, opgediend in een broodje

chef's salad salade van ham, kip, eieren, tomaten, sla en kaas

cherry kers

chestnut tamme kastanje

chicken kip

chicory 1) Brussels lof (GB) 2) andijvie (US)

chili con carne gehakt rundvlees gestoofd met bruine bonen, Spaanse pepers en komijn

chili pepper rode Spaanse pepers

chips 1) patates frites (GB) 2) aardappel chips (US)

chitt(er)lings varkenspens

chive bieslook

chocolate chocolade
  ~ **pudding** 1) chocoladepudding bereid met verkruimelde koekjes, suiker, eieren en bloem (GB) 2) chocolademousse (US)

choice keus

chop kotelet
  ~ **suey** gerecht, bereid uit fijngesneden varkensvlees en kip, groenten en rijst (tjap tjoy)

chopped fijngehakt

chowder dikke soep van vis, schaal- en schelpdieren of kip, met groenten

Christmas pudding speciaal Kerstgebak, soms geflambeerd

chutney sterke Indische kruiderij

cinnamon kaneel

clam steenmossel

club sandwich dubbele sandwich met kip, spek, sla, tomaat en mayonaise

cobbler vruchtenmoes met deeg, soms met ijs

cock-a-leekie soup preisoep met kip

coconut kokosnoot

cod kabeljauw

Colchester oyster beste soort Engelse oester

cold cuts/meat koud vlees

coleslaw koolsla

compote vruchten op sap

condiment kruiderij

consommé heldere soep

cooked gekookt

cookie koekje

corn 1) koren (GB) 2) maïs (US)
  ~ **on the cob** maïskolf

cornflakes maïsvlokken

cottage cheese witte, verse kaas

cottage pie gehakt vlees met uien, bedekt met aardappelpuree in de oven gebakken

course gerecht

cover charge couvert

crab krab

cracker droog beschuit van bladerdeeg

cranberry veenbes
  ~ **sauce** veenbessengelei

crawfish, crayfish 1) rivierkreeft 2) langoest (GB) 3) steurgarnaal (US)

cream 1) room 2) vlaai (dessert) 3) gebonden soep
  ~ **cheese** roomkaas
  ~ **puff** roomsoes

creamed potatoes aardappelen in witte roomsaus

creole op Creoolse wijze bereid; over het algemeen zeer pikant, met tomaten, paprika's en uien, geserveerd met rijst

cress waterkers

crisps chips

croquette kroket

crumpet rond, licht broodje, geroosterd en beboterd

cucumber komkommer

Cumberland ham zeer fijne, gerookte Engelse ham

Cumberland sauce rode bessengelei, op smaak gemaakt met wijn, sinaasappelsap en kruiderijen

cupcake klein rond gebakje

cured gezouten, gerookt, gepekeld (vis en vlees)

currant krent
curried met kerrie
curry kerrie
custard custardvla
cutlet vleeslapje, kotelet
dab schar
Danish pastry soort luchtig koffie-brood
date dadel
Derby cheese gele kaas met pikante smaak
devilled sterk gekruid
devil's food cake machtige chocoladetaart
devils on horseback gekookte pruimen, gevuld met amandelen en ansjovis, omwikkeld met spek, geroosterd en geserveerd op toost
Devonshire cream dikke, klonterige room
diced in dobbelsteentjes gesneden
diet food volgens voedselleer bereid
dill dille
dinner diner, avondeten
dish schotel, gerecht
donut, doughnut soort oliebol
double cream volle room
Dover sole tong uit Dover, in Engeland zeer gewaardeerd
dressing 1) slasaus 2) vulsel voor kalkoen (US)
Dublin Bay prawn steurgarnaal
duck eend
duckling jonge eend
dumpling knoedel
Dutch apple pie appeltaart bedekt met een mengsel van boter en bruine suiker
éclair langwerpig, met chocolade of caramel geglaceerd roomtaartje
eel paling

egg ei
  boiled ~ gekookt
  fried ~ spiegelei
  hard-boiled ~ hardgekookt
  poached ~ gepocheerd
  scrambled ~ roerei
  soft-boiled ~ zachtgekookt
eggplant aubergine, eierplant
endive 1) andijvie (GB) 2) Brussels lof (US)
entrecôte tussenrib
entrée 1) voorgerecht (GB) 2) hoofdgerecht (US)
escalope schnitzel
fennel venkel
fig vijg
filet mignon kalfs- of varkenshaasje
fillet filet van vlees of vis
finnan haddock gerookte schelvis
fish vis
  ~ **and chips** gebakken vis met frites
  ~ **cake** viskoekje
flan vla, ronde taart met vruchten
flapjack (appel)flap
flounder bot
forcemeat farce, gehakt
fowl gevogelte
frankfurter knakworst
French bean slaboon
French bread stokbrood
French dressing 1) slasaus in olie, azijn en tuinkruiden (GB) 2) romige slasaus met ketchup (US)
french fries patates frites
French toast wentelteefje
fresh vers
fricassée ragoût, vleeshachee
fried gebakken in een koekepan of in de olie
fritter beignet, poffertje
frogs' legs kikkerbilletjes

frosting suikerglazuur
fruit vrucht
fry bakken
game wild
gammon gerookte ham
garfish geep (snoekachtige zeevis)
garlic knoflook
garnish garnituur
gherkin augurkje
giblets afval van gevogelte
ginger gember
goose gans
~ **berry** kruisbes
grape druif
~ **fruit** pompelmoes
grated geraspt
gravy vleesjus
grayling vlagzalm
green bean slaboon
green pepper groene paprika
green salad sla
greens groenten
grilled geroosterd
grilse jonge zalm
grouse korhoen
gumbo 1) groente van Afrikaanse afkomst 2) Creools gerecht van vlees, kip of vis, met *okra*zaden, uien, tomaten en kruiden
haddock gerookte schelvis
haggis hart, longen en lever van een schaap fijn gehakt en in de maag gekookt met reuzel, havermeel en uien
hake stokvis
halibut heilbot
ham and eggs spiegeleieren met ham
hamburger gehakt, geroosterd rundvlees opgediend in een broodje
hare haas
haricot bean prinsessenboon, witte boon

hash 1) gehakt of fijngesneden vlees 2) hachee met aardappelen en groenten
hazelnut hazelnoot
heart hart
herb tuinkruid
herring haring
home-made eigengemaakt, van het huis
hominy grits brij van maïsgrutten
honey honing
~ **dew melon** zoete meloen met geelgroen vruchtvlees
hors-d'œuvre voorgerecht (Engeland)
horse-radish mierikswortel
hot 1) heet, warm 2) sterk gekruid
~ **cross bun** fijn broodje gevuld met rozijnen en kruisvormig bedekt met glazuur, wordt in de vastentijd gegeten (brioche)
~ **dog** hot dog, warme worst in een broodje
huckleberry blauwe bosbes
hush puppy beignet van maïsmeel en uien
ice-cream ijs
iced gekoeld
icing suikerglazuur
Idaho baked potato soort bintje, ongeschild in de oven gepoft
Irish stew hutspot van schapevlees, aardappelen en uien
Italian dressing slasaus van olie, azijn en tuinkruiden
jellied in gelei
Jell-O gelatinedessert
jelly jam; gelei
Jerusalem artichoke aardpeer
John Dory zonnevis (zeevis)
jugged hare hazepeper
juice sap
juniper berry jeneverbes
junket gestremde melk (wrongel),

gesuikerd

kale boerenkool

kedgeree stukjes vis met rijst, ei-ren, boter, wordt vaak als warm gerecht aan het ontbijt geser-veerd

kidney nier

kipper bokking

lamb lamsvlees

Lancashire hot pot schotel in de oven van ragoût van lamsvlees en mieren met uien, kruiderijen en aardappelen

larded gelardeerd

lean mager

leek prei

leg bout

lemon citroen

~ **sole** scharretong

lentil linze

lettuce kropsla, veldsla

lima bean tuinboon

lime limoen, kleine groene citroen

liver lever

loaf brood

lobster kreeft

loin lendestuk

Long Island duck eend van Long Island, in de VS zeer goed be-kend staande soort

low-calorie laag caloriegehalte

lox gerookte zalm

macaroon bitterkoekje

mackerel makreel

maize maïs

mandarin mandarijntje

maple syrup ahornstroop

marinated gemarineerd

marjoram marjolein

marmalade marmelade van si-naasappelen of andere citrus-vruchten

marrow beenmerg

~ **bone** mergpijp

marshmallow Amerikaans snoep-goed; *marshmallows* worden vaak aan warme chocola en al-lerlei soorten desserts toege-voegd

marzipan marsepein

mashed potatoes aardappelpuree

meal maaltijd

meat vlees

~ **ball** gehaktbal

~ **loaf** gehaktbrood

~ **pâté** vleespastei

medium (done) net gaar

melon meloen

melted gesmolten

Melton Mowbray pie pastei be-staande uit gehakt vlees en krui-den

meringue schuimgebak, schuimp-je

milk melk

mince fijnhakken

~ **pie** pasteitje met krenten, ro-zijnen, fijngehakte geconfijte vruchten en appelen (met of zonder vlees)

minced fijngehakt

~ **meat** fijngehakt vlees

mint munt (kruid)

minute steak kort gebakken bief-stuk

mixed gemengd

~ **grill** aan een stokje geregen, geroosterde stukjes vlees

molasses melasse, stroop

morel morille, zeer gewaardeerde paddestoelsoort

mousse l) dessert van geklopte eieren en slagroom 2) luchtig pasteitje

mulberry moerbei

mullet harder (vis gelijkend op een karper)

mulligatawny soup zeer sterk ge-

kruide soep van Indische afkomst met wortels, uien, *chutney* en kip met kerrie
mushroom paddestoel
muskmelon meloen
mussel mossel
mustard mosterd
mutton schapevlees
noodle noedel
nut noot
oatmeal (porridge) havermoutpap
oil olie
okra zaad van de *gumbo*, wordt
gebruikt om soepen en ragoût-
sausen aan te dikken
olive olijf
onion ui
orange sinaasappel
ox tongue ossetong
oxtail ossestaart
oyster oester
pancake pannekoek
Parmesan (cheese) Parmezaanse
kaas
parsley peterselie
parsnip pastinaak, witte peen
partridge patrijs
pastry banket, gebakje, taartje
pasty pastei
pea doperwt
peach perzik
peanut olienoot, pinda
~ **butter** pindakaas
pear peer
pearl barley parelgerst
pepper peper
~ **mint** pepermunt
perch baars
persimmon dadelpruim
pheasant fazant
pickerel jonge snoek
pickle 1) groente of geconfijte
vrucht in pekelzuur 2) in het
bijzonder augurkje (US)

pickled in pekel bewaard
pie pastei, vaak met een deksel
van bladerdeeg, gevuld met
vlees, groenten of vruchten
pig varken
pigeon duif
pike snoek
pineapple ananas
plaice schol
plain natuur, zonder iets erin
plate bord, schaal
plum pruim
~ **pudding** speciaal Kerstgebak, soms geflambeerd
poached gepocheerd
popcorn gepofte maïskorrels
popover klein, luchtig broodje
pork varkensvlees
porridge havermoutpap
porterhouse steak biefstuk van de
haas
pot roast met groenten gesmoord
rundvlees
potato aardappel
~ **chips** 1) patates frites (GB)
2) aardappel chips (US)
~ **in its jacket** aardappel in de
schil gekookt en opgediend
potted shrimps garnalen in gesmolten boter, koud opgediend
in een vorm
poultry gevogelte, pluimvee
prawn grote garnaal
prune gedroogde pruim
ptarmigan sneeuwhoen
pudding soepel of stevig beslag
van meel en eieren, gegarneerd
met vlees, vis, groenten of
vruchten, in de oven gebakken
of gaargestoomd; nagerecht
pumpernickel zwart roggebrood
pumpkin pompoen
quail kwartel
quince kweepeer

rabbit konijn
radish radijs
rainbow trout regenboogforel
raisin rozijn
rare ongaar
raspberry framboos
raw rauw
red mullet soort harder (zeevis)
red (sweet) pepper rode paprika
redcurrant rode bes
relish kruiderij gemaakt van fijn-gesneden groente in azijn
rhubarb rabarber
rib (of beef) ribstuk (van het rund)
ribe-eye steak entrecôte
rice rijst
rissole vlees- of viskroket
river trout rivierforel
roast braadstuk
roasted gebraden
Rock Cornish hen piepkuiken
roe viskuit
roll broodje
rollmop herring rolmops, gemari-neerde haringfilet
round steak runderschijf
Rubens sandwich cornedbeef op een toostje, met zuurkool, kaas en slasaus; warm opgediend
rump steak biefstuk
rusk beschuit
rye bread roggebrood
saddle lendestuk
saffron saffraan
sage salie
salad sla
 ~ **bar** verschillende soorten slaatjes, tomaten, prinsessen-bonen
 ~ **cream** slasaus, licht gezoet
 ~ **dressing** slasaus
salmon zalm
 ~ **trout** zalmforel
salt zout

salted gezouten
sardine sardien
sauce saus
sauerkraut zuurkool
sausage worst
sauté(ed) snel in boter, olie of vet gebakken
scallop 1) kamschelp 2) kalfslapje
scampi steurgarnaal
scone zacht broodje, warm geser-veerd, met boter en jam
Scotch broth runder- of schape-bouillon met groenten
Scotch woodcock toost met roerei en ansjovis
sea bass zeebaars
sea kale zeekool
seafood zeebanket
(in) season (in het) seizoen
seasoning kruiderij
service bediening
 ~ **charge** bedieningstarief
 ~ **included** inclusief bediening
 ~ **not included** exclusief bedie-ning
set menu menu van de dag
shad elft (zeevis)
shallot sjalot
shellfish schelp- en schaaldieren
sherbet sorbet
shoulder schouderstuk
shredded wheat gesponnen tarwe, wordt bij het ontbijt gegeten
shrimp garnaal
silverside (of beef) onderste deel van runderschenkel
sirloin steak lendestuk (van het rund)
skewer vleespen
slice sneet(je), plak
sliced in plakken gesneden
sloppy Joe gehakt vlees in scherpe tomatensaus, geserveerd in een broodje

smelt spiering
smoked gerookt
snack hapje, snack
sole tong (vis)
soup soep
sour zuur
soused herring gepekelde haring
spare rib krabbetje
spice kruiderij
spinach spinazie
spiny lobster langoest
(on a) spit (aan het) spit
sponge cake Moscovisch gebak
sprat sprot
squash mergpompoen
starter voorgerecht
steak and kidney pie pastei in bladerdeeg van niertjes en rundvlees
steamed gekookt
stew stoofschotel
Stilton (cheese) een van de beste Engelse kazen, wit of blauw geaderd
strawberry aardbei
string bean slaboon
stuffed gevuld
stuffing vulling
suck(l)ing pig speenvarken
sugar suiker
sugarless zonder suiker
sundae roomijs met vruchten, noten, slagroom en siroop
supper avondmaaltijd
swede knolraap
sweet 1) zoet 2) dessert
  ~ **corn** zoete maïs
  ~ **potato** bataat, knol van een oorspronkelijk tropisch gewas, rijk aan zetmeel en suiker
sweetbread zwezerik
Swiss cheese Emmentaler kaas
Swiss roll opgerold gebak met jam ertussen (koninginnebrood)

Swiss steak met groenten en kruiderijen gestoofde runderlappen
T-bone steak lendestuk van het rund met een T-vormig bot erin
table d'hôte open tafel in een hotel
tangerine mandarijntje
tarragon dragon
tart (vruchten)taart
tenderloin filet van vlees
Thousand Island dressing slasaus, bestaande uit mayonaise met piment, noten, olijven, selderie, uien, peterselie en eieren
thyme tijm
toad-in-the-hole rundvlees (of worstjes) in beslag gedoopt en in de oven gebakken
toast geroosterd brood
toasted getoost
  ~ **cheese** toost met gesmolten kaas
tomato tomaat
tongue tong (vlees)
tournedos ossehaas in dikke plakken
treacle melasse, stroop
trifle cake met amandelen en gelei, in sherry (of brandewijn) gedrenkt, opgediend met vla of slagroom
tripe pens
trout forel
truffle truffel (paddestoel)
tuna, tunny tonijn
turbot tarbot
turkey kalkoen
turnip raap, knol
turnover flap
turtle schildpad
underdone ongaar
vanilla vanille
veal kalfsvlees
  ~ **bird** blinde vink
  ~ **escalope** kalfsoester

vegetable groente
~ **marrow** mergpompoen, courgette
venison wildbraad
vichyssoise preisoep, koud geserveerd
vinegar azijn
Virginia baked ham ham in de oven geroosterd, in inkepingen in het vel worden stukjes ananas, kersen en kruidnagels gestoken waarna de ham met het vruchtesap geglaceerd wordt
wafer wafeltje
waffle warme wafel met boter, stroop of honing
walnut walnoot
water ice sorbet
watercress waterkers

watermelon watermeloen
well-done gaar
Welsh rabbit/rarebit gesmolten kaas op geroosterd brood
whelk kinkhoorn (wulk)
whipped cream slagroom
whitebait witvis
wine list wijnkaart
woodcock (hout)snip
Worcestershire sauce zoetzure saus bestaande uit soja en vele andere ingrediënten
York ham zeer goed bekend staande ham, opgediend in dunne plakken
Yorkshire pudding knappend gebakken deeg, geserveerd met rosbief
zucchini mergpompoen, courgette
zwieback beschuit

Dranken

ale donker, zoetachtig bier, onder hoge temperatuur gegist
bitter ~ bitter bier, nogal zwaar
brown ~ gebotteld, zoetachtig donker bier
light ~ gebotteld licht bier
mild ~ donker bier van het vat met een zeer uitgesproken smaak
pale ~ gebotteld licht bier
applejack Amerikaanse appelbrandewijn
Athol Brose haver vermengd met kokend water, honing en whisky

Bacardi cocktail cocktail van rum en gin met grenadinesiroop en limoensap
barley water frisdrank gemaakt van parelgerst met citroensmaak
barley wine donker bier met hoog alcoholgehalte
beer bier
bottled ~ gebotteld bier
draft, draught ~ getapt bier, bier van het vat
bitters kruidenaperitieven, de spijsvertering bevorderende alcoholische dranken

black velvet champagne met toevoeging van *stout* (vaak ter begeleiding van oesters)

bloody Mary cocktail van wodka, tomatesap en kruiderijen

bourbon Amerikaanse whisky, hoofdzakelijk van mais gestookt

brandy 1) verzamelnaam voor brandewijnsoorten gemaakt van druiven en andere vruchten 2) cognac

~ **Alexander** cocktail van brandewijn, crème de cacao en room

British wines wijnen in Engeland gegist; gemaakt van geïmporteerde druiven (of van geïmporteerd druivesap)

cherry brandy kersenlikeur

chocolate chocolademelk

cider cider

~ **cup** mengsel van cider, kruiderijen, suiker en ijs

claret rode Bordeauxwijn

cobbler *long drink* gemaakt van vruchten, waaraan men wijn of alcohol toevoegt

coffee koffie

~ **with cream** met room

black ~ zonder melk

caffeine-free ~ cafeïnevrij

white ~ half koffie, half melk; koffie verkeerd

cordial hartversterking

cream room

cup verfrissende drank gemaakt van gekoelde wijn, sodawater en een likeur of andere sterkedrank met een schijfje citroen of sinaasappel

daiquiri cocktail van rum, suiker, limoensap

double dubbele portie

Drambuie likeur gemaakt van whisky en honing

dry martini 1) droge vermouth (GB) 2) cocktail van droge vermouth en gin (US)

egg-nog alcoholische drank op basis van rum of andere sterkedrank, vermengd met geklopt eigeel en suiker

gin and it gin met Italiaanse vermouth

gin-fizz gin met citroensap, sodawater en suiker

ginger ale frisdrank met gembersmaak

ginger beer gemberbier

grasshopper cocktail van crème de menthe, crème de cacao en room

Guinness (stout) donker zoetsmakend bier met een hoog moutgehalte en hopgehalte

half pint ongeveer 3 dl

highball alcoholische drank, zoals whisky, vermengd met water, sodawater of *ginger ale*

iced gekoeld, ijskoud

Irish coffee koffie met suiker en slagroom, waaraan men een scheut Ierse whisky toevoegt

Irish Mist Ierse likeur van whisky en honing

Irish whiskey Ierse whisky minder scherp dan Schotse whisky, bevat naast gerst ook rogge, haver en tarwe

juice sap

lager licht bier, koud geserveerd

lemon squash kwast

lemonade limonade

lime juice limoensap

liqueur likeur

liquor sterkedrank

long drink sterkedrank met tonic, sodawater of gewoon water en

ijsblokjes
madeira madera
Manhattan cocktail van Amerikaanse whisky en vermouth met angostura
milk melk
mineral water mineraalwater
mulled wine bisschopswijn; warme, gekruide wijn
neat onvermengd. puur, zonder water of ijs
old-fashioned cocktail van whisky, angostura, sinaasappel schijfje, suiker en maraskijnkersen
on the rocks met ijsblokjes
Ovaltine ovomaltine
Pimm's cup(s) sterkedrank met vruchtesap, eventueel aangelengd met sodawater
~ **No. 1** met gin
~ **No. 2** met whisky
~ **No. 3** met rum
~ **No. 4** met brandewijn
pink champagne roze champagne
pink lady cocktail van eiwit, calvados, citroensap, grenadine en gin
pint ongeveer 6 dl
porter donker, bitter bier
quart 1,14 l (US 0,95 l)
root beer gezoete frisdrank met aromat uit plantenwortels en kruiden
rye (whiskey) whisky uit rogge gestookt; zwaarder en scherper van smaak dan *bourbon*
scotch (whisky) Schotse whisky, een uit gerst en maïs (grain whisky) gestookte sterkedrank,

vaak vermengd met malt whisky, uitsluitend uit gemoute gerst gestookt
screwdriver wodka met sinaasappelsap
shandy *bitter ale* vermengd met limonade of met *ginger beer*
short drink sterkedrank, onverdund gedronken
shot scheut sterkedrank
sloe gin-fizz sleepruimlikeur (vrucht van de sleedoorn) met citroensap en sodawater
soda water sodawater, spuitwater
soft drink frisdrank
spirits spiritualiën, gedistilleerde dranken
stinger cognac en crème de menthe
stout donker bier met veel hop gebrouwen
straight sterkedrank onverdund gedronken, puur
tea thee
toddy grog
Tom Collins *long drink* van gin, citroensap, spuitwater en suiker
tonic (water) tonic, spuitwater met kininesmaak
vodka wodka
whisky sour whisky, citroensap, suiker en sodawater
wine wijn
  dessert ~ zoete
  dry ~ droge
  red ~ rode
  sparkling ~ mousserende
  sweet ~ zoete (dessertwijn)
  white ~ witte

Mini-grammatica

Het lidwoord

Het bepaald lidwoord heeft slechts één vorm: *the*.

the room, the rooms   de kamer, de kamers

Het onbepaald lidwoord heeft twee vormen: *a* voor woorden die met een medeklinker beginnen en *an* voor woorden die met een klinker of stomme h beginnen.

a coat   een jas
an umbrella   een paraplu
an hour   een uur

Het zelfstandig naamwoord

Het meervoud van de meeste zelfstandige naamwoorden wordt gevormd door aan het enkelvoud *-(e)s* toe te voegen.

cup — cups (kopje — kopjes)   **dress — dresses** (jurk — jurken)

N.B. Wanneer een zelfstandig naamwoord op *-y* eindigt en de voorlaatste letter een medeklinker is, wordt de meervoudsuitgang *-ies*; als de voorlaatste letter echter een klinker is dan wordt het meervoud op de normale wijze gevormd.

lady — ladies (dame — dames)   **key — keys** (sleutel — sleutels)

Enkele zelfstandige naamwoorden met een onregelmatig meervoud zijn:

man — men (man — mannen)   **child — children** (kind — kinderen)
woman — women (vrouw — vrouwen)
foot — feet (voet — voeten)

Genitief

1. Als de bezitter een mens is en het zelfstandig naamwoord niet met *-s* eindigt, dan wordt *'s* toegevoegd.

the boy's room   de kamer van de jongen
the children's clothes   de kleren van de kinderen

Eindigt het zelfstandig naamwoord met *-s,* dan wordt alleen een apostrophe (') toegevoegd.

the boys' room   de kamer van de jongens

2. Als de bezitter een ding is, gebruikt men het voorzetsel *of.*

the key of the door   de sleutel van de deur

Het bijvoeglijk naamwoord

De bijvoeglijke naamwoorden staan gewoonlijk voor het zelfstandig naamwoord.

a large brown suitcase   een grote bruine koffer

De vergrotende en overtreffende trap van een bijvoeglijk naamwoord kunnen op twee manieren gevormd worden.

1. Alle bijvoeglijke naamwoorden van één lettergreep en vele van twee lettergrepen krijgen -*(e)r* en -*(e)st*.

small (klein) — **smaller** — **smallest**
pretty (aardig) — **prettier** — **prettiest***

2. Bijvoeglijke naamwoorden van drie of meer lettergrepen en enkele van twee die eindigen op -*ful* en -*less* maken de vergrotende en overtreffende trap met *more* en *most*.

expensive (duur) — **more expensive** — **most expensive**
careful (voorzichtig) — **more careful** — **most careful**

De volgende bijvoeglijke naamwoorden zijn onregelmatig:

good (goed)	**better**	**best**
bad (slecht)	**worse**	**worst**
little (weinig)	**less**	**least**
much/many (veel)	**more**	**most**

Het bijwoord

De meeste bijwoorden worden gemaakt door aan het bijvoeglijk naamwoord -*ly* toe te voegen.

quick/quickly (vlug)   **slow/slowly** (langzaam)
Uitzonderingen:
good/well (goed)   **fast/fast** (snel)

Voornaamwoorden

	persoonlijk voornaamwoord		bezittelijk voornaamwoord	
	onderwerp	lijdend en meew. vw.	1	2
ik	**I**	**me**	**my**	**mine**
jij	**you**	**you**	**your**	**yours**
hij	**he**	**him**	**his**	**his**
zij	**she**	**her**	**her**	**hers**
het	**it**	**it**	**its**	**—**
wij	**we**	**us**	**our**	**ours**
u	**you**	**you**	**your**	**yours**
zij	**they**	**them**	**their**	**theirs**

De vormen onder 1 worden gebruikt vóór een zelfstandig naamwoord, die onder 2 staan op zichzelf.

Where's my key?   Waar is mijn sleutel?
That's not mine.   Dat is niet de mijne.

N.B. Het Engels kent geen onderscheid tussen „jij" en „u", in beide gevallen zegt men *you*.

He came with you.   Hij kwam met jou/u.

---

* *y* wordt *i* als er een medeklinker aan voorafgaat.

Onregelmatige werkwoorden

De onderstaande lijst geeft de Engelse onregelmatige werkwoorden aan. De samengestelde werkwoorden of werkwoorden met een voorvoegsel worden als de grondwerkwoorden vervoegd, bijvoorbeeld: *withdraw* wordt vervoegd als *draw* en *rebuild* als *build*.

Onbepaalde wijs	Onvoltooid verleden tijd	Verleden deelwoord	
arise	arose	arisen	*opstaan*
awake	awoke	awoken	*ontwaken*
be	was	been	*zijn*
bear	bore	borne	*dragen*
beat	beat	beaten	*slaan*
become	became	become	*worden*
begin	began	begun	*aanvangen*
bend	bent	bent	*buigen*
bet	bet	bet	*wedden*
bid	bade/bid	bidden/bid	*verzoeken*
bind	bound	bound	*binden*
bite	bit	bitten	*bijten*
bleed	bled	bled	*bloeden*
blow	blew	blown	*blazen*
break	broke	broken	*breken*
breed	bred	bred	*fokken*
bring	brought	brought	*brengen*
build	built	built	*bouwen*
burn	burnt/burned	burnt/burned	*branden*
burst	burst	burst	*barsten*
buy	bought	bought	*kopen*
can*	could	—	*kunnen*
cast	cast	cast	*werpen*
catch	caught	caught	*vangen*
choose	chose	chosen	*kiezen*
cling	clung	clung	*vastklemmen*
clothe	clothed/clad	clothed/clad	*kleden*
come	came	come	*komen*
cost	cost	cost	*kosten*
creep	crept	crept	*kruipen*
cut	cut	cut	*snijden*
deal	dealt	dealt	*uitdelen*
dig	dug	dug	*graven*
do (he does)	did	done	*doen*
draw	drew	drawn	*trekken*
dream	dreamt/dreamed	dreamt/dreamed	*dromen*
drink	drank	drunk	*drinken*
drive	drove	driven	*rijden*
dwell	dwelt	dwelt	*vertoeven*

* tegenwoordige tijd

eat	ate	eaten	*eten*
fall	fell	fallen	*vallen*
feed	fed	fed	*voeden*
feel	felt	felt	*voelen*
fight	fought	fought	*vechten*
find	found	found	*vinden*
flee	fled	fled	*vluchten*
fling	flung	flung	*werpen*
fly	flew	flown	*vliegen*
forsake	forsook	forsaken	*verzaken*
freeze	froze	frozen	*vriezen*
get	got	got	*krijgen*
give	gave	given	*geven*
go	went	gone	*gaan*
grind	ground	ground	*malen*
grow	grew	grown	*groeien*
hang	hung	hung	*(op)hangen*
have	had	had	*hebben*
hear	heard	heard	*horen*
hew	hewed	hewed/hewn	*hakken*
hide	hid	hidden	*verstoppen*
hit	hit	hit	*slaan*
hold	held	held	*houden*
hurt	hurt	hurt	*pijn doen*
keep	kept	kept	*houden*
kneel	knelt	knelt	*knielen*
knit	knitted/knit	knitted/knit	*breien*
know	knew	known	*weten*
lay	laid	laid	*leggen*
lead	led	led	*leiden*
lean	leant/leaned	leant/leaned	*leunen*
leap	leapt/leaped	leapt/leaped	*springen*
learn	learnt/learned	learnt/learned	*leren*
leave	left	left	*verlaten*
lend	lent	lent	*lenen(aan)*
let	let	let	*laten*
lie	lay	lain	*liggen*
light	lit/lighted	lit/lighted	*aansteken*
lose	lost	lost	*verliezen*
make	made	made	*maken*
may*	might	—	*mogen, kunnen*
mean	meant	meant	*bedoelen*
meet	met	met	*ontmoeten*
mow	mowed	mowed/mown	*maaien*
must*	—	—	*moeten*
ought (to)*	—	—	*moeten*
pay	paid	paid	*betalen*
put	put	put	*zetten*
read	read	read	*lezen*

* tegenwoordige tijd

rid	rid	rid	*zich ontdoen (van)*
ride	rode	ridden	*rijden*
ring	rang	rung	*bellen*
rise	rose	risen	*opstaan*
run	ran	run	*rennen*
saw	sawed	sawn	*zagen*
say	said	said	*zeggen*
see	saw	seen	*zien*
seek	sought	sought	*zoeken*
sell	sold	sold	*verkopen*
send	sent	sent	*verzenden*
set	set	set	*zetten*
sew	sewed	sewed/sewn	*naaien*
shake	shook	shaken	*schudden*
shall*	should	—	*zullen*
shed	shed	shed	*vergieten*
shine	shone	shone	*schijnen*
shoot	shot	shot	*schieten*
show	showed	shown	*tonen*
shrink	shrank	shrunk	*krimpen*
shut	shut	shut	*sluiten*
sing	sang	sung	*zingen*
sink	sank	sunk	*zinken*
sit	sat	sat	*zitten*
sleep	slept	slept	*slapen*
slide	slid	slid	*glijden*
sling	slung	slung	*slingeren*
slink	slunk	slunk	*sluipen*
slit	slit	slit	*opensnijden*
smell	smelled/smelt	smelled/smelt	*ruiken*
sow	sowed	sown/sowed	*zaaien*
speak	spoke	spoken	*spreken*
speed	sped/speeded	sped/speeded	*zich haasten*
spell	spelt/spelled	spelt/spelled	*spellen*
spend	spent	spent	*uitgeven*
spill	spilt/spilled	spilt/spilled	*morsen*
spin	spun	spun	*spinnen*
spit	spat	spat	*spuwen*
split	split	split	*splijten*
spoil	spoilt/spoiled	spoilt/spoiled	*bederven*
spread	spread	spread	*spreiden*
spring	sprang	sprung	*ontspringen*
stand	stood	stood	*staan*
steal	stole	stolen	*stelen*
stick	stuck	stuck	*kleven*
sting	stung	stung	*steken*
stink	stank/stunk	stunk	*stinken*
strew	strewed	strewed/strewn	*strooien*
stride	strode	stridden	*schrijden*

* tegenwoordige tijd

strike	struck	struck/stricken	*slaan*
string	strung	strung	*rijgen*
strive	strove	striven	*streven*
swear	swore	sworn	*zweren*
sweep	swept	swept	*vegen*
swell	swelled	swollen	*zwellen*
swim	swam	swum	*zwemmen*
swing	swung	swung	*slingeren*
take	took	taken	*nemen*
teach	taught	taught	*onderwijzen*
tear	tore	torn	*scheuren*
tell	told	told	*vertellen*
think	thought	thought	*denken*
throw	threw	thrown	*werpen*
thrust	thrust	thrust	*duwen*
tread	trod	trodden	*treden*
wake	woke/waked	woken/waked	*wekken*
wear	wore	worn	*dragen*
weave	wove	woven	*weven*
weep	wept	wept	*huilen*
will*	would	—	*zullen*
win	won	won	*winnen*
wind	wound	wound	*opwinden*
wring	wrung	wrung	*wringen*
write	wrote	written	*schrijven*

* tegenwoordige tijd

Engelse afkortingen

AA	*Automobile Association*	Britse Automobielclub
AAA	*American Automobile Association*	Amerikaanse Automobielclub
ABC	*American Broadcasting Company*	Amerikaanse radio- en televisiemaatschappij
A.D.	*anno Domini*	na Christus
Am.	*America ; American*	Amerika ; Amerikaans
a.m.	*ante meridiem (before noon)*	de tijd tussen 0 en 12 uur
Amtrak	*American railroad corporation*	Amerikaanse spoorwegmaatschappij
AT & T	*American Telephone and Telegraph Company*	Amerikaanse telefoon- en telegraafmaatschappij
Ave.	*avenue*	avenue
BBC	*British Broadcasting Corporation*	Britse radio- en televisie- maatschappij
B.C.	*before Christ*	voor Christus
bldg.	*building*	gebouw
Blvd.	*boulevard*	boulevard
B.R.	*British Rail*	Britse Spoorwegen
Brit.	*Britain ; British*	Groot-Brittannië, Brits
Bros.	*brothers*	gebroeders
¢	*cent*	1/100 van een dollar
Can.	*Canada ; Canadian*	Canada ; Canadees
CBS	*Columbia Broadcasting System*	Amerikaanse radio- en televisiemaatschappij
CID	*Criminal Investigation Department*	afdeling criminele recherche van Scotland Yard
CNR	*Canadian National Railway*	Canadese Nationale Spoorwegen
c/o	*(in) care of*	per adres
Co.	*company*	maatschappij
Corp.	*corporation*	vennootschap
CPR	*Canadian Pacific Railways*	Canadese spoorweg- maatschappij
D.C.	*District of Columbia*	district in de V.S. waarin de hoofdstad Washington ligt
DDS	*Doctor of Dental Science*	doctor in de tandheelkunde
dept.	*department*	departement, afdeling
EEC	*European Economic Community*	EEG, Europese Economische Gemeenschap
e.g.	*for instance*	bijvoorbeeld

Eng.	*England; English*	Engeland; Engels
excl.	*excluding; exclusive*	exclusief
ft.	*foot/feet*	voet
GB	*Great Britain*	Groot-Brittannië
H.E.	*His/Her Excellency;*	Zijne/Hare Excellentie;
	His Eminence	Zijne Eminentie
H.H.	*His Holiness*	Zijne Heiligheid
H.M.	*His/Her Majesty*	Zijne/Hare Majesteit
H.M.S.	*Her Majesty's ship*	Harer Majesteits schip
		(Brits oorlogsschip)
hp	*horsepower*	paardekracht
Hwy	*highway*	autoweg
i.e.	*that is to say*	d.w.z., dat wil zeggen
in.	*inch*	duim (2,54 cm)
Inc.	*incorporated*	naamloze vennootschap
incl.	*including, inclusive*	inclusief
£	*pound sterling*	pond sterling
L.A.	*Los Angeles*	Los Angeles
Ltd.	*limited*	naamloze vennootschap
M.D.	*Doctor of Medicine*	arts
M.P.	*Member of Parliament*	lid van het Lagerhuis
		(Engeland)
mph	*miles per hour*	Engelse mijl per uur
Mr.	*Mister*	meneer
Mrs.	*Missis*	mevrouw
Ms.	*Missis/Miss*	mevrouw/mejuffrouw
nat.	*national*	nationaal
NBC	*National Broadcasting*	Amerikaanse radio- en
	Company	televisiemaatschappij
No.	*number*	nummer
N.Y.C.	*New York City*	New York City
O.B.E.	*Officer (of the Order)*	Officier in de Orde
	of the British Empire	van het Britse Imperium
p.	*page; penny/pence*	bladzijde; 1/100 van een pond
p.a.	*per annum*	per jaar
Ph.D.	*Doctor of Philosophy*	doctor in de wijsbegeerte
p.m.	*post meridiem*	de tijd tussen 12 en 24 uur
	(after noon)	
PO	*Post Office*	postkantoor
POO	*post office order*	postorder
pop.	*population*	bevolking
P.T.O.	*please turn over*	zie ommezijde, a.u.b.
RAC	*Royal Automobile Club*	Koninklijke Britse
		Automobielclub

RCMP	*Royal Canadian Mounted Police*	Koninklijke Canadese Bereden Politie
Rd.	*road*	weg
ref.	*reference*	verwijzing
Rev.	*reverend*	dominee
RFD	*rural free delivery*	landelijke postbus
RR	*railroad*	spoorweg
RSVP	*please reply*	verzoeke gaarne antwoord
$	*dollar*	dollar
Soc.	*society*	maatschappij, genootschap
St.	*saint; street*	sint; straat
STD	*Subscriber Trunk Dialling*	automatisch telefoonverkeer
UN	*United Nations*	V.N., Verenigde Naties
UPS	*United Parcel Service*	Amerikaanse pakketdienst
US	*United States*	Verenigde Staten
USS	*United States Ship*	Amerikaans oorlogsschip
VAT	*value added tax*	B.T.W.
VIP	*very important person*	zeer belangrijke persoon
Xmas	*Christmas*	Kerstmis
yd.	*yard*	yard (91,44 cm)
YMCA	*Young Men's Christian Association*	Christelijke Jongeren Vereniging
YWCA	*Young Women's Christian Association*	Christelijke Meisjes Vereniging
ZIP	*ZIP code*	postnummer

Telwoorden

Hoofdtelwoorden

0	zero
1	one
2	two
3	three
4	four
5	five
6	six
7	seven
8	eight
9	nine
10	ten
11	eleven
12	twelve
13	thirteen
14	fourteen
15	fifteen
16	sixteen
17	seventeen
18	eighteen
19	nineteen
20	twenty
21	twenty-one
22	twenty-two
23	twenty-three
24	twenty-four
25	twenty-five
30	thirty
40	forty
50	fifty
60	sixty
70	seventy
80	eighty
90	ninety
100	a/one hundred
230	two hundred and thirty
1,000	a/one thousand
10,000	ten thousand
100,000	a/one hundred thousand
1,000,000	a/one million

Rangtelwoorden

1st	first
2nd	second
3rd	third
4th	fourth
5th	fifth
6th	sixth
7th	seventh
8th	eighth
9th	ninth
10th	tenth
11th	eleventh
12th	twelfth
13th	thirteenth
14th	fourteenth
15th	fifteenth
16th	sixteenth
17th	seventeenth
18th	eighteenth
19th	nineteenth
20th	twentieth
21st	twenty-first
22nd	twenty-second
23rd	twenty-third
24th	twenty-fourth
25th	twenty-fifth
26th	twenty-sixth
27th	twenty-seventh
28th	twenty-eighth
29th	twenty-ninth
30th	thirtieth
40th	fortieth
50th	fiftieth
60th	sixtieth
70th	seventieth
80th	eightieth
90th	ninetieth
100th	hundredth
230th	two hundred and thirtieth
1,000th	thousandth

Tijd

De Engelsen en Amerikanen gebruiken het twaalf-uren systeem. De uit-drukking *a.m. (ante meridiem)* duidt op de uren tussen middernacht en 12 uur 's middags; *p.m. (post meridiem)* op de uren tussen 12 uur 's middags en middernacht. Engeland gaat momenteel geleidelijk over op het continentale systeem.

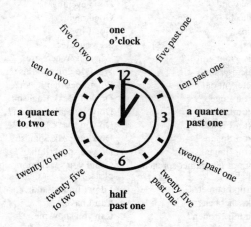

I'll come at seven a.m.   Ik kom om 7 uur 's morgens.
I'll come at two p.m.   Ik kom om 2 uur 's middags.
I'll come at eight p.m.   Ik kom om 8 uur 's avonds.

Dagen van de week

Sunday	zondag	*Thursday*	donderdag
Monday	maandag	*Friday*	vrijdag
Tuesday	dinsdag	*Saturday*	zaterdag
Wednesday	woensdag		

Enkele nuttige zinnen	**Some Basic Phrases**
Alstublieft.	Please.
Hartelijk dank.	Thank you very much.
Niets te danken.	Don't mention it.
Goedemorgen.	Good morning.
Goedemiddag.	Good afternoon.
Goedenavond.	Good evening.
Goedenacht.	Good night.
Tot ziens.	Good-bye.
Tot straks.	See you later.
Waar is/Waar zijn...?	Where is/Where are...?
Hoe noemt u dit?	What do you call this?
Wat betekent dat?	What does that mean?
Spreekt u Engels?	Do you speak English?
Spreekt u Duits?	Do you speak German?
Spreekt u Frans?	Do you speak French?
Spreekt u Spaans?	Do you speak Spanish?
Spreekt u Italiaans?	Do you speak Italian?
Kunt u wat langzamer spreken, alstublieft?	Could you speak more slowly, please?
Ik begrijp het niet.	I don't understand.
Mag ik...hebben?	Can I have...?
Kunt u mij...tonen?	Can you show me...?
Kunt u mij zeggen...?	Can you tell me...?
Kunt u me helpen?	Can you help me, please?
Ik wil graag...	I'd like...
Wij willen graag...	We'd like...
Geeft u me..., alstublieft.	Please give me...
Brengt u me..., alstublieft.	Please bring me...
Ik heb honger.	I'm hungry.
Ik heb dorst.	I'm thirsty.
Ik ben verdwaald.	I'm lost.
Vlug!	Hurry up!
Er is/Er zijn...	There is/There are...
Er is geen/Er zijn geen...	There isn't/There aren't...

Aankomst

Uw paspoort, alstublieft.

Hebt u iets aan te geven?

Nee, helemaal niets.

Kunt u me met mijn bagage helpen, alstublieft?

Waar is de bus naar het centrum?

Hierlangs, alstublieft.

Waar kan ik een taxi krijgen?

Wat kost het naar…?

Breng me naar dit adres, alstublieft.

Ik heb haast.

Arrival

Your passport, please.

Have you anything to declare?

No, nothing at all.

Can you help me with my luggage, please?

Where's the bus to the centre of town, please?

This way, please.

Where can I get a taxi?

What's the fare to…?

Take me to this address, please.

I'm in a hurry.

Hotel

Mijn naam is…

Hebt u gereserveerd?

Ik wil graag een kamer met bad.

Hoeveel kost het per nacht?

Mag ik de kamer zien?

Wat is mijn kamernummer?

Er is geen warm water.

Mag ik de directeur spreken, alstublieft?

Heeft er iemand voor mij opgebeld?

Is er post voor mij?

Mag ik de rekening, alstublieft?

Hotel

My name is…

Have you a reservation?

I'd like a room with a bath.

What's the price per night?

May I see the room?

What's my room number, please?

There's no hot water.

May I see the manager, please?

Did anyone telephone me?

Is there any mail for me?

May I have my bill (check), please?

Uit eten

Hebt u een menu à prix fixe?

Mag ik de spijskaart zien?

Kunt u ons een asbak brengen, alstublieft?

Eating out

Do you have a fixed-price menu?

May I see the menu?

May we have an ashtray, please?

Waar is het toilet?	Where's the toilet, please?
Ik wil graag een voorgerecht.	I'd like an hors d'œuvre (starter).
Hebt u soep?	Have you any soup?
Ik wil graag vis.	I'd like some fish.
Wat voor vis hebt u?	What kind of fish do you have?
Ik wil graag een biefstuk.	I'd like a steak.
Wat voor groenten hebt u?	What vegetables have you got?
Niets meer, dank u.	Nothing more, thanks.
Wat wilt u drinken?	What would you like to drink?
Een pils, alstublieft.	I'll have a beer, please.
Ik wil graag een fles wijn.	I'd like a bottle of wine.
Mag ik de rekening, alstublieft?	May I have the bill (check), please?
Is de bediening inbegrepen?	Is service included?
Dank u, het was een uitstekende maaltijd.	Thank you, that was a very good meal.

Reizen	**Travelling**
Waar is het station?	Where's the railway station, please?
Waar is het loket?	Where's the ticket office, please?
Ik wil graag een kaartje naar...	I'd like a ticket to...
Eerste of tweede klas?	First or second class?
Eerste klas, alstublieft.	First class, please.
Enkele reis of retour?	Single or return (one way or roundtrip)?
Moet ik overstappen?	Do I have to change trains?
Van welk perron vertrekt de trein naar...?	What platform does the train for... leave from?
Waar is het dichtstbijzijnde metrostation?	Where's the nearest underground (subway) station?
Waar is het busstation?	Where's the bus station, please?
Hoe laat vertrekt de eerste bus naar...?	When's the first bus to...?
Wilt u me bij de volgende halte laten uitstappen?	Please let me off at the next stop.

Ontspanning	**Relaxing**
Wat wordt er in de bioscoop gegeven?	What's on at the cinema (movies)?
Hoe laat begint de film?	What time does the film begin?
Zijn er nog plaatsen vrij voor vanavond?	Are there any tickets for tonight?
Waar kunnen we gaan dansen?	Where can we go dancing?

Ontmoetingen	**Meeting people**
Dag mevrouw/juffrouw/mijnheer.	How do you do.
Hoe maakt u het?	How are you?
Uitstekend, dank u. En u?	Very well, thank you. And you?
Mag ik u... voorstellen?	May I introduce...?
Mijn naam is...	My name is...
Prettig kennis met u te maken.	I'm very pleased to meet you.
Hoelang bent u al hier?	How long have you been here?
Het was mij een genoegen.	It was nice meeting you.
Hindert het u als ik rook?	Do you mind if I smoke?
Hebt u een vuurtje, alstublieft?	Do you have a light, please?
Mag ik u iets te drinken aanbieden?	May I get you a drink?
Mag ik u vanavond ten eten uitnodigen?	May I invite you for dinner tonight?
Waar spreken we af?	Where shall we meet?

Winkels en diensten	**Shops, stores and services**
Waar is de dichtstbijzijnde bank?	Where's the nearest bank, please?
Waar kan ik reischeques inwisselen?	Where can I cash some travellers' cheques?
Kunt u me wat kleingeld geven, alstublieft?	Can you give me some small change, please?
Waar is de dichtstbijzijnde apotheek?	Where's the nearest chemist's (pharmacy)?
Hoe kom ik daar?	How do I get there?
Is het te lopen?	Is it within walking distance?

Kunt u mij helpen, alstublieft?	Can you help me, please?
Hoeveel kost dit? En dat?	How much is this? And that?
Het is niet precies wat ik zoek.	It's not quite what I want.
Het bevalt me.	I like it.
Kunt u mij iets tegen zonnebrand aanbevelen?	Can you recommend something for sunburn?
Knippen, alstublieft.	I'd like a haircut, please.
Ik wil een manicure, alstublieft.	I'd like a manicure, please.

De weg vragen

Street directions

Kunt u mij op de kaart aanwijzen waar ik ben?	Can you show me on the map where I am?
U bent op de verkeerde weg.	You are on the wrong road.
Rij/Ga rechtuit.	Go/Walk straight ahead.
Het is aan de linkerkant/aan de rechterkant.	It's on the left/on the right.

Spoedgevallen

Emergencies

Roep vlug een dokter.	Call a doctor quickly.
Roep een ambulance.	Call an ambulance.
Roep de politie, alstublieft.	Please call the police.

dutch-english
_____
nederlands-engels

Introduction

The dictionary has been designed to take account of your practical needs. Unnecessary linguistic information has been avoided. The entries are listed in alphabetical order regardless of whether the entry word is printed in a single word, is hyphened or is in two or more separate words. The only exception to this rule, reflexive verbs, are listed as main entries alphabetically according to the verb, e.g. *zich afvragen* is found under **a**.

When an entry is followed by sub-entries such as expressions and locutions, these, too, have been listed in alphabetical order.

Each main-entry word is followed by a phonetic transcription (see Guide to pronunciation). Following the transcription is the part of speech of the entry word whenever applicable. When an entry word may be used as more then one part of speech, the translations are grouped together after the respective part of speech.

Considering the complexity of the rules for constructing the plural of Dutch nouns, we have supplied the plural form whenever in current use.

Each time an entry word is repeated in plurals or in sub-entries, a tilde (~) is used to represent the full entry word.

In plurals of long words, only the part that changes is written out fully, whereas the unchanged part is represented by a hyphen.

Entry: beker (pl ~s)   Plural: bekers
      kind (pl ~eren)   kinderen
      leslokaal (pl -kalen)   leslokalen

An asterisk (*) in front of a verb indicates that the verb is irregular. For details, refer to the lists of irregular verbs.

Abbreviations

adj	adjective		*p*	past tense
adv	adverb		*pl*	plural
Am	American		*plAm*	plural (American)
art	article		*pp*	past participle
c	common gender		*pr*	present tense
conj	conjunction		*pref*	prefix
n	noun		*prep*	preposition
nAm	noun (American)		*pron*	pronoun
nt	neuter		*v*	verb
num	numeral		*vAm*	verb (American)

Guide to Pronunciation

Each main entry in this part of the dictionary is followed by a phonetic transcription which shows you how to pronounce the words. This transcription should be read as if it were English. It is based on Standard British pronunciation, though we have tried to take account of General American pronunciation also. Below, only those letters and symbols are explained which we consider likely to be ambiguous or not immediately understood.

The syllables are separated by hyphens, and stressed syllables are printed in *italics*.

Of course, the sounds of any two languages are never exactly the same, but if you follow carefully our indications, you should be able to pronounce the foreign words in such a way that you'll be understood. To make your task easier, our transcriptions occasionally simplify slightly the sound system of the language while still reflecting the essential sound differences.

Consonants

g   a g-sound where the tongue doesn't quite close the air passage between itself and the roof of the mouth, so that the escaping air produces audible friction; often fairly hard, so that it resembles **kh**

kh   like **g**, but based on a **k**-sound; therefore hard and voiceless, like **ch** in Scottish lo**ch**

ñ   as in Spanish se**ñ**or, or like **ni** in o**ni**on

s   always hard, as in **s**o

zh   a soft, voiced **sh**, like **s** in plea**s**ure

1) In everyday speech, the **n** in the ending of verbs and plurals of nouns is usually dropped.

2) We use the transcription **v** for two different sounds (written **v** and **w** in Dutch) because the difference between them is often inaudible to foreigners.

Vowels and Diphthongs

aa   long **a**, as in c**a**r, without any **r**-sound

ah   a short version of **aa**; between **a** in c**a**t and **u** in c**u**t

ai   like **air**, without any **r**-sound

Dutch for English:

eh	like **e** in g**e**t
er	as in oth**er**, without any **r**-sound
ew	a "rounded **ee**-sound"; say the vowel sound **ee** (as in s**ee**), and while saying it, round your lips as for **oo** (as in s**oo**n), without moving your tongue; when your lips are in the **oo** position, but your tongue is in the **ee** position, you should be pronouncing the correct sound
ı	like **i** in b**i**t
igh	as in s**igh**
o	always as in h**o**t (British pronunciation)
ou	as in l**ou**d
ur	as in f**ur**, but with rounded lips and no **r**-sound

1) A bar over a vowel symbol (e.g. $\overline{oo}$) shows that this sound is long.

2) Raised letters (e.g. **aa**[ee], **t**[y], [y]**eh**) should be pronounced only fleetingly.

3) Dutch vowels (i.e. not diphthongs) are pure. Therefore, you should try to read a transcription like $\overline{oa}$ without moving tongue or lips while pronouncing the sound.

4) Some Dutch words borrowed from French contain nasal vowels, which we transcribe with a vowel symbol plus ~~ng~~ (e.g. **ahng**). This ~~ng~~ should *not* be pronounced, and serves solely to indicate nasal quality of the preceding vowel. A nasal vowel is pronounced simultaneously through the mouth and the nose.

A

aal (aal) *c* (pl alen) eel

aambeien (*aam*-bay-ern) *pl* haemorrhoids *pl*, piles *pl*

aan (aan) *prep* to; on

aanbetaling (*aam*-ber-taa-ling) *c* (pl ~en) down payment

*__aanbevelen__ (*aam*-ber-vāy-lern) *v* recommend

aanbeveling (*aam*-ber-vāy-ling) *c* (pl ~en) recommendation

aanbevelingsbrief (*aam*-ber-vāy-lings-breef) *c* (pl -brieven) letter of recommendation

*__aanbidden__ (aam-*bi*-dern) *v* worship

*__aanbieden__ (*aam*-bee-dern) *v* offer; present

aanbieding (*aam*-bee-ding) *c* (pl ~en) offer

aanblik (*aam*-blik) *c* sight; appearance

aanbod (*aam*-bot) *nt* offer; supply

aanbranden (*aam*-brahn-dern) *v* *burn

aandacht (*aan*-dahkht) *c* attention; notice, consideration; ~ **besteden aan** attend to

aandeel (*aan*-dāyl) *nt* (pl -delen) share

aandenken (*aan*-dehng-kern) *nt* (pl ~s) remembrance

aandoening (*aan*-dōō-ning) *c* (pl ~en) affection

aandoenlijk (aan-*dōōn*-lerk) *adj* touching

*__aandrijven__ (*aan*-dray-vern) *v* propel

*__aandringen__ (*aan*-dri-ngern) *v* insist

aanduiden (*aan*-dur^(ew)-dern) *v* indicate

*__aangaan__ (*aang*-gaan) *v* concern

aangaande (aang-*gaan*-der) *prep* as regards

aangeboren (aang-ger-*bōa*-rern) *adj* natural

aangelegenheid (aang-ger-*lāy*-gern-hayt) *c* (pl -heden) matter, concern; affair, business

aangenaam (*aang*-ger-naam) *adj* agreeable, pleasing, pleasant

aangesloten (*aang*-ger-slōa-tern) *adj* affiliated

*__aangeven__ (*aang*-gāy-vern) *v* indicate; declare; *give, hand, pass

aangezien (aang-ger-*zeen*) *conj* as, since; because

aangifte (*aang*-gif-ter) *c* (pl ~n) declaration

aangrenzend (aang-*grehn*-zernt) *adj* neighbouring

aanhalen (*aan*-haa-lern) *v* tighten; quote

aanhalingstekens (*aan*-haa-lings-tāy-kerns) *pl* quotation marks

aanhangwagen (*aan*-hahng-vaa-gern) *c* (pl ~s) trailer

aanhankelijk (aan-*hahng*-ker-lerk) *adj*

affectionate

*aanhebben (*aan*-heh-bern) *v* *wear

aanhechten (*aan*-hehkh-tern) *v* attach

aanhoren (*aan*-hōā-rern) *v* listen

*aanhouden (*aan*-hou-dern) *v* insist; aanhoudend constant

aanhouding (*aan*-hou-dɪng) *c* (pl ~en) arrest

*aankijken (*aang*-kay-kern) *v* look at

aanklacht (*aang*-klahkht) *c* (pl ~en) charge

aanklagen (*aang*-klaa-gern) *v* accuse, charge

aankleden (*aang*-klāy-dern) *v* dress; *get dressed

*aankomen (*aang*-kōā-mern) *v* arrive

aankomst (*aang*-komst) *c* arrival

aankomsttijd (*aang*-koms-tayt) *c* (pl ~en) time of arrival

aankondigen (*aang*-kon-der-gern) *v* announce

aankondiging (*aang*-kon-der-gɪng) *c* (pl ~en) notice, announcement

aankoop (*aang*-kōāp) *c* (pl -kopen) purchase

aankruisen (*aang*-krur^(ew)-sern) *v* mark

aanleg (*aan*-lehkh) *c* talent

aanleggen (*aan*-leh-gern) *v* dock

aanleiding (*aan*-lay-dɪng) *c* (pl ~en) cause, occasion

aanlengen (*aan*-leh-ngern) *v* dilute

zich aanmelden (*aan*-mehl-dern) report

aanmerkelijk (aa-*mehr*-ker-lerk) *adj* considerable

aanmerken (aa-*mehr*-kern) *v* comment

aanmoedigen (aa-*mōō*-der-gern) *v* encourage

*aannemen (*aa*-nāy-mern) *v* accept; assume, suppose; adopt; aangenomen dat supposing that

aannemer (aa-*nāy*-merr) *c* (pl ~s) contractor

aanpak (*aam*-pahk) *c* method, approach

aanpassen (*aam*-pah-sern) *v* adapt; suit; adjust

aanplakbiljet (*aam*-plahk-bɪl-^(y)eht) *nt* (pl ~ten) placard

*aanprijzen (*aam*-pray-zern) *v* recommend

*aanraden (*aan*-raa-dern) *v* advise, recommend

aanraken (*aan*-raa-kern) *v* touch

aanraking (*aan*-raa-kɪng) *c* (pl ~en) touch; contact

aanranden (*aan*-rahn-dern) *v* assault

aanrichten (*aan*-rɪkh-tern) *v* cause

aanrijding (*aan*-ray-dɪng) *c* (pl ~en) collision

aanschaffen (*aan*-skhah-fern) *v* *buy

*aansluiten (*aan*-slur^(ew)-tern) *v* connect

aansluiting (*aan*-slur^(ew)-tɪng) *c* (pl ~en) connection

aansporen (*aan*-spōā-rern) *v* incite; urge

aanspraak (*aan*-spraak) *c* (pl -spraken) claim

aansprakelijk (aan-*spraa*-ker-lerk) *adj* liable; responsible

aansprakelijkheid (aan-*spraa*-ker-lerk-hayt) *c* liability; responsibility

*aanspreken (*aan*-sprāy-kern) *v* address

aanstekelijk (aan-*stāy*-ker-lerk) *adj* contagious

*aansteken (*aan*-stāy-kern) *v* *light; infect

aansteker (*aan*-stāy-kerr) *c* (pl ~s) lighter, cigarette-lighter

aanstellen (*aan*-steh-lern) *v* appoint

aanstoot (*aan*-stōāt) *c* offence

aanstootgevend (aan-stōāt-*khāy*-vernt) *adj* offensive

aanstrepen (*aan*-strāy-pern) *v* tick off

aantal (*aan*-tahl) *nt* (pl ~len) number; quantity

aantekenen (aan-tāy-ker-nern) v record; register

aantekening (aan-tāy-ker-ning) c (pl ~en) note

aantonen (aan-tōā-nern) v prove; demonstrate, *show

aantrekkelijk (aan-treh-ker-lerk) adj attractive

*aantrekken** (aan-treh-kern) v attract; tempt; *put on; tighten

aantrekking (aan-treh-king) c attraction

aanvaarden (aan-vaar-dern) v accept

aanval (aan-vahl) c (pl ~len) attack; fit

*aanvallen** (aan-vah-lern) v attack; assault

aanvang (aan-vahng) c beginning

*aanvangen** (aan-vah-ngern) v *begin

aanvankelijk (aan-vahng-ker-lerk) adv originally, at first

aanvaring (aan-vaa-ring) c (pl ~en) collision

aanvoer (aan-vōōr) c supply

aanvoerder (aan-vōōr-derr) c (pl ~s) leader

aanvraag (aan-vraakh) c (pl -vragen) application

aanwezig (aan-vāy-zerkh) adj present

aanwezigheid (aan-vāy-zerkh-hayt) c presence

*aanwijzen** (aan-vay-zern) v point out; designate

aanwijzing (aan-vay-zing) c (pl ~en) indication

aanzetten (aan-zeh-tern) v turn on

aanzien (aan-zeen) nt aspect; esteem; ten ~ van regarding

aanzienlijk (aan-zeen-lerk) adj considerable, substantial

aap (aap) c (pl apen) monkey

aard (aart) c nature

aardappel (aar-dah-perl) c (pl ~s, ~en) potato

aardbei (aart-bay) c (pl ~en) strawberry

aardbeving (aart-bāy-ving) c (pl ~en) earthquake

aardbol (aart-bol) c globe

aarde (aar-der) c earth; soil

aardewerk (aar-der-vehrk) nt crockery, pottery, faience, earthenware, ceramics pl

aardig (aar-derkh) adj pleasant; nice, kind

aardrijkskunde (aar-drayks-kern-der) c geography

aartsbisschop (aarts-bi-skhop) c (pl ~pen) archbishop

aarzelen (aar-zer-lern) v hesitate

aas (aass) nt bait

abces (ahp-sehss) nt (pl ~sen) abscess

abdij (ahb-day) c (pl ~en) abbey

abnormaal (ahp-nor-maal) adj abnormal

abonnee (ah-bo-nāy) c (pl ~s) subscriber

abonnement (ah-bo-ner-mehnt) nt (pl ~en) subscription

abonnementskaart (ah-bo-ner-mehnts-kaart) c (pl ~en) season-ticket

abortus (ah-bor-terss) c (pl ~sen) abortion

abrikoos (ah-bree-kōāss) c (pl -kozen) apricot

absoluut (ahp-sōā-lewt) adj sheer; adv absolutely

abstract (ahp-strahkt) adj abstract

absurd (ahp-serrt) adj absurd

abuis (aa-bur^ew^ss) nt (pl abuizen) mistake

academie (aa-kaa-dāy-mee) c (pl ~s) academy

accent (ahk-sehnt) nt (pl ~en) accent

accepteren (ahk-sehp-tāy-rern) v accept

accessoires (ahk-seh-svaa-rerss) pl accessories pl

accijns (ahk-*sayns*) *c* (pl -cijnzen) Customs duty

accommodatie (ah-ko-mōa-*daa*-tsee) *c* accommodation

accu (*ah*-kēw) *c* (pl ~'s) battery

acht (ahkht) *num* eight

achteloos (*ahkh*-ter-lōass) *adj* careless

achten (*ahkh*-tern) *v* esteem; count

achter (*ahkh*-terr) *prep* behind; after

achteraan (ahkh-ter-*raan*) *adv* behind

achterbuurt (*ahkh*-terr-bēwrt) *c* (pl ~en) slum

achterdochtig (ahkh-terr-*dokh*-terkh) *adj* suspicious

achtergrond (*ahkh*-terr-gront) *c* (pl ~en) background

achterkant (*ahkh*-terr-kahnt) *c* (pl ~en) rear

*****achterlaten** (*ahkh*-terr-laa-tern) *v* *leave behind

achterlicht (*ahkh*-terr-lıkht) *nt* (pl ~en) tail-light, rear-light

achternaam (*ahkh*-terr-naam) *c* (pl -namen) family name, surname

achterstallig (ahkh-terr-*stah*-lerkh) *adj* overdue

achteruit (ahkh-ter-*rur*ᵉʷt) *adv* backwards

*****achteruitrijden** (ahkh-ter-*rur*ᵉʷt-ray-dern) *v* reverse

achterwerk (*ahkh*-terr-vehrk) *nt* (pl ~en) bottom

achting (*ahkh*-tıng) *c* respect, esteem

achtste (*ahkht*-ster) *num* eighth

achttien (*ahkh*-teen) *num* eighteen

achttiende (*ahkh*-teen-der) *num* eighteenth

acne (*ahk*-nāy) *c* acne

acquisitie (ah-kvee-*zee*-tsee) *c* (pl ~s) acquisition

acteur (ahk-*tūrr*) *c* (pl ~s) actor

actie (*ahk*-see) *c* (pl ~s) action

actief (ahk-*teef*) *adj* active

activiteit (ahk-tee-vee-*tayt*) *c* (pl ~en) activity

actrice (ahk-*tree*-ser) *c* (pl ~s) actress

actueel (ahk-tēw-*vāyl*) *adj* topical

acuut (ah-*kēwt*) *adj* acute

adel (*aa*-derl) *c* nobility

adellijk (*aa*-der-lerk) *adj* noble

adem (*aa*-derm) *c* breath

ademen (*aa*-der-mern) *v* breathe

ademhaling (*aa*-derm-haa-lıng) *c* breathing, respiration

adequaat (ah-*dāy*-kvaat) *adj* adequate

ader (*aa*-derr) *c* (pl ~s, ~en) vein

administratie (aht-mee-nee-*straa*-tsee) *c* (pl ~s) administration

administratief (aht-mee-nee-straa-*teef*) *adj* administrative

admiraal (aht-mee-*raal*) *c* (pl ~s) admiral

adopteren (ah-dop-*tāy*-rern) *v* adopt

adres (aa-*drehss*) *nt* (pl ~sen) address

adresseren (aa-dreh-*sāy*-rern) *v* address

advertentie (aht-ferr-*tehn*-see) *c* (pl ~s) advertisement

advies (aht-*feess*) *nt* (pl adviezen) advice

adviseren (aht-fee-*zāy*-rern) *v* advise

advocaat (aht-fōa-*kaat*) *c* (pl -caten) lawyer; barrister; solicitor; attorney

af (ahf) *adv* off; finished; ~ **en toe** occasionally

afbeelding (*ahf*-bāyl-dıng) *c* (pl ~en) picture

afbetalen (*ahf*-ber-taa-lern) *v* *pay on account

afbetaling (*ahf*-ber-taa-lıng) *c* (pl ~en) instalment

*****afblijven** (*ahf*-blay-vern) *v* *keep off

afbraak (*ahf*-braak) *c* demolition

*****afbreken** (*ahf*-brāy-kern) *v* chip

afdaling (*ahf*-daa-lıng) *c* (pl ~en) descent

afdanken (*ahf*-dahng-kern) *v* discard

afdeling (*ahf*-dāy-ling) *c* (pl ~en) division, department; section

*afdingen (*ahf*-dɪ-ngern) *v* bargain

afdrogen (*ahf*-drōa-gern) *v* dry

afdruk (*ahf*-drerk) *c* (pl ~ken) print

*afdwingen (*ahf*-dvɪ-ngern) *v* extort

affaire (ah-*fai*-rer) *c* (pl ~s) deal; affair

affiche (ah-*fee*-sher) *nt* (pl ~s) poster

afgeladen (*ahf*-kher-laa-dern) *adj* packed, replete

afgelegen (*ahf*-kher-lāy-gern) *adj* remote, far-off, out of the way

afgelopen (*ahf*-kher-lōa-pern) *adj* past

afgerond (*ahf*-kher-ront) *adj* rounded

afgevaardigde (*ahf*-kher-vaar-derg-der) *c* (pl ~n) deputy

afgezien van (*ahf*-kher-zeen vahn) apart from

afgod (*ahf*-khot) *c* (pl ~en) idol

afgrijzen (*ahf*-khray-zern) *nt* horror

afgrond (*ahf*-khront) *c* (pl ~en) precipice, abyss

afgunst (*ahf*-khernst) *c* envy

afgunstig (ahf-*khern*-sterkh) *adj* envious

afhalen (*ahf*-haa-lern) *v* collect, fetch

afhandelen (*ahf*-hahn-der-lern) *v* settle

*afhangen van (*ahf*-hah-ngern) depend on

afhankelijk (ahf-*hahng*-ker-lerk) *adj* dependant

afhellend (*ahf*-heh-lernt) *adj* sloping

afkeer (*ahf*-kāyr) *c* dislike; antipathy

afkerig (ahf-*kāy*-rerkh) *adj* averse

afkeuren (*ahf*-kūr-rern) *v* disapprove; reject

afknippen (*ahf*-knɪ-pern) *v* *cut off

afkondigen (*ahf*-kon-der-gern) *v* proclaim

afkorting (*ahf*-kor-tɪng) *c* (pl ~en) abbreviation

afleiden (*ahf*-lay-dern) *v* deduce, infer

afleiding (*ahf*-lay-dɪng) *c* diversion

afleren (*ahf*-lāy-rern) *v* unlearn

afleveren (*ahf*-lāy-ver-rern) *v* deliver

*aflopen (*ahf*-lōa-pern) *v* end; expire

aflossen (*ahf*-lo-sern) *v* relieve; *pay off

afluisteren (*ahf*-lur^{ew}-ster-rern) *v* eavesdrop

afmaken (*ahf*-maa-kern) *v* finish

afmeting (*ahf*-māy-tɪng) *c* (pl ~en) size

*afnemen (*ahf*-nāy-mern) *v* decrease; *take away

afpersing (*ahf*-pehr-sɪng) *c* (pl ~en) extortion

*afraden (*ahf*-raa-dern) *v* dissuade from

afremmen (*ahf*-reh-mern) *v* slow down

Afrika (*aa*-free-kaa) Africa

Afrikaan (aa-free-*kaan*) *c* (pl -kanen) African

Afrikaans (aa-free-*kaans*) *adj* African

afschaffen (*ahf*-skhah-fern) *v* abolish

afscheid (*ahf*-skhayt) *nt* parting

afschrift (*ahf*-skhrɪft) *nt* (pl ~en) copy

afschuw (*ahf*-skhew^{oo}) *c* horror

afschuwelijk (ahf-*skhew*-ver-lerk) *adj* horrible, awful; hideous

*afsluiten (*ahf*-slur^{ew}-tern) *v* *cut off

*afsnijden (*ahf*-snay-dern) *v* *cut off; chip

afspraak (*ahf*-spraak) *c* (pl -spraken) date, appointment; engagement

afstammeling (*ahf*-stah-mer-lɪng) *c* (pl ~en) descendant

afstamming (*ahf*-stah-mɪng) *c* origin

afstand (*ahf*-stahnt) *c* (pl ~en) distance; space, way

afstandsmeter (*ahf*-stahnts-māy-terr) *c* (pl ~s) range-finder

afstellen (*ahf*-steh-lern) *v* adjust

afstemmen (*ahf*-steh-mern) *v* tune in

afstotelijk (ahf-*stōa*-ter-lerk) *adj* repellent

aftekenen (*ahf-tā̄y-ker-nern*) *v* endorse

*aftrekken (*ahf-treh-kern*) *v* deduct; subtract

afvaardiging (*ah-faar-der-gɪng*) *c* (pl ~en) delegation

afval (*ah-fahl*) *nt* garbage, litter, rubbish, refuse

afvegen (*ah-fā̄y-gern*) *v* wipe

afvoer (*ah-fōōr*) *c* drain

zich *afvragen (*ah-fraa-gern*) wonder

afwachten (*ahf-vahkh-tern*) *v* await

afwassen (*ahf-vah-sern*) *v* wash up

afwateren (*ahf-vaa-ter-rern*) *v* drain

afwenden (*ahf-vehn-dern*) *v* avert

afwezig (ahf-*vā̄y*-zerkh) *adj* absent

afwezigheid (ahf-*vā̄y*-zerkh-hayt) *c* absence

*afwijken (*ahf*-vay-kern) *v* deviate

afwijking (*ahf*-vay-kɪng) *c* (pl ~en) aberration

*afwijzen (*ahf*-vay-zern) *v* reject

afwisselen (*ahf*-vɪ-ser-lern) *v* vary; **afwisselend** alternate

afwisseling (*ahf*-vɪ-ser-lɪng) *c* variation

*afzeggen (*ahf*-seh-gern) *v* cancel

afzetting (*ahf*-seh-tɪng) *c* (pl ~en) deposit

afzonderlijk (ahf-*son*-derr-lerk) *adj* individual; separate; *adv* apart

agenda (aa-*gehn*-daa) *c* (pl ~'s) diary; agenda

agent (aa-*gehnt*) *c* (pl ~en) policeman; distributor, agent

agentschap (aa-*gehnt*-skhahp) *nt* (pl ~pen) agency

agrarisch (aa-*graa*-reess) *adj* agrarian

agressief (ah-greh-*seef*) *adj* aggressive

AIDS (eets) *nt* AIDS

akelig (aa-ker-lerkh) *adj* nasty

akker (*ah*-kerr) *c* (pl ~s) field

akkoord (ah-*kōārt*) *nt* (pl ~en) agreement

akte (*ahk*-ter) *c* (pl ~n, ~s) act, cer-

tificate

aktentas (*ahk*-tern-tahss) *c* (pl ~sen) briefcase, attaché case

al (ahl) *adj* all; *adv* already

alarm (aa-*lahrm*) *nt* alarm

alarmeren (aa-lahr-*mā̄y*-rern) *v* alarm

album (*ahl*-berm) *nt* (pl ~s) album

alcohol (*ahl*-kōa-hol) *c* alcohol

alcoholisch (ahl-kōa-*hōā*-leess) *adj* alcoholic

aldoor (*ahl*-dōar) *adv* all the time

alfabet (*ahl*-faa-beht) *nt* alphabet

algebra (*ahl*-ger-braa) *c* algebra

algemeen (ahl-ger-*mā̄yn*) *adj* general; universal, public; **in het ~** in general

Algerije (ahl-ger-*ray*-er) Algeria

Algerijn (ahl-ger-*rayn*) *c* (pl ~en) Algerian

Algerijns (ahl-ger-*rayns*) *adj* Algerian

alhoewel (ahl-hōō-*vehl*) *conj* though

alikruik (aa-lee-krur^ew̄k) *c* (pl ~en) winkle

alimentatie (ah-lee-mehn-*taa*-tsee) *c* alimony

alinea (aa-*lee*-nā̄y-aa) *c* (pl ~'s) paragraph

alledaags (ah-ler-*daakhs*) *adj* ordinary; everyday

alleen (ah-*lā̄yn*) *adv* only; alone

allemaal (ah-ler-*maal*) *num* ALL

allergie (ah-lehr-*gee*) *c* (pl ~ën) allergy

allerlei (*ah*-lerr-lay) *adj* various; all sorts of

alles (*ah*-lerss) *pron* everything

almachtig (ahl-*mahkh*-terkh) *adj* omnipotent

almanak (*ahl*-maa-nahk) *c* (pl ~ken) almanac

als (ahls) *conj* if; when; as, like

alsof (ahl-*zof*) *conj* as if; ***doen ~** pretend

alstublieft (ahl-stew-*bleeft*) here you

are; please

alt (ahlt) *c* (pl ~en) alto

altaar (*ahl*-taar) *nt* (pl altaren) altar

alternatief (ahl-terr-naa-*teef*) *nt* (pl -tieven) alternative

altijd (*ahl*-tayt) *adv* always, ever

amandel (aa-*mahn*-derl) *c* (pl ~en, ~s) almond; **amandelen** tonsils *pl*

amandelontsteking (aa-*mahn*-derl-ont-stãy-king) *c* (pl ~en) tonsilitis

ambacht (*ahm*-bahkht) *nt* (pl ~en) trade

ambassade (ahm-bah-*saa*-der) *c* (pl ~s) embassy

ambassadeur (ahm-bah-saa-*durr*) *c* (pl ~s) ambassador

ambitieus (ahm-bee-*ts* *y* *ūrss*) *adj* ambitious

ambt (ahmt) *nt* (pl ~en) office

ambtenaar (*ahm*-ter-naar) *c* (pl -naren) civil servant

ambulance (ahm-bew-*lahn*-ser) *c* (pl ~s) ambulance

Amerika (aa-*mãy*-ree-kaa) America

Amerikaan (aa-mãy-ree-*kaan*) *c* (pl -kanen) American

Amerikaans (aa-mãy-ree-*kaans*) *adj* American

amethist (ah-mer-*tist*) *c* (pl ~en) amethyst

amicaal (aa-mee-*kaal*) *adj* friendly

ammonia (ah-*mõa*-nee-*y*aa) *c* ammonia

amnestie (ahm-nehss-*tee*) *c* amnesty

amulet (aa-mew-*leht*) *c* (pl ~ten) lucky charm, charm

amusant (aa-mew-*zahnt*) *adj* amusing; entertaining

amusement (aa-mew-zer-*mehnt*) *nt* amusement; entertainment

amuseren (aa-mew-*zãy*-rern) *v* amuse

analfabeet (ahn-ahl-faa-*bãyt*) *c* (pl -beten) illiterate

analist (ah-naa-*list*) *c* (pl ~en) analyst

analyse (ah-naa-*lee*-zer) *c* (pl ~n, ~s) analysis

analyseren (ah-naa-lee-*zãy*-rern) *v* analyse

analyticus (ah-naa-*lee*-tee-kerss) *c* (pl -ci) analyst, psychoanalyst

ananas (*ah*-nah-nahss) *c* (pl ~sen) pineapple

anarchie (ah-nahr-*khee*) *c* anarchy

anatomie (ah-naa-tõa-*mee*) *c* anatomy

ander (*ahn*-derr) *adj* other; different; **een ~** another; **onder andere** among other things

anders (*ahn*-derrs) *adv* else; otherwise

andersom (ahn-derr-*som*) *adv* the other way round

angst (ahngst) *c* (pl ~en) fright, fear; terror

angstig (*ahng*-sterkh) *adj* afraid

angstwekkend (ahngst-*veh*-kernt) *adj* terrifying

animo (aa-nee-mõa) *c* zest

anker (*ahng*-kerr) *nt* (pl ~s) anchor

annexeren (ah-nehk-*sãy*-rern) *v* annex

annonce (ah-*nawng*-ser) *c* (pl ~s) advertisement

annuleren (ah-new-*lãy*-rern) *v* cancel

annulering (ah-new-*lãy*-ring) *c* (pl ~en) cancellation

anoniem (ah-nõa-*neem*) *adj* anonymous

ansichtkaart (*ahn*-zıkht-kaart) *c* (pl ~en) postcard, picture postcard

ansjovis (ahn-*shõa*-viss) *c* (pl ~sen) anchovy

antenne (ahn-*teh*-ner) *c* (pl ~s) aerial

antibioticum (ahn-tee-bee-*y* *õa*-tee-kerm) *nt* (pl -ca) antibiotic

antiek (ahn-*teek*) *adj* antique

antipathie (ahn-tee-paa-*tee*) *c* dislike

antiquair (ahn-tee-*kair*) *c* (pl ~s) antique dealer

antiquiteit (ahn-tee-kvee-*tayt*) *c* (pl ~en) antique

antivries (ahn-tee-*vreess*) *c* antifreeze

antwoord (ahnt-vōart) *nt* (pl ~en) reply, answer; **als ~** in reply

antwoorden (ahnt-vōar-dern) *v* reply, answer

apart (aa-*pahrt*) *adv* apart, separately

aperitief (aa-pāy-ree-*teef*) *nt/c* (pl -tieven) aperitif

apotheek (aa-pōa-*tāyk*) *c* (pl -theken) pharmacy, chemist's; drugstore *nAm*

apotheker (aa-pōa-*tāy*-kerr) *c* (pl ~s) chemist

apparaat (ah-paa-*raat*) *nt* (pl -raten) appliance; machine; apparatus

appartement (ah-pahr-ter-*mehnt*) *nt* (pl ~en) apartment *nAm*

appel (*ah*-perl) *c* (pl ~s) apple

applaudisseren (ah-plou-dee-*sāy*-rern) *v* clap

applaus (ah-*plouss*) *nt* applause

april (ah-*pril*) April

aquarel (aa-kvaa-*rehl*) *c* (pl ~len) water-colour

ar (ahr) *c* (pl ~ren) sleigh

Arabier (aa-raa-*beer*) *c* (pl ~en) Arab

Arabisch (aa-*raa*-beess) *adj* Arab

arbeid (*ahr*-bayt) *c* labour, work

arbeidbesparend (*ahr*-bayt-ber-spaa-rernt) *adj* labour-saving

arbeider (*ahr*-bay-derr) *c* (pl ~s) labourer, workman, worker

arbeidsbureau (*ahr*-bayts-bew-rōa) *nt* (pl ~s) employment exchange

archeologie (ahr-khāy-ōa-lōa-*gee*) *c* archaeology

archeoloog (ahr-khāy-ōa-*lōākh*) *c* (pl -logen) archaeologist

archief (ahr-*kheef*) *nt* (pl -chieven) archives *pl*

architect (ahr-shee-*tehkt*) *c* (pl ~en) architect

architectuur (ahr-shee-tehk-*tewr*) *c* architecture

arena (aa-*rāy*-naa) *c* (pl ~'s) bullring

arend (*aa*-rernt) *c* (pl ~en) eagle

Argentijn (ahr-gern-*tayn*) *c* (pl ~en) Argentinian

Argentijns (ahr-gern-*tayns*) *adj* Argentinian

Argentinië (ahr-gern-*tee*-nee-Yer) Argentina

argument (ahr-gēw-*mehnt*) *nt* (pl ~en) argument

argumenteren (ahr-gēw-mehn-*tāy*-rern) *v* argue

argwaan (*ahrkh*-vaan) *c* suspicion

argwanend (*ahrkh*-vaa-nernt) *adj* suspicious

arm¹ (ahrm) *adj* poor

arm² (ahrm) *c* (pl ~en) arm

armband (*ahrm*-bahnt) *c* (pl ~en) bracelet; bangle

armoede (*ahr*-mōo-der) *c* poverty

armoedig (*ahr*-*mōo*-derkh) *adj* poor

aroma (aa-*rōa*-maa) *nt* aroma

arrestatie (ah-rehss-*taa*-tsee) *c* (pl ~s) arrest

arresteren (ah-rehss-*tāy*-rern) *v* arrest

arrogant (ah-rōa-*gahnt*) *adj* presumptuous

artikel (ahr-*tee*-kerl) *nt* (pl ~en, ~s) article; item

artisjok (ahr-tee-*shok*) *c* (pl ~ken) artichoke

artistiek (ahr-tıss-*teek*) *adj* artistic

arts (ahrts) *c* (pl ~en) doctor

as¹ (ahss) *c* (pl ~sen) axle

as² (ahss) *c* ash

asbak (*ahss*-bahk) *c* (pl ~ken) ashtray

asbest (*ahss*-behst) *nt* asbestos

asfalt (*ahss*-fahlt) *nt* asphalt

asiel (aa-*zeel*) *nt* asylum

aspect (ahss-*pehkt*) *nt* (pl ~en) aspect

asperge (ahss-*pehr*-zher) *c* (pl ~s) asparagus

aspirine (ahss-pee-*ree*-ner) *c* aspirin

assistent (ah-see-*stehnt*) *c* (pl ~en)

assistant

associëren (ah-sōā-*shāy*-rern) v associate

assortiment (ah-sor-tee-*mehnt*) nt (pl ~en) assortment

assurantie (ah-sēw-*rahn*-see) c (pl -ties, -tiën) insurance

astma (*ahss*-maa) nt asthma

atheïst (aa-tāy-*ist*) c (pl ~en) atheist

Atlantische Oceaan (aht-*lahn*-tee-ser ōā-say-*aan*) Atlantic

atleet (aht-*lāyt*) c (pl -leten) athlete

atletiek (aht-lāy-*teek*) c athletics pl

atmosfeer (aht-moss-*fāyr*) c atmosphere

atomisch (aa-*tōā*-meess) adj atomic

atoom (aa-*tōām*) nt (pl atomen) atom; **atoom-** atomic

attent (ah-*tehnt*) adj considerate

attest (ah-*tehst*) nt (pl ~en) certificate

attractie (ah-*trahk*-see) c (pl ~s) attraction

aubergine (ōā-behr-*zhee*-ner) c (pl ~s) eggplant

augustus (ou-*gerss*-terss) August

aula (*ou*-laa) c (pl ~'s) auditorium

Australië (ou-*straa*-lee-Yer) Australia

Australiër (ou-*straa*-lee-Yerr) c (pl ~s) Australian

Australisch (ou-*straa*-leess) adj Australian

auteur (ōā-*tūrr*) c (pl ~s) author

authentiek (ōā-tehn-*teek*) adj authentic

auto (*ōā*-tōā) c (pl ~'s) car; motorcar, automobile

automaat (ōā-tōā-*maat*) c (pl -maten) slot-machine

automatisch (ōā-tōā-*maa*-teess) adj automatic

automatisering (ōā-tōā-maa-tee-*zāy*-ring) c automation

automobielclub (ōā-tōā-mōā-*beel*-klerp) c (pl ~s) automobile club

automobilisme (ōā-tōā-mōā-bee-*liss*-mer) nt motoring

automobilist (ōā-tōā-mōā-bee-*list*) c (pl ~en) motorist

autonoom (ōā-tōā-*nōām*) adj autonomous

autoped (*ōā*-tōā-peht) c (pl ~s) scooter

autopsie (ōā-top-*see*) c autopsy

***autorijden** (*ōā*-tōā-ray-dern) v motor

autorit (*ōā*-tōā-rit) c (pl ~ten) drive

autoritair (ōā-tōā-ree-*tair*) adj authoritarian

autoriteiten (ōā-tōā-ree-*tay*-tern) pl authorities pl

autoverhuur (*ōā*-tōā-verr-*hēwr*) c car hire; car rental Am

autoweg (*ōā*-tōā-vehhk) c (pl ~en) highway nAm

avond c (pl ~en) night, evening

avondeten (*aa*-vernt-*āy*-tern) nt dinner; supper

avondkleding (*aa*-vernt-klāy-ding) c evening dress

avondschemering (*aa*-vernt-skhāy-mer-ring) c dusk

avontuur (aa-von-*tēwr*) nt (pl -turen) adventure

Aziaat (aa-zee-*Yaat*) c (pl Aziaten) Asian

Aziatisch (aa-zee-*Yaa*-teess) adj Asian

Azië (*aa*-zee-Yer) Asia

azijn (aa-*zayn*) c vinegar

B

baai (baa^ee) c (pl ~en) bay

baan (baan) c (pl banen) job

baard (baart) c (pl ~en) beard

baarmoeder (*baar*-mōō-derr) c womb

baars (baars) c (pl baarzen) bass,

perch

baas (baass) c (pl bazen) boss; master

baat (baat) c benefit; profit

babbelen (bah-ber-lern) v chat

babbelkous (bah-berl-kouss) c (pl ~en) chatterbox

babbeltje (bah-berl-tʸer) nt (pl ~s) chat

baby (bā̄y-bee) c (pl ~'s) baby

bacil (bah-sɪl) c (pl ~len) germ

bacterie (bahk-tā̄y-ree) c (pl -riën) bacterium

bad (baht) nt (pl ~en) bath; **een ~ *nemen** bathe

baden (baa-dern) v bathe

badhanddoek (baht-hahn-dō̄ok) c (pl ~en) bath towel

badjas (baht-ʸahss) c (pl ~sen) bathrobe

badkamer (baht-kaa-merr) c (pl ~s) bathroom

badmuts (baht-merts) c (pl ~en) bathing-cap

badpak (baht-pahk) nt (pl ~ken) bathing-suit

badplaats (baht-plaats) c (pl ~en) seaside resort

badstof (baht-stof) c towelling

badzout (baht-sout) nt bath salts

bagage (bah-gaa-zher) c baggage; luggage

bagagedepot (bah-gaa-zher-dā̄y-pō̄a) nt (pl ~s) left luggage office; baggage deposit office Am

bagagenet (bah-gaa-zher-neht) nt (pl ~ten) luggage rack

bagageoverschot (bah-gaa-zher-ō̄a-verr-skhot) nt overweight

bagagerek (bah-gaa-zher-rehk) nt (pl ~ken) luggage rack

bagageruimte (bah-gaa-zher-rurᵉʷm-ter) c (pl ~n, ~s) boot

bagagewagen (bah-gaa-zher-vaa-gern) c (pl ~s) luggage van

bakboord (bahk-bōart) nt port

baken (baa-kern) nt (pl ~s) landmark

bakermat (baa-kerr-maht) c cradle

bakkebaarden (bah-ker-baar-dern) pl whiskers pl, sideburns pl

* **bakken** (bah-kern) v bake; fry

bakker (bah-kerr) c (pl ~s) baker

bakkerij (bah-ker-ray) c (pl ~en) bakery

baksteen (bahk-stāyn) c (pl -stenen) brick

bal¹ (bahl) c (pl ~len) ball

bal² (bahl) nt (pl ~s) ball

balans (bah-lahns) c (pl ~en) balance

baldadig (bahl-daa-derkh) adj rowdy

balie (baa-lee) c (pl ~s) counter

balk (bahlk) c (pl ~en) beam

balkon (bahl-kon) nt (pl ~s) balcony; circle

ballet (bah-leht) nt (pl ~ten) ballet

balling (bah-lɪng) c (pl ~en) exile

ballingschap (bah-lɪng-skhahp) c exile

ballon (bah-lon) c (pl ~s) balloon

ballpoint (bol-poʸnt) c (pl ~s) ballpoint-pen; Biro

bamboe (bahm-bōo) nt bamboo

banaan (baa-naan) c (pl bananen) banana

band (bahnt) c (pl ~en) tape; band; tyre, tire; **lekke ~** flat tyre, puncture

bandenspanning (bahn-der-spah-nɪng) c tyre pressure

bandepech (bahn-der-pehkh) c blowout, puncture

bandiet (bahn-deet) c (pl ~en) bandit

bandrecorder (bahnt-rer-kor-derr) c (pl ~s) tape-recorder, recorder

bang (bahng) adj frightened, afraid

bank (bahngk) c (pl ~en) bank; bench

bankbiljet (bahngk-bɪl-ʸeht) nt (pl ~ten) banknote

banket (bahng-keht) nt (pl ~ten) banquet

banketbakker (bahng-*keht*-bah-kerr) *c* (pl ~s) confectioner

banketbakkerij (bahng-keht-bah-ker-*ray*) *c* (pl ~en) pastry shop

banketzaal (bahng-*keht*-saal) *c* (pl -za-len) banqueting-hall

bankrekening (*bahngk*-rāy-ker-nıng) *c* (pl ~en) bank account

bankroet (bahngk-*rōōt*) *adj* bankrupt

bar (bahr) *c* (pl ~s) bar; saloon

baret (baa-*reht*) *c* (pl ~ten) beret

bariton (*baa*-ree-ton) *c* (pl ~s) bari-tone

barjuffrouw (*bahr*-Yer-frou) *c* (pl ~en) barmaid

barman (*bahr*-mahn) *c* (pl ~nen) bar-tender, barman

barmhartig (bahr-*mahr*-terkh) *adj* mer-ciful

barnsteen (*bahrn*-stāyn) *nt* amber

barok (baa-*rok*) *adj* baroque

barometer (bah-rōa-māy-terr) *c* (pl ~s) barometer

barrière (bah-ree-*Y*ai-rer) *c* (pl ~s) bar-rier

barst (bahrst) *c* (pl ~en) crack

*** barsten** (*bahrs*-tern) *v* crack, *burst, *split; *get cracked

bas (bahss) *c* (pl ~sen) bass

baseren (baa-*zāy*-rern) *v* base

basiliek (baa-zee-*leek*) *c* (pl ~en) ba-silica

basis (*baa*-zerss) *c* (pl bases) basis; base

basiscrème (*baa*-zerss-kraim) *c* (pl ~s) foundation cream

bast (bahst) *c* (pl ~en) bark

bastaard (*bahss*-taart) *c* (pl ~en, ~s) bastard

baten (*baa*-tern) *v* *be of use

batterij (bah-ter-*ray*) *c* (pl ~en) bat-tery

beambte (ber-*ahm*-ter) *c* (pl ~n) clerk

beantwoorden (ber-*ahnt*-vōar-dern) *v* answer

bebost (ber-*bost*) *adj* wooded

bebouwen (ber-*bou*-ern) *v* cultivate

bed (beht) *nt* (pl ~den) bed

bedaard (ber-*daart*) *adj* quiet

bedachtzaam (ber-*dahkht*-saam) *adj* cautious

bedanken (ber-*dahng*-kern) *v* thank

bedaren (ber-*daa*-rern) *v* calm down

beddegoed (*beh*-der-gōōt) *nt* bedding

bedeesd (ber-*dāyst*) *adj* timid

bedekken (ber-*deh*-kern) *v* cover

bedelaar (*bāy*-der-laar) *c* (pl ~s) beg-gar

bedelen (*bāy*-der-lern) *v* beg

*** bedelven** (ber-*dehl*-vern) *v* bury

*** bedenken** (ber-*dehng*-kern) *v* *think of

*** bederven** (ber-*dehr*-vern) *v* *spoil; mess up

bedevaart (*bāy*-der-vaart) *c* (pl ~en) pilgrimage

bediende (ber-*deen*-der) *c* (pl ~n, ~s) domestic, servant; valet; boy

bedienen (ber-*dee*-nern) *v* serve; wait on; attend on

bediening (ber-*dee*-nıng) *c* service

bedieningsgeld (ber-*dee*-nıngs-khehlt) *nt* service charge

bedoelen (ber-*dōō*-lern) *v* *mean; in-tend

bedoeling (ber-*dōō*-lıng) *c* (pl ~en) purpose, intention

bedrag (ber-*drahkh*) *nt* (pl ~en) amount

*** bedragen** (ber-*draa*-gern) *v* amount to

bedreigen (ber-*dray*-gern) *v* threaten

bedreiging (ber-*dray*-gıng) *c* (pl ~en) threat

*** bedriegen** (ber-*dree*-gern) *v* deceive; cheat

bedrijf (ber-*drayf*) *nt* (pl bedrijven)

business, concern; plant; act

bedrijvig (ber-*dray*-verkh) *adj* active

bedroefd (ber-*drōōft*) *adj* sad, sorry

bedroefdheid (ber-*drōōft*-hayt) *c* sadness; grief

bedrog (ber-*drokh*) *nt* deceit; fraud

beëindigen (ber-*ayn*-der-gern) *v* end, finish

beek (bāyk) *c* (pl beken) brook, stream

beeld (bāylt) *nt* (pl ~en) picture, image

beeldhouwer (*bāylt*-hou-err) *c* (pl ~s) sculptor

beeldhouwwerk (*bāylt*-hou-vehrk) *nt* (pl ~en) sculpture

beeldscherm (*bāylt*-skhehrm) *nt* (pl ~en) screen

been[1] (bāyn) *nt* (pl benen) leg

been[2] (bāyn) *nt* (pl beenderen, benen) bone

beer (bāyr) *c* (pl beren) bear

beest (bāyst) *nt* (pl ~en) beast

beestachtig (*bāyst*-ahkh-terkh) *adj* brutal

beet (bāyt) *c* (pl beten) bite

beetje (*bāy*-tᵉer) *nt* bit

*****beetnemen** (*bāyt*-nāy-mern) *v* kid

beetwortel (*bāyt*-vor-terl) *c* (pl ~s, ~en) beetroot

befaamd (ber-*faamt*) *adj* noted

begaafd (ber-*gaaft*) *adj* gifted, talented

*****begaan** (ber-*gaan*) *v* commit

begeerlijk (ber-*gāyr*-lerk) *adj* desirable

begeerte (ber-*gāy*-ter) *c* (pl ~n) desire

begeleiden (ber-ger-*lay*-dern) *v* accompany; conduct

begeren (ber-*gāy*-rern) *v* desire

begin (ber-*gin*) *nt* start, beginning; **begin-** initial

beginneling (ber-*gi*-ner-ling) *c* (pl ~en) learner, beginner

*****beginnen** (ber-*gi*-nern) *v* start, commence, *begin

beginner (ber-*gi*-nerr) *c* (pl ~s) learner

beginsel (ber-*gin*-serl) *nt* (pl ~en, ~s) principle

begraafplaats (ber-*graaf*-plaats) *c* (pl ~en) cemetery

begrafenis (ber-*graa*-fer-niss) *c* (pl ~sen) burial; funeral

*****begraven** (ber-*graa*-vern) *v* bury

*****begrijpen** (ber-*gray*-pern) *v* *understand; *see, *take; **begrijpend** sympathetic

begrip (ber-*grip*) *nt* (pl ~pen) notion; idea, conception; understanding

begroeid (ber-*grōō*ᵉᵉt) *adj* overgrown

begroting (ber-*grōa*-ting) *c* (pl ~en) budget

begunstigde (ber-*gern*-sterkh-der) *c* (pl ~n) payee

begunstigen (ber-*gern*-ster-gern) *v* favour

beha (*bāy*-haa) *c* (pl ~'s) brassiere, bra

behalen (ber-*haa*-lern) *v* obtain

behalve (ber-*hahl*-ver) *prep* but, except; beyond, besides

behandelen (ber-*hahn*-der-lern) *v* treat, handle

behandeling (ber-*hahn*-der-ling) *c* (pl ~en) treatment

behang (ber-*hahng*) *nt* wallpaper

beheer (ber-*hāyr*) *nt* management; administration

beheersen (ber-*hāyr*-sern) *v* master

beheksen (ber-*hehk*-sern) *v* bewitch

zich *behelpen met (ber-*hehl*-pern) *make do with

behendig (ber-*hehn*-derkh) *adj* skilful

beheren (ber-*hāy*-rern) *v* manage

behoedzaam (ber-*hōōt*-saam) *adj* wary

behoefte (ber-*hōōf*-ter) *c* (pl ~n) need, want

behoeven (ber-*hoo*-vern) v need; **ten behoeve van** on behalf of

behoorlijk (ber-*hoar*-lerk) adj proper

behoren (ber-*hoa*-rern) v belong to; *ought

behoudend (ber-*hou*-dernt) adj conservative

beide (*bay*-der) adj both; either; **een van ~** either; **geen van ~** neither

beige (*bai*-zher) adj beige

beïnvloeden (ber-*in*-vloo-dern) v influence; affect

beitel (*bay*-terl) c (pl ~s) chisel

bejaard (ber-*Yaart*) adj aged; elderly

bek (behk) c (pl ~ken) mouth; beak

bekend (ber-*kehnt*) adj well-known

bekende (ber-*kehn*-der) c (pl ~n) acquaintance

bekendmaken (ber-*kehnt*-maa-kern) v announce

bekendmaking (ber-*kehnt*-maa-king) c (pl ~en) announcement

bekennen (ber-*keh*-nern) v admit, confess

bekentenis (ber-*kehn*-ter-niss) c (pl ~sen) confession

beker (*bay*-kerr) c (pl ~s) mug; tumbler; cup

bekeren (ber-*kay*-rern) v convert

*bekijken** (ber-*kay*-kern) v regard, view

bekken (*beh*-kern) nt (pl ~s) basin; pelvis

beklagen (ber-*klaa*-gern) v pity

bekleden (ber-*klay*-dern) v upholster

beklemmen (ber-*kleh*-mern) v oppress

*beklimmen** (ber-*kli*-mern) v ascend

beklimming (ber-*kli*-ming) c (pl ~en) ascent

beknopt (ber-*knopt*) adj concise; brief

zich bekommeren om (ber-*ko*-mer-rern) care about

bekoring (ber-*koa*-ring) c (pl ~en) attraction, charm

bekritiseren (ber-kree-tee-*zay*-rern) v criticize

bekrompen (ber-*krom*-pern) adj narrow-minded

bekronen (ber-*kroa*-nern) v crown

bekwaam (ber-*kvaam*) adj able, capable; skilful

bekwaamheid (ber-*kvaam*-hayt) c (pl -heden) ability, faculty, capacity

bel (behl) c (pl ~len) bell; bubble

belachelijk (ber-*lah*-kher-lerk) adj ridiculous, ludicrous

belang (ber-*lahng*) nt (pl ~en) interest; importance; **van ~ *zijn** matter

belangrijk (ber-*lahng*-rayk) adj important; capital

belangstellend (ber-lahng-*steh*-lernt) adj interested

belangstelling (ber-*lahng*-steh-ling) c interest

belastbaar (ber-*lahst*-baar) adj dutiable

belasten (ber-*lahss*-tern) v charge; tax; **belast met** in charge of

belasting (ber-*lahss*-ting) c (pl ~en) charge; tax; taxation

belastingvrij (ber-lahss-ting-*vray*) adj duty-free; tax-free

beledigen (ber-*lay*-der-gern) v insult; offend; **beledigend** offensive

belediging (ber-*lay*-der-ging) c (pl ~en) insult; offence

beleefd (ber-*layft*) adj polite; civil

belegering (ber-*lay*-ger-ring) c (pl ~en) siege

beleggen (ber-*leh*-gern) v invest

belegging (ber-*leh*-ging) c (pl ~en) investment

beleid (ber-*layt*) nt policy

belemmeren (ber-*leh*-mer-rern) v impede

beletsel (ber-*leht*-serl) nt (pl ~s, ~en) impediment

beletten (ber-*leh*-tern) v prevent

beleven (ber-*lāy*-vern) v experience

Belg (behlkh) c (pl ~en) Belgian

België (*behl*-gee-Yer) Belgium

Belgisch (*behl*-geess) adj Belgian

belichting (ber-*likh*-ting) c exposure

belichtingsmeter (ber-*likh*-tings-māy-terr) c (pl ~s) exposure meter

*****belijden** (beh-*lay*-dern) v *ring

bellen (ber-lern) v *ring

belofte (ber-*lof*-ter) c (pl ~n) promise

belonen (ber-*lōā*-nern) v reward

beloning (ber-*lōā*-ning) c (pl ~en) reward; prize

beloven (ber-*lōā*-vern) v promise

bemachtigen (ber-*mahkh*-ter-gern) v secure

bemanning (ber-*mah*-ning) c (pl ~en) crew

bemerken (ber-*mehr*-kern) v notice; perceive

bemiddelaar (ber-*mı*-der-laar) c (pl ~s) mediator

bemiddeld (ber-*mı*-derlt) adj well-to-do

bemiddelen (ber-*mı*-der-lern) v mediate

bemind (ber-*mınt*) adj beloved

zich bemoeien met (ber-*mōō*ᵉᵉ-ern) interfere with

benadrukken (ber-*naa*-drer-kern) v emphasize, stress

benaming (ber-*naa*-ming) c (pl ~en) denomination

benauwd (ber-*nout*) adj stuffy

bende (*behn*-der) c (pl ~n, ~s) gang

beneden (ber-*nāy*-dern) prep under, below; adv underneath, beneath; below; downstairs; **naar** ~ downwards, down; downstairs

benieuwd (ber-*nee*ᵒᵒt) adj curious

benijden (ber-*nay*-dern) v envy

benoemen (ber-*nōō*-mern) v nominate, appoint

benoeming (ber-*nōō*-ming) c (pl ~en) nomination, appointment

benutten (ber-*ner*-tern) v utilize

benzine (behn-*zee*-ner) c petrol; fuel; gasoline nAm; gas nAm; **loodvrije** ~ unleaded petrol

benzinepomp (behn-*zee*-ner-pomp) c (pl ~en) petrol pump; fuel pump Am; gas pump Am

benzinestation (behn-*zee*-ner-staa-shon) nt (pl ~s) service station, petrol station; gas station Am

benzinetank (behn-*zee*-ner-tehngk) c (pl ~s) petrol tank

beoefenen (ber-*ōō*-fer-nern) v practise

beogen (ber-*ōā*-gern) v aim at

beoordelen (ber-*ōār*-dāy-lern) v judge

beoordeling (ber-*ōār*-dāy-ling) c (pl ~en) judgment

bepaald (ber-*paalt*) adj definite; certain

bepalen (ber-*paa*-lern) v define, determine; stipulate

bepaling (ber-*paa*-ling) c (pl ~en) stipulation; definition

beperken (ber-*pehr*-kern) v limit

beperking (ber-*pehr*-king) c (pl ~en) restriction

beproeven (ber-*prōō*-vern) v attempt

beraad (ber-*raat*) nt deliberation

beraadslagen (ber-*raat*-slaa-gern) v deliberate

beramen (ber-*raa*-mern) v devise

bereid (ber-*rayt*) adj prepared, willing

bereiden (ber-*ray*-dern) v cook

bereidwillig (ber-rayt-*vı*-lerkh) adj cooperative

bereik (ber-*rayk*) nt reach; range

bereikbaar (ber-*rayk*-baar) adj attainable

bereiken (ber-*ray*-kern) v reach; achieve, accomplish, attain

berekenen (ber-*rāy*-ker-nern) v calculate; charge

berekening (ber-*rāy*-ker-nɪng) *c* (pl ~en) calculation

berg (behrkh) *c* (pl ~en) mountain; mount

bergachtig (*behrkh*-ahkh-terkh) *adj* mountainous

bergketen (*behrkh*-kāy-tern) *c* (pl ~s) mountain range

bergkloof (*behrkh*-klōāt) *c* (pl -kloven) glen

bergpas (*behrkh*-pahss) *c* (pl ~sen) mountain pass

bergplaats (*behrkh*-plaats) *c* (pl ~en) depository

bergrug (*behrkh*-rerg) *c* (pl ~gen) ridge

bergsport (*behrkh*-sport) *c* mountaineering

bericht (ber-*rɪkht*) *nt* (pl ~en) message; notice

berispen (ber-*rɪss*-pern) *v* reprimand, scold

berk (behrk) *c* (pl ~en) birch

beroemd (ber-*rōōmt*) *adj* famous

beroep (ber-*rōōp*) *nt* (pl ~en) profession; appeal; **beroeps-** professional

beroerd (ber-*rōōrt*) *adj* miserable

beroerte (ber-*rōōr*-ter) *c* (pl ~n, ~s) stroke

berouw (ber-*rou*) *nt* repentance

beroven (ber-*rōā*-vern) *v* rob

beroving (ber-*rōā*-vɪng) *c* (pl ~en) robbery

berucht (ber-*rerkht*) *adj* notorious

bes (behss) *c* (pl ~sen) berry; currant; **zwarte ~** black-currant

beschaafd (ber-*skhaaft*) *adj* civilized; cultured

beschaamd (ber-*skhaamt*) *adj* ashamed

beschadigen (ber-*skhaa*-der-gern) *v* damage

beschaving (ber-*skhaa*-vɪng) *c* (pl ~en) civilization; culture

bescheiden (ber-*skhay*-dern) *adj* modest

bescheidenheid (ber-*skhay*-dern-hayt) *c* modesty

beschermen (ber-*skhehr*-mern) *v* protect

bescherming (ber-*skhehr*-mɪng) *c* protection

beschikbaar (ber-*skhɪk*-baar) *adj* available

beschikken over (ber-*skhɪ*-kern) dispose of

beschikking (ber-*skhɪ*-kɪng) *c* disposal

beschimmeld (ber-*skhɪ*-merlt) *adj* mouldy

beschouwen (ber-*skhou*-ern) *v* consider; regard; reckon

*****beschrijven** (ber-*skhray*-vern) *v* describe

beschrijving (ber-*skhray*-vɪng) *c* (pl ~en) description

beschuldigen (ber-*skherl*-der-gern) *v* accuse; blame

beschutten (ber-*skher*-tern) *v* shelter

beschutting (ber-*skher*-tɪng) *c* cover, shelter

beseffen (ber-*seh*-fern) *v* realize

beslag (ber-*slahkh*) *nt* batter; **beslag leggen op** impound, confiscate

beslissen (ber-*slɪ*-sern) *v* decide

beslissing (ber-*slɪ*-sɪng) *c* (pl ~en) decision

beslist (ber-*slɪst*) *adv* without fail

besluit (ber-*slur*ᵉʷt) *nt* (pl ~en) decision

*****besluiten** (ber-*slur*ᵉʷ-tern) *v* decide

besmettelijk (ber-*smeh*-ter-lerk) *adj* contagious, infectious

besmetten (ber-*smeh*-tern) *v* infect

besneeuwd (ber-*snāy*ᵒᵒt) *adj* snowy

bespelen (ber-*spāy*-lern) *v* play

bespottelijk (ber-*spo*-ter-lerk) *adj* ridiculous, ludicrous

bespotten (ber-*spo*-tern) v ridicule; mock

*bespreken (ber-*spray*-kern) v engage, reserve; discuss

bespreking (ber-*spray*-king) c (pl ~en) booking; review; discussion

best (behst) adj best

bestaan (ber-*staan*) nt existence

*bestaan (ber-*staan*) v exist; ~ **uit** consist of

bestanddeel (ber-*stahn*-dayl) nt (pl -delen) ingredient; element

besteden (ber-*stay*-dern) v *spend

bestek (ber-*stehk*) nt (pl ~ken) cutlery

bestelauto (ber-*stehl*-oa-toa) c (pl ~'s) van; delivery van, pick-up van

bestelformulier (ber-*stehl*-for-mew-leer) nt (pl ~en) order-form

bestellen (ber-*steh*-lern) v order

bestelling (ber-*steh*-ling) c (pl ~en) order

bestemmen (ber-*steh*-mern) v destine

bestemming (ber-*steh*-ming) c (pl ~en) destination

bestendig (ber-*stehn*-derkh) adj permanent

*bestijgen (ber-*stay*-gern) v mount

bestraten (ber-*straa*-tern) v pave

*bestrijden (ber-*stray*-dern) v combat

besturen (ber-*stew*-rern) v *drive

bestuur (ber-*stewr*) nt (pl besturen) direction; board; rule

bestuurlijk (ber-*stewr*-lerk) adj administrative

bestuursrecht (ber-*stewrs*-rehkht) nt administrative law

betalen (ber-*taa*-lern) v *pay

betaling (ber-*taa*-ling) c (pl ~en) payment

betasten (ber-*tahss*-tern) v *feel

betekenen (ber-*tay*-ker-nern) v *mean

betekenis (ber-*tay*-ker-niss) c (pl ~sen) meaning; sense

beter (*bay*-terr) adj better; superior

beteugelen (ber-*tur*-ger-lern) v curb

betogen (ber-*toa*-gern) v demonstrate

betoging (ber-*toa*-ging) c (pl ~en) demonstration

beton (ber-*ton*) nt concrete

betoveren (ber-*toa*-ver-rern) v bewitch; **betoverend** enchanting, glamorous

betovering (ber-*toa*-ver-ring) c (pl ~en) spell

betrappen (ber-*trah*-pern) v *catch

*betreden (ber-*tray*-dern) v enter

*betreffen (ber-*treh*-fern) v concern; affect, touch; **wat betreft** as regards

betreffende (ber-*treh*-fern-der) prep as regards, regarding, about, concerning

betrekkelijk (ber-*treh*-ker-lerk) adj relative

*betrekken (ber-*treh*-kern) v implicate, *get involved; obtain

betrekking (ber-*treh*-king) c (pl ~en) post, position, job; reference; **met ~ tot** regarding, with reference to

betreuren (ber-*trur*-rern) v regret

betrokken (ber-*tro*-kern) adj cloudy, overcast; concerned, involved

betrouwbaar (ber-*trou*-baar) adj trustworthy, reliable

betuigen (ber-*tur*ew-gern) v express

betwijfelen (ber-*tvay*-fer-lern) v doubt, query

betwisten (ber-*tviss*-tern) v dispute

beu (bur) adj tired of, fed up with

beuk (burk) c (pl ~en) beech

beul (burl) c (pl ~en) executioner

beurs (burrs) c (pl beurzen) purse; stock exchange; fair; grant

beurt (burrt) c (pl ~en) turn

bevaarbaar (ber-*vaar*-baar) adj navigable

*bevallen (ber-*vah*-lern) v please

bevallig (ber-*vah*-lerkh) *adj* graceful

bevalling (ber-*vah*-ling) *c* (pl ~en) delivery, childbirth

***bevaren** (ber-*vaa*-rern) *v* sail

bevatten (ber-*vah*-tern) *v* contain; include

bevel (ber-*vehl*) *nt* (pl ~en) command, order

***bevelen** (ber-*vay*-lern) *v* command, order

bevelhebber (ber-*vehl*-heh-berr) *c* (pl ~s) commander

beven (*bay*-vern) *v* tremble

bever (*bay*-verr) *c* (pl ~s) beaver

bevestigen (ber-*vehss*-ter-gern) *v* acknowledge, confirm; fasten; **bevestigend** affirmative

bevestiging (ber-*vehss*-ter-ging) *c* (pl ~en) confirmation

zich *bevinden (ber-*vin*-dern) *be

bevlieging (ber-*vlee*-ging) *c* (pl ~en) whim

bevochtigen (ber-*vokh*-ter-gern) *v* damp, moisten

bevoegd (ber-*vookht*) *adj* qualified

bevoegdheid (ber-*vookht*-hayt) *c* (pl -heden) qualification

bevolking (ber-*vol*-king) *c* population

bevoorrechten (ber-*voa*-raykh-tern) *v* favour

bevorderen (ber-*vor*-der-rern) *v* promote

bevredigen (ber-*vray*-der-gern) *v* satisfy

bevrediging (ber-*vray*-der-ging) *c* (pl ~en) satisfaction

***bevriezen** (ber-*vree*-zern) *v* *freeze

bevrijding (ber-*vray*-ding) *c* liberation

bevuild (ber-*vur*ʳ*w*⁄*lt*) *adj* soiled

bewaken (ber-*vaa*-kern) *v* guard

bewaker (ber-*vaa*-kerr) *c* (pl ~s) guard; warden

bewapenen (ber-*vaa*-per-nern) *v* arm

bewaren (ber-*vaa*-rern) *v* *hold; preserve; *keep

bewaring (ber-*vaa*-ring) *c* preservation

beweeglijk (ber-*vaykh*-lerk) *adj* mobile

beweegreden (ber-*vaykh*-ray-dern) *c* (pl ~en) cause

***bewegen** (ber-*vay*-gern) *v* move; stir

beweging (ber-*vay*-ging) *c* (pl ~en) movement; motion

beweren (ber-*vay*-rern) *v* claim

bewijs (ber-*vayss*) *nt* (pl bewijzen) proof, evidence; token; voucher

***bewijzen** (ber-*vay*-zern) *v* prove

bewind (ber-*vint*) *nt* rule, government

bewolking (ber-*vol*-king) *c* clouds

bewolkt (ber-*volkt*) *adj* cloudy

bewonderen (ber-*von*-der-rern) *v* admire

bewondering (ber-*von*-der-ring) *c* admiration

bewonen (ber-*voa*-nern) *v* inhabit

bewoner (ber-*voa*-nerr) *c* (pl ~s) inhabitant; occupant

bewoonbaar (ber-*voan*-baar) *adj* habitable, inhabitable

bewust (ber-*verst*) *adj* conscious, aware

bewusteloos (ber-*verss*-ter-loass) *adj* unconscious

bewustzijn (ber-*verst*-sayn) *nt* consciousness

bezem (*bay*-zerm) *c* (pl ~s) broom

bezeren (ber-*zay*-rern) *v* *hurt

bezet (ber-*zeht*) *adj* engaged, occupied

bezetten (ber-*zeh*-tern) *v* occupy

bezetting (ber-*zeh*-ting) *c* (pl ~en) occupation

bezielen (ber-*zee*-lern) *v* inspire

bezienswaardigheid (ber-zeen-*svaar*-derkh-hayt) *c* (pl -heden) sight

bezig (*bay*-zerkh) *adj* engaged, busy

zich *bezighouden met (*bay*-zerkh-hou-dern) attend to

bezinksel (ber-*zingk*-serl) *nt* (pl ~s) deposit

bezit (ber-*zit*) *nt* property; possession

*****bezitten** (ber-*zi*-tern) *v* possess, own

bezitter (ber-*zi*-terr) *c* (pl ~s) owner

bezittingen (ber-*zi*-ting-ern) *pl* belongings *pl*

bezoek (ber-*zōōk*) *nt* (pl ~en) call, visit

*****bezoeken** (ber-*zōō*-kern) *v* visit; call on

bezoeker (ber-*zōō*-kerr) *c* (pl ~s) visitor

bezoekuren (ber-*zōōk*-ēw-rern) *pl* visiting hours

bezonnen (ber-*zo*-nern) *adj* sober

bezorgd (ber-*zorkht*) *adj* anxious, concerned

bezorgdheid (ber-*zorkht*-hayt) *c* worry, anxiety

bezorgen (ber-*zor*-gern) *v* deliver; supply

bezorging (ber-*zor*-ging) *c* delivery

bezwaar (ber-*zvaar*) *nt* (pl bezwaren) objection; ~ *****hebben tegen** object to; mind

*****bezwijken** (ber-*zvay*-kern) *v* collapse; succumb

bibberen (bi-ber-rern) *v* shiver

bibliotheek (bee-blee-Yōa-*tāyk*) *c* (pl -theken) library

*****bidden** (bi-dern) *v* pray

biecht (beekht) *c* (pl ~en) confession

biechten (*beekh*-tern) *v* confess

*****bieden** (*bee*-dern) *v* offer

biefstuk (*beef*-sterk) *c* (pl ~ken) steak

bier (beer) *nt* (pl ~en) beer; ale

bies (beess) *c* (pl biezen) rush

bieslook (*beess*-lōak) *nt* chives *pl*

biet (beet) *c* (pl ~en) beet

big (bikh) *c* (pl ~gen) piglet

bij¹ (bay) *prep* near, at, with, by; to

bij² (bay) *c* (pl ~en) bee

bijbel (*bay*-berl) *c* (pl ~s) bible

bijbetekenis (*bay*-ber-tāy-ker-niss) *c* (pl ~sen) connotation

bijdrage (*bay*-draa-ger) *c* (pl ~n) contribution

bijeen (bay-*āyn*) *adv* together

*****bijeenbrengen** (bay-*āyn*-breh-ngern) *v* assemble

*****bijeenkomen** (bay-*āyng*-kōa-mern) *v* gather

bijeenkomst (bay-*āyng*-komst) *c* (pl ~en) meeting; rally; assembly, congress

bijenkorf (*bay*-er-korf) *c* (pl -korven) beehive

bijgebouw (*bay*-ger-bou) *nt* (pl ~en) annex

bijgeloof (*bay*-ger-lōaf) *nt* superstition

bijgevolg (bay-ger-*volkh*) *adv* consequently

*****bijhouden** (*bay*-hou-dern) *v* *****keep up with

bijknippen (*bay*-kni-pern) *v* trim

bijkomend (*bay*-kōa-mernt) *adj* additional

bijkomstig (bay-*kom*-sterkh) *adj* additional; subordinate

bijl (bayl) *c* (pl ~en) axe

bijlage (*bay*-laa-ger) *c* (pl ~n) annex; enclosure

bijna (*bay*-naa) *adv* nearly, almost

bijnaam (*bay*-naam) *c* (pl -namen) nickname

bijouterie (bee-zhōō-ter-*ree*) *c* jewellery

*****bijsluiten** (*bay*-slur^ew-tern) *v* enclose

*****bijstaan** (*bay*-staan) *v* assist, aid

bijstand (*bay*-stahnt) *c* assistance

*****bijten** (*bay*-tern) *v* *****bite

bijvoegen (*bay*-vōō-gern) *v* attach

bijvoeglijk naamwoord (bay-*vōōkh*-lerk *naam*-vōart) adjective

bijvoorbeeld (ber-*vōar*-bāylt) *adv* for instance, for example

bijwonen (*bay*-vōa-nern) *v* assist at, attend

bijwoord (*bay*-vōart) *nt* (pl ~en) adverb

bijziend (bay-*zeent*) *adj* short-sighted

bijzonder (bee-*zon*-derr) *adj* special, particular; peculiar; **in het ~ in** particular, specially

bijzonderheid (bee-*zon*-derr-hayt) *c* (pl -heden) detail

bil (bɪl) *c* (pl ~len) buttock

biljart (bɪl-*Yahrt*) *nt* billiards *pl*

billijk (*bɪ*-lerk) *adj* right, fair, reasonable

***binden** (*bɪn*-dern) *v* *bind; tie

binnen (*bɪ*-nern) *prep* within, inside; *adv* inside, indoors; in; indoor; **naar ~** inwards; **van ~** within, inside

binnenband (*bɪ*-ner-bahnt) *c* (pl ~en) inner tube

***binnengaan** (*bɪ*-ner-gaan) *v* enter, *go in

binnenkant (*bɪ*-ner-kahnt) *c* interior, inside

***binnenkomen** (*bɪ*-nern-kōa-mern) *v* enter

binnenkomst (*bɪ*-ner-komst) *c* entrance

binnenkort (bɪ-ner-*kort*) *adv* shortly

binnenlands (*bɪ*-ner-lahnts) *adj* domestic

binnenst (*bɪ*-nerst) *adj* inside; **binnenste buiten** *adv* inside out

***binnenvallen** (*bɪ*-ner-vah-lern) *v* invade

biologie (bee-Yōa-lōa-*gee*) *c* biology

bioscoop (bee-Yoss-*kōap*) *c* (pl -scopen) cinema; pictures; movie theater *Am*, movies *Am*

biscuit (bɪss-*kvee*) *nt* (pl ~s) cookie *nAm*

bisschop (*bɪss*-khop) *c* (pl ~pen) bishop

bitter (*bɪ*-terr) *adj* bitter

blaar (blaar) *c* (pl blaren) blister

blaas (blaass) *c* (pl blazen) bladder; blister

blaasontsteking (*blaass*-ont-stāy-kɪng) *c* (pl ~en) cystitis

blad¹ (blaht) *nt* (pl ~eren, blaren) leaf

blad² (blaht) *nt* (pl ~en) sheet; magazine

bladgoud (*blaht*-khout) *nt* gold leaf

bladzijde (*blaht*-say-der) *c* (pl ~n) page

blaffen (*blah*-fern) *v* bark; bay

blanco (*blahng*-kōa) *adj* blank

blank (blahngk) *adj* white

blankvoren (*blahngk*-fōa-rern) *c* (pl ~s) roach

blauw (blou) *adj* blue

***blazen** (*blaa*-zern) *v* *blow

blazer (*blāy*-zerr) *c* (pl ~s) blazer

bleek (blāyk) *adj* pale

bleken (*blāy*-kern) *v* bleach

blessure (bleh-*sēw*-rer) *c* (pl ~s) injury

blij (blay) *adj* glad; happy, joyful

blijkbaar (*blayk*-baar) *adv* apparently

***blijken** (*blay*-kern) *v* prove; appear

blijspel (*blay*-spehl) *nt* (pl ~en) comedy

***blijven** (*blay*-vern) *v* stay, remain; *keep; **blijvend** lasting; permanent

blik (blɪk) *nt* (pl ~ken) tin, can; *c* look; glimpse, glance; **een ~ *werpen** glance

blikopener (*blɪk*-ōa-per-nerr) *c* (pl ~s) tin-opener, can opener

bliksem (*blɪk*-serm) *c* lightning

blind¹ (blɪnt) *nt* (pl ~en) shutter

blind² (blɪnt) *adj* blind

blindedarm (blɪn-der-*dahrm*) *c* (pl ~en) appendix

blindedarmontsteking (blɪn-der-*dahrm*-ont-stāy-king) *c* (pl ~en) appendicitis

***blinken** (*blɪng*-kern) *v* *shine; **blinkend** bright

blocnote (*blok*-nōat) *c* (pl ~s) writing-pad

bloed (blōōt) *nt* blood

bloedarmoede (blōōt-ahr-mōō-der) *c* anaemia

bloeddruk (blōō-drerk) *c* blood pressure

bloeden (blōō-dern) *v* *bleed

bloeding (blōō-dɪng) *c* (pl ~en) haemorrhage

bloedsomloop (blōōt-som-lōap) *c* circulation

bloedvat (blōōt-faht) *nt* (pl ~en) blood-vessel

bloedvergiftiging (blōōt-ferr-gɪf-ter-gɪng) *c* blood-poisoning

bloem[1] (blōōm) *c* flour

bloem[2] (blōōm) *c* (pl ~en) flower

bloemblad (blōōm-blaht) *nt* (pl ~en) petal

bloembol (blōōm-bol) *c* (pl -len) bulb

bloemenwinkel (blōō-mer-vɪng-kerl) *c* (pl ~s) flower-shop

bloemist (blōō-mɪst) *c* (pl ~en) florist

bloemkool (blōōm-kōal) *c* (pl -kolen) cauliflower

bloemlezing (blōōm-lāy-zɪng) *c* (pl ~en) anthology

bloemperk (blōōm-pehrk) *nt* (pl ~en) flowerbed

blok (blok) *nt* (pl ~ken) block; **blokje** *nt* cube

blokkeren (blo-kāy-rern) *v* block

blond (blont) *adj* fair

blondine (blon-dee-ner) *c* (pl ~s) blonde

bloot (blōat) *adj* bare; naked

blootleggen (blōat-leh-gern) *v* uncover

blootstelling (blōat-steh-lɪng) *c* (pl ~en) exposure

blouse (blōō-zer) *c* (pl ~s) blouse

blozen (blōa-zern) *v* blush

blussen (bler-sern) *v* extinguish

bocht (bokht) *c* (pl ~en) turning, bend; curve, turn

bode (bōa-der) *c* (pl ~n, ~s) messenger

bodem (bōa-derm) *c* (pl ~s) bottom; ground; soil

boef (bōōf) *c* (pl boeven) villain

boei (bōōᵉᵉ) *c* (pl ~en) buoy

boeien (bōōᵉᵉ-ern) *v* fascinate

boek (bōōk) *nt* (pl ~en) book

boeken (bōō-kern) *v* book

boekenstalletje (bōō-ker-stah-ler-tʸer) *nt* (pl ~s) bookstand

boeket (bōō-keht) *nt* (pl ~ten) bouquet

boekhandel (bōōk-hahn-derl) *c* (pl ~s) bookstore

boekhandelaar (bōōk-hahn-der-laar) *c* (pl -laren) bookseller

boekwinkel (bōōk-vɪng-kerl) *c* (pl ~s) bookstore

boel (bōōl) *c* lot

boer (bōōr) *c* (pl ~en) farmer; peasant; knave

boerderij (bōōr-der-ray) *c* (pl ~en) farm; farmhouse

boerin (bōō-rɪn) *c* (pl ~nen) farmer's wife

boete (bōō-ter) *c* (pl ~n, ~s) penalty, fine

boetseren (bōōt-sāy-rern) *v* model

bof (bof) *c* mumps

bok (bok) *c* (pl ~ken) goat

boksen (bok-sern) *v* box

bokswedstrijd (boks-veht-strayt) *c* (pl ~en) boxing match

bol (bol) *c* (pl ~len) bulb; sphere

Boliviaan (bōa-lee-vee-ʸaan) *c* (pl -vianen) Bolivian

Boliviaans (bōa-lee-vee-ʸaans) *adj* Bolivian

Bolivië (bōa-lee-vee-ʸer) Bolivia

bom (bom) *c* (pl ~men) bomb

bombarderen (bom-bahr-dāy-rern) *v* bomb

bon (bon) *c* (pl ~nen) coupon; ticket; voucher

bonbon (bom-*bon*) *c* (pl ~s) chocolate

bond (bont) *c* (pl ~en) league, federation

bondgenoot (*bont*-kher-nōat) *c* (pl -noten) associate

bondgenootschap (*bont*-kher-nōat-skhahp) *nt* (pl ~pen) alliance

bons (bons) *c* (pl bonzen) bump

bont (bont) *adj* gay, colourful; *nt* furs

bontjas (*bon*-tⁿahss) *c* (pl ~sen) fur coat

bontwerker (*bon*-tvehr-kerr) *c* (pl ~s) furrier

bonzen (*bon*-zern) *v* bump

boodschap (*bōat*-skhahp) *c* (pl ~pen) errand; message

boodschappentas (*bōat*-skhah-per-tahss) *c* (pl ~sen) shopping bag

boog (bōakh) *c* (pl bogen) arch; bow

boogvormig (*bōakh*-for-merkh) *adj* arched

boom (bōam) *c* (pl bomen) tree

boomgaard (*bōam*-gaart) *c* (pl ~en) orchard

boomkwekerij (bōam-kvāy-ker-*ray*) *c* (pl ~en) nursery

boon (bōan) *c* (pl bonen) bean

boor (bōar) *c* (pl boren) drill

boord (bōart) *nt/c* (pl ~en) collar; **aan boord** aboard; **van boord *gaan** disembark

boordeknoopje (*bōar*-der-knōa-pⁿer) *nt* (pl ~s) collar stud

boos (bōass) *adj* cross

boosaardig (bōa-*zaar*-derkh) *adj* malicious, vicious

boosheid (*bōass*-hayt) *c* anger, temper

boot (bōat) *c* (pl boten) boat

bootje (*bōa*-tⁿer) *nt* (pl ~s) dinghy

boottocht (*bōa*-tokht) *c* (pl ~en) cruise

bord (bort) *nt* (pl ~en) dish, plate; board

bordeel (bor-*dāyl*) *nt* (pl -delen) brothel

borduren (bor-*dēw*-rern) *v* embroider

borduurwerk (bor-*dēwr*-vehrk) *nt* (pl ~en) embroidery

boren (*bōa*-rern) *v* drill, bore

borg (borkh) *c* (pl ~en) guarantor

borgsom (*borkh*-som) *c* (pl ~men) bail

borrel (*boa*-rerl) *c* (pl ~s) drink

borrelhapje (*bo*-rerl-hahp-ⁿer) *nt* (pl ~s) appetizer

borst (borst) *c* (pl ~en) chest; breast, bosom

borstel (*bor*-sterl) *c* (pl ~s) brush

borstelen (*bor*-ster-lern) *v* brush

borstkas (*borst*-kahss) *c* (pl ~sen) chest

bos (boss) *nt* (pl ~sen) forest, wood; *c* bunch

bosje (*bo*-sher) *nt* (pl ~s) grove

boswachter (*boss*-vahkh-terr) *c* (pl ~s) forester

bot¹ (bot) *adj* dull, blunt

bot² (bot) *nt* (pl ~ten) bone

boter (*bōa*-terr) *c* butter

boterham (*bōa*-terr-hahm) *c* (pl ~men) sandwich

botsen (*bot*-sern) *v* bump; collide, crash

botsing (*bot*-sɪng) *c* (pl ~en) collision, crash

bougie (bōō-*zhee*) *c* (pl ~s) sparking-plug

bout (bout) *c* (pl ~en) bolt

boutique (bōō-*teek*) *c* (pl ~s) boutique

bouw (bou) *c* construction

bouwen (*bou*-ern) *v* *build; construct

bouwkunde (*bou*-kern-der) *c* architecture

bouwvallig (bou-*vah*-lerkh) *adj* dilapidated

boven (*bōa*-vern) *prep* above, over;

adv above; upstairs; **naar ~** upwards, up; upstairs

bovendek (bōā-vern-dehk) *nt* main deck

bovendien (bōa-vern-*deen*) *adv* furthermore, moreover, besides

bovenkant (bōā-verng-kahnt) *c* (pl ~en) top side, top

bovenop (bōā-vern-*op*) *prep* on top of

bovenst (bōā-verst) *adj* upper, top

braaf (braaf) *adj* good

braak (braak) *adj* waste

braam (braam) *c* (pl bramen) blackberry

*braden (braa-dern) *v* fry; roast

braken (braa-kern) *v* vomit

brand (brahnt) *c* (pl ~en) fire

brandalarm (brahnt-aa-lahrm) *nt* fire-alarm

brandblusapparaat (brahnt-blerss-ah-paa-raat) *nt* (pl -raten) fire-extinguisher

branden (brahn-dern) *v* *burn

brandkast (brahnt-kahst) *c* (pl ~en) safe

brandmerk (brahnt-mehrk) *nt* (pl ~en) brand

brandpunt (brahnt-pernt) *nt* (pl ~en) focus

brandspiritus (brahnt-spee-ree-terss) *c* methylated spirits

brandstof (brahnt-stof) *c* (pl ~fen) fuel

brandtrap (brahn-trahp) *c* (pl ~pen) fire-escape

brandvrij (brahnt-fray) *adj* fireproof

brandweer (brahn-tvāyr) *c* fire-brigade

brandwond (brahn-tvont) *c* (pl ~en) burn

brasem (braa-serm) *c* (pl ~s) bream

Braziliaan (braa-zee-lee-*Y*aan) *c* (pl -lianen) Brazilian

Braziliaans (braa-zee-lee-*Y*aans) *adj* Brazilian

Brazilië (braa-*zee*-lee-*Y*er) Brazil

breed (brāyt) *adj* broad, wide

breedte (brāy-ter) *c* (pl ~n, ~s) breadth, width

breedtegraad (brāy-ter-graat) *c* (pl -graden) latitude

breekbaar (brāyk-baar) *adj* fragile

breekijzer (brāy-kay-zerr) *nt* (pl ~s) crowbar

breien (bray-ern) *v* *knit

*breken (brāy-kern) *v* *break; *burst, crack; fracture

*brengen (breh-ngern) *v* *bring; *take

bres (brehss) *c* (pl ~sen) gap, breach

bretels (brer-*tehls*) *pl* braces *pl*; suspenders *plAm*

breuk (brurk) *c* (pl ~en) break; fracture; hernia

brief (breef) *c* (pl brieven) letter; **aangetekende ~** registered letter

briefkaart (breef-kaart) *c* (pl ~en) card, postcard

briefopener (breef-ōā-per-nerr) *c* (pl ~s) paper-knife

briefpapier (breef-paa-peer) *nt* notepaper

briefwisseling (breef-vi-ser-ling) *c* correspondence

bries (breess) *c* breeze

brievenbus (bree-ver-berss) *c* (pl ~sen) letter-box, pillar-box; mailbox *nAm*

bril (bril) *c* (pl ~len) spectacles, glasses

briljant (bril-*Y*ahnt) *adj* brilliant

Brit (brit) *c* (pl ~ten) Briton

Brits (brits) *adj* British

broche (bro-sher) *c* (pl ~s) brooch

brochure (bro-*shēw*-rer) *c* (pl ~s) brochure

broeder (brōō-derr) *c* (pl ~s) brother

broederschap (brōō-derr-skhahp) *c*

fraternity
broeikas (*brōō^{ee}*-kahss) *c* (pl ~sen) greenhouse
broek (brōōk) *c* (pl ~en) trousers *pl*, slacks *pl*; pants *plAm*; **korte ~** shorts *pl*
broekpak (*brōōk*-pahk) *nt* (pl ~ken) pant-suit
broer (brōōr) *c* (pl ~s) brother
brok (brok) *nt* (pl ~ken) morsel; lump
bromfiets (*brom*-feets) *c* (pl ~en) moped
brommer (*bro*-merr) *c* (pl ~s) motorbike *nAm*
bron (bron) *c* (pl ~nen) well; fountain, source, spring; **geneeskrachtige ~** spa
bronchitis (brong-*khee*-terss) *c* bronchitis
brons (brons) *nt* bronze
bronzen (*bron*-zern) *adj* bronze
brood (brōāt) *nt* (pl broden) bread; loaf
broodje (*brōā*-t^{y}er) *nt* (pl ~s) roll, bun
broos (brōāss) *adj* fragile
brouwen (*brou*-ern) *v* brew
brouwerij (brou-er-*ray*) *c* (pl ~en) brewery
brug (brerkh) *c* (pl ~gen) bridge
bruid (brur^{ew}t) *c* (pl ~en) bride
bruidegom (*brur^{ew}*-der-gom) *c* (pl ~s) bridegroom
bruikbaar (*brur^{ew}k*-baar) *adj* usable; useful
bruiloft (*brur^{ew}*-loft) *c* (pl ~en) wedding
bruin (brur^{ew}n) *adj* brown
brullen (*brer*-lern) *v* roar
brunette (brēw-*neh*-ter) *c* (pl ~s) brunette
brutaal (brēw-*taal*) *adj* bold, impertinent, insolent
bruto (*brōō*-tōā) *adj* gross
budget (ber-*jeht*) *nt* (pl ~ten, ~s) budget
buffet (bēw-*feht*) *nt* (pl ~ten) buffet
bui (bur^{ew}) *c* (pl ~en) shower; spirit
buidel (*bur^{ew}*-derl) *c* (pl ~s) pouch
buigbaar (*bur^{ew}kh*-baar) *adj* flexible
***buigen** (*bur^{ew}*-gern) *v* *bend; bow
buigzaam (*bur^{ew}kh*-saam) *adj* supple
buik (bur^{ew}k) *c* (pl ~en) belly
buikpijn (*bur^{ew}k*-payn) *c* stomachache
buis (bur^{ew}ss) *c* (pl buizen) tube
buiten (*bur^{ew}*-tern) *prep* outside, out of; *adv* out; outside, outdoors; **naar ~** outwards
buitengewoon (*bur^{ew}*-ter-ger-vōān) *adj* extraordinary, exceptional
buitenhuis (*bur^{ew}*-ter-hur^{ew}ss) *nt* (pl -huizen) cottage
buitenkant (*bur^{ew}*-ter-kahnt) *c* (pl ~en) outside, exterior
in het buitenland (in ert *bur^{ew}*-tern-lahnt) abroad
buitenlander (*bur^{ew}*-ter-lahn-derr) *c* (pl ~s) alien, foreigner
buitenlands (*bur^{ew}*-ter-lahnts) *adj* alien, foreign
buitensporig (bur^{ew}-ter-*spōā*-rerkh) *adj* excessive
buitenwijk (*bur^{ew}*-ter-vayk) *c* (pl ~en) suburb; outskirts *pl*
zich bukken (*ber*-kern) *bend down
Bulgaar (berl-*gaar*) *c* (pl -garen) Bulgarian
Bulgaars (berl-*gaars*) *adj* Bulgarian
Bulgarije (berl-gaa-*ray*-er) Bulgaria
bult (berlt) *c* (pl ~en) lump
bumper (*berm*-perr) *c* (pl ~s) bumper, fender
bundel (*bern*-derl) *c* (pl ~s) bundle
bundelen (*bern*-der-lern) *v* bundle
burcht (berrkht) *c* (pl ~en) stronghold
bureau (bēw-*rōā*) *nt* (pl ~s) agency, office; bureau, desk; **~ voor ge-**

vonden voorwerpen lost property office

bureaucratie (bew-rōa-kraa-tsee) c bureaucracy

burgemeester (berr-ger-*mayss*-terr) c (pl ~s) mayor

burger (*berr*-gerr) c (pl ~s) citizen; civilian; **burger-** civilian, civic

burgerlijk (*berr*-gerr-lerk) adj bourgeois, middle-class; ~ **recht** civil law

bus (berss) c (pl ~sen) coach, bus; tin, canister

buste (*bew*-ster) c (pl ~s, ~n) bust

bustehouder (*bew*-ster-hou-derr) c (pl ~s) brassiere, bra

buur (bewr) c (pl buren) neighbour

buurman (*bewr*-mahn) c neighbour

buurt (bewrt) c (pl ~en) neighbourhood, vicinity

C

cabaret (kaa-baa-*reht*) nt (pl ~s) cabaret

cabine (kaa-*bee*-ner) c (pl ~s) cabin

cadeau (kaa-*dōa*) nt (pl ~s) gift, present

café (kah-*fay*) nt (pl ~s) café; public house, pub

cafetaria (kah-fer-*taa*-ree-ʸaa) c (pl ~s) cafeteria

caissière (kah-*shai*-rer) c (pl ~s) cashier

cake (kayk) c (pl ~s) cake

calcium (*kahl*-see-ʸerm) nt calcium

calorie (kah-lōa-*ree*) c (pl ~ën) calorie

calvinisme (kahl-vee-*niss*-mer) nt Calvinism

camee (kaa-*may*) c (pl ~ën) cameo

campagne (kahm-*pah*-ñer) c (pl ~s) campaign

camping (kehm-ping) c (pl ~s) camping site, camping

Canada (*kaa*-naa-daa) Canada

Canadees (kaa-naa-*dayss*) adj Canadian

capabel (kaa-*paa*-berl) adj able

capaciteit (kaa-paa-see-*tayt*) c (pl ~en) capacity

cape (kayp) c (pl ~s) cape

capitulatie (kah-pee-tew-*laa*-tsee) c (pl ~s) capitulation

capsule (kahp-*sew*-ler) c (pl ~s) capsule

caravan (*keh*-rer-vern) c (pl ~s) caravan

carbonpapier (kahr-*bon*-paa-peer) nt carbon paper

carburateur (kahr-bew-raa-*turr*) c (pl ~s) carburettor

carillon (kaa-ril-*ʸon*) nt (pl ~s) chimes pl

carnaval (*kahr*-naa-vahl) nt carnival

carrière (kah-ree-*ʸai*-rer) c (pl ~s) career

carrosserie (kah-ro-ser-*ree*) c (pl ~ën) coachwork; motor body Am

carter (*kahr*-terr) nt crankcase

casino (kaa-*zee*-nōa) nt (pl ~'s) casino

catacombe (kah-tah-*kom*-ber) c (pl ~n) catacomb

catalogus (kah-*taa*-lōa-gerss) c (pl -gussen, -gi) catalogue

catarre (kaa-*tahr*) c catarrh

catastrofe (kaa-taa-*straw*-fer) c (pl ~s) catastrophe, disaster

categorie (kaa-ter-gōa-*ree*) c (pl ~ën) category

cavia (*kaa*-vee-ʸaa) c (pl ~'s) guinea-pig

cel (sehl) c (pl ~len) cell

celibaat (*say*-lee-*baat*) nt celibacy

cellofaan (seh-loa-*faan*) nt cellophane

celsius (*sehl*-see-ʸerss) centigrade

cement (ser-*mehnt*) nt cement

censuur (sehn-*zewr*) *c* censorship

centimeter (*sehn*-tee-*may*-terr) *c* (pl ~s) centimetre; tape-measure

centraal (sehn-*traal*) *adj* central; ~ **station** central station; **centrale verwarming** central heating

centraliseren (sehn-traa-lee-*zay*-rern) *v* centralize

centrifuge (sehn-tree-*few*-zher) *c* (pl ~s) dryer

centrum (*sehn*-trerm) *nt* (pl centra) centre

ceramiek (*say*-raa-*meek*) *c* ceramics *pl*

ceremonie (*say*-rer-*moa*-nee) *c* (pl -niën, -nies) ceremony

certificaat (*sehr*-tee-fee-*kaat*) *nt* (pl -caten) certificate

chalet (shaa-*leht*) *nt* (pl ~s) chalet

champagne (shahm-*pah*-ñer) *c* (pl ~s) champagne

champignon (shahm-pee-*ñon*) *c* (pl ~s) mushroom

chantage (shahn-*taa*-zher) *c* blackmail

chanteren (shahn-*tay*-rern) *v* blackmail

chaos (*khaa*-oss) *c* chaos

chaotisch (khaa-*oa*-teess) *adj* chaotic

charlatan (*shahr*-laa-tahn) *c* (pl ~s) quack

charmant (shahr-*mahnt*) *adj* charming

charme (*shahr*-mer) *c* (pl ~s) charm; glamour

chartervlucht (*chahr*-terr-vlerkht) *c* (pl ~en) charter flight

chassis (shah-*see*) *nt* (pl ~) chassis

chauffeur (shoa-*fūrr*) *c* (pl ~s) driver, chauffeur

chef (shehf) *c* (pl ~s) boss, manager, chief

chef-kok (shehf-*kok*) *c* (pl ~s) chef

chemie (khay-*mee*) *c* chemistry

chemisch (*khay*-meess) *adj* chemical

cheque (shehk) *c* (pl ~s) cheque; check *nAm*

chequeboekje (shehk-*boo*-kᵞer) *nt* (pl ~s) cheque-book; check-book *nAm*

chic (sheek) *adj* smart

Chileen (shee-*layn*) *c* (pl -lenen) Chilean

Chileens (shee-*layns*) *adj* Chilean

Chili (*shee*-lee) Chile

China (*shee*-naa) China

Chinees (shee-*nayss*) *adj* Chinese

chirurg (shee-*rerrkh*) *c* (pl ~en) surgeon

chloor (khloar) *nt* chlorine

chocola (shoa-koa-*laa*) *c* chocolate

chocolademelk (shoa-koa-*laa*-der-mehlk) *c* chocolate

christelijk (*kriss*-ter-lerk) *adj* Christian

christen (*kriss*-tern) *c* (pl ~en) Christian

Christus (*kriss*-terss) Christ

chronisch (*khroa*-neess) *adj* chronic

chronologisch (khroa-*noa*-*loa*-geess) *adj* chronological

chroom (khroam) *nt* chromium

cijfer (*say*-ferr) *nt* (pl ~s) number, figure; digit; mark

cilinder (see-*lin*-derr) *c* (pl ~s) cylinder

cilinderkop (see-*lin*-derr-kop) *c* (pl ~pen) cylinder head

cipier (see-*peer*) *c* (pl ~s) jailer

circa (*sir*-kaa) *adv* approximately

circulatie (sir-kew-*laa*-tsee) *c* circulation

circus (*sir*-kerss) *nt* (pl ~sen) circus

cirkel (*sir*-kerl) *c* (pl ~s) circle

citaat (see-*taat*) *nt* (pl citaten) quotation

citeren (see-*tay*-rern) *v* quote

citroen (see-*troon*) *c* (pl ~en) lemon

civiel (see-*veel*) *adj* civil

clausule (klou-*sew*-ler) *c* (pl ~s) clause

clavecimbel (klaa-ver-*sim*-berl) *c* (pl ~s) harpsichord

claxon (*klahk*-son) *c* (pl ~s) horn, hooter

claxonneren (klahk-so-*nay*-rern) *v* hoot; toot *vAm*, honk *vAm*

clementie (klay-*mehn*-tsee) *c* mercy

cliënt (klee-*Yehnt*) *c* (pl ~en) customer, client

closetpapier (kloa-*zeht*-pah-peer) *nt* toilet-paper

cocaïne (koa-kaa-*ee*-ner) *c* cocaine

code (*koa*-der) *c* (pl ~s) code

coffeïne (ko-fay-*ee*-ner) *c* caffeine

coffeïnevrij (ko-fay-*ee*-ner-vray) *adj* decaffeinated

cognac (ko-*ñahk*) *c* cognac

coiffure (kvah-*few*-rer) *c* (pl ~s) hair-do

colbert (kol-*bair*) *c* (pl ~s) jacket

collectant (ko-lehk-*tahnt*) *c* (pl ~en) collector

collecteren (ko-lehk-*tay*-rern) *v* collect

collectie (ko-*lehk*-see) *c* (pl ~s) collection

collectief (ko-lehk-*teef*) *adj* collective

collega (ko-*lay*-gaa) *c* (pl ~'s) colleague

college (ko-*lay*-zher) *nt* (pl ~s) lecture

Colombia (koa-*lom*-bee-Yaa) Colombia

Colombiaan (koa-lom-bee-*Yaan*) *c* (pl -bianen) Colombian

Colombiaans (koa-lom-bee-*Yaans*) *adj* Colombian

coma (*koa*-maa) *nt* coma

combinatie (kom-bee-*naa*-tsee) *c* (pl ~s) combination

combineren (kom-bee-*nay*-rern) *v* combine

comfortabel (kom-for-*taa*-berl) *adj* comfortable

comité (ko-mee-*tay*) *nt* (pl ~s) committee

commentaar (ko-mehn-*taar*) *nt* (pl -taren) comment

commercieel (ko-mehr-*shayl*) *adj* commercial

commissie (ko-*mi*-see) *c* (pl ~s) committee; commission

commode (ko-*moa*-der) *c* (pl ~s) bureau *nAm*

commune (ko-*mew*-ner) *c* (pl ~s) commune

communicatie (ko-mew-nee-*kaa*-tsee) *c* communication

communiqué (ko-mew-nee-*kay*) *nt* (pl ~s) communiqué

communisme (ko-mew-*niss*-mer) *nt* communism

compact (kom-*pahkt*) *adj* compact

compact disk (*kom*-pahkt disk) *c* compact disc; ~ **speler** CD-player

compagnon (kom-pah-*ñon*) *c* (pl ~s) partner

compensatie (kom-pehn-*zaa*-tsee) *c* (pl ~s) compensation

compenseren (kom-pehn-*zay*-rern) *v* compensate

compleet (kom-*playt*) *adj* complete

compliment (kom-plee-*mehnt*) *nt* (pl ~en) compliment

componist (kom-poa-*nist*) *c* (pl ~en) composer

compositie (kom-poa-*zee*-tsee) *c* (pl ~s) composition

compromis (kom-proa-*mee*) *nt* (pl ~sen) compromise

computer (kom-*pjoe*-terr) *nt* computer

concentratie (kon-sehn-*traa*-tsee) *c* (pl ~s) concentration

concentreren (kon-sehn-*tray*-rern) *v* concentrate

conceptie (kon-*sehp*-see) *c* conception

concert (kon-*sehrt*) *nt* (pl ~en) concert

concertzaal (kon-*sehrt*-saal) *c* (pl -zalen) concert hall

concessie (kon-*seh*-see) *c* (pl ~s) concession

concierge (kon-*shehr*-zheh) *c* (pl ~s) janitor; caretaker, concierge

conclusie (kong-*klew*-zee) *c* (pl ~s) conclusion

concreet (kong-*krayt*) *adj* concrete

concurrent (kong-kew-*rehnt*) *c* (pl ~en) competitor; rival

concurrentie (kong-kew-*rehn*-tsee) *c* competition; rivalry

conditie (kon-*dee*-tsee) *c* (pl ~s) condition

conditioner (kon-*disj*-er-nerr) *nt* conditioner

condoom (kon-*doom*) *nt* condom

conducteur (kon-derk-*türr*) *c* (pl ~s) conductor; ticket collector

conferencier (kon-fer-rahng-*shay*) *c* (pl ~s) entertainer

conferentie (kon-fer-*rehn*-see) *c* (pl ~s) conference

conflict (kon-*flikt*) *nt* (pl ~en) conflict

congregatie (kong-gray-*gaa*-tsee) *c* (pl ~s) congregation

congres (kong-*grehss*) *nt* (pl ~sen) congress

consequentie (kon-ser-*kvehn*-see) *c* (pl ~s) consequence

conservatief (kon-zerr-vaa-*teef*) *adj* conservative

conserven (kon-*sehr*-vern) *pl* tinned food

consideratie (kon-see-der-*raa*-tsee) *c* consideration

constant (kon-*stahnt*) *adj* even

constateren (koan-staa-*tay*-rern) *v* note, ascertain; diagnose

constipatie (kon-stee-*paa*-tsee) *c* constipation

constructie (kon-*strerk*-see) *c* (pl ~s) construction

construeren (kon-strew^{oo}-*ay*-rern) *v* construct

consulaat (kon-zew-*laat*) *nt* (pl -laten) consulate

consult (kon-*zerlt*) *nt* (pl ~en) consultation

consultatiebureau (kon-zerl-*taa*-tsee-bew-roa) *nt* (pl ~s) health centre

consument (kon-zew-*mehnt*) *c* (pl ~en) consumer

contact (kon-*tahkt*) *nt* (pl ~en) contact; touch

contactlenzen (kon-*tahkt*-lehn-zern) *pl* contact lenses

contanten (kon-*tahn*-tern) *pl* cash

continent (kon-tee-*nehnt*) *nt* (pl ~en) continent

continentaal (kon-tee-nehn-*taal*) *adj* continental

contra (*kon*-traa) *prep* versus

contract (kon-*trahkt*) *nt* (pl ~en) agreement, contract

contrast (kon-*trahst*) *nt* (pl ~en) contrast

controle (kon-*traw*-ler) *c* (pl ~s) control; supervision, inspection

controleren (kon-troa-*lay*-rern) *v* control, check

controlestrook (kon-*traw*-ler-stroak) *c* (-stroken) counterfoil, stub

controversieel (kon-troa-vehr-*zhayl*) *adj* controversial

conversatie (kon-verr-*zaa*-tsee) *c* (pl ~s) conversation

coöperatie (koa-oa-per-*raa*-tsee) *c* (pl ~s) co-operative

coöperatief (koa-oa-per-raa-*teef*) *adj* co-operative

coördinatie (koa-or-dee-*naa*-tsee) *c* co-ordination

coördineren (koa-or-dee-*nay*-rern) *v* co-ordinate

corpulent (kor-pew-*lehnt*) *adj* corpulent, stout

correct (ko-*rehkt*) *adj* correct

correctie (ko-*rehk*-see) *c* (pl ~s) correction

correspondent (ko-rehss-pon-*dehnt*) *c*

(pl ~en) correspondent

correspondentie (ko-rehss-pon-*dehn*-see) *c* correspondence

corresponderen (ko-rehss-pon-*dāy*-rern) *v* correspond

corrigeren (ko-ree-*zhāy*-rern) *v* correct

corrupt (ko-*rerpt*) *adj* corrupt

couchette (kōō-*sheh*-ter) *c* (pl ~s) berth

coupé (kōō-*pāy*) *c* (pl ~s) compartment; ~ **voor rokers** smoking-compartment

couplet (kōō-*pleht*) *nt* (pl ~ten) stanza

coupon (kōō-*pon*) *c* (pl ~s) coupon

crèche (krehsh) *c* (pl ~s) nursery

crediteren (krāy-dee-*tāy*-rern) *v* credit

creëren (krāy-*āy*-rern) *v* create

crematie (krāy-*maa*-tsee) *c* (pl ~s) cremation

crème (kraim) *c* (pl ~s) cream; **vochtinbrengende** ~ moisturizing cream

cremeren (krāy-*māy*-rern) *v* cremate

criminaliteit (kree-mee-naa-lee-*tayt*) *c* criminality

crimineel (kree-mee-*nāyl*) *adj* criminal

crisis (*kree*-serss) *c* (pl -ses) crisis

criticus (*kree*-tee-kerss) *c* (pl -ci) critic

croquant (krōā-*kahnt*) *adj* crisp

Cuba (*kew*-baa) Cuba

Cubaan (kew-*baan*) *c* (pl -banen) Cuban

Cubaans (kew-*baans*) *adj* Cuban

cultuur (kerl-*tewr*) *c* (pl -turen) culture

cursiefschrift (kerr-*zeef*-skhrıft) *nt* italics *pl*

cursus (*kerr*-zerss) *c* (pl ~sen) course

cyclus (*see*-klerss) *c* (pl ~sen) cycle

D

daad (daat) *c* (pl daden) deed, act

daar (daar) *adv* there

daarheen (daar-*hāyn*) *adv* there

daarom (*daa*-rom) *conj* therefore

dadel (*daa*-derl) *c* (pl ~s) date

dadelijk (*daa*-der-lerk) *adv* at once, immediately; presently

dag (dahkh) *c* (pl ~en) day; **dag!** hello!; good-bye!; **per** ~ per day

dagblad (*dahkh*-blaht) *nt* (pl ~en) daily

dagboek (*dahkh*-bōōk) *nt* (pl ~en) diary

dagelijks (*daa*-ger-lerks) *adj* daily

dageraad (*daa*-ger-raat) *c* daybreak, dawn

daglicht (*dahkh*-lıkht) *nt* daylight

dagvaarding (*dahkh*-vaar-dıng) *c* (pl ~en) summons

dak (dahk) *nt* (pl ~en) roof

dakpan (*dahk*-pahn) *c* (pl ~nen) tile

dal (dahl) *nt* (pl ~en) valley

dalen (*daa*-lern) *v* descend

dam (dahm) *c* (pl ~men) dam; dike

dambord (*dahm*-bort) *nt* (pl ~en) draught-board

dame (*daa*-mer) *c* (pl ~s) lady

damestoilet (*daa*-merss-tvah-leht) *nt* (pl ~ten) powder-room, ladies' room

damp (dahmp) *c* (pl ~en) vapour

damspel (*dahm*-spehl) *nt* draughts; checkers *plAm*

dan (dahn) *adv* then; *conj* than; **nu en** ~ occasionally

dankbaar (*dahngk*-baar) *adj* grateful, thankful

dankbaarheid (*dahngk*-baar-hayt) *c* gratitude

danken (*dahng*-kern) *v* thank; **dank u**

thank you; **te ~ *hebben aan** owe

dans (dahns) c (pl ~en) dance

dansen (dahn-sern) v dance

danszaal (dahn-saal) c (pl -zalen) ballroom

dapper (dah-perr) adj brave, courageous

dapperheid (dah-perr-hayt) c courage

darm (dahrm) c (pl ~en) gut, intestine; **darmen** bowels pl

das (dahss) c (pl ~sen) necktie, tie; scarf

dat (daht) pron which; conj that

datum (daa-term) c (pl data) date

dauw (dou) c dew

de (der) art the art

debat (der-baht) nt (pl ~ten) discussion, debate

debatteren (dāy-bah-tāy-rern) v argue

debet (dāy-beht) nt debit

december (dāy-sehm-berr) December

deeg (dāykh) nt dough

deel (dāyl) nt (pl delen) part; share; volume

*deelnemen (dāyl-nāy-mern) v participate

deelnemer (dāyl-nāy-merr) c (pl ~s) participant

deels (dāyls) adv partly

Deen (dāyn) c (pl Denen) Dane

Deens (dāyns) adj Danish

defect[1] (der-fehkt) adj defective, faulty

defect[2] (der-fehkt) nt (pl ~en) fault

defensie (dāy-fehn-zee) c defence

definiëren (dāy-fi-ni-āy-rern) v define

definitie (dāy-fee-nee-tsee) c (pl ~s) definition

degelijk (dāy-ger-lerk) adj thorough; sound

dek (dehk) nt deck

deken (dāy-kern) c (pl ~s) blanket

dekhut (dehk-hert) c (pl ~ten) deck cabin

deksel (dehk-serl) nt (pl ~s) lid; cover, top

dekzeil (dehk-sayl) nt (pl ~en) tarpaulin

delegatie (dāy-ler-gaa-tsee) c (pl ~s) delegation

delen (dāy-lern) v divide; share

delfstof (dehlf-stof) c (pl ~fen) mineral

delicatessen (dāy-lee-kaa-teh-sern) pl delicatessen

delicatessenwinkel (dāy-lee-kaa-teh-ser-ving-kerl) c (pl ~s) delicatessen

delikaat (dāy-lee-kaat) adj delicate

deling (dāy-ling) c (pl ~en) division

delinquent (dāy-ling-kvehnt) c (pl ~en) criminal

*delven (dehl-vern) v *dig

democratie (dāy-mōa-kraa-tsee) c (pl ~ën) democracy

democratisch (dāy-mōa-kraa-teess) adj democratic

demonstratie (dāy-mon-straa-tsee) c (pl ~s) demonstration

demonstreren (dāy-mon-strāy-rern) v demonstrate

den (dehn) c (pl ~nen) fir-tree

Denemarken (dāy-ner-mahr-kern) Denmark

denkbeeld (dehngk-bāyld) nt (pl ~en) idea

denkbeeldig (dehngk-bāyl-derkh) adj imaginary

*denken (dehng-kern) v *think; guess, reckon; **~ aan** *think of

denker (dehng-kerr) c (pl ~s) thinker

denneboom (deh-ner-bōam) c (pl -bomen) fir-tree

deodorant (dāy-yōa-dōa-rahnt) c deodorant

departement (dāy-pahr-ter-mehnt) nt (pl ~en) department

deponeren (dāy-pōa-nāy-rern) v bank

depressie (dāy-preh-see) c (pl ~s) depression

deprimeren (dāy-pree-*māy*-rern) *v* depress

derde (*dehr*-der) *num* third

dergelijk (*dehr*-ger-lerk) *adj* such; similar

dermate (*dehr*-maa-ter) *adv* so

dertien (*dehr*-teen) *num* thirteen

dertiende (*dehr*-teen-der) *num* thirteenth

dertig (*dehr*-terkh) *num* thirty

dertigste (*dehr*-terkh-ster) *num* thirtieth

deserteren (dāy-zehr-*tāy*-rern) *v* desert

deskundig (dehss-*kern*-derkh) *adj* expert

deskundige (dehss-*kern*-der-ger) *c* (pl ~n) expert

dessert (deh-*sair*) *nt* (pl ~s) dessert

detail (dāy-*tigh*) *nt* (pl ~s) detail

detailhandel (dāy-*tigh*-hahn-derl) *c* retail trade

detaillist (dāy-tah-*Yist*) *c* (pl ~en) retailer

detectiveroman (dāy-*tehk*-tıf-rōa-mahn) *c* (pl ~s) detective story

deugd (dūrkht) *c* (pl ~en) virtue

deugniet (*dūrkh*-neet) *c* (pl ~en) rascal

deuk (dūrk) *c* (pl ~en) dent

deur (dūrr) *c* (pl ~en) door

deurbel (*dūrr*-behl) *c* (pl ~len) doorbell

deurwaarder (*dūrr*-vaar-derr) *c* (pl ~s) bailiff

devaluatie (dāy-vaa-lēw-*vaa*-tsee) *c* (pl ~s) devaluation

devalueren (dāy-vaa-lēw-*vāy*-rern) *v* devalue

devies (der-*veess*) *nt* (pl deviezen) motto

deze (*dāy*-zer) *pron* this; these

dia (*dee*-Yaa) *c* (pl ~'s) slide

diabetes (dee-Yaa-*bāy*-terss) *c* diabetes

diabeticus (dee-Yaa-*bāy*-tee-kerss) *c* (pl -ci) diabetic

diagnose (dee-Yahkh-*nōā*-zer) *c* (pl ~n, ~s) diagnosis; **een ~ stellen** diagnose

diagonaal[1] (dee-Yaa-gōā-*naal*) *adj* diagonal

diagonaal[2] (dee-Yaa-gōā-*naal*) *c* (pl -nalen) diagonal

dialect (dee-Yaa-*lehkt*) *nt* (pl ~en) dialect

diamant (dee-Yaa-*mahnt*) *c* (pl ~en) diamond

diarree (dee-Yah-*rāy*) *c* diarrhoea

dicht (dıkht) *adj* dense; thick; closed, shut

dichtbevolkt (dıkht-ber-*volkt*) *adj* populous

dichtbij (dıkht-*bay*) *adj* near

dichtdraaien (*dıkh*-draa^ee-ern) *v* turn off

dichter (*dıkh*-terr) *c* (pl ~s) poet

dichtkunst (*dıkht*-kernst) *c* poetry

***dichtslaan** (*dıkht*-slaan) *v* slam

dictaat (dık-*taat*) *nt* (pl -taten) dictation

dictafoon (dık-taa-*fōān*) *c* (pl ~s) dictaphone

dictator (dık-*taa*-tor) *c* (pl ~s) dictator

dictee (dık-*tāy*) *nt* (pl ~s) dictation

dicteren (dık-*tāy*-rern) *v* dictate

die (dee) *pron* that; those; who

dieet (dee-*Yāyt*) *nt* diet

dief (deef) *c* (pl dieven) robber, thief

diefstal (*deef*-stahl) *c* (pl ~len) robbery, theft

dienblad (*deen*-blaht) *nt* (pl ~en) tray

dienen (*dee*-nern) *v* serve

dienst (deenst) *c* (pl ~en) service; **in ~ *nemen** engage

dienstplichtige (deenst-*plıkh*-ter-ger) *c* (pl ~n) conscript

dienstregeling (*deenst*-rāy-ger-lıng) *c* (pl ~en) schedule, timetable

diep (deep) *adj* deep; low

diepte (*deep*-ter) *c* (pl ~n, ~s) depth

diepvrieskast (*deep*-freess-kahst) *c* (pl ~en) deep-freeze

diepzinnig (deep-*sɪ*-nerkh) *adj* profound

dier (deer) *nt* (pl ~en) animal

dierbaar (*deer*-baar) *adj* dear; precious

dierenarts (*dee*-rern-ahrts) *c* (pl ~en) veterinary surgeon

dierenriem (*dee*-rer-reem) *c* zodiac

dierentuin (*dee*-rer-tur^ew n) *c* (pl ~en) zoological gardens; zoo

diesel (*dee*-serl) *c* diesel

difterie (dɪf-ter-*ree*) *c* diphtheria

digitaal (die-gie-*taal*) *adj* digital

dij (day) *c* (pl ~en) thigh

dijk (dayk) *c* (pl ~en) dike; dam

dik (dɪk) *adj* corpulent; thick; fat, stout, big

dikte (*dɪk*-ter) *c* (pl ~n, ~s) thickness; fatness

dikwijls (*dɪk*-verls) *adv* frequently, often

ding (dɪng) *nt* (pl ~en) thing

dinsdag (*dɪns*-dahkh) *c* Tuesday

diploma (dee-*plōa*-maa) *nt* (pl ~'s) certificate, diploma; **een ~ behalen** graduate

diplomaat (dee-plōa-*maat*) *c* (pl -maten) diplomat

direct (dee-*rehkt*) *adj* direct; *adv* straight away

directeur (dee-rerk-*tūrr*) *c* (pl ~en, ~s) executive, manager, director; headmaster, principal

directie (dee-*rehk*-see) *c* (pl ~s) management

dirigent (dee-ree-*gehnt*) *c* (pl ~en) conductor

dirigeren (dee-ree-*gāy*-rern) *v* conduct

disconto (dɪss-kon-*tōa*) *nt* (pl ~'s) bank-rate

discreet (dɪss-*krāyt*) *adj* modest

discussie (dɪss-*ker*-see) *c* (pl ~s) discussion, argument

discussiëren (dɪss-ker-*shāy*-rern) *v* discuss; argue

distel (*dɪss*-terl) *c* (pl ~s) thistle

district (dɪss-*trɪkt*) *nt* (pl ~en) district

dit (dɪt) *pron* this

divan (*dee*-vahn) *c* (pl ~s) couch

docent (dōa-*sehnt*) *c* (pl ~en) teacher

doch (dokh) *conj* but

dochter (*dokh*-terr) *c* (pl ~s) daughter

doctor (*dok*-tor) *c* (pl ~en, ~s) doctor

document (dōa-kē̄w-*mehnt*) *nt* (pl ~en) document

dodelijk (*dōa*-der-lerk) *adj* mortal, fatal

doden (*dōa*-dern) *v* kill

doek (dōok) *c* (pl ~en) cloth; *nt* curtain

doel (dōol) *nt* (pl ~en) objective, aim, purpose; object, goal, design, target

doelman (*dōol*-mahn) *c* (pl ~nen) goalkeeper

doelmatig (dōol-*maa*-terkh) *adj* efficient

doelpunt (*dōol*-pernt) *nt* (pl ~en) goal

doeltreffend (dōol-*treh*-fernt) *adj* effective

*doen (dōon) *v* *do; cause to

dof (dof) *adj* mat, dim

dok (dok) *nt* (pl ~ken) dock

dokter (*dok*-terr) *c* (pl ~s) doctor, physician

dom[1] (dom) *adj* dumb, stupid

dom[2] (dom) *c* cathedral

dominee (*dōa*-mee-nāy) *c* (pl ~s) clergyman, parson, rector

dompelaar (*dom*-per-laar) *c* (pl ~s) immersion heater

donateur (dōa-naa-*tūrr*) *c* (pl ~s) donor

donder (*don*-derr) *c* thunder

donderdag (*don*-derr-dahkh) *c* Thursday

donderen (*don*-der-rern) *v* thunder

donker (*dong*-kerr) *adj* dark, dim

dons (dons) *nt* down; **donzen dek-bed** eiderdown

dood (dōat) *adj* dead; *c* death

doodstraf (*dōat*-strahf) *c* death penalty

doof (dōaf) *adj* deaf

dooi (dōa^{ee}) *c* thaw

dooien (*dōa^{ee}*-ern) *v* thaw

dooier (*dōa^{ee}*-err) *c* (pl ~s) yolk

doolhof (*dōal*-hof) *nt* (pl -hoven) maze; labyrinth

doop (dōap) *c* baptism, christening

doopsel (*dōap*-serl) *nt* baptism

door (dōar) *prep* through; by

doorboren (dōar-*bōa*-rern) *v* pierce

*__doorbrengen__ (*dōar*-breh-ngern) *v* *spend

doordat (dōar-*daht*) *conj* because

*__doordringen__ (*dōar*-drı-ngern) *v* penetrate

*__doorgaan__ (*dōar*-gaan) *v* continue, *go on; carry on; *go ahead; ~ met *keep on

doorgang (*dōar*-gahng) *c* (pl ~en) passage

doorlichten (*dōar*-lıkh-tern) *v* X-ray

doorlopend (dōar-*lōa*-pernt) *adj* continuous

doormaken (*dōar*-maa-kern) *v* *go through

doorn (dōarn) *c* (pl ~en, ~s) thorn

doorreis (*dōa*-rayss) *c* passage

doorslag (*dōar*-slahkh) *c* (pl ~en) carbon copy

doorweken (dōar-*vāy*-kern) *v* soak

doorzichtig (dōar-*zıkh*-terkh) *adj* transparent, sheer

*__doorzoeken__ (dōar-*zōo*-kern) *v* search

doos (dōass) *c* (pl dozen) box

dop (dop) *c* (pl ~pen) shell

dopen (*dōa*-pern) *v* baptize, christen

dor (dor) *adj* arid

dorp (dorp) *nt* (pl ~en) village

dorst (dorst) *c* thirst

dorstig (*dors*-terkh) *adj* thirsty

dosis (*dōa*-zerss) *c* (pl doses) dose

dossier (do-*shāy*) *nt* (pl ~s) file

douane (dōo-*vaa*-ner) *c* Customs *pl*

douanebeambte (dōo-*vaa*-ner-ber-ahm-ter) *c* (pl ~n) Customs officer

douche (dōosh) *c* (pl ~s) shower

doven (*dōa*-vern) *v* extinguish

dozijn (dōa-*zayn*) *nt* (pl ~en) dozen

draad (draat) *c* (pl draden) thread; wire

draagbaar (*draakh*-baar) *adj* portable

draaglijk (*draakh*-lerk) *adj* tolerable

draai (draa^{ee}) *c* (pl ~en) turn; twist

draaideur (draa^{ee}-*dürr*) *c* (pl ~en) revolving door

draaien (*draa^{ee}*-ern) *v* turn; twist; *spin

draaimolen (*draa^{ee}*-mōa-lern) *c* (pl ~s) merry-go-round

draaiorgel (*draa^{ee}*-or-gerl) *nt* (pl ~s) street-organ

draak (draak) *c* (pl draken) dragon

*__dragen__ (*draa*-gern) *v* carry, *bear; *wear

drager (*draa*-gerr) *c* (pl ~s) bearer

drama (*draa*-maa) *nt* (pl ~'s) drama

dramatisch (draa-*maa*-teess) *adj* dramatic

drang (drahng) *c* urge

drank (drahngk) *c* (pl ~en) drink, beverage; **sterke** ~ spirits, liquor

dreigement (dray-ger-*mernt*) *nt* (pl ~en) threat

dreigen (*dray*-gern) *v* threaten

drek (drehk) *c* muck

drempel (*drehm*-perl) *c* (pl ~s) threshold

dresseren (dreh-*sāy*-rern) *v* train

drie (dree) *num* three

driehoek (*dree*-hōok) *c* (pl ~en) triangle

driehoekig (dree-*hoo*-kerkh) *adj* triangular

driekwart (*dree*-kvahrt) *adj* three-quarter

driemaandelijks (*dree*-maan-der-lerks) *adj* quarterly

drift (drɪft) *c* passion

driftig (*drɪf*-terkh) *adj* quick-tempered; hot-tempered, irascible

drijfkracht (*drayf*-krahkht) *c* driving force

*__drijven__ (*dray*-vern) *v* float

*__dringen__ (*drɪ*-ngern) *v* push; **dringend** pressing, urgent

drinkbaar (*drɪngk*-baar) *adj* for drinking

*__drinken__ (*drɪng*-kern) *v* *drink

drinkwater (*drɪngk*-vaa-terr) *nt* drinking-water

droefheid (*droof*-hayt) *c* sorrow

droevig (*droo*-verkh) *adj* sad

drogen (*droa*-gern) *v* dry

drogisterij (droa-gɪss-ter-*ray*) *c* (pl ~en) pharmacy, chemist's; drugstore *nAm*

dromen (*droa*-mern) *v* *dream

dronken (*drong*-kern) *adj* drunk; intoxicated

droog (droakh) *adj* dry

droogleggen (*droakh*-leh-gern) *v* drain

droogte (*droakh*-ter) *c* drought

droom (droam) *c* (pl dromen) dream

droombeeld (*droam*-baylt) *nt* (pl ~en) illusion

drop (drop) *c* liquorice

druiven (*druɪ*ew-vern) *pl* grapes *pl*

druk (drerk) *adj* busy; crowded; *c* pressure

drukken (*drer*-kern) *v* press; print

drukknop (*drer*-knop) *c* (pl ~pen) push-button

drukte (*drerk*-ter) *c* bustle; fuss, excitement

drukwerk (*drerk*-vehrk) *nt* printed matter

druppel (*drer*-perl) *c* (pl ~s) drop

dubbel (*der*-berl) *adj* double

dubbelzinnig (der-berl-zɪ-nerkh) *adj* ambiguous

duidelijk (*durew*-der-lerk) *adj* distinct, plain, clear; apparent, evident; obvious

duif (durewf) *c* (pl duiven) pigeon

duikbril (*durew*k-brɪl) *c* (pl ~len) goggles *pl*

*__duiken__ (*durew*-kern) *v* dive

duim (durewm) *c* (pl ~en) thumb

duin (durewn) *nt* (pl ~en) dune

duister (*durew*-sterr) *adj* obscure, dark; *nt* gloom

duisternis (*durew*-sterr-nɪss) *c* dark

Duits (durewts) *adj* German

Duitser (*durew*t-serr) *c* (pl ~s) German

Duitsland (*durew*ts-lahnt) Germany

duivel (*durew*-verl) *c* (pl ~s) devil

duizelig (*durew*-zer-lerkh) *adj* giddy, dizzy

duizeligheid (*durew*-zer-lerkh-hayt) *c* giddiness, dizziness

duizeling (*durew*-zer-lɪng) *c* (pl ~en) vertigo

duizend (*durew*-zernt) *num* thousand

dulden (*derl*-dern) *v* *bear

dun (dern) *adj* thin; sheer

dupe (*dew*-per) *c* (pl ~s) victim

duren (*dew*-rern) *v* last

durf (derrf) *c* nerve

durven (*derr*-vern) *v* dare

dus (derss) *conj* so

dutje (*der*-t'er) *nt* (pl ~s) nap

duur (dewr) *adj* dear, expensive; *c* duration

duurzaam (*dewr*-zaam) *adj* lasting, permanent

duw (dewoo) *c* (pl ~en) push

duwen (*dewoo*-ern) *v* push

dwaas¹ (dvaass) *adj* foolish, crazy, silly

dwaas² (dvaass) *c* (pl dwazen) fool

dwalen (*dvaa*-lern) *v* err

dwerg (dvehrkh) *c* (pl ~en) dwarf

*dwingen (*dvı*-ngern) *v* force; compel

dynamo (dee-*naa*-mōā) *c* (pl ~'s) dynamo

dysenterie (dee-sehn-ter-*ree*) *c* dysentery

E

eb (ehp) *c* low tide

ebbehout (*eh*-ber-hout) *nt* ebony

echo (*eh*-khōā) *c* (pl ~'s) echo

echt (ehkht) *adj* genuine, true, authentic, real; *adv* really; *c* matrimony

echtelijk (*ehkh*-ter-lerk) *adj* matrimonial

echter (*ehkh*-terr) *conj* however, yet

echtgenoot (*ehkht*-kher-nōāt) *c* (pl -noten) husband

echtgenote (*ehkht*-kher-nōā-ter) *c* (pl ~n) wife

echtpaar (*ehkht*-paar) *nt* (pl -paren) married couple

echtscheiding (*ehkht*-skhay-dıng) *c* (pl ~en) divorce

economie (āy-kōā-nōā-*mee*) *c* economy

economisch (āy-kōā-*nōā*-meess) *adj* economic

econoom (āy-kōā-*nōām*) *c* (pl -nomen) economist

Ecuador (āy-kvaa-*dor*) Ecuador

Ecuadoriaan (āy-kvaa-dōā-ree-ʸaan) *c* (pl -rianen) Ecuadorian

eczeem (ehk-*sāym*) *nt* eczema

edel (*āy*-derl) *adj* noble

edelmoedigheid (āy-derl-*mōō*-derkh-hayt) *c* generosity

edelsteen (*āy*-derl-stāyn) *c* (pl -stenen) gem, stone

editie (āy-*dee*-tsee) *c* (pl ~s) edition

eed (āyt) *c* (pl eden) oath, vow

eekhoorn (*āyk*-hōārn) *c* (pl ~s) squirrel

eelt (āylt) *nt* callus

een¹ (ern) *art* a art

een² (āyn) *num* one

eenakter (*āyn*-ahk-terr) *c* (pl ~s) one-act play

eend (āynt) *c* (pl ~en) duck

eender (*āyn*-derr) *adj* alike

eenheid (*āyn*-hayt) *c* (pl -heden) unit; unity

eenmaal (*āyn*-maal) *adv* once

eenrichtingsverkeer (āyn-*rıkh*-tıngs-ferr-kāyr) *nt* one-way traffic

eens (āyns) *adv* once; some time, some day; **het ~ *zijn** agree

eentonig (āyn-*tōā*-nerkh) *adj* monotonous

eenvoudig (āyn-*vou*-derkh) *adj* plain, simple; *adv* simply

eenzaam (*āyn*-zaam) *adj* lonely

eenzijdig (āyn-*zay*-derkh) *adj* one-sided

eer (āyr) *c* honour; glory

eerbied (*āyr*-beet) *c* respect

eerbiedig (āyr-*bee*-derkh) *adj* respectful

eerbiedwaardig (āyr-beet-*vaar*-derkh) *adj* venerable

eerder (*āyr*-derr) *adv* before; rather

eergevoel (*āyr*-ger-vōōl) *nt* sense of honour

eergisteren (*āyr*-gıss-ter-rern) *adv* the day before yesterday

eerlijk (*āyr*-lerk) *adj* honest; fair, straight

eerlijkheid (*āyr*-lerk-hayt) *c* honesty

eerst (āyrst) *adj* first; primary, initial; *adv* at first

eersteklas (*āyr*-ster-klahss) *adj* first-class

eersterangs (āyr-ster-rahngs) *adj* first-rate

eerstvolgend (āyrst-*fol*-gernt) *adj* following

eervol (āyr-vol) *adj* honourable

eerzaam (āyr-zaam) *adj* respectable; honourable

eerzuchtig (āyr-*zerkh*-terkh) *adj* ambitious

eetbaar (āyt-baar) *adj* edible

eetkamer (āyt-kaa-merr) *c* (pl ~s) dining-room

eetlepel (āyt-lāy-perl) *c* (pl ~s) tablespoon

eetlust (āyt-lerst) *c* appetite

eetservies (āyt-sehr-veess) *nt* (pl -viezen) dinner-service

eetzaal (āyt-saal) *c* (pl -zalen) dining-room

eeuw (āy^{oo}) *c* (pl ~en) century

eeuwig (āy^{oo}-erkh) *adj* eternal

eeuwigheid (āy^{oo}-erkh-hayt) *c* eternity

effect (eh-*fehkt*) *nt* (pl ~en) effect; **effecten** stocks and shares

effectenbeurs (eh-*fehk*-term-būrrs) *c* (pl -beurzen) stock market, stock exchange

effectief (eh-fehk-*teef*) *adj* effective

effen (eh-fern) *adj* level; smooth, even

efficiënt (eh-fee-*shehnt*) *adj* efficient

egaal (āy-*gaal*) *adj* level

egaliseren (āy-gaa-lee-zāy-rern) *v* level

egel (āy-gerl) *c* (pl ~s) hedgehog

egocentrisch (āy-gōa-*sehn*-treess) *adj* self-centred

egoïsme (āy-gōa-*viss*-mer) *nt* selfishness

egoïstisch (āy-gōa-*viss*-teess) *adj* selfish

Egypte (āy-*gıp*-ter) Egypt

Egyptenaar (āy-*gıp*-ter-naar) *c* (pl -naren) Egyptian

Egyptisch (āy-*gıp*-teess) *adj* Egyptian

ei (ay) *nt* (pl ~eren) egg

eierdooier (ay-err-dōā^{ee}-err) *c* (pl ~s) egg-yolk

eierdopje (ay-err-dop-^yer) *nt* (pl ~s) egg-cup

eigen (ay-gern) *adj* own

eigenaar (ay-ger-naar) *c* (pl ~s, -naren) owner, proprietor

eigenaardig (ay-ger-*naar*-derkh) *adj* singular, peculiar

eigenaardigheid (ay-ger-*naar*-derkh-hayt) *c* (pl -heden) peculiarity

eigendom (ay-gern-dom) *nt* (pl ~men) property; possessions

eigengemaakt (ay-gern-ger-maakt) *adj* home-made

eigenlijk (ay-gern-lerk) *adj* actual; *adv* as a matter of fact, really

eigenschap (ay-gern-skhahp) *c* (pl ~pen) property, quality

eigentijds (ay-gern-*tayts*) *adj* contemporary

eigenwijs (ay-gern-*vayss*) *adj* pig-headed

eik (ayk) *c* (pl ~en) oak

eikel (ay-kerl) *c* (pl ~s) acorn

eiland (ay-lahnt) *nt* (pl ~en) island

einde (ayn-der) *nt* end, finish; ending, issue

eindelijk (ayn-der-lerk) *adv* at last

eindigen (ayn-der-gern) *v* finish

eindpunt (aynt-pernt) *nt* (pl ~en) terminal

eindstreep (aynt-strāyp) *c* (pl -strepen) finish

eis (ayss) *c* (pl ~en) demand, claim

eisen (ay-sern) *v* demand

eiwit (ay-vıt) *nt* (pl ~ten) protein

ekster (ehk-sterr) *c* (pl ~s) magpie

eksteroog (ehk-sterr-ōākh) *nt* (pl -ogen) corn

eland (āy-lahnt) *c* (pl ~en) moose

elastiek (āy-lahss-*teek*) *nt* (pl ~en) rubber band, elastic

elastisch (āy-*lahss*-teess) *adj* elastic
elders (*ehl*-derrs) *adv* elsewhere
elegant (āy-ler-*gahnt*) *adj* elegant
elegantie (āy-ler-*gahnt*-see) *c* elegance
elektricien (āy-lehk-tree-*shang*) *c* (pl ~s) electrician
elektriciteit (āy-lehk-tree-see-*tayt*) *c* electricity
elektriciteitscentrale (āy-lehk-tree-see-*tayt*-sehn-traa-ler) *c* power-station
elektrisch (āy-*lehk*-treess) *adj* electric
elektronisch (āy-lehk-*trōa*-neess) *adj* electronic; ~ **spel** electronic game
element (āy-ler-*mehnt*) *nt* (pl ~en) element
elementair (āy-ler-mehn-*tair*) *adj* primary
elf[1] (ehlf) *num* eleven
elf[2] (ehlf) *c* (pl ~en) elf
elfde (*ehlf*-der) *num* eleventh
elftal (*ehlf*-tahl) *nt* (pl ~len) soccer team
elimineren (āy-lee-mee-*nāy*-rern) *v* eliminate
elk (ehlk) *adj* each, every
elkaar (ehl-*kaar*) *pron* each other
elleboog (*eh*-ler-*bōakh*) *c* (pl -bogen) elbow
ellende (eh-*lehn*-der) *c* misery
ellendig (eh-*lehn*-derkh) *adj* miserable
email (āy-*migh*) *nt* enamel
emailleren (āy-migh-*āy*-rern) *v* glaze
emancipatie (āy-mahn-see-*paa*-tsee) *c* emancipation
embargo (ehm-*bahr*-gōa) *nt* embargo
embleem (ehm-*blāym*) *nt* (pl -blemen) emblem
emigrant (āy-mee-*grahnt*) *c* (pl ~en) emigrant
emigratie (āy-mee-*graa*-tsee) *c* emigration
emigreren (āy-mee-*grāy*-rern) *v* emigrate
eminent (āy-mee-*nehnt*) *adj* outstanding

emmer (*eh*-merr) *c* (pl ~s) bucket, pail
emotie (āy-*mōa*-tsee) *c* (pl ~s) emotion
employé (ahm-plvah-*Yāy*) *c* (pl ~s) employee
en (ehn) *conj* and
encyclopedie (ehn-see-klōa-pāy-*dee*) *c* (pl ~ën) encyclopaedia
endeldarm (*ehn*-derl-dahrm) *c* (pl ~en) rectum
endosseren (ahn-do-*sāy*-rern) *v* endorse
energie (āy-nehr-*zhee*) *c* energy; power
energiek (āy-nehr-*zheek*) *adj* energetic
eng (ehng) *adj* narrow; creepy
engel (*ehn*-gerl) *c* (pl ~en) angel
Engeland (*eh*-nger-lahnt) England; Britain
Engels (*eh*-ngerls) *adj* English; British
Engelsman (*eh*-ngerls-mahn) *c* (pl Engelsen) Englishman; Briton
enig (*āy*-nerkh) *adj* sole, only; *pron* any; **enige** *pron* some
enigszins (*āy*-nerkh-sıns) *adv* somewhat
enkel[1] (*ehng*-kerl) *adj* single; **enkele** *pron* some
enkel[2] (*ehng*-kerl) *c* (pl ~s) ankle
enkeling (*ehng*-ker-lıng) *c* (pl ~en) individual
enkelvoud (*ehng*-kerl-vout) *nt* singular
enorm (āy-*norm*) *adj* tremendous, enormous, huge
enquête (ahng-*kai*-ter) *c* (pl ~s) enquiry
enthousiasme (ahn-tōō-*zhahss*-mer) *nt* enthusiasm
enthousiast (ahn-tōō-*zhahst*) *adj* enthusiastic; keen
entree (ahn-*trāy*) *c* entry; entrance-fee

entresol (ahng-trer-*sol*) *c* (pl ~s) mezzanine

envelop (ahng-ver-*lop*) *c* (pl ~pen) envelope

enzovoort (*ehn*-zōa-vōart) and so on, etcetera

epidemie (ā̄y-pee-der-*mee*) *c* (pl ~ĕn) epidemic

epilepsie (ā̄y-pee-lehp-*see*) *c* epilepsy

epiloog (ā̄y-pee-*lōakh*) *c* (pl -logen) epilogue

episch (*ā̄y*-peess) *adj* epic

episode (ā̄y-pee-*zōa*-der) *c* (pl ~n, ~s) episode

epos (*ā̄y*-poss) *nt* (pl epen, ~sen) epic

equipe (ā̄y-*keep*) *c* (pl ~s) team

equivalent (ā̄y-kvee-vaa-*lehnt*) *adj* equivalent

er (ehr) *adv* there; *pron* of them

erbarmelijk (ehr-*bahr*-mer-lerk) *adj* lamentable

eredienst (*ā̄y*-rer-deenst) *c* (pl ~en) worship

eren (*ā̄y*-rern) *v* honour

erf (ehrf) *nt* (pl erven) yard

erfelijk (*ehr*-fer-lerk) *adj* hereditary

erfenis (*ehr*-fer-niss) *c* (pl ~sen) inheritance; legacy

erg (ehrkh) *adj* bad; *adv* very; **erger** worse; **ergst** worst

ergens (*ehr*-gerns) *adv* somewhere

ergeren (*ehr*-ger-rern) *v* annoy

ergernis (*ehr*-gerr-niss) *c* annoyance

erkennen (ehr-*keh*-nern) *v* recognize; acknowledge

erkenning (ehr-*keh*-ning) *c* (pl ~en) recognition

erkentelijk (ehr-*kehn*-ter-lerk) *adj* grateful

ernst (ehrnst) *c* seriousness; gravity

ernstig (*ehrn*-sterkh) *adj* serious; grave, bad, severe

erts (ehrts) *nt* (pl ~en) ore

*ervaren** (ehr-*vaa*-rern) *v* experience

ervaring (ehr-*vaa*-ring) *c* (pl ~en) experience

erven (*ehr*-vern) *v* inherit

erwt (ehrt) *c* (pl ~en) pea

escorte (ehss-*kor*-ter) *nt* (pl ~s) escort

escorteren (ehss-kor-*tā̄y*-rern) *v* escort

esdoorn (*ehss*-dōarn) *c* (pl ~s) maple

essay (eh-*sā̄y*) *nt* (pl ~s) essay

essentie (eh-*sehn*-see) *c* essence

essentieel (eh-sehn-*shā̄yl*) *adj* vital, essential

etage (ā̄y-*taa*-zher) *c* (pl ~s) floor, storey; apartment *nAm*

etalage (ā̄y-taa-*laa*-zher) *c* (pl ~s) shop-window

etappe (ā̄y-*tah*-per) *c* (pl ~n, ~s) stage

eten (*ā̄y*-tern) *nt* food

*eten** (*ā̄y*-tern) *v* *eat

ether (*ā̄y*-terr) *c* ether

Ethiopië (ā̄y-tee-*Yōa*-pee-Yer) Ethiopia

Ethiopiër (ā̄y-tee-*Yōa*-pee-Yerr) *c* (pl ~s) Ethiopian

Ethiopisch (ā̄y-tee-*Yōa*-peess) *adj* Ethiopian

etiket (ā̄y-tee-*keht*) *nt* (pl ~ten) label, tag

etiketteren (ā̄y-tee-keh-*tā̄y*-rern) *v* label

etmaal (*eht*-maal) *nt* (pl -malen) twenty-four hours

ets (ehts) *c* (pl ~en) etching

ettelijk (*eh*-ter-lerk) *adj* several

etter (*eh*-terr) *c* pus

etui (ā̄y-*tvee*) *nt* (pl ~s) case

Europa (ūr-*rōa*-paa) Europe

Europeaan (ūr-rōa-*pā̄y*-aan) *c* (pl -anen) European

Europees (ūr-rōa-*pā̄yss*) *adj* European

Europese Unie (eur-oo-*peeser* y-nie) European Union

evacueren (ā̄y-vaa-kēw-*vā̄y*-rern) *v* evacuate

evangelie (ā̄y-vahng-*gā̄y*-lee) *nt* (pl- liën, ~s) gospel

even (*āy*-vern) *adj* even; *adv* equally, as

evenaar (*āy*-ver-naar) *c* equator

evenals (*āy*-ver-nahls) *conj* as well as

evenaren (*āy*-ver-naa-rern) *v* equal

eveneens (*āy*-ver-nāyns) *adv* as well, likewise, also

evenredig (*āy*-ver-rāy-derkh) *adj* proportional

eventueel (*āy*-vern-tēw-vāyl) *adj* possible, eventual

evenveel (*āy*-ver-vāyl) *adv* as much

evenwel (*āy*-ver-vehl) *adv* however

evenwicht (*āy*-ver-vikht) *nt* balance

evenwijdig (āy-ver-vay-derkh) *adj* parallel

evenzeer (*āy*-ver-zāyr) *adv* as much

evenzo (*āy*-ver-zōä) *adv* likewise

evolutie (āy-vōä-lēw-tsee) *c* (pl ~s) evolution

exact (ehk-*sahkt*) *adj* precise

examen (ehk-*saa*-mern) *nt* (pl ~s) examination

excentriek (ehk-sehn-*treek*) *adj* eccentric

exces (ehk-*sehss*) *nt* (pl ~sen) excess

exclusief (ehks-klēw-*zeef*) *adj* exclusive

excursie (ehks-*kerr*-zee) *c* (pl ~s) day trip, excursion

excuseren (ehks-kēw-*zāy*-rern) *v* excuse

excuus (ehks-*kēwss*) *nt* (pl excuses) apology, excuse

exemplaar (ehk-serm-*plaar*) *nt* (pl -plaren) specimen; copy

exotisch (ehk-*sōä*-teess) *adj* exotic

expeditie (ehks-per-*dee*-tsee) *c* (pl ~s) expedition

experiment (ehks-pāy-ree-*mehnt*) *nt* (pl ~en) experiment

experimenteren (ehks-pāy-ree-mehn-*tāy*-rern) *v* experiment

expert (ehks-*pair*) *c* (pl ~s) expert

expliciet (ehks-plee-*seet*) *adj* explicit

exploiteren (ehks-plvah-*tāy*-rern) *v* exploit

explosie (ehks-*plōä*-zee) *c* (pl ~s) blast, explosion

explosief (ehks-plōä-*zeef*) *adj* explosive

export (*ehk*-sport) *c* exports *pl*, export

exporteren (ehk-spor-*tāy*-rern) *v* export

expositie (ehk-spōä-*zee*-tsee) *c* (pl ~s) exhibition; display

expresse- (ehk-*spreh*-ser) express; special delivery

extase (ehk-*staa*-zer) *c* ecstasy

extra (*ehk*-straa) *adj* additional, extra; spare

extravagant (ehk-straa-vaa-*gahnt*) *adj* extravagant

extreem (ehk-*strāym*) *adj* extreme

ezel (*āy*-zerl) *c* (pl ~s) ass; donkey

F

faam (faam) *c* fame

fabel (*faa*-berl) *c* (pl ~s, ~en) fable

fabriceren (faa-bree-*sāy*-rern) *v* manufacture

fabriek (faa-*breek*) *c* (pl ~en) factory; mill, works *pl*

fabrikant (faa-bree-*kahnt*) *c* (pl ~en) manufacturer

faciliteit (faa-see-lee-*tayt*) *c* (pl ~en) facility

factor (*fahk*-tor) *c* (pl ~en) factor

factureren (fahk-tēw-*rāy*-rern) *v* bill

factuur (fahk-*tēwr*) *c* (pl -turen) invoice

facultatief (faa-kerl-taa-*teef*) *adj* optional

faculteit (faa-kerl-*tayt*) *c* (pl ~en) faculty

failliet (fah-Yeet) *adj* bankrupt

fakkel (fah-kerl) *c* (pl ~s) torch

falen (faa-lern) *v* fail

familiaar (fah-mee-lee-Yaar) *adj* familiar

familie (faa-*mee*-lee) *c* (pl ~s) family

familielid (faa-*mee*-lee-lɪt) *nt* (pl -leden) relative

fanatiek (faa-naa-*teek*) *adj* fanatical

fanfarekorps (fahm-*faa*-rer-korps) *nt* (pl ~en) brass band

fantasie (fahn-taa-*zee*) *c* (pl ~ën) fantasy, fancy

fantastisch (fahn-*tahss*-teess) *adj* fantastic

farce (fahrs) *c* (pl ~n) farce

farmacologie (fahr-maa-kōa-lōa-*gee*) *c* pharmacology

fascinerend (fah-see-*nāy*-rernt) *adj* glamorous

fascisme (fah-*sɪss*-mer) *nt* fascism

fascist (fah-*sɪst*) *c* (pl ~en) fascist

fascistisch (fah-*sɪss*-teess) *adj* fascist

fase (faa-zer) *c* (pl ~s, ~n) stage, phase

fataal (faa-*taal*) *adj* fatal

fatsoen (faht-*sōōn*) *nt* decency

fatsoenlijk (faht-*sōōn*-lerk) *adj* decent

fauteuil (fōa-*tur*ᵉʷ) *c* (pl ~s) armchair

favoriet (faa-vōa-*reet*) *c* (pl ~en) favourite

fax (faks) *c* fax; **een ~ versturen** send a fax

februari (fāy-brēw-*vaa*-ree) February

federaal (fāy-der-*raal*) *adj* federal

federatie (fāy-der-*raa*-tsee) *c* (pl ~s) federation

fee (fāy) *c* (pl ~ën) fairy

feest (fāyst) *nt* (pl ~en) feast

feestdag (*fāyss*-dahkh) *c* (pl ~en) holiday

feestelijk (*fāy*-ster-lerk) *adj* festive

feestje (*fāy*-sher) *nt* (pl ~s) party

feilloos (*fay*-lōass) *adj* faultless

feit (fayt) *nt* (pl ~en) fact; **in feite** in fact

feitelijk (*fay*-ter-lerk) *adj* factual; *adv* as a matter of fact, actually, in effect

fel (fehl) *adj* fierce

felicitatie (fāy-lee-see-*taa*-tsee) *c* (pl ~s) congratulation

feliciteren (fāy-lee-see-*tāy*-rern) *v* congratulate; compliment

feodaal (fāy-Yōa-*daal*) *adj* feudal

festival (*fehss*-tee-vahl) *nt* (pl ~s) festival

feuilleton (fur*ᵉʷ*-er-*ton*) *nt* (pl ~s) serial

fiasco (fee-Yahss-kōa) *nt* (pl ~'s) failure

fiche (fee-sher) *c* (pl ~s) chip

fictie (*fɪk*-see) *c* (pl ~s) fiction

fiets (feets) *c* (pl ~en) cycle, bicycle

fietser (fee-tserr) *c* (pl ~s) cyclist

figuur (fee-*gēwr*) *c* (pl -guren) figure; diagram

fijn (fayn) *adj* enjoyable; fine; delicate

fijnhakken (*fayn*-hah-kern) *v* mince

*fijnmalen (*fayn*-maa-lern) *v* *grind

fijnproever (*faym*-prōō-verr) *c* (pl ~s) gourmet

fijnstampen (*fayn*-stahm-pern) *v* mash

filiaal (fee-lee-Yaal) *nt* (-ialen) branch

Filippijn (fee-lɪ-*payn*) *c* (pl ~en) Filipino

Filippijnen (fee-lɪ-*pay*-nern) *pl* Philippines *pl*

Filippijns (fee-lɪ-*payns*) *adj* Philippine

film (fɪlm) *c* (pl ~s) film; movie

filmcamera (*fɪlm*-kaa-mer-raa) *c* (pl ~'s) camera

filmen (*fɪl*-mern) *v* film

filmjournaal (*fɪlm*-zhōōr-naal) *nt* newsreel

filosofie (fee-lōa-zōa-*fee*) *c* (pl ~ën) philosophy

filosoof (fee-lōā-*zōāf*) *c* (pl -sofen) philosopher

filter (*fil*-terr) *nt* (pl ~s) filter

Fin (fin) *c* (pl ~nen) Finn

financieel (fee-nahn-*shāyl*) *adj* financial

financiën (fee-*nahn*-see-ᵞern) *pl* finances *pl*

financieren (fee-nahn-*see*-rern) *v* finance

Finland (*fin*-lahnt) Finland

Fins (fins) *adj* Finnish

firma (*fir*-maa) *c* (pl ~'s) company, firm

fitting (*fi*-ting) *c* (pl ~en) socket

fjord (fᵞort) *c* (pl ~en) fjord

flacon (flaa-*kon*) *c* (pl ~s) flask

flamingo (flaa-*ming*-gōā) *c* (pl ~'s) flamingo

flanel (flaa-*nehl*) *nt* flannel

flat (fleht) *c* (pl ~s) flat; apartment *nAm*

flatgebouw (*fleht*-kher-bou) *nt* (pl ~en) block of flats; apartment house *Am*

flauw (flou) *adj* faint

*flauwvallen (*flou*-vah-lern) *v* faint

fles (flehss) *c* (pl ~sen) bottle

flesopener (*fleh*-zōā-per-nerr) *c* (pl ~s) bottle opener

flessehals (*fleh*-ser-hahls) *c* bottleneck

flets (flehts) *adj* dull

flink (flingk) *adj* considerable; brave, plucky

flits (flits) *c* (pl ~en) flash

flitslampje (*flits*-lahm-pᵞer) *nt* (pl ~s) flash-bulb

fluisteren (*flur*ᵉʷss-ter-rern) *v* whisper

fluit (flurᵉʷt) *c* (pl ~en) flute

*fluiten (*flur*ᵉʷ-tern) *v* whistle

fluitje (*flur*ᵉʷ-tᵞer) *nt* (pl ~s) whistle

fluweel (flew-*vāyl*) *nt* velvet

foefje (*fōō*-fᵞer) *nt* (pl ~s) trick

foei! (fōōᵉᵉ) shame!

fok (fok) *c* (pl ~ken) foresail

fokken (*fo*-kern) *v* *breed; raise

folklore (fol-*klōā*-rer) *c* folklore

fonds (fons) *nt* (pl ~en) fund

fonetisch (fōā-*nāy*-teess) *adj* phonetic

fonkelend (*fong*-ker-lernt) *adj* sparkling

fontein (fon-*tayn*) *c* (pl ~en) fountain

fooi (fōāᵉᵉ) *c* (pl ~en) tip; gratuity

foppen (*fo*-pern) *v* fool

forceren (for-*sāy*-rern) *v* strain; force

forel (fōā-*rehl*) *c* (pl ~len) trout

forens (fōā-*rehns*) *c* (pl ~en, forenzen) commuter

formaat (for-*maat*) *nt* (pl -maten) size

formaliteit (for-maa-lee-*tayt*) *c* (pl ~en) formality

formeel (for-*māyl*) *adj* formal

formule (for-*mēw*-ler) *c* (pl ~s) formula

formulier (for-mēw-*leer*) *nt* (pl ~en) form

fornuis (for-*nur*ᵉʷss) *nt* (pl -nuizen) cooker, stove

fors (fors) *adj* robust

fort (fort) *nt* (pl ~en) fort

fortuin (for-*tur*ᵉʷn) *nt* (pl ~en) fortune

foto (*fōā*-tōā) *c* (pl ~'s) photograph, photo

fotocopie (fōā-tōā-kōā-*pee*) *c* (pl ~ën) photocopy

fotograaf (fōā-tōā-*graaf*) *c* (pl -grafen) photographer

fotograferen (fōā-tōā-graa-*fāy*-rern) *v* photograph

fotografie (fōā-tōā-graa-*fee*) *c* photography

fototoestel (*fōā*-tōā-tōō-stehl) *nt* (pl ~len) camera

fotowinkel (*fōā*-tōā-ving-kerl) *c* (pl ~s) camera shop

fouilleren (fōō-ᵞ*āy*-rern) *v* search

fout¹ (fout) *adj* mistaken, wrong

fout² (fout) *c* (pl ~en) error, mistake, fault

foutloos (*fout*-lōass) *adj* faultless

foyer (fvah-*ᵞāy*) *c* (pl ~s) foyer; lobby

fractie (*frahk*-see) *c* (pl ~s) fraction

fragment (frahkh-*mehnt*) *nt* (pl ~en) fragment; extract

framboos (frahm-*bōass*) *c* (pl -bozen) raspberry

franje (*frah*-ñer) *c* (pl ~s) fringe

frankeren (frahng-*kāy*-rern) *v* stamp

frankering (frahng-*kāy*-rıng) *c* (pl ~en) postage

franko (*frahng*-kōa) *adj* postage paid, post-paid

Frankrijk (*frahng*-krayk) France

Frans (frahns) *adj* French

Fransman (*frahns*-mahn) *c* (pl Fransen) Frenchman

frappant (frah-*pahnt*) *adj* striking

fraude (*frou*-der) *c* (pl ~s) fraud

frequent (frer-*kvehnt*) *adj* frequent

frequentie (frer-*kvehn*-tsee) *c* (pl ~s) frequency

fris (friss) *adj* fresh

frisdrank (*friss*-drahngk) *c* soft drink

frites (freet) *pl* chips

fruit (frur^ewt) *nt* fruit

fuif (fur^ewf) *c* (pl fuiven) party

functie (*ferngk*-see) *c* (pl ~s) function

functioneren (ferngk-shōa-*nāy*-rern) *v* work

fundamenteel (fern-daa-mehn-*tāyl*) *adj* fundamental, basic

fusie (*fēw*-zee) *c* (pl ~s) merger

fysica (*fee*-zee-kaa) *c* physics

fysiek (fee-*zeek*) *adj* physical

fysiologie (fee-zee-ᵞōa-lōa-*gee*) *c* physiology

G

***gaan** (gaan) *v* *go; *~ **door** pass through

gaarne (*gaar*-ner) *adv* gladly

gaas (gaass) *nt* gauze

***gadeslaan** (*gaa*-der-slaan) *v* watch

gal (gahl) *c* gall, bile

galblaas (*gahl*-blaass) *c* (pl -blazen) gall bladder

galerij (gah-ler-*ray*) *c* (pl ~en) arcade; gallery

galg (gahlkh) *c* (pl ~en) gallows *pl*

galop (gaa-*lop*) *c* gallop

galsteen (*gahl*-stāyn) *c* (pl -stenen) gallstone

gammel (*gah*-merl) *adj* ramshackle, shaky

gang (gahng) *c* (pl ~en) corridor; gait, pace; course

gangbaar (*gahng*-baar) *adj* current

gangpad (*gahng*-paht) *nt* (pl ~en) aisle

gans (gahns) *c* (pl ganzen) goose

gapen (*gaa*-pern) *v* yawn

garage (gaa-*raa*-zher) *c* (pl ~s) garage

garanderen (gaa-rahn-*dāy*-rern) *v* guarantee

garantie (gaa-*rahn*-tsee) *c* (pl ~s) guarantee

garderobe (gahr-der-*raw*-ber) *c* (pl ~s) wardrobe, cloakroom; checkroom *nAm*

garen (*gaa*-rern) *nt* (pl ~s) thread, yarn; **garen- en bandwinkel** haberdashery

garnaal (gahr-*naal*) *c* (pl -nalen) prawn, shrimp

gas (gahss) *nt* (pl ~sen) gas

gasfabriek (*gahss*-faa-breek) *c* (pl ~en) gasworks

gasfornuis (*gahss*-for-nur^ewss) *nt* (pl

-nuizen) gas cooker

gaskachel (*gahss*-kah-kherl) *c* (pl ~s) gas stove

gaspedaal (*gahss*-per-daal) *nt* (pl -dalen) accelerator

gasstel (*gah*-stehl) *nt* (pl ~len) gas cooker

gast (gahst) *c* (pl ~en) guest

gastheer (*gahst*-hāyr) *c* (pl -heren) host

gastvrij (gahst-*fray*) *adj* hospitable

gastvrijheid (gahst-*fray*-hayt) *c* hospitality

gastvrouw (*gahst*-frou) *c* (pl ~en) hostess

gat (gaht) *nt* (pl ~en) hole

gauw (gou) *adv* soon

gave (*gaa*-ver) *c* (pl ~n) gift, faculty

gazon (gaa-*zon*) *nt* (pl ~s) lawn

geacht (ger-*ahkht*) *adj* esteemed;
    geachte Heer Dear Sir

geadresseerde (ger-ah-dreh-*sāyr*-der) *c* (pl ~n) addressee

geaffecteerd (ger-ah-fehk-*tāyrt*) *adj* affected

gearmd (ger-*ahrmt*) *adv* arm-in-arm

gebaar (ger-*baar*) *nt* (pl gebaren) sign

gebak (ger-*bahk*) *nt* cake, pastry

gebaren (ger-*baa*-rern) *v* gesticulate

gebed (ger-*beht*) *nt* (pl ~en) prayer

gebergte *nt* mountain range

gebeuren (ger-*bur*̄-rern) *v* occur; happen

gebeurtenis (ger-*burr*-ter-niss) *c* (pl ~sen) event; happening, occurrence

gebied (ger-*beet*) *nt* (pl ~en) region; zone, area, field, territory

geblokt (ger-*blokt*) *adj* chequered

gebogen (ger-*bōā*-gern) *adj* curved

geboorte (ger-*bōār*-ter) *c* (pl ~n) birth

geboorteland (ger-*bōār*-ter-lahnt) *nt* native country

geboorteplaats (ger-*bōār*-ter-plaats) *c* place of birth

geboren (ger-*bōā*-rern) *adj* born

gebouw (ger-*bou*) *nt* (pl ~en) construction, building

gebrek (ger-*brehk*) *nt* (pl ~en) deficiency, fault; want, lack, shortage

gebrekkig (ger-*breh*-kerkh) *adj* defective, faulty

gebruik (ger-*brur*̄*ᵉʷk*) *nt* (pl ~en) use, usage; custom

gebruikelijk (ger-*brur*ᵉʷ-ker-lerk) *adj* customary; common, usual

gebruiken (ger-*brur*ᵉʷ-kern) *v* use; employ; apply

gebruiker (ger-*brur*ᵉʷ-kerr) *c* (pl ~s) user

gebruiksaanwijzing (ger-*brur*ᵉʷk-saan-vay-zɪng) *c* (pl ~en) directions for use

gebruiksvoorwerp (ger-*brur*ᵉʷks-fōār-vehrp) *nt* (pl ~en) utensil

gebruind (ger-*brur*ᵉʷnt) *adj* tanned

gebrul (ger-*brerl*) *nt* roar

gecompliceerd (ger-kom-plee-*sāyrt*) *adj* complicated

gedachte (ger-*dahkh*-ter) *c* (pl ~n) thought; idea

gedachtenstreepje (ger-*dahkh*-ter-strāyp-ʸer) *nt* (pl ~s) dash

gedeelte (ger-*dāyl*-ter) *nt* (pl ~n, ~s) part

gedeeltelijk (ger-*dāyl*-ter-lerk) *adj* partial; *adv* partly

gedelegeerde (ger-dāy-ler-*gāyr*-der) *c* (pl ~n) delegate

gedenkteken (ger-*dehngk*-tāy-kern) *nt* (pl ~s) memorial; monument

gedenkwaardig (ger-*dehngk*-*vaar*-derkh) *adj* memorable

gedetailleerd (ger-dāy-tah-ʸ*āyrt*) *adj* detailed

gedetineerde (ger-dāy-tee-*nāyr*-der) *c* (pl ~n) prisoner

gedicht (ger-*dɪkht*) *nt* (pl ~en) poem

geding (ger-*dɪng*) *nt* (pl ~en) lawsuit

gediplomeerd (ger-dee-plōa-*māy*rt) *adj* qualified

gedrag (ger-*drahkh*) *nt* conduct, behaviour

zich *gedragen (ger-*draa*-gern) act, behave

geduld (ger-*derlt*) *nt* patience

geduldig (ger-*derl*-derkh) *adj* patient

gedurende (ger-*deū*-rern-der) *prep* during; for

gedurfd (ger-*derrft*) *adj* daring

geel (gāyl) *adj* yellow

geelkoper (*gāy*l-kōa-perr) *nt* brass

geelzucht (*gāy*l-zerkht) *c* jaundice

geëmailleerd (ger-āy-mah-ʸ*āy*rt) *adj* enamelled

geen (gāyn) *adj* no

geenszins (*gāy*n-sɪns) *adv* by no means

geest (gāyst) *c* (pl ~en) spirit, mind; soul; ghost

geestelijk (gāy-ster-lerk) *adj* spiritual, mental

geestelijke (*gāy*-ster-ler-ker) *c* (pl ~n) clergyman

geestig (*gāy*-sterkh) *adj* witty, humorous

geeuwen (*gāy*ᵒᵒ-ern) *v* yawn

gefluister (ger-*flur*ᵉʷ-sterr) *nt* whisper

gegadigde (ger-*gaa*-derkh-der) *c* (pl ~n) candidate

gegeneerd (ger-zher-*nāy*rt) *adj* embarrassed

gegeven (ger-*gāy*-vern) *nt* (pl ~s) data *pl*

gegrond (ger-*gront*) *adj* well-founded

gehandicapt (ger-hehn-dee-kehpt) *adj* disabled

geheel (ger-*hāy*l) *adj* entire, whole, total; *adv* completely; *nt* whole

geheelonthouder (ger-*hāy*l-ont-hou-derr) *c* (pl ~s) teetotaller

geheim¹ (ger-*haym*) *adj* secret

geheim² (ger-*haym*) *nt* (pl ~en) secret

geheimzinnig (ger-haym-*zɪ*-nerkh) *adj* mysterious

geheugen (ger-*hūr*-gern) *nt* memory

gehoor (ger-*hōar*) *nt* hearing

gehoorzaam (ger-*hōar*-zaam) *adj* obedient

gehoorzaamheid (ger-*hōar*-zaam-hayt) *c* obedience

gehoorzamen (ger-*hōar*-zaa-mern) *v* obey

gehorig (ger-*hōa*-rerkh) *adj* noisy

geïnteresseerd (ger-ɪn-trer-*sāy*rt) *adj* interested

geïsoleerd (ger-ee-zōa-*lāy*rt) *adj* isolated

geit (gayt) *c* (pl ~en) goat

geiteleer (gay-ter-*lāy*r) *nt* kid

gek¹ (gehk) *adj* crazy, mad

gek² (gehk) *c* (pl ~ken) fool

geklets (ger-*klehts*) *nt* chat; rubbish

gekleurd (ger-*klūrt*) *adj* coloured

gekraak (ger-*kraak*) *nt* crack

gekruid (ger-*krur*ᵉʷt) *adj* spiced

gelaatstrek (ger-*laats*-trehk) *c* (pl ~ken) feature

gelach (ger-*lahkh*) *nt* laughter

geld (gehlt) *nt* money; **buitenlands ~** foreign currency; **contant ~** cash

geldautomaat (*gehl*t-oo-too-maat) *c* cash dispenser, ATM

geldbelegging (*gehl*t-ber-leh-gɪng) *c* (pl ~en) investment

*gelden (*gehl*-dern) *v* apply

geldig (*gehl*-derkh) *adj* valid

geldstuk (*gehl*t-sterk) *nt* (pl ~ken) coin

geleden (ger-*lāy*-dern) ago; **kort ~** recently

geleerde (ger-*lāy*r-der) *c* (pl ~n) scholar, scientist

gelegen (ger-*lay*-gern) *adj* situated

gelegenheid (ger-*lāy*-gern-hayt) *c* (pl -heden) occasion, chance, opportunity

gelei (zher-*lay*) *c* (pl ~en) jelly

geleidehond (ger-*lay*-der-hont) *c* (pl ~en) guide-dog

geleidelijk (ger-*lay*-der-lerk) *adj* gradual

gelijk (ger-*layk*) *adj* equal, like, alike; level, even; ~ *hebben* be right; ~ *maken* equalize

gelijkenis (ger-*lay*-ker-niss) *c* (pl ~sen) resemblance, similarity

gelijkgezind (ger-layk-kher-*zint*) *adj* like-minded

gelijkheid (ger-*layk*-hayt) *c* equality

gelijkstroom (ger-*layk*-strōam) *c* direct current

gelijktijdig (ger-layk-*tay*-derkh) *adj* simultaneous

gelijkwaardig (ger-layk-*vaar*-derkh) *adj* equivalent

gelofte (ger-*lof*-ter) *c* (pl ~n) vow

geloof (ger-*lōaf*) *nt* belief; faith

geloofwaardig (ger-lōaf-*vaar*-derkh) *adj* credible

geloven (ger-*lōa*-vern) *v* believe

geluid (ger-*lur*ᵉʷt) *nt* (pl ~en) sound; noise

geluiddicht (ger-lurᵉʷ-*dikht*) *adj* soundproof

geluk (ger-*lerk*) *nt* happiness; luck, fortune

gelukkig (ger-*ler*-kerkh) *adj* happy; fortunate

gelukwens (ger-*lerk*-vehns) *c* (pl ~en) congratulation

gelukwensen (ger-*lerk*-vehn-sern) *v* congratulate, compliment

gemak (ger-*mahk*) *nt* leisure; ease; comfort

gemakkelijk (ger-*mah*-ker-lerk) *adj* easy; convenient

gematigd (ger-*maa*-terkht) *adj* moderate

gember (*gehm*-berr) *c* ginger

gemeen (ger-*mayn*) *adj* foul, mean

gemeenschap (ger-*mayn*-skhahp) *c* (pl ~pen) community

gemeenschappelijk (ger-mayn-*skhah*-per-lerk) *adj* common

gemeente (ger-*mayn*-ter) *c* (pl ~n, ~s) congregation

gemeentebestuur (ger-*mayn*-ter-ber-stēwr) *nt* municipality

gemeentelijk (ger-*mayn*-ter-lerk) *adj* municipal

gemêleerd (ger-meh-*lāyrt*) *adj* mixed

gemengd (ger-*mehngt*) *adj* mixed; miscellaneous

gemiddeld (ger-*mi*-derlt) *adj* average, medium; *adv* on the average

gemiddelde (ger-*mi*-derl-der) *nt* (pl ~n) average, mean

gemis (ger-*miss*) *nt* want, lack

genade (ger-*naa*-der) *c* mercy; grace

geneeskunde (ger-*nāyss*-kern-der) *c* medicine

geneeskundig (ger-*nāyss*-kern-derkh) *adj* medical

geneesmiddel (ger-*nāyss*-mi-derl) *nt* (pl ~en) medicine; remedy, drug

genegen (ger-*nāy*-gern) *adj* inclined

genegenheid (ger-*nāy*-gern-hayt) *c* affection

geneigd (ger-*naykht*) *adj* inclined

generaal (gāy-ner-*raal*) *c* (pl ~s) general

generatie (gāy-ner-*raa*-tsee) *c* (pl ~s) generation

generator (gāy-ner-*raa*-tor) *c* (pl ~en, ~s) generator

***genezen** (ger-*nāy*-zern) *v* heal; cure; recover

genezing (ger-*nāy*-zing) *c* (pl ~en) cure; recovery

genie (zher-*nee*) *nt* (pl ~ën) genius

***genieten van** (ger-*nee*-tern) enjoy

genoeg (ger-*nōōkh*) *adv* enough; sufficient

genoegen (ger-*nōō*-gern) *nt* (pl ~s)

pleasure

genootschap (ger-*nōat*-skhahp) nt (pl ~pen) society; association

genot (ger-*not*) nt joy; delight; enjoyment

geologie (gāy-^yōa-lōa-*gee*) c geology

gepast (ger-*pahst*) adj suitable, proper

gepensioneerd (ger-pehn-shōa-*nāyrt*) adj retired

geraamte (ger-*raam*-ter) nt (pl ~n, ~s) skeleton

geraas (ger-*raass*) nt roar

gerecht (ger-*rehkht*) nt (pl ~en) dish; law court

gerechtigheid (ger-*rehkh*-terkh-hayt) c justice

gereed (ger-*rāyt*) adj ready

gereedschap (ger-*rāyt*-skhahp) nt (pl ~pen) tool; utensil, implement

gereedschapskist (ger-*rāyt*-skhahps-kıst) c (pl ~en) tool kit

geregeld (ger-*rāy*-gerlt) adj regular

gereserveerd (ger-rāy-zehr-*vāyrt*) adj reserved

gerief (ger-*reef*) nt comfort

geriefelijk (ger-*ree*-fer-lerk) adj comfortable, easy; convenient

gering (ger-*rıng*) adj minor; slight, small; **geringst** least

geroddel (ger-*ro*-derl) nt gossip

gerst (gehrst) c barley

gerucht (ger-*rerkht*) nt (pl ~en) rumour

geruit (ger-*rur^{ew}t*) adj chequered

gerust (ger-*rerst*) adj confident

geruststellen (ger-*rerst*-steh-lern) v reassure

gescheiden (ger-*skhay*-dern) adj separate

geschenk (ger-*skhehngk*) nt (pl ~en) gift, present

geschiedenis (ger-*skhee*-der-nıss) c history

geschiedkundig (ger-skheet-*kern*-derkh) adj historical

geschiedkundige (ger-skheet-*kern*-der-ger) c (pl ~n) historian

geschikt (ger-*skhıkt*) adj convenient, suitable, proper, appropriate, fit; ~ *zijn qualify

geschil (ger-*skhıl*) nt (pl ~len) dispute

geslacht (ger-*slahkht*) nt (pl ~en) sex; gender

geslachtsziekte (ger-*slahkht*-seek-ter) c (pl ~n, ~s) venereal disease

gesloten (ger-*slōa*-tern) adj closed, shut

gesp (gehsp) c (pl ~en) buckle

gespannen (ger-*spah*-nern) adj tense

gespierd (ger-*speert*) adj muscular

gespikkeld (ger-*spı*-kerlt) adj spotted

gesprek (ger-*sprehk*) nt (pl ~ken) discussion, conversation, talk; **interlokaal** ~ trunk-call; **lokaal** ~ local call

gestalte (ger-*stahl*-ter) c (pl ~n, ~s) figure

gesticht (ger-*stıkht*) nt (pl ~en) asylum

gestorven (ger-*stor*-vern) adj dead

gestreept (ger-*strāypt*) adj striped

getal (ger-*tahl*) nt (pl ~len) number

getij (ger-*tay*) nt (pl ~en) tide

getrouw (ger-*trou*) adj true

getuige (ger-*tur^{ew}*-ger) c (pl ~n) witness

getuigen (ger-*tur^{ew}*-gern) v testify

getuigschrift (ger-*tur^{ew}kh*-skhrıft) nt (pl ~en) certificate

getypt (ger-*teept*) adj typewritten

geur (gūrr) c (pl ~en) smell, odour; scent

gevaar (ger-*vaar*) nt (pl -varen) danger; risk, peril

gevaarlijk (ger-*vaar*-lerk) adj dangerous; perilous

geval (ger-*vahl*) nt (pl ~len) case; instance; event; **in elk** ~ at any rate, anyway; **in ~ van** in case of

gevangene (ger-*vah*-nger-ner) *c* (pl ~n) prisoner

gevangenis (ger-*vah*-nger-niss) *c* (pl ~sen) prison; gaol, jail

gevangenschap (ger-*vah*-ngern-skhahp) *c* imprisonment

gevarieerd (ger-vaa-ree-*Yāȳrt*) *adj* varied

gevecht (ger-*vehkht*) *nt* (pl ~en) combat, battle, fight

gevel (*gāȳ*-verl) *c* (pl ~s) façade

geveltop (*gāȳ*-verl-top) *c* (pl ~pen) gable

geven (*gāȳ*-vern) *v* *give; ~ **om** mind

gevoel (ger-*vōōl*) *nt* feeling; sensation

gevoelig (ger-*vōō*-lerkh) *adj* sensitive

gevoelloos (ger-*vōō*-lōass) *adj* numb

gevogelte (ger-*vōā*-gerl-ter) *nt* fowl; poultry

gevolg (ger-*volkh*) *nt* (pl ~en) result, consequence; issue, effect; **ten gevolge van** owing to

gevolgtrekking (ger-*volkh*-treh-king) *c* (pl ~en) conclusion

gevorderd (ger-*vor*-derrt) *adj* advanced

gevuld (ger-*verlt*) *adj* stuffed

gewaad (ger-*vaat*) *nt* (pl gewaden) robe

gewaagd (ger-*vaakht*) *adj* risky

gewaarwording (ger-*vaar*-vor-ding) *c* (pl ~en) perception; sensation

gewapend (ger-*vaa*-pernt) *adj* armed

geweer (ger-*vāȳr*) *nt* (pl geweren) rifle, gun

gewei (ger-*vay*) *nt* (pl ~en) antlers *pl*

geweld (ger-*vehlt*) *nt* violence; force

gewelddaad (ger-*vehl*-daat) *c* (pl -daden) outrage

gewelddadig (ger-vehl-*daa*-derkh) *adj* violent

geweldig (ger-*vehl*-derkh) *adj* terrific;

huge

gewelf (ger-*vehlf*) *nt* (pl gewelven) arch, vault

gewend (ger-*vehnt*) *adj* accustomed

gewest (ger-*vehst*) *nt* (pl ~en) province

geweten (ger-*vāȳ*-tern) *nt* conscience

gewicht (ger-*vikht*) *nt* (pl ~en) weight

gewichtig (ger-*vikh*-terkh) *adj* important; big

gewillig (ger-*vi*-lerkh) *adj* co-operative

gewond (ger-*vont*) *adj* injured

gewoon (ger-*vōān*) *adj* normal, ordinary; common, regular, plain, simple; customary, habitual; accustomed; ~ **zijn* **be used to; would

gewoonlijk (ger-*vōān*-lerk) *adj* customary; *adv* as a rule, usually

gewoonte (ger-*vōān*-ter) *c* (pl ~n, ~s) habit; custom

gewoonweg (ger-*vōān*-vehkh) *adv* simply

gewricht (ger-*vrikht*) *nt* (pl ~en) joint

gezag (ger-*zahkh*) *nt* authority

gezagvoerder (ger-*zahkh*-fōōr-derr) *c* (pl ~s) captain

gezamenlijk (ger-*zaa*-mer-lerk) *adj* joint

gezang (ger-*zahng*) *nt* (pl ~en) hymn

gezant (ger-*zahnt*) *c* (pl ~en) envoy

gezellig (ger-*zeh*-lerkh) *adj* cosy

gezelschap (ger-*zehl*-skhahp) *nt* (pl ~pen) company; society

gezet (ger-*zeht*) *adj* corpulent; stout

gezicht (ger-*zikht*) *nt* (pl ~en) face; sight

gezichtscrème (ger-*zikhts*-kraim) *c* (pl ~s) face-cream

gezichtsmassage (ger-*zikhts*-mah-saa-zher) *c* (pl ~s) face massage

gezichtspoeder (ger-*zikhts*-pōō-derr) *nt/c* (pl ~s) face-powder

gezien (ger-*zeen*) *prep* considering

gezin (ger-*zin*) *nt* (pl ~nen) family

gezond (ger-*zont*) *adj* healthy; well; wholesome

gezondheid (ger-*zont*-hayt) *c* health

gezondheidsattest (ger-*zont*-hayts-ah-tehst) *nt* (pl ~en) health certificate

gezwel (ger-*zvehl*) *nt* (pl ~len) tumour, growth

gids (gɪts) *c* (pl ~en) guide; guidebook

giechelen (*gee*-kher-lern) *v* giggle

gier (geer) *c* (pl ~en) vulture

gierig (*gee*-rerkh) *adj* avaricious; stingy

*gieten (*gee*-tern) *v* pour

gietijzer (*gee*-tay-zerr) *nt* cast iron

gift (gɪft) *c* (pl ~en) donation

giftig (*gɪf*-terkh) *adj* poisonous

gijzelaar (*gay*-zer-laar) *c* (pl ~s) hostage

gil (gɪl) *c* (pl ~len) scream, yell, shriek

gillen (*gɪ*-lern) *v* scream, yell, shriek

ginds (gɪns) *adv* over there

gips (gɪps) *nt* plaster

gissen (*gɪ*-sern) *v* guess

gissing (*gɪ*-sɪng) *c* (pl ~en) guess

gist (gɪst) *c* yeast

gisten (*gɪss*-tern) *v* ferment

gisteren (*gɪss*-ter-rern) *adv* yesterday

gitaar (gee-*taar*) *c* (pl -taren) guitar

glad (glaht) *adj* slippery; smooth

glans (glahns) *c* gloss

glanzen (*glahn*-zern) *v* *shine; **glanzend** glossy

glas (glahss) *nt* (pl glazen) glass; **gebrandschilderd** ~ stained glass

glazen (*glaa*-zern) *adj* glass

gletsjer (*gleh"*-sherr) *c* (pl ~s) glacier

gleuf (glÿf) *c* (pl gleuven) slot

glibberig (*glɪ*-ber-rerkh) *adj* slippery

glijbaan (*glay*-baan) *c* (pl -banen) slide

*glijden (*glay*-dern) *v* glide, *slide

glimlach (*glɪm*-lahkh) *c* smile

glimlachen (*glɪm*-lah-khern) *v* smile

glimp (glɪmp) *c* glimpse

globaal (gloa-*baal*) *adj* broad

gloed (gloot) *c* glow

gloeien (*gloōee*-ern) *v* glow

gloeilamp (*gloōee*-lahmp) *c* (pl ~en) light bulb

glooien (*gloā ee*-ern) *v* slope

glooiing (*gloāee*-ɪng) *c* (pl ~en) ramp

glorie (*gloā*-ree) *c* glory

gluren (*glew̄*-rern) *v* peep

gobelin (goa-ber-*lang*) *c* (pl ~s) tapestry

god (got) *c* (pl ~en) god

goddelijk (*go*-der-lerk) *adj* divine

godin (goā-dɪn) *c* (pl ~nen) goddess

godsdienst (gots-deenst) *c* (pl ~en) religion

godsdienstig (gots-*deen*-sterkh) *adj* religious

goed (goōt) *adj* good; right, correct; kind; *adv* well; **goed!** all right!

goederen (*goō*-der-rern) *pl* goods *pl*

goederentrein (*goō*-der-rern-trayn) *c* (pl ~en) goods train; freight-train *nAm*

goedgelovig (goōt-kher-*loā*-verkh) *adj* credulous

goedgestemd (goōt-kher-*stehmt*) *adj* good-tempered

goedhartig (goōt-*hahr*-terkh) *adj* good-natured

goedkeuren (*goōt*-kūr-rern) *v* approve

goedkeuring (*goōt*-kur-rɪng) *c* (pl ~en) approval

goedkoop (goōt-*koāp*) *adj* cheap; inexpensive

gok (gok) *c* chance

golf¹ (golf) *c* (pl golven) wave; gulf

golf² (golf) *nt* golf

golfbaan (*golf*-baan) *c* (pl -banen) golf-links, golf-course

golfclub (*golf*-klerp) *c* (pl ~s) golfclub

golflengte (*golf*-lehng-ter) *c* (pl ~n, ~s) wave-length

golvend (*gol*-vernt) *adj* wavy, undulating

gom (gom) *c*/*nt* (pl ~men) eraser

gondel (*gon*-derl) *c* (pl ~s) gondola

goochelaar (*gōa*-kher-laar) *c* (pl ~s) magician

gooi (gōaee) *c* (pl ~en) throw

gooien (*gōa*ee-ern) *v* *throw; *cast; toss

goot (gōat) *c* (pl goten) gutter

gootsteen (*gōat*-stāyn) *c* (pl -stenen) sink

gordijn (gor-*dayn*) *nt* (pl ~en) curtain

gorgelen (*gor*-ger-lern) *v* gargle

goud (gout) *nt* gold

gouden (*gou*-dern) *adj* golden

goudmijn (*gout*-mayn) *c* (pl ~en) goldmine

goudsmid (*gout*-smɪt) *c* (pl -smeden) goldsmith

gouvernante (gōo-verr-*nahn*-ter) *c* (pl ~s) governess

gouverneur (gōo-verr-*nūrr*) *c* (pl ~s) governor

graad (graat) *c* (pl graden) degree; grade

graaf (graaf) *c* (pl graven) count; earl

graafschap (*graaf*-skhahp) *nt* (pl ~pen) county

graag (graakh) *adv* gladly, willingly

graan (graan) *nt* (pl granen) corn, grain

graat (graat) *c* (pl graten) bone, fishbone

gracht (grahkht) *c* (pl ~en) canal; moat

graf (grahf) *nt* (pl graven) grave; tomb

grafiek (graa-*feek*) *c* (pl ~en) graph, diagram; chart

grafisch (*graa*-feess) *adj* graphic

grafsteen (*grahf*-stāyn) *c* (pl -stenen) ·

tombstone, gravestone

gram (grahm) *nt* (pl ~men) gram

grammatica (grah-*maa*-tee-kaa) *c* grammar

grammaticaal (grah-maa-tee-*kaal*) *adj* grammatical

grammofoonplaat (grah-mōa-*fōan*-plaat) *c* (pl -platen) disc, record

graniet (graa-*neet*) *nt* granite

grap (grahp) *c* (pl ~pen) joke

grappig (*grah*-perkh) *adj* funny, humorous

gras (grahss) *nt* grass

grasspriet (*grahss*-spreet) *c* (pl ~en) blade of grass

grasveld (*grahss*-fehlt) *nt* (pl ~en) lawn

gratie (*graa*-tsee) *c* grace; pardon

gratis (*graa*-terss) *adv* free of charge, free, gratis

grauw (grou) *adj* grey

***graven** (*graa*-vern) *v* *dig

graveren (graa-*vāy*-rern) *v* engrave

graveur (graa-*vūrr*) *c* (pl ~s) engraver

gravin (graa-*vɪn*) *c* (pl ~nen) countess

gravure (graa-*vēw*-rer) *c* (pl ~s, ~n) engraving

grazen (*graa*-zern) *v* graze

greep (grāyp) *c* (pl grepen) grip; grasp, clutch

grendel (*grehn*-derl) *c* (pl ~s) bolt

grens (grehns) *c* (pl grenzen) frontier, border; boundary, bound

grenzeloos (*grehn*-zer-lōass) *adj* unlimited

grenzen (*grehn*-zern) *v* border (on), adjoin; verge

greppel (*greh*-perl) *c* (pl ~s) ditch

Griek (greek) *c* (pl ~en) Greek

Griekenland (*gree*-kern-lahnt) Greece

Grieks (greeks) *adj* Greek

griep (greep) *c* flu, influenza

griet (greet) *c* (pl ~en) brill

griezelig (*gree*-zer-lerkh) *adj* scary,

creepy

grijns (grayns) *c* grin

grijnzen (grayn-zern) *v* grin

*****grijpen** (*gray*-pern) *v* *catch, grip, grasp, seize

grijs (grayss) *adj* grey

gril (gril) *c* (pl ~len) whim, fancy, fad

grind (grint) *nt* gravel

grinniken (gri-ner-kern) *v* chuckle

groef (grōōf) *c* (pl groeven) groove

groei (grōōee) *c* growth

groeien (grōō^{ee}-ern) *v* *grow

groen (grōōn) *adj* green

groente *c* (pl ~n, ~s) greens *pl*, vegetable

groenteboer (grōōn-ter-bōōr) *c* (pl ~en) greengrocer; vegetable merchant

groep (grōōp) *c* (pl ~en) group; bunch, set, party

groet (grōōt) *c* (pl ~en) greeting

groeten (grōō-tern) *v* greet; salute

groeve (grōō-ver) *c* (pl ~n) pit

grof (grof) *adj* gross, coarse; rude

grommen (gro-mern) *v* growl

grond (gront) *c* ground; earth, soil; **begane ~** ground floor

grondig (gron-derkh) *adj* thorough

grondslag (gront-slahkh) *c* (pl ~en) basis, base

grondstof (gront-stof) *c* (pl ~fen) raw material

grondwet (gront-veht) *c* (pl ~ten) constitution

groot (grōāt) *adj* big; great, large, tall; major; **grootst** major, main; **groter** major; superior

*****grootbrengen** (grōāt-breh-ngern) *v* *bring up, raise; rear

Groot-Brittannië (grōāt-bri-*tah*-nee-^yer) Great Britain

groothandel (grōāt-hahn-derl) *c* wholesale

grootmoeder (grōāt-mōō-derr) *c* (pl

~s) grandmother

grootouders (grōāt-ou-derrs) *pl* grandparents *pl*

groots (grōāts) *adj* grand, superb, magnificent

grootte (grōā-ter) *c* (pl ~n, ~s) size

grootvader (grōāt-faa-derr) *c* (pl ~s) grandfather

gros (gross) *nt* (pl ~sen) gross

grossier (gro-*seer*) *c* (pl ~s) wholesale dealer

grot (grot) *c* (pl ~ten) cave; grotto

gruis (grur^{ew}ss) *nt* grit

gruwelijk (grew-ver-lerk) *adj* horrible

gul (gerl) *adj* generous

gulp (gerlp) *c* (pl ~en) fly

gulzig (gerl-zerkh) *adj* greedy

gunnen (ger-nern) *v* grant

gunst (gernst) *c* (pl ~en) favour

gunstig (gern-sterkh) *adj* favourable

guur (gewr) *adj* bleak

gymnast (gim-*nahst*) *c* (pl ~en) gymnast

gymnastiek (gim-nahss-*teek*) *c* gymnastics *pl*

gymnastiekbroek (gim-nahss-*teek*-brōōk) *c* (pl ~en) trunks *pl*

gymnastiekzaal (gim-nahss-*teek*-saal) *c* (pl -zalen) gymnasium

gymschoenen (*gim*-skhōō-nern) *pl* gym shoes, plimsolls *pl*; sneakers *plAm*

gynaecoloog (gee-nāy-kōā-*lōākh*) *c* (pl -logen) gynaecologist

H

haai (haa^{ee}) *c* (pl ~en) shark

haak (haak) *c* (pl haken) hook; **tussen twee haakjes** by the way

haalbaar (*haal*-baar) *adj* attainable, realizable

haan (haan) *c* (pl hanen) cock

haar¹ (haar) *nt* (pl haren) hair

haar² (haar) *pron* her

haarborstel (*haar*-bor-sterl) *c* (pl ~s) hairbrush

haarcrème (*haar*-kraim) *c* (pl ~s) hair cream

haard (haart) *c* (pl ~en) hearth, fireplace

haardroger (*haar*-drōa-gerr) *c* (pl ~s) hair-dryer

haargel (*haar*-zhel) *c* hair gel

haarlak (*haar*-lahk) *c* (pl ~ken) hairspray

haarnetje (*haar*-neh-t^yer) *nt* (pl ~s) hair-net

haarspeld (*haar*-spehlt) *c* (pl ~en) hairpin, hair-grip; bobby pin *Am*

haarstukje (*haar*-ster-k^yer) *nt* (pl ~s) hair piece

haarversteviger (*haar*-verr-stāy-ver-gerr) *c* setting lotion

haas (haass) *c* (pl hazen) hare

haast¹ (haast) *adv* nearly, almost

haast² (haast) *c* haste, hurry

zich haasten (*haass*-tern) hasten, rush, hurry

haastig (*haass*-terkh) *adj* hasty; *adv* in a hurry

haat (haat) *c* hatred, hate

hachelijk (*hah*-kher-lerk) *adj* precarious, critical

hagel (*haa*-gerl) *c* hail

hak (hahk) *c* (pl ~ken) heel

haken (*haa*-kern) *v* crochet

hakken (*hah*-kern) *v* chop

hal (hahl) *c* (pl ~len) lobby, hall

halen (*haa*-lern) *v* *get, fetch; *make; *catch; *laten ~ *send for

half (hahlf) *adj* half; semi-; *adv* half

hallo! (hah-*lōa*) hello!

hals (hahls) *c* (pl halzen) throat; neck

halsband (*hahls*-bahnt) *c* (pl ~en) collar

halsketting (*hahls*-keh-tıng) *c* (pl ~en) necklace

halt! (hahlt) stop!

halte (*hahl*-ter) *c* (pl ~n, ~s) stop

halveren (hahl-*vāy*-rern) *v* halve

halverwege (*hahl*-verr-vāy-ger) *adv* halfway

ham (hahm) *c* (pl ~men) ham

hamer (*haa*-merr) *c* (pl ~s) hammer; **houten ~** mallet

hand (hahnt) *c* (pl ~en) hand; **hand-** manual; **met de ~ gemaakt** handmade

handbagage (*hahnt*-bah-gaa-zher) *c* hand luggage; hand baggage *Am*

handboeien (*hahnt*-bōo^ee-ern) *pl* handcuffs *pl*

handboek (*hahnt*-bōōk) *nt* (pl ~en) handbook

handcrème (*hahnt*-kraim) *c* (pl ~s) hand cream

handdoek (*hahn*-dōōk) *c* (pl ~en) towel

handdruk (*hahn*-drerk) *c* handshake

handel (*hahn*-derl) *c* commerce, trade; business; ~ *drijven trade; **handels-** commercial

handelaar (*hahn*-der-laar) *c* (pl ~s, -laren) tradesman, merchant; dealer, trader

handelen (*hahn*-der-lern) *v* act

handeling (*hahn*-der-lıng) *c* (pl ~en) action; deed, plot

handelsmerk (*hahn*-derls-mehrk) *nt* (pl ~en) trademark

handelsrecht (*hahn*-derls-rehkht) *nt* commercial law

handelswaar (*hahn*-derls-vaar) *c* merchandise

handenarbeid (*hahn*-der-nahr-bayt) *c* handicraft

handhaven (*hahnt*-haa-vern) *v* maintain

handig (*hahn*-derkh) *adj* handy

handkoffertje (*hahnt*-ko-ferr-t^yer) *nt* (pl ~s) grip *nAm*

handpalm (*hahnt*-pahlm) *c* (pl ~en) palm

handrem (*hahnt*-rehm) *c* (pl ~men) hand-brake

handschoen (*hahnt*-skhōōn) *c* (pl ~en) glove

handschrift (*hahnt*-skhrıft) *nt* (pl ~en) handwriting

handtas (*hahn*-tahss) *c* (pl ~sen) handbag, bag

handtekening (*hahn*-tāy-ker-nıng) *v* (pl ~en) signature

handvat (*hahnt*-faht) *nt* (pl ~ten) handle

handvol (*hahnt*-fol) *c* handful

handwerk (*hahnt*-vehrk) *nt* handwork, handicraft; needlework

hangbrug (*hahng*-brerkh) *c* (pl ~gen) suspension bridge

*****hangen** (*hah*-ngern) *v* *hang

hangmat (*hahng*-maht) *c* (pl ~ten) hammock

hangslot (*hahng*-slot) *nt* (pl ~en) padlock

hanteerbaar (hahn-*tāyr*-baar) *adj* manageable

hanteren (hahn-*tāy*-rern) *v* handle

hap (hahp) *c* (pl ~pen) bite

hard (hahrt) *adj* hard; loud

harddraverij (hahr-draa-ver-*ray*) *c* (pl ~en) horserace

hardnekkig (hahrt-*neh*-kerkh) *adj* obstinate, dogged, stubborn

hardop (hahrt-*op*) *adv* aloud

harig (*haa*-rerkh) *adj* hairy

haring (*haa*-rıng) *c* (pl ~en) herring

hark (hahrk) *c* (pl ~en) rake

harmonie (hahr-mōa-*nee*) *c* harmony

harnas (*hahr*-nahss) *nt* (pl ~sen) armour

harp (hahrp) *c* (pl ~en) harp

hars (hahrs) *nt/c* resin

hart (hahrt) *nt* (pl ~en) heart

hartaanval (*hahr*-taan-vahl) *c* (pl ~len) heart attack

hartelijk (*hahr*-ter-lerk) *adj* hearty, cordial; sympathetic

harteloos (*hahr*-ter-lōass) *adj* heartless

hartklopping (*hahrt*-klo-pıng) *c* (pl ~en) palpitation

hartstocht (*hahrts*-tokht) *c* passion

hartstochtelijk (hahrts-*tokh*-ter-lerk) *adj* passionate

hatelijk (*haa*-ter-lerk) *adj* spiteful

haten (*haa*-tern) *v* hate

haven (*haa*-vern) *c* (pl ~s) port, harbour

havenarbeider (*haa*-vern-ahr-bay-derr) *c* (pl ~s) docker

haver (*haa*-verr) *c* oats *pl*

havik (*haa*-vık) *c* (pl ~en) hawk

hazelnoot (*haa*-zerl-nōat) *c* (pl -noten) hazelnut

hazewind (haa-zer-*vınt*) *c* (pl ~en) greyhound

*****hebben** (*heh*-bern) *v* *have

Hebreeuws (hāy-brāy^{ōō}ss) *nt* Hebrew

hebzucht (*hehp*-serkht) *c* greed

hebzuchtig (hehp-*serkh*-terkh) *adj* greedy

hechten (*hehkh*-tern) *v* attach; sew up

hechtenis (*hehkh*-ter-nıss) *c* custody

hechting (*hehkh*-tıng) *c* (pl ~en) stitch

hechtpleister (*hehkht*-play-sterr) *c* (pl ~s) adhesive tape

heden (*hāy*-dern) *nt* present

hedendaags (*hāy*-dern-daakhs) *adj* contemporary

heel (hāyl) *adj* entire, whole; unbroken; *adv* quite

heelal (hāy-*lahl*) *nt* universe

heelhuids (*hāyl*-hur^{ew}ts) *adj* unhurt

*****heengaan** (*hāyng*-gaan) *v* depart

heer (hāyr) *c* (pl heren) gentleman

heerlijk (*hāyr*-lerk) *adj* lovely, wonderful; delightful, delicious

heerschappij (hāyr-skhah-*pay*) c (pl ~en) rule; dominion

heersen (*hāyr*-sern) v rule

heerser (*hāyr*-serr) c (pl ~s) ruler

hees (hāyss) *adj* hoarse

heet (hāyt) *adj* hot; warm

hefboom (hehf-*bōam*) c (pl -bomen) lever

*heffen (*heh*-fern) v raise

heftig (*hehf*-terkh) *adj* violent

heg (hehkh) c (pl ~gen) hedge

heide (*hay*-der) c (pl ~n) heath; moor; heather

heiden (*hay*-dern) c (pl ~en) heathen, pagan

heidens (*hay*-derns) *adj* heathen, pagan

heiig (*hay*-erkh) *adj* hazy

heilbot (*hayl*-bot) c (pl ~ten) halibut

heilig (*hay*-lerkh) *adj* holy, sacred

heiligdom (*hay*-lerkh-dom) *nt* (pl ~men) shrine

heilige (*hay*-ler-ger) c (pl ~n) saint

heiligschennis (*hay*-lerkh-skheh-nerss) c sacrilege

heimwee (*haym*-vāy) *nt* homesickness

hek (hehk) *nt* (pl ~ken) fence; gate; railing

hekel (*hāy*-kerl) c dislike; **een ~ *hebben aan** hate, dislike

heks (hehks) c (pl ~en) witch

hel (hehl) c hell

helaas (*hāy*-*laass*) *adv* unfortunately

held (hehlt) c (pl ~en) hero

helder (*hehl*-derr) *adj* clear; serene; bright

heleboel (*hāy*-ler-*bōōl*) c plenty

helemaal (*hāy*-ler-maal) *adv* entirely, altogether, completely, wholly; quite; at all

helft (hehlft) c (pl ~en) half

hellen (*heh*-lern) v slant; **hellend** slanting

helling (*heh*-lɪng) c (pl ~en) slope; hillside; gradient, incline

helm (hehlm) c (pl ~en) helmet

*helpen (*hehl*-pern) v help; assist, aid

helper (*hehl*-perr) c (pl ~s) helper

hem (hehm) *pron* him

hemd (hehmt) *nt* (pl ~en) shirt; vest; undershirt

hemel (*hāy*-merl) c (pl ~s, ~en) sky; heaven

hen[1] (hehn) *pron* them

hen[2] (hehn) c (pl ~nen) hen

hendel (*hehn*-derl) c (pl ~s) lever

hengel (*heh*-ngerl) c (pl ~s) fishing rod

hengelen (*heh*-nger-lern) v angle, fish

hennep (*heh*-nerp) c hemp

herberg (*hehr*-behrkh) c (pl ~en) hostel, tavern, inn

herbergen (*hehr*-behr-gern) v lodge

herbergier (hehr-behr-*geer*) c (pl ~s) inn-keeper

herdenking (hehr-*dehng*-kɪng) c (pl ~en) commemoration

herder (*hehr*-derr) c (pl ~s) shepherd

herenhuis (*hāy*-rern-hur[ew]ss) *nt* (pl -huizen) mansion, manor-house

herenigen (heh-*rāy*-ner-gern) v reunite

herentoilet (*hāy*-rern-tvah-leht) *nt* (pl ~ten) men's room

herfst (hehrfst) c autumn; fall *nAm*

herhalen (hehr-*haa*-lern) v repeat

herhaling (hehr-*haa*-lɪng) c (pl ~en) repetition

herinneren (heh-*rɪ*-ner-rern) v remind; **zich ~** remember, recollect, recall

herinnering (heh-*rɪ*-ner-rɪng) c (pl ~en) memory; remembrance

herkennen (hehr-*keh*-nern) v recognize

herkomst (*hehr*-komst) c origin

hernia (*hehr*-nee-[y]aa) c slipped disc

herrie (*heh*-ree) c noise; fuss

*herroepen (heh-*rōō*-pern) v recall

hersenen (*hehr*-ser-nern) *pl* brain

hersenschudding (*hehr*-sern-skher-dıng) *c* (pl ~en) concussion

herstel (hehr-*stehl*) *nt* repair; recovery; revival

herstellen (hehr-*steh*-lern) *v* repair, mend; **zich ~** recover

hert (hehrt) *nt* (pl ~en) deer

hertog (*hehr*-tokh) *c* (pl ~en) duke

hertogin (hehr-tōā-*gın*) *c* (pl ~nen) duchess

hervatten (hehr-*vah*-tern) *v* resume, recommence

*herzien (hehr-*zeen*) *v* revise

herziening (hehr-*zee*-nıng) *c* (pl ~en) revision

het (heht, ert) *art* the; *pron* it

*heten (*hāy*-tern) *v* *be called

heteroseksueel (hāy-ter-rōā-sehk-sew-*vāyl*) *adj* heterosexual

hetzij ... hetzij (heht-*say*) either ... or

heup (hūrp) *c* (pl ~en) hip

heuvel (*hūr*-verl) *c* (pl ~s) hill; mound

heuvelachtig (*hūr*-ver-lahkh-terkh) *adj* hilly

heuveltop (*hūr*-verl-top) *c* (pl ~pen) hilltop

hevig (*hāy*-verkh) *adj* severe, violent; intense

hiel (heel) *c* (pl ~en) heel

hier (heer) *adv* here

hiërarchie (hee-ᵞer-rahr-*khee*) *c* (pl ~ën) hierarchy

hij (hay) *pron* he

hijgen (*hay*-gern) *v* pant

*hijsen (*hay*-sern) *v* hoist

hijskraan (*hayss*-kraan) *c* (pl -kranen) crane

hik (hık) *c* hiccup

hinderen (*hın*-der-rern) *v* hinder; bother, embarrass

hinderlaag (*hın*-derr-laakh) *c* (pl -lagen) ambush

hinderlijk (*hın*-derr-lerk) *adj* annoying

hindernis (*hın*-derr-nıss) *c* (pl ~sen) obstacle

hinken (*hıng*-kern) *v* limp

historisch (hee-*stōā*-reess) *adj* historic

hitte (*hı*-ter) *c* heat

hobbelig (*ho*-ber-lerkh) *adj* bumpy

hobby (*ho*-bee) *c* (pl ~'s) hobby

hoe (hōō) *adv* how; **~ ... hoe** the ... the; **~ dan ook** anyhow, any way; at any rate

hoed (hōōt) *c* (pl ~en) hat

hoede (*hōō*-der) *c* custody

zich hoeden (*hōō*-dern) beware

hoef (hōōf) *c* (pl hoeven) hoof

hoefijzer (*hōōf*-ay-zerr) *nt* (pl ~s) horseshoe

hoek (hōōk) *c* (pl ~en) corner; angle

hoer (hōōr) *c* (pl ~en) whore

hoes (hōōss) *c* (pl hoezen) sleeve

hoest (hōōst) *c* cough

hoesten (*hōōss*-tern) *v* cough

hoeveel (hōō-*vāyl*) *pron* how much; how many

hoeveelheid (hōō-*vāyl*-hayt) *c* (pl -heden) quantity; amount

hoeven (*hōō*-vern) *v* need

hoewel (hōō-*vehl*) *conj* although, though

hof (hof) *nt* (pl hoven) court

hoffelijk (*ho*-fer-lerk) *adj* courteous

hokje (*ho*-kᵞer) *nt* (pl ~s) booth

hol¹ (hol) *nt* (pl ~en) den; cavern

hol² (hol) *adj* hollow

Holland (*ho*-lahnt) Holland

Hollander (*ho*-lahn-derr) *c* (pl ~s) Dutchman

Hollands (*ho*-lahnts) *adj* Dutch

holte (*hol*-ter) *c* (pl ~s, ~n) cavity

homoseksueel (hōā-mōā-sehk-sew-*vāyl*) *adj* homosexual

hond (hont) *c* (pl ~en) dog

hondehok (*hon*-der-hok) *nt* (pl ~ken) kennel

honderd (*hon*-derrt) *num* hundred

hondsdolheid (honts-*dol*-hayt) *c* rabies

Hongaar (hong-*gaar*) *c* (pl -garen) Hungarian

Hongaars (hong-*gaars*) *adj* Hungarian

Hongarije (hong-gaa-*ray*-er) Hungary

honger (*ho*-ngerr) *c* hunger

hongerig (*ho*-nger-rerkh) *adj* hungry

honing (*hōā*-ning) *c* honey

honkbal (*hongk*-bahl) *nt* baseball

honorarium (hōā-nōā-*raa*-ree-ᵛerm) *nt* (pl -ria) fee

hoofd (hōāft) *nt* (pl ~en) head; **het ~ *bieden aan** face; **hoofd-** primary, main, chief; cardinal, capital; **over het ~ *zien** overlook; **uit het ~** by heart; **uit het ~ leren** memorize

hoofdkussen (*hōāft*-ker-sern) *nt* (pl ~s) pillow

hoofdkwartier (*hōāft*-kvahr-teer) *nt* (pl ~en) headquarters *pl*

hoofdleiding (*hōāft*-lay-ding) *c* (pl ~en) mains *pl*

hoofdletter (*hōāft*-leh-terr) *c* (pl ~s) capital letter

hoofdlijn (*hōāft*-layn) *c* (pl ~en) main line

hoofdonderwijzer (*hōāft*-on-derr-vay-zerr) *c* (pl ~s) head teacher

hoofdpijn (*hōāft*-payn) *c* headache

hoofdstad (*hōāft*-staht) *c* (pl -steden) capital

hoofdstraat (*hōāft*-straat) *c* (pl -straten) main street, thoroughfare

hoofdweg (*hōāft*-vehkh) *c* (pl ~en) main road, thoroughfare; highway

hoofdzakelijk (hōāft-*saa*-ker-lerk) *adv* mainly

hoog (hōākh) *adj* high; tall; **hoger** upper; superior; **hoogst** foremost, extreme

hooghartig (hōākh-*hahr*-terkh) *adj* haughty

hoogleraar (hōākh-*lāy*-raar) *c* (pl -lera-ren, ~s) professor

hoogmoedig (hōākh-*mōō*-derkh) *adj* proud

hoogovens (*hōākh*-ōā-verns) *pl* iron-works

hoogseizoen (*hōākh*-say-zōōn) *nt* high season, peak season

hoogstens (*hōākh*-sterns) *adv* at most

hoogte (*hōākh*-ter) *c* (pl ~n, ~s) height; altitude

hoogtepunt (*hōākh*-ter-pernt) *nt* (pl ~en) height

hooguit (*hōākh*-ur-ewt) *adv* at most

hoogvlakte (*hōākh*-flahk-ter) *c* (pl ~n, ~s) uplands *pl*; plateau

hooi (hōā-ee) *nt* hay

hooikoorts (*hōā-ee*-kōārts) *c* hay fever

hoon (hōān) *c* scorn

hoop¹ (hōāp) *c* (pl hopen) heap, lot

hoop² (hōāp) *c* hope

hoopvol (*hōāp*-fol) *adj* hopeful

hoorbaar (*hōār*-baar) *adj* audible

hoorn (*hōā*-rern) *c* (pl ~en, ~s) horn

hop (hop) *c* hop

hopeloos (*hōā*-per-lōāss) *adj* hopeless

hopen (*hōā*-pern) *v* hope

horen (*hōā*-rern) *v* *hear

horizon (*hōā*-ree-zon) *c* horizon

horizontaal (hōā-ree-zon-*taal*) *adj* horizontal

horloge (hor-*lōā*-zher) *nt* (pl ~s) watch

horlogebandje (hor-*lōā*-zher-bahn-tᵛer) *nt* (pl ~s) watch-strap

horlogemaker (hor-*lōā*-zher-maa-kerr) *c* (pl ~s) watch-maker

hors d'œuvre (awr-*dūr*-vrer) *c* (pl ~s) hors-d'œuvre

hospes (*hoss*-perss) *c* (pl ~sen) land-lord

hospita (*hoss*-pee-taa) *c* (pl ~'s) land-lady

hospitaal (*hoss*-pee-taal) *nt* (pl -talen) hospital

hotel (hōa-*tehl*) *nt* (pl ~s) hotel

***houden** (*hou*-dern) *v* *hold; *keep; ~ **van** love; like, care for, *be fond of; **niet ~ van** dislike

houding (*hou*-dɪng) *c* (pl ~en) position; attitude

hout (hout) *nt* wood

houtblok (*hout*-blok) *nt* (pl ~ken) log

houten (*hou*-tern) *adj* wooden

houtskool (*houts*-kōal) *c* charcoal

***houtsnijden** (*hout*-snay-dern) *v* carve

houtsnijwerk (*hout*-snay-vehrk) *nt* wood-carving

houtzagerij (hout-saa-ger-*ray*) *c* (pl ~en) saw-mill

houvast (hou-*vahst*) *nt* grip

houweel (hou-*vāyl*) *nt* (pl -welen) pick-axe

huichelaar (*hur*ew-kher-laar) *c* (pl ~s) hypocrite

huichelachtig (*hur*ew-kherl-ahkh-terkh) *adj* hypocritical

huichelarij (hur*ew*-kher-laa-*ray*) *c* hypocrisy

huichelen (*hur*ew-kher-lern) *v* simulate

huid (hur*ew*t) *c* (pl ~en) skin; hide

huidcrème (*hur*ew*t*-kraim) *c* (pl ~s) skin cream

huidig (*hur*ew-derkh) *adj* current

huiduitslag (*hur*ew*t*-ur*ew*t-slahkh) *c* rash

huilen (*hur*ew-lern) *v* cry, *weep

huis (hur*ew*ss) *nt* (pl huizen) house; home; **naar ~** home

huisarts (*hur*ew*ss*-ahrts) *c* (pl ~en) general practitioner

huisbaas (*hur*ew*ss*-baass) *c* (pl -bazen) landlord

huisdier (*hur*ew*ss*-deer) *nt* (pl ~en) pet

huiselijk (*hur*ew-ser-lerk) *adj* domestic

huishouden (*hur*ew*ss*-hou-dern) *nt* (pl ~s) household; housework, housekeeping

huishoudster (*hur*ew*ss*-hout-sterr) *c* (pl ~s) housekeeper

huiskamer (*hur*ew*ss*-kaa-merr) *c* (pl ~s) living-room

huisonderwijzer (*hur*ew*ss*-on-derr-vay-zerr) *c* (pl ~s) tutor

huissleutel (*hur*ew*ss*-slur-terl) *c* (pl ~s) latchkey

huisvrouw (*hur*ew*ss*-frou) *c* (pl ~en) housewife

huizenblok (*hur*ew-zern-blok) *nt* (pl ~ken) house block *Am*

hulde (*herl*-der) *c* tribute, homage

huldigen (*herl*-der-gern) *v* honour

hulp (herlp) *c* help; assistance, aid; **eerste ~** first-aid; **eerste hulppost** first-aid post

hulpvaardig (herlp-*faar*-derkh) *adj* helpful

humeur (hew-*mŭrr*) *nt* (pl ~en) mood

humor (*hew*-mor) *c* humour

humoristisch (hew-mōa-*rɪss*-teess) *adj* humorous

hun (hern) *pron* their

huppelen (*her*-per-lern) *v* hop, skip

huren (*hew*-rern) *v* hire, rent; lease

hut (hert) *c* (pl ~ten) hut; cabin

huur (hewr) *c* (pl huren) rent; **te ~** for hire

huurcontract (*hewr*-kon-trahkt) *nt* (pl ~en) lease

huurder (*hewr*-derr) *c* (pl ~s) tenant

huurkoop (*hewr*-kōap) *c* hire-purchase

huwelijk (*hew*-ver-lerk) *nt* (pl ~en) wedding, marriage

huwelijksreis (*hew*-ver-lerks-rayss) *c* (pl -reizen) honeymoon

huwen (*hew*ᵒᵒ-ern) *v* marry

hygiëne (hee-gee-*ʸāy*-ner) *c* hygiene

hygiënisch (hee-gee-*ʸāy*-neess) *adj* hygienic

hypocriet (hee-pōa-*kreet*) *adj* hypocritical

hypotheek (hee-pōa-*tāyk*) *c* (pl -theken) mortgage

hysterisch (hee-*stāy*-reess) *adj* hysterical

I

ideaal[1] (ee-dāy-ˠaal) *adj* ideal
ideaal[2] (ee-dāy-ˠaal) *nt* (pl idealen) ideal
idee (ee-*dāy*) *nt/c* (pl ~ën, ~s) idea
identiek (ee-dehn-*teek*) *adj* identical
identificatie (ee-dehn-tee-fi-*kaa*-tsee) *c* identification
identificeren (ee-dehn-tee-fee-*sāy*-rern) *v* identify
identiteit (ee-dehn-ti-*tayt*) *c* identity
identiteitskaart (ee-dehn-tee-*tayts*-kaart) *c* (pl ~en) identity card
idiomatisch (ee-dee-ˠ*ōa*-*maa*-teess) *adj* idiomatic
idioom (ee-dee-ˠ*ōām*) *nt* (pl idiomen) idiom
idioot[1] (ee-dee-ˠ*ōāt*) *adj* idiotic
idioot[2] (ee-dee-ˠ*ōāt*) *c* (pl idioten) idiot
idool (ee-*dōāl*) *nt* (pl idolen) idol
ieder (*ee*-derr) *pron* each, every; everyone
iedereen (ee-der-*rāyn*) *pron* everyone, everybody; anyone
iemand (*ee*-mahnt) *pron* someone, somebody
iep (eep) *c* (pl ~en) elm
Ier (eer) *c* (pl ~en) Irishman
Ierland (*eer*-lahnt) Ireland
Iers (eers) *adj* Irish
iets (eets) *pron* something; some
ijdel (*ay*-derl) *adj* vain; idle
ijs (ayss) *nt* ice; ice-cream
ijsbaan (*ayss*-baan) *c* (pl -banen) skating-rink
ijsje (*ay*-sher) *nt* (pl ~s) ice-cream
ijskast (*ayss*-kahst) *c* (pl ~en) fridge,

refrigerator
ijskoud (*ayss*-kout) *adj* freezing
IJsland (*ayss*-lahnt) Iceland
IJslander (*ayss*-lahn-derr) *c* (pl ~s) Icelander
IJslands (*ayss*-lahnts) *adj* Icelandic
ijswater (*ayss*-vaa-terr) *nt* iced water
ijver (*ay*-verr) *c* zeal; diligence
ijverig (*ay*-ver-rerkh) *adj* zealous; diligent
ijzer (*ay*-zerr) *nt* iron
ijzerdraad (*ay*-zerr-draat) *nt* wire
ijzeren (*ay*-zer-rern) *adj* iron
ijzerwaren (*ay*-zerr-vaa-rern) *pl* hardware
ik (ɪk) *pron* I
ikoon (ee-*kōān*) *c* (pl ikonen) icon
illegaal (ee-ler-*gaal*) *adj* illegal
illusie (ɪ-*lēw*-zee) *c* (pl ~s) illusion
illustratie (ɪ-lēw-*straa*-tsee) *c* (pl ~s) illustration
illustreren (ɪ-lēw-*strāy*-rern) *v* illustrate
imitatie (ee-mee-*taa*-tsee) *c* (pl ~s) imitation
imiteren (ee-mee-*tāy*-rern) *v* imitate
immigrant (ɪ-mee-*grahnt*) *c* (pl ~en) immigrant
immigratie (ɪ-mee-*graa*-tsee) *c* immigration
immigreren (ɪ-mee-*grāy*-rern) *v* immigrate
immuniteit (ɪ-mēw-nee-*tayt*) *c* immunity
impliceren (ɪm-plee-*sāy*-rern) *v* imply, involve
imponeren (ɪm-pōa-*nāy*-rern) *v* impress
impopulair (ɪm-pōa-pēw-*lair*) *adj* unpopular
import (*ɪm*-port) *c* import
importeren (ɪm-por-*tāy*-rern) *v* import
importeur (ɪm-por-*tūrr*) *c* (pl ~s) importer

impotent (ɪm-pōā-*tehnt*) *adj* impotent

impotentie (ɪm-pōā-*tehn*-see) *c* impotence

improviseren (ɪm-prōā-vee-*sāy*-rern) *v* improvise

impuls (ɪm-*perls*) *c* (pl ~en) impulse

impulsief (ɪm-perl-*zeef*) *adj* impulsive

in (ɪn) *prep* in; into, inside; at

inademen (*ɪn*-aa-der-mern) *v* inhale

inbegrepen (ɪn-ber-*grāy*-pern) *adj* included; **alles ~** all in

inboorling (*ɪm*-bōar-lɪng) *c* (pl ~en) native

***inbreken** (*ɪm*-brāy-kern) *v* burgle

inbreker (*ɪm*-brāy-kerr) *c* (pl ~s) burglar

incasseren (ɪng-kah-*sāy*-rern) *v* cash

incident (ɪn-see-*dehnt*) *nt* (pl ~en) incident

inclusief (ɪng-klew-*zeef*) *adv* inclusive

incompleet (ɪng-kom-*plāyt*) *adj* incomplete

indelen (*ɪn*-dāy-lern) *v* classify

zich *indenken (*ɪn*-dehng-kern) imagine

inderdaad (ɪn-derr-*daat*) *adv* indeed

index (*ɪn*-dehks) *c* (pl ~en) index

India (*ɪn*-dee-ʸah) India

Indiaan (ɪn-dee-ʸaan) *c* (pl Indianen) Indian

Indiaans (ɪn-dee-ʸaans) *adj* Indian

indien (ɪn-*deen*) *conj* in case, if

Indiër (*ɪn*-dee-ʸerr) *c* (pl ~s) Indian

indigestie (ɪn-dee-*gehss*-tee) *c* indigestion

indirect (*ɪn*-dee-rehkt) *adj* indirect

Indisch (*ɪn*-deess) *adj* Indian

individu (ɪn-dee-vee-*dēw*) *nt* (pl ~en, ~'s) individual

individueel (ɪn-dee-vee-dēw-*vāyl*) *adj* individual

Indonesië (ɪn-dōā-*nāy*-zee-ʸer) Indonesia

Indonesiër (ɪn-dōā-*nāy*-zee-ʸerr) *c* (pl ~s) Indonesian

Indonesisch (ɪn-dōā-*nāy*-zeess) *adj* Indonesian

indringer (*ɪn*-drɪ-ngerr) *c* (pl ~s) trespasser

indruk (*ɪn*-drerk) *c* (pl ~ken) impression; **~ maken op** impress

indrukken (*ɪn*-drer-kern) *v* press

indrukwekkend (ɪn-drerk-*veh*-kernt) *adj* impressive, imposing

industrie (ɪn-derss-*tree*) *c* (pl ~ën) industry

industrieel (ɪn-derss-tree-ʸāyl) *adj* industrial

industriegebied (ɪn-derss-*tree*-ger-beet) *nt* (pl ~en) industrial area

ineens (ɪ-*nāyns*) *adv* suddenly; at once

inenten (*ɪn*-ehn-tern) *v* vaccinate, inoculate

inenting (*ɪn*-ehn-tɪng) *c* (pl ~en) vaccination, inoculation

infanterie (*ɪn*-fahn-ter-ree) *c* infantry

infectie (ɪn-*fehk*-see) *c* (pl ~s) infection

inferieur (ɪn-fāy-ree-ʸūrr) *adj* inferior

inflatie (ɪn-*flaa*-tsee) *c* inflation

informatie (ɪn-for-*maa*-tsee) *c* (pl ~s) information; enquiry; **~ *inwinnen** *v* inquire

informatiebureau (ɪn-for-*maa*-tsee-bēw-rōā) *nt* (pl ~s) inquiry office

informeel (ɪn-for-*māyl*) *adj* informal

informeren (ɪn-for-*māy*-rern) *v* enquire; inform

infrarood (*ɪn*-fraa-rōāt) *adj* infra-red

***ingaan** (*ɪng*-gaan) *v* enter; *take effect

ingang (*ɪng*-gahng) *c* (pl ~en) entrance, way in; entry; **met ~ van** as from

ingenieur (ɪn-zhern-ʸūrr) *c* (pl ~s) engineer

ingenomen (*ɪng*-ger-nōā-mern) *adj*

pleased

ingevolge (ing-ger-*vol*-ger) *prep* in accordance with

ingewanden (ing-ger-vahn-dern) *pl* bowels *pl*, intestines, insides

ingewikkeld (ing-ger-vi-kerlt) *adj* complicated; complex

ingrediënt (ing-grāy-dee-^yehnt) *nt* (pl ~en) ingredient

***ingrijpen** (*ing*-gray-pern) *v* intervene

inhalen (*in*-haa-lern) *v* *overtake; pass *vAm*; ~ **verboden** no overtaking; no passing *Am*

inham (*in*-hahm) *c* (pl ~men) creek, inlet

inheems (in-*hāyms*) *adj* native

inhoud (*in*-hout) *c* contents *pl*

***inhouden** (*in*-hou-dern) *v* contain; imply; restrain

inhoudsopgave (*in*-houts-op-khaa-ver) *c* (pl ~n) table of contents

initiatief (ee-nee-shaa-*teef*) *nt* (pl -tieven) initiative

injectie (in-^yehk-see) *c* (pl ~s) shot, injection

inkomen (*ing*-kōä-mern) *nt* (pl ~s) revenue, income

inkomsten (*ing*-kom-stern) *pl* earnings *pl*

inkomstenbelasting (*ing*-kom-ster-ber-lahss-ting) *c* income-tax

inkt (ingkt) *c* ink

inleiden (*in*-lay-dern) *v* introduce; **inleidend** preliminary

inleiding (*in*-lay-ding) *c* (pl ~en) introduction

inlichten (*in*-likh-tern) *v* inform

inlichting (*in*-likh-ting) *c* (pl ~en) information

inlichtingenkantoor (*in*-likh-ti-nger-kahn-tōar) *nt* (pl -toren) information bureau

inmaken (*in*-maa-kern) *v* preserve

inmenging (*in*-mehng-ing) *c* (pl ~en) interference

inmiddels (in-*mi*-derls) *adv* in the meantime

***innemen** (*i*-nāy-mern) *v* *take up; occupy; capture

inneming (*i*-nāy-ming) *c* capture

innen (*i*-nern) *v* cash

inpakken (*im*-pah-kern) *v* wrap; pack up, pack

inrichten (*in*-rikh-tern) *v* furnish

inrichting (*in*-rikh-ting) *c* (pl ~en) institution

inschakelen (*in*-skhaa-ker-lern) *v* switch on; plug in

***inschenken** (*in*-skhehng-kern) *v* pour

inschepen (*in*-skhāy-pern) *v* embark

inscheping (*in*-skhāy-ping) *c* embarkation

***inschrijven** (*in*-skhray-vern) *v* enter, book; **zich** ~ register, check in

inschrijvingsformulier (*in*-skhray-vings-for-mēw-leer) *nt* (pl ~en) registration form

inscriptie (in-*skrip*-see) *c* (pl ~s) inscription

insekt (in-*sehkt*) *nt* (pl ~en) insect; bug *nAm*

insekticide (in-sehk-tee-*see*-der) *c* (pl ~n) insecticide

inslikken (*in*-sli-kern) *v* swallow

***insluiten** (*in*-slur^{ew}-tern) *v* *shut in; encircle; include; enclose

inspanning (*in*-spah-ning) *c* (pl ~en) strain, effort

inspecteren (in-spehk-*tāy*-rern) *v* inspect

inspecteur (in-spehk-*turr*) *c* (pl ~s) inspector

inspectie (in-*spehk*-see) *c* (pl ~s) inspection

***inspuiten** (*in*-spur^{ew}-tern) *v* inject

installatie (in-stah-*laa*-tsee) *c* (pl ~s) installation

installeren (in-stah-*lāy*-rern) *v* install

instappen (ın-stah-pern) *v* *get on;
embark

instellen (ın-steh-lern) *v* institute

instelling (ın-steh-lıng) *c* (pl ~en) institution, institute

instemmen (ın-steh-mern) *v* consent;
~ **met** approve of

instemming (ın-steh-mıng) *c* approval, consent

instinct (ın-stıngkt) *nt* (pl ~en) instinct

instituut (ın-stee-tewt) *nt* (pl -tuten)
institute

instorten (ın-stor-tern) *v* collapse

instructie (ın-strerk-see) *c* (pl ~s) direction

instrument (ın-strew-mehnt) *nt* (pl
~en) instrument

intact (ın-tahkt) *adj* intact

integendeel (ın-tāy-gern-dāyl) on the
contrary

intellect (ın-ter-lehkt) *nt* intellect

intellectueel (ın-ter-lehk-tew-vāyl) *adj*
intellectual

intelligent (ın-ter-lee-gehnt) *adj* clever, intelligent

intelligentie (ın-ter-lee-gehn-see) *c* intelligence

intens (ın-tehns) *adj* intense

interessant (ın-ter-rer-sahnt) *adj* interesting

interesse (ın-ter-reh-ser) *c* interest

interesseren (ın-ter-reh-sāy-rern) *v* interest

intermezzo (ın-terr-mehd-zōa) *nt* (pl
~'s) interlude

intern (ın-tehrn) *adj* internal; resident

internaat (ın-terr-naat) *nt* (pl -naten)
boarding-school

internationaal (ın-terr-naht-shōa-naal)
adj international

intiem (ın-teem) *adj* intimate

introduceren (ın-trōa-dew-sāy-rern) *v*
introduce

intussen (ın-ter-sern) *adv* meanwhile

inval (ın-vahl) *c* (pl ~len) brain-wave,
idea; raid, invasion

invalide[1] (ın-vaa-lee-der) *adj* disabled,
invalid

invalide[2] (ın-vaa-lee-der) *c* (pl ~n) invalid

invasie (ın-vaa-zee) *c* (pl ~s) invasion

inventaris (ın-vehn-taa-rerss) *c* (pl
~sen) inventory

investeerder (ın-vehss-tāyr-derr) *c* (pl
~s) investor

investeren (ın-vehss-tāy-rern) *v* invest

investering (ın-vehss-tāy-rıng) *c* (pl
~en) investment

inviteren (ın-vee-tāy-rern) *v* invite

invloed (ın-vlōōt) *c* (pl ~en) influence

invloedrijk (ın-vlōōt-rayk) *adj* influential

invoegen (ın-vōō-gern) *v* insert

invoer (ın-vōōr) *c* import

invoeren (ın-vōō-rern) *v* introduce;
import

invoerrecht (ın-vōō-rehkht) *nt* (pl
~en) duty, import duty

invullen (ın-ver-lern) *v* fill in; fill out
Am

inwendig (ın-vehn-derkh) *adj* inner;
internal

inwilligen (ın-vı-ler-gern) *v* grant

inwoner (ın-vōa-nerr) *c* (pl ~s) inhabitant; resident

inzet (ın-zeht) *c* (pl ~ten) bet

inzetten (ın-zeh-tern) *v* launch

inzicht (ın-zıkht) *nt* (pl ~en) insight

*inzien (ın-zeen) *v* *see

Iraaks (ee-raaks) *adj* Iraqi

Iraans (ee-raans) *adj* Iranian

Irak (ee-raak) Iraq

Irakees (ee-raa-kāyss) *c* (pl -kezen)
Iraqi

Iran (ee-raan) Iran

Iraniër (ee-raa-nee-ᵛerr) *c* (pl ~s) Iranian

ironie (ee-rōā-*nee*) *c* irony

ironisch (ee-*rōā*-neess) *adj* ironical

irriteren (ɪ-ree-*tāy*-rern) *v* annoy, irritate

isolatie (ee-zōa-*laa*-tsee) *c* insulation; isolation

isolator (ee-zōa-*laa*-tor) *c* (pl ~en, ~s) insulator

isolement (ee-zōa-ler-*mehnt*) *nt* isolation

isoleren (ee-zōa-*lāy*-rern) *v* insulate; isolate

Israël (*ɪss*-raa-ehl) Israel

Israëliër (ɪss-raa-*āy*-lee-ʸerr) *c* (pl ~s) Israeli

Israëlisch (ɪss-raa-*āy*-leess) *adj* Israeli

Italiaan (ee-taa-lee-*ʸaan*) *c* (pl -lianen) Italian

Italiaans (ee-taa-lee-*ʸaans*) *adj* Italian

Italië (ee-*taa*-lee-ʸer) Italy

ivoor (ee-*vōār*) *nt* ivory

J

ja (ʸaa) yes

jaar (ʸaar) *nt* (pl jaren) year

jaarboek (*ʸaar*-bōōk) *nt* (pl ~en) annual

jaargetijde (*ʸaar*-ger-tay-der) *nt* (pl ~n) season

jaarlijks (*ʸaar*-lerks) *adj* annual, yearly; *adv* per annum

jacht¹ (ʸahkht) *c* hunt; chase

jacht² (ʸahkht) *nt* (pl ~en) yacht

jachthuis (*ʸahkht*-hurᵉʷss) *nt* (pl -huizen) lodge

jade (*ʸaa*-der) *nt/c* jade

jagen (*ʸaa*-gern) *v* hunt

jager (*ʸaa*-gerr) *c* (pl ~s) hunter

jaloers (ʸa-*lōōrs*) *adj* envious, jealous

jaloezie (ʸaa-lōō-*zee*) *c* (pl ~ën) jealousy; blind

jam (zhehm) *c* jam

jammer! (*ʸah*-merr) what a pity!

janboel (*ʸahn*-bōōl) *c* mess, shambles

janken (*ʸahn*-kern) *v* yelp; whine, whimper

januari (ʸah-new-*vaa*-ree) January

Japan (ʸaa-*pahn*) Japan

Japanner (ʸaa-*pah*-nerr) *c* (pl ~s) Japanese

Japans (ʸaa-*pahns*) *adj* Japanese

japon (ʸaa-*pon*) *c* (pl ~nen) dress; gown

jarretelgordel (zhah-rer-*tehl*-gor-derl) *c* (pl ~s) suspender belt; garter belt *Am*

jas (ʸahss) *c* (pl ~sen) coat

jasje (*ʸah*-sher) *nt* (pl ~s) jacket

jassenhanger (*ʸass*-en-hahng-err) *c* coathanger

je (ʸer) *pron* you; yourself; yourselves

jegens (*ʸāy*-gerns) *prep* towards

jeugd (ʸūrkht) *c* youth

jeugdherberg (*ʸūrkht*-hehr-behrkh) *c* (pl ~en) youth hostel

jeugdig (*ʸūrkh*-derkh) *adj* juvenile

jeuk (ʸūrk) *c* itch

jeuken (*ʸūr*-kern) *v* itch

jicht (ʸɪkht) *c* gout

jij (ʸay) *pron* you

joch (ʸokh) *nt* boy, lad

jodium (*ʸōā*-dee-ʸerm) *nt* iodine

jong (ʸong) *adj* young; **jonger** junior

jongen (*ʸo*-ngern) *c* (pl ~s) boy; lad

jood (ʸōāt) *c* (pl joden) Jew

joods (ʸōāts) *adj* Jewish

Jordaans (ʸor-*daans*) *adj* Jordanian

Jordanië (ʸor-*daa*-nee-ʸer) Jordan

Jordaniër (ʸor-*daa*-nee-ʸerr) *c* (pl ~s) Jordanian

jou (ʸou) *pron* you

journaal (zhōōr-*naal*) *nt* news

journalist (zhōōr-naa-*lɪst*) *c* (pl ~en) journalist

journalistiek (zhoor-naa-liss-*teek*) c
journalism

jouw (You) *pron* your

jubileum (Yu-bee-*lāy*-Yerm) *nt* (pl ~s,
-lea) jubilee

juffrouw (Yer-frou) c (pl ~en) miss

juichen (Yur^{ew}-khern) v cheer

juist (Yur^{ew}st) *adj* right, correct, just;
proper, appropriate

juistheid (Yur^{ew}st-hayt) c correctness

juk (Yerk) *nt* (pl ~ken) yoke

jukbeen (Yerk-bāyn) *nt* (pl ~deren,
-benen) cheek-bone

juli (Yēw-lee) July

jullie (Yer-lee) *pron* you; your

juni (Yēw-nee) June

juridisch (Yēw-ree-deess) *adj* legal

jurist (Yēw-rıst) c (pl ~en) lawyer

jurk (Yerrk) c (pl ~en) frock, robe,
dress

jury (zhēw-ree) c (pl ~'s) jury

jus (zhew) c gravy

juweel (Yēw-vāyl) *nt* (pl -welen) jewel; gem; **juwelen** jewellery

juwelier (Yēw-ver-*leer*) c (pl ~s) jeweller

K

kaak (kaak) c (pl kaken) jaw

kaal (kaal) *adj* bald; naked, bare

kaap (kaap) c (pl kapen) cape

kaars (kaars) c (pl ~en) candle

kaart (kaart) c (pl ~en) map; card;
groene ~ green card

kaartenautomaat (*kaar*-tern-ōa-tōa-
maat) c (pl -maten) ticket machine

kaartje (*kaar*-t^yer) *nt* (pl ~s) ticket

kaas (kaass) c (pl kazen) cheese

kabaal (kaa-*baal*) *nt* racket

kabel (*kaa*-berl) c (pl ~s) cable

kabeljauw (kah-berl-You) c (pl ~en)
cod

kabinet (kaa-bee-*neht*) *nt* (pl ~ten)
cabinet

kachel (*kah*-kherl) c (pl ~s) heater;
stove

kade (*kaa*-der) c (pl ~n) quay; embankment; dock, wharf

kader (*kaa*-derr) *nt* (pl ~s) cadre

kajuit (kaa-Yur^{ew}t) c (pl ~en) cabin

kaki (*kaa*-kee) *nt* khaki

kalender (kaa-*lehn*-derr) c (pl ~s) calendar

kalf (kahlf) *nt* (pl kalveren) calf

kalfsleer (*kahlfs*-lāyr) *nt* calf skin

kalfsvlees (*kahlfs*-flāyss) *nt* veal

kalk (kahlk) c lime

kalkoen (kahl-*kōōn*) c (pl ~en) turkey

kalm (kahlm) *adj* calm; sedate, quiet,
serene

kalmeren (kahl-*māy*-rern) v calm
down

kam (kahm) c (pl ~men) comb

kameel (kaa-*māyl*) c (pl kamelen)
camel

kamer (*kaa*-merr) c (pl ~s) room;
chamber

kameraad (kah-mer-*raat*) c (pl -raden)
comrade

kamerbewoner (*kaa*-merr-ber-vōa-nerr)
c (pl ~s) lodger

kamerjas (*kaa*-merr-Yahss) c (pl ~sen)
dressing-gown

kamerlid (*kaa*-merr-lıt) *nt* (pl -leden)
Member of Parliament

kamermeisje (*kaa*-merr-may-sher) *nt*
(pl ~s) chambermaid

kamertemperatuur (*kaa*-merr-tehm-
per-raa-tēwr) c room temperature

kamgaren (*kahm*-gaa-rern) *nt* worsted

kammen (*kah*-mern) v comb

kamp (kahmp) *nt* (pl ~en) camp

kampeerder (kahm-*pāyr*-derr) c (pl
~s) camper

kampeerterrein (kahm-*pāyr*-teh-rayn)

nt (pl ~en) camping site

kampeerwagen (kahm-*pāyr*-vaa-gern) *c* (pl ~s) trailer *nAm*

kamperen (kahm-*pāy*-rern) *v* camp

kampioen (kahm-pee-*ᵞōōn*) *c* (pl ~en) champion

kan (kahn) *c* (pl ~nen) jug

kanaal (kaa-*naal*) *nt* (pl kanalen) canal; channel; **het Kanaal** English Channel

kanarie (kaa-*naa*-ree) *c* (pl ~s) canary

kandelaber (kahn-der-*laa*-berr) *c* (pl ~s) candelabrum

kandidaat (kahn-dee-*daat*) *c* (pl -daten) candidate

kaneel (kaa-*nāyl*) *c* cinnamon

kangoeroe (*kahng*-ger-rōō) *c* (pl ~s) kangaroo

kanker (*kahng*-kerr) *c* cancer

kano (*kaa*-nōa) *c* (pl ~'s) canoe

kanon (kaa-*non*) *nt* (pl ~nen) gun

kans (kahns) *c* (pl ~en) chance; opportunity

kansel (*kahn*-serl) *c* (pl ~s) pulpit

kant¹ (kahnt) *c* (pl ~en) side; way; edge; **aan de andere ~ van** across

kant² (kahnt) *nt* lace

kantine (kahn-*tee*-ner) *c* (pl ~s) canteen

kantlijn (*kahnt*-layn) *c* (pl ~en) margin

kantoor (kahn-*tōar*) *nt* (pl -toren) office

kantoorbediende (kahn-*tōar*-ber-deen-der) *c* (pl ~n, ~s) clerk

kantoorboekhandel (kahn-*tōar*-bōōk-hahn-derl) *c* (pl ~s) stationer's

kantooruren (kahn-*tōar*-ēw-rern) *pl* business hours, office hours

kap (kahp) *c* (pl ~pen) hood

kapel (kaa-*pehl*) *c* (pl ~len) chapel

kapelaan (kah-per-*laan*) *c* (pl ~s) chaplain

kapen (*kaa*-pern) *v* hijack

kaper (*kaa*-perr) *c* (pl ~s) hijacker

kapitaal (kah-pee-*taal*) *nt* capital

kapitalisme (kah-pee-taa-*liss*-mer) *nt* capitalism

kapitein (kah-pee-*tayn*) *c* (pl ~s) captain

kapot (kaa-*pot*) *adj* broken

kapper (*kah*-perr) *c* (pl ~s) barber; hairdresser

kapsel (*kahp*-serl) *nt* (pl ~s) hair-do

kapstok (*kahp*-stok) *c* (pl ~ken) hat rack

kar (kahr) *c* (pl ~ren) cart

karaat (kaa-*raat*) *nt* carat

karaf (kaa-*rahf*) *c* (pl ~fen) carafe

karakter (kaa-*rahk*-terr) *nt* (pl ~s) character

karakteristiek (kaa-rahk-ter-riss-*teek*) *adj* characteristic

karaktertrek (kaa-*rahk*-terr-trehk) *c* (pl ~ken) characteristic

karamel (kaa-raa-*mehl*) *c* (pl ~s, ~len) caramel

karbonade (kahr-bōa-*naa*-der) *c* (pl ~s) cutlet, chop

kardinaal¹ (kahr-dee-*naal*) *c* (pl -nalen) cardinal

kardinaal² (kahr-dee-*naal*) *adj* cardinal

karper (*kahr*-perr) *c* (pl ~s) carp

karton (kahr-*ton*) *nt* cardboard

kartonnen (kahr-*to*-nern) *adj* cardboard; ~ **doos** carton

karwei (kahr-*vay*) *nt* (pl ~en) job

kas (kahss) *c* (pl ~sen) greenhouse

kasjmier (*kahsh*-meer) *nt* cashmere

kassa (*kah*-saa) *c* (pl ~'s) pay-desk; box-office

kassier (kah-*seer*) *c* (pl ~s) cashier

kast (kahst) *c* (pl ~en) cupboard, closet

kastanje (kahss-*tah*-ñer) *c* (pl ~s) chestnut

kastanjebruin (kahss-*tah*-ñer-brur^(ew)n) *adj* auburn

kasteel (kahss-*tāyl*) *nt* (pl -telen) castle

kat (kaht) *c* (pl ~ten) cat

kathedraal (kaa-tāy-*draal*) *c* (pl -dralen) cathedral

katholiek (kaa-tōa-*leek*) *adj* catholic

katoen (kaa-*tōōn*) *nt/c* cotton

katoenen (kaa-*tōō*-nern) *adj* cotton

katoenfluweel (kaa-*tōōn*-flew-*vāyl*) *nt* velveteen

katrol (kaa-*trol*) *c* (pl ~len) pulley

kattekwaad (*kah*-ter-kvaat) *nt* mischief

kauwen (*kou*-ern) *v* chew

kauwgom (*kou*-gom) *c/nt* chewing-gum

kaviaar (kaa-vee-*Yaar*) *c* caviar

kazerne (kaa-*zehr*-ner) *c* (pl ~s, ~n) barracks *pl*

keel (kāyl) *c* (pl kelen) throat

keelontsteking (*kāyl*-ont-stāy-kıng) *c* (pl ~en) laryngitis

keelpijn (*kāyl*-payn) *c* sore throat

keer (kāyr) *c* (pl keren) time

keerpunt (*kāyr*-pernt) *nt* (pl ~en) turning-point

keerzijde (*kāyr*-zay-der) *c* (pl ~n) reverse

kegelbaan (*kāy*-gerl-baan) *c* (pl -banen) bowling alley

kegelspel (*kāy*-gerl-spehl) *nt* bowling

keizer (*kay*-zerr) *c* (pl ~s) emperor

keizerin (kay-zer-rın) *c* (pl ~nen) empress

keizerlijk (*kay*-zer-lerk) *adj* imperial

keizerrijk (*kay*-zer-rayk) *nt* (pl ~en) empire

kelder (*kehl*-derr) *c* (pl ~s) cellar

kelner (*kehl*-nerr) *c* (pl ~s) waiter

kenmerk (*kehn*-mehrk) *nt* (pl ~en) characteristic, feature

kenmerken (*kehn*-mehr-kern) *v* characterize, mark; **kenmerkend** characteristic, typical

kennel (*keh*-nerl) *c* (pl ~s) kennel

kennen (*keh*-nern) *v* *know

kenner (*keh*-nerr) *c* (pl ~s) connoisseur

kennis[1] (*keh*-nerss) *c* knowledge

kennis[2] (*keh*-nerss) *c* (pl ~sen) acquaintance

kenteken (*kehn*-tāy-kern) *nt* (pl ~s) registration number; licence number *Am*

Kenya (*kāy*-nee-Yaa) Kenya

kerel (*kāy*-rerl) *c* (pl ~s) fellow

keren (*kāy*-rern) *v* turn

kerk (kehrk) *c* (pl ~en) church; chapel

kerkhof (*kehrk*-hof) *nt* (pl -hoven) cemetery, graveyard, churchyard

kerktoren (*kehrk*-tōa-rern) *c* (pl ~s) steeple

kermis (*kehr*-merss) *c* (pl ~sen) fair

kern (kehrn) *c* (pl ~en) nucleus; heart, core; essence; **kern-** nuclear

kernenergie (*kehrn*-āy-nehr-zhee) *c* nuclear energy

kerrie (*keh*-ree) *c* curry

kers (kehrs) *c* (pl ~en) cherry

Kerstmis (*kehrs*-merss) Xmas, Christmas

kerven (*kehr*-vern) *v* carve

ketel (*kāy*-terl) *c* (pl ~s) kettle

keten (*kāy*-tern) *c* (pl ~s, ~en) chain

ketting (*keh*-tıng) *c* (pl ~en) chain

keuken (*kūr*-kern) *c* (pl ~s) kitchen

keurig (*kūr*-rerkh) *adj* neat

keus (kūrss) *c* (keuzen) pick, choice

keuze (*kūr*-zer) *c* (pl ~n) selection, choice

kever (*kāy*-verr) *c* (pl ~s) beetle; bug

kiekje (*keek*-Yer) *nt* (pl ~s) snapshot

kiel (keel) *c* (pl ~en) keel

kiem (keem) *c* (pl ~en) germ

kier (keer) *c* (pl ~en) chink

kies (keess) *c* (pl kiezen) molar

kiesdistrict (*keess*-dıss-trıkt) *nt* (pl

~en) constituency

kieskeurig (keess-*kūr*-rerkh) *adj* particular

kiesrecht (*keess*-rehkht) *nt* franchise, suffrage

kietelen (*kee*-ter-lern) *v* tickle

kieuw (kee∞) *c* (pl ~en) gill

kievit (*kee*-veet) *c* (pl ~en) pewit

kiezel (*kee*-zerl) *c* (pl ~s) pebble; gravel

***kiezen** (*kee*-zern) *v* *choose; pick; elect

***kijken** (*kay*-kern) *v* look; ~ **naar** look at; watch

kijker (*kay*-kerr) *c* (pl ~s) spectator

kijkje (*kayk*-Yer) *nt* (pl ~s) look

kikker (*kɪ*-kerr) *c* (pl ~s) frog

kil (kɪl) *adj* chilly

kilo (*kee*-lōā) *nt* (pl ~'s) kilogram

kilometer (*kee*-lōā-māy-terr) *c* (pl ~s) kilometre

kilometertal (*kee*-lōā-māy-terr-tahl) *nt* distance in kilometres

kim (kɪm) *c* horizon

kin (kɪn) *c* (pl ~nen) chin

kind (kɪnt) *nt* (pl ~eren) child; kid

kinderjuffrouw (*kɪn*-derr-Yer-frou) *c* (pl ~en) nurse

kinderkamer (*kɪn*-derr-kaa-merr) *c* (pl ~s) nursery

kinderverlamming (*kɪn*-derr-verr-lah-mɪng) *c* polio

kinderwagen (*kɪn*-derr-vaa-gern) *c* (pl ~s) pram; baby carriage *Am*

kinine (kee-*nee*-ner) *c* quinine

kiosk (kee-*Yosk*) *c* (pl ~en) kiosk

kip (kɪp) *c* (pl ~pen) hen; chicken

kippevel (*kɪ*-per-vehl) *nt* goose-flesh

kist (kɪst) *c* (pl ~en) chest

klaar (klaar) *adj* ready

klaarblijkelijk (klaar-*blay*-ker-lerk) *adv* apparently

klaarmaken (*klaar*-maa-kern) *v* prepare; cook

klacht (klahkht) *c* (pl ~en) complaint

klachtenboek (*klahkh*-tern-bōōk) *nt* (pl ~en) complaints book

klagen (*klaa*-gern) *v* complain

klank (klahngk) *c* (pl ~en) sound; tone

klant (klahnt) *c* (pl ~en) customer; client

klap (klahp) *c* (pl ~pen) blow; smack, slap

klappen (*klah*-pern) *v* clap

klaproos (*klahp*-rōāss) *c* (pl -rozen) poppy

klas (klahss) *c* (pl ~sen) class; form

klasgenoot (*klahss*-kher-nōāt) *c* (pl -noten) class-mate

klasse (*klah*-ser) *c* (pl ~n) class

klassiek (klah-*seek*) *adj* classical

klauw (klou) *c* (pl ~en) claw

klaver (*klaa*-verr) *c* (pl ~s) clover; shamrock

zich kleden (*klāy*-dern) dress

kleding (*klāy*-ding) *c* clothes *pl*

kleedhokje (*klāyt*-hok-Yer) *nt* (pl ~s) cabin

kleedje (*klāy*-tYer) *nt* (pl ~s) rug

kleedkamer (*klāyt*-kaa-merr) *c* (pl ~s) dressing-room

kleerborstel (*klāyr*-bor-sterl) *c* (pl ~s) clothes-brush

kleerhanger (*klāyr*-hah-ngerr) *c* (pl ~s) hanger, coat-hanger

kleerkast (*klāyr*-kahst) *c* (pl ~en) closet *nAm*

kleermaker (*klāyr*-maa-kerr) *c* (pl ~s) tailor

klei (klay) *c* clay

klein (klayn) *adj* little, small; minor, petty, short; **kleiner** minor; **kleinst** least

kleindochter (*klayn*-dokh-terr) *c* (pl ~s) granddaughter

kleingeld (*klayn*-gehlt) *nt* change, petty cash

kleinhandel (*klayn*-hahn-derl) *c* retail trade

kleinhandelaar (*klayn*-hahn-der-laar) *c* (pl -laren, ~s) retailer

kleinood (*klay*-nōat) *nt* (pl -noden) gem

kleinzoon (*klayn*-zōan) *c* (pl -zonen) grandson

klem (klehm) *c* (pl ~men) clamp

klemschroef (*klehm*-skhrōōf) *c* (pl -schroeven) clamp

kleren (*klāy*-rern) *pl* clothes *pl*

klerenhaak (*klāy*-rern-haak) *c* (pl -haken) peg

klerenkast (*klāy*-rer-kahst) *c* (pl ~en) wardrobe

klerk (klehrk) *c* (pl ~en) clerk

kletsen (*kleht*-sern) *v* chat; talk rubbish

kleur (klurr) *c* (pl ~en) colour

kleurecht (*klūr*-ehkht) *adj* fast-dyed

kleurenblind (*klūr*-rerm-blint) *adj* colour-blind

kleurenfilm (*klūr*-rer-film) *c* (pl ~s) colour film

kleurrijk (*klūr*-rayk) *adj* colourful

kleurstof (*klūr*-stof) *c* (pl ~fen) colourant

kleuter (*klūr*-terr) *c* (pl ~s) tot

kleuterschool (*klūr*-terr-skhōal) *c* (pl -scholen) kindergarten

kleven (*klāy*-vern) *v* *stick

kleverig (*klāy*-ver-rerkh) *adj* sticky

klier (kleer) *c* (pl ~en) gland

klimaat (klee-*maat*) *nt* (pl -maten) climate

***klimmen** (*kli*-mern) *v* climb

klimop (kli-*mop*) *c* ivy

kliniek (klee-*neek*) *c* (pl ~en) clinic

***klinken** (*kling*-kern) *v* sound

klinker (*kling*-kerr) *c* (pl ~s) vowel

klip (klip) *c* (pl ~pen) cliff

klok (klok) *c* (pl ~ken) clock; bell

klokhuis (*klok*-hur^ewss) *nt* (pl -huizen) core

klomp (klomp) *c* (pl ~en) wooden shoe

klont (klont) *c* (pl ~en) lump

klonterig (*klon*-ter-rerkh) *adj* lumpy

kloof (klōaf) *c* (pl kloven) cleft; chasm

klooster (*klōa*-sterr) *nt* (pl ~s) monastery; convent, cloister

klop (klop) *c* (pl ~pen) knock, tap

kloppen (*klo*-pern) *v* knock, tap; whip

klucht (klerkht) *c* (pl ~en) farce

kluis (klur^ewss) *c* (pl kluizen) safe, vault

knaap (knaap) *c* (pl knapen) boy

knalpot (*knahl*-pot) *c* (pl ~ten) silencer; muffler *nAm*

knap (knahp) *adj* smart, clever; pretty, handsome, good-looking

knappend (*knah*-pernt) *adj* crisp

knapzak (*knahp*-sahk) *c* (pl ~ken) knapsack

kneuzen (*knūr*-zern) *v* bruise

kneuzing (*knūr*-zing) *c* (pl ~en) bruise

knie (knee) *c* (pl ~ën) knee

knielen (*knee*-lern) *v* *kneel

knieschijf (*knee*-skhayf) *c* (pl -schijven) kneecap

***knijpen** (*knay*-pern) *v* pinch

knik (knik) *c* nod

knikken (*kni*-kern) *v* nod

knikker (*kni*-kerr) *c* (pl ~s) marble

knippen (*kni*-pern) *v* *cut

knoflook (*knof*-lōak) *nt/c* garlic

knokkel (*kno*-kerl) *c* (pl ~s) knuckle

knoop (knōap) *c* (pl knopen) button; knot

knooppunt (*knōa*-pernt) *nt* (pl ~en) junction

knoopsgat (*knōa*ps-khaht) *nt* (pl ~en) buttonhole

knop (knop) *c* (pl ~pen) bud; knob

knopen (*knōa*-pern) *v* button; tie, knot

knots (knots) *c* (pl ~en) club

knuffelen (*kner*-fer-lern) *v* cuddle

knuppel (*kner*-perl) *c* (pl ~s) club; cudgel

knus (knerss) *adj* cosy

koe (kōō) *c* (pl koeien) cow

koeiehuid (*kōō*ᵉᵉ-er-hurᵉʷt) *c* (pl ~en) cow-hide

koek (kōōk) *c* (pl ~en) cake

koekepan (*kōō*-ker-pahn) *c* (pl ~nen) frying-pan

koekje (*kōōk*-ʸer) *nt* (pl ~s) biscuit; cracker *nAm*

koekoek (*kōō*-kōōk) *c* (pl ~en) cuckoo

koel (kōōl) *adj* cool

koelkast (*kōōl*-kahst) *c* (pl ~en) fridge, refrigerator

koelsysteem (*kōōl*-see-stāym) *nt* (pl -temen) cooling system

koeltas (*kōōl*-tahss) *c* (pl ~sen) ice-bag

koepel (*kōō*-perl) *c* (pl ~s) dome

koers (kōōrs) *c* (pl ~en) exchange rate; course

koets (kōōts) *c* (pl ~en) carriage, coach

koffer (*ko*-ferr) *c* (pl ~s) case, suit-case, bag; trunk

kofferruimte (*ko*-fer-rurᵉʷm-ter) *c* trunk *nAm*

koffie (*ko*-fee) *c* coffee

kogel (*kōā*-gerl) *c* (pl ~s) bullet

kok (kok) *c* (pl ~s) cook

koken (*kōā*-kern) *v* cook; boil

kokosnoot (*kōā*-koss-nōāt) *c* (pl -noten) coconut

kolen (*kōā*-lern) *pl* coal

kolom (kōā-*lom*) *c* (pl ~men) column

kolonel (kōā-lōā-*nehl*) *c* (pl ~s) colonel

kolonie (kōā-*lōā*-nee) *c* (pl ~s, -niën) colony

kolonne (kōā-*lo*-ner) *c* (pl ~s) column

kom (kom) *c* (pl ~men) basin

komedie (kōā-*māy*-dee) *c* (pl ~s) comedy

*****komen** (*kōā*-mern) *v* *come

komfort (koam-*fōār*) *nt* comfort

komiek (kōā-*meek*) *c* (pl ~en) comedian

komisch (*kōā*-meess) *adj* comic

komkommer (kom-*ko*-merr) *c* (pl ~s) cucumber

komma (*ko*-maa) *c* (pl ~'s) comma

kompas (kom-*pahss*) *nt* (pl ~sen) compass

komplot (kom-*plot*) *nt* (pl ~ten) plot, intrigue

komst (komst) *c* coming; arrival

konijn (kōā-*nayn*) *nt* (pl ~en) rabbit

koning (*kōā*-nıng) *c* (pl ~en) king

koningin (kōā-nı-*ngın*) *c* (pl ~nen) queen

koninklijk (*kōā*-nıng-klerk) *adj* royal

koninkrijk (*kōā*-nıng-krayk) *nt* (pl ~en) kingdom

kooi (kōāᵉᵉ) *c* (pl ~en) cage; bunk, berth

kookboek (*kōāk*-bōōk) *nt* (pl ~en) cookery-book; cookbook *nAm*

kool (kōāl) *c* (pl kolen) cabbage

koop (kōāp) *c* purchase; **te ~** for sale

koophandel (*kōāp*-hahn-derl) *c* trade

koopje (*kōāp*-ʸer) *nt* (pl ~s) bargain

koopman (*kōāp*-mahn) *c* (pl koopheden) dealer, merchant

koopprijs (*kōā*-prayss) *c* (pl -prijzen) purchase price

koopwaar (*kōāp*-vaar) *c* merchandise

koor (kōār) *nt* (pl koren) choir

koord (kōārt) *nt* (pl ~en) cord

koorts (kōārts) *c* fever

koortsig (*kōārt*-serkh) *adj* feverish

kop (kop) *c* (pl ~pen) head; headline

*****kopen** (*kōā*-pern) *v* *buy; purchase

koper¹ (*kōā*-perr) *nt* brass; copper

koper² (*kōā*-perr) *c* (pl ~s) buyer, purchaser

koperwerk (kōā-perr-vehrk) nt brass-ware

kopie (kōā-pee) c (pl ~ën) copy

kopiëren (kōā-pee-Yāy-rern) v copy

kopje (kop-Yer) nt (pl ~s) cup

koplamp (kop-lahmp) c (pl ~en) headlight, headlamp

koppeling (ko-per-ling) c clutch

koppelteken (ko-perl-tāy-kern) nt (pl ~s) hyphen

koppig (ko-perkh) adj obstinate, headstrong

koraal (kōā-raal) c (pl -ralen) coral

koren (kōā-rern) nt corn, grain

korenveld (kōā-rer-vehlt) nt (pl ~en) cornfield

korhoen (kor-hōōn) nt (pl ~ders) grouse

korrel (ko-rerl) c (pl ~s) corn, grain

korset (kor-seht) nt (pl ~ten) corset

korst (korst) c (pl ~en) crust

kort (kort) adj brief, short

korting (kor-ting) c (pl ~en) discount, reduction, rebate

kortsluiting (kort-slur^ew-ting) c short circuit

kortstondig (kort-ston-derkh) adj momentary

kosmetica (koss-māy-tee-kaa) pl cosmetics pl

kost (kost) c food, fare; livelihood; ~ en inwoning room and board, board and lodging, bed and board

kostbaar (kost-baar) adj precious, valuable, expensive

kostbaarheden (kost-baar-hāy-dern) pl valuables pl

kosteloos (koss-ter-lōāss) adj free of charge

kosten (koss-tern) v *cost; pl cost, expenditure

koster (koss-terr) c (pl ~s) sexton

kostganger (kost-khah-ngerr) c (pl ~s) boarder

kostuum (koss-tewm) nt (pl ~s) suit

kotelet (kōā-ter-leht) c (pl ~ten) chop

kou (kou) c cold; ~ vatten catch a cold

koud (kout) adj cold

kous (kouss) c (pl ~en) stocking

kraag (kraakh) c (pl kragen) collar

kraai (kraa^ee) c (pl ~en) crow

kraakbeen (kraak-bāyn) nt cartilage

kraal (kraal) c (pl kralen) bead

kraam (kraam) c (pl kramen) stand, stall; booth

kraan (kraan) c (pl kranen) tap; faucet nAm

krab (krahp) c (pl ~ben) crab

krabben (krah-bern) v scratch

kracht (krahkht) c (pl ~en) force, strength; energy, power

krachtig (krahkh-terkh) adj strong

kraken (kraa-kern) v creak, crack

kralensnoer (kraa-ler-snōōr) nt (pl ~en) beads pl

kramp (krahmp) c (pl ~en) cramp; convulsion

krankzinnig (krahngk-sı-nerkh) adj insane; lunatic, crazy, mad

krankzinnige (krahngk-sı-ner-ger) c (pl ~n) lunatic

krankzinnigheid (krahngk-sı-nerkh-hayt) c lunacy

krant (krahnt) c (pl ~en) newspaper, paper

krantenkiosk (krahn-ter-kee-Yosk) c (pl ~en) newsstand

krantenverkoper (krahn-ter-verr-kōā-perr) c (pl ~s) newsagent

krap (krahp) adj tight

kras (krahss) c (pl ~sen) scratch

krassen (krah-sern) v scratch

krat (kraht) nt (pl ~ten) crate

krater (kraa-terr) c (pl ~s) crater

krediet (krer-deet) nt (pl ~en) credit

kredietbrief (krer-deet-breef) c (pl -brieven) letter of credit

kreeft (kräyft) c (pl ~en) lobster

kreek (kräyk) c (pl kreken) creek

kreet (kräyt) c (pl kreten) cry

krekel (kräy-kerl) c (pl ~s) cricket

krenken (krehng-kern) v offend, injure

krent (krehnt) c (pl ~en) currant

kreuken (krūr-kern) v crease

kreunen (krūr-nern) v moan, groan

kreupel (krūr-perl) adj lame, crippled

kribbe (krı-ber) c (pl ~n) manger

kriebel (kree-berl) c (pl ~s) itch

***krijgen** (kray-gern) v *get; receive

krijgsgevangene (kraykhs-kher-vah-nger-ner) c (pl ~n) prisoner of war

krijgsmacht (kraykhs-mahkht) c (pl ~en) military force

krijt (krayt) nt chalk

krik (krık) c (pl ~ken) jack

***krimpen** (krım-pern) v *shrink

krimpvrij (krımp-vray) adj shrinkproof

kring (krıng) c (pl ~en) ring, circle

kringloop (krıng-lōap) c (pl -lopen) cycle

kristal (krıss-tahl) nt (pl ~len) crystal

kristallen (krıss-tah-lern) adj crystal

kritiek (kree-teek) adj critical; c criticism

kritisch (kree-teess) adj critical

kroeg (krōokh) c (pl ~en) public house; pub

kroes (krōoss) c (pl kroezen) mug

krokodil (krōā-kōā-dıl) c (pl ~len) crocodile

krom (krom) adj crooked; curved, bent

kromming (kro-mıng) c (pl ~en) curve, bend

kronen (krōā-nern) v crown

kronkelen (krong-ker-lern) v *wind

kronkelig (krong-ker-lerkh) adj winding

kroon (krōān) c (pl kronen) crown

kruid (krurᵉwt) nt (pl ~en) herb; **kruiden** spices; v flavour

kruidenier (krurᵉw-der-neer) c (pl ~s) grocer

kruidenierswaren (krurᵉw-der-neers-vaa-rern) pl groceries pl

kruidenierswinkel (krurᵉw-der-neers-vıng-kerl) c (pl ~s) grocer's

kruier (krurᵉw-err) c (pl ~s) porter

kruik (krurᵉwk) c (pl ~en) pitcher

kruimel (krurᵉw-merl) c (pl ~s) crumb

***kruipen** (krurᵉw-pern) v *creep, crawl

kruis (krurᵉwss) nt (pl ~en) cross

kruisbeeld (krurᵉwss-bäylt) nt (pl ~en) crucifix

kruisbes (krurᵉwss-behss) c (pl ~sen) gooseberry

kruisigen (krurᵉw-ser-gern) v crucify

kruisiging (krurᵉw-ser-gıng) c (pl ~en) crucifixion

kruising (krurᵉw-sıng) c (pl ~en) crossing, junction

kruispunt (krurᵉwss-pernt) nt (pl ~en) crossroads, intersection

kruissnelheid (krurᵉw-snehl-hayt) c cruising speed

kruistocht (krurᵉwss-tokht) c (pl ~en) crusade

kruit (krurᵉwt) nt gunpowder

kruiwagen (krurᵉw-vaa-gern) c (pl ~s) wheelbarrow

kruk (krerk) c (pl ~ken) crutch

krukas (krerk-ahss) c crankshaft

krul (krerl) c (pl ~len) curl

krullen (krer-lern) v curl; **krullend** curly

krulspeld (krerl-spehlt) c (pl ~en) curler

krultang (krerl-tahng) c (pl ~en) curling-tongs pl

kubus (kew-berss) c (pl ~sen) cube

kudde (ker-der) c (pl ~n, ~s) herd, flock

kuiken (kurᵉw-kern) nt (pl ~s) chicken

kuil (kurᵉwl) c (pl ~en) hole; pit

kuis (kurᵉwss) adj chaste

kuit[1] (kur^{ew}t) *c* roe

kuit[2] (kur^{ew}t) *c* (pl ~en) calf

kundig (*kern*-derkh) *adj* capable

***kunnen** (*ker*-nern) *v* *can, *be able to; *might, *may

kunst (kernst) *c* (pl ~en) art; **schone kunsten** fine arts

kunstacademie (*kernst*-ah-kaa-*dāy*-mee) *c* (pl ~s) art school

kunstenaar (*kern*-ster-naar) *c* (pl ~s) artist

kunstenares (kern-ster-naa-*rehss*) *c* (pl ~sen) artist

kunstgalerij (*kernst*-khah-ler-ray) *c* (pl ~en) art gallery

kunstgebit (*kernst*-kher-bıt) *nt* (pl ~ten) denture, false teeth

kunstgeschiedenis (*kernst*-kher-skhee-der-nıss) *c* art history

kunstijsbaan (*kernst*-ayss-baan) *c* (pl -banen) skating-rink

kunstje (*kern*-sher) *nt* (pl ~s) trick

kunstmatig (kernst-*maa*-terkh) *adj* artificial

kunstnijverheid (kernst-*nay*-verr-hayt) *c* arts and crafts

kunsttentoonstelling (*kerns*-tern-tōan-steh-lıng) *c* (pl ~en) art exhibition

kunstverzameling (*kernst*-ferr-zaa-mer-lıng) *c* (pl ~en) art collection

kunstwerk (*kernst*-vehrk) *nt* (pl ~en) work of art

kunstzijde (*kernst*-say-der) *c* rayon

kunstzinnig (kernst-*sı*-nerkh) *adj* artistic

kurk (kerrk) *c* (pl ~en) cork

kurketrekker (*kerr*-ker-treh-kerr) *c* (pl ~s) corkscrew

kus (kerss) *c* (pl ~sen) kiss

kussen[1] (*ker*-sern) *v* kiss

kussen[2] (*ker*-sern) *nt* (pl ~s) cushion; pillow; **kussentje** *nt* pad

kussensloop (*ker*-ser-slōap) *c/nt* (pl -slopen) pillow-case

kust (kerst) *c* (pl ~en) coast, shore; seaside, seashore

kuur (kēwr) *c* (pl kuren) cure

kwaad[1] (kvaat) *adj* angry, cross; mad; ill

kwaad[2] (kvaat) *nt* (pl kwaden) evil; mischief, harm

kwaadaardig (kvaa-*daar*-derkh) *adj* malignant

kwaal (kvaal) *c* (pl kwalen) ailment

kwadraat (kvaa-*draat*) *nt* (pl -draten) square

kwakzalver (*kvahk*-sahl-verr) *c* (pl ~s) quack

kwal (kvahl) *c* (pl ~len) jelly-fish

kwalijk ***nemen** (kvaa-lerk *nāy*-mern) resent; **neem me niet kwalijk!** sorry!

kwaliteit (kvaa-lee-*tayt*) *c* (pl ~en) quality

kwart (kvahrt) *nt* (pl ~en) quarter

kwartaal (kvahr-*taal*) *nt* (pl -talen) quarter

kwartel (*kvahr*-terl) *c* (pl ~s) quail

kwartier (kvahr-*teer*) *nt* quarter of an hour

kwast (kvahst) *c* (pl ~en) brush

kweken (*kvāy*-kern) *v* cultivate, *grow

kwellen (*kveh*-lern) *v* torment

kwelling (*kveh*-lıng) *c* (pl ~en) torment

kwestie (*kvehss*-tee) *c* (pl ~s) matter, question, issue

kwetsbaar (*kvehts*-baar) *adj* vulnerable

kwetsen (*kveht*-sern) *v* injure; *hurt, wound

kwijtraken (*kvayt*-raa-kern) *v* *lose; *mislay

kwik (kvık) *nt* mercury

kwistig (*kvıss*-terkh) *adj* lavish

kwitantie (kvee-*tahn*-see) *c* (pl ~s) receipt

L

la (laa) *c* (pl ~den) drawer

laag[1] (laakh) *adj* low; **lager** *adj* inferior

laag[2] (laakh) *c* (pl lagen) layer

laagland (*laakh*-lahnt) *nt* lowlands *pl*

laan (laan) *c* (pl lanen) avenue

laars (laars) *c* (pl laarzen) boot

laat (laat) *adj* late; **laatst** *adj* last; ultimate, final; *adv* lately; **later** *adv* afterwards; **te** ~ late; overdue

labiel (laa-*beel*) *adj* unstable

laboratorium (laa-bōa-raa-tōā-ree-Yerm) *nt* (pl -ria) laboratory

lach (lahkh) *c* laugh

*lachen (*lah*-khern) *v* laugh

ladder (*lah*-derr) *c* (pl ~s) ladder

lade (*laa*-der) *c* (pl ~n) drawer

*laden (*laa*-dern) *v* load; charge

ladenkast (*laa*-der-kahst) *c* (pl ~en) chest of drawers

lading (*laa*-dɪng) *c* (pl ~en) charge, load; freight, cargo

laf (lahf) *adj* cowardly

lafaard (*lah*-faart) *c* (pl ~s) coward

lagune (laa-*gēw*-ner) *c* (pl ~s) lagoon

lak (lahk) *c* (pl ~ken) lacquer, varnish

laken (*laa*-kern) *nt* (pl ~s) sheet

lakken (*lah*-kern) *v* varnish

lam[1] (lahm) *adj* lame

lam[2] (lahm) *nt* (pl ~meren) lamb

lambrizering (lahm-bree-*zāy*-rɪng) *c* panelling

lamp (lahmp) *c* (pl ~en) lamp

lampekap (*lahm*-per-kahp) *c* (pl ~pen) lampshade

lamsvlees (*lahms*-flāyss) *nt* lamb

lanceren (lahn-*sāy*-rern) *v* launch

land (lahnt) *nt* (pl ~en) country, land; **aan** ~ ashore; **aan** ~ ***gaan** land

landbouw (*lahnt*-bou) *c* agriculture; **landbouw-** agrarian

landen (*lahn*-dern) *v* land

landengte (*lahnt*-ehng-ter) *c* (pl ~n, ~s) isthmus

landgenoot (*lahnt*-kher-nōāt) *c* (pl -noten) countryman

landgoed (*lahnt*-khōōt) *nt* (pl ~eren) estate

landhuis (*lahnt*-hur^(ew)ss) *nt* (pl -huizen) country house

landkaart (*lahnt*-kaart) *c* (pl ~en) map

landloper (*lahnt*-lōā-perr) *c* (pl ~s) tramp

landloperij (lahnt-lōā-per-*ray*) *c* vagrancy

landschap (*lahnt*-skhahp) *nt* (pl ~pen) scenery, landscape

landsgrens (*lahnts*-khrehns) *c* (pl -grenzen) boundary

landtong (*lahn*-tong) *c* (pl ~en) headland

lang (lahng) *adj* long; tall

langdurig (lahng-*dēw*-rerkh) *adj* long

langs (lahngs) *prep* along; past

langspeelplaat (*lahng*-spāyl-plaat) *c* (pl -platen) long-playing record

langwerpig (lahng-*vehr*-perkh) *adj* oblong

langzaam (*lahng*-zaam) *adj* slow

langzamerhand (lahng-zaa-merr-*hahnt*) *adv* gradually

lantaarn (lahn-*taa*-rern) *c* (pl ~s) lantern

lantaarnpaal (lahn-*taa*-rerm-paal) *c* (pl -palen) lamp-post

las (lahss) *c* (pl ~sen) joint

lassen (*lah*-sern) *v* weld

last (lahst) *c* (pl ~en) charge; load, burden; trouble, nuisance, bother

laster (*lahss*-terr) *c* slander

lastig (*lahss*-terkh) *adj* troublesome, inconvenient; difficult

*laten (*laa*-tern) *v* *let; allow to;

*leave ; *have

Latijns-Amerika (lah-tayn-zaa-*máy*-ree-kaa) Latin America

Latijns-Amerikaans (lah-tayn-zaa-máy-ree-*kaans*) *adj* Latin-American

lauw (lou) *adj* lukewarm, tepid

lawaai (laa-*vaa*ᵉᵉ) *nt* noise

lawaaierig (laa-*vaa*ᵉᵉ-er-rerkh) *adj* noisy

lawine (laa-*vee*-ner) *c* (pl ~s, ~n) avalanche

laxeermiddel (lahk-*sáyr*-mı-derl) *nt* (pl ~en) laxative

ledemaat (*láy*-der-maat) *c* (pl maten) limb

lederen (*láy*-der-rern) *adj* leather

ledigen (*láy*-der-gern) *v* empty

leed (láyt) *nt* affliction, sorrow

leeftijd (*láyf*-tayt) *c* (pl ~en) age

leeg (láykh) *adj* empty

leek (láyk) *c* (pl leken) layman

leer¹ (láyr) *c* teachings *pl*

leer² (láyr) *nt* leather

leerboek (*láyr*-bōok) *nt* (pl ~en) textbook

leerling (*láyr*-lıng) *c* (pl ~en) pupil ; scholar

leerzaam (*láyr*-zaam) *adj* instructive

leesbaar (*láyss*-baar) *adj* legible

leeslamp (*láyss*-lahmp) *c* (pl ~en) reading-lamp

leeszaal (*láy*-saal) *c* (pl -zalen) reading-room

leeuw (láyᵒᵒ) *c* (pl ~en) lion

leeuwerik (*láy*ᵒᵒ-er-rık) *c* (pl ~en) lark

lef (lehf) *nt* guts

legalisatie (láy-gaa-lee-*zaa*-tsee) *c* legalization

legatie (ler-*gaa*-tsee) *c* (pl ~s) legation

leger (*láy*-gerr) *nt* (pl ~s) army

leggen (*leh*-gern) *v* *lay, *put

legpuzzel (*lehkh*-per-zerl) *c* (pl ~s) jigsaw puzzle

lei (lay) *nt* slate

leiden (*lay*-dern) *v* head, direct ; guide, *lead, conduct

leider (*lay*-derr) *c* (pl ~s) leader

leiderschap (*lay*-derr-skhahp) *nt* leadership

leiding¹ (*lay*-dıng) *c* lead

leiding² (*lay*-dıng) *c* (pl ~en) pipe

lek¹ (lehk) *adj* leaky ; punctured

lek² (lehk) *nt* (pl ~ken) leak

lekken (*leh*-kern) *v* leak

lekker (*leh*-kerr) *adj* good ; nice, enjoyable, delicious, tasty

lekkernij (leh-kerr-*nay*) *c* (pl ~en) delicacy

lelie (*láy*-lee) *c* (pl ~s) lily

lelijk (*láy*-lerk) *adj* ugly

lemmet (*leh*-mert) *nt* (pl ~en) blade

lenen (*láy*-nern) *v* *lend ; borrow

lengte (*lehng*-ter) *c* (pl ~n, ~s) length ; **in de ~** lengthways

lengtegraad (*lehng*-ter-graat) *c* (pl -graden) longitude

lenig (*láy*-nerkh) *adj* supple

lening (*láy*-nıng) *c* (pl ~en) loan

lens (lehns) *c* (pl lenzen) lens

lente (*lehn*-ter) *c* (pl ~s) spring

lepel (*láy*-perl) *c* (pl ~s) spoon ; spoonful

lepra (*láy*-praa) *c* leprosy

leraar (*láy*-raar) *c* (pl leraren, ~s) master, teacher ; instructor

lerares (*láy*-raa-*rehss*) *c* (pl ~sen) teacher

leren¹ (*láy*-rern) *v* *teach ; *learn

leren² (*láy*-rern) *adj* leather

les (lehss) *c* (pl ~sen) lesson

leslokaal (*lehss*-lōa-kaal) *nt* (pl -kalen) classroom

lessenaar (*leh*-ser-naar) *c* (pl ~s) desk

letsel (*leht*-serl) *nt* (pl ~s) injury

letten op (*leh*-tern) attend to, *pay attention to ; watch, mind

letter (*leh*-terr) *c* (pl ~s) letter

lettergreep (leh-terr-grāyp) c (pl -grepen) syllable

letterkundig (leh-terr-kern-derkh) adj literary

leugen (lūr-gern) c (pl ~s) lie

leuk (lūrk) adj enjoyable; funny, jolly

leunen (lūr-nern) v *lean

leuning (lūr-nɪng) c (pl ~en) arm; rail

leunstoel (lūrn-stōōl) c (pl ~en) easy chair, armchair

leus (lūrss) c (pl leuzen) slogan

leven¹ (lāy-vern) v live; **levend** alive; live

leven² (lāy-vern) nt (pl ~s) life; lifetime; **in ~** alive

levendig (lāy-vern-derkh) adj lively; brisk, vivid

levensmiddelen (lāy-verns-mɪ-der-lern) pl foodstuffs pl

levensstandaard (lāy-vern-stahn-daart) c standard of living

levensverzekering (lāy-verns-ferr-zāy-ker-rɪng) c (pl ~en) life insurance

lever (lāy-verr) c (pl ~s) liver

leveren (lāy-ver-rern) v furnish, provide, supply

levering (lāy-ver-rɪng) c (pl ~en) delivery, supply

***lezen** (lāy-zern) v *read

lezing (lāy-zɪng) c (pl ~en) lecture

Libanees¹ (lee-baa-nāyss) adj Lebanese

Libanees² (lee-bah-nāyss) c (pl -nezen) Lebanese

Libanon (lee-baa-non) Lebanon

liberaal (lee-ber-raal) adj liberal

Liberia (lee-bāy-ree-ʸaa) Liberia

Liberiaan (lee-bāy-ree-ʸaan) c (pl -rianen) Liberian

Liberiaans (lee-bāy-ree-ʸaans) adj Liberian

licentie (lee-sehn-see) c (pl ~s) licence

lichaam (lɪ-khaam) nt (pl lichamen) body

licht¹ (lɪkht) adj light; pale; gentle, slight

licht² (lɪkht) nt (pl ~en) light

lichtbruin (lɪkht-brurᵉʷn) adj fawn

lichtgevend (lɪkht-kher-vernt) adj luminous

lichting (lɪkh-tɪng) c (pl ~en) collection

lichtpaars (lɪkht-paars) adj mauve

lid (lɪt) nt (pl leden) member; associate

lidmaatschap (lɪt-maat-skhahp) nt membership

lidwoord (lɪt-vōart) nt (pl ~en) article

lied (leet) nt (pl ~eren) song

lief (leef) adj dear; sweet; affectionate, adorable

liefdadigheid (leef-daa-derkh-hayt) c charity

liefde (leef-der) c (pl ~s) love

liefdesgeschiedenis (leef-derss-kher-skhee-der-nɪss) c (pl ~sen) love-story

***liefhebben** (leef-heh-bern) v love

liefhebberij (leef-heh-ber-ray) c (pl ~en) hobby

liefje (leef-ʸer) nt (pl ~s) sweetheart

***liegen** (lee-gern) v lie

lies (leess) c (pl liezen) groin

lieveling (lee-ver-lɪng) c (pl ~en) darling, sweetheart; favourite, pet; **lievelings-** favourite, pet

liever (lee-verr) adv sooner, rather; **~ *hebben** prefer

lift (lɪft) c (pl ~en) lift; elevator nAm

liften (lɪf-tern) v hitchhike

lifter (lɪf-terr) c (pl ~s) hitchhiker

***liggen** (lɪ-gern) v *lie; ***gaan ~** *lie

ligging (lɪ-gɪng) c location; situation, site

ligstoel (lɪkh-stōōl) c (pl ~en) deck chair

lijden (lay-dern) nt suffering

*lijden (*lay*-dern) v suffer

lijf (layf) nt (pl lijven) body

lijfwacht (*layf*-vahkht) c (pl ~en) bodyguard

lijk (layk) nt (pl ~en) corpse

*lijken (lay-kern) v seem, appear; look; ~ op resemble

lijm (laym) c glue, gum

lijn (layn) c (pl ~en) line; leash

lijnboot (*layn*-bōat) c (pl -boten) liner

lijst (layst) c (pl ~en) list; frame

lijster (*lay*-sterr) c (pl ~s) thrush

lijvig (*lay*-verkh) adj bulky

likdoorn (*lı*k-dōa-rern) c (pl ~s) corn

likeur (lee-*kürr*) c (pl ~en) liqueur

likken (*lı*-kern) v lick

limiet (lee-*meet*) c (pl ~en) limit

limoen (lee-*mōon*) c (pl ~en) lime

limonade (lee-mōa-*naa*-der) c (pl ~s) lemonade

linde (*lın*-der) c (pl ~n) limetree, lime

lingerie (lang-zher-*ree*) c lingerie

liniaal (lee-nee-*Yaal*) c (pl -alen) ruler

links (lıngks) adj left; left-hand

linkshandig (lıngks-*hahn*-derkh) adj left-handed

linnen (*lı*-nern) nt linen

linnengoed (*lı*-ner-gōōt) nt linen

lint (lınt) nt (pl ~en) ribbon; tape

lip (lıp) c (pl ~pen) lip

lippenboter (*lı*-per-bōa-terr) c lipsalve

lippenstift (*lı*-per-stıft) c lipstick

list (lıst) c (pl ~en) ruse, artifice

listig (*lıss*-terkh) adj sly

liter (*lee*-terr) c (pl ~s) litre

literair (lee-ter-*rair*) adj literary

literatuur (lee-ter-raa-*tewr*) c literature

lits-jumeaux (lee-zhēw-*mōa*) nt twin beds

litteken (*lı*-tāy-kern) nt (pl ~s) scar

locomotief (lōa-kōa-mōa-*teef*) c (pl -tieven) engine, locomotive

loeien (*lōōee*-ern) v roar

lof (lof) c glory, praise

logé (lōa-*zhāy*) c (pl ~'s) guest

logeerkamer (lōa-*zhāyr*-kaa-merr) c (pl ~s) spare room, guest-room

logeren (lōa-*zhāy*-rern) v stay

logica (*lōa*-gee-kaa) c logic

logies (lōa-*zheess*) nt lodgings pl, accommodation; ~ en ontbijt bed and breakfast

logisch (*lōa*-geess) adj logical

lokaal (lōa-*kaal*) adj local

lol (lol) c fun

lonen (*lōa*-nern) v *pay

long (long) c (pl ~en) lung

longontsteking (*long*-ont-stāy-kıng) c (pl ~en) pneumonia

lont (lont) c (pl ~en) fuse

lood (lōat) nt lead

loodgieter (*lōat*-khee-terr) c (pl ~s) plumber

loodrecht (*lōat*-rehkht) adj perpendicular

loods (lōats) c (pl ~en) pilot

loon (lōan) nt (pl lonen) wages pl; salary, pay

loonsverhoging (*lōans*-ferr-hōa-gıng) c (pl ~en) raise nAm

loop (lōap) c course; gait, walk

loopbaan (*lōa*-baan) c (pl -banen) career

loopplank (*lōa*-plahngk) c (pl ~en) gangway

*lopen (*lōa*-pern) v walk; *go

los (loss) adj loose

losgeld (*loass*-khehlt) nt (pl ~en) ransom

losknopen (*loss*-knōa-pern) v unbutton; untie

losmaken (*loss*-maa-kern) v unfasten, *undo, detach; loosen

losschroeven (*lo*-skhrōō-vern) v unscrew

lossen (*lo*-sern) v unload, discharge

lot[1] (lot) nt lot, fortune, destiny, fate

lot[2] (lot) nt (pl ~en) lot

loterij (lōa-ter-*ray*) *c* (pl ~en) lottery

lotion (lōa-*shon*) *c* (pl ~s) lotion

loyaal (lōa-*Yaal*) *adj* loyal

lucht (lerkht) *c* air; breath; sky

luchtdicht (*lerkh*-dıkht) *adj* airtight

luchtdruk (*lerkh*-drerk) *c* atmospheric pressure

luchten (*lerkh*-tern) *v* air, ventilate

luchtfilter (*lerkht*-fıl-terr) *nt* (pl ~s) air-filter

luchthaven (*lerkht*-haa-vern) *c* (pl ~s) airport

luchtig (*lerkh*-terkh) *adj* airy

luchtpost (*lerkht*-post) *c* airmail

luchtvaartmaatschappij (*lerkht*-faart-maat-skhah-pay) *c* (pl ~en) airline

luchtverversing (*lerkht*-ferr-vehr-sıng) *c* air-conditioning, ventilation

luchtziekte (*lerkht*-seek-ter) *c* air-sickness

lucifer (*lēw*-see-fehr) *c* (pl ~s) match

lucifersdoosje (*lēw*-see-fehrs-dōa-sher) *nt* (pl ~s) match-box

lui (lur*ew*) *adj* lazy; idle

luid (lur*ew*t) *adj* loud

luidspreker (*lur*ewt-sprāy-kerr) *c* (pl ~s) loud-speaker

luier (*lur*ew-err) *c* (pl ~s) nappy; diaper *nAm*

luik (lur*ew*k) *nt* (pl ~en) hatch; shutter

luis (lur*ew*ss) *c* (pl luizen) louse

luisteraar (*lur*ewss-ter-raar) *c* (pl ~s) listener

luisteren (*lur*ewss-ter-rern) *v* listen

luisterrijk (*lur*ewss-ter-rayk) *adj* magnificent

lukken (*ler*-kern) *v* succeed

lunch (lernsh) *c* (pl ~es) lunch

lus (lerss) *c* (pl ~sen) loop

lusten (*lerss*-tern) *v* like; fancy

luxe (*lēw*k-ser) *c* luxury

luxueus (lēwk-sēw-*ūrss*) *adj* luxurious

M

maag (maakh) *c* (pl magen) stomach; **maag-** gastric

maagd (maakht) *c* (pl ~en) virgin

maagpijn (*maakh*-payn) *c* stomachache

maagzuur (*maakh*-sēwr) *nt* heartburn

maagzweer (*maakh*-svāyr) *c* (pl -zweren) gastric ulcer

maal[1] (maal) *nt* (pl malen) meal

maal[2] (maal) *c* (pl malen) time

maal[3] (maal) *prep* times

maaltijd (*maal*-tayt) *c* (pl ~en) meal; **warme ~** dinner

maan (maan) *c* (pl manen) moon

maand (maant) *c* (pl ~en) month

maandag (*maan*-dahkh) *c* Monday

maandblad (*maant*-blaht) *nt* (pl ~en) monthly magazine

maandelijks (*maan*-der-lerks) *adj* monthly

maandverband (*maant*-ferr-bahnt) *nt* sanitary towel

maanlicht (*maan*-lıkht) *nt* moonlight

maar (maar) *conj* but; yet; *adv* only

maart (maart) March

maas (maass) *c* (pl mazen) mesh

maat (maat) *c* (pl maten) size, measure; **extra grote ~** outsize; **op ~ gemaakt** tailor-made; made to order

maatregel (*maat*-rāy-gerl) *c* (pl ~en, ~s) measure

maatschappelijk (maat-*skhah*-per-lerk) *adj* social

maatschappij (maat-skhah-*pay*) *c* (pl ~en) company; society

maatstaf (*maat*-stahf) *c* (pl -staven) standard

machine (mah-*shee*-ner) *c* (pl ~s) engine, machine

machinerie (mah-shee-ner-*ree*) *c* machinery

macht (mahkht) *c* (pl ~en) power; force, might; authority

machteloos (*mahkh*-ter-lōass) *adj* powerless

machtig (*mahkh*-terkh) *adj* powerful, mighty

machtiging (*mahkh*-ter-gɪng) *c* (pl ~en) authorization

magazijn (maa-gaa-*zayn*) *nt* (pl ~en) store-house, warehouse

mager (*maa*-gerr) *adj* lean, thin

magie (maa-*gee*) *c* magic

magistraat (maa-gɪss-*traat*) *c* (pl -straten) magistrate

magneet (mahkh-*nāyt*) *c* (pl -neten) magnet

magnetisch (mahkh-*nāy*-teess) *adj* magnetic

maillot (maa-*Yōa*) *c* (pl ~s) tights *pl*

maïs (mighss) *c* maize

maïskolf (*mighss*-kolf) *c* (pl -kolven) corn on the cob

maître d'hôtel (mai-trer-dōa-*tehl*) head-waiter

maîtresse (meh-*tray*-ser) *c* (pl ~s, ~n) mistress

majoor (maa-*Yōar*) *c* (pl ~s) major

mak (mahk) *adj* tame

makelaar (*maa*-ker-laar) *c* (pl ~s) broker, house agent

maken (*maa*-kern) *v* *make; **te ~ *hebben met** *deal with

makreel (maa-*krāyl*) *c* (pl -relen) mackerel

mal (mahl) *adj* foolish, silly

malaria (maa-*laa*-ree-Yaa) *c* malaria

Maleis (maa-*layss*) *nt* Malay

Maleisië (maa-*lay*-zee-Yer) Malaysia

Maleisisch (maa-*lay*-zeess) *adj* Malaysian

*malen (*maa*-lern) *v* *grind

mals (mahls) *adj* tender

mammoet (*mah*-mōot) *c* (pl ~en, ~s) mammoth

man (mahn) *c* (pl ~nen) man; husband

manchet (mahn-*sheht*) *c* (pl ~ten) cuff

manchetknopen (mahn-*sheht*-knōa-pern) *pl* cuff-links *pl*

mand (mahnt) *c* (pl ~en) hamper, basket

mandaat (mahn-*daat*) *nt* (pl -daten) mandate

mandarijn (mahn-daa-*rayn*) *c* (pl ~en) mandarin, tangerine

manege (maa-*nāy*-zher) *c* (pl ~s) riding-school

manicure (maa-nee-*kēw*-rer) *c* (pl ~s) manicure

manicuren (maa-nee-*kēw*-rern) *v* manicure

manier (maa-*neer*) *c* (pl ~en) manner; way, fashion

mank (mahngk) *adj* lame

mannelijk (*mah*-ner-lerk) *adj* male; masculine

mannequin (mah-ner-*kang*) *c* (pl ~s) model, mannequin

mantel (*mahn*-terl) *c* (pl ~s) coat, cloak

manufacturier (mah-nēw-fahk-tēw-reer) *c* (pl ~s) draper

manuscript (maa-nerss-*krɪpt*) *nt* (pl ~en) manuscript

marcheren (mahr-*shāy*-rern) *v* march

margarine (mahr-gaa-*ree*-ner) *c* margarine

marge (*mahr*-zher) *c* (pl ~s) margin

marine (maa-*ree*-ner) *c* navy; **marine-** naval

maritiem (mah-ree-*teem*) *adj* maritime

markt (mahrkt) *c* (pl ~en) market; **zwarte ~** black market

marktplein (*mahrkt*-playn) *nt* (pl ~en) market-place

marmelade (mahr-mer-*laa*-der) *c* (pl ~s, ~n) marmalade

marmer (*mahr*-merr) *nt* marble

Marokkaan (mah-ro-*kaan*) *c* (pl -ka-nen) Moroccan

Marokkaans (mah-ro-*kaans*) *adj* Moroccan

Marokko (maa-*ro*-kōa) Morocco

mars (mahrs) *c* (pl ~en) march

martelaar (*mahr*-ter-laar) *c* (pl ~s, -la-ren) martyr

martelen (*mahr*-ter-lern) *v* torture

marteling (*mahr*-ter-lıng) *c* (pl ~en) torture

mascara (mahss-*kaa*-raa) *c* mascara

masker (*mahss*-kerr) *nt* (pl ~s) mask

massa (*mah*-saa) *c* (pl ~'s) bulk, mass; crowd

massage (mah-*saa*-zher) *c* (pl ~s) massage

massaproduktie (*mah*-saa-prōa-derk-see) *c* mass production

masseren (mah-*sāy*-rern) *v* massage

masseur (mah-*sūrr*) *c* (pl ~s) masseur

massief (mah-*seef*) *adj* solid, massive

mast (mahst) *c* (pl ~en) mast

mat¹ (maht) *adj* dull, mat, dim

mat² (maht) *c* (pl ~ten) mat

materiaal (maa-tree-*Yaal*) *nt* (pl -ria-len) material

materie (mah-*tāy*-ree) *c* (pl -riën, ~s) matter

materieel (maa-tree-*Yāyl*) *adj* material

matig (*maa*-terkh) *adj* moderate

matras (maa-*trahss*) *c* (pl ~sen) mattress

matroos (maa-*trōass*) *c* (pl matrozen) sailor

mausoleum (mou-sōa-*lāy*-Yerm) *nt* (pl ~s, -lea) mausoleum

mazelen (*maa*-zer-lern) *pl* measles

me (mer) *pron* me; myself

mechanisch (māy-*khaa*-neess) *adj* mechanical

mechanisme (māy-khaa-*nıss*-mer) *nt* (pl ~n) mechanism; machinery

medaille (māy-*dah*-Yer) *c* (pl ~s) medal

mededelen (*māy*-der-dāy-lern) *v* notify, communicate, inform

mededeling (*māy*-der-dāy-lıng) *c* (pl ~en) communication, information

medegevoel (*māy*-der-ger-vōol) *nt* sympathy

medelijden (*māy*-der-lay-dern) *nt* pity; ~ *hebben met* pity

medeplichtige (māy-der-*plıkh*-ter-ger) *c* (pl ~n) accessary

medewerking (*māy*-der-vehr-kıng) *c* co-operation

medisch (*māy*-deess) *adj* medical

mediteren (māy-dee-*tāy*-rern) *v* meditate

*meebrengen (*māy*-breh-ngern) *v* *bring

meedelen (*māy*-dāy-lern) *v* communicate

meel (māyl) *nt* flour

meemaken (*māy*-maa-kern) *v* *go through

*meenemen (*māy*-nāy-mern) *v* *take away

meer¹ (māyr) *adj* more; ~ *dan* over; *niet* ~ no longer

meer² (māyr) *nt* (pl meren) lake

meerderheid (*māyr*-derr-hayt) *c* majority; bulk

meerderjarig (māyr-derr-*Yaa*-rerkh) *adj* of age

meervoud (*māyr*-vout) *nt* (pl ~en) plural

meest (māyst) *adj* most

meestal (māy-*stahl*) *adv* mostly

meester (*māy*-sterr) *c* (pl ~s) master; schoolmaster, teacher

meesteres (māy-ster-*rehss*) *c* (pl ~sen) mistress

meesterwerk (*māy*-sterr-vehrk) *nt* (pl

~en) masterpiece

meetellen (*māy*-teh-lern) v count

meetkunde (*māyt*-kern-der) c geometry

meeuw (māy^oo) c (pl ~en) gull; seagull

mei (may) May

meid (mayt) c (pl ~en) housemaid, maid

meineed (*may*-nāyt) c (pl -eden) perjury

meisje (*may*-sher) nt (pl ~s) girl

meisjesnaam (*may*-sherss-naam) c (pl -namen) maiden name

mejuffrouw (mer-^Yer-frou) miss

melden (*mehl*-dern) v report

melding (*mehl*-dıng) c (pl ~en) mention

melk (mehlk) c milk

melkboer (*mehlk*-bōōr) c (pl ~en) milkman

melodie (māy-lōā-*dee*) c (pl ~ën) melody; tune

melodieus (māy-lōā-dee-^Yūrss) adj tuneful

melodrama (māy-lōā-*draa*-maa) nt (pl ~'s) melodrama

meloen (mer-*lōōn*) c (pl ~en) melon

memorandum (māy-mōā-*rahn*-derm) nt (pl -randa) memo

men (mehn) pron one

meneer (mer-*nāyr*) mister; sir

menen (*māy*-nern) v consider; *mean

mengen (*meh*-ngern) v mix

mengsel (*mehng*-serl) nt (pl ~s) mixture

menigte (*māy*-nerkh-ter) c (pl ~n, ~s) crowd

mening (*māy*-nıng) c (pl ~en) opinion; view; **van ~ verschillen** disagree

mens (mehns) c (pl ~en) man; **mensen people** pl

menselijk (*mehn*-ser-lerk) adj human;

~ **wezen** human being

mensheid (*mehns*-hayt) c humanity, mankind

menstruatie (mehn-strēw-*vaa*-tsee) c menstruation

menukaart (mer-*nēw*-kaart) c (pl ~en) menu

merel (*māy*-rerl) c (pl ~s) blackbird

merg (mehrkh) nt marrow

merk (mehrk) nt (pl ~en) brand

merkbaar (*mehrk*-baar) adj noticeable, perceptible

merken (*mehr*-kern) v notice; mark

merkteken (*mehrk*-tāy-kern) nt (pl ~s) mark

merrie (*meh*-ree) c (pl ~s) mare

mes (mehss) nt (pl ~sen) knife

messing (*meh*-sıng) nt brass

mest (mehst) c dung, manure

mesthoop (*mehst*-hōāp) c (pl -hopen) dunghill

met (meht) prep with; by

metaal (māy-*taal*) nt (pl metalen) metal

metalen (māy-*taa*-lern) adj metal

meteen (mer-*tāyn*) adv at once, straight away, immediately, instantly; presently

***meten** (*māy*-tern) v measure

meter (*māy*-terr) c (pl ~s) metre; meter; gauge

metgezel (*meht*-kher-zehl) c (pl ~len) companion

methode (māy-*tōā*-der) c (pl ~n, ~s) method

methodisch (māy-*tōā*-deess) adj methodical

metrisch (*māy*-treess) adj metric

metro (*māy*-trōā) c (pl ~'s) underground

metselaar (*meht*-ser-laar) c (pl ~s) bricklayer

metselen (*meht*-ser-lern) v *lay bricks

meubilair (mūr-bee-*lair*) nt furniture

meubileren (mūr-bee-lā̄y-rern) v furnish

mevrouw (mer-*vrou*) madam

Mexicaan (mehk-see-*kaan*) c (pl -canen) Mexican

Mexicaans (mehk-see-*kaans*) adj Mexican

Mexico (*mehk*-see-kōā) Mexico

microfoon (mee-krōā-*fōān*) c (pl ~s) microphone

middag (*mı*-dahkh) c (pl ~en) afternoon; midday; noon

middageten (*mı*-dahkh-āȳ-tern) nt luncheon, lunch; dinner

middel[1] (*mı*-derl) nt (pl ~en) means; remedy; **antiseptisch** ~ antiseptic; **insektenwerend** ~ insect repellent; **kalmerend** ~ tranquilliser, sedative; **pijnstillend** ~ anaesthetic; **stimulerend** ~ stimulant; **verdovend** ~ drug

middel[2] (*mı*-derl) nt (pl ~s) waist

middeleeuwen (*mı*-derl-āȳ°°-ern) pl Middle Ages

middeleeuws (*mı*-derl-āȳ°°ss) adj mediaeval

Middellandse Zee (*mı*-der-lahnt-ser-zā̄y) Mediterranean

middelmatig (*mı*-derl-*maa*-terkh) adj moderate; medium

middelpunt (*mı*-derl-pernt) nt (pl ~en) centre

middelst (*mı*-derlst) adj middle

midden (*mı*-dern) nt midst, middle; **midden-** medium-; ~ **in** amid; **te** ~ **van** amid; among

middernacht (*mı*-derr-*nahkht*) c midnight

midzomer (mıt-*sōā*-merr) c midsummer

mier (meer) c (pl ~en) ant

mierikswortel (*mee*-rıks-vor-terl) c (pl ~s) horseradish

migraine (mee-*grai*-ner) c migraine

mijl (mayl) c (pl ~en) mile

mijlpaal (*mayl*-paal) c (pl -palen) milestone; landmark

mijn[1] (mayn) pron my

mijn[2] (mayn) c (pl ~en) mine

mijnbouw (*mayn*-bou) c mining

mijnheer (mer-*nā̄yr*) c mister

mijnwerker (*mayn*-vehr-kerr) c (pl ~s) miner

mikken op (*mı*-kern) aim at

mikpunt (*mık*-pernt) nt (pl ~en) target

mild (mılt) adj liberal

milieu (meel-*ᵞūr*) nt (pl ~s) milieu; environment

militair[1] (mee-lee-*tair*) adj military

militair[2] (mee-lee-*tair*) c (pl ~en) soldier

miljoen (mıl-*ᵞōōn*) nt million

miljonair (mıl-ᵞōā-*nair*) c (pl ~s) millionaire

min (mın) prep minus

minachting (*mın*-ahkh-tıng) c contempt

minder (*mın*-derr) adv less

minderheid (*mın*-derr-hayt) c (pl -heden) minority

minderjarig (mın-derr-*ᵞaa*-rerkh) adj under age

minderjarige (mın-derr-*ᵞaa*-rer-ger) c (pl ~n) minor

minderwaardig (mın-derr-*vaar*-derkh) adj inferior

mineraal (mee-ner-*raal*) nt (pl -ralen) mineral

mineraalwater (mee-ner-*raal*-vaa-terr) nt mineral water

miniatuur (mee-nee-ᵞaa-*tewr*) c (pl -turen) miniature

minimum (*mee*-nee-merm) nt (pl -ma) minimum

minister (mee-*nıss*-terr) c (pl ~s) minister

ministerie (mee-nıss-*tā̄y*-ree) nt (pl

~s) ministry

minnaar (*mı-naar*) *c* (pl ~s) lover

minst (mınst) *adj* least

minstens (*mın-sterns*) *adv* at least

minuscuul (mee-nerss-*kewl*) *adj* tiny, minute

minuut (mee-*newt*) *c* (pl minuten) minute

mis (mıss) *c* (pl ~sen) Mass

misbruik (*mıss*-brur^{ew}k) *nt* misuse, abuse

misdaad (*mıss*-daat) *c* (pl -daden) crime

misdadig (mıss-*daa*-derkh) *adj* criminal

misdadiger (mıss-*daa*-der-gerr) *c* (pl ~s) criminal

zich *misdragen (mıss-*draa*-gern) *mis-behave*

misgunnen (mıss-*kher*-nern) *v* grudge

mishagen (mıss-*haa*-gern) *v* displease

miskraam (*mıss*-kraam) *c* (pl -kramen) miscarriage

mislukking (mıss-*ler*-kıng) *c* (pl ~en) failure

mislukt (mıss-*lerkt*) *adj* unsuccessful

mismaakt (mıss-*maakt*) *adj* deformed

misplaatst (mıss-*plaatst*) *adj* mis-placed

misschien (mı-*skheen*) *adv* perhaps; maybe

misselijk (*mı*-ser-lerk) *adj* sick; dis-gusting

misselijkheid (*mı*-ser-lerk-hayt) *c* nau-sea, sickness

missen (*mı*-sern) *v* lack; miss; spare

misstap (*mı*-stahp) *c* (pl ~pen) slip

mist (mıst) *c* fog, mist

mistig (*mıss*-terkh) *adj* foggy, misty

mistlamp (*mıst*-lahmp) *c* (pl ~en) fog-lamp

***misverstaan** (*mıss*-ferr-staan) *v* *mis-understand

misverstand (*mıss*-ferr-stahnt) *nt* (pl ~en) misunderstanding

misvormd (mıss-*formt*) *adj* deformed

mits (mıts) *conj* provided that

mobiel (mōā-*beel*) *adj* mobile

modder (*mo*-derr) *c* mud

modderig (*mo*-der-rerkh) *adj* muddy

mode (*mōā*-der) *c* (pl ~s) fashion

model (mōā-*dehl*) *nt* (pl ~len) model

modelleren (mōā-deh-*lāy*-rern) *v* model

modern (mōā-*dehrn*) *adj* modern

modieus (mōā-dee-^y*ürss*) *adj* fashion-able

modiste (mōā-*diss*-ter) *c* (pl ~s) mil-liner

moe (mōō) *adj* tired; weary

moed (mōōt) *c* courage

moeder (*mōō*-derr) *c* (pl ~s) mother

moedertaal (*mōō*-derr-taal) *c* native language, mother tongue

moedig (*mōō*-derkh) *adj* brave, coura-geous

moeilijk (*mōō^{ee}*-lerk) *adj* difficult; hard

moeilijkheid (*mōō^{ee}*-lerk-hayt) *c* (pl -heden) difficulty

moeite (*mōō^{ee}*-ter) *c* (pl ~n) trouble; pains, difficulty; **de ~ waard *zijn** *be worth-while; ~ *doen bother

moer (mōōr) *c* (pl ~en) nut

moeras (mōō-*rahss*) *nt* (pl ~sen) swamp; bog, marsh

moerassig (mōō-*rah*-serkh) *adj* marshy

moerbei (*mōōr*-bay) *c* (pl ~en) mul-berry

moestuin (*mōōss*-tur^{ew}n) *c* (pl ~en) kitchen garden

***moeten** (*mōō*-tern) *v* *must; *have to; need to, *ought to, *be obliged to, *should

mogelijk (*mōā*-ger-lerk) *adj* possible

mogelijkheid (*mōā*-ger-lerk-hayt) *c* (pl -heden) possibility

***mogen** (*mōā*-gern) *v* *be allowed;

*may; like

mogendheid (*mōa*-gernt-hayt) *c* (pl -heden) power

mohair (*mōa*-hair) *nt* mohair

molen (*mōa*-lern) *c* (pl ~s) mill; windmill

molenaar (*mōa*-ler-naar) *c* (pl ~s) miller

mollig (*mo*-lerkh) *adj* plump

moment (*mōa*-mehnt) *nt* (pl ~en) moment

momentopname (*mōa*-mehnt-op-naa-mer) *c* (pl ~n) snapshot

monarchie (*mōa*-nahr-*khee*) *c* (pl ~ën) monarchy

mond (mont) *c* (pl ~en) mouth

mondeling (*mon*-der-lıng) *adj* oral, verbal

monding (*mon*-dıng) *c* (pl ~en) mouth

mondspoeling (*mont*-spōō-lıng) *c* mouthwash

monetair (*mōa*-nāy-*tair*) *adj* monetary

monnik (*mo*-nerk) *c* (pl ~en) monk

monoloog (*mōa*-nōa-*lōakh*) *c* (pl -logen) monologue

monopolie (*mōa*-nōa-*pōa*-lee) *nt* (pl ~s) monopoly

monster (*mon*-sterr) *nt* (pl ~s) sample

monteren (*mon*-*tāy*-rern) *v* assemble

monteur (*mon*-*tūrr*) *c* (pl ~s) mechanic

montuur (*mon*-*tewr*) *nt* (pl -turen) frame

monument (*mōa*-*new*-*mehnt*) *nt* (pl ~en) monument

mooi (*mōa*ee) *adj* beautiful; pretty, fine; nice, lovely, fair

moord (*mōart*) *c* (pl ~en) assassination, murder

moordenaar (*mōar*-der-naar) *c* (pl ~s) murderer

mop (mop) *c* (pl ~pen) joke

mopperen (*mo*-per-rern) *v* grumble

moraal (*mōa*-*raal*) *c* moral

moraliteit (*mōa*-raa-lee-*tayt*) *c* morality

moreel (*mōa*-*rāyl*) *adj* moral

morfine (*mor*-*fee*-ner) *c* morphine, morphia

morgen¹ (*mor*-gern) *adv* tomorrow

morgen² (*mor*-gern) *c* (pl ~s) morning

morsen (*mor*-sern) *v* *spill

mos (moss) *nt* (pl ~sen) moss

moskee (moss-*kāy*) *c* (pl ~ën) mosque

mossel (*mo*-serl) *c* (pl ~s, ~en) mussel

mosterd (*moss*-terrt) *c* mustard

mot (mot) *c* (pl ~ten) moth

motel (*mōa*-*tehl*) *nt* (pl ~s) motel

motie (*mōa*-tsee) *c* (pl ~s) motion

motief (*mōa*-*teef*) *nt* (pl motieven) motive; pattern

motor (*mōa*-terr) *c* (pl ~en, ~s) engine, motor

motorboot (*mōa*-terr-bōat) *c* (pl -boten) motor-boat

motorfiets (*mōa*-terr-feets) *c* (pl ~en) motor-cycle

motorkap (*mōa*-terr-kahp) *c* (pl ~pen) bonnet; hood *nAm*

motorpech (*mōa*-terr-pehkh) *c* breakdown

motorschip (*mōa*-terr-skhıp) *nt* (pl -schepen) launch

motregen (*mot*-rāy-gern) *c* drizzle

mousseline (*mōō*-ser-*lee*-ner) *c* muslin

mousserend (*mōō*-*sāy*-rernt) *adj* sparkling

mouw (mou) *c* (pl ~en) sleeve

mozaïek (*mōa*-zaa-*eek*) *nt* (pl ~en) mosaic

mug (merkh) *c* (pl ~gen) mosquito

muil (*mur*ewl) *c* (pl ~en) mouth

muildier (*mur*ewl-deer) *nt* (pl ~en) mule

muilezel (*mur^ewl*-āy-zerl) *c* (pl ~s) mule

muis (mur^ewss) *c* (pl muizen) mouse

muiterij (mur^ew-ter-*ray*) *c* (pl ~en) mutiny

mul (merl) *c* mullet

munt (mernt) *c* (pl ~en) coin; token; mint

munteenheid (mernt-āyn-hayt) *c* (pl -heden) monetary unit

muntstuk (mernt-sterk) *nt* (pl ~ken) coin

mus (merss) *c* (pl ~sen) sparrow

museum (mew-*zāy*-Yerm) *nt* (pl ~s, -sea) museum

musical (*m^Yōō*-zɪ-kerl) *c* (pl ~s) musical comedy, musical

musicus (mew-zee-kerss) *c* (pl -ci) musician

muskiet (merss-*keet*) *c* (pl ~en) mosquito

muskietennet (merss-*kee*-ter-neht) *nt* (pl ~ten) mosquito-net

muts (merts) *c* (pl ~en) cap

muur (mewr) *c* (pl muren) wall

muziek (mew-*zeek*) *c* music

muziekinstrument (mew-*zeek*-ɪn-strēw-mehnt) *nt* (pl ~en) musical instrument

muzikaal (mew-zee-*kaal*) *adj* musical

mysterie (mee-*stāy*-ree) *nt* (pl ~s) mystery

mysterieus (mee-stāy-ree-*Yūrss*) *adj* mysterious

mythe (*mee*-ter) *c* (pl ~n) myth

N

na (naa) *prep* after

naad (naat) *c* (pl naden) seam

naadloos (*naat*-lōass) *adj* seamless

naaien (*naa^ee*-ern) *v* sew

naaimachine (*naa^ee*-mah-shee-ner) *c* (pl ~s) sewing-machine

naaister (*naa^ee*-sterr) *c* (pl ~s) dressmaker

naakt (naakt) *adj* nude, naked; bare

naaktstrand (*naakt*-strahnt) *nt* (pl ~en) nudist beach

naald (naalt) *c* (pl ~en) needle

naam (naam) *c* (pl namen) name; reputation; denomination; **in ~ van** on behalf of

naar¹ (naar) *prep* to, towards; at, for

naar² (naar) *adj* nasty, unpleasant

naast (naast) *prep* next to, beside

nabij (naa-*bay*) *adj* near, close

nabijheid (naa-*bay*-hayt) *c* vicinity

nabijzijnd (naa-*bay*-zaynt) *adj* nearby

nabootsen (naa-*bōat*-sern) *v* imitate

naburig (naa-*bōō*-rerkh) *adj* neighbouring

nacht (nahkht) *c* (pl ~en) night; **'s nachts** by night; overnight

nachtclub (*nahkht*-klerp) *c* (pl ~s) nightclub, cabaret

nachtcrème (*nahkht*-kraim) *c* (pl ~s) night-cream

nachtegaal (*nahkh*-ter-gaal) *c* (pl -galen) nightingale

nachtelijk (*nahkh*-ter-lerk) *adj* nightly

nachtjapon (*nahkht*-Yaa-pon) *c* (pl ~nen) nightdress

nachttarief (*nahkh*-taa-reef) *nt* (pl -rieven) night rate

nachttrein (*nahkht*-trayn) *c* (pl ~en) night train

nachtvlucht (*nahkht*-flerkht) *c* (pl ~en) night flight

nadat (naa-*daht*) *conj* after

nadeel (naa-*dāyl*) *nt* (pl -delen) disadvantage

nadelig (naa-*dāy*-lerkh) *adj* harmful

***nadenken** (naa-*dehng*-kern) *v* *think; **nadenkend** thoughtful

nader (*naa*-derr) *adj* further

naderen (*naa*-der-rern) *v* approach;
naderend oncoming

naderhand (naa-derr-*hahnt*) *adv* afterwards

nadien (naa-*deen*) *adv* afterwards

nadruk (*naa*-drerk) *c* stress; accent

nagedachtenis (*naa*-ger-dahkh-ter-niss) *c* memory

nagel (*naa*-gerl) *c* (pl ~s) nail

nagelborstel (*naa*-gerl-bors-terl) *c* (pl ~s) nailbrush

nagellak (*naa*-ger-lahk) *c* nail-polish

nagelschaar (*naa*-gerl-skhaar) *c* (pl -scharen) nail-scissors *pl*

nagelvijl (*naa*-gerl-vayl) *c* (pl ~en) nail-file

naïef (naa-*eef*) *adj* naïve

najaar (*naa*-Yaar) *nt* autumn

*****najagen** (*naa*-Yaa-gern) *v* chase

*****nakijken** (*naa*-kay-kern) *v* check

*****nalaten** (*naa*-laa-tern) *v* fail

nalatig (naa-*laa*-terkh) *adj* neglectful

namaak (*naa*-maak) *c* imitation

namaken (*naa*-maa-kern) *v* copy

namelijk (*naa*-mer-lerk) *adv* namely

namens (*naa*-merns) *adv* on behalf of, in the name of

namiddag (naa-*mı*-dahkh) *c* (pl ~en) afternoon

narcis (nahr-*siss*) *c* (pl ~sen) daffodil

narcose (nahr-*kōā*-zer) *c* narcosis

narcoticum (nahr-*kōā*-tee-kerm) *nt* (pl -ca) narcotic

narigheid (*naa*-rerkh-hayt) *c* (pl -heden) misery

naseizoen (*naa*-say-zōōn) *nt* low season

nastreven (*naa*-strāy-vern) *v* aim at, pursue

nat (naht) *adj* wet; damp, moist

natie (*naa*-tsee) *c* (pl ~s) nation

nationaal (naa-tshōā-*naal*) *adj* national; **nationale klederdracht** national dress

nationaliseren (naa-tshōā-naa-lee-*zāy*-rern) *v* nationalize

nationaliteit (naa-tshōā-naa-lee-*tayt*) *c* (pl ~en) nationality

natuur (naa-*tewr*) *c* nature

natuurkunde (naa-*tewr*-kern-der) *c* physics

natuurkundige (naa-tewr-*kern*-der-ger) *c* (pl ~n) physicist

natuurlijk (naa-*tewr*-lerk) *adj* natural; *adv* of course, naturally

natuurreservaat (naa-*tewr*-rāy-zerr-vaat) *nt* (pl -vaten) national park

nauw (nou) *adj* narrow; tight

nauwelijks (*nou*-er-lerks) *adv* hardly; scarcely, barely

nauwkeurig (nou-*kūr*-rerkh) *adj* accurate; precise, careful, exact

navel (*naa*-verl) *c* (pl ~s) navel

navigatie (naa-vee-*gaa*-tsee) *c* navigation

navraag (*naa*-vraakh) *c* inquiry; demand

*****navragen** (*naa*-vraa-gern) *v* query, inquire

*****nazenden** (*naa*-zehn-dern) *v* forward

nederig (*nāy*-der-rerkh) *adj* humble

nederlaag (*nāy*-derr-laakh) *c* (pl -lagen) defeat

Nederland (*nāy*-derr-lahnt) the Netherlands

Nederlander (*nāy*-derr-lahn-derr) *c* (pl ~s) Dutchman

Nederlands (*nāy*-derr-lahnts) *adj* Dutch

nee (nāy) no

neef (nāyf) *c* (pl neven) cousin; nephew

neen (nāyn) no

neer (nāyr) *adv* down; downwards

*****neerlaten** (*nāyr*-laa-tern) *v* lower

*****neerslaan** (*nāyr*-slaan) *v* knock down

neerslachtig (nāyr-*slahkh*-terkh) *adj*

down, low, blue, depressed

neerslachtigheid (nāyr-slahkh-terkh-hayt) c depression

neerslag (nāyr-slahkh) c precipitation

neerstorten (nāyr-stor-tern) v crash

negatief (nāy-gaa-teef) adj negative

negen (nāy-gern) num nine

negende (nāy-gern-der) num ninth

negentien (nāy-gern-teen) num nineteen

negentiende (nāy-gern-teen-der) num nineteenth

negentig (nāy-gern-terkh) num ninety

neger (nāy-gerr) c (pl ~s) Negro

negeren (ner-gāy-rern) v ignore

negligé (nāy-glee-zhāy) nt (pl ~s) negligee

neigen (nay-gern) v *be inclined to; ~ tot v tend to

neiging (nay-gɪng) c (pl ~en) inclination, tendency; de ~ *hebben tend

nek (nehk) c (pl ~ken) nape of the neck

***nemen** (nāy-mern) v *take; op zich ~ *take charge of

neon (nāy-Yon) nt neon

nergens (nehr-gerns) adv nowhere

nerts (nehrts) nt (pl ~en) mink

nerveus (nehr-vūrss) adj nervous

nest (nehst) nt (pl ~en) nest; litter

net[1] (neht) adj tidy, neat

net[2] (neht) nt (pl ~ten) net

netnummer (neht-ner-merr) nt (pl ~s) area code

netto (neh-tōa) adj net

netvlies (neht-fleess) nt (pl -vliezen) retina

netwerk (neht-vehrk) nt (pl ~en) network

neuriën (nūr-ree-Yern) v hum

neurose (nūr-rōā-zer) c (pl ~n, ~s) neurosis

neus (nūrss) c (pl neuzen) nose

neusbloeding (nūrss-blōō-dɪng) c (pl ~en) nosebleed

neusgat (nūrss-khaht) nt (pl ~en) nostril

neushoorn (nūrss-hōārn) c (pl ~s) rhinoceros

neutraal (nūr-traal) adj neutral

nevel (nāy-verl) c (pl ~s, ~en) haze, mist

nicht (nɪkht) c (pl ~en) cousin; niece

nicotine (nee-kōā-tee-ner) c nicotine

niemand (nee-mahnt) pron nobody, no one

nier (neer) c (pl ~en) kidney

niet (neet) adv not

nietig (nee-terkh) adj petty, insignificant; void

nietje (nee-tYer) nt (pl ~s) staple

niets (neets) pron nothing; nil

nietsbetekenend (neets-ber-tāy-ker-nernt) adj insignificant

nietszeggend (neet-seh-gernt) adj meaningless

niettemin (nee-ter-mɪn) adv nevertheless

nieuw (nee∞) adj new

nieuwjaar (nee∞-Yaar) New Year

nieuws (nee∞ss) nt news; tidings pl

nieuwsberichten (nee∞ss-ber-rɪkh-tern) pl news

nieuwsgierig (nee∞-skhee-rerkh) adj curious, inquisitive

nieuwsgierigheid (nee∞-skhee-rerkh-hayt) c curiosity

Nieuw-Zeeland (nee∞-zāy-lahnt) New Zealand

niezen (nee-zern) v sneeze

Nigeria (nee-gāy-ree-Yaa) Nigeria

Nigeriaan (nee-gāy-ree-Yaan) c (pl -rianen) Nigerian

Nigeriaans (nee-gāy-ree-Yaans) adj Nigerian

nijptang (nayp-tahng) c (pl ~en) pincers pl

nikkel (nɪ-kerl) nt nickel

niks (nɪks) *pron* nothing

nimmer (nɪ-merr) *adv* never

niveau (nee-*voa*) *nt* (pl ~s) level

nivelleren (nee-ver-*lay*-rern) *v* level

noch … noch (nokh) neither … nor

nodig (*noa*-derkh) *adj* necessary; ~ *hebben need

noemen (*noo*-mern) *v* call; name, mention

nog (nokh) *adv* still, yet; ~ **een** another; ~ **eens** once more; ~ **wat** some more

noga (*noa*-gaa) *c* nougat

nogal (*no*-gahl) *adv* pretty, fairly, rather, quite

nogmaals (*nokh*-maals) *adv* once more

nokkenas (*no*-ker-nahss) *c* (pl ~sen) camshaft

nominaal (*noa*-mee-*naal*) *adj* nominal

nominatie (*noa*-mee-*naa*-tsee) *c* (pl ~s) nomination

non (non) *c* (pl ~nen) nun

nonnenklooster (*no*-ner-kloass-terr) *nt* (pl ~s) nunnery

nood (noat) *c* (pl noden) distress; misery; need

noodgedwongen (*noat*-kher-*dvo*-ngern) *adv* by force

noodgeval (*noat*-kher-vahl) *nt* (pl ~len) emergency

noodlot (*noat*-lot) *nt* destiny, fate

noodlottig (noat-*lo*-terkh) *adj* fatal

noodsein (*noat*-sayn) *nt* (pl ~en) distress signal

noodtoestand (*noa*-tōō-stahnt) *c* emergency

nooduitgang (*noat*-ur^ewt-khahng) *c* (pl ~en) emergency exit

noodzaak (*noat*-saak) *c* need, necessity

noodzakelijk (noat-*saa*-ker-lerk) *adj* necessary

noodzaken (*noat*-saa-kern) *v* force

nooit (noa^eet) *adv* never

Noor (noar) *c* (pl Noren) Norwegian

noord (noart) *c* north

noordelijk (*noar*-der-lerk) *adj* northern, northerly, north

noorden (*noar*-dern) *nt* north

noordoosten (noart-*oass*-tern) *nt* north-east

noordpool (*noart*-poal) *c* North Pole

noordwesten (noart-*vehss*-tern) *nt* north-west

Noors (noars) *adj* Norwegian

Noorwegen (*noa*-vehm-gern) Norway

noot (noat) *c* (pl noten) nut; note

nootmuskaat (*noat*-merss-*kaat*) *c* nutmeg

norm (norm) *c* (pl ~en) standard

normaal (nor-*maal*) *adj* normal, regular

nota (*noa*-taa) *c* (pl ~'s) bill

notaris (*noa*-*taa*-rerss) *c* (pl ~sen) notary

notedop (*noa*-ter-dop) *c* (pl ~pen) nutshell

notekraker (*noa*-ter-kraa-kerr) *c* (pl ~s) nutcrackers *pl*

noteren (noa-*tay*-rern) *v* note; list

notie (*noa*-tsee) *c* notion

notitie (noa-*tee*-tsee) *c* (pl ~s) note

notitieboek (noa-*tee*-tsee-bōōk) *nt* (pl ~en) notebook

notulen (*noa*-tēw-lern) *pl* minutes

nou (nou) *adv* now

november (noa-*vehm*-berr) November

nu (nēw) *adv* now; ~ **en dan** now and then; **tot** ~ **toe** so far

nuance (nēw-*ahng*-ser) *c* (pl ~s, ~n) nuance

nuchter (*nerkh*-terr) *adj* sober; down-to-earth, matter-of-fact

nucleair (nēw-klay-^yair) *adj* nuclear

nul (nerl) *c* (pl ~len) nought, zero

nummer (*ner*-merr) *nt* (pl ~s) number; act

nummerbord (*ner*-merr-bort) *nt* (pl ~en) registration plate; licence plate *Am*

nut (nert) *nt* utility, use

nutteloos (*ner*-ter-lōass) *adj* useless

nuttig (*ner*-terkh) *adj* useful

nylon (*nay*-lon) *nt* nylon

O

oase (ōa-*vaa*-zer) *c* (pl ~n, ~s) oasis

ober (*ōa*-berr) *c* (pl ~s) waiter

object (op-*Y*ehkt) *nt* (pl ~en) object

objectief (op-*Y*ehk-*teef*) *adj* objective

obligatie (ōa-blee-*gaa*-tsee) *c* (pl ~s) bond

obsceen (op-*sāyn*) *adj* obscene

obscuur (op-*skewr*) *adj* obscure

observatie (op-sehr-*vaa*-tsee) *c* (pl ~s) observation

observatorium (op-sehr-vaa-*tōa*-ree-*Y*erm) *nt* (pl -ria) observatory

observeren (op-sehr-*vāy*-rern) *v* observe

obsessie (op-*seh*-see) *c* (pl ~s) obsession

obstipatie (op-stee-*paa*-tsee) *c* constipation

oceaan (ōa-sāy-*Y*aan) *c* (pl oceanen) ocean

ochtend (*okh*-ternt) *c* (pl ~en) morning

ochtendblad (*okh*-ternt-blaht) *nt* (pl ~en) morning paper

ochtendeditie (*okh*-ternt-āy-dee-tsee) *c* (pl ~s) morning edition

ochtendschemering (*okh*-ternt-skhāy-mer-ring) *c* dawn

octopus (*ok*-tōa-perss) *c* (pl ~sen) octopus

octrooi (ok-*trōa*^ee) *nt* (pl ~en) patent

oefenen (*ōō*-fer-nern) *v* practise, exercise

oefening (*ōō*-fer-nrng) *c* (pl ~en) exercise

oeroud (*ōōr*-out) *adj* ancient

oerwoud (*ōōr*-vout) *nt* (pl ~en) jungle

oester (*ōōss*-terr) *c* (pl ~s) oyster

oever (*ōō*-verr) *c* (pl ~s) river bank; bank, shore

of (of) *conj* or; whether; ~ ... **of** either ... or; whether ... or

offensief[1] (o-fehn-*seef*) *adj* offensive

offensief[2] (o-fehn-*seef*) *nt* (pl -sieven) offensive

offer (*o*-ferr) *nt* (pl ~s) sacrifice

officieel (o-fee-*shāyl*) *adj* official

officier (o-fee-*seer*) *c* (pl ~en, ~s) officer

officieus (o-fee-*shūrss*) *adj* unofficial

ofschoon (of-*skhōan*) *conj* although, though

ogenblik (*ōa*-germ-blik) *nt* (pl ~ken) moment, instant

ogenblikkelijk (*ōa*-germ-*bli*-ker-lerk) *adv* instantly

ogenschaduw (*ōa*-ger-skhaa-dew^oo) *c* eye-shadow

oktober (ok-*tōa*-berr) October

olie (*ōa*-lee) *c* oil

olieachtig (*ōa*-lee-ahkh-terkh) *adj* oily

oliebron (*ōa*-lee-bron) *c* (pl ~nen) oil-well

oliedruk (*ōa*-lee-drerk) *c* oil pressure

oliefilter (*ōa*-lee-fil-terr) *nt* (pl ~s) oil filter

oliën (*ōa*-lee-*Y*ern) *v* lubricate

olieraffinaderij (*ōa*-lee-rah-fee-naa-der-ray) *c* (pl ~en) oil-refinery

olieverfschilderij (*ōa*-lee-vehrf-skhil-der-ray) *nt* (pl ~en) oil-painting

olifant (*ōa*-lee-fahnt) *c* (pl ~en) elephant

olijf (ōa-*layf*) *c* (pl olijven) olive

olijfolie (ōa-*layf*-ōa-lee) *c* olive oil

om (om) *prep* round, about, around;

~ **te** to, in order to

oma (*ōā*-maa) *c* (pl ~'s) grandmother

***ombrengen** (*om*-breh-ngern) *v* kill

omcirkelen (om-*sir*-ker-lern) *v* encircle

omdat (om-*daht*) *conj* because; as

omdraaien (*om*-draa^ee^-ern) *v* turn; invert; **zich** ~ turn round

omelet (ōā-mer-*leht*) *nt* (pl ~ten) omelette

***omgaan met** (*om*-gaan) associate with, mix with

omgang (*om*-gahng) *c* intercourse

omgekeerd (om-ger-*kāyrt*) *adj* reverse

***omgeven** (om-*gāy*-vern) *v* surround, circle

omgeving (om-*gāy*-ving) *c* environment, surroundings *pl*; setting

omheen (om-*hāyn*) *adv* about

omheining (om-*hay*-ning) *c* (pl ~en) fence

omhelzen (om-*hehl*-zern) *v* hug, embrace

omhelzing (om-*hehl*-zing) *c* (pl ~en) hug, embrace

omhoog (om-*hōākh*) *adv* up; ~ ***gaan** ascend

omkeer (*om*-kāyr) *c* reverse

omkeren (*om*-kāy-rern) *v* turn over, turn, turn round

***omkomen** (*om*-kōā-mern) *v* perish

***omkopen** (*om*-kōā-pern) *v* bribe, corrupt

omkoping (*om*-kōā-ping) *c* (pl ~en) bribery, corruption

omlaag (om-*laakh*) *adv* down

omleiding (*om*-lay-ding) *c* (pl ~en) detour

omliggend (*om*-li-gernt) *adj* surrounding

omloop (*om*-lōāp) *c* circulation

omrekenen (*om*-rāy-ker-nern) *v* convert

omrekentabel (om-rāy-ker-taa-behl) *c* (pl ~len) conversion chart

omringen (om-*ring*-ern) *v* encircle, surround, circle

***omschrijven** (oam-*skhray*-vern) *v* define

omslag (*om*-slahkh) *c/nt* (pl ~en) cover, jacket

omslagdoek (*om*-slahkh-dōōk) *c* (pl ~en) shawl

omstandigheid (om-*stahn*-derkh-hayt) *c* (pl -heden) circumstance; condition

omstreden (om-*strāy*-dern) *adj* controversial

omstreeks (om-*strāyks*) *adv* about

omtrek (*om*-trehk) *c* (pl ~ken) contour, outline

omtrent (om-*trehnt*) *prep* about, concerning

omvang (*om*-vahng) *c* bulk, size; extent

omvangrijk (om-*vahng*-rayk) *adj* bulky, big; extensive

omvatten (om-*vah*-tern) *v* comprise

omver (om-*vehr*) *adv* down, over

omweg (*om*-vehkh) *c* (pl ~en) detour

omwenteling (*om*-vehn-ter-ling) *c* (pl ~en) revolution

omwisselen (*om*-vi-ser-lern) *v* switch

omzet (*om*-zeht) *c* (pl ~ten) turnover

omzetbelasting (*om*-zeht-ber-lahss-ting) *c* turnover tax; sales tax

onaangenaam (on-*aan*-ger-naam) *adj* unpleasant, disagreeable

onaanvaardbaar (on-aan-*vaart*-baar) *adj* unacceptable

onaardig (on-*aar*-derkh) *adj* unkind

onafgebroken (on-*ahf*-kher-brōā-kern) *adj* continuous

onafhankelijk (on-ahf-*hahng*-ker-lerk) *adj* independent

onafhankelijkheid (on-ahf-*hahng*-ker-lerk-hayt) *c* independence

onbeantwoord (om-ber-*ahnt*-vōārt) *adj* unanswered

onbebouwd (om-ber-*bout*) *adj* uncultivated

onbeduidend (om-ber-*dur^ew*-dernt) *adj* petty, insignificant

onbegaanbaar (om-ber-*gaam*-baar) *adj* impassable

onbegrijpelijk (om-ber-*gray*-per-lerk) *adj* puzzling

onbehaaglijk (om-ber-*haakh*-lerk) *adj* uneasy

onbekend (om-ber-*kehnt*) *adj* unfamiliar, unknown

onbekwaam (om-ber-*kvaam*) *adj* unable, incompetent, incapable

onbelangrijk (om-ber-*lahng*-rayk) *adj* unimportant; insignificant

onbeleefd (om-ber-*layft*) *adj* impolite

onbemind (om-ber-*mint*) *adj* unpopular

onbepaald (om-ber-*paalt*) *adj* indefinite; **onbepaalde wijs** infinitive

onbeperkt (om-ber-*pehrkt*) *adj* unlimited

onbeschaamd (om-ber-*skhaamt*) *adj* impudent, impertinent, insolent

onbeschaamdheid (om-ber-*skhaamt*-hayt) *c* impertinence, insolence

onbescheiden (om-ber-*skhay*-dern) *adj* immodest

onbeschermd (om-ber-*skhehrmt*) *adj* unprotected

onbeschoft (oam-ber-*skhoft*) *adj* impertinent

onbetrouwbaar (om-ber-*trou*-baar) *adj* untrustworthy, unreliable

onbevoegd (om-ber-*vōōkht*) *adj* unqualified; unauthorized

onbevredigend (om-ber-*vrāy*-der-gernt) *adj* unsatisfactory

onbewoonbaar (om-ber-*vōām*-baar) *adj* uninhabitable

onbewoond (om-ber-*vōānt*) *adj* uninhabited

onbewust (om-ber-*verst*) *adj* unaware

onbezet (om-ber-*zeht*) *adj* unoccupied

onbezonnen (om-ber-*zo*-nern) *adj* rash

onbezorgd (om-ber-*zorkht*) *adj* carefree

onbillijk (om-b*ı*-lerk) *adj* unfair

onbreekbaar (om-*brāyk*-baar) *adj* unbreakable

ondankbaar (on-*dahngk*-baar) *adj* ungrateful

ondanks (*on*-dahngks) *prep* despite, in spite of

ondenkbaar (on-*dehngk*-baar) *adj* inconceivable

onder (*on*-derr) *prep* under; beneath, below; among, amid

onderaan (on-der-*raan*) *adv* below

***onderbreken** (on-derr-*brāy*-kern) *v* interrupt

onderbreking (on-derr-*brāy*-king) *c* (pl ~en) interruption

***onderbrengen** (*on*-derr-breh-ngern) *v* accommodate

onderbroek (*on*-derr-brōōk) *c* (pl ~en) briefs *pl*, pants *pl*, panties *pl*; shorts *plAm*; underpants *plAm*

onderdaan (on-derr-daan) *c* (pl -danen) subject

onderdak (*on*-derr-dahk) *nt* accommodation

onderdeel (*on*-derr-dāyl) *nt* (pl -delen) spare part

onderdrukken (on-derr-*drer*-kern) *v* suppress

***ondergaan** (on-derr-*gaan*) *v* suffer

ondergang (*on*-derr-gahng) *c* destruction; ruination, ruin

ondergeschikt (on-derr-ger-*skhıkt*) *adj* subordinate; secondary, minor

ondergetekende (on-derr-ger-*tāy*-kern-der) *c* (pl ~n) undersigned

ondergoed (*on*-derr-gōōt) *nt* underwear

ondergronds (on-derr-*gronts*) *adj* underground

ondergrondse (on-derr-*gron*-tser) *c* subway *nAm*

onderhandelen (on-derr-*hahn*-der-lern) *v* negotiate

onderhandeling (on-derr-*hahn*-der-lıng) *c* (pl ~en) negotiation

onderhevig aan (on-derr-*hay*-verkh aan) subject to; liable to; **aan bederf onderhevig** perishable

onderhoud (*on*-derr-hout) *nt* upkeep; maintenance

* **onderhouden** (on-derr-*hou*-dern) *v* entertain

onderling (*on*-derr-lıng) *adj* mutual

* **ondernemen** (on-derr-*nay*-mern) *v* *undertake

onderneming (on-derr-*nay*-mıng) *c* (pl ~en) enterprise, undertaking; concern, company

onderrichten (on-der-*rıkh*-tern) *v* instruct

onderrok (*on*-derr-rok) *c* (pl ~ken) slip

onderschatten (on-derr-*skhah*-tern) *v* underestimate

onderscheid (*on*-derr-skhayt) *nt* distinction; difference; ~ **maken** distinguish

* **onderscheiden** (on-derr-*skhay*-dern) *v* distinguish

onderst (*on*-derrst) *adj* bottom

ondersteboven (on-derr-ster-*boa*-vern) *adv* upside-down

ondersteunen (on-derr-*stur*-nern) *v* *hold up, support

onderstrepen (on-derr-*stray*-pern) *v* underline

onderstroom (*on*-derr-stroam) *c* (pl -stromen) undercurrent

ondertekenen (on-derr-*tay*-ker-nern) *v* sign

ondertitel (*on*-derr-tee-terl) *c* (pl ~s) subtitle

ondertussen (on-derr-*ter*-sern) *adv* in

the meantime, meanwhile

* **ondervinden** (on-derr-*vın*-dern) *v* experience

ondervoeding (on-derr-*voo*-dıng) *c* malnutrition

* **ondervragen** (on-derr-*vraa*-gern) *v* interrogate

onderwerp (*on*-derr-vehrp) *nt* (pl ~en) subject; topic, theme

* **onderwerpen** (on-derr-*vehr*-pern) *v* subject; **zich** ~ submit

onderwijs (*on*-derr-vayss) *nt* tuition; education, instruction

* **onderwijzen** (on-derr-*vay*-zern) *v* *teach

onderwijzer (on-derr-*vay*-zerr) *c* (pl ~s) schoolteacher, schoolmaster, master, teacher

onderzoek (*on*-derr-zook) *nt* (pl ~en) enquiry, investigation, inquiry; check-up, examination; research

* **onderzoeken** (on-derr-*zoo*-kern) *v* enquire, investigate, examine; explore

ondeugend (on-*dur*-gernt) *adj* naughty, mischievous

ondiep (on-*deep*) *adj* shallow

ondoeltreffend (on-*dool*-treh-fehnt) *adj* inefficient

ondraaglijk (on-*draakh*-lerk) *adj* unbearable

onduidelijk (on-*dur^{ew}*-der-lerk) *adj* ambiguous

onecht (on-*ehkht*) *adj* false

het oneens *zijn** (ert on-*ayns* zayn) disagree

oneerlijk (on-*ayr*-lerk) *adj* crooked, dishonest; unfair

oneetbaar (on-*ayt*-baar) *adj* inedible

oneffen (on-*eh*-fern) *adj* uneven

oneindig (on-*ayn*-derkh) *adj* infinite, endless; immense

onenigheid (on-*ay*-nerkh-hayt) *c* (pl -heden) dispute

onervaren (on-ehr-*vaa*-rern) *adj* inexperienced

oneven (on-*āy*-vern) *adj* odd

onevenwichtig (on-*āy*-ver-*vikh*-terkh)
adj unsteady

onfatsoenlijk (om-faht-*sōōn*-lerk) *adj*
indecent

ongeacht (ong-ger-*ahkht*) *prep* in
spite of

ongebruikelijk (ong-ger-*brur*ᵉʷ-ker-
lerk) *adj* unusual

ongeduldig (ong-ger-*derl*-derkh) *adj*
impatient; eager

ongedurig (ong-ger-*dēw*-rerkh) *adj*
restless

ongedwongen (ong-ger-*dvo*-ngern)
adj casual

ongedwongenheid (ong-ger-*dvo*-nger-
hayt) *c* ease

ongeldig (ong-*gehl*-derkh) *adj* invalid

ongelegen (ong-ger-*lāy*-gern) *adj* inconvenient

ongelijk (ong-ger-*layk*) *adj* unequal;
uneven; ~ *hebben *be wrong

ongelofelijk (ong-ger-*lōā*-fer-lerk) *adj*
incredible

ongeluk (*ong*-ger-lerk) *nt* (pl ~ken)
accident; misfortune

ongelukkig (ong-ger-*ler*-kerkh) *adj* unhappy; unlucky, unfortunate

ongelukkigerwijs (ong-ger-ler-ker-gerr-
vayss) *adv* unfortunately

ongemak (*ong*-ger-mahk) *nt* (pl ~ken)
inconvenience

ongemakkelijk (ong-ger-*mah*-ker-lerk)
adj uncomfortable

ongemeubileerd (ong-ger-mūr-bee-
*lāy*rt) *adj* unfurnished

ongeneeslijk (ong-ger-*nāyss*-lerk) *adj*
incurable

ongepast (ong-ger-*pahst*) *adj* unsuitable; improper

ongerief (*ong*-ger-reef) *nt* inconvenience

ongerijmd (ong-ger-*raymt*) *adj* absurd

ongerust (ong-ger-*rerst*) *adj* worried;
zich ~ **maken** worry

ongeschikt (ong-ger-*skhikt*) *adj* unfit

ongeschoold (ong-ger-*skhōālt*) *adj* uneducated; unskilled

ongetrouwd (ong-ger-*trout*) *adj* single

ongetwijfeld (ong-ger-*tvay*-ferlt) *adv*
undoubtedly

ongeval (*ong*-ger-vahl) *nt* (pl ~len)
accident

ongeveer (ong-ger-*vāyr*) *adv* about,
approximately

ongevoelig (ong-ger-*vōō*-lerkh) *adj* insensitive

ongewenst (ong-ger-*vehnst*) *adj* undesirable

ongewoon (ong-ger-*vōān*) *adj* uncommon, unusual

ongezond (ong-ger-*zont*) *adj* unhealthy, unsound

ongunstig (ong-*gerns*-terkh) *adj* unfavourable

onhandig (on-*hahn*-derkh) *adj* clumsy,
awkward

onheil (*on*-hayl) *nt* calamity, disaster;
mischief

onheilspellend (on-hayl-*speh*-lernt)
adj sinister; ominous

onherroepelijk (on-heh-*rōō*-per-lerk)
adj irrevocable

onherstelbaar (on-hehr-*stehl*-baar) *adj*
irreparable

onjuist (oñ-*ur*ᵉʷst) *adj* incorrect

onkosten (*ong*-koss-tern) *pl* expenses
pl

onkruid (*ong*-krur*ᵉʷ*t) *nt* weed

onlangs (*on*-lahngs) *adv* recently;
lately

onleesbaar (on-*lāyss*-baar) *adj* illegible

onmetelijk (o-*māy*-ter-lerk) *adj* vast,
immense

onmiddellijk (o-*mi*-der-lerk) *adj* immediate, prompt; *adv* immediately,

instantly

onmogelijk (o-*mōā*-ger-lerk) *adj* impossible

onnauwkeurig (o-nou-*kūr*-rerkh) *adj* inaccurate; incorrect

onnodig (o-*nōā*-derkh) *adj* unnecessary

onontbeerlijk (on-ont-*bāyr*-lerk) *adj* essential

onopvallend (on-op-*fah*-lernt) *adj* inconspicuous

onopzettelijk (on-op-*seh*-ter-lerk) *adj* unintentional

onoverkomelijk (on-*ōā*-verr-*kōā*-mer-lerk) *adj* prohibitive

onovertroffen (on-*ōā*-verr-*tro*-fern) *adj* unsurpassed

onpartijdig (om-pahr-*tay*-derkh) *adj* impartial

onpersoonlijk (om-pehr-*sōān*-lerk) *adj* impersonal

onplezierig (om-pler-*zee*-rerkh) *adj* unpleasant

onrecht (*on*-rehkht) *nt* injustice; wrong; ~ ***aandoen** wrong

onrechtvaardig (on-rehkht-*faar*-derkh) *adj* unjust

onredelijk (on-*rāy*-der-lerk) *adj* unreasonable

onregelmatig (on-rāy-gerl-*maa*-terkh) *adj* irregular

onrein (on-*rayn*) *adj* unclean

onrust (*on*-rerst) *c* unrest

onrustig (on-*rerss*-terkh) *adj* restless

ons (ons) *pron* our; us; ourselves

onschadelijk (on-*skhaa*-der-lerk) *adj* harmless

onschatbaar (on-*skhaht*-baar) *adj* priceless

onschuld (*on*-skherlt) *c* innocence

onschuldig (on-*skherl*-derkh) *adj* innocent

ontbijt (ont-*bayt*) *nt* breakfast

***ontbinden** (ont-*bın*-dern) *v* dissolve

***ontbreken** (ont-*brāy*-kern) *v* fail; **ontbrekend** missing

ontdekken (on-*deh*-kern) *v* detect, discover

ontdekking (on-*deh*-kıng) *c* (pl ~en) discovery

ontdooien (on-*dōā*ᵉᵉ-ern) *v* thaw

ontevreden (on-ter-*vrāy*-dern) *adj* dissatisfied; discontented

***ontgaan** (ont-*khaan*) *v* escape

ontglippen (ont-*khlı*-pern) *v* slip

onthaal (ont-*haal*) *nt* reception

***ontheffen** (ont-*heh*-fern) *v* exempt; ~ **van** discharge of

***onthouden** (ont-*hou*-dern) *v* remember; deny; **zich ~ van** abstain from

onthullen (ont-*her*-lern) *v* reveal

onthulling (ont-*her*-lıng) *c* (pl ~en) revelation

onthutsen (ont-*hert*-sern) *v* overwhelm

ontkennen (ont-*keh*-nern) *v* deny; **ontkennend** negative

ontkoppelen (ont-*ko*-per-lern) *v* disconnect

ontkurken (ont-*kerr*-kern) *v* uncork

ontleden (ont-*lāy*-dern) *v* analyse; ***break down**

ontlenen (ont-*lāy*-nern) *v* borrow

ontmoeten (ont-*mōō*-tern) *v* encounter; ***meet**

ontmoeting (ont-*mōō*-tıng) *c* (pl ~en) encounter, meeting

***ontnemen** (ont-*nāy*-mern) *v* deprive of

ontoegankelijk (on-*tōō*-*gahng*-ker-lerk) *adj* inaccessible

ontploffen (ont-*plo*-fern) *v* explode

ontplooien (ont-*plōā*ᵉᵉ-ern) *v* expand

ontroeren (oant-*rōō*-rern) *v* move

ontroering (oant-*rōō*-rıng) *c* emotion

ontrouw (*on*-trou) *adj* unfaithful

ontruimen (ont-*rur*ᵉʷ-mern) *v* vacate

ontschepen (ont-*skhāy*-pern) *v* disembark

*ontslaan (ont-*slaan*) v dismiss, fire

ontslag *nemen (ont-*slahkh nāy*-mern) resign

ontslagneming (ont-*slahkh*-nāy-ming) c resignation

ontsmetten (ont-*smeh*-tern) v disinfect

ontsmettingsmiddel (ont-*smeh*-tings-mi-derl) nt (pl ~en) disinfectant

ontsnappen (ont-*snah*-pern) v escape

ontsnapping (ont-*snah*-ping) c (pl ~en) escape

ontspannen (ont-*spah*-nern) adj easygoing

zich ontspannen (ont-*spah*-nern) relax

ontspanning (ont-*spah*-ning) c relaxation; recreation

*ontstaan (ont-*staan*) v *arise

*ontsteken (ont-*stāy*-kern) v *become septic

ontsteking (ont-*stāy*-king) c (pl ~en) ignition; ignition coil; inflammation

ontstemmen (ont-*steh*-mern) v displease

*ontvangen (ont-*fah*-ngern) v receive; entertain

ontvangst (ont-*fahngst*) c (pl ~en) receipt; reception

ontvlambaar (ont-*flahm*-baar) adj inflammable

ontvluchten (ont-*flerkh*-tern) v escape

ontvouwen (ont-*fou*-ern) v unfold

ontwaken (ont-*vaa*-kern) v wake up

ontwerp (ont-*vehrp*) nt (pl ~en) design

*ontwerpen (ont-*vehr*-pern) v design

*ontwijken (ont-*vay*-kern) v avoid

ontwikkelen (ont-*vi*-ker-lern) v develop

ontwikkeling (ont-*vi*-ker-ling) c (pl ~en) development

ontwricht (ont-*frikht*) adj dislocated

ontzag (ont-*sahkh*) nt respect

*ontzeggen (ont-*seh*-gern) v deny

ontzettend (ont-*seh*-ternt) adj dreadful, terrible

onuitstaanbaar (on-ur^ewt-*staam*-baar) adj intolerable

onvast (on-*vahst*) adj unsteady

onveilig (on-*vay*-lerkh) adj unsafe

onverdiend (on-verr-*deent*) adj unearned

onverklaarbaar (on-verr-*klaar*-baar) adj unaccountable

onvermijdelijk (on-verr-*may*-der-lerk) adj unavoidable, inevitable

onverschillig (on-verr-*skhi*-lerkh) adj indifferent

onverstandig (on-verr-*stahn*-derkh) adj unwise

onverwacht (on-verr-*vahkht*) adj unexpected

onvoldoende (on-vol-*dōōn*-der) adj insufficient; inadequate

onvolledig (on-vo-*lāy*-derkh) adj incomplete

onvolmaakt (on-vol-*maakt*) adj imperfect

onvoorwaardelijk (on-vōar-*vaar*-der-lerk) adj unconditional

onvoorzien (on-vōar-*zeen*) adj unexpected

onvriendelijk (on-*vreen*-der-lerk) adj unkind, unfriendly

onwaar (on-*vaar*) adj untrue, false

onwaarschijnlijk (on-vaar-*skhayn*-lerk) adj unlikely, improbable

onweer (on-*vāyr*) nt thunderstorm

onweerachtig (on-*vāyr*-ahkh-terkh) adj thundery

onwel (on-*vehl*) adj unwell

onwerkelijk (on-*vehr*-ker-lerk) adj unreal

onwetend (on-*vāy*-ternt) adj ignorant

onwettig (on-*veh*-terkh) adj unlawful, illegal

onwillig (on-*vi*-lerkh) *adj* unwilling

onyx (*ōa*-niks) *nt* onyx

onzeker (on-*zāy*-kerr) *adj* doubtful, uncertain

onzelfzuchtig (on-zehlf-*serkh*-terkh) *adj* unselfish

onzichtbaar (on-*zıkht*-baar) *adj* invisible

onzijdig (on-*zay*-derkh) *adj* neuter

onzin (*on*-zın) *c* nonsense, rubbish

oog (ōakh) *nt* (pl ogen) eye

oogarts (*ōakh*-ahrts) *c* (pl ~en) oculist

ooggetuige (*ōa*-kher-tur*ew*-ger) *c* (pl ~n) eye-witness

ooglid (*ōakh*-lıt) *nt* (pl -leden) eyelid

oogst (ōakhst) *c* (pl ~en) harvest; crop

ooievaar (*ōa*ᵉᵉ-er-vaar) *c* (pl ~s) stork

ooit (*ōa*ᵉᵉt) *adv* ever

ook (ōak) *adv* also, too; as well

oom (ōam) *c* (pl ~s) uncle

oor (*ōar*) *nt* (pl oren) ear

oorbel (*ōar*-behl) *c* (pl ~len) earring

oordeel (*ōar*-dāyl) *nt* (pl -delen) judgment

oordelen (*ōar*-dāy-lern) *v* judge

oorlog (*ōar*-lokh) *c* (pl ~en) war

oorlogsschip (*ōar*-lokh-skhıp) *nt* (pl -schepen) man-of-war

oorpijn (*ōar*-payn) *c* earache

oorsprong (*ōar*-sprong) *c* (pl ~en) origin

oorspronkelijk (*ōar*-*sprong*-ker-lerk) *adj* original

oorzaak (*ōar*-zaak) *c* (pl -zaken) cause; reason

oost (ōast) *c* east; oost- eastern

oostelijk (*o*-ster-lerk) *adj* eastern, easterly

oosten (*ōa*-stern) *nt* east

Oostenrijk (*ōa*-stern-rayk) Austria

Oostenrijker (*ōa*-stern-ray-kerr) *c* (pl ~s) Austrian

Oostenrijks (*ōa*-stern-rayks) *adj* Austrian

oosters (*ōa*-sterrs) *adj* oriental

op (op) *prep* on, upon; at, in; *adv* up; finished

opa (*ōa*-paa) *c* (pl ~'s) grandfather, granddad

opaal (ōa-*paal*) *c* (pl opalen) opal

opbellen (*o*-beh-lern) *v* call, ring up, phone; call up *Am*

*opbergen (*o*-behr-gern) *v* *put away

opblaasbaar (o-*blaass*-baar) *adj* inflatable

*opblazen (o-*blaa*-zern) *v* inflate

opbouw (*o*-bou) *c* construction

opbouwen (o-bou-ern) *v* erect; construct

opbrengst (*o*-brehngst) *c* (pl ~en) produce

opdat (ob-*daht*) *conj* so that

opdracht (*op*-drahkht) *c* (pl ~en) order; assignment

*opdragen aan (*oap*-draa-gern) assign to

opeens (op-*āyns*) *adv* suddenly

opeisen (*op*-ay-sern) *v* claim

open (*ōa*-pern) *adj* open

openbaar (ōa-*perm*-*baar*) *adj* public

openbaren (ōa-*perm*-*baa*-rern) *v* reveal

opendraaien (*ōa*-per-draa*ee*ern) *v* turn on

openen (*ōa*-per-nern) *v* unlock; open

openhartig (ōa-per-*hahr*-terkh) *adj* open

opening (*ōa*-per-nıng) *c* (pl ~en) opening

openingstijden (*ōa*-per-nıngs-tay-dern) *pl* business hours

opera (*ōa*-per-raa) *c* (pl ~'s) opera; opera house

operatie (ōa-per-*raa*-tsee) *c* (pl ~s) operation, surgery

opereren (ōa-per-*rāy*-rern) *v* operate

operette (ōa-per-*reh*-ter) *c* (pl ~s) operetta

*opgaan (op-khaan) v *rise

opgeruimd (op-kher-rur^{ew}mt) adj good-humoured

opgetogen (oap-kher-tōa-gern) adj delighted

*opgeven (oap-khāy-vern) v declare; *give up

opgewekt (op-kher-vehkt) adj cheerful

opgraving (op-khraa-ving) c (pl ~en) excavation

ophaalbrug (op-haal-brerkh) c (pl ~gen) drawbridge

ophalen (op-haa-lern) v collect, pick up

*ophangen (op-hah-ngern) v *hang

ophanging (op-hah-nging) c suspension

ophef (op-hehf) c fuss

*opheffen (op-heh-fern) v discontinue

ophelderen (op-hehl-der-rern) v clarify

*ophouden (op-hou-dern) v cease; ~ met stop; quit

opinie (ōa-pee-nee) c (pl ~s) opinion

opkomst (op-komst) c rise; attendance

oplage (op-laa-ger) c (pl ~n) issue

opleiden (op-lay-dern) v educate

opletten (op-leh-tern) v *pay attention; oplettend attentive

oplichten (op-likh-tern) v cheat, swindle

oplichter (op-likh-terr) c (pl ~s) swindler

*oplopen (op-lōa-pern) v increase; contract

oplosbaar (op-loss-baar) adj soluble

oplossen (op-lo-sern) v dissolve; solve

oplossing (op-lo-sing) c (pl ~en) solution

opmerkelijk (op-mehr-ker-lerk) adj remarkable; noticeable, striking

opmerken (op-mehr-kern) v notice, note; remark

opmerking (op-mehr-king) c (pl ~en) remark

opname (op-naa-mer) c (pl ~n) recording; shot

*opnemen (op-nāy-mern) v *draw

opnieuw (op-nee^{oo}) adv again

opofferen (op-o-fer-rern) v sacrifice

oponthoud (op-ont-hout) nt delay

oppassen (o-pah-sern) v look out, beware

oppasser (o-pah-serr) c (pl ~s) attendant

opperhoofd (o-perr-hōaft) nt (pl ~en) chieftain

oppervlakkig (o-perr-vlah-kerkh) adj superficial

oppervlakte (o-perr-vlahk-ter) c (pl ~n, ~s) surface; area

oppositie (o-pōa-see-tsee) c (pl ~s) opposition

oprapen (op-raa-pern) v pick up

oprecht (op-rehkht) adj honest, sincere

oprichten (op-rikh-tern) v found; erect

*oprijzen (op-ray-zern) v *arise

oproer (op-rōor) nt revolt, rebellion

opruimen (op-rur^{ew}-mern) v tidy up

opruiming (op-rur^{ew}-ming) c clearance sale

opscheppen (op-skheh-pern) v boast

*opschieten (op-skhee-tern) v hurry

opschorten (op-skhor-tern) v *put off

*opschrijven (op-skhray-vern) v *write down

*opslaan (op-slaan) v store

opslag¹ (op-slahkh) c storage

opslag² (op-slahkh) c rise; raise nAm

opslagplaats (op-slahkh-plaats) c (pl ~en) depot

*opsluiten (op-slur^{ew}-tern) v lock up

opsporen (op-spōa-rern) v trace

*opstaan (op-staan) v *get up, *rise

opstand (op-stahnt) c (pl ~en) rising, revolt, rebellion; in ~ *komen revolt

opstapelen (*op*-staa-per-lern) *v* pile

opstel (*op*-stehl) *nt* (pl ~len) essay

opstellen (*op*-steh-lern) *v* *draw up, *make up

***opstijgen** (*op*-stay-gern) *v* ascend

optellen (*op*-teh-lern) *v* add; count

optelling (*op*-teh-lɪng) *c* (pl ~en) addition

opticien (op-tee-*shang*) *c* (pl ~s) optician

optillen (*op*-tɪ-lern) *v* lift; raise

optimisme (op-tee-*mɪss*-mer) *nt* optimism

optimist (op-tee-*mɪst*) *c* (pl ~en) optimist

optimistisch (op-tee-*mɪss*-teess) *adj* optimistic

optocht (*op*-tokht) *c* (pl ~en) parade

optreden (*op*-trāy-dern) *nt* (pl ~s) appearance

***optreden** (*op*-trāy-dern) *v* act; appear

***opvallen** (*op*-fah-lern) *v* attract attention; **opvallend** striking

opvatten (*op*-fah-tern) *v* conceive

opvatting (*op*-fah-tɪng) *c* (pl ~en) view

opvoeden (*op*-fōō-dern) *v* *bring up, educate

opvoeding (*op*-fōō-dɪng) *c* education

opvolgen (*op*-fol-gern) *v* succeed

***opvouwen** (*op*-fou-ern) *v* fold

opvrolijken (*op*-frōa-ler-kern) *v* cheer up

opvullen (*op*-fer-lern) *v* fill up

***opwinden** (*op*-vɪn-dern) *v* *wind; excite

opwinding (*op*-vɪn-dɪng) *c* excitement

opzettelijk (op-*seh*-ter-lerk) *adj* deliberate, intentional; on purpose

opzicht (*op*-sɪkht) *nt* (pl ~en) respect

opzichter (*op*-sɪkh-terr) *c* (pl ~s) supervisor; warden

opzienbarend (op-seen-*baa*-rernt) *adj* sensational

opzij (op-*say*) *adv* aside; sideways

***opzoeken** (*op*-sōō-kern) *v* look up

oranje (ōā-*rah*-ñer) *adj* orange

orde¹ (*or*-der) *c* order; method; **in ~** in order; **in orde!** okay!, all right!

orde² (*or*-der) *c* (pl ~n, ~s) congregation

ordenen (*or*-der-nern) *v* arrange

ordinair (or-dee-*nair*) *adj* common, vulgar

orgaan (or-*gaan*) *nt* (pl organen) organ

organisatie (or-gaa-nee-*zaa*-tsee) *c* (pl ~s) organization

organisch (or-*gaa*-neess) *adj* organic

organiseren (or-gaa-nee-*zāy*-rern) *v* organize

orgel (*or*-gerl) *nt* (pl ~s) organ

zich oriënteren (ōā-ree-ᵞehn-*tāy*-rern) orientate

origine (ōā-ree-*zhee*-ner) *c* origin

origineel (ōā-ree-zhee-*nāyl*) *adj* original

orkaan (or-*kaan*) *c* (pl orkanen) hurricane

orkest (or-*kehst*) *nt* (pl ~en) orchestra; band

orlon (*or*-lon) *nt* orlon

ornamenteel (or-naa-mehn-*tāyl*) *adj* ornamental

orthodox (or-tōā-*doks*) *adj* orthodox

os (oss) *c* (pl ~sen) ox

oud (out) *adj* old; ancient; aged; **ouder** elder; **oudst** eldest, elder

oudbakken (out-*bah*-kern) *adj* stale

ouderdom (*ou*-derr-dom) *c* age; old age

ouders (*ou*-derrs) *pl* parents *pl*

ouderwets (ou-derr-*vehts*) *adj* old-fashioned, ancient; out of date; quaint

oudheden (*out*-hāy-dern) *pl* antiquities *pl*

Oudheid (*out*-hayt) *c* antiquity

oudheidkunde (*out*-hayt-kern-der) *c* archaeology

ouverture (ōō-verr-*te̅w̅*-rer) *c* (pl ~s, ~n) overture

ouvreuse (ōō-*vrūr*-zer) *c* (pl ~s) usherette

ovaal (ōā-*vaal*) *adj* oval

oven (*ōā*-vern) *c* (pl ~s) oven; furnace; **mikrogolf ~** microwave oven

over (*ōā*-verr) *prep* about; over; across; in; *adv* over

overal (*ōā*-verr-*ahl*) *adv* everywhere; anywhere, throughout

overall (ōā-ver-*rahl*) *c* (pl ~s) overalls *pl*

overblijfsel (*ōā*-verr-*blayf*-serl) *nt* (pl ~s, ~en) remnant

*****overblijven** (ōā-verr-*blay*-vern) *v* remain

overbodig (ōā-verr-*bōā*-derkh) *adj* superfluous; redundant

*****overbrengen** (*ōā*-verr-*breh*-ngern) *v* transfer

overdag (ōā-verr-*dahkh*) *adv* by day

*****overdenken** (ōā-verr-*dehng*-kern) *v* *think over

*****overdrijven** (ōā-verr-*dray*-vern) *v* exaggerate; **overdreven** extravagant

*****overeenkomen** (ōā-verr-*rayng*-kōā-mern) *v* agree; correspond

overeenkomst (ōā-ver-*rayng*-komst) *c* (pl ~en) agreement, settlement

overeenkomstig (ōā-ver-*rayng*-*kom*-sterkh) *adj* similar; *prep* according to

overeenstemming (ōā-ver-*rayn*-steh-mɪng) *c* agreement

overeind (ōā-ver-*raynt*) *adv* upright; erect

overgang (*ōā*-verr-gahng) *c* (pl ~en) transition

overgave (*ōā*-verr-gaa-ver) *c* surrender

*****overgeven** (*ōā*-verr-*gāy*-vern) *v* vomit; **zich *overgeven** surrender

overhaast (ōā-verr-*haast*) *adj* rash

overhalen (*ōā*-verr-haa-lern) *v* persuade

overheersing (ōā-verr-*hāyr*-sɪng) *c* domination

overheid (*ōā*-verr-hayt) *c* (pl -heden) authorities *pl*

overhemd (*ōā*-verr-hehmt) *nt* (pl ~en) shirt

overig (*ōā*-ver-rerkh) *adj* remaining

overigens (*ōā*-ver-rer-gerns) *adv* though

overjas (*ōā*-verr-ᵞahss) *c* (pl ~sen) topcoat, overcoat

aan de overkant (aan der *ōā*-verr-kahnt) across

overleg (ōā-verr-*lehkh*) *nt* deliberation

overleggen (ōā-verr-*leh*-gern) *v* deliberate

overleven (ōā-verr-*lāy*-vern) *v* survive

overleving (ōā-verr-*lāy*vɪng) *c* survival

*****overlijden** (ōā-verr-*lay*-dern) *v* depart, die

overmaken (*ōā*-verr-maa-kern) *v* remit

overmoedig (ōā-verr-*mōō*-derkh) *adj* presumptuous

*****overnemen** (*ōā*-verr-*nāy*-mern) *v* *take over

overreden (ōā-ver-*rāy*-dern) *v* persuade

overschot (*ōā*-verr-skhot) *nt* (pl ~ten) surplus

*****overschrijden** (ōā-verr-*skhray*-dern) *v* exceed

overschrijving (*ōā*-verr-skhray-vɪng) *c* (pl ~en) money order

*****overslaan** (*ōā*-verr-slaan) *v* skip

overspannen (ōā-verr-*spah*-nern) *adj* overstrung

overstappen (*ōā*-verr-stah-pern) *v* change

oversteekplaats (*ōā*-verr-*stāyk*-plaats) *c* (pl ~en) crossing

*oversteken (ōa-verr-stay-kern) v cross

overstroming (ōa-verr-strōa-ming) c (pl ~en) flood

overstuur (ōa-verr-stewr) adj upset

overtocht (ōa-verr-tokht) c (pl ~en) crossing, passage

*overtreden (ōa-verr-tray-dern) v offend

overtreding (ōa-verr-tray-ding) c (pl ~en) offence

*overtreffen (ōa-verr-treh-fern) v *outdo, exceed

overtuigen (ōa-verr-tur^ew-gern) v convince; persuade

overtuiging (ōa-verr-tur^ew-ging) c (pl ~en) conviction; persuasion

overval (ōa-verr-vahl) c (pl ~len) hold-up

oververmoeid (ōa-verr-verr-mōo^eet) adj over-tired

overvloed (ōa-verr-vlōot) c abundance; plenty

overvloedig (ōa-verr-vlōo-derkh) adj abundant, plentiful

overvol (ōa-verr-vol) adj crowded

overweg (ōa-verr-vehkh) c (pl ~en) level crossing, crossing

*overwegen (ōa-verr-vay-gern) v consider

overweging (ōa-verr-vay-ging) c (pl ~en) consideration

overweldigen (ōa-verr-vehl-der-gern) v overwhelm

zich overwerken (ōa-verr-vehr-kern) overwork

*overwinnen (ōa-verr-vi-nern) v conquer; *overcome

overwinning (ōa-verr-vi-ning) c (pl ~en) victory

overzees (ōa-verr-zayss) adj overseas

overzicht (ōa-verr-zikht) nt (pl ~en) survey

P

paal (paal) c (pl palen) post, pole

paar (paar) nt (pl paren) pair; couple

paard (paart) nt (pl ~en) horse

paardebloem (paar-der-blōōm) c (pl ~en) dandelion

paardekracht (paar-der-krahkht) c horsepower

paardesport (paar-der-sport) c riding

*paardrijden (paart-ray-dern) v *ride

paarlemoer (paar-ler-mōōr) nt mother-of-pearl

paars (paars) adj purple

pacht (pahkht) c (pl ~en) lease

pacifisme (pah-see-fiss-mer) nt pacifism

pacifist (pah-see-fist) c (pl ~en) pacifist

pacifistisch (pah-see-fiss-teess) adj pacifist

pad¹ (paht) nt (pl ~en) path; lane, trail

pad² (paht) c (pl ~den) toad

paddestoel (pah-der-stōōl) c (pl ~en) toadstool; mushroom

padvinder (paht-fin-derr) c (pl ~s) scout, boy scout

padvindster (paht-fint-sterr) c (pl ~s) girl guide

pagina (paa-gee-naa) c (pl ~'s) page

pak (pahk) nt (pl ~ken) package

pakhuis (pahk-hur^ewss) nt (pl -huizen) warehouse

Pakistaan (paa-kee-staan) c (pl -stanen) Pakistani

Pakistaans (paa-kee-staans) adj Pakistani

Pakistan (paa-kiss-tahn) Pakistan

pakje (pahk-Yer) nt (pl ~s) parcel, packet

pakken (pah-kern) v *take

pakket (pah-*keht*) *nt* (pl ~ten) parcel

pakpapier (*pahk*-paa-peer) *nt* wrapping paper

paleis (paa-*layss*) *nt* (pl paleizen) palace .

paling (*paa*-ling) *c* (pl ~en) eel

palm (pahlm) *c* (pl ~en) palm

pan (pahn) *c* (pl ~nen) pan

pand (pahnt) *nt* (pl ~en) security; house, premises *pl*

pandjesbaas (*pahn*-t^{y}erss-baass) *c* (pl -bazen) pawnbroker

paneel (paa-*nāyl*) *nt* (pl panelen) panel

paniek (paa-*neek*) *c* panic

panne (*pah*-ner) *c* breakdown

pantoffel (pahn-*to*-ferl) *c* (pl ~s) slipper

panty (*pehn*-tee) *c* (pl panties) pantyhose

papa (*pah*-paa) *c* (pl ~'s) daddy

papaver (paa-*paa*-verr) *c* (pl ~s) poppy

papegaai (pah-per-*gaa*^{ee}) *c* (pl ~en) parrot

papier (paa-*peer*) *nt* (pl ~en) paper

papieren (paa-*pee*-rern) *adj* paper; ~ **servet** paper napkin; ~ **zak** paper bag; ~ **zakdoek** tissue

parade (paa-*raa*-der) *c* (pl ~s) parade

paraferen (paa-raa-*fāy*-rern) *v* initial

paragraaf (paa-raa-*graaf*) *c* (pl -grafen) paragraph

parallel (paa-raa-*lehl*) *adj* parallel

paraplu (paa-raa-*plēw*) *c* (pl ~'s) umbrella

parasol (paa-raa-*sol*) *c* (pl ~s) sunshade

pardon! (pahr-*don*) sorry!

parel (*paa*-rerl) *c* (pl ~s, ~en) pearl

parfum (pahr-*ferm*) *nt* (pl ~s) perfume

park (pahrk) *nt* (pl ~en) park

parkeermeter (pahr-*kāyr*-māy-terr) *c* (pl ~s) parking meter

parkeerplaats (pahr-*kāyr*-plaats) *c* (pl ~en) car park; parking lot *Am*

parkeertarief (pahr-*kāyr*-taa-reef) *nt* (pl -tarieven) parking fee

parkeerzone (pahr-*kāyr*-zaw-ner) *c* (pl ~s) parking zone

parkeren (pahr-*kāy*-rern) *v* park

parkiet (pahr-*keet*) *c* (pl ~en) parakeet

parlement (pahr-ler-*mehnt*) *nt* (pl ~en) parliament

parlementair (pahr-ler-mehn-*tair*) *adj* parliamentary

parochie (pah-*ro*-khee) *c* (pl ~s) parish

particulier (pahr-tee-kēw-*leer*) *adj* private

partij (pahr-*tay*) *c* (pl ~en) party; side; batch

partijdig (pahr-*tay*-derkh) *adj* partial

partner (*pahrt*-nerr) *c* (pl ~s) partner; associate

pas[1] (pahss) *c* (pl ~sen) step

pas[2] (pahss) *adv* just

Pasen (*paa*-sern) Easter

pasfoto (*pahss*-fōa-tōa) *c* (pl ~'s) passport photograph

paskamer (*pahss*-kaa-merr) *c* (pl ~s) fitting room

paspoort (*pahss*-pōart) *nt* (pl ~en) passport

paspoortcontrole (*pahss*-pōart-kon-traw-ler) *c* passport control

passage (pah-*saa*-zher) *c* (pl ~s) excerpt; passage

passagier (pah-saa-*zheer*) *c* (pl ~s) passenger

passen (*pah*-sern) *v* try on; fit; ~ **bij** match; **passend** appropriate; convenient, adequate, proper; ~ **op** look after; attend to

passeren (pah-*sāy*-rern) *v* pass; bypass, pass by

passie (*pah*-see) *c* passion

passief (pah-*seef*) *adj* passive

pasta (*pahss*-taa) *c* (pl ~'s) paste

pastorie (pahss-tō̄a-*ree*) *c* (pl ~ën) parsonage, vicarage, rectory

patent (paa-*tehnt*) *nt* (pl ~en) patent

pater (*paa*-terr) *c* (pl ~s) father

patient (paa-*shehnt*) *c* (pl ~en) patient

patrijs (paa-*trayss*) *c* (pl patrijzen) partridge

patrijspoort (paa-*trayss*-pōart) *c* (pl ~en) porthole

patriot (paa-tree-ᵛ*ot*) *c* (pl ~ten) patriot

patroon (paa-*trōan*) *nt* (pl patronen) pattern; *c* cartridge

patrouille (paa-*troō̄*-ᵛer) *c* (pl ~s) patrol

patrouilleren (paa-troō̄-ᵛ*ay*-rern) *v* patrol

paus (pouss) *c* (pl ~en) pope

pauw (pou) *c* (pl ~en) peacock

pauze (*pou*-zer) *c* (pl ~s) pause; break; interval, intermission

pauzeren (pou-*zay*-rern) *v* pause

paviljoen (paa-vil-ᵛ*ōon*) *nt* (pl ~en, ~s) pavilion

pech (pehkh) *c* bad luck

pedaal (per-*daal*) *nt/c* (pl pedalen) pedal

peddel (*peh*-derl) *c* (pl ~s) paddle

pedicure (pāy-dee-*kew̄*-rer) *c* (pl ~s) pedicure, chiropodist

peen (pāyn) *c* (pl penen) carrot

peer (pāyr) *c* (pl peren) pear; light bulb

pees (pāyss) *c* (pl pezen) sinew, tendon

peetvader (*pāyt*-faa-derr) *c* (pl ~s) godfather

peil (payl) *nt* (pl ~en) level

pelgrim (*pehl*-grim) *c* (pl ~s) pilgrim

pelikaan (pāy-lee-*kaan*) *c* (pl -kanen) pelican

pels (pehls) *c* (pl pelzen) fur

pen (pehn) *c* (pl ~nen) pen

penicilline (pāy-nee-see-*lee*-ner) *c* penicilline

penningmeester (*peh*-nɪng-māyss-terr) *c* (pl ~s) treasurer

penseel (pehn-*sāyl*) *nt* (pl -selen) paint-brush

pensioen (pehn-*shōōn*) *nt* (pl ~en) pension

pension (pehn-*shon*) *nt* (pl ~s) board; boarding-house, guest-house, pension; **vol** ~ full board, board and lodging, bed and board

peper (*pāy*-perr) *c* pepper

pepermunt (*pāy*-perr-*mernt*) *c* peppermint

per (pehr) *prep* by

perceel (pehr-*sāyl*) *nt* (pl -celen) plot

percentage (pehr-sehn-*taa*-zher) *nt* (pl ~s) percentage

percolator (pehr-kōa-*laa*-tor) *c* (pl ~s) percolator

perfectie (pehr-*fehk*-see) *c* perfection

periode (pāy-ree-ᵛ*ōa*-der) *c* (pl ~s, ~n) period; term

periodiek (pāy-ree-ᵛōa-*deek*) *adj* periodical

permanent (pehr-maa-*nehnt*) *adj* permanent; *c* permanent wave

permissie (pehr-*mɪ*-see) *c* permission

perron (peh-*ron*) *nt* (pl ~s) platform

perronkaartje (peh-*ron*-kaar-tᵛer) *nt* (pl ~s) platform ticket

Pers (pehrs) *c* (pl Perzen) Persian

pers (pehrs) *c* press

persconferentie (*pehrs*-kon-fer-rehn-tsee) *c* (pl ~s) press conference

persen (*pehr*-sern) *v* press

personeel (pehr-sōa-*nāyl*) *nt* personnel

personentrein (pehr-*sōa*-ner-trayn) *c* (pl ~en) passenger train

persoon (pehr-*sōan*) *c* (pl -sonen) person; **per** ~ per person

persoonlijk (pehr-sōān-lerk) adj personal; private

persoonlijkheid (pehr-sōān-lerk-hayt) c (pl -heden) personality

perspectief (pehr-spehk-teef) nt (pl -tieven) perspective

Perzië (pehr-zee-Yer) Persia

perzik (pehr-zɪk) c (pl ~en) peach

Perzisch (pehr-zeess) adj Persian

pessimisme (peh-see-mɪss-mer) nt pessimism

pessimist (peh-see-mɪst) c (pl ~en) pessimist

pessimistisch (peh-see-mɪss-teess) adj pessimistic

pet (peht) c (pl ~ten) cap

peterselie (pāy-terr-sāy-lee) c parsley

petitie (per-tee-tsee) c (pl ~s) petition

petroleum (pāy-trōā-lāy-Yerm) c petroleum; kerosene, paraffin

peuter (pūr-terr) c (pl ~s) toddler

pianist (pee-Yaa-nɪst) c (pl ~en) pianist

piano (pee-Yaa-nōā) c (pl ~s) piano

piccolo (pee-kōā-lōā) c (pl ~'s) page-boy, bellboy

picknick (pɪk-nɪk) c (pl ~s) picnic

picknicken (pɪk-nɪ-kern) v picnic

pick-up (pɪk-erp) c (pl ~s) record-player

pienter (peen-terr) adj bright, smart, clever

pier (peer) c (pl ~en) pier, jetty

pijl (payl) c (pl ~en) arrow

pijn (payn) c (pl ~en) ache, pain; ~ *doen *hurt; ache

pijnlijk (payn-lerk) adj sore, painful; embarrassing, awkward

pijnloos (payn-lōāss) adj painless

pijp (payp) c (pl ~en) pipe; tube

pijpestoker (pay-per-stōā-kerr) c (pl ~s) pipe cleaner

pijptabak (payp-taa-bahk) c pipe to-

bacco

pikant (pee-kahnt) adj spicy; savoury

pil (pɪl) c (pl ~len) pill

pilaar (pee-laar) c (pl pilaren) column, pillar

piloot (pee-lōāt) c (pl piloten) pilot

pils (pɪls) nt beer

pincet (pɪn-seht) c (pl ~ten) tweezers pl

pinda (pɪn-daa) c (pl ~'s) peanut

pinguin (pɪn-gvɪn) c (pl ~s) penguin

pink (pɪngk) c (pl ~en) little finger

Pinksteren (pɪngk-ster-rern) Whitsun

pion (pee-Yon) c (pl ~nen) pawn

pionier (pee-Yōā-neer) c (pl ~s) pioneer

piraat (pee-raat) c (pl piraten) pirate

piste (peess-ter) c (pl ~s) ring

pistool (peess-tōāl) nt (pl pistolen) pistol

pit (pɪt) c (pl ~ten) stone, pip

pittoresk (pee-tōā-rehsk) adj picturesque

plaag (plaakh) c (pl plagen) plague

plaat (plaat) c (pl platen) plate, sheet; picture

plaats (plaats) c (pl ~en) place; spot, locality, site; seat; room; **in** ~ **van** instead of

plaatselijk (plaat-ser-lerk) adj local; regional

plaatsen (plaat-sern) v *lay, *put, place; locate

*plaatshebben (plaats-heh-bern) v *take place

plaatskaartenbureau (plaats-kaar-ter-bēw-rōā) nt (pl ~s) box-office

plaatsvervanger (plaats-ferr-vah-ngerr) c (pl ~s) deputy, substitute

plafond (plaa-font) nt (pl ~s) ceiling

plagen (plaa-gern) v tease

plakband (plahk-bahnt) nt scotch tape, adhesive tape

plakboek (plahk-bōōk) nt (pl ~en)

scrap-book

plakken (*plah*-kern) v *stick; paste

plan (plahn) nt (pl ~nen) plan; project, scheme; **van ~ *zijn** intend

planeet (plaa-*nayt*) c (pl -neten) planet

planetarium (plaa-ner-*taa*-ree-Yerm) nt (pl ~s, -ria) planetarium

plank (plahngk) c (pl ~en) board, plank; shelf

plannen (*pleh*-nern) v plan

plant (plahnt) c (pl ~en) plant

plantage (plahn-*taa*-zher) c (pl ~s) plantation

planten (*plahn*-tern) v plant

plantengroei (*plahn*-ter-grōō^ee^) c vegetation

plantkunde (*plahnt*-kern-der) c botany

plantsoen (plahnt-*sōōn*) nt (pl ~en) public garden

plas (plahss) c (pl ~sen) puddle

plastic (*pleh*-stık) adj plastic

plat (plaht) adj flat; even, level

platenspeler (*plaa*-ter-spāy-lerr) c (pl ~s) record-player

platina (*plaa*-tee-naa) nt platinum

plattegrond (plah-ter-*gront*) c (pl ~en) map, plan

platteland (plah-ter-*lahnt*) nt countryside, country; **plattelands-** rural

platzak (*plaht*-sahk) adj broke

plaveien (plaa-*vay*-ern) v pave

plaveisel (plaa-*vay*-serl) nt pavement

plechtig (*plehkh*-terkh) adj solemn

pleegouders (*plāykh*-ou-derrs) pl foster-parents pl

plegen (*plāy*-gern) v commit

pleidooi (play-*dōā*^ee^) nt (pl ~en) plea

plein (playn) nt (pl ~en) square

pleister[1] (*play*-sterr) c (pl ~s) plaster

pleister[2] (*play*-sterr) nt plaster

pleiten (*play*-tern) v plead

plek (plehk) c (pl ~ken) spot; **blauwe ~** bruise; **zere ~** sore

plezier (pler-*zeer*) nt pleasure; fun

plicht (plıkht) c (pl ~en) duty

ploeg[1] (plōōkh) c (pl ~en) plough

ploeg[2] (plōōkh) c (pl ~en) team; shift; gang

ploegen (*plōō*-gern) v plough

plooi (plōā^ee^) c (pl ~en) crease

plooihoudend (plōā^ee^-*hou*-dernt) adj permanent press

plotseling (*plot*-ser-lıng) adj sudden

plukken (*pler*-kern) v pick

plus (plerss) prep plus

pneumatisch (pnūr-*maa*-teess) adj pneumatic

pocketboek (*po*-kert-bōōk) nt (pl ~en) paperback

poeder (*pōō*-derr) nt/c (pl ~s) powder

poederdons (*pōō*-derr-dons) c (pl -donzen) powder-puff

poederdoos (*pōō*-derr-dōāss) c (pl -dozen) powder compact

poelier (*pōō*-leer) c (pl ~s) poulterer

poes (pōōss) c (pl poezen) pussy-cat

poetsen (*pōō*-tsern) v brush; polish

pogen (*pōā*-gern) v try

poging (*pōā*-gıng) c (pl ~en) try, attempt; effort

pokken (*po*-kern) pl smallpox

Polen (*pōā*-lern) Poland

polio (*pōā*-lee-Yōā) c polio

polis (*pōā*-lerss) c (pl ~sen) policy

politicus (pōā-*lee*-tee-kerss) c (pl -ci) politician

politie (pōā-*lee*-tsee) c police pl

politieagent (pōā-*lee*-tsi-aa-gehnt) c (pl ~en) policeman

politiebureau (pōā-*lee*-tsee-bēw-rōā) nt (pl ~s) police-station

politiek (pōā-lee-*teek*) adj political; c policy; politics

pols (pols) c (pl ~en) wrist; pulse

polshorloge (*pols*-hor-lōā-zher) nt (pl ~s) wrist-watch

polsslag (*pol*-slahkh) c pulse

pomp (pomp) *c* (pl ~en) pump

pompelmoes (*pom*-perl-mōōss) *c* (pl -moezen) grapefruit

pompen (*pom*-pern) *v* pump

pond (pont) *nt* pound

Pool (pōal) *c* (pl Polen) Pole

Pools (pōals) *adj* Polish

poort (pōart) *c* (pl ~en) gate

poosje (*pōa*-sher) *nt* while

poot (pōat) *c* (pl poten) leg; paw

pop (pop) *c* (pl ~pen) doll

popeline (pōa-per-*lee*-ner) *nt/c* poplin

popmuziek (*pop*-mēw-zeek) *c* pop music

poppenkast (*po*-per-kahst) *c* puppet-show

populair (pōa-pēw-*lair*) *adj* popular

porselein (por-seh-*layn*) *nt* porcelain, china

portefeuille (por-ter-*fur*ew-Yer) *c* (pl ~s) pocket-book, wallet

portemonnee (por-ter-mo-*nāy*) *c* (pl ~s) purse

portie (*por*-see) *c* (pl ~s) portion; helping

portier (por-*teer*) *c* (pl ~s) doorman, door-keeper, porter

portret (por-*treht*) *nt* (pl ~ten) portrait

Portugal (*por*-tēw-gahl) Portugal

Portugees (por-tēw-*gāyss*) *adj* Portuguese

positie (pōa-*zee*-tsee) *c* (pl ~s) position

positief (pōa-zee-*teef*) *adj* positive

post¹ (post) *c* mail, post

post² (post) *c* (pl ~en) entry

postbode (*post*-bōa-der) *c* (pl ~s, ~n) postman

postcode (*post*-kōa-der) *c* (pl ~s) zip code *Am*

posten (*poss*-tern) *v* mail, post

poste restante (post-rehss-*tahnt*) poste restante

posterijen (poss-ter-*ray*-ern) *pl* postal service

postkantoor (*post*-kahn-tōar) *nt* (pl -toren) post-office

postwissel (*post*-vi-serl) *c* (pl ~s) postal order; mail order *Am*

postzegel (*post*-sāy-gerl) *c* (pl ~s) postage stamp, stamp

postzegelautomaat (*post*-sāy-gerl-ōa-tōa-maat) *c* (pl -maten) stamp machine

pot (pot) *c* (pl ~ten) pot; jar

potlood (*pot*-lōat) *nt* (pl -loden) pencil

praatje (*praa*-tYer) *nt* (pl ~s) chat

pracht (prahkht) *c* splendour

prachtig (*prahkh*-terkh) *adj* lovely, wonderful, marvellous; splendid, gorgeous, fine

praktijk (prahk-*tayk*) *c* (pl ~en) practice

praktisch (*prahk*-teess) *adj* practical

praten (*praa*-tern) *v* talk

precies (prer-*seess*) *adj* precise, very, exact; *adv* exactly; just

predikant (prāy-dee-*kahnt*) *c* (pl ~en) clergyman, minister, vicar, rector

preek (prāyk) *c* (pl preken) sermon

preekstoel (*prāyk*-stōōl) *c* (pl ~en) pulpit

preken (*prāy*-kern) *v* preach

premie (*prāy*-mee) *c* (pl ~s) premium

premier (prer-m*Yāy*) *c* (pl ~s) premier, Prime Minister

prent (prehnt) *c* (pl ~en) picture; print, engraving

prentbriefkaart (*prehnt*-breef-kaart) *c* (pl ~en) picture postcard

president (prāy-zee-*dehnt*) *c* (pl ~en) president

prestatie (prehss-*taa*-tsee) *c* (pl ~s) achievement; feat

presteren (prehss-*tāy*-rern) *v* achieve

prestige (prehss-*tee*-zher) *nt* prestige

pret (preht) *c* fun; gaiety, pleasure

prettig (*preh*-terkh) *adj* enjoyable, pleasant; nice

preventief (*pray*-vehn-*teef*) *adj* preventive

priester (*pree*-sterr) *c* (pl ~s) priest

prijs (prayss) *c* (pl prijzen) price-list; charge, cost, rate; prize, award; **op ~ stellen** appreciate

prijsdaling (*prayss*-daa-lıng) *c* (pl ~en) slump

prijslijst (*prayss*-layst) *c* (pl ~en) price list

prijzen (*pray*-zern) *v* price

***prijzen** (*pray*-zern) *v* praise

prijzig (*pray*-zerkh) *adj* expensive

prik[1] (prık) *c* (pl ~ken) sting

prik[2] (prık) *c* fizz

prikkel (*prı*-kerl) *c* (pl ~s) impulse

prikkelbaar (*prı*-kerl-baar) *adj* irritable

prikkelen (*prı*-ker-lern) *v* irritate

prikken (*prı*-kern) *v* prick

prima (*pree*-maa) *adj* first-rate

primair (*pree*-mair) *adj* primary

principe (prın-*see*-per) *nt* (pl ~s) principle

prins (prıns) *c* (pl ~en) prince

prinses (prın-*sehss*) *c* (pl ~sen) princess

prioriteit (*pree*-Yōa-ree-*tayt*) *c* (pl ~en) priority

privé (pree-*vāy*) *adj* private

privéleven (pree-*vāy*-lāy-vern) *nt* privacy

proberen (prōa-*bāy*-rern) *v* try; attempt; test

probleem (prōa-*blāym*) *nt* (pl -blemen) problem

procédé (prōa-ser-*dāy*) *nt* (pl ~s) process

procedure (prōa-ser-*dēw*-rer) *c* (pl ~s) procedure

procent (prōa-*sehnt*) *nt* (pl ~en) percent

proces (prōa-*sehss*) *nt* (pl ~sen) process; lawsuit

processie (prōa-*seh*-see) *c* (pl ~s) procession

producent (prōa-dēw-*sehnt*) *c* (pl ~en) producer

produceren (prōa-dēw-*sāy*-rern) *v* produce

produkt (prōa-*derkt*) *nt* (pl ~en) product; produce

produktie (prōa-*derk*-see) *c* (pl ~s) production; output

proef (prōof) *c* (pl proeven) experiment; trial, test

proeven (*prōo*-vern) *v* taste

profeet (prōa-*fāyt*) *c* (pl -feten) prophet

professor (prōa-*feh*-sor) *c* (pl ~en, ~s) professor

profiteren (prōa-fee-*tāy*-rern) *v* profit, benefit

programma (prōa-*grah*-maa) *nt* (pl ~'s) programme

progressief (prōa-greh-*seef*) *adj* progressive

project (prōa-*Yehkt*) *nt* (pl ~en) project

promenade (pro-mer-*naa*-der) *c* (pl ~s) esplanade, promenade

promotie (prōa-*mōa*-tsee) *c* (pl ~s) promotion

prompt (prompt) *adj* prompt

propaganda (prōa-paa-*gahn*-daa) *c* propaganda

propeller (prōa-*peh*-lerr) *c* (pl ~s) propeller

proportie (prōa-*por*-see) *c* (pl ~s) proportion

prospectus (pro-*spehk*-terss) *c* (pl ~sen) prospectus

prostituée (pro-stee-tēw-*vāy*) *c* (pl ~s) prostitute

protest (prōa-*tehst*) *nt* (pl ~en) protest

protestants (prōa-terss-*tahnts*) *adj*

Protestant
protesteren (prōa-tehss-*tāy*-rern) *v* protest
provinciaal (prōa-vın-*shaal*) *adj* provincial
provincie (prōa-*vın*-see) *c* (pl ~s) province
provisiekast (prōa-*vee*-zee-kahst) *c* (pl ~en) larder
pruik (prur^ewk) *c* (pl ~en) wig
pruim (prur^ewm) *c* (pl ~en) plum; prune
prullenmand (*prer*-ler-mahnt) *c* (pl ~en) wastepaper-basket
psychiater (psee-khee-*Yaa*-terr) *c* (pl ~s) psychiatrist
psychisch (*psee*-kheess) *adj* psychic
psychologie (psee-khōa-lōa-*gee*) *c* psychology
psychologisch (psee-khōa-*lōa*-geess) *adj* psychological
psycholoog (psee-khōa-*lōakh*) *c* (pl -logen) psychologist
publiceren (pēw-blee-*sāy*-rern) *v* publish
publiek (pēw-*bleek*) *adj* public; *nt* audience, public
publikatie (pēw-blee-*kaa*-tsee) *c* (pl ~s) publication
puimsteen (*pur^ew*m-stāyn) *nt* pumice stone
puistje (*pur^ew*-sher) *nt* (pl ~s) pimple
punaise (pēw-*nai*-zer) *c* (pl ~s) drawing-pin; thumbtack *nAm*
punctueel (perngk-tēw-*vāyl*) *adj* punctual
punt (pernt) *nt* (pl ~en) point; item, issue; *c* full stop, period; tip
puntenslijper (*pern*-ter-slay-perr) *c* (pl ~s) pencil-sharpener
puntkomma (pernt-*ko*-maa) *c* semicolon
put (pert) *c* (pl ~ten) well
puur (pēwr) *adj* neat; sheer

puzzel (*per*-zerl) *c* (pl ~s) puzzle
pyjama (pee-*Yaa*-maa) *c* (pl ~'s) pyjamas *pl*

Q

quarantaine (kaa-rahn-*tai*-ner) *c* quarantine
quota (*kvōa*-taa) *c* (pl ~'s) quota

R

raad¹ (raat) *c* advice, counsel
raad² (raat) *c* (pl raden) council
raadplegen (*raat*-plāy-gern) *v* consult
raadpleging (*raat*-plāy-gıng) *c* (pl ~en) consultation
raadsel (*raat*-serl) *nt* (pl ~s, ~en) riddle, puzzle; mystery, enigma
raadslid (*raats*-lıt) *nt* (pl -leden) councillor
raadsman (*raats*-mahn) *c* (pl -lieden) counsellor; solicitor
raaf (raaf) *c* (pl raven) raven
raam (raam) *nt* (pl ramen) window
raar (raar) *adj* curious, odd, strange, queer, quaint
rabarber (raa-*bahr*-berr) *c* rhubarb
racket (*reh*-kert) *nt* (pl ~s) racquet
* **raden** (*raa*-dern) *v* guess
radiator (raa-dee-*Yaa*-tor) *c* (pl ~s, ~en) radiator
radicaal (raa-dee-*kaal*) *adj* radical
radijs (raa-*dayss*) *c* (pl radijzen) radish
radio (raa-dee-*Yōa*) *c* (pl ~'s) wireless, radio
rafelen (*raa*-fer-lern) *v* fray
raffinaderij (rah-fee-naa-der-*ray*) *c* (pl ~en) refinery
rage (*raa*-zher) *c* (pl ~s) craze

raken (*raa*-kern) *v* *hit

raket (raa-*keht*) *c* (pl ~ten) rocket

ramp (rahmp) *c* (pl ~en) calamity, disaster

rampzalig (rahm-*psaa*-lerkh) *adj* disastrous

rand (rahnt) *c* (pl ~en) edge, border; brim, rim, verge

rang (rahng) *c* (pl ~en) rank; class

rangschikken (*rahng*-skhı-kern) *v* arrange; sort, grade

rantsoen (rahnt-*sōōn*) *nt* (pl ~en) ration

ranzig (*rahn*-zerkh) *adj* rancid

rapport (rah-*port*) *nt* (pl ~en) report

rapporteren (rah-por-*tāy*-rern) *v* report

rariteit (raa-ree-*tayt*) *c* (pl ~en) curio

ras (rahss) *nt* (pl ~sen) race; breed; **rassen-** racial

rasp (rahsp) *c* (pl ~en) grater

raspen (*rahss*-pern) *v* grate

rat (raht) *c* (pl ~ten) rat

rauw (rou) *adj* raw

ravijn (raa-*vayn*) *nt* (pl ~en) gorge

razen (*raa*-zern) *v* rage

razend (*raa*-zernt) *adj* furious

razernij (raa-zerr-*nay*) *c* rage

reactie (rāy-*Yahk*-see) *c* (pl ~s) reaction

reageren (rāy-*Yah-gāy*-rern) *v* react

recent (rer-*sehnt*) *adj* recent

recept (rer-*sehpt*) *nt* (pl ~en) recipe; prescription

receptie (rer-*sehp*-see) *c* (pl ~s) reception office

receptioniste (rer-sehp-shōa-*nıss*-ter) *c* (pl ~s) receptionist

recht[1] (rehkht) *nt* (pl ~en) right; law, justice

recht[2] (rehkht) *adj* straight

rechtbank (*rehkht*-bahngk) *c* (pl ~en) court

rechtdoor (rehkh-*dōar*) *adv* straight on, straight ahead

rechter[1] (*rehkh*-terr) *adj* right-hand

rechter[2] (*rehkh*-terr) *c* (pl ~s) judge

rechthoek (*rehkht*-hōōk) *c* (pl ~en) oblong, rectangle

rechtopstaand (rehkh-*top*-staant) *adj* erect, upright

rechts (rehkhts) *adj* right-hand, right

rechtschapen (rehkht-*skhaa*-pern) *adj* honourable

rechtstreeks (*rehkh*-strāyks) *adj* direct

rechtszaak (*rehkht*-saak) *c* (pl -zaken) trial

rechtuit (rehkh-*turᵉwt*) *adv* straight ahead

rechtvaardig (raykht-*faar*-derkh) *adj* just, righteous, right

rechtvaardigheid (rehkht-*faar*-derkh-hayt) *c* justice

reclame (rer-*klaa*-mer) *c* advertising

reclamespot (rer-*klaa*-mer-spot) *c* (pl ~s) commercial

record (rer-*kawr*) *nt* (pl ~s) record

recreatie (rāy-krāy-*Yaa*-tsee) *c* recreation

recreatiecentrum (rāy-krāy-*Yaa*-tsee-sehn-trerm) *nt* (pl -tra) recreation centre

rector (*rehk*-tor) *c* (pl ~en, ~s) headmaster, principal

reçu (rer-*sew*) *nt* (pl ~'s) receipt

recycleerbar (ree-sie-*kleer*-bar) *adj* recyclable

recycleren (ree-sie-*klee*-rern) *v* recycle

redakteur (rāy-dahk-*tūrr*) *c* (pl ~en, ~s) editor

redden (*reh*-dern) *v* save, rescue

redder (*reh*-derr) *c* (pl ~s) saviour

redding (*reh*-dıng) *c* (pl ~en) rescue

reddingsgordel (*reh*-dıngs-khor-derl) *c* (pl ~s) lifebelt

rede[1] (*rāy*-der) *c* sense; reason

rede[2] (*rāy*-der) *c* (pl ~s) speech

redelijk (*rāy*-der-lerk) *adj* reasonable

reden (*rāy*-dern) *c* (pl ~en) reason

redeneren (rāy-der-nāy-rern) v reason

reder (rāy-derr) c (pl ~s) shipowner

redetwisten (rāy-der-tvīss-tern) v argue

reduceren (rāy-dēw-sāy-rern) v reduce

reductie (rer-derk-see) c (pl ~s) discount, reduction, rebate

reeds (rāyts) adv already

reekalf (rāy-kahlf) nt (pl -kalveren) fawn

reeks (rāyks) c (pl ~en) series; sequence

referentie (rer-fer-rehn-tsee) c (pl ~s) reference

reflector (rer-flehk-tor) c (pl ~s, ~en) reflector

reformatie (rāy-for-maa-tsee) c reformation

regel (rāy-gerl) c (pl ~s) line; rule; **in de** ~ as a rule

regelen (rāy-ger-lern) v arrange; settle; regulate

regeling (rāy-ger-līng) c (pl ~en) arrangement; settlement; regulation

regelmatig (rāy-gerl-maa-terkh) adj regular

regen (rāy-gern) c rain

regenachtig (rāy-gern-ahkh-terkh) adj rainy

regenboog (rāy-ger-bōākh) c (pl -bogen) rainbow

regenbui (rāy-ger-burew) c (pl ~en) shower

regenen (rāy-ger-nern) v rain

regenjas (rāy-ger-ʸahss) c (pl ~sen) mackintosh, raincoat

regeren (rer-gāy-rern) v rule, govern, reign

regering (rer-gāy-rīng) c (pl ~en) government; reign

regie (rer-gee) c (pl ~s) direction

regime (rer-zheem) nt (pl ~s) régime

regisseren (rāy-gee-sāy-rern) v direct

regisseur (rāy-gee-surr) c (pl ~s) director

register (rer-gīss-terr) nt (pl ~s) record; index

registratie (rāy-gīss-traa-tsee) c registration

reglement (rāy-gler-mehnt) nt (pl ~en) regulation

rein (rayn) adj pure

reinigen (ray-ner-gern) v clean; **chemisch** ~ dry-clean

reiniging (ray-ner-gīng) c cleaning

reinigingsmiddel (ray-ner-gīngs-mi-derl) nt (pl ~en) cleaning fluid

reis (rayss) c (pl reizen) journey; trip, voyage

reisagent (rayss-aa-gehnt) c (pl ~en) travel agent

reisbureau (rayss-bēw-rōā) nt (pl ~s) travel agency

reischeque (ray-shehk) c (pl ~s) traveller's cheque

reiskosten (rayss-koss-tern) pl fare

reisplan (rayss-plahn) nt (pl ~nen) itinerary

reisroute (rayss-rōō-ter) c (pl ~s, ~n) itinerary

reisverzekering (rayss-ferr-zāy-ker-rīng) c travel insurance

reiswieg (rayss-veekh) c (pl ~en) carry-cot

reizen (ray-zern) v travel

reiziger (ray-zer-gerr) c (pl ~s) traveller

rek (rehk) c elasticity

rekbaar (rehk-baar) adj elastic

rekenen (rāy-ker-nern) v reckon

rekening (rāy-ker-nīng) c (pl ~en) account; bill; check nAm

rekenkunde (rāy-kerng-kern-der) c arithmetic

rekenmachine (ree-kern-ma-sjiner) c calculator

rekken (reh-kern) v stretch

rekruut (rer-krēwt) c (pl rekruten) recruit

rel (rehl) *c* (pl ~len) riot

relatie (rer-*laa*-tsee) *c* (pl ~s) relation; connection

relatief (rer-laa-*teef*) *adj* relative; comparative

reliëf (rerl-*Yehf*) *nt* (pl ~s) relief

relikwie (rer-ler-*kvee*) *c* (pl ~ën) relic

reling (*rāy*-lıng) *c* (pl ~en) rail

rem (rehm) *c* (pl ~men) brake

remlichten (*rehm*-lıkh-tern) *pl* brake lights

remtrommel (*rehm*-tro-mehl) *c* (pl ~s) brake drum

renbaan (*rehn*-baan) *c* (pl -banen) race-course; track; race-track

rendabel (rehn-*daa*-berl) *adj* paying

rendier (*rehn*-deer) *nt* (pl ~en) reindeer

rennen (*reh*-nern) *v* *run

renpaard (*rehn*-paart) *nt* (pl ~en) race-horse

rente (*rehn*-ter) *c* (pl ~n, ~s) interest

reparatie (rāy-paa-*raa*-tsee) *c* (pl ~s) reparation

repareren (rāy-paa-*rāy*-rern) *v* repair, fix; mend

repertoire (rer-pehr-*tvaar*) *nt* (pl ~s) repertory

repeteren (rer-per-*tāy*-rern) *v* rehearse

repetitie (rer-per-*tee*-tsee) *c* (pl ~s) rehearsal

representatief (rer-prāy-zehn-taa-*teef*) *adj* representative

reproduceren (rāy-prōa-dēw-*sāy*-rern) *v* reproduce

reproduktie (rāy-prōa-*derk*-see) *c* (pl ~s) reproduction

reptiel (rehp-*teel*) *nt* (pl ~en) reptile

republiek (rāy-pēw-*bleek*) *c* (pl ~en) republic

republikeins (rāy-pēw-blee-*kayns*) *adj* republican

reputatie (rāy-pēw-*taa*-tsee) *c* reputa-

tion; fame

reserve (rer-*zehr*-ver) *c* (pl ~s) reserve; **reserve-** spare

reserveband (rer-*zehr*-ver-bahnt) *c* (pl ~en) spare tyre

reserveren (rer-zehr-*vāy*-rern) *v* reserve; book

reservering (rer-zehr-*vāy*-rıng) *c* (pl ~en) reservation; booking

reservewiel (rer-*zehr*-ver-veel) *nt* (pl ~en) spare wheel

reservoir (rer-zerr-*vvaar*) *nt* (pl ~s) reservoir; container

resoluut (rāy-zōā-*lōōt*) *adj* resolute

respect (reh-*spehkt*) *nt* respect; esteem, regard

respectabel (reh-spehk-*taa*-berl) *adj* respectable

respecteren (reh-spehk-*tāy*-rern) *v* respect

respectievelijk (reh-spehk-*tee*-ver-lerk) *adj* respective

rest (rehst) *c* (pl ~en) rest; remainder; remnant

restant (rehss-*tahnt*) *nt* (pl ~en) remainder; remnant

restaurant (reh-stōā-*rahnt*) *nt* (pl ~s) restaurant

restauratiewagen (rehss-tōā-*raa*-tsee-vaa-gern) *c* (pl ~s) dining-car

restrictie (rer-*strık*-see) *c* (pl ~s) qualification

resultaat (rāy-zerl-*taat*) *nt* (pl -taten) result; outcome, issue

resulteren (rāy-zerl-*tāy*-rern) *v* result

resumé (rāy-zēw-*māy*) *nt* (pl ~s) summary

retour (rer-*tōōr*) round trip *Am*

retourvlucht (rer-*tōōr*-vlerkht) *c* (pl ~en) return flight

reumatiek (rūr-maa-*teek*) *c* rheumatism

reus (rūrss) *c* (pl reuzen) giant

reusachtig (rūr-*zahkh*-terkh) *adj* huge;

gigantic, enormous, immense

revalidatie (rāy-vaa-lee-*daa*-tsee) c rehabilitation

revers (rer-*vair*) c (pl ~) lapel

reviseren (rāy-vee-*zāy*-rern) v overhaul

revolutie (rāy-vōā-*lēw*-tsee) c (pl ~s) revolution

revolutionair (rāy-vōā-lēw-tshōā-*nair*) adj revolutionary

revolver (rer-*vol*-verr) c (pl ~s) gun, revolver

revue (rer-*vēw*) c (pl ~s) revue

rib (rɪp) c (pl ~ben) rib

ribfluweel (*rɪp*-flew-vāyl) nt corduroy

richten (*rɪkh*-tern) v direct; ~ **op** aim at

richting (*rɪkh*-tɪng) c (pl ~en) direction; way

richtingaanwijzer (*rɪkh*-tɪng-aan-vay-zerr) c (pl ~s) trafficator, indicator; directional signal Am

richtlijn (*rɪkht*-layn) c (pl ~en) directive

ridder (*rɪ*-derr) c (pl ~s) knight

riem (reem) c (pl ~en) belt; strap; lead

riet (reet) nt reed; cane

rif (rɪf) nt (pl ~fen) reef

rij (ray) c (pl ~en) row, rank; line; file, queue; **in de ~ *staan** queue; stand in line Am

rijbaan (*ray*-baan) c (pl -banen) carriageway; roadway nAm

rijbewijs (*ray*-ber-vayss) nt driving licence

*rijden (*ray*-dern) v *drive; *ride

*rijgen (*ray*-gern) v thread

rijk¹ (rayk) adj rich; wealthy

rijk² (rayk) nt (pl ~en) kingdom, empire; **rijks-** imperial

rijkdom (*rayk*-dom) c (pl ~men) wealth, riches pl

rijm (raym) nt (pl ~en) rhyme

rijp (rayp) adj ripe, mature

rijpheid (*rayp*-hayt) c maturity

rijst (rayst) c rice

rijstrook (*ray*-strōāk) c (pl -stroken) lane

rijtuig (*ray*-tur^{ew}g) nt (pl ~en) carriage; coach

rijweg (*ray*-vehkh) c drive

rijwiel (*ray*-veel) nt (pl ~en) cycle; bicycle

rillen (*rɪ*-lern) v shiver; tremble

rillerig (*rɪ*-ler-rerkh) adj shivery

rilling (*rɪ*-lɪng) c (pl ~en) chill; shiver, shudder

rimpel (*rɪm*-perl) c (pl ~s) wrinkle

ring (rɪng) c (pl ~en) ring

ringweg (*rɪng*-vehkh) c (pl ~en) by-pass

riool (ree-^yōāl) nt (pl riolen) sewer

risico (*ree*-zee-kōā) nt (pl ~'s) risk; chance, hazard

riskant (rɪss-*kahnt*) adj risky

rit (rɪt) c (pl ~ten) ride

ritme (*rɪt*-mer) nt (pl ~n) rhythm

ritssluiting (*rɪt*-slur^{ew}-tɪng) c (pl ~en) zipper, zip

rivaal (ree-*vaal*) c (pl rivalen) rival

rivaliseren (ree-vaa-lee-*zāy*-rern) v rival

rivaliteit (ree-vaa-lee-*tayt*) c rivalry

rivier (ree-*veer*) c (pl ~en) river

riviermonding (ree-*veer*-mon-dɪng) c (pl ~en) estuary

rivieroever (ree-*veer*-ōō-verr) c (pl ~s) riverside

rob (rop) c (pl ~ben) seal

robijn (rōā-*bayn*) c (pl ~en) ruby

roddelen (*ro*-der-lern) v gossip

roede (*rōō*-der) c (pl ~n) rod

roeiboot (*rōō^{ee}*-bōāt) c (pl -boten) rowing-boat

roeien (*rōō^{ee}*-ern) v row

roeiriem (*rōō^{ee}*-reem) c (pl ~en) oar

roem (rōōm) c glory; celebrity, fame

Roemeen (rōō-*māyn*) c (pl -menen)

Rumanian

Roemeens (rōō-*māyns*) *adj* Rumanian

Roemenië (rōō-*māy*-nee-Yer) Rumania

roep (rōōp) *c* call, cry

***roepen** (*rōō*-pern) *v* call; cry, shout

roer (rōōr) *nt* rudder, helm

roeren (*rōō*-rern) *v* stir

roerend (*rōō*-rernt) *adj* movable

roest (rōōst) *nt* rust

roestig (*rōōss*-terkh) *adj* rusty

rok (rok) *c* (pl ~ken) skirt

roken (*rōā*-kern) *v* smoke

roker (*rōā*-kerr) *c* (pl ~s) smoker

rol (rol) *c* (pl ~len) roll

rolgordijn (*rol*-gor-dayn) *nt* (pl ~en) blind

rollen (*ro*-lern) *v* roll

rolstoel (*rol*-stōōl) *c* (pl ~en) wheel-chair

roltrap (*rol*-trahp) *c* (pl ~pen) escalator

roman (rōā-*mahn*) *c* (pl ~s) novel

romance (rōā-*mahng*-ser) *c* (pl ~s, ~n) romance

romanschrijver (rōā-*mahn*-skhray-verr) *c* (pl ~s) novelist

romantisch (rōā-*mahn*-teess) *adj* romantic

romig (*rōā*-merkh) *adj* creamy

rommel (*ro*-merl) *c* mess; litter; trash, junk

rond (ront) *adj* round; *prep* around

ronde (*ron*-der) *c* (pl ~n, ~s) round

rondom (ront-*om*) *adv* around; *prep* round

rondreis (*ront*-rayss) *c* (pl -reizen) tour

rondreizend (*ront*-ray-zernt) *adj* itinerant

***rondtrekken** (*ront*-treh-kern) *v* tramp

***rondzwerven** (*ront*-svehr-vern) *v* wander

röntgenfoto (*rernt*-gern-fōā-tōā) *c* (pl ~'s) X-ray

rood (rōāt) *adj* red

roodborstje (*rōāt*-bor-sher) *nt* (pl ~s) robin

roodkoper (*rōāt*-kōā-perr) *nt* copper

roof (rōāf) *c* robbery

roofdier (*rōāf*-deer) *nt* (pl ~en) beast of prey

rook (rōāk) *c* smoke

rookcoupé (*rōā*-kōō-pay) *c* (pl ~s) smoker

rookkamer (*rōā*-kaa-merr) *c* smoking-room

room (rōām) *c* cream

roomkleurig (rōām-*klūr*-rerkh) *adj* cream

rooms-katholiek (rōāms-kah-tōā-*leek*) *adj* Roman Catholic

roos[1] (rōāss) *c* (pl rozen) rose

roos[2] (rōāss) *c* dandruff

rooster (*rōā*-sterr) *nt* (pl ~s) grate; schedule

roosteren (*rōā*-ster-rern) *v* grill, roast

rot (rot) *adj* rotten

rotan (*rōā*-tahn) *nt* rattan

rotonde (rōā-*ton*-der) *c* (pl ~s) round-about

rots (rots) *c* (pl ~en) rock; cliff

rotsachtig (*rot*-sahkh-terkh) *adj* rocky

rotsblok (*rots*-blok) *nt* (pl ~ken) boulder

rouge (rōō-zher) *c/nt* rouge

roulette (rōō-*leh*-ter) *c* roulette

route (*rōō*-ter) *c* (pl ~s) route

routine (rōō-*tee*-ner) *c* routine

rouw (rou) *c* mourning

royaal (rōā-Yaal) *adj* generous; liberal

roze (*raw*-zer) *adj* rose, pink

rozenkrans (*rōā*-zer-krahns) *c* (pl ~en) rosary, beads *pl*

rozijn (rōā-*zayn*) *c* (pl ~en) raisin

rubber (*rer*-berr) *nt* rubber

rubriek (rēw-*breek*) *c* (pl ~en) column

rug (rerkh) *c* (pl ~gen) back

ruggegraat (*rer*-ger-graat) *c* spine, backbone

rugpijn (*rerkh*-payn) *c* backache

rugzak (*rerkh*-sahk) *c* (pl ~ken) rucksack

***ruiken** (*rur*ew-kern) *v* *smell

ruil (rurew**l**) *c* exchange

ruilen (*rur*ew-lern) *v* exchange; swap

ruim[1] (rurew**m**) *adj* broad, large; roomy, spacious

ruim[2] (rurew**m**) *nt* (pl ~en) hold

ruimte (*rur*ew**m**-ter) *c* room, space

ruïne (rēw-*vee*-ner) *c* (pl ~s) ruins

ruïneren (rēw-vee-*nāy*-rern) *v* ruin

ruit (rurew**t**) *c* (pl ~en) check; pane

ruitenwisser (*rur*ew-ter-vi-serr) *c* (pl ~s) windscreen wiper; windshield wiper *Am*

ruiter (*rur*ew-terr) *c* (pl ~s) horseman; rider

ruk (rerk) *c* (pl ~ken) tug, wrench

rumoer (rēw-*mōor*) *nt* noise

rundvlees (*rernt*-flāyss) *nt* beef

Rus (rerss) *c* (pl ~sen) Russian

Rusland (*rerss*-lahnt) Russia

Russisch (*rer*-seess) *adj* Russian

rust (rerst) *c* rest; quiet; half-time

rusteloosheid (rerss-ter-*lōass*-hayt) *c* unrest

rusten (*rerss*-tern) *v* rest

rusthuis (*rerst*-hur ewss) *nt* (pl -huizen) rest-home

rustiek (rerss-*teek*) *adj* rustic

rustig (*rerss*-terkh) *adj* calm, quiet; restful, tranquil

ruw (rēw oo) *adj* rough, harsh

ruzie (*rēw*-zee) *c* (pl ~s) row, quarrel, dispute; ~ **maken** quarrel

S

saai (saa ee) *adj* dull, boring

sacharine (sah-khaa-*ree*-ner) *c* saccharin

saffier (sah-*feer*) *nt* sapphire

salaris (saa-*laa*-rıss) *nt* (pl ~sen) salary; pay

saldo (*sahl*-dōā) *nt* (pl ~'s, saldi) balance

salon (saa-*lon*) *c* (pl ~s) drawing-room, lounge; salon

samen (*saa*-mern) *adv* together

***samenbinden** (*saa*-mer-bın-dern) *v* bundle

***samenbrengen** (*saa*-mer-breh-ngern) *v* combine

samenhang (*saa*-mer-hahng) *c* coherence

samenleving (*saa*-mer-lāy-vıng) *c* (pl ~en) community

samenloop (*saa*-mer-lōap) *c* concurrence

samenstellen (*saa*-mer-steh-lern) *v* compose, compile

samenstelling (*saa*-mer-steh-lıng) *c* (pl ~en) composition

***samenvallen** (*saa*-mer-vah-lern) *v* coincide

samenvatting (*saa*-mer-vah-tıng) *c* (pl ~en) résumé, summary

samenvoegen (*saa*-mer-vōō-gern) *v* join

samenwerking (*saa*-mer-vehr-kıng) *c* co-operation

***samenzweren** (*saa*-mer-zvāy-rern) *v* conspire

samenzwering (*saa*-mer-zvāy-rıng) *c* (pl ~en) plot

sanatorium (saa-naa-*tōā*-ree- yerm) *nt* (pl ~s, -ria) sanatorium

sandaal (sahn-*daal*) *c* (pl -dalen) sandal

sanitair (saa-nee-*tair*) *adj* sanitary

Saoedi-Arabië (saa-ōō-dee-aa-*raa*-bee- yer) Saudi Arabia

Saoedi-Arabisch (saa-ōō-dee-aa-*raa*-beess) *adj* Saudi Arabian

sap (sahp) *nt* (pl ~pen) juice

sappig (*sah*-perkh) *adj* juicy

sardine (sahr-*dee*-ner) *c* (pl ~s) sardine

satelliet (saa-ter-*leet*) *c* (pl ~en) satellite

satijn (saa-*tayn*) *nt* satin

sauna (*sou*-naa) *c* (pl ~'s) sauna

saus (souss) *c* (pl sauzen) sauce

Scandinavië (skahn-dee-*naa*-vee-ᵞer) Scandinavia

Scandinaviër (skahn-dee-*naa*-vee-ᵞerr) *c* (pl ~s) Scandinavian

Scandinavisch (skahn-dee-*naa*-veess) *adj* Scandinavian

scène (*sai*-ner) *c* (pl ~s) scene

schaafwond (*skhaaf*-vont) *c* (pl ~en) graze

schaak! (skhaak) check!

schaakbord (*skhaak*-bort) *nt* (pl ~en) checkerboard *nAm*

schaakspel (*skhaak*-spehl) *nt* chess

schaal (skhaal) *c* (pl schalen) dish; bowl; scale

schaaldier (*skhaal*-deer) *nt* (pl ~en) shellfish

schaamte (*skhaam*-ter) *c* shame

schaap (skhaap) *nt* (pl schapen) sheep

schaar (skhaar) *c* (pl scharen) scissors *pl*

schaars (skhaars) *adj* scarce

schaarste (*skhaar*-ster) *c* scarcity

schaats (skhaats) *c* (pl ~en) skate

schaatsen (*skhaat*-sern) *v* skate

schade (*skhaa*-der) *c* damage; harm, mischief

schadelijk (*skhaa*-der-lerk) *adj* harmful; hurtful

schadeloosstelling (*skhaa*-der-lōa-steh-lıng) *c* (pl ~en) indemnity

schaden (*skhaa*-dern) *v* harm

schadevergoeding (*skhaa*-der-verr-gōo-dıng) *c* (pl ~en) compensation, indemnity

schaduw (*skhaa*-dēw°°) *c* (pl ~en) shade; shadow

schaduwrijk (*skhaa*-dēw°°-rayk) *adj* shady

schakel (*skhaa*-kerl) *c* (pl ~s) link

schakelaar (*skhaa*-ker-laar) *c* (pl ~s) switch

schakelbord (*skhaa*-kerl-bort) *nt* switchboard

schakelen (*skhaa*-ker-lern) *v* change gear

zich schamen (*skhaa*-mern) *be ashamed

schandaal (skhahn-*daal*) *nt* (pl -dalen) scandal

schande (*skhahn*-deh) *c* disgrace, shame

schapevlees (*skhaa*-per-vlāyss) *nt* mutton

scharnier (skhahr-*neer*) *nt* (pl ~en) hinge

schat (skhaht) *c* (pl ~ten) treasure; darling

schatkist (*skhaht*-kıst) *c* treasury

schatten (*skhah*-tern) *v* evaluate, estimate, value; appreciate

schatting (*skhah*-tıng) *c* (pl ~en) estimate; appreciation

schedel (*skhāy*-derl) *c* (pl ~s) skull

scheef (skhāyf) *adj* slanting

scheel (skhāyl) *adj* cross-eyed

scheepswerf (*skhāyps*-vehrf) *c* (pl -werven) shipyard

scheepvaart (*skhāyp*-faart) *c* navigation

scheepvaartlijn (*skhāyp*-faart-layn) *c* (pl ~en) shipping line

scheerapparaat (*skhāyr*-ah-paa-raat) *nt* (pl -raten) safety-razor, electric razor, shaver

scheercrème (*skhāyr*-kraim) *c* (pl ~s) shaving-cream

scheerkwast (*skhāyr*-kvahst) *c* (pl ~en) shaving-brush

scheermesje (*skhāyr*-meh-sher) *nt* (pl

~s) razor-blade

scheerzeep (*skhayr-zayp*) c shaving-soap

***scheiden** (*skhay-dern*) v separate; divide, part; divorce

scheiding (*skhay-ding*) c (pl ~en) division; parting

scheidsrechter (*skhayts-rehkh-terr*) c (pl ~s) umpire

scheikunde (*skhay-kern-der*) c chemistry

scheikundig (skhay-*kern*-derkh) adj chemical

***schelden** (*skhehl-dern*) v scold

schelm (skhehlm) c (pl ~en) rascal

schelp (skhehlp) c (pl ~en) shell

schelvis (*skhehl*-viss) c haddock

schema (*skhay*-maa) nt (pl ~'s, ~ta) diagram; scheme

schemering (*skhay*-mer-ring) c twilight

schending (*skhehn*-ding) c (pl ~en) violation

***schenken** (*skhehng*-kern) v pour; donate

schenking (*skhehng*-king) c (pl ~en) donation

***scheppen** (*skheh*-pern) v create

schepsel (*skhehp*-serl) nt (pl ~s) creature

zich ***scheren** (*skhay*-rern) shave

scherm (skhehrm) nt (pl ~en) screen

schermen (*skhehr*-mern) v fence

scherp (skhehrp) adj sharp; keen

schets (skhehts) c (pl ~en) sketch

schetsboek (*skhehts*-book) nt (pl ~en) sketch-book

schetsen (*skheht*-sern) v sketch

scheur (skhurr) c (pl ~en) tear

scheuren (*skhur*-rern) v rip, *tear

schiereiland (*skheer*-ay-lahnt) nt peninsula

***schieten** (*skhee*-tern) v *shoot, fire

schietschijf (*skheet*-skhayf) c (pl

-schijven) mark

schijf (skhayf) c (pl schijven) disc

schijn (skhayn) c semblance

schijnbaar (*skhaym*-baar) adj apparent

***schijnen** (*skhay*-nern) v appear, seem; *shine

schijnheilig (skhayn-*hay*-lerkh) adj hypocritical

schijnwerper (*skhayn*-vehr-perr) c (pl ~s) spotlight, searchlight

schikken (*skhi*-kern) v suit

schikking (*skhi*-king) c (pl ~en) settlement

schil (skhil) c (pl ~len) skin; peel

schilder (*skhil*-derr) c (pl ~s) painter

schilderachtig (*skhil*-derr-ahkh-terkh) adj scenic, picturesque

schilderen (*skhil*-der-rern) v paint

schilderij (skhil-der-*ray*) nt (pl ~en) painting, picture

schildpad (*skhilt*-paht) c (pl ~den) turtle

schilfer (*skhil*-ferr) c (pl ~s) chip

schillen (*skhi*-lern) c peel

schimmel (*skhi*-merl) c (pl ~s) mildew

schip (skhip) nt (pl schepen) ship; boat, vessel

schitterend (*skhi*-ter-rernt) adj brilliant, splendid

schittering (*skhi*-ter-ring) c (pl ~en) glare

schoeisel (*skhooee*-serl) nt footwear

schoen (skhoon) c (pl ~en) shoe

schoenmaker (*skhoon*-maa-kerr) c (pl ~s) shoemaker

schoensmeer (*skhoon*-smayr) c shoe polish

schoenveter (*skhoon*-fay-terr) c (pl ~s) shoe-lace

schoenwinkel (*skhoon*-ving-kerl) c (pl ~s) shoe-shop

schoft (skhoft) c (pl ~en) bastard

schok (skhok) c (pl ~ken) shock

schokbreker (*skhok*-brāy-kerr) *c* (pl
~s) shock absorber

schokken (*skho*-kern) *v* shock

schol (skhol) *c* (pl ~len) plaice

schommel (*skho*-merl) *c* (pl ~s) swing

schommelen (*skho*-mer-lern) *v* rock,
*swing

school (skhōal) *c* (pl scholen) school;
college; **middelbare** ~ secondary
school

schoolbank (*skhōal*-bahngk) *c* (pl
~en) desk

schoolbord (*skhōal*-bort) *nt* (pl ~en)
blackboard

schoolhoofd (*skhōal*-hōaft) *nt* (pl
~en) headmaster, head teacher

schooljongen (*skhōal*-Yo-ngern) *c* (pl
~s) schoolboy

schoolmeester (*skhōal*-māyss-terr) *c*
(pl ~s) teacher

schoolmeisje (*skhōal*-may-sher) *nt* (pl
~s) schoolgirl

schoolslag (*skhōal*-slahkh) *c* breaststroke

schooltas (*skhōal*-tahss) *c* (pl ~sen)
satchel

schoon (skhōan) *adj* clean

schoonheid (*skhōan*-hayt) *c* (pl -he-
den) beauty

schoonheidsbehandeling (*skhōan*-
hayts-ber-hahn-der-lıng) *c* (pl ~en)
beauty treatment

schoonheidsmasker (*skhōan*-hayts-
mahss-kerr) *nt* (pl ~s) face-pack

schoonheidsmiddelen (*skhōan*-hayts-
mı-der-lern) *pl* cosmetics *pl*

schoonheidssalon (*skhōan*-hayts-saa-
lon) *c* (pl ~s) beauty salon, beauty
parlour

schoonmaak (*skhōa*-maak) *c* cleaning

schoonmaken (*skhōa*-maa-kern) *v*
clean

schoonmoeder (*skhōa*-mōo-derr) *c* (pl
~s) mother-in-law

schoonouders (*skhōan*-ou-derrs) *pl*
parents-in-law *pl*

schoonvader (*skhōan*-vaa-derr) *c* (pl
~s) father-in-law

schoonzoon (*skhōan*-zōan) *c* (pl -zo-
nen) son-in-law

schoonzuster (*skhōan*-zerss-terr) *c* (pl
~s) sister-in-law

schoorsteen (*skhōar*-stāyn) *c* (pl -ste-
nen) chimney

schop (skhop) *c* (pl ~pen) kick;
spade, shovel

schoppen (*skho*-pern) *v* kick

schor (skhor) *adj* hoarse

schorsen (*skhor*-sern) *v* suspend

schort (skhort) *c* (pl ~en) apron

Schot (skhot) *c* (pl ~ten) Scot

schot (skhot) *nt* (pl ~en) shot

schotel (*skhōa*-terl) *c* (pl ~s) dish;
schoteltje *nt* saucer

Schotland (*skhot*-lahnt) Scotland

Schots (skhots) *adj* Scottish, Scotch

schouder (*skhou*-derr) *c* (pl ~s) shoulder

schouwburg (*skhou*-berrkh) *c* (pl ~en)
theatre

schouwspel (*skhou*-spehl) *nt* (pl ~en)
spectacle

schram (skhrahm) *c* (pl ~men)
scratch

schrappen (*skhrah*-pern) *v* scrape

schrede (*skhrāy*-der) *c* (pl ~n) pace

schreeuw (skhrāy⁰⁰) *c* (pl ~en)
scream, cry, shout

schreeuwen (*skhrāy⁰⁰*-ern) *v* scream,
cry, shout

schriftelijk (*skhrif*-ter-lerk) *adj* written; *adv* in writing

schrijfbehoeften (*skhrayf*-ber-hōof-
tern) *pl* stationery

schrijfblok (*skhrayf*-blok) *nt* (pl ~ken)
writing-pad

schrijfmachine (*skhrayf*-mah-shee-ner)
c (pl ~s) typewriter

schrijfmachinepapier (*skhrayf*-mah-shee-ner-paa-peer) *nt* typing paper

schrijfpapier (*skhrayf*-paa-peer) *nt* notepaper; writing-paper

schrijftafel (*skhrayf*-taa-ferl) *c* (pl ~s) bureau

schrijn (skhrayn) *c* (pl ~en) shrine

*****schrijven** (*skhray*-vern) *v* *write

schrijver (*skhray*-vehr) *c* (pl ~s) author, writer

schrik (skhrɪk) *c* fright, scare; ~ *****aanjagen** terrify

schrikkeljaar (*skhrɪ*-kerl-ᵞaar) *nt* leap-year

*****schrikken** (*skhrɪ*-kern) *v* *be frightened; *****doen** ~ frighten, scare

schrobben (*skhro*-bern) *v* scrub

schroef (skhrōōf) *c* (pl schroeven) screw; propeller

schroefsleutel (*skhrōōf*-slūr-terl) *c* (pl ~s) spanner

schroevedraaier (*skhrōō*-ver-draa-ᵞerr) *c* (pl ~s) screw-driver

schroeven (*skhrōō*-vern) *v* screw

schroot (skhrōāt) *nt* scrap-iron

schub (skherp) *c* (pl ~ben) scale

schudden (*skher*-dern) *v* *shake; shuffle

schuifdeur (*skhurᵉʷf*-dūrr) *c* (pl ~en) sliding door

schuilplaats (*skhurᵉʷl*-plaats) *c* (pl ~en) cover; shelter

schuim (skhurᵉʷm) *nt* froth, lather, foam

schuimen (*skhurᵉʷ*-mern) *v* foam

schuimrubber (*skhurᵉʷm*-rer-berr) *nt* foam-rubber

schuin (skhurᵉʷn) *adj* slanting

*****schuiven** (*skhurᵉʷ*-vern) *v* push

schuld¹ (skherlt) *c* guilt; fault, blame; **de** ~ *****geven aan** blame

schuld² (skherlt) *c* (pl ~en) debt

schuldeiser (*skherlt*-ay-serr) *c* (pl ~s) creditor

schuldig (*skherl*-derkh) *adj* guilty; ~ *****bevinden** convict; ~ *****zijn** owe

schuur (skhewr) *c* (pl schuren) barn; shed

schuurpapier (*skhewr*-paa-peer) *nt* sandpaper

schuw (skhewᵒᵒ) *adj* shy

scoren (*skōā*-rern) *v* score

seconde (ser-*kon*-der) *c* (pl ~n) second

secretaresse (sɪ-krer-taa-*reh*-ser) *c* (pl ~n) secretary

secretaris (sɪ-krer-*taa*-rerss) *c* (pl ~sen) secretary; clerk

sectie (*sehk*-see) *c* (pl ~s) section

secundair (*sāy*-kern-*dair*) *adj* secondary

secuur (ser-*kewr*) *adj* precise

sedert (*sāy*-derrt) *prep* since

sein (sayn) *nt* (pl ~en) signal

seinen (*say*-nern) *v* signal

seizoen (say-*zōōn*) *nt* (pl ~en) season; **buiten het** ~ off season

seksualiteit (sehk-sēw-vaa-lee-*tayt*) *c* sexuality

seksueel (sehk-sēw-*vāyl*) *adj* sexual

selderij (*sehl*-der-ray) *c* celery

select (ser-*lehkt*) *adj* select

selecteren (*sāy*-lehk-*tāy*-rern) *v* select

selectie (*sāy*-lehk-see) *c* selection

senaat (ser-*naat*) *c* senate

senator (ser-*naa*-tor) *c* (pl ~en) senator

seniel (ser-*neel*) *adj* senile

sensatie (sehn-*zaa*-tsee) *c* (pl ~s) sensation

sensationeel (sehn-zaa-tshōā-*nāyl*) *adj* sensational

sentimenteel (sehn-tee-mehn-*tāyl*) *adj* sentimental

september (sehp-*tehm*-berr) September

septisch (*sehp*-teess) *adj* septic

serie (*sāy*-ree) *c* (pl ~s) series

serieus (sāy-ree-ᵛūrss) *adj* serious

serum (sāy-rerm) *nt* (pl ~s, sera) serum

serveerster (sehr-vāyr-sterr) *c* (pl ~s) waitress

servet (sehr-veht) *nt* (pl ~ten) napkin, serviette

sfeer (sfāyr) *c* atmosphere; sphere

shag (shehk) *c* cigarette tobacco

shampoo (shahm-pōa) *c* shampoo

Siam (see-ᵞahm) Siam

Siamees (see-ᵞaa-māyss) *adj* Siamese

sifon (see-fon) *c* (pl ~s) syphon, siphon

sigaar (see-gaar) *c* (pl sigaren) cigar

sigarenwinkel (see-gaa-rer-ving-kerl) *c* (pl ~s) cigar shop

sigarenwinkelier (see-gaa-rer-ving-ker-leer) *c* (pl ~s) tobacconist

sigaret (see-gaa-reht) *c* (pl ~ten) cigarette

sigarettenkoker (see-gaa-reh-ter-kōa-kehr) *c* (pl ~s) cigarette-case

sigarettepijpje (see-gaa-reh-ter-payp-ᵞer) *nt* (pl ~s) cigarette-holder

signaal (see-ñaal) *nt* (pl ñalen) signal

signalement (see-ñaa-ler-mehnt) *nt* (pl ~en) description

simpel (sim-perl) *adj* simple

sinaasappel (see-naa-sah-perl) *c* (pl ~en, ~s) orange

sinds (sins) *conj* since

sindsdien (sins-deen) *adv* since

singel (si-ngerl) *c* (pl ~s) canal

sirene (see-rāy-ner) *c* (pl ~s) siren

siroop (see-rōap) *c* syrup

situatie (see-tēw-vaa-tsee) *c* (pl ~s) situation

sjaal (shaal) *c* (pl ~s) shawl; scarf

skelet (sker-leht) *nt* (pl ~ten) skeleton

ski (skee) *c* (pl ~'s) ski

skibroek (skee-brōōk) *c* (pl ~en) ski pants

skiën (skee-ᵞern) *v* ski

skiër (skee-ᵞerr) *c* (pl ~s) skier

skilift (skee-lift) *c* (pl ~en) ski-lift

skischoenen (skee-skhōō-nern) *pl* ski boots

skistokken (skee-sto-kern) *pl* ski sticks; ski poles *Am*

sla (slaa) *c* lettuce; salad

slaaf (slaaf) *c* (pl slaven) slave

****slaan** (slaan) *v* *beat; *hit, *strike; smack, slap

slaap[1] (slaap) *c* sleep; **in ~** asleep

slaap[2] (slaap) *c* (pl slapen) temple

slaapkamer (slaap-kaa-merr) *c* (pl ~s) bedroom

slaappil (slaa-pil) *c* (pl ~len) sleeping-pill

slaapwagen (slaap-vaa-gern) *c* (pl ~s) sleeping-car

slaapzaal (slaap-saal) *c* (pl -zalen) dormitory

slaapzak (slaap-sahk) *c* (pl ~ken) sleeping-bag

slachtoffer (slahkht-o-ferr) *nt* (pl ~s) victim; casualty

slag[1] (slahkh) *c* (pl ~en) blow; battle

slag[2] (slahkh) *nt* sort

slagader (slahkh-aa-derr) *c* (pl ~s) artery

slagboom (slahkh-bōam) *c* (pl -bomen) barrier

slagen (slaa-gern) *v* manage, succeed; pass

slager (slaa-gerr) *c* (pl ~s) butcher

slagzin (slahkh-sin) *c* (pl ~nen) slogan

slak (slahk) *c* (pl ~ken) snail

slang (slahng) *c* (pl ~en) snake

slank (slahngk) *adj* slim, slender

slaolie (slaa-ōā-lee) *c* salad-oil

slap (slahp) *adj* limp; weak

slapeloos (slaa-per-lōass) *adj* sleepless

slapeloosheid (slaa-per-lōass-hayt) *c* insomnia

****slapen** (slaa-pern) *v* *sleep

slaperig (slaa-per-rerkh) *adj* sleepy

slecht (slehkht) *adj* bad; poor; ill; wicked, evil; **slechter** worse; **slechtst** worst

slechts (slehkhts) *adv* only, merely

slede (*slāy*-der) *c* (pl ~n) sledge

slee (slāy) *c* (pl ~ën) sleigh, sledge

sleepboot (*slāy*-bōat) *c* (pl -boten) tug

slepen (*slāy*-pern) *v* drag, haul; tug, tow

sleutel (*slūr*-terl) *c* (pl ~s) key; wrench

sleutelbeen (*slūr*-terl-bāyn) *nt* (pl -beenderen, -benen) collarbone

sleutelgat (*slūr*-terl-gaht) *nt* (pl ~en) keyhole

*slijpen (*slay*-pern) *v* sharpen

slijterij (slay-ter-*ray*) *c* (pl ~en) off-licence

slikken (*slı*-kern) *v* swallow

slim (slım) *adj* clever

slip (slıp) *c* (pl ~s) briefs *pl*; panties *pl*

slippen (*slı*-pern) *v* slip; skid

slof (slof) *c* (pl ~fen) slipper; carton

slokje (*slok*-ʏer) *nt* (pl ~s) sip

sloot (slōat) *c* (pl sloten) ditch

slopen (*slōa*-pern) *v* demolish

slordig (*slor*-derkh) *adj* untidy; slovenly, sloppy, careless

slot¹ (slot) *nt* (pl ~en) lock; castle; **op ~ *doen** lock

slot² (slot) *nt* end, issue

sluier (*slur*ᵉʷ-err) *c* (pl ~s) veil

sluipschutter (*slur*ᵉʷp-skher-terr) *c* (pl ~s) sniper

sluis (slurᵉʷss) *c* (pl sluizen) lock, sluice

*sluiten (*slur*ᵉʷ-tern) *v* close, *shut; fasten

sluiting (*slur*ᵉʷ-tıng) *c* (pl ~en) fastener

sluw (slēwᵒᵒ) *adj* cunning

smaak (smaak) *c* (pl smaken) taste; flavour

smakelijk (smaa-ker-lerk) *adj* savoury, tasty; appetizing

smakeloos (smaa-ker-lōass) *adj* tasteless

smaken (smaa-kern) *v* taste

smal (smahl) *adj* narrow

smaragd (smaa-*rahkht*) *nt* emerald

smart (smahrt) *c* (pl ~en) grief

smartlap (*smahrt*-lahp) *c* (pl ~pen) tear-jerker

smeerolie (*smāyr*-ōa-lee) *c* lubrication oil

smeersysteem (*smāyr*-see-stāym) *nt* lubrication system

smeken (*smāy*-kern) *v* beg

*smelten (*smehl*-tern) *v* melt

smeren (*smāy*-rern) *v* lubricate, grease

smerig (*smāy*-rerkh) *adj* dirty; foul, filthy

smering (*smāy*-rıng) *c* lubrication

smet (smeht) *c* (pl ~ten) blot

smid (smıt) *c* (pl smeden) smith, blacksmith

smoking (*smōa*-kıng) *c* (pl ~s) dinner-jacket; tuxedo *nAm*

smokkelen (*smo*-ker-lern) *v* smuggle

snaar (snaar) *c* (pl snaren) string

snavel (*snaa*-verl) *c* (pl ~s) beak

snee (snāy) *c* (pl ~ën) cut; slice

sneeuw (snāyᵒᵒ) *c* snow

sneeuwen (*snāy*ᵒᵒ-ern) *v* snow

sneeuwslik (*snāy*ᵒᵒ-slık) *nt* slush

sneeuwstorm (*snāy*ᵒᵒ-storm) *c* (pl ~en) snowstorm, blizzard

snel (snehl) *adj* fast, swift, rapid

snelheid (*snehl*-hayt) *c* (pl -heden) speed; **maximum ~** speed limit

snelheidsbeperking (*snehl*-hayts-ber-pehr-kıng) *c* speed limit

snelheidsmeter (*snehl*-hayts-māy-terr) *c* speedometer

snelheidsovertreding (*snehl*-hayts-ōa-verr-trāy-dıng) *c* speeding

snelkookpan (*snehl*-kōak-pahn) *c* (pl

~nen) pressure-cooker

snellen (*sneh*-lern) *v* dash

sneltrein (*snehl*-trayn) *c* (pl ~en) express train

snelweg (*snehl*-vehhk) *c* (pl ~en) motorway

*****snijden** (*snay*-dern) *v* *cut; carve

snijwond (*snay*-vont) *c* (pl ~en) cut

snipper (*sni*-perr) *c* (pl ~s) scrap

snoek (snook) *c* (pl ~en) pike

snoep (snoop) *nt* sweets; candy *nAm*

snoepgoed (*snoop*-khoot) *nt* sweets; candy *nAm*

snoepje (*snoop*-Yer) *nt* (pl ~s) sweet; candy *nAm*

snoepwinkel (*snoop*-ving-kerl) *c* (pl ~s) sweetshop; candy store *Am*

snoer (snoor) *nt* (pl ~en) line, cord; flex; electric cord

snor (snor) *c* (pl ~ren) moustache

snorkel (*snor*-kerl) *c* (pl ~s) snorkel

snugger (*sner*-gerr) *adj* bright

snuit (snur^{ew}t) *c* (pl ~en) snout

snurken (*snerr*-kern) *v* snore

sociaal (*soa*-*shaal*) *adj* social

socialisme (*soa*-shaa-*liss*-mer) *nt* socialism

socialist (*soa*-shaa-*list*) *c* (pl ~en) socialist

socialistisch (*soa*-shaa-*liss*-teess) *adj* socialist

sociëteit (*soa*-see-Yer-*tayt*) *c* (pl ~en) club

sodawater (*soa*-daa-vaa-terr) *nt* soda-water

soep (soop) *c* (pl ~en) soup

soepbord (*soo*-bort) *nt* (pl ~en) soup-plate

soepel (*soo*-perl) *adj* supple, flexible

soeplepel (*soop*-lāy-perl) *c* (pl ~s) soup-spoon

sofa (*soa*-faa) *c* (pl ~'s) sofa

sok (sok) *c* (pl ~ken) sock

soldaat (sol-*daat*) *c* (pl -daten) soldier

soldeerbout (sol-*dāyr*-bout) *c* (pl ~en) soldering-iron

solderen (sol-*dāy*-rern) *v* solder

solide (soa-*lee*-der) *adj* (pl ~en) solid

solitair (*soa*-lee-*tehr*) *adj* solitary

sollicitatie (so-lee-see-*taa*-tsee) *c* (pl ~s) application

solliciteren (so-lee-see-*tāy*-rern) *v* apply

som (som) *c* (pl ~men) sum; amount; **ronde** ~ lump sum

somber (*som*-berr) *adj* gloomy, sombre

sommige (*so*-mer-ger) *pron* some

soms (soms) *adv* sometimes

soort (sōart) *c*/*nt* (pl ~en) sort, kind; breed, species

sorteren (sor-*tāy*-rern) *v* assort, sort

sortering (sor-*tāy*-ring) *c* (pl ~en) assortment

souterrain (*soo*-ter-rang) *nt* (pl ~s) basement

souvenir (soo-ver-*neer*) *nt* (pl ~s) souvenir; **souvenirwinkel** souvenir shop

spaak (spaak) *c* (pl spaken) spoke

Spaans (spaans) *adj* Spanish

spaarbank (*spaar*-bahngk) *c* (pl ~en) savings bank

spaargeld (*spaar*-gehlt) *nt* savings *pl*

spaarzaam (*spaar*-zaam) *adj* economical

spade (*spaa*-der) *c* (pl ~n) spade

spalk (spahlk) *c* (pl ~en) splint

Spanjaard (spah-ñaart) *c* (pl ~en) Spaniard

Spanje (*spah*-ñer) Spain

spannend (*spah*-nernt) *adj* exciting

spanning (*spah*-ning) *c* (pl ~en) tension; pressure, strain, stress

sparen (*spaa*-rern) *v* save; economize

spat (spaht) *c* (pl ~ten) stain, spot, speck

spatader (*spaht*-aa-derr) *c* (pl ~s,

~en) varicose vein

spatbord (*spaht*-bort) *nt* (pl ~en) mud-guard

spatiëren (spaa-*tshāy*-rern) *v* space

spatten (*spah*-tern) *v* splash

specerij (spāy-ser-*ray*) *c* (pl ~en) spice

speciaal (spāy-*shaal*) *adj* special; particular, peculiar

zich specialiseren (spāy-shaa-lee-*zāy*-rern) specialize

specialist (spāy-shaa-*list*) *c* (pl ~en) specialist

specialiteit (spāy-shaa-lee-*tayt*) *c* (pl ~en) speciality

specifiek (spāy-see-*feek*) *adj* specific

specimen (*spāy*-see-mehn) *nt* (pl ~s) specimen

speculeren (spāy-kēw-*lāy*-rern) *v* speculate

speeksel (*spāyk*-serl) *nt* spit

speelgoed (*spāyl*-gōot) *nt* toy

speelgoedwinkel (*spāyl*-gōot-ving-kerl) *c* (pl ~s) toyshop

speelkaart (*spāyl*-kaart) *c* (pl ~en) playing-card

speelplaats (*spāyl*-plaats) *c* (pl ~en) playground

speelterrein (*spāyl*-teh-rayn) *nt* (pl ~en) recreation ground

speer (spāyr) *c* (pl speren) spear

spek (spehk) *nt* bacon

spel[1] (spehl) *nt* (pl ~en) game

spel[2] (spehl) *nt* (pl ~len) play

speld (spehlt) *c* (pl ~en) pin

spelen (*spāy*-lern) *v* play

speler (*spāy*-lerr) *c* (pl ~s) player

spellen (*speh*-lern) *v* *spell

spelling (*speh*-ling) *c* spelling

spelonk (spāy-*longk*) *c* (pl ~en) cave

spiegel (*spee*-gerl) *c* (pl ~s) looking-glass, mirror

spiegelbeeld (*spee*-gerl-bāylt) *nt* (pl ~en) reflection

spier (speer) *c* (pl ~en) muscle

spijbelen (*spay*-ber-lern) *v* play truant

spijker (*spay*-kerr) *c* (pl ~s) nail

spijkerbroek (*spay*-kerr-brōōk) *c* (pl ~en) jeans *pl*

spijskaart (*spayss*-kaart) *c* (pl ~en) menu

spijsvertering (*spayss*-ferr-tāy-ring) *c* digestion

spijt (spayt) *c* regret

spin (spin) *c* (pl ~nen) spider

spinazie (spee-*naa*-zee) *c* spinach

* **spinnen** (*spi*-nern) *v* *spin

spinneweb (*spi*-ner-vehp) *nt* (pl ~ben) spider's web, cobweb

spion (spee-*Yon*) *c* (pl ~nen) spy

spiritusbrander (*spee*-ree-terss-brahn-derr) *c* (pl ~s) spirit stove

spit[1] (spit) *nt* (pl ~ten) spit

spit[2] (spit) *nt* lumbago

spits[1] (spits) *adj* pointed

spits[2] (spits) *c* (pl ~en) peak; spire

spitsuur (*spits*-ēwr) *nt* (pl -uren) rush-hour, peak hour

* **splijten** (*splay*-tern) *v* *split

splinter (*splin*-terr) *c* (pl ~s) splinter

splinternieuw (*splin*-terr-nee∞) *adj* brand-new

zich splitsen (*split*-sern) fork

spoed (spōot) *c* haste, speed

spoedcursus (*spōōt*-kerr-zerss) *c* (pl ~sen) intensive course

spoedgeval (*spōōt*-kher-vahl) *nt* (pl ~len) emergency

spoedig (*spōō*-derkh) *adv* soon, shortly

spoel (spōōl) *c* (pl ~en) spool

spoelen (*spōō*-lern) *v* rinse

spoeling (*spōō*-ling) *c* (pl ~en) rinse

spons (spons) *c* (pl sponzen) sponge

spook (spōak) *nt* (pl spoken) ghost, phantom; spook

spoor (spōar) *nt* (pl sporen) trace; trail, track

spoorbaan (*spōar*-baan) *c* (pl -banen)

railway; railroad *nAm*

spoorweg (*spōar*-vehkh) *c* (pl ~en)
railway; railroad *nAm*

sport (sport) *c* sport

sportjasje (*sport*-Yah-sher) *nt* (pl ~s)
sports-jacket, blazer

sportkleding (*sport*-klāy-dɪng) *c*
sportswear

sportman (*sport*-mahn) *c* (pl ~en)
sportsman

sportwagen (*sport*-vaa-gern) *c* (pl ~s)
sports-car

spot (spot) *c* mockery

spraak (spraak) *c* speech; **ter sprake
*brengen** *bring up

spraakzaam (*spraak*-saam) *adj* talkative

sprakeloos (*spraa*-ker-lōass) *adj*
speechless

spreekkamer (*sprāy*-kaa-merr) *c* (pl
~s) surgery

spreekuur (*sprāy*-ēwr) *nt* (pl -uren)
consultation hours

spreekwoord (*sprāyk*-vōart) *nt* (pl
~en) proverb

spreeuw (sprāy⁰⁰) *c* (pl ~en) starling

sprei (spray) *c* (pl ~en) counterpane,
quilt

spreiden (*spray*-dern) *v* *spread

*spreken (*sprāy*-kern) *v* *speak, talk

*springen (*sprɪ*-ngern) *v* jump; *leap

springstof (*sprɪng*-stof) *c* (pl ~fen) explosive

sprinkhaan (*sprɪngk*-haan) *c* (pl -ha-
nen) grasshopper

sproeier (*sprōō*ee-err) *c* (pl ~s) atomizer

sprong (sprong) *c* (pl ~en) jump;
hop, leap

sprookje (*sprōāk*-Yer) *nt* (pl ~s) fairytale

spruitjes (*sprur*ᵉʷ-tYerss) *pl* sprouts *pl*

spuit (spur*ᵉʷ*t) *c* (pl ~en) syringe

spuitbus (*spur*ᵉʷt-berss) *c* (pl ~sen)

atomizer

spuitwater (*spur*ᵉʷt-vaa-terr) *nt* sodawater

spuug (speᵂkh) *nt* spit

spuwen (speᵂ⁰⁰-ern) *v* *spit

staal (staal) *nt* steel; **roestvrij ~**
stainless steel

*staan (staan) *v* *stand; **goed ~** *become; suit

staart (staart) *c* (pl ~en) tail

staat (staat) *c* (pl staten) state; **in ~
stellen** enable; **in ~ *zijn om** *be
able to; **staats-** national

staatsburgerschap (*staats*-berr-gerr-
skhahp) *nt* citizenship

staatshoofd (*staats*-hōaft) *nt* (pl ~en)
head of state

staatsman (*staats*-mahn) *c* (pl -lieden)
statesman

stabiel (staa-*beel*) *adj* stable

stad (staht) *c* (pl steden) town; city

stadhuis (staht-*hur*ᵉʷss) *nt* (pl -hui-
zen) town hall

stadion (*staa*-dee-Yon) *nt* (pl ~s) stadium

stadium (*staa*-dee-Yerm) *nt* (pl stadia)
stage

stadscentrum (*staht*-sehn-trerm) *nt* (pl
-tra) town centre

stadslicht (*stahts*-lɪkht) *nt* (pl ~en)
parking light

stadsmensen (*stahts*-mehn-sern) *pl*
townspeople *pl*

staf (stahf) *c* staff

staken (*staa*-kern) *v* *strike; stop, discontinue

staking (*staa*-kɪng) *c* (pl ~en) strike

stal (stahl) *c* (pl ~len) stable

stallen (*stah*-lern) *v* garage

stalles (*stah*-lerss) *pl* stall; orchestra
seat *Am*

stam (stahm) *c* (pl ~men) trunk;
tribe

stamelen (*staa*-mer-lern) *v* falter

stampen (*stahm*-pern) *v* stamp, thump

stampvol (*stahmp*-fol) *adj* packed

stand (stahnt) *c* score; **tot ~ *bren-gen** realize

standbeeld (*stahnt*-bāylt) *nt* (pl ~en) statue

standpunt (*stahnt*-pernt) *nt* (pl ~en) point of view

standvastig (stahnt-*fahss*-terkh) *adj* steadfast

stang (stahng) *c* (pl ~en) rod, bar

stap (stahp) *c* (pl ~pen) step; pace; move

stapel (*staa*-perl) *c* (pl ~s) stack, heap, pile

stappen (*stah*-pern) *v* step

staren (*staa*-rern) *v* gaze, stare

start (stahrt) *c* take-off

startbaan (*stahrt*-baan) *c* runway

starten (*stahr*-tern) *v* *take off

startmotor (*stahrt*-mōā-terr) *c* starter motor

statiegeld (*staa*-tsee-gehlt) *nt* deposit

station (staa-*shon*) *nt* (pl ~s) station; depot *nAm*

stationschef (staa-*shon*-shehf) *c* (pl ~s) station-master

statistiek (staa-tiss-*teek*) *c* (pl ~en) statistics *pl*

stedelijk (*stāy*-der-lerk) *adj* urban

steeds (stāyts) *adv* continually

steeg (stāykh) *c* (pl stegen) alley, lane

steek (stāyk) *c* (pl steken) stitch; sting, bite

steel (stāyl) *c* (pl stelen) stem; handle

steelpan (*stāyl*-pahn) *c* (pl ~nen) saucepan

steen (stāyn) *c* (pl stenen) stone; brick

steengroeve (*stāyn*-grōō-ver) *c* (pl ~n) quarry

steenpuist (*stāyn*-pur^ewst) *c* (pl ~en) boil

steigers (*stay*-gerrs) *pl* scaffolding

steil (stayl) *adj* steep

stekelvarken (*stāy*-kerl-vahr-kern) *nt* (pl ~s) porcupine

***steken** (*stāy*-kern) *v* *sting

stekker (*steh*-kerr) *c* (pl ~s) plug

stel (stehl) *nt* (pl ~len) set

***stelen** (*stāy*-lern) *v* *steal

stellen (*steh*-lern) *v* *put

stelling (*steh*-lɪng) *c* (pl ~en) thesis

stelsel (*stehl*-serl) *nt* (pl ~s) system; **tientallig ~** decimal system

stem (stehm) *c* (pl ~men) voice; vote

stemmen (*steh*-mern) *v* vote

stemming[1] (*steh*-mɪng) *c* mood; atmosphere; spirits

stemming[2] (*steh*-mɪng) *c* (pl ~en) vote

stempel (*stehm*-perl) *c* (pl ~s) stamp

stemrecht (*stehm*-rehkht) *nt* suffrage

stenen (*stāy*-nern) *adj* stone

stenograaf (stāy-nōā-*graaf*) *c* (pl -grafen) stenographer

stenografie (stāy-nōā-graa-*fee*) *c* shorthand

step-in (stehp-*ɪn*) *c* (pl ~s) girdle

ster (stehr) *c* (pl ~ren) star

sterfelijk (*stehr*-fer-lerk) *adj* mortal

steriel (ster-*reel*) *adj* sterile

steriliseren (stāy-ree-li-*zāy*-rern) *v* sterilize

sterk (stehrk) *adj* powerful, strong; **sterke drank** spirits

sterkte (*stehrk*-ter) *c* strength

sterrenkunde (*steh*-rer-kern-der) *c* astronomy

***sterven** (*stehr*-vern) *v* die

steun (stūrn) *c* assistance, support; relief

steunen (*stūr*-nern) *v* support

steunkousen (*stūrn*-kou-sern) *pl* support hose

steurgarnaal (*stūrr*-gahr-naal) *c* (pl -nalen) prawn

stevig (*stāy*-verkh) *adj* solid, firm

stichten (*stɪkh*-tern) *v* found

stichting (*stɪkh*-tɪng) *c* (pl ~en) foundation

stiefkind (*steef*-kɪnt) *nt* (pl ~eren) stepchild

stiefmoeder (*steef*-mōō-derr) *c* (pl ~s) stepmother

stiefvader (*stee*-faa-derr) *c* (pl ~s) stepfather

stier (steer) *c* (pl ~en) bull

stierengevecht (*stee*-rer-ger-vehkht) *nt* (pl ~en) bullfight

stijf (stayf) *adj* stiff

stijfsel (*stayf*-serl) *nt* starch

stijgbeugel (*staykh*-būr-gerl) *c* (pl ~s) stirrup

*stijgen (*stay*-gern) *v* *rise; climb

stijging (*stay*-gɪng) *c* (pl ~en) rise; climb, ascent

stijl (stayl) *c* (pl ~en) style

*stijven (*stay*-vern) *v* starch

stikken (*stɪ*-kern) *v* choke

stikstof (*stɪk*-stof) *c* nitrogen

stil (stɪl) *adj* silent; quiet; still

Stille Oceaan (*stɪ*-ler ōā-*sāy*-aan) Pacific Ocean

stilstaand (*stɪl*-staant) *adj* stationary

stilte (*stɪl*-ter) *c* (pl ~s) silence; stillness, quiet

stimuleren (stee-mēw-*lāy*-rern) *v* stimulate

*stinken (*stɪng*-kern) *v* *smell; *stink; **stinkend** smelly

stipt (stɪpt) *adj* punctual

stoel (stōōl) *c* (pl ~en) chair; seat

stoep (stōōp) *c* (pl ~en) sidewalk *nAm*

stoet (stōōt) *c* (pl ~en) procession

stof¹ (stof) *nt* dust

stof² (stof) *c* (pl ~fen) fabric, cloth, material; matter; **stoffen** drapery; **vaste ~** solid

stoffelijk (*sto*-fer-lerk) *adj* substantial, material

stoffig (*sto*-ferkh) *adj* dusty

stofzuigen (*stof*-sur^{ew}-gern) *v* hoover; vacuum *vAm*

stofzuiger (*stof*-sur^{ew}-gerr) *c* (pl ~s) vacuum cleaner

stok (stokl) *c* (pl ~ken) stick; cane

stokpaardje (*stok*-paar-t^yer) *nt* (pl ~s) hobby-horse

stola (*stōā*-laa) *c* (pl ~'s) stole

stollen (*sto*-lern) *v* coagulate

stom (stom) *adj* mute, dumb

stomerij (*stōā*-mer-*ray*) *c* (pl ~en) dry-cleaner's

stomp (stomp) *adj* blunt

stompen (*stom*-pern) *v* punch

stookolie (*stōāk*-ōā-lee) *c* fuel oil

stoom (stōām) *c* steam

stoomboot (*stōām*-bōāt) *c* (pl boten) steamer

stoot (stōāt) *c* (pl stoten) bump

stop (stop) *c* (pl ~pen) stopper, cork

stopgaren (*stop*-khaa-rern) *nt* darning wool

stoplicht (*stop*-lɪkht) *nt* (pl ~en) traffic light

stoppen (*sto*-pern) *v* stop, halt; *put; darn

stoptrein (*stop*-trayn) *c* (pl ~en) stopping train, local train

storen (*stōā*-rern) *v* disturb; trouble

storing (*stōā*-rɪng) *c* (pl ~en) disturbance

storm (storm) *c* (pl ~en) storm; gale, tempest

stormachtig (*storm*-ahkh-terkh) *adj* stormy

stormlamp (*storm*-lahmp) *c* (pl ~en) hurricane lamp

stortbui (*stort*-bur^{ew}) *c* (pl ~en) downpour

storten (*stor*-tern) *v* *shed; deposit

storting (*stor*-tɪng) *c* (pl ~en) remittance, deposit

*stoten (*stōā*-tern) *v* bump

stout (stout) *adj* naughty, bad

stoutmoedig (stout-*mōō*-derkh) *adj* bold

straal (straal) *c* (pl stralen) squirt, spout, jet; ray, beam; radius

straalvliegtuig (*straal*-vleekh-tur^ewkh) *nt* (pl ~en) turbojet, jet

straat (straat) *c* (pl straten) street; road

straatweg (*straat*-vehkh) *c* (pl ~en) causeway

straf (strahf) *c* (pl ~fen) punishment; penalty

straffen (*strah*-fern) *v* punish

strafrecht (*strahf*-rehkht) *nt* criminal law

strafschop (*strahf*-skhop) *c* (pl ~pen) penalty kick

strak (strahk) *adj* tight; **strakker maken** tighten

straks (strahks) *adv* in a moment

strand (strahnt) *nt* (pl ~en) beach

streek (strāȳk) *c* (pl streken) region; district, country, area; trick

streep (strāȳp) *c* (pl strepen) line; stripe

streng (strehng) *adj* strict, harsh; severe

stretcher (*streht*-sherr) *c* (pl ~s) camp-bed; cot *nAm*

streven (*strāȳ*-vern) *v* aspire

strijd (strayt) *c* fight, combat, battle; struggle, strife, contest

*****strijden** (*stray*-dern) *v* *fight; struggle

strijdkrachten (*strayt*-krahkh-tern) *pl* armed forces

*****strijken** (*stray*-kern) *v* iron; *strike, lower

strijkijzer (*strayk*-ay-zerr) *nt* (pl ~s) iron

strikje (*strik*-^Yer) *nt* (pl ~s) bow tie

strikt (strikt) *adj* strict

stripverhaal (*strip*-ferr-haal) *nt* (pl -ha-

len) comics *pl*

stro (strōa) *nt* straw

strodak (*strōa*-dahk) *nt* (pl ~en) thatched roof

stromen (*strōa*-mern) *v* stream, flow

stroming (*strōa*-ming) *c* (pl ~en) current

strook (strōak) *c* (pl stroken) strip

stroom (strōam) *c* (pl stromen) stream; current

stroomafwaarts (strōam-*ahf*-vaarts) *adv* downstream

stroomopwaarts (strōam-*op*-vaarts) *adv* upstream

stroomverdeler (*strōam*-verr-dāȳ-lerr) *c* distributor

stroomversnelling (*strōam*-verr-sneh-ling) *c* (pl ~en) rapids *pl*

stroop (strōap) *c* syrup

stropen (*strōa*-pern) *v* poach

structuur (strerk-*tēwr*) *c* (pl -turen) structure; fabric, texture

struik (strur^ewk) *c* (pl ~en) scrub, bush, shrub

struikelen (*strur^ew*-ker-lern) *v* stumble

struisvogel (*strurss*-fōa-gerl) *c* (pl ~s) ostrich

studeerkamer (stew-*dāȳr*-kaa-merr) *c* study

student (stēw-*dehnt*) *c* (pl ~en) student

studente (stēw-*dehn*-ter) *c* (pl ~s) student

studeren (stēw-*dāȳ*-rern) *v* study

studie (*stēw*-dee) *c* (pl ~s) study

studiebeurs (*stēw*-dee-bērrs) *c* (pl -beurzen) scholarship

stuitend (*stur^ew*-ternt) *adj* revolting

stuk¹ (sterk) *adj* broken; ~ *****gaan** *break down

stuk² (sterk) *nt* (pl ~ken) part, piece; lump, chunk; fragment; stretch

sturen (*stēw*-rern) *v* *send; navigate

stuurboord (*stēwr*-bōart) *nt* starboard

stuurkolom (*stewr*-kōa-lom) *c* steering-column

stuurman (*stewr*-mahn) *c* (pl -lieden, -lui) steersman, helmsman

stuurwiel (*stewr*-veel) *nt* steering-wheel

subsidie (serp-*see*-dee) *c* (pl ~s) subsidy

substantie (serp-*stahn*-see) *c* (pl ~s) substance

subtiel (serp-*teel*) *adj* subtle

succes (serk-*sehss*) *nt* (pl ~sen) success

succesvol (serk-*sehss*-fol) *adj* successful

suède (sew-*vai*-der) *nt/c* suede

suf (serf) *adj* dumb

suiker (*surew*-kerr) *c* sugar

suikerklontje (*surew*-kerr-klon-tᵞer) *nt* (pl ~s) lump of sugar

suikerzieke (*surew*-kerr-zee-ker) *c* (pl ~n) diabetic

suikerziekte (*surew*-kerr-zeek-ter) *c* diabetes

suite (*svee*-ter) *c* (pl ~s) suite

summier (ser-*meer*) *adj* concise

superieur (sew-per-ree-ᵞūrr) *adj* superior

superlatief (sew-perr-laa-*teef*) *c* (pl -tieven) superlative

supermarkt (*sew*-perr-mahrkt) *c* (pl ~en) supermarket

supplement (ser-pler-*mehnt*) *nt* (pl ~en) supplement

suppoost (ser-*pōast*) *c* (pl ~en) custodian, usher

surfplank (*serrf*-plahngk) *c* (pl ~en) surf-board

surveilleren (serr-vay-ᵞai-rern) *v* patrol

Swahili (svaa-*hee*-lee) *nt* Swahili

symbool (sim-*bōal*) *nt* (pl -bolen) symbol

symfonie (sim-tōa-*nee*) *c* (pl ~ën) symphony

sympathie (sim-paa-*tee*) *c* (pl ~ën) sympathy

sympathiek (sim-paa-*teek*) *adj* nice

symptoom (sim-*tōam*) *nt* (pl -tomen) symptom

synagoge (see-naa-*gōa*-ger) *c* (pl ~n) synagogue

synoniem (see-nōa-*neem*) *nt* (pl ~en) synonym

synthetisch (sin-*tāy*-teess) *adj* synthetic

Syrië (*see*-ree-ᵞer) Syria

Syriër (*see*-ree-ᵞerr) *c* (pl ~s) Syrian

Syrisch (*see*-reess) *adj* Syrian

systeem (seess-*tāym*) *nt* (pl -temen) system

systematisch (seess-tāy-*maa*-teess) *adj* systematic

T

taai (taaᵉᵉ) *adj* tough

taak (taak) *c* (pl taken) task; duty

taal (taal) *c* (pl talen) language; speech

taalgids (*taal*-gits) *c* (pl ~en) phrase-book

taart (taart) *c* (pl ~en) cake

tabak (taa-*bahk*) *c* tobacco

tabakswinkel (taa-*bahks*-ving-kerl) *c* (pl ~s) tobacconist's

tabakszak (taa-*bahk*-sahk) *c* (pl ~ken) tobacco pouch

tabel (taa-*behl*) *c* (pl ~len) chart, table

tablet (taa-*bleht*) *nt* (pl ~ten) tablet

taboe (taa-*bōō*) *nt* (pl ~s) taboo

tachtig (*tahkh*-terkh) *num* eighty

tactiek (tahk-*teek*) *c* (pl ~en) tactics *pl*

tafel (*taa*-ferl) *c* (pl ~s) table

tafellaken (*taa-*fer-laa-kern) *nt* (pl ~s) table-cloth

tafeltennis (*taa-*ferl-teh-nerss) *nt* table tennis, ping-pong

taille (*tah-*Yer) *c* (pl ~s) waist

tak (tahk) *c* (pl ~ken) branch, bough

talenpracticum (*taa-*ler-prahk-tee-kerm) *nt* (pl -tica) language laboratory

talent (taa-*lehnt*) *nt* (pl ~en) faculty, talent

talkpoeder (*tahlk-*pōō-derr) *nt/c* talc powder

talrijk (*tahl-*rayk) *adj* numerous

tam (tahm) *adj* tame

tamelijk (*taa-*mer-lerk) *adv* pretty, fairly, quite, rather

tampon (tahm-*pon*) *c* (pl ~s) tampon

tand (tahnt) *c* (pl ~en) tooth

tandarts (*tahn-*dahrts) *c* (pl ~en) dentist

tandenborstel (*tahn-*der-bors-terl) *c* (pl ~s) toothbrush

tandestoker (*tahn-*der-stōā-kerr) *c* (pl ~s) toothpick

tandpasta (*tahnt-*pahss-taa) *c/nt* (pl ~'s) toothpaste

tandpijn (*tahnt-*payn) *c* toothache

tandpoeder (*tahnt-*pōō-derr) *nt/c* toothpowder

tandvlees (*tahnt-*flāyss) *nt* gum

tang (tahng) *c* (pl ~en) tongs *pl*, pliers *pl*

tank (tehngk) *c* (pl ~s) tank

tankschip (*tehnk-*skhip) *nt* (pl -schepen) tanker

tante (*tahn-*ter) *c* (pl ~s) aunt

tapijt (taa-*payt*) *nt* (pl ~en) carpet

tarief (taa-*reef*) *nt* (pl tarieven) rate, tariff; fare

tarwe (*tahr-*ver) *c* wheat

tas (tahss) *c* (pl ~sen) bag

tastbaar (*tahst-*baar) *adj* palpable; tangible

tastzin (*tahst-*sin) *c* touch

taxeren (tahk-*sāy-*rern) *v* estimate

taxi (*tahk-*see) *c* (pl ~'s) cab, taxi

taxichauffeur (*tahk-*see-shōā-fūrr) *c* (pl ~s) cab-driver, taxi-driver

taximeter (*tahk-*see-may-terr) *c* taximeter

taxistandplaats (*tahk-*see-stahnt-plaats) *c* (pl ~en) taxi rank; taxi stand *Am*

te (ter) *adv* too

technicus (*tehkh-*nee-kerss) *c* (pl -ci) technician

techniek (tehkh-*neek*) *c* (pl ~en) technique

technisch (*tehkh-*neess) *adj* technical

technologie (tehkh-nōā-lōā-*gee*) *c* technology

teder (*tāy-*derr) *adj* delicate, tender

teef (tāyf) *c* (pl teven) bitch

teen (tāyn) *c* (pl tenen) toe

teer (tāyr) *adj* gentle, tender; *c/nt* tar

tegel (*tāy-*gerl) *c* (pl ~s) tile

tegelijk (ter-ger-*layk*) *adv* at the same time; at once

tegelijkertijd (ter-ger-lay-kerr-*tayt*) *adv* simultaneously

tegemoetkomend (ter-ger-*mōōt-*kōā-mernt) *adj* oncoming

tegemoetkoming (ter-ger-*mōōt-*kōā-ming) *c* (pl ~en) concession

tegen (*tāy-*gern) *prep* against

tegendeel (*tāy-*ger-dāyl) *nt* contrary, reverse

tegengesteld (*tāy-*ger-ger-stehlt) *adj* contrary, opposite

*__tegenkomen__ (*tāy-*ger-kōā-mern) *v* *come across, *meet; run into

tegenover (*tāy-*ger-*nōā-*verr) *prep* opposite, facing

tegenslag (*tāy-*ger-slahkh) *c* (pl ~en) misfortune; reverse

*__tegenspreken__ (*tāy-*ger-sprāy-kern) *v* contradict

tegenstander (tāy-ger-stahn-derr) c (pl ~s) opponent

tegenstelling (tāy-ger-steh-lıng) c (pl ~en) contrast

tegenstrijdig (tāy-ger-stray-derkh) adj contradictory

*__tegenvallen__ (tāy-ger-vah-lern) v *be disappointing

*__tegenwerpen__ (tāy-ger-vehr-pern) v object

tegenwerping (tāy-ger-vehr-pıng) c (pl ~en) objection

tegenwoordig (tāy-ger-vōar-derkh) adj present; adv nowadays

tegenwoordigheid (tāy-ger-vōar-derkh-hayt) c presence

tegenzin (tāy-ger-zın) c aversion

tehuis (ter-hur^{ew}ss) nt (pl tehuizen) home; asylum

teint (taint) c complexion

teken (tāy-kern) nt (pl ~s, ~en) sign; indication, signal; token

tekenen (tāy-ker-nern) v *draw, sketch; sign

tekenfilm (tāy-ker-film) c (pl ~s) cartoon

tekening (tāy-ker-nıng) c (pl ~en) drawing, sketch

tekort (ter-kort) nt (pl ~en) shortage; deficit; ~ *__schieten__ fail

tekortkoming (ter-kort-kōa-mıng) c (pl ~en) shortcoming

tekst (tehkst) c (pl ~en) text

tel (tehl) c (pl ~len) second

telefoneren (tay-ler-fōa-nāy-rern) v phone

telefoniste (tāy-ler-fōa-nıss-ter) c (pl ~n, ~s) operator, telephonist

telefoon (tay-ler-fōan) c (pl ~s) phone, telephone

telefoonboek (tāy-ler-fōan-bōok) nt (pl ~en) telephone directory; telephone book Am

telefooncel (tāy-ler-fōan-sehl) c (pl ~len) telephone booth

telefooncentrale (tāy-ler-fōan-sehn-traa-ler) c (pl ~s) telephone exchange

telefoongesprek (tāy-ler-fōan-ger-sprehk) nt (pl ~ken) telephone call

telefoongids (tay-ler-fōan-gıts) c (pl ~en) telephone directory; telephone book Am

telefoonhoorn (tāy-ler-fōan-hōa-rern) c (pl ~s) receiver

telefoontje (tāy-ler-fōan-t^yer) nt (pl ~s) call

telegraferen (tay-ler-graa-fāy-rern) v cable, telegraph

telegram (tāy-ler-grahm) nt (pl ~men) cable, telegram

telelens (tāy-ler-lehns) c (pl -lenzen) telephoto lens

telepathie (tāy-lāy-paa-tee) c telepathy

teleurstellen (ter-lūrr-steh-lern) v disappoint; *let down

teleurstelling (ter-lūrr-steh-lıng) c (pl ~en) disappointment

televisie (tāy-ler-vee-zee) c television; **cabel-~** cable tv; **satelliet-~** satellite tv

televisietoestel (tāy-ler-vee-zee-tōo-stehl) nt (pl ~len) television set

telex (tāy-lehks) c (pl ~en) telex

telkens (tehl-kerns) adv again and again

tellen (teh-lern) v count

telwoord (tehl-vōart) nt (pl ~en) numeral

temmen (teh-mern) v tame

tempel (tehm-perl) c (pl ~s) temple

temperatuur (tehm-per-raa-tēwr) c (pl -turen) temperature

tempo (tehm-pōa) nt pace

tendens (tehn-dehns) c (pl -denzen) tendency

tenminste (ter-mın-ster) adv at least

tennis (*teh*-nerss) *nt* tennis

tennisbaan (*teh*-nerss-baan) *c* (pl -banen) tennis-court

tennisschoenen (*teh*-ner-skhoo-nern) *pl* tennis shoes

tenslotte (tehn-*slo*-ter) *adv* at last

tent (tehnt) *c* (pl ~en) tent

tentdoek (*tehn*-dook) *nt* canvas

tentoonstellen (tehn-*toan*-steh-lern) *v* exhibit; *show

tentoonstelling (tehn-*toan*-steh-ling) *c* (pl ~en) exposition, exhibition; display, show

tenzij (tehn-*zay*) *conj* unless

teraardebestelling (tehr-*aar*-der-bersteh-ling) *c* (pl ~en) burial

terecht (ter-*rehkht*) *adj* just; *adv* rightly

terechtstelling (ter-*rehkht*-steh-ling) *c* (pl ~en) execution

terloops (tehr-*loaps*) *adj* casual

term (tehrm) *c* (pl ~en) term

termijn (tehr-*mayn*) *c* (pl ~en) term

terpentijn (tehr-pern-*tayn*) *c* turpentine

terras (teh-*rahss*) *nt* (pl ~sen) terrace

terrein (teh-*rayn*) *nt* (pl ~en) terrain; grounds

terreur (teh-*rurr*) *c* terrorism

terrorisme (teh-ro-*riss*-mer) *nt* terrorism

terrorist (teh-*roa*-rist) *c* (pl ~en) terrorist

terug (ter-*rerkh*) *adv* back

terugbetalen (ter-*rerkh*-ber-taa-lern) *v* *repay; reimburse, refund

terugbetaling (terrerkh-ber-taa-ling) *c* (pl ~en) repayment, refund

***terugbrengen** (ter-*rerkh*-brehng-ern) *v* *bring back

***teruggaan** (ter-*rer*-khaan) *v* *go back, *get back

teruggang (ter-*rer*-khahng) *c* depression, recession

terugkeer (ter-*rerkh*-kayr) *c* return

terugkeren (ter-*rerkh*-kay-rern) *v* return; turn back

***terugkomen** (ter-*rerkh*-koa-mern) *v* return

terugreis (ter-*rerkh*-rayss) *c* return journey

***terugroepen** (ter-*rerkh*-roo-pern) *v* recall

terugsturen (ter-*rerkh*-stew-rern) *v* *send back

***terugtrekken** (ter-*rerkh*-treh-kern) *v* *withdraw

***terugvinden** (ter-*rerkh*-fin-dern) *v* recover

terugweg (ter-*rerkh*-vehkh) *c* way back

***terugzenden** (ter-*rerkh*-sehn-dern) *v* *send back

terwijl (terr-*vayl*) *conj* whilst, while

terylene (*teh*-ree-layn) *nt* terylene

terzijde (tehr-*zay*-der) *adv* aside

test (tehst) *c* (pl ~s) test

testament (tehss-taa-*mehnt*) *nt* (pl ~en) will

testen (*tehss*-tern) *v* test

tevens (*tay*-verns) *adv* also

tevergeefs (ter-verr-*gayfs*) *adv* in vain

tevoren (ter-*voa*-rern) *adv* before; **van ~** in advance

tevreden (ter-*vray*-dern) *adj* satisfied, content

tewaterlating (ter-*vaa*-terr-laa-ting) *c* launching

***teweegbrengen** (ter-*vaykh*-brehngern) *v* effect

tewerkstellen (ter-*vehrk*-steh-lern) *v* employ

tewerkstelling (ter-*vehrk*-steh-ling) *c* (pl ~en) employment

textiel (tehks-*teel*) *c/nt* textile

Thailand (*tigh*-lahnt) Thailand

Thailander (*tigh*-lahn-derr) *c* (pl ~s) Thai

Thailands (*tigh*-lahnts) *adj* Thai

thans (tahns) *adv* now

theater (tāy-ᵞaa-terr) *nt* (pl ~s) theatre

thee (tāy) *c* tea

theedoek (tāy-dōōk) *c* (pl ~en) teacloth

theekopje (tāy-kop-ᵞay) *nt* (pl ~s) teacup

theelepel (tāy-lāy-perl) *c* (pl ~s) teaspoon

theepot (tāy-pot) *c* (pl ~ten) teapot

theeservies (tāy-sehr-veess) *nt* (pl -viezen) tea-set

thema (tāy-maa) *nt* (pl ~'s) theme; exercise

theologie (tāy-ᵞōa-lōa-gee) *c* theology

theoretisch (tāy-ᵞōa-rāy-teess) *adj* theoretical

theorie (tāy-ᵞōa-ree) *c* (pl ~ën) theory

therapie (tāy-raa-pee) *c* (pl ~ën) therapy

thermometer (tehr-mōa-māy-terr) *c* (pl ~s) thermometer

thermosfles (tehr-moss-flehss) *c* (pl ~sen) vacuum flask, thermos flask

thermostaat (tehr-moss-taat) *c* (pl -staten) thermostat

thuis (tur^ewss) *adv* home, at home

tien (teen) *num* ten

tiende (teen-der) *num* tenth

tiener (tee-nerr) *c* (pl ~s) teenager

tijd (tayt) *c* (pl ~en) time; **de laatste ~** lately; **op ~** in time; **vrije ~** spare time, leisure

tijdbesparend (tayt-ber-spaa-rernt) *adj* time-saving

tijdelijk (tay-der-lerk) *adj* temporary

tijdens (tay-derns) *prep* during

tijdgenoot (tayt-kher-nōāt) *c* (pl -noten) contemporary

tijdperk (tayt-pehrk) *nt* (pl ~en) period

tijdschrift (tayt-skhrift) *nt* (pl ~en) review, periodical, journal

tijger (tay-gerr) *c* (pl ~s) tiger

tijm (taym) *c* thyme

tikken (ti-kern) *v* type

timmerhout (ti-merr-hout) *nt* timber

timmerman (ti-merr-mahn) *c* (pl -lieden, -lui) carpenter

tin (tin) *nt* tin, pewter

tiran (tee-rahn) *c* (pl ~nen) tyrant

titel (tee-terl) *c* (pl ~s) title; heading; degree

toch (tokh) *adv* still; *conj* yet

tocht (tokht) *c* draught

toe (tōō) *adj* closed

toebehoren (tōō-ber-hōā-rern) *v* belong; *pl* accessories *pl*

toedienen (tōō-dee-nern) *v* administer

toegang (tōō-gahng) *c* admittance, admission, access; entry, entrance; approach

toegankelijk (tōō-*gahng*-ker-lerk) *adj* accessible

****toegeven** (tōō-gāy-vern) *v* admit, acknowledge; *give in, indulge

toehoorder (tōō-hōār-derr) *c* (pl ~s) auditor

toekennen (tōō-keh-nern) *v* award

toekomst (tōō-komst) *c* future

toekomstig (tōō-*kom*-sterkh) *adj* future

toelage (tōō-laa-ger) *c* (pl ~n) allowance, grant

****toelaten** (tōō-laa-tern) *v* admit

toelating (tōō-laa-ting) *c* (pl ~en) admission

toelichten (tōō-likh-tern) *v* elucidate

toelichting (tōō-likh-ting) *c* (pl ~en) explanation

toen (tōōn) *conj* when; *adv* then

toename (tōō-naa-mer) *c* increase

****toenemen** (tōō-nāy-mern) *v* increase; **toenemend** progressive

toenmalig (tōōn-maa-lerkh) *adj* contemporary

toepassen (tōō-pah-sern) *v* apply

toepassing (*toō-pah-sıng*) *c* (pl ~en) application

toereikend (*toō-ray-kernt*) *adj* adequate

toerisme (toō-*riss*-mer) *nt* tourism

toerist (toō-*rist*) *c* (pl ~en) tourist

toeristenklasse (toō-*riss*-ter-klah-ser) *c* tourist class

toernooi (toōr-*nōᵃᵉᵉ*) *nt* (pl ~en) tournament

toeschouwer (*toō*-skhou-err) *c* (pl ~s) spectator

*****toeschrijven aan** (*toō*-skhray-vern) assign to

*****toeslaan** (*toō*-slaan) *v* *strike

toeslag (*toō*-slahkh) *c* (pl ~en) surcharge

toespraak (*toō*-spraak) *c* (pl -spraken) speech

*****toestaan** (*toō*-staan) *v* allow, permit

toestand (*toō*-stahnt) *c* (pl ~en) state; condition

toestel (*toō*-stehl) *nt* (pl ~len) apparatus, appliance; aircraft; extension

toestemmen (*toō*-steh-mern) *v* agree, consent

toestemming (*toō*-steh-mıng) *c* authorization, permission; consent

toetje (*toō*-tᵞer) *nt* (pl ~s) sweet

toeval (*toō*-vahl) *nt* chance; luck

toevallig (toō-*vah*-lerkh) *adj* accidental, casual, incidental; *adv* by chance

toevertrouwen (*toō*-verr-trou-ern) *v* commit

toevoegen (*toō*-vōō-gern) *v* add

toevoeging (*toō*-vōō-gıng) *c* (pl ~en) addition

toewijden (*toō*-vay-dern) *v* dedicate

*****toewijzen** (*toō*-vay-zern) *v* allot

toezicht (*toō*-zıkht) *nt* supervision; ~ *****houden op** supervise

toffee (to-*fay*) *c* (pl ~s) toffee

toilet (tvah-*leht*) *nt* (pl ~ten) toilet, lavatory, bathroom; washroom *nAm*

toiletbenodigdheden (tvah-*leht*-ber-nōā-derkht-hāy-dern) *pl* toiletry

toiletpapier (tvah-*leht*-paa-peer) *nt* toilet-paper

toilettafel (tvah-*leh*-taa-ferl) *c* (pl ~s) dressing-table

toilettas (tvah-*leh*-tahss) *c* (pl ~sen) toilet case

tol (tol) *c* toll

tolk (tolk) *c* (pl ~en) interpreter

tolken (*tol*-kern) *v* interpret

tolweg (*tol*-verkh) *c* (pl ~en) turnpike *nAm*

tomaat (tōā-*maat*) *c* (pl tomaten) tomato

ton (ton) *c* (pl ~nen) cask, barrel; ton

toneel (tōā-*nāyl*) *nt* drama; stage

toneelkijker (tōā-*nāyl*-kay-kerr) *c* (pl ~s) binoculars *pl*

toneelschrijver (tōā-*nāyl*-skhray-verr) *c* (pl ~s) dramatist, playwright

toneelspeelster (tōā-*nāyl*-spāyl-sterr) *c* (pl ~s) actress

toneelspelen (tōā-*nāyl*-spāy-lern) *v* act

toneelspeler (tōā-*nāyl*-spāy-lerr) *c* (pl ~s) actor; comedian

toneelstuk (tōā-*nāyl*-sterk) *nt* (pl ~ken) play

tonen (*tōā*-nern) *v* *show; display

tong (tong) *c* (pl ~en) tongue; sole

tonicum (*tōā*-nee-kerm) *nt* (pl -ca, ~s) tonic

tonijn (tōā-*nayn*) *c* (pl ~en) tuna

toon (tōān) *c* (pl tonen) tone; note

toonbank (*tōām*-bahngk) *c* (pl ~en) counter

toonladder (*tōān*-lah-derr) *c* (pl ~s) scale

toonzaal (*tōān*-zaal) *c* (pl -zalen) showroom

toorn (*tōā*-rern) *c* anger

top (top) *c* (pl ~pen) peak; top, summit

toppunt (*to*-pernt) *nt* (pl ~en) height; zenith

toren (*tō̄a*-rern) *c* (pl ~s) tower

tot (tot) *prep* until, to, till; *conj* till; ~ **aan** till; ~ **zover** so far

totaal[1] (tō̄a-*taal*) *adj* total, overall; utter

totaal[2] (tō̄a-*taal*) *nt* (pl totalen) total; **in** ~ altogether

totalisator (tō̄a-taa-lee-*zaa*-tor) *c* (pl ~s) totalizator

totalitair (tō̄a-taa-lee-*tair*) *adj* totalitarian

totdat (to-*daht*) *conj* till

touw (tou) *nt* (pl ~en) twine, rope, string

toverkunst (*tō̄a*-verr-kernst) *c* magic

traag (traakh) *adj* slow; slack

traan (traan) *c* (pl tranen) tear

trachten (*trahkh*-tern) *v* try, attempt

tractor (*trahk*-tor) *c* (pl ~en, ~s) tractor

traditie (traa-*dee*-tsee) *c* (pl ~s) tradition

traditioneel (traa-dee-shō̄a-*nāyl*) *adj* traditional

tragedie (traa-*gāy*-dee) *c* (pl ~s) tragedy

tragisch (*traa*-geess) *adj* tragic

trainen (*trāy*-nern) *v* drill, train

tralie (*traa*-lee) *c* (pl ~s) bar

tram (trehm) *c* (pl ~s) tram; streetcar *nAm*

transactie (trahn-*zahk*-see) *c* (pl ~s) deal, transaction

transatlantisch (trahn-zaht-*lahn*-teess) *adj* transatlantic

transformator (trahns-for-*maa*-tor) *c* (pl ~en, ~s) transformer

transpiratie (trahn-spee-*raa*-tsee) *c* perspiration

transpireren (trahn-spee-*rāy*-rern) *v* perspire

transport (trahn-*sport*) *nt* (pl ~en) transportation

transporteren (trahn-spor-*tāy*-rern) *v* transport

trap (trahp) *c* (pl ~pen) stairs *pl*, staircase; kick

trapleuning (*trahp*-lūr-nıng) *c* (pl ~en) banisters *pl*

trappen (*trah*-pern) *v* kick

trechter (*trehkh*-terr) *c* (pl ~s) funnel

trede (*trāy*-der) *c* (pl ~n) step

treffen (*treh*-fern) *v* *hit; *strike

trefpunt (*trehf*-pernt) *nt* (pl ~en) meeting-place

trein (trayn) *c* (pl ~en) train; **doorgaande** ~ through train

trek[1] (trehk) *c* (pl ~ken) trait

trek[2] (trehk) *c* appetite

trekken (*treh*-kern) *v* pull; *draw; extract; hike

trekker (*treh*-kerr) *c* (pl ~s) trigger

trekking (*treh*-kıng) *c* (pl ~en) draw

treuren (*trūr*-rern) *v* grieve

treurig (*trūr*-rerkh) *adj* sad

treurspel (*trūrr*-spehl) *nt* (pl ~en) drama

tribune (tree-*bēw*-ner) *c* (pl ~s) stand

tricotgoederen (tree-*kō̄a*-gōō-der-rern) *pl* hosiery

triest (treest) *adj* depressing

trillen (trı-lern) *v* tremble; vibrate

triomf (tree-ᵛ*omf*) *c* (pl ~en) triumph

triomfantelijk (tree-ᵛom-*fahn*-ter-lerk) *adj* triumphant

troepen (*trōō*-pern) *pl* troops *pl*

trommel (*tro*-merl) *c* (pl ~s) canister; drum

trommelvlies (*tro*-merl-vleess) *nt* (pl -vliezen) ear-drum

trompet (trom-*peht*) *c* (pl ~ten) trumpet

troon (trō̄an) *c* (pl tronen) throne

troost (trō̄ast) *c* comfort

troosten (*trō̄ass*-tern) *v* comfort

troostprijs (*trōast*-prayss) *c* (pl -prijzen) consolation prize

tropen (*trōa*-pern) *pl* tropics *pl*

tropisch (*trōa*-peess) *adj* tropical

trots (trots) *adj* proud; *c* pride

trottoir (tro-*tvaar*) *nt* (pl ~s) pavement; sidewalk *nAm*

trottoirband (tro-*tvaar*-bahnt) *c* (pl ~en) curb

trouw (trou) *adj* true, faithful

trouwen (*trou*-ern) *v* marry

trouwens (*trou*-erns) *adv* besides

trouwring (*trou*-rɪng) *c* (pl ~en) wedding-ring

trui (truɪᵉʷ) *c* (pl ~en) jersey

Tsjech (tsⁱehkh) *c* (pl ~en) Czech

Tsjechisch (tsⁱeh-kheess) *adj* Czech

tube (*tēw*-ber) *c* (pl ~s) tube

tuberculose (tēw-behr-kēw-*lōa*-zer) *c* tuberculosis

tuchtigen (tukh-*tɪ*-gern) *v* chastise, punish

tuin (turᵉʷn) *c* (pl ~en) garden

tuinbouw (*turᵉʷm*-bou) *c* horticulture

tuinman (*turᵉʷn*-mahn) *c* (pl -lieden, -lui) gardener

tuit (turᵉʷt) *c* (pl ~en) nozzle

tulp (terlp) *c* (pl ~en) tulip

tumor (*tēw*-mor) *c* (pl ~s) tumour

Tunesië (tēw-*nāy*-zee-ʸer) Tunisia

Tunesiër (tēw-*nāy*-zee-ʸerr) *c* (pl ~s) Tunisian

Tunesisch (tēw-*nāy*-zeess) *adj* Tunisian

tuniek (tēw-*neek*) *c* (pl ~en) tunic

tunnel (*ter*-nerl) *c* (pl ~s) tunnel

turbine (terr-*bee*-ner) *c* (pl ~s) turbine

Turk (terrk) *c* (pl ~en) Turk

Turkije (terr-*kay*-er) Turkey

Turks (terrks) *adj* Turkish; ~ **bad** Turkish bath

tussen (*ter*-sern) *prep* between; among, amid

tussenbeide °komen (ter-serm-*bay*-der *kōa*-mern) interfere

tussenpersoon (ter-ser-pehr-*sōan*) *c* (pl -sonen) intermediary

tussenpoos (ter-ser-*pōass*) *c* (pl -pozen) interval

tussenruimte (ter-ser-rur*ᵉʷm*-ter) *c* (pl ~n, ~s) space

tussenschot (ter-ser-skhot) *nt* (pl ~ten) partition; diaphragm

tussentijd (ter-ser-tayt) *c* interim

twaalf (tvaalf) *num* twelve

twaalfde (tvaalf-der) *num* twelfth

twee (tvāy) *num* two

tweede (*tvāy*-der) *num* second

tweedehands (tvāy-der-*hahnts*) *adj* second-hand

tweedelig (tvāy-*dāy*-lerkh) *adj* two-piece

tweeling (*tvāy*-lɪng) *c* (pl ~en) twins *pl*

tweemaal (*tvāy*-maal) *adv* twice

tweesprong (*tvāy*-sprong) *c* (pl ~en) fork, road fork

tweetalig (tvāy-*taa*-lerkh) *adj* bilingual

twijfel (tvay-ferl) *c* (pl ~s) doubt

twijfelachtig (tvay-ferl-ahkh-terkh) *adj* doubtful

twijfelen (tvay-fer-lern) *v* doubt

twijg (tvaykh) *c* (pl ~en) twig

twintig (tvɪn-terkh) *num* twenty

twintigste (tvɪn-terkh-ster) *num* twentieth

twist (tvɪst) *c* (pl ~en) quarrel

twisten (*tvɪss*-tern) *v* quarrel, dispute

tyfus (tee-ferss) *c* typhoid

type (tee-per) *nt* (pl ~n, ~s) type

typen (tee-pern) *v* type

typisch (tee-peess) *adj* typical

typiste (tee-*pɪ*-ster) *c* (pl ~s, ~n) typist

U

u (ēw) *pron* you

ui (ur^(ew)) *c* (pl ~en) onion

uil (ur^(ew)l) *c* (pl ~en) owl

uit (ur^(ew)t) *prep* from, out of; for; *adv* out

uitademen (ur^(ew)t-aa-der-mern) *v* expire, exhale

uitbarsting (ur^(ew)t-bahr-stern) *c* (pl ~en) outbreak

uitbenen (ur^(ew)t-bāy-nern) *v* bone

*uitblinken (ur^(ew)t-bling-kern) *v* excel

uitbreiden (ur^(ew)t-bray-dern) *v* extend, enlarge, expand

uitbreiding (ur^(ew)t-bray-dɪng) *c* (pl ~en) extension

uitbuiten (ur^(ew)t-bur-tern) *v* exploit

uitbundig (ur^(ew)t-*bern*-derkh) *adj* exuberant

uitdagen (ur^(ew)-daa-gern) *v* dare, challenge

uitdaging (ur^(ew)-daa-gɪng) *c* (pl ~en) challenge

uitdelen (ur^(ew)-dāy-lern) *v* distribute; *deal

*uitdoen (ur^(ew)-dōōn) *v* *put out

uitdrukkelijk (ur^(ew)-*drer*-ker-lerk) *adj* express, explicit

uitdrukken (-ur^(ew)-drer-kern) *v* express

uitdrukking (ur^(ew)-drer-kɪng) *c* (pl ~en) expression; phrase

uiteindelijk (ur^(ew)t-*ayn*-der-lerk) *adj* eventual; *adv* at last

uiten (ur^(ew)-tern) *v* express; utter

uiteraard (ur^(ew)-ter-*raart*) *adv* of course, naturally

uiterlijk (ur^(ew)-terr-lerk) *adj* outward, external, exterior; *nt* outside; look

uiterst (ur^(ew)-terrst) *adj* extreme; utmost, very

uiterste (ur^(ew)-terr-ster) *nt* (pl ~n) extreme

*uitgaan (ur^(ew)t-khaan) *v* *go out

uitgang (ur^(ew)t-khahng) *c* (pl ~en) way out, exit; issue

uitgangspunt (ur^(ew)t-khahngs-pernt) *nt* (pl ~en) starting-point

uitgave (ur^(ew)t-khaa-ver) *c* (pl ~n) expense, expenditure; edition, issue

uitgebreid (ur^(ew)t-kher-brayt) *adj* comprehensive, extensive

uitgelezen (ur^(ew)t-kher-lāy-zern) *adj* select

uitgestrekt (ur^(ew)t-kher-strehkt) *adj* vast

*uitgeven (ur^(ew)t-khāy-vern) *v* *spend; publish, issue

uitgever (ur^(ew)t-khāy-verr) *c* (pl ~s) publisher

uitgezonderd (ur^(ew)t-kher-zon-derrt) *prep* except

uitgifte (ur^(ew)t-khɪf-ter) *c* (pl ~n) issue

*uitglijden (ur^(ew)t-khlay-dern) *v* slip

uithoudingsvermogen (ur^(ew)t-hou-dɪngs-ferr-mōā-gern) *nt* stamina

uiting (ur^(ew)-tɪng) *c* (pl ~en) expression

*uitkiezen (ur^(ew)t-kee-zern) *v* select

*uitkijken (ur^(ew)t-kay-kern) *v* watch out, look out; ~ **naar** watch for

zich uitkleden (ur^(ew)t-klāy-dern) undress

*uitkomen (ur^(ew)t-kōā-mern) *v* *come out; *come true; *be convenient; ~ **op** open on

uitkomst (ur^(ew)t-komst) *c* (pl ~en) issue

uitlaat (ur^(ew)t-laat) *c* (pl -laten) exhaust

uitlaatgassen (ur^(ew)t-laat-khah-sern) *pl* exhaust gases

uitlaatpijp (ur^(ew)t-laat-payp) *c* (pl ~en) exhaust

*uitladen (ur^(ew)t-laa-dern) *v* unload, discharge

uitleg (ur*ew*t-lehkh) *c* explanation

uitleggen (ur*ew*t-leh-gern) *v* explain

uitlenen (ur*ew*t-lāy-nern) *v* *lend

uitleveren (ur*ew*t-lāy-ver-rern) *v* extradite

uitmaken (ur*ew*t-maa-kern) *v* matter; determine; *put out

uitnodigen (ur*ew*t-nōā-der-gern) *v* invite; ask

uitnodiging (ur*ew*t-nōā-der-ging) *c* (pl ~en) invitation

uitoefenen (ur*ew*t-ōō-fer-nern) *v* exercise

uitpakken (ur*ew*t-pah-kern) *v* unpack; unwrap

uitputten (ur*ew*t-per-tern) *v* exhaust

uitrekenen (ur*ew*t-rāy-ker-nern) *v* calculate

uitrit (ur*ew*t-rit) *c* (pl ~ten) exit

uitroep (ur*ew*t-rōōp) *c* (pl ~en) exclamation

* **uitroepen** (ur*ew*t-rōō-pern) *v* exclaim

uitrusten (ur*ew*t-rerss-tern) *v* rest; equip

uitrusting (ur*ew*t-rerss-ting) *c* (pl ~en) equipment; gear, kit, outfit

uitschakelen (ur*ew*t-skhaa-ker-lern) *v* switch off; disconnect

* **uitscheiden** (ur*ew*t-skhay-dern) *v* quit

* **uitschelden** (ur*ew*t-skhehl-dern) *v* call names

uitslag (ur*ew*t-slahkh) *c* (pl ~en) result; rash

* **uitsluiten** (ur*ew*t-slur*ew*-tern) *v* exclude

uitsluitend (ur*ew*t-slur*ew*-ternt) *adv* solely, exclusively

uitspraak (ur*ew*t-spraak) *c* (pl -spraken) pronunciation; verdict

uitspreiden (ur*ew*t-spray-dern) *v* expand

* **uitspreken** (ur*ew*t-sprāy-kern) *v* pronounce

uitstapje (ur*ew*t-stahp-ʸer) *nt* (pl ~s) trip, excursion

uitstappen (ur*ew*t-stah-pern) *v* *get off

uitstekend (ur*ew*t-*stāy*-kernt) *adj* fine, excellent

uitstel (ur*ew*t-stehl) *nt* delay; respite

uitstellen (ur*ew*t-steh-lern) *v* delay, postpone; adjourn

* **uittrekken** (ur*ew*t-treh-kern) *v* extract

uitverkocht (ur*ew*t-ferr-kokht) *adj* sold out

uitverkoop (ur*ew*t-ferr-kōap) *c* sales

* **uitvinden** (ur*ew*t-fin-dern) *v* invent

uitvinder (ur*ew*t-fin-derr) *c* (pl ~s) inventor

uitvinding (ur*ew*t-fin-ding) *c* (pl ~en) invention

uitvoer (ur*ew*t-fōōr) *c* exportation

uitvoerbaar (ur*ew*t-*fōōr*-baar) *adj* feasible

uitvoeren (ur*ew*t-fōō-rern) *v* carry out; implement, perform, execute; export

uitvoerend (ur*ew*t-*fōō*-rernt) *adj* executive; **uitvoerende macht** executive

uitvoerig (ur*ew*t-*fōō*-rerkh) *adj* detailed

uitwerken (ur*ew*t-vehr-kern) *v* elaborate

* **uitwijzen** (ur*ew*t-vay-zern) *v* expel

uitwisselen (ur*ew*t-vi-ser-lern) *v* exchange

* **uitzenden** (ur*ew*t-sehn-dern) *v* *broadcast, transmit

uitzending (ur*ew*t-sehn-ding) *c* (pl ~en) broadcast, transmission

uitzicht (ur*ew*t-sikht) *nt* (pl ~en) view

uitzondering (ur*ew*t-son-der-ring) *c* (pl ~en) exception

uitzonderlijk (ur*ew*t-*son*-derr-lerk) *adj* exceptional

* **uitzuigen** (ur*ew*t-sur*ew*-gern) *v* *bleed

ultraviolet (erl-traa-vee-ʸōā-*leht*) *adj* ultraviolet

unaniem (ēw-naa-*neem*) *adj* unanimous

unie (ēw-nee) c (pl ~s) union

uniek (ēw-neek) adj unique

uniform¹ (ēw-nee-form) adj uniform

uniform² (ēw-nee-form) nt/c (pl ~en) uniform

universeel (ēw-nee-vehr-zāyl) adj universal

universiteit (ēw-nee-vehr-zee-tayt) c (pl ~en) university

urgent (err-gehnt) adj pressing

urgentie (err-gehn-see) c urgency

urine (ēw-ree-ner) c urine

Uruguay (ōō-rōō-gvigh) Uruguay

Uruguayaan (ōō-rōō-gvah-ᵞaan) c (pl -yanen) Uruguayan

Uruguayaans (ōō-rōō-gvah-ᵞaans) adj Uruguayan

uur (ēwr) nt (pl uren) hour; **om ... ~** at ... o'clock; **uur-** hourly

uw (ēwᵒᵒ) pron your

V

vaag (vaakh) adj vague; faint; dim

vaak (vaak) adv often

vaandel (vaan-derl) nt (pl ~s) banner

vaardig (vaar-derkh) adj skilled, skilful

vaardigheid (vaar-derkh-hayt) c (pl -heden) skill; art

vaart (vaart) c speed

vaartuig (vaar-turᵉwkh) nt (pl ~en) vessel

vaarwater (vaar-vaa-terr) nt waterway

vaas (vaass) c (pl vazen) vase

vaatje (vaa-tᵞer) nt (pl ~s) keg

vaatwerk (vaat-vehrk) nt crockery

vacant (vaa-kahnt) adj vacant

vacature (vah-kah-tēw-rer) c (pl ~s) vacancy

vacuüm (vaa-kēw-erm) nt vacuum

vader (vaa-derr) c (pl ~s) father; dad

vaderland (vaa-derr-lahnt) nt native country, fatherland

vagebond (vaa-ger-bont) c (pl ~en) tramp

vak (vahk) nt (pl ~ken) profession, trade; section

vakantie (vaa-kahn-see) c (pl ~s) holiday, vacation; **met ~** on holiday

vakantiekamp (vaa-kahn-see-kahmp) nt (pl ~en) holiday camp

vakantieoord (vaa-kahn-see-ōart) nt (pl ~en) holiday resort

vakbond (vahk-bont) c (pl ~en) trade-union

vakkundig (vah-kern-derkh) adj skilled

vakman (vahk-mahn) c (pl -lieden) expert

val¹ (vahl) c fall

val² (vahl) c (pl ~len) trap

valk (vahlk) c (pl ~en) hawk

vallei (vah-lay) c (pl ~en) valley

***vallen** (vah-lern) v *fall; ***laten ~** drop

vals (vahls) adj false

valuta (vaa-lēw-taa) c (pl ~'s) currency

van (vahn) prep of; from; off; with

vanaf (vah-nahf) prep from, as from

vanavond (vah-naa-vernt) adv tonight

vandaag (vahn-daakh) adv today

***vangen** (vah-ngern) v *catch; capture

vangrail (vahng-rāyl) c (pl ~s) crash barrier

vangst (vahngst) c (pl ~en) capture

vanille (vaa-nee-ᵞer) c vanilla

vanmiddag (vah-mɪ-dahkh) adv this afternoon

vanmorgen (vah-mor-gern) adv this morning

vannacht (vah-nahkht) adv tonight

vanwege (vahn-vāy-ger) prep on account of, for, owing to, because of

vanzelfsprekend (vahn-zehlf-sprāy-kernt) adj self-evident

*varen (vaa-rern) v sail, navigate

variëren (vaa-ree-Yáy-rern) v vary

variététheater (vaa-ree-Yáy-táy-táy-Yaa-terr) nt (pl ~s) variety theatre; music-hall

variétévoorstelling (vaa-ree-Yáy-táy-vóar-steh-ling) c (pl ~en) variety show

varken (vahr-kern) nt (pl ~s) pig

varkensleer (vahr-kerss-láyr) nt pig-skin

varkensvlees (vahr-kerss-fláyss) nt pork

vaseline (vaa-zer-lee-ner) c vaseline

vast (vahst) adj fixed, firm; steady, permanent; adv tight; ~ **menu** set menu

vastberaden (vahss-ber-raa-dern) adj resolute

vastbesloten (vahss-ber-slóa-tern) adj determined

vasteland (vahss-ter-lahnt) nt mainland; continent

*vasthouden (vahst-hou-dehn) v *hold; **zich** ~ *hold on

vastmaken (vahst-maa-kern) v fasten; attach

vastomlijnd (vahss-tom-laynt) adj definite

vastspelden (vahst-spehl-dern) v pin

vaststellen (vahst-steh-lern) v establish, determine

vat (vaht) nt (pl ~en) cask, barrel; vessel

*vechten (vehkh-tern) v *fight; combat, battle

vee (váy) nt cattle pl

veearts (váy-ahrts) c (pl ~en) veterinary surgeon

veel (váyl) adj much, many; adv much, far

veelbetekenend (váyl-ber-táy-ker-nernt) adj significant

veelomvattend (váyl-om-vah-ternt)

adj extensive

veelvuldig (váyl-verl-derkh) adj frequent

veelzijdig (váyl-zay-derkh) adj all-round

veen (váyn) nt moor

veer (váyr) c (pl veren) feather; spring

veerboot (váyr-bóat) c (pl -boten) ferry-boat

veertien (váyr-teen) num fourteen; ~ **dagen** fortnight

veertiende (váyr-teen-der) num fourteenth

veertig (váyr-terkh) num forty

vegen (váy-gern) v *sweep; wipe

vegetariër (váy-ger-taa-ree-Yerr) c (pl ~s) vegetarian

veilig (vay-lerkh) adj safe; secure

veiligheid (vay-lerkh-hayt) c safety; security

veiligheidsgordel (vay-lerkh-hayts-khor-derl) c (pl ~s) safety-belt; seat-belt

veiligheidsspeld (vay-lerkh-hayt-spehlt) c (pl ~en) safety-pin

veiling (vay-ling) c (pl ~en) auction

vel (vehl) nt (pl ~len) skin

veld (vehlt) nt (pl ~en) field

veldbed (vehlt-beht) nt (pl ~den) camp-bed

veldkijker (vehlt-kay-kerr) c (pl ~s) field glasses

velg (vehlkh) c (pl ~en) rim

Venezolaan (váy-náy-zóa-laan) c (pl -lanen) Venezuelan

Venezolaans (váy-náy-zóa-laans) adj Venezuelan

Venezuela (váy-náy-zéw-váy-laa) Venezuela

vennoot (ver-nóat) c (pl -noten) associate

vensterbank (vehn-sterr-bahngk) c (pl ~en) window-sill

vent (vehnt) *c* chap, guy

ventiel (vehn-*teel*) *nt* (pl ~en) valve

ventilatie (vehn-tee-*laa*-tsee) *c* (pl ~s) ventilation

ventilator (vehn-ti-*laa*-tor) *c* (pl ~s, ~en) ventilator, fan

ventilatorriem (vehn-tee-*laa*-to-reem) *c* (pl ~en) fan belt

ventileren (vehn-tee-*lāy*-rern) *v* ventilate

ver (vehr) *adj* far; remote, far-away, distant

verachten (verr-*ahkh*-tern) *v* scorn, despise

verachting (verr-*ahkh*-ting) *c* scorn, contempt

verademing (verr-*aa*-der-ming) *c* relief

veranda (ver-*rahn*-daa) *c* (pl ~'s) veranda

veranderen (verr-*ahn*-der-rern) *v* change; alter, transform; vary; ~ **in** turn into

verandering (verr-*ahn*-der-ring) *c* (pl ~en) change; alteration; variation

veranderlijk (verr-*ahn*-derr-lerk) *adj* variable

verantwoordelijk (verr-ahnt-*vōar*-der-lerk) *adj* responsible

verantwoordelijkheid (verr-ahnt-*vōar*-der-lerk-hayt) *c* (pl -heden) responsibility

verantwoorden (verr-*ahnt*-vōar-dern) *v* account for

verband (verr-*bahnt*) *nt* (pl ~en) connection, relation; bandage

verbandkist (verr-*bahnt*-kist) *c* (pl ~en) first-aid kit

verbazen (verr-*baa*-zern) *v* astonish, amaze, surprise; **zich** ~ marvel

verbazing (verr-*baa*-zing) *c* astonishment, amazement, surprise

zich verbeelden (verr-*bāyl*-dern) fancy, imagine

verbeelding (verr-*bāyl*-ding) *c* imagination

***verbergen** (verr-*behr*-gern) *v* *hide; conceal

verbeteren (verr-*bāy*-ter-rern) *v* improve; correct

verbetering (verr-*bāy*-ter-ring) *c* (pl ~en) improvement; correction

***verbieden** (verr-*bee*-dern) *v* prohibit, *forbid

***verbinden** (verr-*bin*-dern) *v* link, connect, join; dress; **zich** ~ engage

verbinding (verr-*bin*-ding) *c* (pl ~en) link; connection; **zich in** ~ **stellen met** contact

verbindingsstuk (verr-*bin*-ding-sturk) *nt* adaptor

verblijf (verr-*blayf*) *nt* (pl -blijven) stay

verblijfsvergunning (verr-*blayfs*-ferr-ger-ning) *c* (pl ~en) residence permit

***verblijven** (verr-*blay*-vern) *v* stay

verblinden (verr-*blin*-dern) *v* blind; **verblindend** glaring

verbod (verr-*bot*) *nt* (pl ~en) prohibition

verboden (verr-*bōa*-dern) *adj* prohibited; ~ **te parkeren** no parking; ~ **te roken** no smoking; ~ **toegang** no entry, no admittance; ~ **voor voetgangers** no pedestrians

verbond (verr-*bont*) *nt* (pl ~en) union

verbranden (verr-*brahn*-dern) *v* *burn

verbruiken (verr-*brur^{ew}*-kern) *v* use up

verbruiker (verr-*brur^{ew}*-kerr) *c* (pl ~s) consumer

verdacht (verr-*dahkht*) *adj* suspicious

verdachte (verr-*dahkh*-teh) *c* (pl ~n) suspect; accused

verdampen (verr-*dahm*-pern) *v* evaporate

verdedigen (verr-*dāy*-der-gern) *v* defend

verdediging (verr-*dāy*-der-ging) *c* defence

verdelen (verr-*dāy*-lern) *v* divide

*__verdenken__ (verr-*dehng*-kern) *v* suspect

verdenking (verr-*dehng*-kɪng) *c* (pl ~en) suspicion

verder (*vehr*-derr) *adj* further; *adv* beyond; ~ **dan** beyond

verdienen (verr-*dee*-nern) *v* earn; *make; deserve, merit

verdienste (verr-*deens*-ter) *c* (pl ~n) merit; **verdiensten** *pl* earnings *pl*

verdieping (verr-*dee*-pɪng) *c* (pl ~en) storey, floor

verdikken (verr-*dɪ*-kern) *v* thicken

verdoving (verr-*dōā*-vɪng) *c* (pl ~en) anaesthesia

verdraaien (verr-*draa*ᵉᵉ-ern) *v* wrench

verdrag (verr-*drahkh*) *nt* (pl ~en) treaty

*__verdragen__ (verr-*draa*-gern) *v* endure, *bear; sustain

verdriet (verr-*dreet*) *nt* grief, sorrow

verdrietig (verr-*dree*-terkh) *adj* sad

*__verdrijven__ (verr-*dray*-vern) *v* chase

*__verdrinken__ (verr-*drɪng*-kern) *v* drown; *be drowned

verdrukken (verr-*drer*-kern) *v* oppress

verduidelijken (verr-*dur*ᵉʷ-der-ler-kern) *v* clarify

verduistering (verr-*dur*ᵉʷss-ter-rehn) *c* (pl ~en) eclipse

verdunnen (verr-*der*-nern) *v* dilute

verdwaald (verr-*dvaalt*) *adj* lost

*__verdwijnen__ (verr-*dvay*-nern) *v* vanish, disappear

vereisen (verr-*ay*-sern) *v* demand, require; **vereist** requisite

vereiste (verr-*ayss*-ter) *c* (pl ~n) requirement

Verenigde Staten (verr-*āy*-nerkh-der-*staa*-tern) United States, the States

verenigen (verr-*āy*-ner-gern) *v* join; unite; **verenigd** joint

vereniging (verr-*āy*-ner-gɪng) *c* (pl ~en) association; union, society, club

verf (vehrf) *c* (pl verven) paint; dye

verfdoos (*vehrf*-dōāss) *c* (pl -dozen) paint-box

verfrissen (verr-*frɪ*-sern) *v* refresh

verfrissing (verr-*frɪ*-sɪng) *c* (pl ~en) refreshment

vergadering (verr-*gaa*-der-rɪng) *c* (pl ~en) meeting; assembly

vergeefs (verr-*gāyfs*) *adj* vain; *adv* in vain

vergeetachtig (verr-*gāyt*-ahkh-terkh) *adj* forgetful

*__vergelijken__ (vehr-ger-*lay*-kern) *v* compare

vergelijking (vehr-ger-*lay*-kɪng) *c* (pl ~en) comparison

*__vergeten__ (verr-*gāy*-tern) *v* *forget

*__vergeven__ (verr-*gāy*-vern) *v* *forgive

zich vergewissen van (verr-ger-*vɪ*-sern) ascertain

vergezellen (verr-ger-*zeh*-lern) *v* accompany

vergiet (verr-*geet*) *nt* (pl ~en) strainer

vergif (verr-*gɪf*) *nt* poison

vergiffenis (verr-*gɪ*-fer-nɪss) *c* pardon

vergiftig (verr-*gɪf*-terkh) *adj* toxic

vergiftigen (verr-*gɪf*-teh-gern) *v* poison

zich vergissen (verr-*gɪ*-sern) *be mistaken; err

vergissing (verr-*gɪ*-sɪng) *c* (pl ~en) oversight; error, mistake

vergoeden (verr-*gōō*-dern) *v* *make good, reimburse; remunerate

vergoeding (verr-*gōō*-dɪng) *c* (pl ~en) remuneration

vergrootglas (verr-*grōāt*-khlahss) *nt* (pl -glazen) magnifying glass

vergroten (verr-*grōā*-tern) *v* enlarge

vergroting (verr-*grōā*-tɪng) *c* (pl ~en) enlargement

verguld (verr-*gerlt*) *adj* gilt

vergunning (verr-*ger*-nɪng) *c* (pl ~en)

licence, permit, permission; **een ~ verlenen** license

verhaal (verr-*haal*) *nt* (pl -halen) story; tale

verhandeling (verr-*hahn*-der-ling) *c* (pl ~en) essay

verheugd (verr-*hūrkht*) *adj* glad

verhinderen (verr-*hin*-der-rern) *v* prevent

verhogen (verr-*hōa*-gern) *v* raise

verhoging (verr-*hōa*-ging) *c* (pl ~en) rise, increase

verhoor (verr-*hōar*) *nt* (pl -horen) examination, interrogation

verhouding (verr-*hou*-ding) *c* (pl ~en) affair

verhuizen (verr-*hur*ᵉʷ-zern) *v* move

verhuizing (verr-*hur*ᵉʷ-zing) *c* (pl ~en) move

verhuren (verr-*hēw̄*-rern) *v* *let; lease

verifiëren (vāy-ree-fee-*ʸāy*-rern) *v* verify

vering (*vāy*-ring) *c* suspension

verjaardag (verr-*ʸaar*-dahkh) *c* (pl ~en) birthday; anniversary

***verjagen** (verr-*ʸaa*-gern) *v* chase

verkeer (verr-*kāyr*) *nt* traffic

verkeerd (verr-*kāyrt*) *adj* false, wrong

verkeersbureau (verr-*kāyrs*-bēw̄-rōa) *nt* (pl ~s) tourist office

verkeersopstopping (verr-*kāyrz*-op-sto-ping) *c* (pl ~en) traffic jam

verkennen (verr-*keh*-nern) *v* explore

***verkiezen** (verr-*kee*-zern) *v* elect

verkiezing (verr-*kee*-zing) *c* (pl ~en) election

verklaarbaar (verr-*klaar*-baar) *adj* accountable

verklaren (verr-*klaa*-rern) *v* state, declare; explain

verklaring (verr-*klaa*-ring) *c* (pl ~en) statement, declaration; explanation

zich verkleden (verr-*klāy*-dern) change

verkleuren (verr-*klūr*-rern) *v* fade; dis-

colour

verknoeien (verr-*knōō*ᵉᵉ-ern) *v* muddle

verkoop (*vehr*-kōap) *c* sale

verkoopbaar (verr-*kōā*-baar) *adj* saleable

verkoopster (verr-*kōāp*-sterr) *c* (pl ~s) salesgirl; shop assistant

***verkopen** (verr-*kōā*-pern) *v* *sell; **in het klein ~** retail

verkoper (verr-*kōā*-perr) *c* (pl ~s) salesman; shop assistant

verkorten (verr-*kor*-tern) *v* shorten

verkoudheid (verr-*kout*-hayt) *c* cold

verkrachten (verr-*krahkh*-tern) *v* rape

verkrijgbaar (verr-*kraykh*-baar) *adj* obtainable, available

***verkrijgen** (verr-*kray*-gern) *v* obtain

verlagen (verr-*laa*-gern) *v* lower, reduce; *cut

verlammen (verr-*lah*-mern) *v* paralise

verlangen[1] (verr-*lah*-ngern) *v* wish, desire; **~ naar** long for

verlangen[2] (verr-*lah*-ngern) *nt* (pl ~s) wish; longing

verlaten (verr-*laa*-tern) *adj* desert

***verlaten** (verr-*laa*-tern) *v* *leave; desert

verleden (verr-*lāy*-dern) *adj* previous; *nt* past

verlegen (verr-*lāy*-gern) *adj* shy; embarrassed

verlegenheid (verr-*lāy*-gern-hayt) *c* shyness, timidity; **in ~ *brengen** embarrass

verleiden (verr-*lay*-dern) *v* seduce

verleiding (verr-*lay*-ding) *c* (pl ~en) temptation

verlenen (verr-*lāy*-nern) *v* grant; extend

verlengen (verr-*leh*-ngern) *v* lengthen; extend; renew

verlenging (verr-*leh*-nging) *c* (pl ~en) extension

verlengsnoer (verr-*lehng*-snoŏr) *nt* (pl ~en) extension cord

verlichten (verr-*lıkh*-tern) *v* illuminate; relieve

verlichting (verr-*lıkh*-ting) *c* lighting, illumination; relief

verliefd (verr-*leeft*) *adj* in love

verlies (verr-*leess*) *nt* (pl -liezen) loss

*****verliezen** (verr-*lee*-zern) *v* *lose

verlof (verr-*lof*) *nt* (pl -loven) leave; permission

verloofd (verr-*loāft*) *adj* engaged

verloofde (verr-*loāf*-der) *c* (pl ~n) fiancé; fiancée

verlossen (verr-*lo*-sern) *v* deliver; redeem

verlossing (verr-*lo*-sing) *c* (pl ~en) delivery

verloving (verr-*loā*-ving) *c* (pl ~en) engagement

verlovingsring (verr-*loā*-vings-ring) *c* (pl ~en) engagement ring

vermaak (verr-*maak*) *nt* entertainment, amusement

vermageren (verr-*maa*-ger-rern) *v* slim

vermakelijk (verr-*maa*-ker-lerk) *adj* entertaining

vermaken (verr-*maa*-kern) *v* entertain, amuse

vermeerderen (verr-*maȳr*-der-rern) *v* increase

vermelden (verr-*mehl*-dern) *v* mention

vermelding (verr-*mehl*-ding) *c* (pl ~en) mention

vermenigvuldigen (verr-*maȳ*-nerkh-ferl-der-gern) *v* multiply

vermenigvuldiging (verr-*maȳ*-nerkh-ferl-der-ging) *c* (pl ~en) multiplication

*****vermijden** (verr-*may*-dern) *v* avoid

verminderen (verr-*mın*-der-rern) *v* decrease, lessen, reduce

vermindering (verr-*mın*-der-ring) *c* (pl ~en) decrease

vermiste (verr-*mıss*-ter) *c* (pl ~n) missing person

vermoedelijk (verr-*moō*-der-lerk) *adj* presumable, probable

vermoeden (verr-*moō*-dern) *v* suspect

vermoeien (verr-*moō*ᵉᵉ-ern) *v* tire; **vermoeid** weary, tired

vermogen (verr-*moā*-gern) *nt* (pl ~s) ability, faculty; capacity

zich vermommen (verr-*mo*-mern) disguise

vermomming (verr-*mo*-ming) *c* (pl ~en) disguise

vermoorden (verr-*moār*-dern) *v* murder

vernielen (verr-*nee*-lern) *v* wreck, destroy

vernietigen (verr-*nee*-ter-gern) *v* destroy

vernietiging (verr-*nee*-ter-ging) *c* destruction

vernieuwen (verr-*nee*ᵒᵒ-ern) *v* renew

vernis (verr-*nıss*) *nt/c* varnish

veronderstellen (verr-on-derr-*steh*-lern) *v* assume, suppose

verontreiniging (verr-ont-*ray*-ner-ging) *c* (pl ~en) pollution

verontschuldigen (verr-ont-*skherl*-der-gern) *v* excuse; **zich** ~ apologize

verontschuldiging (verr-ont-*skherl*-der-ging) *c* (pl ~en) apology

verontwaardiging (verr-ont-*vaar*-der-ging) *c* indignation

veroordeelde (verr-*oār*-daȳl-der) *c* (pl ~n) convict

veroordelen (verr-*oār*-daȳ-lern) *v* sentence

veroordeling (verr-*oār*-daȳ-ling) *c* (pl ~en) conviction

veroorloven (verr-*oār*-loā-vern) *v* allow, permit; **zich** ~ afford

veroorzaken (verr-*oār*-zaa-kern) *v* cause

veroveraar (verr-*oā*-ver-raar) *c* (pl ~s)

conqueror

veroveren (verr-*ōā*-ver-rern) v conquer

verovering (verr-*ōā*-ver-ring) c (pl ~en) conquest

verpachten (verr-*pahkh*-tern) v lease

verpakking (verr-*pah*-king) c (pl ~en) packing

verpanden (verr-*pahn*-dern) v pawn

verplaatsen (verr-*plaat*-sern) v move

verpleegster (verr-*plāykh*-sterr) c (pl ~s) nurse

verplegen (verr-*plāy*-gern) v nurse

verplicht (verr-*plikht*) adj obligatory, compulsory; ~ *zijn om* *be obliged to

verplichten (verr-*plikh*-tern) v oblige

verplichting (verr-*plikh*-ting) c (pl ~en) engagement

verraad (ver-*raat*) nt treason

*verraden (ver-*raa*-dern) v betray

verrader (ver-*raa*-derr) c (pl ~s) traitor

verrassen (ver-*rah*-sern) v surprise

verrassing (ver-*rah*-sing) c (pl ~en) surprise

verrekijker (*veh*-rer-kay-kerr) c (pl ~s) binoculars pl

verreweg (*veh*-rer-vehkh) adv by far

verrichten (ver-*rikh*-tern) v perform

verrukkelijk (ver-*rer*-ker-lerk) adj delightful, wonderful

verrukking (ver-*rer*-king) c (pl ~en) delight; **in ~** *brengen delight

vers¹ (vehrs) adj fresh

vers² (vehrs) nt (pl verzen) verse

verschaffen (verr-*skhah*-fern) v furnish, provide

verscheidene (verr-*skhay*-der-ner) num various; several

verscheidenheid (verr-*skhay*-dern-hayt) c (pl -heden) variety

verschepen (verr-*skhāy*-pern) v ship

*verschieten (verr-*skhee*-tern) v fade

*verschijnen (verr-*skhay*-nern) v appear

verschijning (verr-*skhay*-ning) c (pl ~en) apparition

verschijnsel (verr-*skhayn*-serl) nt (pl ~en, ~s) phenomenon

verschil (verr-*skhil*) nt (pl ~len) difference; distinction, contrast

verschillen (verr-*skhi*-lern) v differ; vary

verschillend (verr-*skhi*-lernt) adj unlike, different; distinct

verschrikkelijk (verr-*skhri*-ker-lerk) adj terrible; horrible, frightful, awful

verschuldigd (verr-*skherl*-derkht) adj due; ~ *zijn* owe

versie (*vehr*-zee) c (pl ~s) version

versiering (verr-*see*-ring) c (pl ~en) decoration

versiersel (verr-*seer*-serl) nt (pl ~s, ~en) ornament

*verslaan (verr-*slaan*) v defeat, *beat

verslag (verr-*slahkh*) nt (pl ~en) report, account

verslaggever (verr-*slah*-khāy-verr) c (pl ~s) reporter

zich ***verslapen** (verr-*slaa*-pern) *oversleep

versleten (verr-*slāy*-tern) adj worn-out, worn, threadbare

*verslijten (verr-*slay*-tern) v wear out

versnellen (verr-*sneh*-lern) v accelerate

versnelling (verr-*sneh*-ling) c (pl ~en) gear

versnellingsbak (verr-*sneh*-lings-bahk) c (pl ~ken) gear-box

versnellingspook (verr-*sneh*-lings-pōā) c gear lever

versperren (verr-*speh*-rern) v block

verspillen (verr-*spi*-lern) v waste

verspilling (verr-*spi*-ling) c waste

verspreiden (verr-*spray*-dern) v scatter, *shed

*verstaan (verr-*staan*) v *understand

verstand (verr-*stahnt*) nt brain; wits

pl, reason; **gezond** ~ sense

verstandig (verr-*stahn*-derkh) *adj* sensible

verstellen (verr-*steh*-lern) *v* patch

verstijfd (verr-*stayft*) *adj* numb

verstoppen (verr-*sto*-pern) *v* *hide

verstoren (verr-*stoā*-rern) *v* disturb; upset

*****verstrijken** (verr-*stray*-kern) *v* expire

verstuiken (verr-*stur*ew-kern) *v* sprain

verstuiking (verr-*stur*ew-king) *c* (pl ~en) sprain

verstuiver (verr-*stur*ew-verr) *c* (pl ~s) atomizer

versturen (verr-*stew*-rern) *v* *send off, dispatch

vertalen (verr-*taa*-lern) *v* translate

vertaler (verr-*taa*-lerr) *c* (pl ~s) translator

vertaling (verr-*taa*-ling) *c* (pl ~en) translation; version

verteerbaar (verr-*tāyr*-baar) *adj* digestible

vertegenwoordigen (verr-*tāy*-ger-*vōar*-der-gern) *v* represent

vertegenwoordiger (verr-*tāy*-ger-*vōar*-der-gerr) *c* (pl ~s) agent

vertegenwoordiging (verr-*tāy*-ger-*vōar*-der-ging) *c* (pl ~en) representation; agency

vertellen (verr-*ter*-lern) *v* *tell; relate

vertelling (verr-*teh*-ling) *c* (pl ~en) tale

verteren (verr-*tāy*-rern) *v* digest

verticaal (vehr-tee-*kaal*) *adj* vertical

vertolken (verr-*tol*-kern) *v* interpret

vertonen (verr-*tōā*-nern) *v* exhibit; display

vertragen (verr-*traa*-gern) *v* delay, slow down

vertraging (verr-*traa*-ging) *c* (pl ~en) delay

vertrek[1] (verr-*trehk*) *nt* departure

vertrek[2] (verr-*trehk*) *nt* (pl ~ken) room

*****vertrekken** (verr-*treh*-kern) *v* *leave; depart, *set out, pull out

vertrektijd (verr-*trehk*-tayt) *c* (pl ~en) time of departure

vertrouwd (verr-*trout*) *adj* familiar

vertrouwelijk (verr-*trou*-er-lerk) *adj* confidential

vertrouwen (verr-*trou*-ern) *nt* confidence, trust, faith; *v* trust; ~ **op** rely on

vervaardigen (verr-*vaar*-der-gern) *v* manufacture

vervaldag (verr-*vahl*-dahkh) *c* expiry

vervallen (verr-*vah*-lern) *adj* expired; due

*****vervallen** (verr-*vah*-lern) *v* expire

vervalsen (verr-*vahl*-sern) *v* forge; counterfeit

vervalsing (verr-*vahl*-sing) *c* (pl ~en) fake

*****vervangen** (verr-*vah*-ngern) *v* replace, substitute

vervanging (verr-*vah*-nging) *c* substitute

vervelen (verr-*vāy*-lern) *v* bore; bother

vervelend (verr-*vāy*-lernt) *adj* dull, boring, annoying; unpleasant

verven (*vehr*-vern) *v* paint; dye

vervloeken (verr-*vlōō*-kern) *v* curse

vervoer (verr-*vōōr*) *nt* transport

vervolg (verr-*volkh*) *nt* (pl ~en) sequel

vervolgen (verr-*vol*-gern) *v* continue; pursue

vervolgens (verr-*vol*-gerss) *adv* then

vervuiling (verr-*vur*ew-ling) *c* pollution

verwaand (verr-*vaant*) *adj* conceited, snooty

verwaarlozen (verr-*vaar*-lōā-zern) *v* neglect

verwaarlozing (verr-*vaar*-lōā-zing) *c* neglect

verwachten (verr-*vahkh*-tern) *v* expect; anticipate

verwachting (verr-*vahkh*-ting) *c* (pl ~en) expectation; outlook; **in ~** pregnant

verwant (verr-*vahnt*) *adj* related

verwante (verr-*vahn*-ter) *c* (pl ~n) relation

verward (verr-*vahrt*) *adj* confused

verwarmen (verr-*vahr*-mern) *v* heat, warm

verwarming (verr-*vahr*-ming) *c* heating

verwarren (verr-*vah*-rern) *v* confuse; *mistake

verwarring (verr-*vah*-ring) *c* confusion; disturbance; **in ~ brengen** embarrass

verwekken (verr-*veh*-kern) *v* generate

verwelkomen (verr-*vehl*-kōa-mern) *v* welcome

verwennen (verr-*veh*-nern) *v* *spoil

*verwerpen** (verr-*vehr*-pern) *v* turn down, reject

*verwerven** (verr-*vehr*-vern) *v* acquire

verwezenlijken (verr-*vāy*-zer-ler-kern) *v* realize

verwijden (verr-*vay*-dern) *v* widen

verwijderen (verr-*vay*-der-rern) *v* remove

verwijdering (verr-*vay*-der-ring) *c* removal

verwijt (verr-*vayt*) *nt* (pl ~en) reproach; blame

*verwijten** (verr-*vay*-tern) *v* reproach

*verwijzen naar** (verr-*vay*-zern) refer to

verwijzing (verr-*vay*-zing) *c* (pl ~en) reference

verwonden (verr-*von*-dern) *v* wound, injure

verwonderen (verr-*von*-der-rern) *v* amaze

verwondering (verr-*von*-der-ring) *c* wonder

verwonding (verr-*von*-ding) *c* (pl ~en) injury

verzachten (verr-*zahkh*-tern) *v* soften

verzamelaar (verr-*zaa*-mer-laar) *c* (pl ~s) collector

verzamelen (verr-*zaa*-mer-lern) *v* gather; collect

verzameling (verr-*zaa*-mer-ling) *c* (pl ~en) collection

verzekeren (verr-*zāy*-ker-rern) *v* assure; insure

verzekering (verr-*zāy*-ker-ring) *c* (pl ~en) insurance

verzekeringspolis (verr-*zāy*-ker-rings-pōa-lerss) *c* (pl ~sen) insurance policy

*verzenden** (verr-*zehn*-dern) *v* despatch, dispatch

verzending (verr-*zehn*-ding) *c* expedition

verzet (verr-*zeht*) *nt* resistance

zich verzetten (verr-*zeh*-tern) oppose

verzilveren (verr-*zil*-ver-rern) *v* cash

*verzinnen** (verr-*zi*-nern) *v* invent

verzinsel (verr-*zin*-serl) *nt* (pl ~s) fiction

verzoek (verr-*zōōk*) *nt* (pl ~en) request

*verzoeken** (verr-*zōō*-kern) *v* request, ask

verzoening (verr-*zōō*-ning) *c* (pl ~en) reconciliation

verzorgen (verr-*zor*-gern) *v* look after, *take care of; tend

verzorging (verr-*zor*-ging) *c* care

verzwikken (verr-*zvi*-kern) *v* sprain

vest (vehst) *nt* (pl ~en) cardigan; waistcoat, jacket; vest *nAm*

vestigen (*vehss*-ter-gern) *v* establish; **zich ~** settle down

vesting (*vehss*-ting) *c* (pl ~en) fortress

vet[1] (veht) *adj* fat; greasy

vet[2] (veht) *nt* (pl ~ten) fat; grease

veter (*vāy*-terr) *c* (pl ~s) lace

vettig (veh-terkh) adj greasy, fatty

vezel (vay-zerl) c (pl ~s) fibre

vibratie (vee-braa-tsee) c (pl ~s) vibration

video camera (vie-dee-oo kaa-mee-raa) c video camera

video cassette (vie-dee-oo ka-seter) c video cassette

video recorder (vie-dee-oo rie-kor-derr) c video recorder

vier (veer) num four

vierde (veer-der) num fourth

vieren (vee-rern) v celebrate

viering (vee-ring) c (pl ~en) celebration

vierkant (veer-kahnt) adj square; nt square

vies (veess) adj dirty

vijand (vay-ahnt) c (pl ~en) enemy

vijandig (vay-ahn-derkh) adj hostile

vijf (vayf) num five

vijfde (vayf-der) num fifth

vijftien (vayf-teen) num fifteen

vijftiende (vayf-teen-der) num fifteenth

vijftig (vayf-terkh) num fifty

vijg (vaykh) c (pl ~en) fig

vijl (vayl) c (pl ~en) file

vijver (vay-verr) c (pl ~s) pond

villa (vee-laa) c (pl ~'s) villa

vilt (vilt) nt felt

*****vinden** (vin-dern) v *find; *come across; consider

vindingrijk (vin-ding-rayk) adj inventive

vinger (vi-ngerr) c (pl ~s) finger

vingerafdruk (vi-ngerr-ahf-drerk) c (pl ~ken) fingerprint

vingerhoed (vi-ngerr-hōot) c (pl ~en) thimble

violet (vee-ᵞōa-leht) adj violet

viool (vee-ᵞōal) c (pl violen) violin

viooltje (vee-ᵞōal-tᵞer) nt (pl ~s) violet

vis (viss) c (pl ~sen) fish

visakte (viss-ahk-ter) c (pl ~n, ~s) fishing licence

visgraat (viss-khraat) c (pl -graten) fishbone

vishaak (viss-haak) c (pl -haken) fishing hook

visie (vee-zee) c vision

visite (vee-zee-ter) c (pl ~s) visit; call

visitekaartje (vi-zee-ter-kaar-tᵞer) nt (pl ~s) visiting-card

viskuit (viss-kurᵉʷt) c roe

vislijn (viss-layn) c (pl ~en) fishing line

visnet (viss-neht) nt (pl ~ten) fishing net

vissen (vi-sern) v fish

visser (vi-serr) c (pl ~s) fisherman

visserij (vi-ser-ray) c fishing industry

vistuig (viss-turᵉʷkh) nt fishing tackle, fishing gear

visum (vee-zerm) nt (pl visa) visa

viswinkel (viss-ving-kerl) c (pl ~s) fish shop

vitamine (vee-taa-mee-ner) c (pl ~n, ~s) vitamin

vitrine (vee-tree-ner) c (pl ~s) showcase

vlag (vlahkh) c (pl ~gen) flag

vlak (vlahk) adj flat; smooth; level, plane

vlakgom (vlahk-khom) c/nt (pl ~men) rubber

vlakte (vlahk-ter) c (pl ~n, ~s) plain

vlam (vlahm) c (pl ~men) flame

vlees (vlāyss) nt meat; flesh

vlek (vlehk) c (pl ~ken) stain, spot, blot

vlekkeloos (vleh-ker-lōass) adj stainless, spotless

vlekken (vleh-kern) v stain

vlekkenwater (vleh-ker-vaa-terr) nt stain remover

vleugel (vlūr-gerl) c (pl ~s) wing;

grand piano

vlieg (vleekh) c (pl ~en) fly

*vliegen (vlee-gern) v *fly

vliegramp (vleekh-rahmp) c (pl ~en) plane crash

vliegtuig (vleekh-tur^{ew}kh) nt (pl ~en) aircraft, aeroplane, plane; airplane nAm

vliegveld (vleekh-fehlt) nt (pl ~en) airfield

vlijt (vlayt) c diligence

vlijtig (vlay-terkh) adj industrious; diligent

vlinder (vlın-derr) c (pl ~s) butterfly

vlinderdasje (vlın-derr-dah-sher) nt (pl ~s) bow tie

vlinderslag (vlın-derr-slahkh) c butterfly stroke

vloed (vloōt) c flood

vloeibaar (vloō^{ee}-baar) adj liquid, fluid

vloeien (vloō^{ee}-ern) v flow; **vloeiend** fluent

vloeipapier (vloō^{ee}-paa-peer) nt blotting paper

vloeistof (vloō^{ee}-stof) c (pl ~fen) fluid

vloek (vloōk) c (pl ~en) curse

vloeken (vloō-kern) v curse, *swear

vloer (vloōr) c (pl ~en) floor

vloerkleed (vloōr-klāyt) nt (pl -kleden) carpet

vloot (vloāt) c (pl vloten) fleet

vlot (vlot) nt (pl ~ten) raft

vlotter (vlo-terr) c (pl ~s) float

vlucht (vlerkht) c (pl ~en) flight

vluchten (vlerkh-tern) v escape

vlug (vlerkh) adj fast, quick, rapid; adv soon

vocaal (voā-kaal) adj vocal

vocabulaire (voā-kaa-bew-lair) nt vocabulary

vocht (vokht) nt damp

vochtig (vokh-terkh) adj humid, moist; damp, wet

vochtigheid (vokh-terkh-hayt) c humidity, moisture

vod (vot) nt (pl ~den) rag

voeden (voō-dern) v *feed

voedsel (voōt-serl) nt food; fare

voedselvergiftiging (voōt-serl-verr-gıf-ter-gıng) c food poisoning

voedzaam (voōt-saam) adj nutritious, nourishing

zich voegen bij (voō-gern) join

voelen (voō-lern) v *feel; sense

voeren (voō-rern) v carry

voering (voō-rıng) c (pl ~en) lining

voertuig (voōr-tur^{ew}kh) nt (pl ~en) vehicle

voet (voōt) c (pl ~en) foot; **te ~** on foot, walking

voetbal (voōt-bahl) nt soccer

voetbalwedstrijd (voōt-bahl-veht-strayt) c (pl ~en) football match

voetganger (voōt-khah-ngerr) c (pl ~s) pedestrian

voetpad (voōt-paht) nt (pl ~en) footpath

voetrem (voōt-rehm) c foot-brake

vogel (voā-gerl) c (pl ~s) bird

vol (vol) adj full; full up

volbloed (vol-bloōt) adj thoroughbred

*volbrengen (vol-breh-ngern) v accomplish

voldaan (vol-daan) adj satisfied

voldoende (vol-doōn-der) adj sufficient, enough; **~ *zijn** *do, suffice

voldoening (vol-doō-nıng) c satisfaction

volgen (vol-gern) v follow; **volgend** subsequent, next, following

volgens (vol-gerns) prep according to

volgorde (vol-gor-der) c order, sequence

*volhouden (vol-hou-dern) v *keep up; insist

volk (volk) *nt* (pl ~en, ~eren) people; nation; folk; **volks-** national; popular; vulgar

volkomen (voal-*kōa*-mern) *adj* perfect; *adv* completely

volkorenbrood (vol-*kōa*-rerm-brōat) *nt* wholemeal bread

volksdans (*volks*-dahns) *c* (pl ~en) folk-dance

volkslied (*volks*-leet) *nt* (pl ~eren) folk song; national anthem

volledig (vo-*lāy*-derkh) *adj* complete

volmaakt (vol-*maakt*) *adj* perfect

volmaaktheid (vol-*maakt*-hayt) *c* perfection

volslagen (vol-*slaa*-gern) *adj* total, utter

volt (volt) *c* volt

voltage (vol-*taa*-zher) *c/nt* (pl ~s) voltage

voltooien (vol-*tōa*ee-ern) *v* complete

volume (vōa-*lēw*-mer) *nt* (pl ~n, ~s) volume

volwassen (vol-*vah*-sern) *adj* adult; grown-up

volwassene (vol-*vah*-ser-ner) *c* (pl ~n) adult; grown-up

vonk (vongk) *c* (pl ~en) spark

vonnis (*vo*-nerss) *nt* (pl ~sen) verdict, sentence

voogd (vōakht) *c* (pl ~en) tutor, guardian

voogdij (vōakh-*day*) *c* custody

voor (vōar) *prep* before; ahead of, in front of; for; to

vooraanstaand (vōar-*aan*-staant) *adj* leading, outstanding

*voorafgaan (vōar-*ahf*-khaan) *v* precede

voorai (vōa-*rahl*) *adv* essentially, especially, most of all

voorbarig (vōar-*baa*-rerkh) *adj* premature

voorbeeld (vōar-*bāy*lt) *nt* (pl ~en) example, instance

voorbehoedmiddel (vōar-ber-*hōot*-mi-derl) *nt* (pl ~en) contraceptive

voorbehoud (vōar-ber-hout) *nt* qualification

voorbereiden (vōar-ber-ray-dern) *v* prepare

voorbereiding (vōar-ber-ray-ding) *c* (pl ~en) preparation

voorbij (vōar-*bay*) *adj* past, over; *prep* past, beyond

*voorbijgaan (vōar-*bay*-gaan) *v* pass

voorbijganger (vōar-*bay*-gah-ngerr) *c* (pl ~s) passer-by

voordat (vōar-daht) *conj* before

voordeel (vōar-dāyl) *nt* (pl -delen) advantage; profit, benefit

voordelig (vōar-*dāy*-lerkh) *adj* advantageous; cheap

zich *voordoen (vōar-dōon) occur

voorgaand (vōar-khaant) *adj* previous, preceding

voorganger (vōar-gah-ngerr) *c* (pl ~s) predecessor

voorgerecht (vōar-ger-rehkht) *nt* (pl ~en) hors-d'œuvre

voorgrond (vōar-gront) *c* foreground

voorhanden (vōar-*hahn*-dern) *adj* available

voorheen (vōar-*hāyn*) *adv* formerly

voorhoofd (vōar-hōaft) *nt* (pl ~en) forehead

voorjaar (vōar-ʸaar) *nt* springtime, spring

voorkant (vōar-kahnt) *c* front

voorkeur (vōar-kūrr) *c* preference; **de ~ *geven aan** prefer

voorkomen[1] (vōar-*kōa*-mern) *nt* look, appearance

*voorkomen[2] (vōar-kōa-mern) *v* occur, happen

*voorkomen[3] (vōar-*kōa*-mern) *v* prevent; anticipate

voorkomend (vōar-*kōa*-mernt) *adj* obliging

voorletter (*vōar*-leh-terr) *c* (pl ~s) initial

voorlopig (vōar-*lōa*-perkh) *adj* provisional, temporary; preliminary

voormalig (vōar-*maa*-lerkh) *adj* former

voorman (*vōar*-mahn) *c* (pl ~nen) foreman

voornaam¹ (vōar-*naam*) *adj* distinguished; **voornaamst** *adj* principal, main, leading, chief

voornaam² (*vōar*-naam) *c* (pl -namen) first name, Christian name

voornaamwoord (*vōar*-naam-vōart) *nt* (pl ~en) pronoun

voornamelijk (vōar-*naa*-mer-lerk) *adv* especially

vooroordeel (*vōar*-ōar-dāyl) *nt* (pl -delen) prejudice

vooroorlogs (vōar-*ōar*-lokhs) *adj* prewar

voorraad (*vōa*-raat) *c* (pl -raden) stock, store, supply; provisions *pl*; **in ~ *hebben** stock

voorrang (*vōa*-rahng) *c* priority; right of way

voorrecht (*vōa*-rehkht) *nt* (pl ~en) privilege

voorruit (*vōa*-rur^(ew)t) *c* (pl ~en) windscreen; windshield *nAm*

*voorschieten (*vōar*-skhee-tern) *v* advance

voorschot (*vōar*-skhot) *nt* (pl ~ten) advance

voorschrift (*vōar*-skhrift) *nt* (pl ~en) regulation

*voorschrijven (*vōar*-skhray-vern) *v* prescribe

voorspellen (vōar-*speh*-lern) *v* predict, forecast

voorspelling (vōar-*speh*-ling) *c* (pl ~en) forecast

voorspoed (*vōar*-spōot) *c* prosperity

voorsprong (*vōar*-sprong) *c* lead

voorstad (*vōar*-staht) *c* (pl -steden) suburb

voorstander (*vōar*-stahn-derr) *c* (pl ~s) advocate

voorstel (*vōar*-stehl) *nt* (pl ~len) proposition, proposal; suggestion

voorstellen (*vōar*-steh-lern) *v* propose, suggest; present, introduce; represent; **zich ~** conceive, fancy, imagine

voorstelling (*vōar*-steh-ling) *c* (pl ~en) show, performance

voortaan (*vōar*-taan) *adv* henceforth

voortduren (*vōar*-dēw-rern) *v* continue; **voortdurend** continuous, continual

*voortgaan (*vōart*-khaan) *v* continue; proceed

voortreffelijk (vōar-*treh*-fer-lerk) *adj* excellent; exquisite

voorts (vōarts) *adv* moreover

voortzetten (*vōart*-seh-tern) *v* carry on, continue

vooruit (vōa-*rur^(ew)t*) *adv* ahead, forward; in advance

vooruitbetaald (vōa-*rur^(ew)t*-ber-taalt) *adj* prepaid

*vooruitgaan (vōa-*rur^(ew)t*-khaan) *v* advance

vooruitgang (vōa-*rur^(ew)t*-khahng) *c* progress, advance

vooruitstrevend (vōa-rur^(ew)t-*strāy*-vernt) *adj* progressive

vooruitzicht (vōa-*rur^(ew)t*-sikht) *nt* (pl ~en) prospect

voorvader (*vōar*-vaa-derr) *c* (pl ~s, ~en) ancestor

voorvechter (*vōar*-vehkh-terr) *c* (pl ~s) champion

voorvoegsel (*vōar*-vōokh-serl) *nt* (pl ~s) prefix

voorwaarde (*vōar*-vaar-der) *c* (pl ~n) condition; term

voorwaardelijk (vōar-*vaar*-der-lerk) *adj*

conditional

voorwaarts (*vōar*-vaarts) *adv* onwards, forward

voorwenden (*vōar*-vehn-dern) *v* pretend

voorwendsel (*vōar*-vehnt-serl) *nt* (pl ~s, ~en) pretext, pretence

voorwerp (*vōar*-vehrp) *nt* (pl ~en) object; **gevonden voorwerpen** lost and found

voorzetsel (*vōar*-zeht-serl) *nt* (pl ~s) preposition

voorzichtig (*vōar*-zıkh-terkh) *adj* careful; gentle

voorzichtigheid (*vōar*-zıkh-terkh-hayt) *c* caution

*****voorzien** (vōar-*zeen*) *v* anticipate; ~ **van** furnish with

voorzitter (*vōar*-zı-terr) *c* (pl ~s) chairman, president

voorzorg (*vōar*-zorkh) *c* (pl ~en) precaution

voorzorgsmaatregel (*vōar*-zorkhs-maat-rāy-gerl) *c* (pl ~en) precaution

vorderen (vor-der-rern) *v* *get on; confiscate, claim

vorig (*vōa*-rerkh) *adj* last; past

vork (vork) *c* (pl ~en) fork

vorm (vorm) *c* (pl ~en) shape; form

vormen (*vor*-mern) *v* shape; form

vorming (*vor*-mıng) *c* background

vorst[1] (vorst) *c* (pl ~en) ruler, monarch, sovereign

vorst[2] (vorst) *c* frost

vos (voss) *c* (pl ~sen) fox

vouw (vou) *c* (pl ~en) fold; crease

*****vouwen** (*vou*-ern) *v* fold

vraag (vraakh) *c* (pl vragen) question; inquiry, query

vraaggesprek (*vraa*-kher-sprehk) *nt* (pl ~ken) interview

vraagstuk (*vraakh*-sterk) *nt* (pl ~ken) problem, question

vraagteken (*vraakh*-tāy-kern) *nt* (pl

~s) question mark

vracht (vrahkht) *c* (pl ~en) freight, cargo

vrachtwagen (*vrahkht*-vaa-gern) *c* (pl ~s) lorry; truck *nAm*

*****vragen** (*vraa*-gern) *v* ask; beg; **vragend** interrogative

vrede (*vrāy*-der) *c* peace

vreedzaam (*vrāyt*-saam) *adj* peaceful

vreemd (vrāymt) *adj* strange; odd, queer; foreign

vreemde (*vrāym*-der) *c* (pl ~n) stranger

vreemdeling (*vrāym*-der-lıng) *c* (pl ~en) foreigner; stranger, alien

vrees (vrāyss) *c* dread, fear

vreselijk (*vrāy*-ser-lerk) *adj* terrible; horrible, dreadful, frightful

vreugde (*vrūrkh*-der) *c* (pl ~n) gladness, joy

vrezen (*vrāy*-zern) *v* dread, fear

vriend (vreent) *c* (pl ~en) friend

vriendelijk (*vreen*-der-lerk) *adj* friendly; kind

vriendschap (*vreent*-skhahp) *c* (pl ~pen) friendship

vriendschappelijk (vreent-*skhah*-per-lerk) *adj* friendly

vriespunt (*vreess*-pernt) *nt* freezing-point

*****vriezen** (*vree*-zern) *v* *freeze

vrij (vray) *adj* free; *adv* pretty, fairly, quite, rather

vrijdag (*vray*-dahkh) *c* Friday

vrijgevig (vray-*gāy*-verkh) *adj* liberal

vrijgezel (vray-ger-*zehl*) *c* (pl ~len) bachelor

vrijheid (*vray*-hayt) *c* (pl -heden) freedom, liberty

vrijkaart (*vray*-kaart) *c* (pl ~en) free ticket

vrijpostig (vray-*poss*-terkh) *adj* bold

vrijspraak (*vray*-spraak) *c* acquittal

vrijstellen (*vray*-steh-lern) *v* exempt;

vrijgesteld exempt

vrijstelling (*vray*-steh-lıng) *c* (pl ~en) exemption

vrijwel (*vray*-vehl) *adv* practically

vrijwillig (vray-*vı*-lerkh) *adj* voluntary

vrijwilliger (vray-*vı*-ler-gerr) *c* (pl ~s) volunteer

vroedvrouw (*vrōōt*-frou) *c* (pl ~en) midwife

vroeg (vrōōkh) *adj* early

vroeger (*vrōō*-gerr) *adj* prior, previous, former; *adv* formerly

vrolijk (*vrōā*-lerk) *adj* gay, cheerful, merry, joyful

vrolijkheid (*vrōā*-lerk-hayt) *c* gaiety

vroom (vrōām) *adj* pious

vrouw (vrou) *c* (pl ~en) woman; wife

vrouwelijk (*vrou*-er-lerk) *adj* female; feminine

vrouwenarts (*vrou*-ern-ahrts) *c* (pl ~en) gynaecologist

vrucht (vrerkht) *c* (pl ~en) fruit

vruchtbaar (*vrerkht*-baar) *adj* fertile

vruchtensap (*vrerkh*-ter-sahp) *nt* (pl ~pen) squash

vuil (vur^ewl) *adj* filthy, dirty; *nt* dirt

vuilnis (*vur^ewl*-nıss) *nt* garbage

vuilnisbak (*vur^ewl*-nıss-bahk) *c* (pl ~ken) rubbish-bin, dustbin; trash can *Am*

vuist (vur^ewst) *c* (pl ~en) fist

vuistslag (*vur^ewst*-slahkh) *c* (pl ~en) punch

vulgair (verl-*gair*) *adj* vulgar

vulkaan (verl-*kaan*) *c* (pl -kanen) volcano

vullen (*ver*-lern) *v* fill

vulling (*ver*-lıng) *c* (pl ~en) stuffing, filling; refill

vulpen (*verl*-pehn) *c* (pl ~nen) fountain-pen

vuur (vewr) *nt* (pl vuren) fire

vuurrood (*vewr*-rōāt) *adj* scarlet, crimson

vuursteen (*vewr*-stāyn) *c* (pl -stenen) flint

vuurtoren (*vewr*-tōā-rern) *c* (pl ~s) lighthouse

vuurvast (*vewr*-vahst) *adj* fireproof

W

***waaien** (*vaa^ee*-ern) *v* *blow

waaier (*vaa^ee*-err) *c* (pl ~s) fan

waakzaam (*vaak*-saam) *adj* vigilant

waanzin (*vaan*-zın) *c* madness

waanzinnig (vaan-*zı*-nerkh) *adj* mad

waar[1] (vaar) *adj* true; very

waar[2] (vaar) *adv* where; *conj* where; ~ **dan ook** anywhere; ~ **ook** wherever

waarborg (*vaar*-borkh) *c* (pl ~en) guarantee

waard (vaart) *adj* worthy of; ~ *zijn *be worth

waarde (*vaar*-der) *c* (pl ~n) worth, value

waardeloos (vaar-der-lōāss) *adj* worthless

waarderen (vaar-*dāy*-rern) *v* appreciate

waardering (vaar-*dāy*-rıng) *c* appreciation

waardevol (*vaar*-der-vol) *adj* valuable

waardig (*vaar*-derkh) *adj* dignified

waarheid (*vaar*-hayt) *c* (pl -heden) truth

waarheidsgetrouw (*vaar*-hayts-kher-trou) *adj* truthful

***waarnemen** (*vaar*-nāy-mern) *v* observe

waarneming (*vaar*-nāy-mıng) *c* (pl ~en) observation

waarom (vaa-*rom*) *adv* why; what for

waarschijnlijk (vaar-*skhayn*-lerk) *adj* probable, likely; *adv* probably

waarschuwen (*vaar*-skhew⁰⁰-ern) *v* warn ; caution ; notify

waarschuwing (*vaar*-skhew⁰⁰-ing) *c* (pl ~en) warning

waas (vaass) *nt* haze

wachten (*vahkh*-tern) *v* wait ; ~ **op** await

wachtkamer (*vahkht*-kaa-merr) *c* (pl ~s) waiting-room

wachtlijst (*vahkht*-layst) *c* (pl ~en) waiting-list

wachtwoord (*vahkht*-voart) *nt* (pl ~en) password

waden (*vaa*-dern) *v* wade

wafel (*vaa*-ferl) *c* (pl ~s) waffle, wafer

wagen¹ (*vaa*-gern) *c* (pl ~s) cart

wagen² (*vaa*-gern) *v* dare, venture, risk

wagon (vaa-*gon*) *c* (pl ~s) carriage, waggon ; passenger car *Am*

wakker (*vah*-kerr) *adj* awake ; ~ *worden wake up

walgelijk (*vahl*-ger-lerk) *adj* revolting, disgusting

walnoot (*vahl*-noat) *c* (pl -noten) walnut

wals (vahls) *c* (pl ~en) waltz

walvis (*vahl*-viss) *c* (pl ~sen) whale

wand (vahnt) *c* (pl ~en) wall

wandelaar (*vahn*-der-laar) *c* (pl ~s) walker

wandelen (*vahn*-der-lern) *v* stroll, walk

wandeling (*vahn*-der-ling) *c* (pl ~en) stroll, walk

wandelstok (*vahn*-derl-stok) *c* (pl ~ken) walking-stick

wandkleed (*vahnt*-klayt) *nt* (pl -kleden) tapestry

wandluis (*vahnt*-lur^ew ss) *c* (pl -luizen) bug

wang (vahng) *c* (pl ~en) cheek

wanhoop (*vahn*-hoap) *c* despair

wanhopen (*vahn*-hoa-pern) *v* despair

wanhopig (vahn-*hoa*-perkh) *adj* desperate

wankel (*vahn*-kerl) *adj* unsteady

wankelen (*vahn*-ker-lern) *v* falter

wanneer (vah-*nayr*) *adv* when ; *conj* when ; ~ **ook** whenever

wanorde (*vahn*-or-der) *c* disorder

want (vahnt) *conj* for

wanten (*vahn*-tern) *pl* mittens *pl*

wantrouwen (*vahn*-trou-ern) *nt* suspicion ; *v* mistrust

wapen (*vaa*-pern) *nt* (pl ~s, ~en) weapon, arm

warboel (*vahr*-bool) *c* muddle, mess

waren (*vaa*-rern) *pl* goods *pl*, wares *pl*

warenhuis (*vaa*-rer-hur^ew ss) *nt* (pl -huizen) department store

warm (vahrm) *adj* warm ; hot ; ~ *eten dine

warmte (*vahrm*-ter) *c* warmth ; heat

warmwaterkruik (vahrm-*vaa*-terr-krur^ew k) *c* (pl ~en) hot-water bottle

was¹ (vahss) *c* laundry, washing

was² (vahss) *c* wax

wasbaar (*vahss*-baar) *adj* washable

wasbekken (*vahss*-beh-kern) *nt* (pl ~s) wash-basin

wasecht (vahss-*ehkht*) *adj* fast-dyed

wasgoed (*vahss*-khoot) *nt* washing

wasmachine (*vahss*-mah-shee-ner) *c* (pl ~s) washing-machine

wasmiddel (*vahss*-mi-derl) *nt* (pl ~en) detergent

waspoeder (*vahss*-poo-derr) *nt* (pl ~s) washing-powder

*wassen (*vah*-sern) *v* wash

wassenbeeldenmuseum (vah-ser-*bayl*-der-mew-zay-^yerm) *nt* (pl ~s, -musea) waxworks *pl*

wasserette (vah-ser-*reh*-ter) *c* (pl ~s) launderette

wasserij (vah-ser-*ray*) *c* (pl ~en) laundry

wastafel (*vahss*-taa-ferl) *c* (pl ~s)

wash-stand

wasverzachter (*vahss*-ferr-zahkh-terr) *c* (pl ~s) water-softener

wat (vaht) *pron* what; *adv* how; ~ **dan ook** whatever; anything

water (*vaa*-terr) *nt* water; **hoog** ~ high tide; **laag** ~ low tide; **stromend** ~ running water; **zoet** ~ fresh water

waterdicht (*vaa*-terr-dıkht) *adj* rainproof, waterproof

waterkers (*vaa*-terr-kehrs) *c* watercress

watermeloen (*vaa*-terr-mer-lōōn) *c* (pl ~en) watermelon

waterpas (*vaa*-terr-pahss) *c* (pl ~sen) level

waterpokken (*vaa*-terr-po-kern) *pl* chickenpox

waterpomp (*vaa*-terr-pomp) *c* (pl ~en) water pump

waterski (*vaa*-terr-skee) *c* (pl ~'s) water ski

waterstof (*vaa*-terr-stof) *c* hydrogen

waterstofperoxyde (*vaa*-terr-stof-pehr-ok-see-der) *nt* peroxide

waterval (*vaa*-terr-vahl) *c* (pl ~len) waterfall

waterverf (*vaa*-terr-vehrf) *c* water-colour

watten (*vah*-tern) *pl* cotton-wool

wazig (*vaa*-zerkh) *adj* hazy

we (ver) *pron* we

wedden (*veh*-dern) *v* *bet

weddenschap (*veh*-der-skhahp) *c* (pl ~pen) bet

wederverkoper (*vāy*-derr-verr-kōā-perr) *c* (pl ~s) retailer

wederzijds (vāy-derr-*zayts*) *adj* mutual

wedijveren (*veht*-ay-ver-rern) *v* compete

wedloop (*veht*-lōap) *c* (pl -lopen) race

wedstrijd (*veht*-strayt) *c* (pl ~en) competition, contest; match

weduwe (*vāy*-dew°°-er) *c* (pl ~n) widow

weduwnaar (*vāy*-dew°°-naar) *c* (pl ~s) widower

weeën (*vāy*-ern) *pl* labour

weefsel (*vāyf*-serl) *nt* (pl ~s) tissue

weegschaal (*vāykh*-skhaal) *c* (pl -schalen) weighing-machine, scales *pl*

week (vāyk) *c* (pl weken) week

weekdag (*vāyk*-dahkh) *c* (pl ~en) weekday

weekend (*vee*-kehnt) *nt* (pl ~s) week-end

weemoed (*vāy*-mōōt) *c* melancholy

weer[1] (vāyr) *nt* weather

weer[2] (vāyr) *adv* again

weerbericht (*vāyr*-ber-rıkht) *nt* (pl ~en) weather forecast

*weerhouden (vāyr-*hou*-dern) *v* restrain

weerkaatsen (vāyr-*kaat*-sern) *v* reflect

weerkaatsing (vāyr-*kaat*-sıng) *c* reflection

weerklank (*vāyr*-klahngk) *c* echo

weerzinwekkend (vāyr-zın-*veh*-kernt) *adj* repulsive, repellent, revolting

wees (vāyss) *c* (pl wezen) orphan

weg[1] (vehkh) *adv* gone, away; lost; off

weg[2] (vehkh) *c* (pl ~en) way; road; **doodlopende** ~ cul-de-sac; **op** ~ **naar** bound for

*wegen (*vāy*-gern) *v* weigh

wegenkaart (*vāy*-ger-kaart) *c* (pl ~en) road map

wegennet (*vāy*-ger-neht) *nt* (pl ~ten) road system

wegens (*vāy*-gerns) *prep* because of, for

*weggaan (*veh*-khaan) *v* *go away

wegkant (*vehkh*-kahnt) *c* (pl ~en) roadside, wayside

*weglaten (*vehkh*-laa-tern) *v* omit, *leave out

*wegnemen (*vehkh*-nāy-mern) *v* *take out, *take away

wegomlegging (*vaykh*-om-leh-ging) *c* (pl ~en) diversion

wegrestaurant (*vehkh*-rehss-tōa-raht) *nt* (pl ~s) roadhouse; roadside restaurant

wegwerp- (*vehkh*-vehrp) disposable

wegwijzer (*vehkh*-vay-zerr) *c* (pl ~s) milepost, signpost

*wegzenden (*vehkh*-sehn-dern) *v* dismiss

wei (vay) *c* (pl ~den) meadow

weigeren (*vay*-ger-rern) *v* refuse; deny

weigering (*vay*-ger-ring) *c* (pl ~en) refusal

weiland (*vay*-lahnt) *nt* (pl ~en) pasture

weinig (*vay*-nerkh) *adj* little; few

wekelijks (*vāy*-ker-lerks) *adj* weekly

weken (*vāy*-kern) *v* soak

wekken (*veh*-kern) *v* *awake, *wake

wekker (*veh*-kerr) *c* (pl ~s) alarm-clock

weldra (*vehl*-draa) *adv* soon, shortly

welk (vehlk) *pron* which; ~ **ook** whichever

welkom (*vehl*-kom) *adj* welcome; *nt* welcome

wellicht (veh-*likht*) *adv* perhaps

wellust (*veh*-lerst) *c* (pl ~en) lust

welnu! (vehl-*nēw*) well!

welvaart (*vehl*-vaart) *c* prosperity

welvarend (vehl-*vaa*-rernt) *adj* prosperous

welwillendheid (vehl-*vi*-lernt-hayt) *c* goodwill

welzijn (*vehl*-zayn) *nt* welfare

wending (*vehn*-ding) *c* (pl ~en) turn

wenk (vehngk) *c* (pl ~en) sign

wenkbrauw (*vehngk*-brou) *c* (pl ~en) eyebrow

wenkbrauwstift (*vehngk*-brou-stift) *c* (pl ~en) eye-pencil

wennen (*veh*-nern) *v* accustom

wens (vehns) *c* (pl ~en) wish, desire

wenselijk (*vehn*-ser-lerk) *adj* desirable

wensen (*vehn*-sern) *v* wish, desire; want

wereld (*vāy*-rerlt) *c* (pl ~en) world

wereldberoemd (*vāy*-rerlt-ber-rōōmt) *adj* world-famous

wereldbol (*vāy*-rerlt-bol) *c* globe

werelddeel (*vāy*-rerl-dāyl) *nt* (pl -delen) continent

wereldomvattend (*vāy*-rerlt-om-vah-ternt) *adj* global, world-wide

wereldoorlog (*vāy*-rerlt-ōar-lokh) *c* (pl ~en) world war

werk (vehrk) *nt* work; labour; occupation, employment; business; **te ~ *gaan** proceed; ~ **in uitvoering** road up

werkdag (*vehrk*-dahkh) *c* (pl ~en) working day

werkelijk (*vehr*-ker-lerk) *adj* actual, true; substantial, very; *adv* really

werkelijkheid (*vehr*-ker-lerk-hayt) *c* reality

werkeloos (*vehr*-ker-lōass) *adj* unemployed; idle

werkeloosheid (vehr-ker-*lōass*-hayt) *c* unemployment

werken (*vehr*-kern) *v* work; operate

werkgever (*vehrk*-khāy-verr) *c* (pl ~s) employer

werking (*vehr*-king) *c* operation, working; **buiten ~** out of order

werknemer (*vehrk*-nāy-merr) *c* (pl ~s) employee

werkplaats (*vehrk*-plaats) *c* (pl ~en) workshop

werktuig (*vehrk*-tur^{ew}kh) *nt* (pl ~en) tool; utensil, implement

werkvergunning (*vehrk*-ferr-ger-ning) *c* (pl ~en) work permit; labor permit *Am*

werkwoord (*vehrk*-voārt) *nt* (pl ~en) verb

*werpen (*vehr*-pern) *v* *cast, *throw

wesp (vehsp) *c* (pl ~en) wasp

west (vehst) *c* west

westelijk (*vehss*-ter-lerk) *adj* westerly

westen (*vehss*-tern) *nt* west

westers (*vehss*-terrs) *adj* western

wet (veht) *c* (pl ~ten) law

*weten (*vā̄y*-tern) *v* *know

wetenschap (*vā̄y*-ter-skhahp) *c* (pl ~pen) science

wetenschappelijk (vā̄y-ter-*skhah*-per-lerk) *adj* scientific

wettelijk (*veh*-ter-lerk) *adj* legal

wettig (*veh*-terkh) *adj* legal, lawful; legitimate

*weven (*vā̄y*-vern) *v* *weave

wever (*vā̄y*-verr) *c* (pl ~s) weaver

wezen¹ (*vā̄y*-zern) *nt* (pl ~s) creature, being

wezen² (*vā̄y*-zern) *nt* essence

wezenlijk (*vā̄y*-zer-lerk) *adj* essential

wie (vee) *pron* who; whom; ~ **dan ook** anybody; ~ **ook** whoever

wieg (veekh) *c* (pl ~en) cradle

wiel (veel) *nt* (pl ~en) wheel

wielrijder (*veel*-ray-derr) *c* (pl ~s) cyclist

wierook (*vee*-rōak) *c* incense

wig (vikh) *c* (pl ~gen) wedge

wijd (vayt) *adj* broad, wide

wijden (*vay*-dern) *v* devote

wijk (vayk) *c* (pl ~en) quarter, district

wijn (vayn) *c* (pl ~en) wine

wijngaard (*vayn*-gaart) *c* (pl ~en) vineyard

wijnkaart (*vayng*-kaart) *c* (pl ~en) wine-list

wijnkelder (*vayng*-kehl-derr) *c* (pl ~s) wine-cellar

wijnkelner (*vayng*-kehl-nerr) *c* (pl ~s) wine-waiter

wijnkoper (*vayng*-kōa-perr) *c* (pl ~s) wine-merchant

wijnoogst (*vayn*-ōākhst) *c* (pl ~en) vintage

wijnstok (*vayn*-stok) *c* (pl ~ken) vine

wijs¹ (vayss) *adj* wise

wijs² (vayss) *c* (pl wijzen) tune

wijsbegeerte (*vayss*-ber-gā̄yr-ter) *c* philosophy

wijsgeer (*vayss*-khā̄yr) *c* (pl -geren) philosopher

wijsheid (*vayss*-hayt) *c* (pl -heden) wisdom

wijsvinger (*vayss*-fı-ngerr) *c* (pl ~s) index finger

wijting (*vay*-tıng) *c* (pl ~en) whiting

wijze (*vay*-zer) *c* (pl ~n) manner, way

*wijzen (*vay*-zern) *v* point; direct

wijzigen (*vay*-zer-gern) *v* change, alter, modify

wijziging (*vay*-zer-gıng) *c* (pl ~en) change, alteration

wil (vıl) *c* will

wild (vılt) *adj* wild; savage, fierce; *nt* game

wildpark (*vılt*-pahrk) *nt* (pl ~en) game reserve

willekeurig (vı-ler-*kūr*-rerkh) *adj* arbitrary

*willen (*vı*-lern) *v* want; *will

wilskracht (*vıls*-krahkht) *c* will-power

wimper (*vım*-perr) *c* (pl ~s) eyelash

wind (vınt) *c* (pl ~en) wind

*winden (*vın*-dern) *v* *wind; twist

winderig (*vın*-der-rerkh) *adj* windy, gusty

windmolen (*vınt*-mōa-lern) *c* (pl ~s) windmill

windstoot (*vınt*-stōat) *c* (pl -stoten) gust

windvlaag (*vınt*-flaakh) *c* (pl -vlagen) blow

winkel (*vıng*-kerl) *c* (pl ~s) store, shop

winkelcentrum (*vıng*-kerl-sehn-trerm) *nt* (pl -tra) shopping centre

winkelen (*ving*-ker-lern) *v* shop
winkelier (ving-ker-*leer*) *c* (pl ~s) shopkeeper
winnaar (*vi*-naar) *c* (pl ~s) winner
***winnen** (*vi*-nern) *v* *win; gain
winst (vinst) *c* (pl ~en) profit; gain, winnings *pl*, benefit
winstgevend (vinst-*khāy*-vernt) *adj* profitable
winter (*vin*-terr) *c* (pl ~s) winter
wintersport (*vin*-terr-sport) *c* winter sports
wip (vip) *c* (pl ~pen) seesaw
wirwar (*vir*-vahr) *c* muddle
wiskunde (*viss*-kern-der) *c* mathematics
wiskundig (viss-*kern*-derkh) *adj* mathematical
wissel (*vi*-serl) *c* (pl ~s) draft
wisselen (*vi*-ser-lern) *v* change; exchange
wisselgeld (*vi*-serl-gehlt) *nt* change
wisselkantoor (*vi*-serl-kahn-tōar) *nt* (pl -toren) money exchange, exchange office
wisselkoers (*vi*-serl-kōōrs) *c* (pl ~en) exchange rate
wisselstroom (*vi*-serl-strōam) *c* alternating current
wit (vit) *adj* white
wittebroodsweken (*vi*-ter-brōats-vāy-kern) *pl* honeymoon
witvis (*vit*-fiss) *c* (pl ~sen) whitebait
woede (*vōō*-der) *c* anger, rage
woeden (*vōō*-dern) *v* rage
woedend (*vōō*-dernt) *adj* furious
woensdag (*vōōns*-dahkh) *c* Wednesday
woest (vōōst) *adj* wild, fierce; desert
woestijn (vōōss-*tayn*) *c* (pl ~en) desert
wol (vol) *c* wool
wolf (volf) *c* (pl wolven) wolf
wolk (volk) *c* (pl ~en) cloud

wolkbreuk (*volk*-brŭrk) *c* (pl ~en) cloud-burst
wolkenkrabber (*vol*-ker-krah-berr) *c* (pl ~s) skyscraper
wollen (*vo*-lern) *adj* woollen
wond (vont) *c* (pl ~en) wound
wonder (*von*-derr) *nt* (pl ~en) wonder, miracle; marvel
wonderbaarlijk (von-derr-*baar*-lerk) *adj* miraculous
wonen (*vōa*-nern) *v* live; reside
woning (*vōa*-ning) *c* (pl ~en) house
woonachtig (vōan-*ahkh*-terkh) *adj* resident
woonboot (*vōan*-bōat) *c* (pl -boten) houseboat
woonkamer (*vōang*-kaa-merr) *c* (pl ~s) living-room
woonplaats (*vōam*-plaats) *c* (pl ~en) domicile, residence
woonwagen (*vōan*-vaa-gern) *c* (pl ~s) caravan
woord (vōart) *nt* (pl ~en) word
woordenboek (*vōar*-der-bōōk) *nt* (pl ~en) dictionary
woordenlijst (*vōar*-der-layst) *c* (pl ~en) vocabulary
woordenschat (*vōar*-der-skhaht) *c* vocabulary
woordenwisseling (*vōar*-der-vi-ser-ling) *c* (pl ~en) argument
***worden** (*vor*-dern) *v* *become; *go, *get, *grow
worm (vorm) *c* (pl ~en) worm
worp (vorp) *c* (pl ~en) cast
worst (vorst) *c* (pl ~en) sausage
worstelen (*vor*-ster-lern) *v* struggle
worsteling (*voar*-ster-ling) *c* (pl ~en) struggle
wortel (*vor*-terl) *c* (pl ~s, ~en) root; carrot
woud (vout) *nt* (pl ~en) forest
wraak (vraak) *c* revenge
wrak (vrahk) *nt* (pl ~ken) wreck

wreed (vrāyt) *adj* harsh, cruel

*****wrijven** (*vray*-vern) *v* rub

wrijving (*vray*-vɪng) *c* (pl ~en) friction

wurgen (*verr*-gern) *v* strangle, choke

Z

zaad (zaat) *nt* (pl zaden) seed

zaag (zaakh) *c* (pl zagen) saw

zaagsel (*zaakh*-serl) *nt* sawdust

zaaien (*zaaee*-ern) *v* *sow

zaak (zaak) *c* (pl zaken) cause; case, matter; business

zaal (zaal) *c* (pl zalen) hall

zacht (zahkht) *adj* soft; gentle, smooth, mild, mellow

zadel (*zaa*-derl) *nt* (pl ~s) saddle

zak (zahk) *c* (pl ~ken) pocket; sack, bag

zakdoek (*zahk*-dōōk) *c* (pl ~en) handkerchief; **papieren** ~ tissue

zakelijk (*zaa*-ker-lerk) *adj* business-like

zaken (*zaa*-kern) *pl* business; **voor** ~ on business; ~ *doen met *deal with

zakenman (*zaa*-ker-mahn) *c* (pl -lieden, -lui) businessman

zakenreis (*zaa*-ker-rayss) *c* (pl -reizen) business trip

zakhorloge (*zahk*-hor-lōā-zher) *nt* (pl ~s) pocket-watch

zakkam (*zah*-kahm) *c* (pl ~men) pocket-comb

zakken (*zah*-kern) *v* fail

zaklantaarn (*zahk*-lahn-taa-rern) *c* (pl ~s) torch, flash-light

zakmes (*zahk*-mehss) *nt* (pl ~sen) pocket-knife, penknife

zalf (zahlf) *c* (pl zalven) ointment, salve

zalm (zahlm) *c* (pl ~en) salmon

zand (zahnt) *nt* sand

zanderig (*zahn*-der-rerkh) *adj* sandy

zanger (*zah*-ngerr) *c* (pl ~s) vocalist, singer

zangeres (zah-nger-*rehss*) *c* (pl ~sen) singer

zaterdag (*zaa*-terr-dahkh) *c* Saturday

ze (zer) *pron* she; they

zebra (*zāy*-braa) *c* (pl ~'s) zebra

zebrapad (*zāy*-braa-paht) *nt* (pl ~en) pedestrian crossing; crosswalk *nAm*

zedelijk (*zāy*-der-lerk) *adj* moral

zeden (*zāy*-dern) *pl* morals

zee (zāy) *c* (pl ~ĕn) sea

zeeëgel (*zāy*-āy-gerl) *c* (pl ~s) sea-urchin

zeef (zāyf) *c* (pl zeven) sieve

zeegezicht (*zāy*-ger-zɪkht) *nt* (pl ~en) seascape

zeehaven (*zāy*-haa-vern) *c* (pl ~s) sea-port

zeehond (*zāy*-hont) *c* (pl ~en) seal

zeekaart (*zāy*-kaart) *c* (pl ~en) chart

zeekust (*zāy*-kerst) *c* (pl ~en) sea-coast

zeeman (*zāy*-mahn) *c* (pl -lieden, -lui) seaman

zeemeermin (*zāy*-māyr-mɪn) *c* (pl ~nen) mermaid

zeemeeuw (*zāy*-māyoo) *c* (pl ~en) seagull

zeep (zāyp) *c* soap

zeeppoeder (*zāy*-pōō-derr) *nt* soap powder

zeer (zāyr) *adj* sore; *adv* very, quite

zeeschelp (*zāy*-skhehlp) *c* (pl ~en) sea-shell

zeevogel (*zāy*-vōā-gerl) *c* (pl ~s) sea-bird

zeewater (*zāy*-vaa-terr) *nt* sea-water

zeeziek (*zāy*-zeek) *adj* seasick

zeeziekte (*zāy*-zeek-ter) *c* seasickness

zegel (*zāy*-gerl) *nt* (pl ~s) seal

zegen (*zāy*-gern) *c* blessing

zegenen (*zāy*-ger-nern) *v* bless

zegevieren (zāy-ger-vee-rern) v triumph

*zeggen (zeh-gern) v *say; *tell

zeil (zayl) nt (pl ~en) sail

zeilboot (zayl-bōat) c (pl -boten) sailing-boat

zeilclub (zayl-klerp) c (pl ~s) yacht-club

zeilsport (zayl-sport) c yachting

zeker (zāy-kerr) adv surely; adj certain, sure; ~ **niet** by no means

zekering (zāy-ker-rıng) c (pl ~en) fuse

zelden (zehl-dern) adv seldom, rarely

zeldzaam (zehlt-saam) adj rare; uncommon, infrequent

zelf (zehlf) pron myself; yourself; himself; herself; oneself; ourselves; yourselves; themselves

zelfbediening (zehlf-ber-dee-nıng) c self-service

zelfbedieningsrestaurant (zehlf-ber-dee-nıngs-rehss-tōa-rahnt) nt (pl ~s) self-service restaurant

zelfbestuur (zehlf-ber-stēwr) nt self-government

zelfde (zehlf-der) adj same

zelfmoord (zehlf-mōart) c (pl ~en) suicide

zelfs (zehlfs) adv even

zelfstandig (zehlf-stahn-derkh) adj independent; self-employed; ~ **naamwoord** noun

zelfstrijkend (zehlf-stray-kernt) adj drip-dry, wash and wear

zelfzuchtig (zehlf-serkh-terkh) adj egoistic

*zenden (zehn-dern) v *send

zender (zehn-derr) c (pl ~s) transmitter

zending (zehn-dıng) c (pl ~en) consignment

zenit (zāy-nıt) nt zenith

zenuw (zay-nēw⁰⁰) c (pl ~en) nerve

zenuwachtig (zāy-nēw⁰⁰-ahkh-terkh) adj nervous

zenuwpijn (zāy-nēw⁰⁰-payn) c (pl ~en) neuralgia

zes (zehss) num six

zesde (zehss-der) num sixth

zestien (zehss-teen) num sixteen

zestiende (zehss-teen-der) num sixteenth

zestig (zehss-terkh) num sixty

zet (zeht) c (pl ~ten) move; push

zetel (zāy-terl) c (pl ~s) chair; seat

zetpil (zeht-pıl) c (pl ~len) suppository

zetten (zeh-tern) v place; *lay, *set, *put; **in elkaar** ~ assemble

zeurpiet (zūrr-peet) c (pl ~en) bore

zeven¹ (zāy-vern) num seven

zeven² (zāy-vern) v strain, sift, sieve

zevende (zāy-vern-der) num seventh

zeventien (zāy-vern-teen) num seventeen

zeventiende (zāy-vern-teen-der) num seventeenth

zeventig (zāy-vern-terkh) num seventy

zich (zıkh) pron himself; herself; themselves

zicht (zıkht) nt sight; visibility; **op** ~ on approval

zichtbaar (zıkht-baar) adj visible

ziek (zeek) adj ill, sick

ziekenauto (zee-kern-ōa-tōa) c (pl ~'s) ambulance

ziekenhuis (zee-ker-hur⁵ᵂss) nt (pl -huizen) hospital

ziekenzaal (zee-ker-zaal) c (pl -zalen) infirmary

ziekte (zeek-ter) c (pl ~n, ~s) disease; ailment, illness, sickness

ziel (zeel) c (pl ~en) soul

*zien (zeen) v *see; notice; **er uit** ~ look; *laten ~ *show

zienswijze (zeens-vay-zer) c (pl ~n) outlook

zigeuner (zee-gūr-nerr) c (pl ~s) gipsy

zijbeuk (*zay*-būrk) *c* (pl ~en) aisle

zijde[1] (*zay*-der) *c* silk

zijde[2] (*zay*-der) *c* (pl ~n) side

zijden (*zay*-dern) *adj* silken

zijlicht (*zay*-likht) *nt* sidelight

zijn (zayn) *pron* his

***zijn** (zayn) *v* *be

zijrivier (*zay*-ree-veer) *c* (pl ~en) tributary

zijstraat (*zay*-straat) *c* (pl -straten) side-street

zilver (*zil*-verr) *nt* silver

zilveren (*zil*-ver-rern) *adj* silver

zilverpapier (*zil*-verr-paa-peer) *nt* tinfoil

zilversmid (*zil*-verr-smit) *c* (pl -smeden) silversmith

zilverwerk (*zil*-verr-vehrk) *nt* silverware

zin[1] (zin) *c* sense; desire; ~ *hebben in *feel like, fancy

zin[2] (zin) *c* (pl ~nen) sentence

***zingen** (*zi*-ngern) *v* *sing

zink (zingk) *nt* zinc

***zinken** (*zing*-kern) *v* *sink

zinloos (*zin*-lōass) *adj* senseless

zintuig (*zin*-tur^{ew}kh) *nt* (pl ~en) sense

zitkamer (*zit*-kaa-merr) *c* (pl ~s) sitting-room

zitplaats (*zit*-plaats) *c* (pl ~en) seat

***zitten** (*zi*-tern) *v* *sit; ***gaan** ~ *sit down

zitting (*zi*-ting) *c* (pl ~en) session

zitvlak (*zit*-flahk) *nt* bottom

zo (zōa) *adv* so, thus; such; **zo'n** such a

zoals (zōa-*ahls*) *conj* like, as; such as

zodat (zōa-*daht*) *conj* so that

zodra (zōa-*draa*) *conj* as soon as

***zoeken** (*zōō*-kern) *v* look for; *seek, search; hunt for

zoeker (*zōō*-kerr) *c* (pl ~s) view-finder

zoen (zōōn) *c* (pl ~en) kiss

zoet (zōōt) *adj* sweet; good; ~ ma-

ken sweeten

zoetzuur (*zōōt*-se^ūwr) *nt* pickles *pl*

zogen (*zōa*-gern) *v* nurse

zogenaamd (*zōa*-ger-*naamt*) *adj* so-called

zolder (*zol*-derr) *c* (pl ~s) attic

zomer (*zōa*-merr) *c* (pl ~s) summer

zomertijd (*zōa*-merr-tayt) *c* summer time

zon (zon) *c* (pl ~nen) sun

zondag (*zon*-dahkh) *c* Sunday

zonde (*zon*-der) *c* (pl ~n) sin

zondebok (*zon*-der-bok) *c* (pl ~ken) scapegoat

zonder (*zon*-derr) *prep* without

zonderling (*zon*-derr-ling) *adj* funny, queer

zone (*zaw*-ner) *c* (pl ~s) zone

zonlicht (*zon*-likht) *nt* sunlight

zonnebaden (*zo*-ner-baa-dern) *v* sunbathe

zonnebrand (*zo*-ner-brahnt) *c* sunburn

zonnebrandolie (*zo*-ner-brahnt-ōa-lee) *c* suntan oil

zonnebril (*zo*-ner-bril) *c* (pl ~len) sunglasses *pl*

zonnescherm (*zo*-ner-skhehrm) *nt* (pl ~en) awning

zonneschijn (*zo*-ner-skhayn) *c* sunshine

zonnesteek (*zo*-ner-stāyk) *c* sunstroke

zonnig (*zo*-nerkh) *adj* sunny

zonsondergang (zons-*on*-derr-gahng) *c* (pl ~en) sunset

zonsopgang (zons-*op*-khahng) *c* (pl ~en) sunrise

zoogdier (*zōa*kh-deer) *nt* (pl ~en) mammal

zool (zōal) *c* (pl zolen) sole

zoölogie (zōa-ōa-lōa-*gee*) *c* zoology

zoom (zōam) *c* (pl zomen) hem

zoon (zōan) *c* (pl zonen) son

zorg (zorkh) *c* (pl ~en) concern, worry, care; trouble

zorgen voor (*zor*-gern) look after, *take care of; see to

zorgvuldig (zorkh-*ferl*-derkh) *adj* careful

zorgwekkend (zorkh-*veh*-kernt) *adj* critical

zorgzaam (*zorkh*-saam) *adj* thoughtful

zout (zout) *nt* salt; *adj* salty

zoutvaatje (*zout*-faa-t^{y}er) *nt* (pl ~s) salt-cellar

zoveel (*zoa*-vāyl) *adv* so much

zowel ... als (*zoa-veh*...ahls) both ... and

zuid (zur^{ew}t) *c* south

Zuid-Afrika (zur^{ew}t-*aa*-free-kaa) South Africa

zuidelijk (*zur^{ew}*-der-lerk) *adj* southern, southerly

zuiden (*zur^{ew}*-dern) *nt* south

zuidoosten (zur^{ew}t-*ōass*-tern) *nt* southeast

zuidpool (*zur^{ew}*t-pōal) *c* South Pole

zuidwesten (zur^{ew}t-*vehss*-tern) *nt* south-west

zuigeling (*zur^{ew}*-ger-lιng) *c* (pl ~en) infant

*zuigen** (*zur^{ew}*-gern) *v* suck

zuiger (*zur^{ew}*-gerr) *c* (pl ~s) piston

zuigerring (*zur^{ew}*-ger-rιng) *c* (pl ~en) piston ring

zuigerstang (*zur^{ew}*-gerr-stahng) *c* (pl ~en) piston-rod

zuil (zur^{ew}l) *c* (pl ~en) column, pillar

zuilengang (*zur^{ew}*-ler-gahng) *c* (pl ~en) arcade

zuinig (*zur^{ew}*-nerkh) *adj* economical, thrifty

zuivelwinkel (*zur^{ew}*-verl-vιng-kerl) *c* (pl ~s) dairy

zuiver (*zur^{ew}*-verr) *adj* pure, clean

zulk (zerlk) *adj* such

*zullen** (*zer*-lern) *v* *will, *shall

zus (zerss) *c* (pl ~sen) sister

zuster (*zerss*-terr) *c* (pl ~s) sister; nurse

zuur[1] (zēwr) *adj* sour

zuur[2] (zēwr) *nt* (pl zuren) acid

zuurstof (*zēwr*-stof) *c* oxygen

zwaaien (*zvaa^{ee}*-ern) *v* *swing; wave

zwaan (zvaan) *c* (pl zwanen) swan

zwaar (zvaar) *adj* heavy

zwaard (zvaart) *nt* (pl ~en) sword

zwaartekracht (*zvaar*-ter-krahkht) *c* gravity

zwager (*zvaa*-gerr) *c* (pl ~s) brother-in-law

zwak (zvahk) *adj* feeble, weak; faint; dim

zwakheid (*zvahk*-hayt) *c* (pl -heden) weakness

zwaluw (*zvaa*-lēw^{oo}) *c* (pl ~en) swallow

zwanger (*zvah*-ngerr) *adj* pregnant

zwart (zvahrt) *adj* black

Zweden (*zvāy*-dern) Sweden

Zweed (zvāyt) *c* (pl Zweden) Swede

Zweeds (zvāyts) *adj* Swedish

zweefvliegtuig (*zvāy*-fleekh-tur^{ew}kh) *nt* (pl ~en) glider

zweep (zvāyp) *c* (pl zwepen) whip

zweer (zvāyr) *c* (pl zweren) ulcer, sore

zweet (zvāyt) *nt* sweat, perspiration

*zwellen** (*zveh*-lern) *v* *swell

zwelling (*zveh*-lιng) *c* (pl ~en) swelling

zwembad (*zvehm*-baht) *nt* (pl ~en) swimming pool

zwembroek (*zvehm*-brōok) *c* (pl ~en) swimming-trunks, bathing-trunks, bathing-suit

*zwemmen** (*zveh*-mern) *v* *swim

zwemmer (*zveh*-merr) *c* (pl ~s) swimmer

zwempak (*zvehm*-pahk) *nt* (pl ~ken) swim-suit

zwemsport (*zvehm*-sport) *c* swimming

zwendelarij (zvehn-der-laa-*ray*) *c* (pl ~en) swindle

*zweren (*zvāy*-rern) *v* *swear, vow

*zwerven (*zvehr*-vern) *v* roam, wander

zweten (*zvāy*-tern) *v* sweat, perspire

*zwijgen (*zvay*-gern) *v* *be silent, *keep quiet; tot ~ *brengen silence; zwijgend silent

zwijn (zvayn) *nt* (pl ~en) pig

Zwitser (*zvit*-serr) *c* (pl ~s) Swiss

Zwitserland (*zvit*-serr-lahnt) Switzerland

Zwitsers (*zvit*-serrs) *adj* Swiss

zwoegen (*zvoo*-gern) *v* labour

Food

aalbes redcurrant

aardappel potato

~ **puree** mashed potatoes

aardbei strawberry

abrikoos apricot

amandel almond

~ **broodje** a sweet roll with al-mond-paste filling

ananas pineapple

andijvie endive (US chicory)

~ **stamppot** mashed potato and endive casserole

anijs aniseed

ansjovis anchovy

appel apple

~ **beignet** fritter

~ **bol** dumpling

~ **flap** puff-pastry containing an apple slice

~ **gebak** cake

~ **moes** sauce

Ardense pastei rich pork mixture cooked in a pastry crust, served cold in slices

artisjok artichoke

asperge asparagus

~ **punt** tip

aubergine aubergine (US egg-plant)

augurk gherkin (US pickle)

avondeten dinner, supper

azijn vinegar

baars perch

babi pangang slices of roast suck-(l)ing pig, served with a sweet-and-sour sauce

bami goreng a casserole of noodles, vegetables, diced pork and shrimps

banaan banana

banketletter pastry with an al-mond-paste filling

basilicum basil

bediening service

belegd broodje roll with a variety of garnishes

belegen kaas pungent-flavoured cheese

biefstuk fillet of beef

~ **van de haas** small round fillet of beef

bieslook chive

bitterbal small, round breaded meatball served as an appetizer

blinde vink veal bird; thin slice of veal rolled around stuffing

bloedworst black pudding (US blood sausage)

~ **met appelen** with cooked ap-ples

bloemkool cauliflower

boerenkool met worst kale mixed with mashed potatoes and served with smoked sausage

boerenomelet omelet with diced vegetables and bacon

bokking bloater

boon bean

borrelhapje appetizer

borststuk breast, brisket

bosbes bilberry (US blueberry)

bot 1) flounder 2) bone

boter butter

boterham slice of buttered bread

bouillon broth

braadhaantje spring chicken

braadworst frying sausage

braam blackberry

brasem bream

brood bread

~ **maaltijd** bread served with cold meat, eggs, cheese, jam or other garnishes

~ **pudding** kind of bread pudding with eggs, cinnamon and rum flavouring

broodje roll

~ **halfom** buttered roll with liver and salted beef

~ **kaas** buttered roll with cheese

bruine bonen met spek red kidney beans served with bacon

Brussels lof chicory (US endive)

caramelpudding caramel mould

caramelvla caramel custard

champignon mushroom

chocola(de) chocolate

citroen lemon

cordon bleu veal scallop stuffed with ham and cheese

dadel date

dagschotel day's special

dame blanche vanilla ice-cream

with hot chocolate sauce

dille dill

doperwt green pea

dragon tarragon

drie-in-de-pan small, fluffy pancake filled with currants

druif grape

duif pigeon

Duitse biefstuk hamburger steak

Edam, Edammer kaas firm, mild-flavoured yellow cheese, coated with red wax

eend duck

ei egg

eierpannekoek egg pancake

erwt pea

erwtensoep met kluif pea soup with diced, smoked sausages, pork fat, pig's trotter (US feet), parsley, leeks and celery

exclusief not included

fazant pheasant

filet fillet

~ **américain** steak tartare

flensje small, thin pancake

foe yong hai omelet with leeks, onions, and shrimps served in a sweet-and-sour sauce

forel trout

framboos raspberry

Friese nagelkaas cheese made from skimmed milk, flavoured with cloves

frikadel meatball

frites, frieten chips (US french fries)

gaar well-done

gans goose

garnaal shrimp, prawn

gebak pastry, cake

gebakken fried

gebonden soep cream soup

gebraden roasted

gedroogde pruim prune

gehakt 1) minced 2) minced meat
~**bal** meatball
gekookt boiled
gekruid seasoned
gemarineerd marinated
gember ginger
~**koek** gingerbread
gemengd assorted, mixed
gepaneerd breaded
gepocheerd ei poached egg
geraspt grated
gerecht course, dish
gerookt smoked
geroosterd brood toast
gerst barley
gestoofd braised
gevogelte fowl
gevuld stuffed
gezouten salted
Goudakaas, Goudse kaas a renowned Dutch cheese, similar to *Edam*, large, flat and round; it gains in flavour with maturity
griesmeel semolina
~**pudding** semolina pudding
griet brill
groente vegetable
Haagse bluf dessert of whipped egg-whites, served with redcurrant sauce
haantje cockerel
haas hare
hachee hash of minced meat, onions and spices
half, halve half
hardgekookt ei hard-boiled egg
haring herring
hart heart
havermoutpap (oatmeal) porridge
hazelnoot hazelnut
heilbot halibut
heldere soep consommé, clear soup
hersenen brains

hete bliksem potatoes, bacon and apples, seasoned with butter, salt and sugar
Hollandse biefstuk loin section of a porterhouse or T-bone steak
Hollandse nieuwe freshly caught, filleted herring
honing honey
houtsnip 1) woodcock 2) cheese sandwich on rye bread
hutspot met klapstuk hotch-potch of mashed potatoes, carrots and onions served with boiled beef
huzarensla salad of potatoes, hard-boiled eggs, cold meat, gherkins, beetroot and mayonnaise
ijs ice, ice-cream
inclusief included
Italiaanse salade mixed salad with tomatoes, olives and tunny fish
jachtschotel a casserole of meat, onions and potatoes, often served with apple sauce
jonge kaas fresh cheese
jus gravy
kaas cheese
~**balletje** baked cheese ball
kabeljauw cod
kalfslapje, kalfsoester veal cutlet
kalfsrollade roast veal
kalfsvlees veal
kalkoen turkey
kapucijners met spek peas served with fried bacon, boiled potatoes, onions and green salad
karbonade chop, cutlet
karper carp
kastanje chestnut
kaviaar caviar
kerrie curry
kers cherry
kievitsei plover's egg
kip chicken

kippeborst breast of chicken
kippebout leg of chicken
knakworst small frankfurter sausage
knoflook garlic
koek 1) cake 2) gingerbread
koekje biscuit (US cookie)
koffietafel light lunch consisting of bread and butter with a variety of garnishes, served with coffee
kokosnoot coconut
komijnekaas cheese flavoured with cumin seeds
komkommer cucumber
konijn rabbit
koninginnesoep cream of chicken
kool cabbage
~ **schotel met gehakt** casserole of meatballs and cabbage
kotelet chop, cutlet
koud cold
~ **vlees** cold meat (US cold cuts)
krab crab
krabbetje spare rib
krent currant
kroepoek large, deep-fried shrimp wafer
kroket croquette
kruiderij herb, seasoning
kruidnagel clove
kruisbes gooseberry
kwark fresh white cheese
kwartel quail
kweepeer quince
lamsbout leg of lamb
lamsvlees lamb
langoest spiny lobster
Leidse kaas cheese flavoured with cumin seeds
lekkerbekje fried, filleted haddock or plaice
lendestuk sirloin
lever liver

linze lentil
loempia spring roll (US egg roll)
maïskolf corn on the cob
makreel mackerel
mandarijntje tangerine
marsepein marzipan
meikaas a creamy cheese with high fat content
meloen melon
menu van de dag set menu
mossel mussel
mosterd mustard
nagerecht dessert
nasi goreng a casserole of rice, fried onions, meat, chicken, shrimps, vegetables and seasoning, usually topped with a fried egg
nier kidney
~ **broodje** roll filled with kidneys and chopped onions
noot nut
oester oyster
olie oil
~ **bol** fritter with raisins
olijf olive
omelet fines herbes herb omelet
omelet met kippelevertjes chicken liver omelet
omelet nature plain omelet
ongaar underdone (US rare)
ontbijt breakfast
~ **koek** honey cake
~ **spek** bacon, rasher
ossehaas fillet of beef
ossestaart oxtail
oude kaas any mature and strong cheese
paddestoel mushroom
paling eel
~ **in 't groen** braised in white sauce garnished with chopped parsley and other greens
pannekoek pancake

~ **met stroop** pancake served with treacle (US syrup)

pap porridge

paprika green or red (sweet) pepper

patates frites chips (US french fries)

pastei pie, pasty

patrijs partridge

peer pear

pekeltong salt(ed) tongue

pekelvlees slices of salted meat

peper pepper

~ **koek** gingerbread

perzik peach

peterselie parsley

piccalilly pickle

pinda peanut

~ **kaas** peanut butter

pisang goreng fried banana

poffertje fritter served with sugar and butter

pompelmoes grapefruit

portie portion

postelein purslane (edible plant)

prei leek

prinsessenboon French bean (US green bean)

pruim plum

rabarber rhubarb

radijs radish

rauw raw

reebout, reerug venison

reine-claude greengage

rekening bill

ribstuk rib of beef

rijst rice

~ **tafel** an Indonesian preparation composed of some 30 dishes including stewed vegetables, spit-roasted meat and fowl, served with rice, various sauces, fruit, nuts and spices

rivierkreeft crayfish

rode biet beetroot

rode kool red cabbage

roerei scrambled egg

roggebrood rye bread

rolmops Bismarck herring

rolpens fried slices of spiced and pickled minced beef and tripe, topped with an apple slice

rookspek smoked bacon

rookworst smoked sausage

roomboter butter

roomijs ice-cream

rosbief roast beef

rozemarijn rosemary

runderlap beefsteak

rundvlees beef

Russische eieren Russian eggs; hard-boiled egg-halves garnished with mayonnaise, herring, shrimps, capers, anchovies and sometimes caviar; served on lettuce

salade salad

sambal kind of spicy paste consisting mainly of ground pimentos, usually served with *rijsttafel*, *bami* or *nasi goreng*

sardien sardine

saté, sateh skewered pieces of meat covered with a spicy peanut sauce

saucijzebroodje sausage roll

saus sauce, gravy

schaaldier shellfish

schapevlees mutton

scharretong lemon sole

schelvis haddock

schildpadsoep turtle soup

schnitzel cutlet

schol plaice

schuimomelet fluffy dessert omelet

selderij celery

sinaasappel orange

sjaslik skewered chunks of meat, grilled, then braised in a spicy sauce of tomatoes, onions and bacon

sla salad, lettuce

slaboon French bean (US green bean)

slagroom whipped cream

slak snail

sneeuwbal kind of cream puff, sometimes filled with currants and raisins

snijboon sliced French bean

soep soup

  ~ van de dag soup of the day

sorbet water ice (US sherbet)

speculaas spiced almond biscuit

spek bacon

sperzieboon French bean (US green bean)

spiegelei fried egg

spijskaart menu, bill of fare

spinazie spinach

sprits a kind of shortbread

spruitje brussels sprout

stamppot a stew of vegetables and mashed potatoes

steur sturgeon

stokvis stockfish (dried cod)

stroop treacle (US syrup)

suiker sugar

taart cake

tarbot turbot

tartaar steak tartare

  ~ speciaal extra-large portion, of prime quality

tijm thyme

tjap tjoy chop suey; a dish of fried meat and vegetables served with rice

toeristenmenu tourist menu

tomaat tomato

tong 1) tongue 2) sole

tonijn tunny (US tuna)

toost toast

tosti grilled cheese-and-ham sandwich

tournedos thick round fillet cut of prime beef (US rib or rib-eye steak)

truffel truffle

tuinboon broad bean

ui onion

uitsmijter two slices of bread garnished with ham or roast beef and topped with two fried eggs

vanille vanilla

varkenshaas pork tenderloin

varkenslapje pork fillet

varkensvlees pork

venkel fennel

vermicellisoep consommé with thin noodles

vers fresh

vijg fig

vis fish

vla custard

vlaai fruit tart

Vlaamse karbonade small slices of beef and onions braised in broth, with beer sometimes added

vlees meat

voorgerecht starter or first course

vrucht fruit

vruchtensalade fruit salad

wafel wafer

walnoot walnut

warm hot

waterkers watercress

waterzooi chicken poached in white wine and shredded vegetables, cream and egg-yolk

wentelteefje French toast; slice of white bread dipped in egg batter and fried, then sprinkled with cinnamon and sugar

wijnkaart wine list

wijting whiting
wild game
  ~ zwijn wild boar
wilde eend wild duck
witlof chicory (US endive)
  ~ op zijn Brussels chicory rolled in a slice of ham and oven-browned with cheese sauce

worst sausage
wortel carrot
zachtgekookt ei soft-boiled egg
zalm salmon
zeekreeft lobster
zeevis saltwater fish
zout salt
zuurkool sauerkraut
zwezerik sweetbread

Drinks

advocaat egg liqueur
ananassap pineapple juice
aperitief aperitif
bessenjenever blackcurrant gin
bier beer
bisschopswijn mulled wine
bittertje bitter-tasting aperitif
boerenjongens Dutch brandy with raisins
boerenmeisjes Dutch brandy with apricots
borrel shot
brandewijn brandy
cassis blackcurrant liqueur
chocolademelk, chocomel(k) chocolate drink
citroenbrandewijn lemon brandy
citroenjenever lemon-flavoured gin
citroentje met suiker brandy flavoured with lemon peel, with sugar added
cognac brandy, cognac
donker bier porter; dark sweet-tasting beer
druivesap grape juice

frisdrank soft drink
gekoeld iced
genever see *jenever*
Geuzelambiek a strong Flemish bitter beer brewed from wheat and barley
jenever Dutch gin
jonge jenever/klare young Dutch gin
karnemelk buttermilk
kersenbrandewijn kirsch; spirit distilled from cherries
koffie coffee
  ~ met melk with milk
  ~ met room with cream
  ~ met slagroom with whipped cream
  ~ verkeerd white coffee; equal quantity of coffee and hot milk
  zwarte ~ black
Kriekenlambiek a strong Brussels bitter beer flavoured with morello cherries
kwast hot or cold lemon squash
licht bier lager; light beer
likeur liqueur

limonade lemonade
melk milk
mineraalwater mineral water
oude jenever/klare Dutch gin
aged in wood casks, yellowish in
colour and more mature than
jonge jenever
oranjebitter orange-flavoured bitter
pils general name for beer
sap juice
sinas orangeade
spuitwater soda water
sterkedrank liquor, spirit
tafelwater mineral water

thee tea
~ **met citroen** with lemon
~ **met suiker en melk** with sugar and milk
trappistenbier malt beer brewed
(originally) by Trappist monks
vieux brandy bottled in Holland
vruchtesap fruit juice
warme chocola hot chocolate
wijn wine
droge ~ dry
rode ~ red
witte ~ white
zoete ~ sweet
wodka vodka

Mini-Grammar

Articles

Dutch nouns are either common gender (originally separate masculine and feminine) or neuter.

1. Definite article (the)

The definite article in Dutch is either **de** or **het**. **De** is used with roughly two thirds of all common-gender singular nouns as well as with all plural nouns, while **het** is mainly used with neuter singular nouns and all diminutives:

de straat   the street   **het huis**   the house   **het katje**   the kitten

2. Indefinite article (a; an)

The indefinite article is **een** for both genders, always unstressed and pronounced like *an* in the English word "another". As in English there is no plural. When it bears accent marks (**één**) it means "one" and is pronounced rather like a in "late", but a pure vowel, not a diphthong.

een man	a man	**een vrouw**	a woman	**een kind**	a child
mannen	men	**vrouwen**	women	**kinderen**	children

Plural

The most common sign of the plural in Dutch is an **-en** ending:

krant	newspaper	**woord**	word	**dag**	day
kranten	newspapers	**woorden**	words	**dagen**	days

a) In nouns with a double vowel, one vowel is dropped when **-en** is added:

uur	hour	**boot**	boat	**jaar**	year
uren	hours	**boten**	boats	**jaren**	years

b) most nouns ending in **-s** or **-f** change this letter into **-z** and **-v** respectively, when **-en** is added:

prijs	the price	**brief**	letter
prijzen	prices	**brieven**	letters

Another common plural ending in Dutch is **-s**. Nouns ending in an unstressed **-el**, **-em**, **-en**, **-aar** as well as **-je** (diminutives) take an **-s** in the plural:

tafel/tafels	table(s)	**winnaar/winnaars**	winner(s)
deken/dekens	blanket(s)	**kwartje/kwartjes**	25-cent piece(s)

Some exceptions:

stad/steden	town(s)	**auto/auto's**	car(s)
ship/schepen	ship(s)	**paraplu/paraplu's**	umbrella(s)
kind/kinderen	child(ren)	**foto/foto's**	photo(s)
ei/eieren	egg(s)	**musicus/musici**	musician(s)

Adjectives

When the adjective stands immediately before the noun, it usually takes the ending **-e**:

de jonge vrouw	the young woman
een prettige reis	a pleasant trip
aardige mensen	nice people

However, no ending is added to the adjective in the following cases:

1) When the adjective follows the noun:

De stad is groot.	The city is big.
De zon is heet.	The sun is hot.

2) When the noun is neuter singular and preceded by **een** (a/an), or when the words **elk/ieder** (each), **veel** (much), **zulk** (such) and **geen** (no) precede the adjective:

een wit huis	a white house
elk goed boek	each good book
veel vers fruit	much fresh fruit
zulk mooi weer	such good weather
geen warm water	no hot water

Demonstrative adjectives (this/that):

this	**deze**	(with nouns of common gender)
	dit	(with nouns of neuter gender)
that	**die (daar)**	(with nouns of common gender)
	dat	(with nouns of neuter gender)
these	**deze**	(with all plural nouns)
those	**die (daar)**	(with all plural nouns)

Deze stad is groot.	This city is big.
Dat huis is wit.	That house is white.

Personal pronouns

Subject		Object	
I	**ik**	me	**mij** or **me**
you	**jij** or **je** (fam.)	you	**jou** or **je** (fam.)
you	**u** (pol.)	you	**u** (pol.)
he	**hij**	him	**hem**
she	**zij** or **ze**	her	**haar**
it	**het**	it	**het**
we	**wij** or **we**	us	**ons**
you	**jullie** (fam.)	you	**jullie** (fam.)
they	**zij** or **ze**	them	**hen**

Possessive adjectives

my	**mijn**
your	**jouw** (fam.)
your	**uw** (pol.)
his	**zijn**
her	**haar**
its	**zijn**
our	**ons** (with singular neuter nouns)
	onze (with singular nouns of common gender and all plurals)
you	**jullie** (fam.)
their	**hun**

Verbs

First a few handy irregular verbs. If you learn only these, or even only the "I" and polite "you" forms of them, you'll have made a useful start.

1) The indispensible verbs **hebben** (to have) and **zijn** (to be) in the present:

I have	**ik heb**	I am	**ik ben**
you have	**jij hebt**	you are	**jij bent**
you have	**u hebt**	you are	**u bent**
he/she/it has	**hij/zij/het heeft**	he/she/it is	**hij/zij/het is**
we have	**wij hebben**	we are	**wij zijn**
you have	**jullie hebben**	you are	**jullie zijn**
they have	**zij hebben**	they are	**zij zijn**

2) Some more useful irregular verbs (in the present):

Infinitive		**willen** (to want)	**kunnen** (can)	**gaan** (to go)	**doen** (to do)	**weten** (to know)
I	**ik**	**wil**	**kan**	**ga**	**doe**	**weet**
you	**jij**	**wilt**	**kunt**	**gaat**	**doet**	**weet**
you	**u**	**wilt**	**kunt**	**gaat**	**doet**	**weet**
he	**hij**	**wil**	**kan**	**gaat**	**doet**	**weet**
she	**zij**	**wil**	**kan**	**gaat**	**doet**	**weet**
it	**het**	**wil**	**kan**	**gaat**	**doet**	**weet**
we	**wij**	**willen**	**kunnen**	**gaan**	**doen**	**weten**
you	**jullie**	**willen**	**kunnen**	**gaan**	**doen**	**weten**
they	**zij**	**willen**	**kunnen**	**gaan**	**doen**	**weten**

3) Infinitive and verb stem:

In Dutch verbs, the infinitive generally ends in **-en**: **noemen** (to name).

As the verb stem is usually the base for forming tenses, you need to know how to obtain it. The general rule is: the infinitive less **-en**:

infinitive: **noemen**   stem: **noem**

4) Present and past tenses:

First find the stem of the verb (see under 3 above).

Them add the appropriate endings, where applicable, according to the models given below for present and past tenses.

Note: in forming the past tense, the **-de/-den** endings shown in our example are added after most verb stems. However, if the stem ends in **p, t, k, f, s**, or **ch**, add **te/-ten** instead.

Present tense		Past tense	
ik noem	I name	**ik noemde**	I named
jij noemt	you name	**jij noemde**	you named
u noemt	you name	**u noemde**	you named
hij/zij/het noemt	he/she/it names	**hij/zij/het noemde**	he/she/it named
wij noemen	we name	**wij noemden**	we named
jullie noemen	you name	**jullie noemden**	you named
zij noemen	they name	**zij noemden**	they named

5) Past perfect (e.g.: "I have built"):

This tense is generally formed, as in English, by the verb "to have" (**hebben**) (see page 339) + the past participle.

To form the past participle, start with the verb stem, and add **ge-** to the front of it and **-d** or **-t** to the end:

infinitive:	**bouwen** (to build)
verb stem:	**bouw**
past participle:	**gebouwd**

The past participle must be placed *after* the object of the sentence:

Ik heb een huis gebouwd.	I have built a house.

Note: Verbs prefixed by **be-, er-, her-, ont-** and **ver-** do not take **ge-** in the past participle.

Instead of **hebben**, the verb **zijn** (to be) is used with verbs expressing motion (if the destination is specified or implied) or a change of state:

Wij zijn naar Parijs gevlogen.	We have flown to Paris.
Hij is rijk geworden.	He has become rich.

Negatives

To put a verb into the negative, place **niet** (not) after the verb, or after the direct object if there is one:

Ik rook.	I smoke.	**Ik heb de kaartjes.**	I have the tickets.
Ik rook niet.	I don't smoke.	**Ik heb de kaartjes niet.**	I don't have the tickets.

Questions

In Dutch, questions are formed by placing the subject after the verb:

Hij reist.	He travels.	**Ik betaal.**	I pay.
Reist hij?	Does he travel?	**Betaal ik?**	Do I pay?

Questions are also introduced by the following **interrogative pronouns:**

Wie (who)	Who says so?	**Wie zegt dat?**
	Whose house is that?	**Van wie is dat huis?**
Wat (what)	What does he do?	**Wat doet hij?**
Waar (where)	Where is the hotel!	**Waar is het hotel?**
Hoe (how)	How are you?	**Hoe gaat het met u?**

Irregular verbs

The following list contains the most common strong and irregular verbs. If a compound verb or a verb with a prefix (*be-, con-, dis-, im-, in-, mis-, om-, on-, ont-, ver-,* etc.) is not listed, its forms may be found by looking up the basic verb, e.g. *verbinden* is conjugated as *binden*.

Infinitive	Past	Past participle	
bakken	bakte	gebakken	*bake*
barsten	barstte	gebarsten	*burst, crack*
bederven	bedierf	bedorven	*spoil*
bedriegen	bedroog	bedrogen	*deceive*
beginnen	begon	begonnen	*begin*
bergen	borg	geborgen	*put*
bevelen	beval	bevolen	*order*
bewegen	bewoog	bewogen	*move*
bezwijken	bezweek	bezweken	*succumb*
bidden	bad	gebeden	*pray*
bieden	bood	geboden	*offer*
bijten	beet	gebeten	*bite*
binden	bond	gebonden	*tie*
blazen	blies	geblazen	*blow*
blijken	bleek	gebleken	*prove to be*
blijven	bleef	gebleven	*remain*
blinken	blonk	geblonken	*shine*
braden	braadde	gebraden	*fry*
breken	brak	gebroken	*break*
brengen	bracht	gebracht	*bring*
buigen	boog	gebogen	*bow*
delven	delfde/dolf	gedolven	*dig up*
denken	dacht	gedacht	*think*
dingen	dong	gedongen	*compete (for)*
doen	deed	gedaan	*do*
dragen	droeg	gedragen	*wear*
drijven	dreef	gedreven	*float*
dringen	drong	gedrongen	*push*
drinken	dronk	gedronken	*drink*
druipen	droop	gedropen	*drip*
duiken	dook	gedoken	*dive*
dwingen	dwong	gedwongen	*force*
eten	at	gegeten	*eat*
fluiten	floot	gefloten	*whistle*
gaan	ging	gegaan	*go*
gelden	gold	gegolden	*be valid*
genezen	genas	genezen	*heal*
genieten	genoot	genoten	*enjoy*
geven	gaf	gegeven	*give*
gieten	goot	gegoten	*pour*
glijden	gleed	gegleden	*slide*
glimmen	glom	geglommen	*shine*
graven	groef	gegraven	*dig*

grijpen	greep	gegrepen	*catch*
hangen	hing	gehangen	*hang*
hebben	had	gehad	*have*
heffen	hief	geheven	*raise*
helpen	hielp	geholpen	*help*
heten	heette	geheten	*be called*
hijsen	hees	gehesen	*hoist*
houden	hield	gehouden	*keep*
jagen	jaagde/joeg	gejaagd	*chase*
kiezen	koos	gekozen	*choose*
kijken	keek	gekeken	*look*
klimmen	klom	geklommen	*climb*
klinken	klonk	geklonken	*sound*
knijpen	kneep	geknepen	*pinch*
komen	kwam	gekomen	*come*
kopen	kocht	gekocht	*buy*
krijgen	kreeg	gekregen	*get*
krimpen	kromp	gekrompen	*shrink*
kruipen	kroop	gekropen	*creep*
kunnen	kon	gekund	*can*
lachen	lachte	gelachen	*laugh*
laden	laadde	geladen	*load*
laten	liet	gelaten	*let*
lezen	las	gelezen	*read*
liegen	loog	gelogen	*tell lies*
liggen	lag	gelegen	*lie*
lijden	leed	geleden	*suffer*
lijken	leek	geleken	*seem*
lopen	liep	gelopen	*walk*
malen	maalde	gemalen	*grind*
meten	mat	gemeten	*measure*
moeten	moest	gemoeten	*must*
mogen	mocht	gemogen/gemoogd	*may*
nemen	nam	genomen	*take*
prijzen	prees	geprezen	*praise*
raden	raadde/ried	geraden	*guess*
rijden	reed	gereden	*ride*
rijgen	reeg	geregen	*thread*
rijzen	rees	gerezen	*rise*
roepen	riep	geroepen	*call*
ruiken	rook	geroken	*smell*
scheiden	scheidde	gescheiden	*separate*
schelden	schold	gescholden	*call names*
schenken	schonk	geschonken	*pour*
scheppen	schiep	geschapen	*create*
scheren	schoor	geschoren	*shave*
schieten	schoot	geschoten	*shoot*
schijnen	scheen	geschenen	*shine, seem to be*
schrijden	schreed	geschreden	*stride*
schrijven	schreef	geschreven	*write*
schrikken	schrok	geschrokken	*be frightened*

schuiven	schoof	geschoven	*shove*
slaan	sloeg	geslagen	*hit*
slapen	sliep	geslapen	*sleep*
slijpen	sleep	geslepen	*sharpen*
slijten	sleet	gesleten	*wear down*
sluipen	sloop	geslopen	*sneak*
sluiten	sloot	gesloten	*close*
smelten	smolt	gesmolten	*melt*
snijden	sneed	gesneden	*cut*
spinnen	spon	gesponnen	*spin*
splijten	spleet	gespleten	*split*
spreken	sprak	gesproken	*speak*
springen	sprong	gesprongen	*jump*
spuiten	spoot	gespoten	*squirt*
staan	stond	gestaan	*stand*
steken	stak	gestoken	*sting*
stelen	stal	gestolen	*steal*
sterven	stierf	gestorven	*die*
stijgen	steeg	gestegen	*rise*
stijven	steef	gesteven	*starch*
stinken	stonk	gestonken	*stink*
stoten	stootte/stiet	gestoten	*push*
strijden	streed	gestreden	*fight*
strijken	streek	gestreken	*iron*
treden	trad	getreden	*tread*
treffen	trof	getroffen	*hit*
trekken	trok	getrokken	*pull*
vallen	viel	gevallen	*fall*
vangen	ving	gevangen	*catch*
varen	voer	gevaren	*sail*
vechten	vocht	gevochten	*fight*
verbergen	verborg	verborgen	*hide*
verdwijnen	verdween	verdwenen	*disappear*
vergeten	vergat	vergeten	*forget*
verliezen	verloor	verloren	*lose*
vermijden	vermeed	vermeden	*avoid*
verslinden	verslond	verslonden	*devour*
vinden	vond	gevonden	*find*
vliegen	vloog	gevlogen	*fly*
voortspruiten	sproot voort	voortgesproten	*result*
vouwen	vouwde	gevouwen	*fold*
vragen	vroeg	gevraagd	*ask*
vriezen	vroor	gevroren	*freeze*
waaien	waaide/woei	gewaaid	*blow*
wassen	waste	gewassen	*wash*
wegen	woog	gewogen	*weigh*
werpen	wierp	geworpen	*throw*
werven	wierf	geworven	*recruit*
weten	wist	geweten	*know*
weven	weefde	geweven	*weave*
wijken	week	geweken	*yield*

wijten	weet	geweten	*impute*
wijzen	wees	gewezen	*show*
willen	wilde/wou	gewild	*want*
winden	wond	gewonden	*wind*
winnen	won	gewonnen	*win*
worden	werd	geworden	*become*
wreken	wreekte	gewroken	*revenge*
wrijven	wreef	gewreven	*rub*
zeggen	zei	gezegd	*say*
zenden	zond	gezonden	*send*
zien	zag	gezien	*see*
zijn	was	geweest	*be*
zingen	zong	gezongen	*sing*
zinken	zonk	gezonken	*sink*
zinnen	zon	gezonnen	*brood*
zitten	zat	gezeten	*sit*
zoeken	zocht	gezocht	*seek*
zuigen	zoog	gezogen	*suck*
zullen	zou	—	*shall, will*
zwellen	zwol	gezwollen	*swell*
zwemmen	zwom	gezwommen	*swim*
1) zweren	zwoer	gezworen	*swear*
2) zweren	zweerde/zwoor	gezworen	*ulcerate*
zwerven	zwierf	gezworven	*wander*
zwijgen	zweeg	gezwegen	*be silent*

Dutch Abbreviations

A°	*anno*	(built) in the year
afd.	*afdeling*	department
alg.	*algemeen*	general
A.N.W.B.	*Algemene Nederlandse Wielrijdersbond*	Dutch Touring Association
a.s.	*aanstaande*	next
a.u.b.	*alstublieft*	please
Bfr.	*Belgische frank*	Belgian franc
b.g.	*begane grond*	ground floor
b.g.g.	*bij geen gehoor*	if no answer
blz.	*bladzijde*	page
B.R.T.	*Belgische Radio en Televisie*	Belgian Broadcasting Company
B.T.W.	*Belasting Toegevoegde Waarde*	VAT, value added tax
b.v.	*bijvoorbeeld*	e.g.
B.V.	*besloten vennootschap*	limited liability company
C.S.	*Centraal Station*	main railway station
ct.	*cent*	1/100 of the guilder
dhr.	*de heer*	Mr.
drs.	*doctorandus*	Master of Arts
d.w.z.	*dat wil zeggen*	i.e.
EEG	*Europese Economische Gemeenschap*	EEC, European Economic Community (Common Market)
E.H.B.O.	*Eerste Hulp bij Ongelukken*	first aid
enz.	*enzovoort*	etc.
excl.	*exclusief*	exclusive, not included
fl/f	*gulden*	guilder
geb.	*geboren*	born
H.K.H.	*Hare Koninklijke Hoogheid*	Her Royal Highness
H.M.	*Hare Majesteit*	His/Her Majesty
hs	*huis*	ground floor
incl.	*inclusief*	inclusive, included
i.p(l).v.	*in plaats van*	in the place of
ir.	*ingenieur*	engineer
jl.	*jongstleden*	last
K.A.C.B.	*Koninklijke Automobielclub van België*	Royal Automobile Association of Belgium
km/u	*kilometer per uur*	kilometres per hour
K.N.A.C.	*Koninklijke Nederlandse Automobielclub*	Royal Dutch Automobile Association

K.N.M.I.	*Koninklijk Nederlands Meteorologisch Instituut*	Royal Dutch Meteorological Institute
m.a.w.	*met andere woorden*	in other words
Mej.	*mejuffrouw*	Miss
Mevr.	*mevrouw*	Mrs.
Mij.	*maatschappij*	company
Mr.	*meester in de rechten; mijnheer*	barrister, lawyer; Mr.
N.A.V.O.	*Noordatlantische Verdragsorganisatie*	NATO
N.B.T.	*Nederlands Bureau voor Toerisme*	Dutch National Tourist Office
n.Chr.	*na Christus*	A.D.
nl.	*namelijk*	namely
n.m.	*namiddag*	afternoon
N.M.B.S.	*Nationale Maatschappij der Belgische Spoorwegen*	Belgian National Railways
N.P.	*niet parkeren*	no parking
N.S.	*Nederlandse Spoorwegen*	Dutch National Railways
N.V.	*naamloze vennootschap*	Ltd. or Inc.
p.a.	*per adres*	in care of
pk	*paardekracht*	horsepower
r.-k./R.-K.	*rooms-katholiek*	Roman Catholic
t.e.m.	*tot en met*	up to and including
t.o.v.	*ten opzichte van*	with regard to
v.a.	*volgens anderen, vanaf*	from
V.A.B.	*Vlaamse Automobilistenbond*	Flemish Automobile Association
v.Chr.	*voor Christus*	B.C.
v.m.	*voormiddag*	morning
V.N.	*Verenigde Naties*	UN
V.S.	*Verenigde Staten*	USA
V.T.B.	*Vlaamse Toeristenbond*	Flemish Tourist Association
V.V.V.	*Vereniging voor Vreemdelingenverkeer*	tourist-information office
zgn.	*zogenaamd*	so-called
Z.K.H.	*Zijne Koninklijke Hoogheid*	His Royal Highness
z.o.z.	*zie ommezijde*	pto, please turn over

Numerals

Cardinal numbers		Ordinal numbers	
0	nul	1e	eerste
1	een	2e	tweede
2	twee	3e	derde
3	drie	4e	vierde
4	vier	5e	vijfde
5	vijf	6e	zesde
6	zes	7e	zevende
7	zeven	8e	achtste
8	acht	9e	negende
9	negen	10e	tiende
10	tien	11e	elfde
11	elf	12e	twaalfde
12	twaalf	13e	dertiende
13	dertien	14e	veertiende
14	veertien	15e	vijftiende
15	vijftien	16e	zestiende
16	zestien	17e	zeventiende
17	zeventien	18e	achttiende
18	achttien	19e	negentiende
19	negentien	20e	twintigste
20	twintig	21e	eenentwintigste
21	eenentwintig	22e	tweeëntwintigste
22	tweeëntwintig	23e	drieëntwintigste
23	drieëntwintig	24e	vierentwintigste
24	vierentwintig	25e	vijfentwintigste
30	dertig	26e	zesentwintigste
40	veertig	30e	dertigste
50	vijftig	40e	veertigste
60	zestig	50e	vijftigste
70	zeventig	60e	zestigste
80	tachtig	70e	zeventigste
90	negentig	80e	tachtigste
100	honderd	90e	negentigste
101	honderdeen	100e	honderdste
230	tweehonderddertig	101e	honderdeerste
1000	duizend	230e	tweehonderddertigste
1001	duizendeen	1000e	duizendste
1100	elfhonderd	1001e	duizendeerste
2000	tweeduizend	1100e	elfhonderdste
1 000 000	een miljoen	2000e	tweeduizendste

Time

Although official time in Holland and Belgium is based on the 24-hour clock, the 12-hour system is used in conversation.

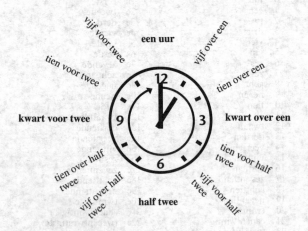

To avoid confusion, you can make use of the terms *'s morgens* (morning), and *'s middags* (afternoon) or *'s avonds* (evening).

Ik kom om vier uur 's morgens.	I'll come at 4 a.m.
Ik kom om vier uur 's middags.	I'll come at 4 p.m.
Ik kom om acht uur 's avonds.	I'll come at 8 p.m.

Days of the Week

zondag	Sunday	*donderdag*	Thursday
maandag	Monday	*vrijdag*	Friday
dinsdag	Tuesday	*zaterdag*	Saturday
woensdag	Wednesday		